The Inner Science of Buddhist Practice

The Tsadra Foundation Series

published by Snow Lion Publications

Tsadra Foundation is a U.S.-based non-profit organization that was founded in 2000 in order to support the activities of advanced Western students of Tibetan Buddhism, specifically those with significant contemplative experience. Taking its inspiration from the nineteenth-century nonsectarian Tibetan scholar and meditation master Jamgön Kongtrül Lodrö Tayé, Tsadra Foundation is named after his hermitage in eastern Tibet, Tsadra Rinchen Drak. The Foundation's various program areas reflect his values of excellence in both scholarship and contemplative practice, and the recognition of their mutual complementarity.

This publication is part of Tsadra Foundation's Translation Program, which aims to make authentic and authoritative texts from the Tibetan traditions available in English. The Foundation is honored to present the work of its fellows and grantees, individuals of confirmed contemplative and intellectual integrity; however, their views do not necessarily reflect those of the Foundation.

Tsadra Foundation is delighted to ally with Snow Lion Publications in making these important texts available in the English language.

The Inner Science of Buddhist Practice

Vasubandhu's *Summary of the Five Heaps*
with Commentary by Sthiramati

Artemus B. Engle

Snow Lion Publications
ITHACA, NEW YORK

Snow Lion Publications
P.O. Box 6483
Ithaca, New York 14851 USA
607-273-8519
www.snowlionpub.com

Printed in USA on acid-free recycled paper.

ISBN-10: 1-55939-322-X
ISBN-13: 978-1-55939-322-5

Design by Gopa & Ted2, Inc.

Library of Congress Cataloging-in-Publication Data

Engle, Artemus B., 1948-
The inner science of Buddhist practice : Vasubandhu's Summary of the five heaps with commentary by Sthiramati / Artemus B. Engle.
p. cm. — (The Tsadra Foundation series)
Includes Tibetan and Sanskrit texts and translations into English.
Includes bibliographical references and index.
ISBN-13: 978-1-55939-322-5 (alk. paper)
ISBN-10: 1-55939-322-X (alk. paper)
1. Lam-rim. 2. Vasubandhu. Pañcaskandhaprakarana. 3. Sthiramati. Pañcaskandhaprakaranavibhasya. I. Vasubandhu. Pañcaskandhaprakarana. Polyglot. II. Sthiramati. Pañcaskandhaprakaranavibhasya. English. III. Title.
BQ7645.L35E65 2009
294.3'420423—dc22

2008054131

Contents

The Tathāgata taught the causes
Of entities that are causally produced;
The Great Ascetic is also the one who revealed
The manner of their cessation.

ये धर्मा हेतुप्रभवा हेतुं तेषां तथागतो ह्यवदात् ।
तेषां च यो निरोध एवं वादी महाश्रमणः ॥

ye dharmā hetuprabhavā hetuṃ teṣāṃ tathāgato hyavadāt /
teṣāṃ ca yo nirodha evaṃ vādī mahāśramaṇaḥ //

ཆོས་རྣམས་གང་དག་རྒྱུས་བྱུང་དེ་དག་ནི།།
རྒྱུ་དང་དེ་ལ་འགོག་པ་གང་ཡིན་པ།།
དེ་བཞིན་གཤེགས་པ་ཉིད་ཀྱིས་བཀའ་སྩལ་པ།།
དེ་སྐད་གསུངས་པའི་ཚུལ་ཅན་དགེ་སྦྱོང་ཆེ།།

Preface

IN THE SPRING of 1972, after having studied Tibetan for barely a year, it was my immense good fortune to meet a truly extraordinary Tibetan Buddhist teacher and almost immediately begin receiving from him an explanation of Vasubandhu's renowned *Abhidharmakośabhāṣyam* (T: *Chos mngon pa'i mdzod kyi bshad pa*), or *Commentary to the Treasury of Higher Learning*. Part of a translation project that lasted for three years, this instruction was in many ways my introduction to the Buddha Dharma.

My teacher, known then as Geshe Lobsang Tharchin, had studied at the Mey College of Sera Monastery near Lhasa, Tibet and earned the Lharampa Geshe title with honors in 1953. He also completed Tantric studies at Gyumed College before escaping to India in 1959. I was his first Dharma student in the United States and maintained a close and ongoing relationship with him that lasted more than thirty years, until his passing in December 2004. If I have learned anything about the teachings of Lord Buddha, it is due almost exclusively to the kindness of this lama.

During the three-year period that I first studied Vasubandhu's great work, I developed a particular interest in a subject that can best be described as Buddhist psychology. In Tibetan it is called *sem sem jung* (T: *sems sems byung*), or "mind and mental factors." My attraction stemmed from the recognition that an understanding of this material brings a greater awareness of the workings of one's own mind, making it a powerful tool in learning to develop mindfulness—*apramāda* in Sanskrit and *bak yö* (T: *bag yod*) in Tibetan—a quality that is central to Buddhist spiritual practice.

I soon also became acquainted with a native Tibetan work on this same topic written by Tsechok Ling Yongzin Yeshe Gyeltsen (1713–1793), an important Gelukpa scholar who served as tutor to the eighth Dalai Lama. Entitled *A Necklace for Those of Clear Mind: An Elucidation of Mind and*

Mental Factors, this work is distinguished by the way that it relates the descriptions of mind and mental factors to the instructions of the teaching system known as *Lamrim*, or Stages of the Path, which is revered for its effectiveness in enabling practitioners of all levels to develop the spiritual attitudes that lie at the heart of the Buddhist Mahāyāna tradition.

Off and on from the late 1980s to 2001, I worked on a translation of a series of edited oral teachings on Lamrim practice that were given by the influential Gelukpa lama Kyabje Pabongka Rinpoche (1878–1941). The effort to translate this work, entitled *Liberation in Our Hands*, engendered a long-standing interest in the extensive body of Indian and Tibetan literature that relates to the Lamrim tradition, as well as a personal devotion to the system of spiritual practice that it elucidates.

Finally, over the years I have found the writings of the Indian Buddhist scholar Sthiramati—such as his commentary on Vasubandhu's *Summary of the Five Heaps*—to be among the most detailed sources on the topic of mind and mental factors. This is one of the main reasons that Vasubandhu's root text and Sthiramati's commentary, which appear in Part Two of this book, were chosen for translation.

A primary aim of this book is to examine the importance of Abhidharma literature, which seems to be largely unappreciated by contemporary Western Buddhist practitioners, particularly those who are drawn to any of the Tibetan Buddhist traditions. Often viewed as little more than a dry and uninspiring catalog of lists and definitions, this material is in fact a repository of the fundamental concepts and ideas that inform all of the major Buddhist philosophical schools and traditions. Great Mahāyāna figures like Nāgārjuna and Asaṅga should properly be seen as presenting a critical analysis of the early realist tendencies in Buddhist thought, rather than positing views that reject the very framework on which all Buddhist philosophical theories are constructed. On a more practical level, Abhidharma literature contains the subject matter that allows one to investigate and learn with minute precision every aspect of the three Buddhist trainings of morality, one-pointed concentration, and wisdom.

Teachers of the Lamrim tradition viewed learning at least some Abhidharma material as essential to one's spiritual practice. In his *Great Treatise on the Stages of the Path*, Je Tsongkapa makes a passing reference to Sthiramati's work when he states, "I have explained these ten mental afflictions according to the descriptions that are found in *The Compendium of Higher Learning* [i.e., Asaṅga's *Abhidharmasamuccayaḥ*], *The Levels of Spiritual*

Practice [Asaṅga's *Yogācārabhūmiḥ*], and [Sthiramati's] commentary to the *Summary of the Five Heaps*." Je Tsongkapa also quotes the early Kadampa teacher Gönbawa Wangchuk Gyeltsen (1016–1082) as saying, in part, "To learn the essential characteristics of the mental afflictions, you must listen to teachings on the Abhidharma. At a minimum, you must receive instruction on *A Summary of the Five Heaps*."

While there are several English and French translations of Vasubandhu's *Summary of the Five Heaps*, Sthiramati's commentary on this root text has not been available in English before now. It is hoped that his explanations will be a useful contribution to the body of Buddhist writings available to Western readers. For the benefit of those who read Tibetan and/or Sanskrit, the appendix contains both a critical edition of Vasubandhu's work in its Tibetan translation and a reconstruction of the original Sanskrit text.

As this book was about to go to press, I obtained a copy of *Vasubandhu's Pañcaskhandhaka*, a work published jointly by the China Tibetology Publishing House and the Austrian Academy of Sciences Press. Their critical edition of the Sanskrit to Vasubandhu's *Summary of the Five Heaps* is based on a twelfth-century manuscript that was found in the Potala Palace in Lhasa, Tibet. Although I did not have time to examine the text at length, the language of the manuscript appears to differ slightly in a few places from the version that was used for the Tibetan translations that are found in the various Tibetan Tengyur editions. Nevertheless, the differences are only minor and I did rely on it to make a number of last-minute revisions to the text that appears in the appendix. I must, therefore, readily acknowledge that my attempt to reconstruct a Sanskrit version of Vasubandhu's text was greatly improved from having had access to this publication. Any errors that remain are my own.

I would like to express my deep gratitude and appreciation to the Tsadra Foundation, which made it possible for me to prepare these two translations, along with the presentation of my views on their importance. Thanks also go to those friends who read the first draft of the manuscript and offered valuable suggestions for how it might be improved. Lastly, it would be unforgivable not to acknowledge the longstanding support of my dear wife, Bali.

Introduction

I bow with utmost respect to the feet of the Holy Lamas.
May they watch over me throughout this and all my future lives.

AT ITS HEART, Buddhism is a system of spiritual practice that teaches individuals how to transform themselves from a condition of unhappiness and confusion to progressively higher states of virtue and knowledge. Potentially, at least, it has the ability to lead them to the attainment of enlightenment itself. Indeed, the path that the Buddha revealed to his followers is understood to be the very one that he himself traversed. The challenge for those who seek to follow this path is first to learn what it consists of and then to integrate it into their lives. Put another way, study and practice are the main tools by which every Buddhist should endeavor to bring about his or her spiritual development.

When someone first turns his or her attention to Buddhism, it is usually prompted by a sense of disquiet or lack of personal fulfillment. This can stem from such factors as a realization that material prosperity and the pursuit of ordinary pleasures do not provide genuine or lasting satisfaction. From the perspective of the Dharma this kind of reaction is not only understandable, it is essential; without it we would never feel any need to escape from the bewilderment of samsaric life.

The first teaching that the Buddha made following his enlightenment was to a group of five religious ascetics just outside the ancient city of Varanasi. These individuals had been companions of the Buddha during a period before his enlightenment in which they had all engaged in severe forms of physical hardship and privation. The Blessed One began his famous discourse on the Four Noble Truths[1] by observing that a religious ascetic should avoid these two extremes: devotion to indulgence in sense pleasures and devotion to self-mortification. Clearly, the Buddha was telling these spiritual seekers that it was fruitless to engage in the kind of self-inflicted physical torment that they had been practicing.

The modern Westerner, man or woman, cannot easily identify with the austere life that is typically followed by homeless ascetics. However, not all of the Buddha's disciples were individuals who had renounced the householder's life and were embarked upon a search for spiritual salvation. In fact, the Buddha's very next convert was the young son of a wealthy merchant in Varanasi who simply woke up one night and found himself overcome by a deep sense of despair. Having set out from his home not knowing where he was headed or what he would do, he happened upon the Buddha, presumably within days of when he had turned the wheel of the Dharma for the first time. This incident is described in the Vinaya scriptures[2] and although it took place more than two thousand years ago, one can easily imagine how similar circumstances might befall any of us today. It reveals how the Blessed One dealt skillfully with a troubled youth, first calming his mind and uplifting his spirits, and then guiding him to a point where he was ready to comprehend the Four Noble Truths. At the end of the encounter, Yasha attains the status of an Arhat.[3] The passage concludes with the assertion, expressed in verse,[4] that even someone clothed in the finery of worldly society—that is, even a layperson—can and should develop virtuous qualities and follow the basic principles of a spiritual life.

From the very earliest days, Lord Buddha welcomed and gave Dharma instruction to persons who were living the ordinary life of a householder. After giving Yasha the instruction that brought about his liberation, the Blessed One accepted an invitation to receive a meal at the home of his family. While there, he gave a discourse on the Dharma to Yasha's mother and his former wife that inspired the two to become the first women to take refuge in the Three Jewels. Soon, four of Yasha's close friends and then some fifty more young men from well-to-do families in the region followed him into the Sangha, or religious community of monks.

These novices would certainly have been introduced to the Buddha's teachings in a gradual manner. Only when their understanding had developed sufficiently would they have been taught the more profound elements of instruction that are meant to bring complete liberation from any further samsaric rebirth. Here is the description from the Vinaya scriptures of how the Tathāgata instructed Yasha:

> Yasha, son of Kula Shresthi, then went to the Komitra River. At this time, the Blessed One was on the far side of the Komitra River, out in the open outside a hall, at times sitting and at other times walking about. From a distance, Yasha, son of Kula Shresthi, saw the Blessed One walking by the edge of the Komitra River, and cried out in anguish, "O ascetic, I am tormented; O ascetic, I am in distress." Then the Blessed One said to Yasha, son of Kula Shresthi, "Come here, son. This is a place where you can be freed of torment and distress."
>
> So Yasha, son of Kula Shresthi, removed his jewel slippers worth a vast sum by the bank of the Komitra River and, after crossing the river, approached the Blessed One. He bowed his head to the feet of the Blessed One and sat down nearby. The Blessed One brought Yasha, son of Kula Shresthi, to a sheltered area and, once there, the two seated themselves. After taking a seat, the Blessed One rightly taught and instructed Yasha, son of Kula Shresthi, with conversation relating to Dharma, and rightly uplifted his spirits and caused him to feel happy.
>
> The Buddhas give as their first Dharma instruction a discussion on generosity, morality, and the celestial realms. They explain at length the meager value and disadvantages of sensory pleasures, the nature of affliction and purification, renunciation, the benefits of living in solitude, and those qualities that are conducive to purification.
>
> When the Blessed One realized that Yasha had become happy in mind, virtuous in mind, satisfied in mind, that his mind was free of obstacles, that he had become pious and was able to understand the most excellent Dharma if it were taught to him, the Blessed One then taught him at length the Buddhas' most excellent teaching on the Four Noble Truths—that is, suffering, origination, cessation and the path. And just as a clean and dirt-free cloth that has been rendered suitable for dyeing is able to properly hold fast the dye, Yasha, son of Kula Shresthi, was able to realize the Four Noble Truths of suffering, origination, cessation and the path.

In Tibetan Buddhism, such a step-by-step approach underlies the teaching system known as *Lamrim*, or "Stages of the Path." The nature of this process of transformation from an ordinary secular person to a disciplined spiritual practitioner capable of pursuing liberation and even supreme enlightenment is the main topic explored in Part One of this book.

The teacher who introduced the Lamrim teaching in Tibet, Atiśa Dīpaṃkāra Śrījñāna, was born into a prosperous, royal family of East Bengal around the year 982 C.E. A lay practitioner during his early years, he received ordination as a *bhikṣu* or monk, at the age of twenty-nine. His dedication to Buddhist learning and practice led him to travel to what many believe was the island of Sumatra, where he studied for some twelve years with a teacher known popularly as Suvarṇadvīpa Guru, or Master from the Golden Isles. Lord Atiśa revered this guru more than any of his one hundred and fifty-two spiritual teachers, because it was under his tutelage that Atiśa was able to develop genuine enlightenment mind. After returning to India, he successfully defended the faith on a number of occasions in debates with followers of non-Buddhist traditions. With the growth of his reputation as an erudite and authoritative scholar, he was offered a teaching position under the royal patronage of King Mahīpāla (c. 995–1043 C.E.) at Vikramaśīla Monastery, an important center of Buddhist learning that was situated about 50 kilometers east of the present-day city of Bhagalpur in the state of Bihar.

Aspiring Tibetans scholars had been traveling to Vikramaśīla to pursue their studies for some time. It was while Lord Atiśa was in residence here that Jangchub Wö, a king from the Ngari region of western Tibet, invited him to come to Tibet to spread the Buddha's teaching. He was officially welcomed by the king at Toding Temple around the year 1037. Although he originally planned to teach only a few years and then return to India, Lord Atiśa remained in Tibet for the rest of his life, passing away in the town of Nyetang near Lhasa at the age of seventy-two in the fall of the Horse Year (1054), according to his earliest and most authoritative biography.

It was while in residence at Toding Temple that Lord Atiśa composed the sixty-eight-verse poem entitled *Lamp of the Path to Enlightenment*, which is considered the root text of the widely influential Lamrim tradition. Almost a thousand years have gone by since Lord Atiśa began teaching this instruction in Tibet. Over the centuries the tradition has not merely survived, it has thrived greatly and spawned a prodigious body of native Tibetan religious literature devoted to its propagation. Of this literature, no work has been more important than the *Great Treatise on the Stages of the Path to Enlightenment*, which was composed by the great Tibetan lama Tsongkapa Losang Drakpa (1357–1419) at the age of forty-six in the Water Horse Year (1402). The life-long spiritual activities of this illustrious figure led to the formation of the Gelukpa tradition, one of the four major schools of Tibetan Buddhism. Je Tsongkapa was already an accomplished scholar by the time that he first received several lineages of instruction on the Lamrim teachings. Nevertheless, in a letter to one of his own lamas he described why he felt this teaching system was so important:

> It is clear that this instruction [introduced] by Dīpaṃkara Śrījñāna on the stages of the path to enlightenment . . . teaches [the meanings contained in] all the canonical scriptures, their commentaries, and related instruction by combining them into a single graded path. One can see that when taught by a capable teacher and put into practice by able listeners it brings order, not just to some minor instruction, but to the entire [body of] canonical scriptures. Therefore, I have not taught a wide variety of [other] instructions.[5]

Thus, a key point to recognize about the Lamrim teaching is that at its heart it is a systematic collection of oral instructions that make use of the entire range of Buddhist literature to present a comprehensive program for spiritual transformation. In addition to copious citations from traditional Indian Buddhist literature, Je Tsongkapa's *Great Treatise* includes many pithy and insightful sayings of the early Tibetan teachers known as followers of the Kadampa School. The instructions begin with the most fundamental elements of Buddhist doctrine and then gradually introduce the student to the requisite meditation practices that will enable him or her eventually to become fully engaged in the vast and profound tradition that is Mahāyāna Buddhism.

The Translations

Two translations are presented in Part Two: Vasubandhu's *Summary of the Five Heaps* and Sthiramati's *Detailed Commentary on the Summary of the Five Heaps*. Sthiramati states in the opening portion of his commentary that the purpose of the root text is "to make known the general and specific characteristics of entities." He then offers several reasons for composing such an abbreviated treatment of this material. The one that is most relevant for the modern Western reader states: "Because householders are involved in a great many activities, they are unable to apply themselves to the study of a large work," such as Asaṅga's *Levels of Spiritual Practice*. In short, Vasubandhu's root text is an introduction to the fundamental elements of Buddhist philosophical thought, with some attention given to the unique tenets of the Mind Only School. Thus, it provides a concise overview for those who have only a limited opportunity to learn about the Abhidharma. However, it can also be seen as a starting point for those who intend to pursue a more extensive and wide-ranging study of Buddhist philosophy.

The great Indian scholar and teacher Vasubandhu is believed to have been born in the early part of the fourth century in the city that is now called Peshawar, the capital of the North-West Frontier Province in Pakistan. What little is known about his life is based mainly on differing accounts found in several Chinese and Tibetan sources.[6] One thing that can be said with confidence is that, aside from his elder brother Asaṅga, he is the most important proponent of the Buddhist Mind Only School. Tibetans refer to him as a "second Buddha" and count him as one of six "ornaments" among Indian Buddhist scholars.

Of his many writings, the *Treasury of Higher Learning* (S: *Abhidharma-kośaḥ*, T: *Chos mngon pa'i mdzod*), a work that is written in verse, along with its autocommentary have exerted a great influence on Tibetan Buddhism. Considered one of his earlier works, the root text is essentially a compendium of the Abhidharma views formulated by proponents of an early Buddhist realist tradition known as the Vaibhāṣika School. Vasubandhu's works on the Mind Only School include commentaries to three of Maitreya's Five Dharma Teachings: *The Ornament of Mahāyāna Sutras* (S: *Mahāyānasūtrālaṃkāraḥ*), *The Treatise That Distinguishes the Middle Way from Extreme Views* (S: *Madhyāntavibhāgaḥ*), and *The Treatise That Distinguishes Phenomena and Their Ultimate Nature* (S: *Dharmadharmatāvibhāgaḥ*). In addition to the *Summary of the Five Heaps* and a number of other original works, he also wrote commentaries to Asaṅga's *Summary of the Mahāyāna Tradition* (S: *Mahāyānasaṃgrahaḥ*) and to such Mahāyāna sutras as the *Diamond-cutter* (S: *Vajracchedikā*), the *Teachings of Akṣayamati* (S: *Akṣayamatinirdeśaḥ*), and the *Ten Levels* [*of an Ārya Bodhisattva*] (S: *Daśabhūmikā*).

Even less is known about the life of Sthiramati than that of Vasubandhu. The Tibetan scholars Butön Rinchen Drup and Taranatha give more or less similar accounts; however, even Butön expresses some reservations about their authenticity. Both writers cite the legend that in his previous life he was a dove who listened to Vasubandhu recite the hundred-thousand-line version of the *Perfection of Wisdom Sutra*, and indicate that he studied with the Master at an early age. Other sources identify him as having mainly been a disciple of Guṇamati. Modern scholars generally believe that he flourished in the mid-sixth century.

Tibetan tradition describes Sthiramati as having surpassed Vasubandhu in his knowledge of the Abhidharma. The Tengyur collection contains a commentary by him on Vasubandhu's *Treasury of Higher Learning.* He wrote a number of commentaries on other works by Vasubandhu, and is recognized principally for this effort. Writing in a style that is both lucid and straightforward, his subcommentaries on the *Ornament of Mahāyāna Sutras* and the *Treatise That Distinguishes the Middle Way from Extreme Views* are especially valuable resources that provide extensive explanations of Buddhist doctrine. I consider his *Detailed Commentary on the Summary of the Five Heaps* to be one of the most informative works on the topic of mind and mental factors.

It is true that the form in which the Lamrim instructions are usually taught does not rely heavily on the complex explanations that are the province of Abhidharma literature. One benefit of this fact is that the teachings are for the most part quite accessible even to the layperson with limited exposure to Buddhist philosophy. At the same time, it is also stated a number of times in Pabongka Rinpoche's *Liberation in Our Hands* that certain points are assumed to be familiar to those who have studied the "great treatises"[7] but too difficult to explain to the unschooled listener. Tibetan lamas can be heard to make similar remarks today when they are giving a teaching on the Lamrim instruction.

Perhaps the simplicity and directness of the language used in this teaching system is a reflection of the devotional aspect of the practice, which places the greatest emphasis on bringing about spiritual transformation. Commentaries typically use such expressions as "develop a mental change" (T: *yid 'gyur skye ba*) or "elicit an experiential awareness" (T: *myong ba thon pa*) to describe the immediate goal of any given meditation topic. Everyone knows that scholarship alone, untempered by such virtues as faith and humility, can easily lead to the very antithesis of spirituality. On the other hand, the discussions that follow attempt to make the case that gaining at least some knowledge of the closely reasoned explanations found in Buddhist philosophical literature has the very real potential of enabling one's spiritual endeavors to achieve a depth and strength that might not otherwise be possible.

Part One

An examination of how the subject matter contained in Vasubandhu's *Summary of the Five Heaps* can enhance one's ability to practice the Mahāyāna Buddhist instruction known as the "Stages of the Path"

Prologue

TO REACH the main Buddhist goals of liberation and supreme enlightenment, one must develop two forms of transcendent awareness: a direct realization of the insubstantiality of the person (S: *pudgalanairātmyam*, T: *gang zag gi bdag med*) and a direct realization of the insubstantiality of entities (S: *dharmanairātmyam*, T: *chos kyi bdag med*). The objects of these two forms of awareness are often referred to as "the nonexistence of a self" (S: *anātman*, T: *bdag med*) and "emptiness" (S: *śūnyatā*, T: *stong pa nyid*), respectively. Buddhist philosophy is concerned with explaining the nature of these two realizations, as well as how to attain them, because they represent the sole means of eradicating two types of obstacles, called "the obscurations of the mental afflictions" (S: *kleśāvaraṇam*, T: *nyon mongs pa'i sgrib pa*) and "the obscurations to objects of knowledge" (S: *jñeyāvaraṇam*, T: *shes bya'i sgrib pa*). The former obstacle is the principal cause of samsaric existence, and its complete removal marks the attainment of liberation or nirvana. The latter obstacle is distinct from the mental afflictions and more subtle in nature. Its essence is the indisposition of the mind that impedes one from gaining the perfect awareness of a Buddha.

In a more immediate sense, these two types of obstacles cause the samsaric being to misinterpret both the nature of his or her personal being and that of the world in which he or she lives. According to Buddhist doctrine, the mind of an ordinary person, even at birth, is nothing like a "clean slate." Deeply ingrained predispositions built up over countless past lives lead us to perceive the elements of our everyday experience wrongly and to believe, for instance, that entities persist through time, that the pleasures we pursue are genuinely satisfying, that our own personal being is governed by a real self, and that all physical and mental phenomena have a distinct, independent, and real essence. Our everyday language and ordinary society only serve to reinforce and deepen these erring notions.

A fundamental aim of the Buddhist teaching is to reveal to its followers how to reject these flawed beliefs and replace them with a model that not only is a more accurate representation of our experience but also is indispensable to the pursuit of the two just-mentioned forms of transcendent realization. The ability to accomplish this task rests largely with learning the unique vocabulary and explanations found in Abhidharma literature, since that is how we will discover what is mistaken about our untutored beliefs and where we will gain the intellectual skills that are needed to construct a new and more refined "conceptual infrastructure."

The most concise presentation of what we need to know in order to develop a proper Buddhist world-view is the doctrine of the five heaps, which makes up the principal subject matter of Vasubandhu's *Summary of the Five Heaps.* The term "heap" (S: *skandhaḥ*, T: *phung po*)—which other translators have rendered as "aggregate"—refers to the entities that make up the entire natural world in general, and especially the physical and mental constituents of our own individual existence. Lord Buddha referred to each of five categories of causally produced entities as "heaps" to indicate that they are collections of transitory phenomena occurring in a variety of forms.

The first heap, called "form" (S: *rūpam*, T: *gzugs*), includes all entities that are physical in nature. The second and third heaps—called "feeling" (S: *vedanā*, T: *tshor ba*) and "conception" (S: *saṃjñā*, T: *'du shes*), respectively—are each made up of a single mental factor, because of the great influence that they exert on beings' lives. As Vasubandhu states in his *Commentary to the Treasury of Higher Learning,* "Through the relishing of feelings, [beings] develop attachment for the sense objects and, through erring conceptions, [they develop attachment] for [mistaken] views. Therefore, these two [mental factors—i.e., feelings and conceptions] are principal causes of samsara."[8] The fourth heap, called "formations" (S: *saṃskārāḥ*, T: *'du byed rnams*), includes all the remaining mental factors that can accompany consciousness, as well as a collection of non-mental entities that are mentioned in Buddhist sutras and discussed at some length in Abhidharma literature. The fifth and final heap, called "consciousness" (S: *vijñānam*, T: *rnam par shes pa*), is made up of the various types of basic awareness, which typically are said to number six but in the Mind Only school are considered to have eight forms.

"Heap"[9] is the expression that Buddha Śākyamuni used to describe the collection of momentary physical and mental phenomena that make up the totality of a sentient being. As the often-quoted sutra passage states, "O monks, whatever ascetics or brahmins perceive a self, they all perceive nothing but these five grasping heaps."[10] Concerning the number of heaps, Sthiramati notes in the opening portion of his *Detailed Commentary on the Summary of the Five Heaps*:

> The heaps are exactly five in number, neither more nor less, because they were taught as the entities that constitute the basis for grasping an "I" and a "mine." Most immature beings grasp consciousness as an "I," and the remaining heaps as "mine."[11]

Sthiramati describes the term "grasping" in the following manner in his discussion of "egoistic pride,"[12] one of seven forms of pride mentioned in the root text:

> The term "grasping"[13] refers to aspiration and desire. Aspiration means desire for a future existence. Desire is attachment. Thus, you grasp at a future existence in the sense of having aspiration for it, and you grasp at your present heaps in the sense that your desire for them makes you not want to give them up. Therefore, these two attitudes are called "grasping." The heaps that are associated with them are the grasping heaps.

And, as part of the discussion on the root mental affliction of desire, Sthiramati observes:

> Craving is referred to as "grasping" either because it causes a being to take birth in [any of] the three levels of [samsaric] existence or because it takes hold of the karma that brings rebirth.[14]

In the same section, he also presents a description that is an abridgement of a passage from the first chapter of Vasubandhu's *Commentary to the Treasury of Higher Learning*:

> The term "grasping heaps" is interpreted as meaning either that the impure heaps originate from grasping, or that they are governed by grasping, or that grasping arises from them.[15]

In short, the Tathāgata taught the doctrine of the five heaps both to describe how we should correctly understand the momentary phenomena that make up our ordinary experience and as the foundation for explaining how a deluded person wrongly believes that his or her existence is governed by a real personal self. Sthiramati discusses the mistaken belief in a real self at some length in relation to the root mental affliction known by the technical term "perishable collection view" (S: *satkāyadṛṣṭiḥ*, T: *'jig tshogs la lta ba*).

The form of transcendent awareness referred to above as "the realization of the insubstantiality of the person" is the antithesis of, and the ultimate antidote for, the perishable collection view. What both states of mind have in common is that they are largely defined in terms of the five heaps. For instance, the perishable collection view variously takes some aspect of the five heaps, individually or collectively, as constituting a real self, being an attribute of such a real self, or possessing some real relation with such a self. By contrast, the realization of the insubstantiality of the person is gained by establishing that no such self actually exists. Classic Buddhist arguments assert that if the self were real, it would either have to be identical with some element of the five heaps or entirely distinct from them. By refuting both possibilities, we can conclude that the self is merely a nominal entity whose existence is dependently ascribed in relation to the five heaps. However, before we can comprehend these arguments properly, we must develop an adequate grasp of how the five heaps are meant to be understood.

How Knowledge of the Five Heaps Can Enhance One's Spiritual Practice

In *The Lamp of the Path to Enlightenment*, Lord Atiśa presents the Lamrim teachings within the framework of three types of practitioner, called lesser, middling, and supreme. The main characteristics of each of these types are described in Chapter One, while subsequent chapters focus on elements of the *Lamrim* instruction that relate to each of these three types of practitioner. The focus of Part One is to identify three kinds of "correct view" that are intimately linked with the three groups of instruction, and to examine the areas of Buddhist doctrine that must be pursued in order to establish the justification for these three valid forms of knowledge. The scriptural basis for this approach is a passage from a work by the Indian scholar Kamalaśīla that is cited in Chapter One. The three forms of knowledge identified in this passage represent the means of overcoming three main types of error that are the underlying cause of all the torment and suffering that beings repeatedly undergo from one lifetime to the next. These errors are (1) a lack of understanding regarding karma and its results; (2) the belief in a real, personal self; and (3) the belief that the objects of ordinary experience possess self-existent or real, independent essences.

The central form of knowledge for practitioners of lesser capacity is referred to as the "worldly correct view." Described as the belief that regards the relationship between karma and its results correctly, this attitude is both the foundation of Buddhist morality and the main practice that enables one to achieve the temporary goal of a favorable rebirth.

The principal theme of Chapter Two is that a Buddhist practitioner's faith will remain at risk unless he or she examines the justification for believing in the existence of past and future lives, the hell realms and beings described as "hungry ghosts," as well as the Buddha's teachings on karma. However, we cannot understand fully the arguments that Buddhist scholars have put forth in support of these doctrines without first learning about the five heaps and the Four Noble Truths. This point is investigated at length in relation to the classic Buddhist proof that a Buddha's statements about the nature and workings of karma are authoritative and trustworthy.

Chapter Three examines two topics that are associated with practitioners of middling capacity: (1) the requirements for developing genuine "renunciation," which is defined as the mind that seeks to achieve liberation, and (2) the practice of the "four closely placed recollections," which serves to counteract four erroneous beliefs and bring about an experiential awareness of the Four Noble Truths. The knowledge that is central to both of these topics is the form of "transcendent correct view" that realizes the insubstantiality of the person.

The four erroneous beliefs are deeply ingrained predispositions that cause ordinary beings to mistakenly regard (1) what is impure as pure, (2) what is impermanent as permanent, (3) what is unsatisfactory [i.e., suffering] as a state of well being, and (4) what is not a real self as constituting a real self. The object of all of these beliefs is the same: the five "grasping"—that is, samsaric—heaps. These mistaken judgments are largely responsible for perpetuating our attachment to samsaric existence. However, for us to simply acknowledge that our assumptions about the nature of ordinary experience are flawed does little to alter them; to overcome these mistaken beliefs we must cultivate a rigorous and systematic program of mental training. Using the subject matter and terminology that relate to the doctrine of the five heaps, this training is explored in relation to the practice known as "the four closely placed recollections."

Chapter Four examines how an understanding of the five heaps and the Four Noble Truths is essential to developing the two central Mahāyāna attitudes of *bodhicitta*, or "enlightenment mind," and the wisdom that realizes the insubstantiality of entities, or "emptiness." While the preceding chapter explains that one must understand the five heaps to undertake an in-depth study of the Four Noble Truths, and that both topics are necessary to develop genuine renunciation, this final chapter of Part One considers how the practitioner who has only a limited understanding of these two topics will also be unable to develop the great compassion that is the root of a Bodhisattva's enlightenment mind. The wisdom that realizes emptiness represents the third form of essential knowledge identified by Kamalaśīla, and in Mahāyāna Buddhism it is also recognized as a second type of "transcendent correct view."

With regard to gaining a realization of emptiness, several passages from the writings of Nāgārjuna and Candrakīrti are cited to show that this topic is taught by relying upon the doctrine of two truths, often described as "conventional truth" and "ultimate truth." Conventional truth refers to the entities that make up our ordinary experience. As already noted, a correct understanding of this subject is gained by learning about the five heaps. Ultimate truth is a synonym for emptiness. Since the nature of emptiness is established through applying a critical analysis to such conventional-truth entities as the five heaps, a clear understanding of the latter topic is indispensable to any attempt at gaining a realization of ultimate truth.

Part One ends with a summary of two specific forms of Mahāyāna practice. The first is an aspect of the Perfection of Wisdom—or *prajñāpāramitā*—that is called the "knowledge of entities." The discussion examines how an understanding of the five heaps can contribute to one's ability to develop all three of the spiritual attitudes of renunciation, enlightenment mind, and a realization of emptiness. The final topic addresses how the Mahāyāna practice of the four closely placed recollections differs from the way it is taught in the Listeners' Vehicle.

At its heart, Buddhism is a religious tradition that emphasizes practice and training as the means of bringing about the spiritual transformation that leads to genuine happiness. However, the ability to carry out the practice requires that we receive instruction on how to do so from a qualified teacher. This instruction is especially crucial for the novice. With it, we can begin to recognize the forms of error and afflictive emotions that not only are the source of all our misfortune but also are the formidable obstacles that severely impede all our attempts to cultivate the path and achieve the spiritual goals. Therefore, the immediate power of proper instruction is the knowledge that it gives us to hold in check the coarsest forms of the nonvirtuous attitudes. This, in turn, greatly enhances our efforts to put the Buddha's holy teachings into practice effectively. This is the spirit with which I have sought to clarify the value of learning the subject matter contained in Ācārya Vasubandhu's short treatise and the commentary on it by the illustrious scholar Sthiramati.

The Lamrim Teaching and Its Three Essential Forms of Knowledge 1

AN OVERVIEW OF THE LAMRIM TRADITION

THE VARIOUS lineages of Tibetan Buddhist teachings provide numerous examples of distinct bodies of instruction that have been developed and preserved since the time of the Buddha. They are clear, precise, and most important of all, provide the means of bringing about a radical and profound transformation in a person's psyche when put into practice correctly. At the same time, it is incumbent upon all spiritual seekers to carefully investigate a particular teaching before deciding to follow it. Concerning this issue, the Gelukpa lama Pabongka Rinpoche makes the following remarks:

> There are several points you should initially make sure of when considering a Dharma teaching to practice. First, it should be a Dharma taught by the Buddha. Second, it should be one whose meaning has been explained with exactness by scholarly pandits. Finally, the great and accomplished spiritual masters should have achieved realizations of its meaning through meditation. Otherwise, however long we meditate on some other supposedly profound instruction, which was neither spoken by the Buddha nor understood by any pandits or adepts, the only result we are likely to achieve is one that no Buddha or any other accomplished practitioner ever attained.[16]
>
> Thus, before undertaking to practice any Dharma teaching, we must first make a general investigation. As Lord Sakya Pandita[17] said:
>
> > When [worldly persons] buy and sell
> > Common things like a horse or jewels,

> They question everyone and examine [the items] closely.
> We can observe these efforts being made
> In the petty affairs of this life.
> Yet, though the happiness of all our future lives
> Depends on the Holy Dharma,
> [The foolish] act like dogs with food.
> Without examining its merits in any way,
> They revere whatever they happen to find.[18]

> When buying and selling horses, for instance, we customarily make a thorough investigation, seeking the advice of a lama and inquiring of many other people, as well. Or take a humble monk who is considering buying some tea. He will repeatedly examine its color, weight, and shape, carefully scrutinize whether it has been damaged by water, and ask others what they might know. But even if he makes a mistake, the worst that can happen is he will lose the price of several cups of tea.
>
> We often see this sort of detailed investigation in matters of temporary concern. But when it comes to the basis for attaining the ultimate goal of all our lives—the Dharma we intend to practice—seldom is any kind of examination carried out. Like a dog with food, we are satisfied with whatever we happen to find. This is a terrible mistake; for to be wrong about the Dharma means to be wrong about the ultimate aim for all our lives.[19]

The role of the spiritual teacher in perpetuating the instruction cannot be overemphasized. The lamas and teachers who disseminate the instruction today are part of an unbroken lineage that goes back literally to the time of the Buddha. For example, in the opening pages of his *Great Treatise on the Stages Path to Enlightenment*, Je Tsongkapa singles out two figures in particular:

> In a broad sense, this [Lamrim] instruction represents the instruction contained in the *Ornament of Realizations*,[20] which was taught by the Supreme Lord Maitreya. More specifically, the [main] treatise upon which this [text] is based is the *Lamp of the Path to Enlightenment;* therefore, [in a sense] the creator of that [work] should also be recognized as the creator of this one.[21]

The reference to Maitreya's work is meant to indicate that the Lamrim teaching is heavily influenced by the Indian commentarial tradition associated with that treatise. In describing Lord Atiśa as the principal author who inspired his own work, Je Tsongkapa is of course paying tribute to the essential role that this figure played in bringing the teaching system to Tibet. In addition, Je Tsongkapa composed an important supplication prayer that identifies all the lineage lamas of the Lamrim reaching as far as his own direct teachers.[22] *Liberation in Our Hands* also states:

> However, this teaching—the Stages of the Path to Enlightenment—is the creation of neither the great Je Rinpoche nor Lord Atiśa. It has come down to us through a lineage originating with the fully enlightened Buddha himself. Once you have an understanding of this teaching, you will recognize all the scriptures as instructions on the stages of the path, whether or not the phrase "stages of the path" appears in their title.[23]

While Atiśa's biography[24] reports that he was a holder of a great many different Sutra and Tantra teaching lineages, the two principal ones that relate to the Lamrim instruction are known as the Lineage of Extensive Activities[25] and the Lineage of the Profound View.[26] The former is described as originating with the current Buddha's successor, the supreme Bodhisattva Maitreya, who first transmitted teachings to Asaṅga. Among the most important texts that relate to this lineage are the five Maitreya Teachings[27] and Asaṅga's Five Sections on Levels.[28] The Lineage of the Profound View originated with the Bodhisattva Mañjuśrī, who transmitted it to Nāgārjuna, the founder of the Mādhyamika School. The major texts of this lineage are Nāgārjuna's Six Works on Reasoning[29] and the writings of Candrakīrti. Another figure whose two principal works—*Engaging in Bodhisattva Activities*[30] and *Compendium of Training*[31]—are essential sources of instruction for the Lamrim teachings is the eighth-century Indian teacher Śāntideva. Although not formally listed among the Indian teachers who make up the two main Lamrim lineages, he is a major figure within a third lineage, called the Lineage of Powerful Activities,[32] which is largely associated with the Lojong or Mind Training tradition.

The followers of Atiśa in Tibet before the time of Je Tsongkapa were known as the Kadampas,[33] a term that literally means these disciples regarded all forms of the Buddha's speech as spiritual instruction. Je

Tsongkapa received the Lamrim instruction of three separate Kadampa lineages from two of his own spiritual teachers. Since then, the tradition of his followers—known as the Gelukpa[34] School—has produced a vast body of literature devoted to the Lamrim teachings. In modern times, eight works are viewed as representing the most important writings of this genre and are referred to as the Eight Great Lamrim Manuals.[35]

While the term *Lamrim* is familiar to Western Buddhists and many individuals have listened to teachings on this subject at one time or another, relatively few have tried to put the instruction into practice. Nor is this true only of Western Buddhists. In addressing an audience made up almost exclusively of ordained Tibetan monks and nuns, including many lamas and geshes, Kyabje Pabongka Rinpoche made the following observation:

> We regard having to actually meditate on the Lamrim teachings as almost more terrifying than death itself. Most of us would rather spend our lives reading scriptures, studying Buddhist philosophy, or reciting prayers. But this attitude stems from a lack of understanding about the most crucial elements of the Dharma.[36]

The Lamrim is described as containing the teachings that are "common" to both the Sutra and Tantra forms of Mahāyāna Buddhism. For example, one frequently hears it said in the Gelukpa tradition that a prospective Tantric practitioner must be someone who has become "trained in [the practices that relate to] the common path."[37] This means that a certain level of proficiency in the Lamrim tradition is necessary before one is qualified to undertake the Mantrayāna practice. However, it would be wrong to conclude that the Lamrim instructions are something only to be practiced until one is allowed to enter the Tantric Vehicle. These instructions are the essence of the complete body of teachings contained in the Vehicle of the Perfections.[38] Since they represent the path that all the Buddhas of the three times complete in order to attain supreme enlightenment, they are not something to be pursued only for a limited period and then put aside. Indeed, the teaching system that Je Tsongkapa formulated is also known as one that "unites [the practices of] Sutra and Tantra."[39] Therefore, the Lamrim instruction should rightly be perceived as a form of spiritual training that needs to be practiced continually, even after entering the Mantrayāna, if one hopes to attain the special qualities that are unique to that tradition. As Pabongka Rinpoche notes:

> Even the profound aspects of the secret Mantrayāna depend on the Lamrim teaching, for the power of the mantra path to grant us Buddhahood within a single lifetime cannot be realized without first generating knowledge of the three principal elements of the path.[40]

In all three of Je Tsongkapa's Lamrim works that were referenced earlier, the Lamrim practitioner is said to benefit from the teaching's four qualities of greatness.[41] He or she will (1) realize that all the Buddha's teachings are free of contradiction; (2) recognize all the scriptures as personal instruction; (3) easily comprehend the Conqueror's underlying thought; and (4) spontaneously terminate great misdeeds.

The first of these qualities means that the Lamrim teaching will enable us to realize that all the Buddha's teachings—both those of the three Sūtrayāna traditions and those of the four divisions of Tantrayāna—represent elements of one and the same path to enlightenment. Because of this, a Mahayanist should understand that he or she must also learn the teachings of the so-called Lesser Vehicle[42] because they include the fundamental Buddhist teachings that prepare one to undertake the practices that are unique to the Mahāyāna. We will return to this point again later on, in the context of considering how this relates specifically to the subject matter contained in Vasubandhu's *Summary of the Five Heaps*. A Mahayanist must also learn the teachings of the Listeners' Vehicle in order to be able to benefit others, since a Bodhisattva must be prepared to teach others whatever Dharma instruction is most suitable for them, and certain individuals may not yet have developed the capacity to pursue the ultimate goal of Buddhahood. Furthermore, it is wrong to believe that there is any conflict between the Sūtrayāna and the Tantrayāna teachings, since it is frequently mentioned in tantric scriptures that enlightenment mind[43] and the six perfections are never to be abandoned, and the tantric vows specifically require that the practitioner must uphold all forms of the Holy Dharma, which is described as including the "outer" and "secret" teachings as well as those of the three vehicles.[44]

Je Tsongkapa begins his explanation of the second quality of greatness by observing that there is no greater personal instruction than the word of the Buddha. Next, he notes that the commentaries of such great Buddhist scholars as Nāgārjuna, Asaṅga, and their principal disciples represent the best means of gaining insight into the meaning of the Buddha's word.

Finally, he identifies the role of the Lamrim instruction as that of collecting all the essential points contained in the Sutras and their commentaries, and presenting them to the practitioner in a graduated and systematic manner. One result of learning and meditating on this well-ordered body of instruction is that the practitioner will come to recognize all the Sutras and their commentaries as personal instruction. This means that the words of virtually any scripture will be understood in such a way that they seem to speak to the reader directly and in a very personal manner. This type of awareness has an aesthetic quality that is deeply moving and represents a sign of spiritual progress. The present study seeks to clarify several of the main factors that are essential to this process.

Kyabje Pabongka Rinpoche explains the nature of this greatness as follows:

> Neljorpa Jangchup Rinchen[45] declared, "To gain realization of the instruction does not mean simply to comprehend the meaning of some small manual that fits in the palm of the hand. It means to understand all the scriptures as instruction."[46] This statement should be understood according to the above explanations; indeed, it is regarded as the source that inspired them.
>
> What, then, does it take to gain this recognition of all the scriptures as instruction? Though you might think it will do merely to have listened to the Lamrim teachings, here is what is actually required.
>
> We must comprehend how the subject matter of all the scriptures and their commentaries can be subsumed within this teaching on the stages of the path—which begins with the correct method of serving a spiritual teacher and ends with quiescence and insight. And regardless of the detail in which the individual topics are explained, we must have a thorough grasp of the full body of instruction in the sense that we know how to put [all the elements of] it into practice. Specifically, this means we must know how to apply analytic meditation to the topics requiring that method of practice and how to apply stabilizing meditation to the topics requiring that method.[47] Once this level of understanding is reached, we can readily associate any scripture we might examine with the appropriate meditation topic in our practice. This represents the true measure of being able to recognize all the scriptures as personal instruction.[48]

The third greatness asserts that the Lamrim instruction is particularly appropriate for beginning practitioners because it greatly facilitates the process of learning the deeper meanings of the great Sutras and their commentaries. The fourth greatness emphasizes the point that a relatively untrained practitioner runs the risk of dismissing those Buddhist teachings that he or she may mistakenly perceive as unimportant. Such an attitude is identified as resulting in the serious misdeed of rejecting the Dharma. Because a proper understanding of the Lamrim instruction reverses this tendency, it automatically puts an end to this misdeed.

To achieve these four greatnesses it is first necessary to hear the instruction. This means that the Lamrim should be learned under the tutelage of a qualified teacher and not merely by trying to read English translations of the instruction on one's own. Indeed, the most effective way to learn the Buddhist teachings is through direct and personal contact with a spiritual teacher. This is why Je Tsongkapa begins his *Great Treatise on the Stages of the Path* with the topic of how to cultivate a proper relationship with a spiritual teacher. In the opening portion of this discussion, the following remark by the Kadampa Geshe Potowa Rinchen Sel[49] is cited:

> Nothing is more important than a lama for the pursuit of liberation. If it is essential to have a teacher even for the activities of this life that can be learned by direct observation,[50] how could it be possible for someone who has just come from the lower realms to travel to a place he has never been before without a lama?[51]

In introducing the Lamrim instruction in this way, Je Tsongkapa was following the approach taken by Drolungpa Lodrö Jung-ne in his *Great Treatise on the Stages of the Teaching*,[52] an extensive and detailed work that served as an important source for much of the instruction contained in Je Tsongkapa's own *Great Treatise*. This was not, however, the only method that Lamrim teachers adopted for introducing the instruction. Historical accounts indicate that Kadampa teachers also began the instruction with such topics as (1) the practices for a "middling" person,[53] (2) the varieties of spiritual lineage,[54] (3) the process by which samsara is set in motion and brought to an end,[55] (4) recollection of the Buddha,[56] (5) the difficulty of finding a rebirth possessing leisure and fortune,[57] and (6) the twelve limbs of dependent origination.[58]

Before addressing the instruction itself, however, we need to consider the attitude that a student should maintain when seeking to learn the instruction. Unquestionably, Buddhism is a spiritual tradition that is meant to be put into practice. Anyone who limits his or her efforts to listening to a teacher's oral instruction or to reading Buddhist scriptures will certainly fail to appreciate or experience its true purpose and value. Consider this verse from the *Collection of Uplifting Sayings*:

> Though he recites well-reasoned words extensively,
> The heedless man will fail to put them into practice.
> Like a herdsman who keeps count of others' cattle,
> He gains no share of the spiritual life's true worth.[59]

At the same time, it is equally important and necessary to learn an instruction sufficiently well before attempting to put it into practice. As a well-known Tibetan proverb states:

> A person without learning [who tries to be] a great meditator
> Is like a man without hands [who tries to] climb a rocky cliff.[60]

The amount of learning that an individual needs and the length of time it must be pursued cannot be quantified in a categorical manner. The central concern, however, is that we must acquire a clear and complete understanding not only of the substance of an instruction but also of the correct method of putting it into practice. Otherwise, we may well set out to meditate on the instruction only to reach a point where we no longer know how to proceed. Generally speaking, the more extensive our learning, the more effectively we will be able to reflect on the various topics. And the more extensively we reflect on each topic, the more easily we will be able to develop genuine experiential realizations of their meaning. Though the process of learning the instruction represents only a preparatory stage, it is crucially important to get this right, since everything that follows will depend upon it. Needless to say, the importance of receiving sufficient instruction also reflects on the equally important issue of finding the ideal spiritual teacher, as well as the necessity for there to exist a favorable environment in which the process of learning can occur.

The Buddhist term for learning is literally "listening"[61] and is included among seven spiritual riches.[62] As Nāgārjuna stated in his *Letter to a Friend:*

> The Muni taught that faith, morality,
> Untainted learning, generosity, shame,

Abashment, and wisdom are the seven riches.
View other riches as secondary and meaningless.[63]

It is especially important for the Mahāyāna practitioner not to regard learning as an activity that needs to be pursued for only a relatively short period of time and then can be discontinued. The Perfection of Wisdom Sutras describe a series of purifying acts[64] that must be cultivated on each of the ten Ārya Bodhisattva stages. Among the five associated with the third Bodhisattva stage, the first one is to maintain an insatiable desire for extensive learning.[65] This quality is also described in the following passage from the *Sutra on the Ten Levels:*

> Disillusioned in this way by the nature of all conditioned things, with careful regard toward all sentient beings, recognizing the beneficial qualities of omniscience, relying on the knowledge of the Tathāgatas, and intent upon saving all sentient beings, [the third stage Bodhisattva] reflects in the following way: "By what means might it be possible to raise up these beings who have fallen into such a state of extensive suffering and affliction, and then place them in the perfect bliss of nirvana and enable them to achieve freedom from doubt concerning all things?"
>
> Then the following thoughts occur to the Bodhisattva: "This can only be found in the state of unobstructed knowledge and liberation. And this state of unobstructed knowledge and liberation can only be found in the realization of all entities as they truly are. The realization of all entities as they truly are can only be found in the wisdom that experiences nothing as coming forth or arising [as a real entity]. The vision present in that wisdom can only be found in the determinations that are gained through applying discerning analysis during skillful meditative practice. The determinations reached by applying discerning analysis during skillful meditative practice can only be found through exercising skillfulness in learning."
>
> With the understanding gained by such reflection, he [or she] becomes increasingly more diligent about seeking the Holy Dharma. Day and night he [or she] is intent upon hearing the Dharma. Because of this quest for the Buddha's Teaching, his [or her] desire for Dharma is unceasing and unquenchable. He [or she] delights in the Dharma and is devoted to the Dharma, he [or she]

> relies upon the Dharma as a refuge, he [or she] is dedicated to the Dharma, he [or she] is strongly disposed toward the Dharma, he [or she] has a deep propensity for the Dharma, he [or she] is wholly engaged in the Dharma, he [or she] adheres to the Dharma, the Dharma is his [or her] protection, and he [or she] practices the successive Dharma-knowledge.
>
> While he [or she] is thus dedicated to his [or her] quest for the Buddha Dharma, there is no manner of object, storehouse of grain, or repository of wealth—whether of gold, silver, gem, pearl, diamond, cat's eye, conch shell, camphor, coral, beautiful ivory figures—or even all of his [or her] very own limbs and appendages that he [or she] would not give away because of his [or her] desire for Dharma. Nor does he [or she] regard these as difficult acts; he [or she] only regards it as difficult to find a Dharma teacher who will teach him [or her] a single Dharma statement.[66]

The ultimate purpose of pursuing spiritual learning is to enable one to engage in a systematic program of contemplative practice. By failing to put the teachings into practice, one risks falling victim to a fault described as becoming "hardened to the Dharma."[67] This expression refers to a condition in which the mind of an individual with some literary knowledge of the teaching becomes callous and insensitive to the Dharma because he or she did not put that knowledge into practice. The following passage from *Liberation in Our Hands* explains this fault:

> Some listen to the Dharma extensively but fail to practice it. Others devote their efforts only to the words of the Dharma and try to accumulate as many different teachings as possible. However, as the *Sutra Encouraging a Superior Attitude* declares, they are like a person who wants to experience the inner sweetness of sugarcane but who, because of his [or her] attachment to its skin, eats only that:
>
> The skin of sugarcane has no taste at all;
> That most delightful essence lies within.
> By eating the skin one cannot obtain
> The sugarcane's excellent taste.
> As is the skin, just so is speech.
> As is the essence, just so is meaningful reflection.[68]

The same sutra also compares such persons to an actor who only imitates the deeds of others:

> Like an actor who stands in the middle of a theater
> Proclaiming the virtues of heroes other than himself,
> One's own practice will become inferior.
> These are the faults of delighting in speech.[69]

Because of this, we must devote ourselves to practicing Dharma and not merely to hearing it. Otherwise, our efforts may only serve to make us insensitive to the Dharma. There is a saying, "Frequent listening with infrequent meditating can cause you to become hardened to the Dharma."[70] When we first listen to Dharma, it seems to benefit our mind somewhat. But if we don't follow up our listening with continued reflection and meditation, when we listen to Dharma again this positive effect will become weaker and weaker. Eventually, no matter how profound the instruction, we come to think that we already know everything we hear and, as a result, listening to Dharma brings us no mental benefit at all. When that happens, we have become hardened to Dharma and reached a most reprehensible state.[71]

In the Gelukpa tradition, the antidote for the fault of becoming hardened to Dharma is "analytic meditation."[72] Je Tsongkapa considered this a crucial form of practice and discusses it repeatedly at various points throughout his *Great Treatise*. Kyabje Pabongka Rinpoche composed a poem that explains how to cultivate this practice in relation to a series of earlier Lamrim topics. The following excerpt appears at the beginning of Kyabje Pabongka Rinpoche's poem:

> When we are proud of our wide learning, our efforts at teaching and studying,
> And we are even sure that we could explain a hundred scriptures,
> Though our minds have not improved the least bit spiritually,
> It is because we lack the analytic meditation that combines understanding with experience.
>
> A mere semblance of listening, study, and understanding can generate
> Both strong faith and listening wisdom[73] about the topics of leisure

and fortune,
Impermanence, aversion,[74] and so on; but they have not arisen through analytic meditation.
Such wisdom is nothing more than right belief,[75] and so eventually it fades away.

You run a risk by failing to generate soon after this wisdom
The genuine experience that comes from reflection.
Many persons become insensitive to Dharma when they allow
The former awareness to fade away before they can generate the latter.[76]

Once overcome by insensitivity to Dharma, your mind stream
Becomes ruined and you are incapable of being tamed,
Even by the Lamrim or the blessed words of your lama.
So apply yourself to the profound method for avoiding insensitivity to Dharma.

That's achieved through combining the blessings of your guru's speech
With your own efforts to listen to Dharma properly.
But it's vital as well that any understanding gained through hearing Dharma
Be followed soon after by development of the understanding gained through reflection.

How, then, do you generate the understanding that comes from reflection?
Analytic meditation is the exercise of eliciting experiential realizations
By contemplating a particular meditation topic from every standpoint
And in every way, using scriptural citations and sharp reasoning.[77]

The Lamrim instruction is organized into three major divisions associated with three types of practitioner, which are referred to as "lesser," "intermediate," and "great" persons.[78] The great Lord Atiśa Dīpaṃkara Śrījñāna describes them in his *Lamp of the Path to Enlightenment*, a work that is regarded as the root text of the Lamrim tradition:

There are three persons that should be known:
The lesser, the middling, and the supreme.

These types can be explained
By revealing their main attributes.

Whoever, by various means,
Seeks only to gain the happiness
Of samsara for himself
Is known as a lesser person.

Having turned away from samsara's happiness
With a nature that avoids evil deeds,
One who seeks peace only for himself
Is called a middling person.

A supreme person is one who,
Through his own suffering,
Dearly wants to end completely
All the suffering of others.[79]

THE THREE ESSENTIAL FORMS OF KNOWLEDGE

A series of meditation topics is associated with each of the three types of Lamrim practitioner. Traditionally, these three types of "person" are defined in terms of the principal motivation that guides their particular form of practice. The lesser person seeks to gain the temporary happiness of escaping rebirth in the lower states. The middling person is dedicated to achieving the peace that comes with permanent liberation from all samsaric suffering. The supreme person is someone who pursues the Māhayāna ideal of attaining the complete enlightenment of a Buddha in order to lead all other beings to that same ultimate state of supreme happiness. For each level of motivation, there is a particular type of knowledge or right view that a Lamrim practitioner must develop in order to be able to cultivate the complete range of meditation topics with deep and unwavering conviction. These three forms of knowledge are mentioned in the following passage from Kamalaśīla's *Explanation of the Difficult Points in the Compendium of Views on the Nature of Reality*:

> That is, the attainment of a high station and the ultimate good are said to be what benefits mankind. And the cause of these two is

> the absence of error, since all the mental afflictions are rooted in error and the benefit of the world depends upon the reversal of the mental afflictions. Therefore, the reversal of the cause of the mental afflictions stands as the cause that brings about the benefit of the world. Moreover, the absence of error refers to the belief that regards the relationship between karma and its results correctly, as well as an unerring realization of the insubstantiality of the person and [an unerring realization of the insubstantiality] of entities.[80]

By clarifying a number of terms that appear in this passage, its larger implications can be more fully understood. To take them in the order that they occur: While the original Sanskrit for the expression "high station"[81] has a range of meanings, its use here is intended to indicate rebirth as a human being or a samsaric god. Such a rebirth is commonly referred to by an expression that means literally "happy state"[82] and is often rendered in English as "rebirth in the higher realms." This is to be contrasted with rebirth in the "lower realms"[83] or "unhappy states"[84]—meaning those of a denizen of one of the hell regions, a hungry ghost, or an animal. In short, the term "high station" represents a temporary goal of Buddhist practice, which is to avoid being reborn in the lower states in one's future lives. This is what Atiśa meant when he described a lesser person as someone who "seeks only to gain the happiness of samsara for himself."

The term "ultimate good"[85] refers both to the Hīnayāna goal of complete liberation from samsara and to the Mahāyāna goal of perfect enlightenment or Buddhahood. Liberation from samsara represents the aim of the middling practitioner who, as Atiśa writes, "seeks peace (i.e., Hīnayāna nirvana) only for himself," while the complete enlightenment of Buddhahood is the goal of the supreme practitioner. Both of these goals are ultimate in the sense that they are not subject to reversal. That is, once the liberation of Hīnayāna nirvana is attained, one can never again be subject to samsaric rebirth. Similarly, the ultimate enlightenment of Buddhahood constitutes the permanent removal of not only the mental afflictions, but the more subtle obstructions to objects of knowledge[86] as well. These three goals—one temporary and two ultimate—are what Kamalaśīla describes as "the benefit of mankind."[87]

Kamalaśīla's next point is that the main cause for achieving these goals is the "absence of error." The term "error"[88] refers mainly to a kind of judgment that wrongly ascribes some quality or nature to its object that that object doesn't possess. Buddhist literature often identifies four main forms: (1) the error that regards what is impure as pure, (2) the error that regards what is impermanent as permanent, (3) the error that regards what is unsatisfactory (i.e., suffering) as a state of well-being, and (4) the error that regards what is not a [real] self as constituting a [real] self. *The Treasury of Higher Learning* identifies three necessary conditions that apply to these mistaken beliefs: they conceive of their object in a completely erroneous manner[89]; they involve the forming of a judgment[90] about their object; and they falsely attribute[91] to their object some quality or nature that it does not possess.

Kamalaśīla further notes that the mental afflictions are "rooted" in these forms of error, which is to say that the mental afflictions arise from them. Of the ten mental afflictions, five are views and five are not. The five that are not views are desire, hatred, ignorance, pride, and doubt. The five views are the perishable collection view, the view that grasps an extreme, wrong view, the consideration that views are supreme, and the consideration that morality and asceticism are supreme.[92] As Vasubandhu explains in *The Treasury of Higher Learning*, the four erroneous beliefs can be identified as forms of three of the five views. More specifically, two of the four errors—the error that regards what is impure as pure and the error that regards what is unsatisfactory as a state of well-being—are forms of the consideration that views are supreme.[93] The error that regards what is impermanent as permanent is a form of the view that grasps an extreme—in particular, the extreme that regards the self as existing eternally.[94] The error that regards what is not a real self as constituting a real self is a form of the perishable collection view.[95]

How, then, are we to understand the phrase that "all the mental afflictions are rooted in error"? It is a common tenet of all Buddhist philosophical schools, regardless of whether they belong to the Hīnayāna or Mahāyāna traditions, that the main source of all the mental afflictions is the perishable collection view. For instance, Candrakīrti writes in his *Introduction to the Middle Way*:

> Seeing with his mind that all mental afflictions and adversities
> Without remainder originate from the perishable collection view,
> And having realized that the self is the object of that [view],
> The yogi must undertake to refute the self.[96]

The renowned Buddhist epistemologist Dharmakīrti expresses the same idea in his *Extensive Treatise on Knowledge:*

The notion of "other" occurs when that of a self exists.
From the conception of self and other, attachment and hatred arise.
Those who are bound by these two [mental afflictions],
Give rise to all the [other mental] faults.[97]

Thus, all the mental afflictions are ultimately generated on the basis of the error that regards what is not a real self as constituting a real self. The specific antidote for this erroneous belief is "the unerring realization of the insubstantiality of the person,"[98] one of the three forms of "absence of error" or correct view that Kamalaśīla mentions in the above passage. This realization is the most important element of the last of the Four Noble Truths, the Truth of the Path. It is the main practice that is cultivated by the person of middling capacity, since it has the power to destroy all the seeds of all the mental afflictions and that is what enables one to achieve the peace of Hīnayāna nirvana.

A second form of unerring view that Kamalaśīla mentions is "the belief that regards the relationship between karma and its results correctly,"[99] which is also known as the "worldly correct view."[100] This understanding is the foundation of the spiritual practice that is cultivated by a person of lesser capacity. It represents the awareness that enables one to achieve the temporary goal of a "high station." Nāgārjuna makes reference both to the worldly correct view and to the transcendent correct view[101] in his *Letter to a Friend:*

If you desire the higher states and liberation,
You must cultivate right view.[102]

The Sakya Lama Rendawa Shönu Lodrö[103] explains these lines as follows:

The right view that is meant here is of two types; one has relative truth as its object and the other has ultimate truth as its object. The first is the belief that there is a connection between deeds and their future results. The second is the wisdom that realizes the emptiness that is the true nature of entities. The first right view is the cause for attaining the higher states; the second is the cause for attaining liberation. Therefore, if you desire the temporary happiness of rebirth in the higher states[104] and the ultimate happiness of liberation, you must continually meditate upon the two forms of right view that

> were just mentioned—the one that has relative truth as its object and the one that has ultimate truth as its object.[105]

Kyabje Pabongka Rinpoche also makes the following remarks about the worldly correct view in *Liberation in Our Hands*:

> Therefore, the first thing to do when practicing meditation is to correct one's motivation; the first topic of the Lamrim teachings is leisure and fortune; and the first element of Dharma practice is to observe the principles of karma and its results. The last of these [three] is also called the worldly correct view. The term "worldly" here refers to an ordinary person,[106] meaning that for ordinary persons this is the most important view.
>
> Nowadays, many persons show great interest in the transcendent correct view. But for beginning practitioners it is more important to develop faith in the principles of karma, and then to correctly pursue a course of performing right actions and abandoning wrong ones. There are some who believe they are being mindful of the Dharma when they spend all their time mumbling prayers. Others try to develop mental equipoise by pretending to meditate on an understanding of emptiness. But these persons are merely showing that they don't know what it means to practice Dharma.[107]

The third and final type of correct view that Kamalaśīla's passage mentions is "the unerring realization of the insubstantiality of entities."[108] The term "entities" refers mainly, though not exclusively, to the five heaps; therefore, this particular form of unerring realization is represented by the understanding that the five heaps lack any inherently real essence. Kamalaśīla mentions this wisdom because it represents one of the two main elements of the path that leads to the "ultimate good" of unsurpassed enlightenment or Buddhahood. In *The Lamp of the Path to Enlightenment* Atiśa describes the supreme practitioner as someone who "wants to end completely all the suffering of others." This phrase is a reference to the other main element of the Mahāyāna path—the altruistic attitude of a Bodhisattva. These two forms of spiritual awareness are also known as ultimate enlightenment mind and conventional enlightenment mind,[109] respectively. Candrakīrti alludes to both of these minds in the following verse:

With his great white wings of the conventional and ultimate
outstretched,
The goose king[110] glides at the forefront of a multitude of geese
Toward that supreme far shore of the Victorious Ones' ocean of
good qualities,
Carried along by the swift wind currents of virtuous activities.[111]

To summarize, the first of the three forms of knowledge that a Lamrim practitioner needs to develop is the belief that regards the relationship between karma and its results correctly. This type of correct view is the mainstay of the instruction for persons of lesser capacity. It provides the means of overcoming the specific mental affliction of being attached to this life, as well as the impetus for holding in check the great variety of misdeeds that are responsible for bringing about undesirable rebirths in the future. When coupled with the act of taking refuge, Je Tsongkapa describes a spiritual practice that is based on this knowledge as "the method for achieving happiness in future lives."[112] However, the ability to develop such a practice depends largely on gaining a deep conviction about the truthfulness of Buddha's teachings on the subject of karma, as well as the related doctrine of past and future lives. In the next chapter, we will examine a number of ways in which an understanding of the five heaps contributes to the development of such a conviction.

The second type of knowledge that needs to be gained, which Kamalaśīla describes as "the unerring realization of the insubstantiality of the person," is taken up in Chapter Three. The goal of the instruction for "middling" persons is to engender an appreciation of the unsatisfactoriness of all forms of samsaric existence so that one can develop the aspiration to free oneself from that condition. One method for developing this attitude, known as "renunciation," is to learn and reflect upon the Four Noble Truths. The central tenet of this teaching is the insubstantiality of the person. A related topic is the role that the doctrine of the five heaps plays in this overall discussion.

The final chapter of Part One addresses two elements that lie at the heart of the Mahāyāna path, the compassion that is the root of conventional enlightenment mind and the wisdom that is known as ultimate enlightenment mind. This latter awareness, which Kamalaśīla refers to as "the unerring realization of the insubstantiality of entities," represents the last of the three essential forms of knowledge that a practitioner of the Lamrim teachings must develop.

The Fundamentals 2

THE LAMRIM INSTRUCTIONS that are identified with so-called "lesser" persons are presented within these four topics: (1) recalling one's impermanence in the form of death, (2) contemplating the suffering of the lower states, (3) developing the central Buddhist practice of taking refuge, and (4) cultivating principles of morality that are based on the doctrine of karma. The central aim of these instructions is to overcome the tendency to remain attached to the concerns of this life and replace that with a concern for cultivating the spiritual practices that will bring about a favorable rebirth in the future. We will discuss the role that the worldly correct view plays in relation to these instructions and examine how knowledge of the doctrine of the five heaps is essential if we are to develop a strong conviction about the validity of this view. The two most important elements of this discussion involve a review of classic Buddhist arguments in support of the doctrines of rebirth and karma. Lastly, we will address how the ability to identify virtuous and nonvirtuous mental factors can enhance one's effort to develop and maintain mindfulness. But first it is important to point out how this portion of the instruction is considered to fit into the overall body of the Lamrim teaching.

UNDERSTANDING THE STRUCTURE OF THE LAMRIM TEACHING

After summarizing the three main divisions of Lamrim instruction, Je Tsongkapa's *Great Treatise*[113] asserts that the first two categories—those associated with "lesser" and "middling" persons—are meant to be subsumed within the third category of "supreme" or "great" persons—that is to say, Mahāyāna practitioners. In other words, the first two categories of instruction should properly be understood as forming components of the Mahāyāna path. Modern teachers typically explain this point by saying that the first two categories of instruction represent "the path that is *held in common* with lesser and middling persons; it is not the *actual* path for lesser and middling persons."[114] The principal argument in support of this notion is that the instruction nominally identified with lesser and middling practitioners is essential to the central practice of developing conventional enlightenment mind, and developing that awareness represents the sole and exclusive means of entering the Mahāyāna path. The explanation is expressed in the following manner:

> Thus, those who wish to enter the Mahāyāna system of practice must generate that [enlightenment] mind by applying themselves strenuously to a number of spiritual practices. In particular, the *Compendium of Training* and *Engaging in the Bodhisattva Activities*[115]—those supreme texts for teaching the stages of a Bodhisattva's path—state that to generate enlightenment mind you must be someone who has meditated on the benefits of generating it until you develop a strong and heartfelt eagerness to gain those benefits, and you also need to cultivate the practice of taking refuge in combination with the seven-limb prayer.[116]

Je Tsongkapa continues by describing the benefits of enlightenment mind as falling into two categories: temporary and ultimate. The temporary benefit is that you will avoid falling into the lower realms and attain rebirth in the higher realms. Enlightenment mind accomplishes the former by enabling you to purify yourself of nonvirtuous deeds committed in the past and by overcoming any tendency you might have to commit new misdeeds. Similarly, it accomplishes the latter goal by strengthening the virtuous deeds that you carried out in the past and by endowing new virtues that you accomplish with the ability to generate positive results, not just once but perpetually. As for the ultimate benefit of enlightenment mind, the text simply asserts that it will enable the practitioner to achieve with ease the goals of liberation and omniscience.

To put the matter succinctly, the purpose of the instructions for practitioners of lesser and middling capacity is to enable the student to appreciate what is meant by the temporary goal of being reborn in the higher realms and the ultimate goal of achieving liberation from samsara. This will encourage him or her to engender a sincere aspiration to achieve the enlightenment mind that is unsurpassed for its ability to enable the practitioner to gain those benefits. Je Tsongkapa describes the consequence of failing to gain this understanding in the following words:

> If you don't develop beforehand a genuine aspiration to gain the temporary and ultimate benefits of enlightenment mind, since those benefits derive from having generated that mind, although you may claim that you will strive to generate it, this will be mere words. If you examine this point within your own mind, it will become exceedingly clear.[117]

Once you decide to cultivate the actual instruction for generating enlightenment mind, it is essential that you develop the two root causes of loving-kindness and great compassion. And the ability to develop these two attitudes depends upon your having already contemplated how you yourself lack genuine happiness and are oppressed by every manner of samsaric suffering, since the failure to do so will leave you unmoved by the fact that others are subject to this same condition. Again, Je Tsongkapa writes:

> Therefore, with the instructions for a lesser person, you reflect how you personally are subject to the harm of the suffering that exists in the lower states. And with the instructions for a middling person, you reflect how, even in the higher states, you must still undergo suffering and there is no opportunity of finding the happiness that comes from having quelled such suffering. Then, as the means of developing loving-kindness and compassion, you meditate again on this same suffering that you previously considered in relation to yourself, only now you do so in relation to all sentient beings, whom you regard as close family relatives. Since enlightenment mind arises on the basis of those two attitudes,[118] training yourself in the attitudes that are held in common with lesser and middling persons is an integral part of the overall method for developing genuine enlightenment mind; it does not represent a form of practice in which a disciple is led on some separate path.[119]

Only a few lines later, this issue is stressed one final time:

> At this point, a lama should inform his disciples effectively about the manner in which the teachings identified with lesser and

> middling persons are an integral element in the process of developing unsurpassed enlightenment mind. For their part, the disciples should also gain a strong conviction about this point and, each time they meditate on this portion of the Lamrim teaching, they should recall that understanding and maintain the highest regard for the fact that they are training themselves in the factors that contribute to the development of enlightenment mind.
>
> If you fail to do this, your efforts will represent a path that is unrelated to and distinct from the path of a great person. As a result, you will not gain any definite understanding of enlightenment mind until you reach the portion of Lamrim teaching that addresses the actual path of a great person. This means that the efforts made during this earlier period could obstruct the development of enlightenment mind, or at least fail to contribute toward that great aim. Therefore, you should be particularly diligent about this matter.[120]

Je Tsongkapa concludes this discussion by asking rhetorically why the instructions need to be divided into separate categories that are identified with three types of person. If the entire body of instructions is properly intended for Mahāyāna practitioners, it would seem adequate simply to describe it as a system of practice for "great" persons. His response is that the threefold distinction serves two purposes. The first is that it will prevent the practitioner who has not yet developed a genuine realization of the instructions that are held in common with lesser and middling persons from mistakenly believing that he or she has attained the level of a great person. Such an unwarranted belief stems from a form of "exaggerated pride"[121] that would impede a practitioner from gaining the full benefits of the overall teaching. The unique potential of the Lamrim teaching to bring about spiritual development effectively represents the second purpose of its structure. That is to say, by classifying the instructions into these three divisions, practitioners of all levels of development are able to acquire the benefits of each section in the most expeditious manner.

THE WORLDLY CORRECT VIEW

As important as it is to recognize that the instructions associated with lesser and middling persons are integral to the central aim of developing enlightenment mind, our main purpose here is to consider how each of the three sections of the teaching is closely tied to a particular form of correct understanding. For the instructions that are associated with so-called "lesser" persons, this understanding is "the belief that regards the relationship between karma and its results correctly," to repeat the language from Kamalaśīla's passage that was quoted in the previous chapter. This belief, which is also described as the worldly correct view, encompasses the following premises:

(1) Every ordinary being's existence is made up of a beginningless series of lives that is fundamentally unsatisfactory in nature and that will continue indefinitely unless its causes are destroyed.

(2) Fully enlightened beings, such as Buddha Śākyamuni, are what they and their followers declare them to be: the sole, infallible sources of a unique teaching that not only can free us permanently and irreversibly from our samsaric condition but—from the Mahāyāna perspective—can also lead us to the same state of omniscience and immortality that the Buddhas themselves enjoy.

(3) Although ordinary beings cannot directly verify for themselves the truthfulness of the teachings on karma and its results, they must gain a strong conviction regarding their validity and heed their admonitions with utmost scrupulousness.

Note that Kamalaśīla describes the view regarding karma and its results as a "belief"[122] rather than a "realization,"[123] which is the word he uses to describe the other two forms of unmistaken view. The term "belief" is meant to indicate that adherence to this view relies principally on the authority and trustworthiness of a Buddha's word. Indeed it is readily acknowledged—both in the canonical sutras and in philosophical writings—that only a Buddha has the ability to know directly and unerringly the workings of karma in all its limitless variety and detail. This does not mean, however, that Buddha's followers are required to accept the doctrine of karma with unquestioning faith, or that reason has no role to play in providing the justification for accepting it. In fact, Buddhist scholars accord belief in karma the status of inference based on infallible testimony,[124] and regard it as a form of epistemologically valid knowledge.[125] By contrast, they also assert that an ordinary person can rely on his or her own powers of ordinary inferential reasoning to develop certain knowledge about the existence of past and future lives. Works such as Dharmakīrti's *Extensive Treatise on Knowledge* and Śāntarakṣita's *Compendium of Views on the Nature of Reality* construct a logical rationale for believing that a Buddha is an infallible source of knowledge concerning those subjects that lie beyond the comprehension of ordinary beings. We will have more to say about these points later.

RECOLLECTION OF DEATH

The first of the four topics that make up the initial division of the Lamrim instruction is called "impermanence in the form of death."[126] While its validity also hinges on that of the three premises just outlined, as a specific form of practice it is presented as an antidote to a rough form of the mistaken view that regards what is impermanent as permanent. Meditation on one's own impending death, or "rough impermanence,"[127] is crucially important and its implications extend far beyond the initial steps of the spiritual path. Je Tsongkapa makes the following cautionary statement:

> The mind's tendency to adhere to the notion that one is not going to die is the source of all misfortune. The antidote to that attitude—recollection of death—is the source of all excellence. Therefore, you should not think, "This is a practice for those who do not have any profound teaching to meditate upon," or "This is a genuine topic to meditate upon, but only briefly at the beginning [of my spiritual training]; it does not merit being made part of my regular practice." Instead, you should undertake to meditate on this topic only after having developed the deep conviction that it is necessary at the beginning, middle, and end [of your entire career of spiritual training].[128]

Indeed, recollection of death is represented as the one practice that can ensure our spiritual efforts do not become tainted by the eight worldly concerns and attachment to this life. The following excerpt from Kyabje Pabongka Rinpoche's *Liberation in Our Hands* provides a concise explanation of this point:

> Unless we recall death, we won't be able to abandon our attachment for this life. And if we fail to do this, we will become pleased when we gain something of material value and upset when we don't. We will also react in this same inappropriate way toward well-being and suffering, fame and disrepute, and praise and scorn—that is, we will come under the influence of the eight worldly concerns. Nāgārjuna described the eight worldly concerns with these lines:

> Gain and loss, pleasure and pain,
> Fame and dishonor, praise and scorn—
> World-knower, be indifferent to these eight
> Worldly concerns and bar them from your mind.[129]

A few lines later, Kyabje Pabongka Rinpoche points out that even learned scholars and meditation practitioners can fall victim to one of the eight worldly concerns in particular:

> Of the three main objects for which we most often have attachment—food, clothing, and reputation—some persons are bound by their attachment to one, some by their attachment to two, and some by all three of them. Among the three, however, the most difficult one to abandon is desire for reputation. It doesn't matter if one is a scholar, a well-disciplined monk, a teacher, or a meditator; there are many such persons who desire fame and a good reputation. (Kyabje Rinpoche then quoted a lengthy passage by Gyer Drowey Gönpo[130] that includes these lines:
>
> > The great learned and disciplined meditators who are
> > attached to this life
> > Want to become known as learned and disciplined for this
> > life's sake.
> > They are great meditators who refuse to meet with anyone;
> > They go into retreat and write admonitions above the
> > door.
> > These great meditators want to be known as devout for this
> > life's sake.[131])

As with all the mental afflictions, attachment to this life derives ultimately from the erroneous belief in a real self. However, because it is extremely difficult to gain a genuine understanding of the nonexistence of such a self, particularly during the early stages of practice, it is crucial to cultivate the rough impermanence that is represented by one's impending death as the most effective means of ensuring that one's efforts to pursue the Dharma remain pure. In a section entitled "the disadvantages of failing to meditate on the recollection of death,"[132] Je Tsongkapa presents a series of harmful consequences that follow naturally from the erroneous assumption that one need not regard one's death as imminent. This passage drives home in quite poignant language why meditating on impermanence in the form of death is such an essential practice. Kyabje Pabongka Rinpoche's modern presentation of Lamrim oral instruction formulates this same topic in terms of six separate disadvantages. The following list is a paraphrase of the points that appear in Je Tsongkapa's *Great Treatise:*

(1) By failing to counteract the tendency to believe that you aren't going to die any time soon,[133] you will constantly think only about acquiring the things that are necessary to insure your happiness during this life. This will prevent you from considering how you might devote yourself to the Dharma.

(2) Any virtuous Dharma activities that you might decide to undertake will be inherently weak, because they will have been done for the sake of this life.

(3) Since your spiritual activities tend to be accompanied by various kinds of misdeeds, they are likely to be intermingled with the [karmic] causes that bring rebirth in the lower states.

(4) Even if you devote yourself to the aim of your future lives, you will be unable to overcome the laziness that procrastinates about pursuing a spiritual practice. Also, by wasting time and being distracted with useless activities, you will be unable to pursue a spiritual practice correctly and with great effort.

(5) Deceived by the expectation that you will continue living for a long time, you will continually develop powerful mental afflictions. For example, you will feel strong attachment for the eight worldly concerns and strong hatred toward those you perceive as impeding your efforts; you will continue to perpetuate the ignorance that fails to recognize the faults of these two root mental afflictions; and you will generate other root and secondary mental afflictions that arise from this attachment, hatred, and ignorance, such as pride and jealousy.

(6) As you continue to develop these mental afflictions over time, the potential for carrying out every kind of misdeed will become progressively stronger. This will simultaneously lead you farther and farther away from the Dharma that counteracts these misdeeds and provides the opportunity for you to pursue temporary and ultimate spiritual goals. When death finally comes, you will experience great remorse as you realize that you have failed to accomplish anything of true value during your

life and you now face the prospect of having to endure the suffering that comes with being reborn in the lower states.

The Buddhist teaching on impermanence asserts that all the entities that comprise an individual's five impure heaps do not exist longer than an instant, which is defined as the smallest unit of time. Having been produced by the momentary causes that preceded them, this collection of impermanent entities in turn serves as the set of causes for the next moment of equally evanescent heaps. While the point is not often emphasized, gaining an understanding of this subtle impermanence is an important step in the process that leads ultimately to a realization of selflessness.[134] Because this subtle impermanence is imperceptible to the ordinary person's mind, the similarity of succeeding moments in the series of the five heaps leads to the false notion that it possesses various degrees of constancy. For example, we have a sense that the individual who wakes up today is identical to the one who was active yesterday. This misunderstanding is the ultimate source of the erroneous belief that an unchanging self or soul survives from one life to the next.

The instruction for "lesser" persons essentially remains at a level of ordinary language in which the individual is regarded as a nominally existent person that is born, experiences suffering, commits deeds, dies, and is reborn. While the precise nature of this nominally existent person is of great philosophical import, such discussions are deferred until a later stage in the instruction.

THE SUFFERING OF THE LOWER STATES

Contemplation of the variety of physical and mental suffering that occurs in the hells, the hungry ghost realm, and the world of animals constitutes the next topic in the instruction for "lesser" persons. Needless to say, except for the experiences of animals, these states are beyond the awareness of ordinary humans. The force of this instruction derives from several propositions, the most fundamental of which, once again, is the validity of the teachings on karma. Since the average person is unable to verify even the very existence of these realms, much less the exact nature of how one comes to be born there, the basis for believing in them must be the trustworthiness of those scriptures in which they are described. Once that premise has been established, the purpose of the instruction is to motivate the practitioner by pointing out that we are all powerless to escape the effects of our deeds as long as we have not gained control over our own minds. The recognition of this helplessness is an essential factor in the fundamental Buddhist practice of taking refuge in the Three Jewels, the next topic in this part of the instruction.

Je Tsongkapa introduces the presentation of the lower realms' suffering with the following brief remarks:

> As just described, in view of the certainty that death is near at hand, we should recognize that we do not have the opportunity to remain very long in this life. Moreover, following our death we do not just disappear; we will have to take birth again. And, since there is no other place to be born except among the two types of migrating beings,[135] we will be reborn either in one of the pleasurable states of existence or in one of the lower states.
>
> Because we do not have the freedom to choose where we will be reborn and we are, in fact, under the control of our own karma, we will be born according to the propelling force of our white and black karma. Therefore, we should contemplate the suffering of the lower states in such a way that we ask ourselves, "What sort of experiences will I have to undergo if I am reborn in the lower states?"[136]

In terms of practicing the instruction, it is not enough to become familiar with these descriptions and consider them to be true. The practitioner must avoid regarding the lower states in an impersonal and detached manner and assuming that there is no great likelihood of being reborn there. This is accomplished largely by understanding that we all possess the karmic seeds that have the potential to bring about our rebirth in states of great suffering. Initially, the experiences that occur in the lower states should be contemplated on their own. This will naturally lead us to wonder how we can protect ourselves from having to be reborn there. This desire is crucial for the practice of taking refuge. Over the longer term, contemplating the suffering of the lower states is also necessary for developing the compassion that leads to enlightenment mind. As Kyabje Pabongka Rinpoche explains:

> We also should not approach this description of how someone might take birth in the lower states as if it were a far-removed spectacle that did not involve us personally. If we do approach the instruction in this way, it won't help us to develop renunciation. As Nāgārjuna stated:

Each day the hells should be recalled,
Both the hot ones and the cold ones.[137]

The proper way to meditate on the suffering of the lower states is similar to the way we meditate on a tutelary deity in the generation stage of Anuttarayoga Tantra. We must imagine that we have actually been born in each of the regions that make up the lower states and then generate a vivid sense of what it would be like for us to undergo the experiences that occur there. We must continue to reflect in this way until the meditation produces in us a genuine feeling of terror.

Typically, we have a high regard for the practice of meditating on the physical form of a tutelary deity. But, for the time being at least, it is more beneficial for us to meditate on the body of a hell being. This is because the first moment that we generate a genuine spiritual realization in connection with the suffering of the hot hells, we will have begun to develop the initial stages of renunciation. To accomplish this represents a very meaningful result. There are other great benefits to be derived from this practice as well. For example, the discontent associated with renunciation enables us to dispel the arrogance of pride. As Śāntideva said:

And suffering's other benefits are
Loss of pride through discontent,
Compassion for samsara's beings,
Dread of evil, and love of good.[138]

The principal cause, then, for developing both renunciation and compassion is to meditate on suffering. Since the leisure and fortune we possess in our present physical form allow us to develop these two attitudes with relative ease, it is very important that we meditate on suffering.[139]

Kyabje Pabongka Rinpoche's poem on the practice of analytic meditation describes how to reflect on the suffering of the lower states:

Although the topic of meditating on the suffering of the lower states
Is taught separately from how to perform the act of taking refuge,

The ideal way in which to practice them is to take refuge
Right after reflecting on each aspect of the lower states.

Still, a powerful and effective instruction for the novice practitioner
Is to meditate initially on the suffering of the lower states alone,
Separately from the act of taking refuge. Then, after gaining the first stages
Of experiential realization, you should cultivate the two practices jointly.

Among the areas of the three lower states, begin by meditating on
The suffering of Revivals, which is the first of the hot hells.
After generating the perception that you have actually taken birth there,
Contemplate its forms of suffering as though you are really experiencing them.

You may think, "It would be agonizing to take birth in such a place;
But I am only imagining this. It is not a real experience."
Though it is just your imagination and not a real experience,
Your mind contains the seeds of accumulated and undiminished karma
That have the power to hurl you into the Revivals hell.

So have no doubt; when these seeds are activated and rendered potent
In the limb called "existence,"[140] you will definitely fall into that place.
If it frightens you now merely to contemplate such a place,
What will you do when you are actually born there?
Consider whether you could bear that kind of suffering
And whether you could endure such a life span for that long.

So meditate alternately and with conviction on these two ideas:
That you have actually been born there and that you are certain to be born there.
When you develop an intense desire to seek immediately
A means of liberation and a refuge that can save you from this peril,
And this brings on such great apprehension that you even
Lose your appetite for food, this is the measure of having generated
An experiential awareness of the suffering in the lower states.[141]

ARGUMENTS IN SUPPORT OF THE DOCTRINE OF REBIRTH

Although the traditional Lamrim literature doesn't address the justification for believing in the existence of past and future lives in any rigorous way, this doctrine obviously plays a fundamental role in all levels of Buddhist practice. Those who have the opportunity to study the classic Buddhist arguments in favor of the doctrine of rebirth gain a powerful tool that can be directly applied to their spiritual practice. One of the most important literary sources is a section from the second chapter of Dharmakīrti's *Extensive Treatise on Knowledge.*[142] Śāntarakṣita's *Compendium of Views on the Nature of Reality* also devotes a chapter to this topic that covers many of the same ideas found in Dharmakīrti's work.

At the beginning of his commentary to Dharmakīrti's second chapter, Khedrup Gelek Pelsang,[143] one of Je Tsongkapa's principal disciples, presents a lengthy overview and analysis of the arguments presented in that chapter. The topic of past and future lives forms part of a larger discussion that sets out the necessary causes a Bodhisattva must cultivate over countless lives in order to reach the ultimate goal of Buddhahood. Dharmakīrti articulates the Buddhist justification for the doctrine of rebirth against the backdrop of refuting the position of the Indian materialist tradition known as the Cārvaka School,[144] which held that mind is solely and entirely a product of the body. In essence, adherents of this school argued that, since the mind arises from the body, it did not exist prior to one's current life nor will it continue to exist after this life comes to an end.

From the Buddhist perspective, such a belief represents a form of wrong view.[145] Wrong view is included among the ten nonvirtuous karmic paths that form a central topic in Buddhist morality and it is also identified as one of the ten root mental afflictions that are the principal cause of samsaric existence. Wrong view is described as a particularly grave fault in that it destroys one's capacity to develop positive moral qualities, referred to as "roots of virtue."[146] Asaṇga describes the action of wrong view as follows:

> Its action is to completely destroy the roots of virtue and to support the continued strength of the roots of nonvirtue. Alternatively, its action is to [cause one to] engage in nonvirtuous deeds and to prevent [one from] engaging in virtuous deeds."[147]

The sutras also state that adhering to wrong view represents one of eight "inopportune states."[148] A person who holds wrong views is incapable of pursuing the Dharma because he or she rejects all spiritual matters as either meaningless or untrue. Beyond the outright denial of past and future lives, even developing uncertainty about this doctrine can become a serious obstacle. If such uncertainty leads an individual to question the validity of his or her spiritual efforts, then it takes on the nature of doubt, which is yet another root mental affliction. Such doubt concerning the true spiritual path is identified as one of three major obstacles to the pursuit of liberation.[149] Moreover, the prevailing secular view in contemporary Western societies is that a person's entire existence is circumscribed by his or her present life. Modern science, as well, holds a largely materialistic position on the status of the mind. Against such a backdrop, here are some observations that Khedrup Je makes concerning the importance of gaining conviction about the existence of past and future lives:

> Only certain non-Buddhists who follow a distinct philosophical system such as the one formulated by the Lokāyata School can possess the overt conceptual mistaken belief that denies the existence of past and future lives.[150] Nevertheless, the seeds of such a misconception are possessed by virtually all ordinary persons[151] on the strength of having heard philosophical tenets and scriptural traditions like those of the Lokāyata School in previous lives, an event that causes traces of this mistaken belief to be planted in their minds. If this were not so, it could not be established that the minds of those ordinary persons who have not been influenced by philosophical thought [in this life] possess the seeds of any other mistaken beliefs developed on the basis of doctrinal tenets. And it would then follow incorrectly that the minds of ordinary persons who have not been influenced by philosophical thought do not possess any of the obstacles that are abandoned by the Seeing Path.[152]
>
> Moreover, virtually no common "ordinary persons"[153] possess the kind of knowledge that directly perceives past and future lives, nor can they possess inferential knowledge of past and future lives until they have come to understand a correct reason that establishes their existence. And since it is impossible for them to develop a sure understanding regarding the existence of past and future lives if they lack either of these two forms of knowledge, they will also not be able to counteract any tendency they might have for developing the overt form of the misconception that denies the existence

> of past and future lives. Accordingly, as long as you have not generated the certain understanding that past and future lives do exist, you cannot possibly gain a conviction about having to meditate on compassion and other related paths[154] over the course of a great many lifetimes and you will be unable to eliminate any misconception that may develop about the impossibility of cultivating such practices over many lifetimes.
>
> Therefore, as long as you have not gained a certain understanding about past and future lives on the basis of a correct reason that proves their existence, it will be impossible for you to develop a genuine form of the enlightenment mind in which you resolve, "I shall attain Buddhahood for the sake of all sentient beings." Moreover, it will also be impossible for you to develop a sure understanding about the process of abandoning misdeeds and cultivating virtue because you fear falling into the lower realms and you wish to attain the status of a human being or a god in your future lives. Thus, as long as you have not gained a conviction about the existence of past and future lives on the strength of correct reasoning, the door to all the paths that lead to a high station and the ultimate good will remain closed. For this reason, at the very outset of your efforts to meditate on the path it is extremely important that you gain a sure understanding about this topic and eliminate the mistaken belief that denies the existence past and future lives. . . .[155]

Dharmakīrti's arguments in support of rebirth appear in a section of the second chapter of his *Extensive Treatise on Knowledge* that spans some eighty-six verses.[156] The general aim of his presentation is to demonstrate how mind consciousness can arise, function, and continue to exist in a manner that is not determined solely or even principally by the body. He notes that while the mind can be influenced by the body in a variety of ways, the opposite is equally true. The principal thesis underlying the overall discussion is that mind consciousness in particular operates in a manner that is fundamentally autonomous. Dharmakīrti also refutes the materialist claim that the mind's existence is derived from the body or that it is a property of the body. Because such Buddhist doctrines as the five heaps, impermanence, and selflessness, as well as Buddhist views on the nature of causation inform many of the arguments that are put forward, a basic understanding of these topics is essential for anyone who wants to fully appreciate the methodology of Dharmakīrti's presentation.

At the beginning of his commentary on this section of Dharmakīrti's root text, Khedrup Je provides an overview and analysis of the discussion. He opens the summary with the following words:

> Moreover, what is being refuted here[157] is the belief of the Lokāyata School that the existence of mind[158] depends exclusively on the physical body that is composed of the four elements. The aim is to demonstrate that, if the mind does not depend exclusively on the body, this will undermine and bring into question the proposition that the mind must cease to exist when the body perishes. That is the reason for the term "solely" in the verse that states:
>
> > When an individual takes birth,
> > The breath, sense faculties, and mind
> > Do not arise solely from the body,
> > With no relation to entities of the same kind.[159]

The Buddhist position implicit in this verse is that the breath, sense faculties, and mind which occur at the very beginning of this life must have as their respective material causes[160] the same kind of entities as they themselves are—which is to say, previous instances of the breath, sense faculties, and mind. If this is true, the only possible cause for such entities would be those instances of them that occurred in a former life. This is the essence of the argument for the existence of past lives. The main support for this claim is drawn from the direct observation that any given moment of consciousness that we currently experience arises out of the states of awareness that immediately preceded it. Kamalaśīla presents the argument in his *Explanation of the Difficult Points in the Compendium of Views on the Nature of Reality:*

> The form [of the argument] is [as follows]: Those entities that have the nature of four [of the five] heaps—namely, consciousness, feelings, conceptions, and [the mental] formations—arise on the strength of their own [individual] material causes, because their nature is that of consciousness, and the rest, just as with that very same group of four heaps that exist during the stages [of life] of being a youth, and so forth. The collection of the mind and the rest that exist at the beginning of life also have the nature of being consciousness and the rest.[161]

The implied conclusion of this argument is that because "the collection of the mind and the rest that exists at the beginning of life also has the nature of being consciousness and the rest," these entities, too, must "arise on the strength of their own material causes." And if that is true, there must have existed instances of them before the first moment of this life, which means that there must have existed a previous life.

Khedrup Je also notes that the effort to refute that the mind arises from the body should be understood as seeking to disprove principally that the body is the material cause of the mind. A material cause is defined as having a nature that governs every quality without remainder that exists in the effect. This means that the effect is unable to undergo any change without some modification having occurred in the material cause. Buddhists argue that since the mind *can* undergo modification without any change having taken place in the body, the body does not represent the material cause of the mind. For example, without the body undergoing any modification, a person's mind can take on a state of unhappiness simply by recalling misdeeds that were committed at some time in the past. Similarly, such earlier modifications of the mind as fear or grief can bring about later modifications of the mind, without the body having undergone any change. Conversely, alterations of the body do not necessarily bring about a corresponding modification of the mind.

Dharmakīrti acknowledges later in the same chapter that the body does play an instrumental role in the process of continued samsaric existence since much of our craving occurs in relation to the body, but he again rejects that the body should be considered as the mind's material cause.[162] In the following verse, he also states what he does believe to be the nature of the relationship that exists between the mind and body:

> The same is true of mind and body.
> They coexist with each one's cause assisting
> In the arising of the other's result,
> Like fire and the liquidity of copper.[163]

The central point of this verse is that the influence of the mind on the body and that of the body on the mind represent forms of mutual interaction and coexistence. This process is described using an analogy of copper that is melted by its proximity to fire. When fire melts copper, the earlier moments of the solid copper are the material cause for its later molten state. Likewise, the earlier moments of fire are the material cause for the succeeding moments of fire, as well as the efficient cause[164] for the molten copper. Similarly, the mind that is closely connected with the body arises from a previous moment of mind. That earlier moment of the mind was also accompanied by a state of the body that functioned as an efficient cause for the later moment of the mind. The fully formed body also has the various stages of the fetus as its material cause, and it continues to come into being with the mind functioning as an efficient cause. Mind and body coexist in this way throughout a particular being's life.

On the other hand, Dharmakīrti argues, even if the body does occasionally serve as an efficient cause for the arising of the mind, this does not mean that the mind must cease to exist when this life's body ceases to function, or that another life's body cannot be formed, which will then again coexist with the mind for some finite period of time. He cites as an analogy the fire that helps to cure a pot. Even when the fire is extinguished at the end of this process, the pot does not cease to exist.

> Even granting that occasionally [the body]
> Is an assisting factor for the mental continuum,
> That alone does not cause its disappearance,
> As fire, etc., does not for a pot, and the like.[165]

Traditional accounts describe proponents of the Indian Cārvaka School as having three different views of the central relationship between body and mind. They are identified in the following verse from Prajñākaragupta's commentary to the *Pramāṇavārttika*:

> Based on the three views that mind
> Is the same nature as the body, a result
> Of the body, or an attribute of the body,
> There is no possibility for repeated practice.[166]

Buddhist scholars address the third view, that the mind is an attribute of the body, in a variety of ways. One interpretation is that the materialists believe the relation between the body and mind to be one in which the two entities arise simultaneously, but with the body acting as the necessary support for the mind.[167] This relation is compared to that which exists between a lamp and the light that emanates from it. Just as the light from a lamp is extinguished when the lamp ceases to function or undergoes destruction, the mind that is an attribute of the body will cease to exist when the body perishes, without there being any possibility of a subsequent rebirth.

Dharmakīrti rejects this position on the strength of the observation that it is the action of the mind itself and not the body that is responsible for an increase or decrease in such purely mental qualities as wisdom. For instance, skill in a particular craft and a high degree of spiritual knowledge are achieved through repeated practice and the long-term pursuit of extensive learning, respectively. These actions are essentially forms of mental training, suggesting that such development of the mind takes place in a way that is largely independent of the body.

At the same time, it is recognized that the health and well-being of the body can play a limited role in the development of such mental traits. Nevertheless, this physical influence is seen by Buddhists to be one that does not represent a direct link between mind and body. Tibetan commentaries explain that the body directly affects a person's body consciousness through the body faculty, which is physical in nature. This first level of influence is responsible for generating a form of body consciousness that is accompanied by a favorable physical sensation. This distinct body consciousness then induces a state of mental well-being that directly enables such positive qualities as wisdom and the like to improve more easily. These points are expressed in the following verses:

> Moreover, the increase and decrease
> Of wisdom and the like take place
> Through differing actions of the mind,
> Without any increase or decrease in the body.
>
> This is not found in dependent relations
> Like those between a lamp and light.
> Even where the improvement of one is due to the other,
> It is not without the mind's assistance.[168]

The mind-body relation is further addressed by considering an objection that argues in favor of a more direct influence between the two. This claim asserts that the relative strength of the body is observed to influence the arising of other mental states, such as desire or anger. Dharmakīrti's response is that even though there is some evidence that this effect does occur, it is not one that is inevitable. It can, in fact, be mitigated by one who has developed knowledge.

The key factor that leads to the arising of such mental afflictions as desire is identified as improper attention.[169] But when a practitioner cultivates the meditation practice of unattractiveness,[170] for instance, he or she can weaken or even completely overcome the habitual tendencies that would otherwise trigger desire. Moreover, desire and anger are more directly linked to pleasant and unpleasant feelings, respectively, than they are to some strength or weakness of the body. It is those two types of feeling that directly lead to desire and anger. The body only serves as the inner object for the arising of such feelings; it is not the basis that forms the direct cause of desire or anger. Buddhist texts further point out that the occurrence of pleasant and unpleasant feelings does not always result in the arising of the mental afflictions. This result is only "occasional" in the sense that while the mental afflictions of desire, hatred, and ignorance can be generated by pleasant, unpleasant, and even neutral feelings, the connection between feelings and the mental afflictions is not one in which the occurrence of the former necessarily leads to the arising of the latter. For example, a skillful practitioner can reflect on suffering in ways that lead to such qualities as patience, humility, renunciation, and compassion.[171] Dharmakīrti's root text continues:

> The growth of desire, etc., due to physical strength, and so forth,
> Is [only] occasional and arises from pleasure and suffering.
> The latter two, in turn, derive from the presence of inner objects,
> Such as a balance of the elements, and the like.[172]

This point is underscored by citing two more instances that are said to conform to this analysis and therefore provide further support for the claim that the mind itself is the direct and principal factor in circumstances where a significant alteration of consciousness occurs. The first is a state of delirium and other extreme symptoms that can accompany such illnesses as a severe physiological imbalance or high fever. A person who is suffering from such a condition can become disoriented and lose the ability to reason clearly or recognize his or her surroundings. Although the root text uses a term that translates literally as "memory loss," this is not meant to refer to amnesia. Dharmakīrti asserts that this type of alteration of a sick person's mind consciousness is directly caused by another aspect of the mind—namely, the individual's body consciousness. This body consciousness has taken on an abnormal aspect because it is experiencing an extraordinary inner sensation that is due to a profound physiological imbalance.

The body consciousness then affects the mind continuum in such a way that extreme symptoms will arise.

> This explains the memory loss, and the like,
> Brought on by a disorder [of the humors], etc.;
> For this change is caused by the mind itself,
> Which has arisen from a particular inner object.[173]

A second example further reinforces the claim that the body is not the direct cause of such mental states by describing how certain persons' perception of objects that lie outside their bodies can induce intense mental states like fainting spells. In such situations it is beyond dispute that these external objects could be the material cause of a mental reaction. Nevertheless, as the objects of a sensory perception, they can serve as indirect factors that bring about an intense emotional state. Dharmakīrti specifically mentions the sound of a tiger's roar or the sight of another being's blood as being capable of causing a timid person to faint, or at the very least to experience strong fear or repulsion. The larger point of this entire series of verses is to demonstrate that mind alone is the material cause of an individual's mind consciousness, and that, therefore, consciousness does not have to cease with the perishing of the physical body.

> For example, fainting[174] and the like can arise
> In the continuum of one who is highly sensitive,
> Through the hearing of a tiger
> Or the seeing of blood, and so forth.
>
> Therefore, mind is the sole formative factor
> To which [the mind] necessarily conforms
> And without which it cannot occur.
> For these reasons, [mind] is dependent upon mind.[175]

The argument for the existence of future lives relies on the principle that a preceding moment of consciousness is the sole necessary and sufficient material cause for the arising of a future moment of consciousness. This type of causation is referred to in the commentaries as "a special cause that [by its absence] would prevent [a result from occurring]."[176] This phrase implicitly suggests that consciousness does not simply have the capacity or the potential to produce a particular result; its presence insures that another consciousness will arise with absolute necessity.[177] Dharmakīrti describes this as a relation in which the presence of the cause is efficacious in the sense that it is *always* followed by its corresponding result. He further equates this with two formulations of causality that were expressed by Lord Buddha. One states: "When this is present, that comes into being."[178] The first clause of this statement indicates the presence of a cause with the seventh, or locative, grammatical case. The second formulation states: "From the arising of that, this arises."[179] The latter description identifies a cause using the fifth, or ablative, grammatical case, which expresses the source from which something is derived.

> That cause whose presence is beneficial
> In that it is always followed [by a result]
> Describes both the [causal] seventh case
> And the phrase "from the arising of that."[180]

By establishing that such a relation exists between prior and succeeding moments of consciousness, Buddhist scholars feel justified in asserting that the final moment of awareness in the life of a person who remains subject to desire must serve as the type of direct cause that cannot be precluded from generating a subsequent state of awareness as its result. The certainty that such a future moment of consciousness will occur represents the basis for proving the existence of a future life. Once again, Kamalaśīla provides the formal language of this argument:

> A mind that is associated with desire has the ability to generate another mind as its "object to be grasped,"[181] because it is associated with desire, like the minds that existed at earlier stages [in a person's life]. And the mind at the moment of death is one that is associated with desire.[182]

The aim of the above discussion has been to identify and describe several of the main issues that lie at the core of the Buddhist arguments in support of past and future lives. In a broad sense, the Buddhist teaching seeks to draw the untutored individual away from the everyday perspective in which unwarranted importance is given to the physical aspect of one's being and replace it with a frame of reference in which there is a greater awareness of the mental components. Learning about the range of mental states that is presented in the *Summary of the Five Heaps* can help to bring a clearer understanding of the complexity of mental phenomena. This goal is also greatly enhanced by personal instruction from an experienced spiritual teacher; however, it is ultimately achieved through personal introspection. Knowledge of the Buddhist theory of mind should thus be seen as indispensable for anyone who wants to investigate the classic arguments that underlie the doctrine of rebirth.

TAKING REFUGE

Taking refuge and observing the principles of karma are the final two topics of the instructions that are held in common with "lesser" persons. In Je Tsongkapa's *Great Treatise*, both of these topics are subsumed under the heading "Pursuing the methods of achieving happiness in future lives,"[183] which indicates that they represent the actual means of attaining the temporary goal of a favorable rebirth.

The explanation of the practice of taking refuge is based mainly on Asaṅga's *Collection of Determinations*[184] and the oral instruction of Lamrim lineage teachers. According to the personal instruction associated with the Lamrim tradition, this practice is what determinates whether or not one can legitimately call oneself a Buddhist. The first of eight benefits that derive from taking refuge is that such a person "enters the inner faith of Buddhism."[185] Here is Je Tsongkapa's explanation of this benefit:

> While it is evident, in a general sense, that there are many ways of identifying [the characteristics that distinguish] the inner faith and outer faiths, it is widely recognized that Lord [Atiśa] and Śāntarakṣita distinguished them on the basis of [the act of] taking refuge. Therefore, [a Buddhist] is defined as someone who has accomplished the refuge act and has not forsaken it [at some later time]. As such, the initial step of entering the Buddhist faith requires a person to hold from the bottom of his or her heart that, of the Three Jewels, [the Buddha Jewel] is the [supreme] Teacher, and so forth.[186] Without having done this, a person will not become a Buddhist no matter what virtuous acts he or she may carry out.[187]

Among the explanations that relate to the topic of taking refuge, none is more important than the causes that form the basis for this act, since in their absence the practice cannot be done correctly and in a genuine manner. Je

Tsongkapa identifies the two principal causes of fear and faith in the following introductory statement:

> In short, [the causes for taking refuge] are two: (1) our own fear of the lower states and the like,[188] and (2) our belief that the Triple Gem has the power to save us from that [source of fear]. For this reason, if these two causes are understood merely in words, our refuge practice will be the same. However, if these two become powerful and firm, our refuge practice will be one in which our mind has been properly transformed. Therefore, we should strive to cultivate these two causes.[189]

The type of fear that represents the first cause was described earlier in the section on contemplating the suffering of the lower states. The second cause, the belief that the Triple Gem has the power to save us, represents one of three kinds of faith that Vasubandhu identifies in his root text. Sthiramati's commentary describes it in relation to belief in karma and the first two of the Four Noble Truths. However, this faith also includes the firm conviction that the Buddha, Dharma, and Sangha exist in the sense that they possess the spiritual qualities that are ascribed to them in the scriptures. Sthiramati describes faith in the Three Jewels in terms of a second kind of faith, which is referred to as "clarity of mind."[190] For instance, he states in relation to the Buddha:

> Faith in Lord Buddha is the clarity of mind that is demonstrated by a bristling of the body hair or the flowing of tears and is felt toward that object which has perfected all virtuous qualities and completely removed all faults.[191]

Je Tsongkapa's instructions on how to develop these two types of faith toward the Three Jewels is based on principles that are outlined in Asaṅga's *Collection of Determinations*. Je Tsongkapa clarifies these principles in the *Great Treatise* using citations from sutras and a variety of devotional works. However, the Lamrim tradition does not seem to place much emphasis on providing a logical justification for these assertions. Thus, for many, belief in the Three Jewels stems mainly from a determination that the instruction explained by a spiritual teacher is trustworthy and deserves to be believed. Such a view is founded more on intuition than reason. Nevertheless, even the Buddhist Abhidharma tradition recognizes two basic kinds of practitioner:

one who proceeds on the basis of faith and one who proceeds on the basis of the Dharma.[192] The former type of practitioner initially relies primarily on instruction received from a trusted teacher. The latter type relies on an understanding of the Dharma that is gained on one's own.

In the scholastic curriculum of the major Gelukpa monasteries, the principal text that forms the basis for undertaking a more comprehensive and detailed study of the Three Jewels is the *Ornament of Realizations*. The Three Jewels are one of ten topics of instruction identified in the first chapter of this work. The commentarial literature related to this text provides a general overview of the Three Jewels that draws principally on a series of verses from the *Higher Science of the Mahāyāna*.[193] The act of taking refuge is also examined in connection with this discussion of the Three Jewels. The *Ornament of Realizations* itself also contains numerous explanations that enable a practitioner to gain valid knowledge regarding this topic.

It is particularly important for Western Buddhists to examine the reasons supporting the belief that Buddhas have actually attained a state of unsurpassed enlightenment. This is because the relative scarcity of knowledgeable and qualified teachers—and, as a direct consequence, the number of learned students—limits the possibilities for those practitioners who rely primarily on instruction received from a trusted teacher.

The second chapter of Dharmakīrti's *Extensive Treatise on Knowledge* provides a unique and powerful antidote to these challenges. The entire chapter is devoted to a detailed analysis of the statement of homage that appears in the following verse composed by the master Dignāga, who is credited with having had the greatest influence on Dharmakīrti and his writings on epistemology:

> Having bowed to the One who became a true authority, the One who desires to help the world,
> The Teacher, the One who has gone well, and the Savior,
> I will collect together here numerous points dispersed throughout my works
> In order to prove what the nature of knowledge is.[194]

In the first half of this verse Buddha Śākyamuni is described with five epithets. The first of these, "One who became a true authority,"[195] identifies the main thesis of the chapter, which is that a Buddha is a being who attained the status of an infallible authority regarding the spiritual aims of all those who seek liberation. The remaining epithets are explained in relation to the following points. A Buddha achieves this status by cultivating two main causes: (1) the ultimate intention[196] of great compassion and (2) the ultimate practice[197] of the wisdom that perceives the insubstantiality of persons and entities. The ultimate intention is represented by the epithet "One who desires to help the world,"[198] and the ultimate practice is represented by the epithet "Teacher."[199]

These two causes are what make it possible to achieve the result of enlightenment, which is described in terms of two qualities: the perfection of one's own aims[200] and the perfection of others' aims.[201] The perfection of one's own aims is a Buddha's wisdom body and is represented by the epithet "Sugata," which translates literally, if somewhat awkwardly, as "One who has gone well."[202] The perfection of others' aims is a Buddha's physical body and is represented by the epithet "Savior."[203]

Most of Dharmakīrti's second chapter discusses these two pairs of causes and results in two separate discussions. The first presentation, which addresses the two causes followed by the two results, is referred to as the presentation that proceeds in the original order,[204] which means the order in which they occur in Dignāga's verse of homage. Following that, the same four epithets are discussed again, but in a reverse order—that is, the two results followed by the two causes. Khedrup Je provides the following brief explanation of the purpose of these two presentations:

> The statement of homage that appears in *The Compendium of Knowledge* describes in their entirety both the stages of the path to omniscience and the stages of the path that is the common vehicle.[205] The former is the path that the Lord himself traversed in order to achieve the status of a perfect and fully enlightened Buddha, and the latter represents the instruction that he taught following his enlightenment as the means by which his followers could achieve liberation. Since these are the two principal topics that seekers of liberation must [first] become aware of and [then] meditate upon, this chapter—which explains the statement of homage [that appears in Dignāga's] *Compendium of Knowledge*—was composed in order to eliminate all mistaken understanding and generate an unerring knowledge of the paths to liberation and omniscience, along with their results.[206]

Several pages later, Khedrup Je goes on to explain how these two discussions enable practitioners to develop a deep and unshakable conviction about the nature of the Three Jewels and the significance that this conviction holds for the practice of taking refuge. In the following paragraph, he describes how the first presentation of the four epithets identifies the Three Jewels in the Mahāyāna tradition:

> Thus, the discussion [of the four epithets] in the original order establishes accurately the Three Jewels as understood in the Mahāyāna tradition, because the Buddha Jewel is represented by the state of omniscience and the essence body that possesses three forms of abandonment[207]; the Sangha Jewel is represented by the Bodhisattvas who are motivated by the great compassion that wishes to liberate all beings and who cultivate over a extended period of time the wisdom[208] that directly realizes selflessness in combination with those practices described as the means aspect of the Mahāyāna path; and the Dharma Jewel is represented by the wisdom that directly realizes selflessness and is supported by those elements of the Mahāyāna path described as excellent means, such as great compassion and the aspiration to achieve unsurpassed enlightenment.

This analysis of how the Three Jewels are taught in Dharmakīrti's text is one that must be inferred from what the root text explicitly states. The phrase "state of omniscience" is a reference to the epithet "Savior" in that a Buddha possesses both the knowledge that enables him to reveal the path to others and the unselfish compassion that obligates him to exercise that ability accurately and truthfully. This represents the essence of a Buddha's wisdom body,[209] which Khedrup Tenba Dargye defines in his *Overview of the Perfection of Wisdom* as "the ultimate and immaculate wisdom that has been transformed beyond [all states of] impurity."[210] While other works, such as the *Ornament of Mahāyāna Sūtras*[211] and the *Ornament of Realizations*,[212] provide more detailed explanations of the nature of the wisdom body, the principal aim of Dharmakīrti's *Extensive Treatise* is to present logical proofs for the possibility of achieving this state.

The phrase "three forms of abandonment" is a reference to the epithet "Sugata," or "One who has gone well." The prefix *su* in "Sugata" generally serves as an adjective or adverb that means "good" or "well." The first explanation of this epithet is that it refers to a Buddha's ultimate Truth of Cessation—which is to say, the condition of having completely abandoned the two types of obscurations. As Khedrup Je mentions, this represents a Buddha's essence body.[213] Dharmakīrti follows an established tradition by explaining that a Buddha's ultimate cessation represents three types of goodness. First, a Buddha's ultimate cessation is "excellent"[214] in that it is superior to the accomplishments of non-Buddhist practitioners, since none of them have ever achieved the transcendent realization of selflessness. Second, this ultimate cessation insures that samsaric rebirth and the mental afflictions "will not recur,"[215] to distinguish it from the cessation achieved by those Hīnayāna Āryas who have not yet abandoned all the mental afflictions. Finally, it is a condition in which all the obscurations have been destroyed "without remainder,"[216] to indicate that a Buddha is not subject to the subtle obstacles that Hīnayāna Arhats do not abandon. These two qualities identify principal elements of the Buddha Jewel as understood in the Mahāyāna tradition.

The phrase "great compassion" is a reference to the epithet "One who desires to help the world." As describe above, this phrase is used to describe the "ultimate intention" that motivates a Bodhisattva to pursue Buddhahood so that he or she can achieve the ability to benefit others in the highest way possible. Thus, it represents an essential quality of the Mahāyāna Sangha Jewel. The phrase "wisdom that directly realizes selflessness" is meant to indicate the epithet "Teacher." As noted earlier, this stands for the "ultimate practice" of wisdom that Bodhisattvas must perfect to achieve enlightenment, and therefore represents another essential quality of the Mahāyāna Sangha. These same two elements also indicate the nature of the Mahāyāna Dharma Jewel, in that they are qualities associated with the Truth of Cessation and the Truth of the Path, both of which are present to some degree in the minds of all Mahāyāna Āryas.

In seeking to establish the possibility of attaining the enlightenment represented by the perfection of the two aims, the first presentation addresses two conditions that must be met if one is to complete their two causes. The first condition is the existence of past and future lives, which establishes the possibility of cultivating the path over countless lifetimes until one has achieved the ultimate goal. This topic was discussed in the previous section. The second condition is that it must be possible for spiritual qualities such as compassion and wisdom to be developed until they reach a state of perfection.

The latter point centers on the proposition that the improvement of spiritual qualities is not innately subject to any limitation. The arguments that Dharmakīrti presents in favor of this thesis are meant to counter the common-sense notion that, although mental qualities can be improved to a certain degree, these improvements cannot be developed beyond the boundaries of human nature. Concordant examples for such a view are the physical limit to how far an athlete can jump and the natural limit to how hot water can be heated.

The main Buddhist argument that is put forward to counter this belief is called "a reason that relates to special qualities."[217] There are two special qualities: (1) the mind is a "stable basis"[218] that permits improvements to occur continuously over an indefinite period of time, and (2) such improvements "occur naturally,"[219] making it possible for them to reach a state of perfection. Heated water is an example of an unstable basis, both because its temperature cannot rise above the boiling point and because, if the heat is maintained continuously, it will eventually evaporate. Similarly, the act of jumping may be improved through continuous training, but subsequent effort does not indefinitely continue to produce jumps of ever greater distances.

By contrast, the mind is not subject to either of these restrictions. Spiritual qualities like compassion, wisdom, etc., respond to repeated practice[220] in such a way that each improvement of a particular quality is retained in the mind without disappearing. Therefore, whatever level of attainment one has achieved previously, the quality will continue to arise naturally and effortlessly. It is likened to the way in which, when a log of wood has been ignited, the fire will continue to burn spontaneously until the wood has burned completely. In the case of mental qualities, a direct consequence of this characteristic is that each new effort to cultivate compassion, etc., provides an opportunity for those qualities to be developed to an ever higher degree. This is what is meant by saying that the improvement of mental qualities can "occur naturally." Tibetan commentaries explain that the mind is a "stable basis" in the sense that its essential nature of luminous awareness[221] promotes the continuous development of compassion, etc., since these spiritual qualities arise with the same essential nature as the mind itself.

Dharmakīrti presents the key elements of this view in the following verses:

> In the same way that fire, and the like, [act] upon
> Such objects as wood, mercury, and gold,
> The compassion, etc., that arise from repeated practice
> Continue to be produced in the mind naturally.
>
> Therefore, that which has come about through those [repeated
> exercises]
> Arises as a quality having the nature [of mind];

And each effort subsequent to that [former practice]
Is able to bring about an [ever greater] improvement.

Moreover, since compassion, and the like, are mental states
That grow from prior seeds that are the same class [of entity],
When repeated practice of those [qualities] occurs,
Why would they remain fixed [in an unchanged state]?[222]

The ultimate intention of compassion is the motivating factor that urges a Bodhisattva to pursue the ultimate practice of wisdom, since that wisdom, by destroying the mental obstacles, gives one the ability to liberate other beings. It also insures that one will continue to develop this wisdom until enlightenment has been reached, rather than seeking merely to terminate one's own suffering. This is how the two ultimate causes lead to the attainment of the perfection of the two aims.

After providing a description of how the Three Jewels of the Hīnayāna tradition are implicitly taught in Dharmakīrti's second explanation of the four epithets, Khedrup Je concludes his introductory remarks by describing a series of benefits that are gained by developing an understanding of the Three Jewels that derives from valid cognition. He contrasts this with the shortcomings of an understanding that is based solely upon the acceptance of another person's word:

> When a practitioner uses the type of valid inference that is based upon the nature of entities[223] to correctly ascertain in the manner described the various aspects of the cognitional Teaching, as well as the Teacher who revealed it and the Sangha who practice it, he also recognizes by means of valid knowledge[224] that the Sugata's scriptural Teaching, which contains the verbal descriptions of these topics, deserves to be viewed [with deep reverence] as the wondrous place where all seekers of liberation must begin their spiritual activities. He further acquires an unshakable devotion toward the Teacher and his Teaching that neither Mara nor any proponent of a rival system could persuade him to relinquish. Since this quality derives from "faith born of insight," it is free of such shortcomings as doubt, unsubstantiated belief,[225] or a belief embraced merely to please someone else, or out of the desire to achieve fame, praise, gain, or honor. In addition, the individual who possesses this quality will succeed in further increasing the strength of his spiritual lineage.[226]

> Thus, once you succeed in eliciting a true certainty about the validity of the Three Jewels on the basis of valid knowledge, every form of meditation practice that you undertake—from a single instance of taking refuge to all those that follow—has the power to demolish the mountain of samsara. On the other hand, as long as your efforts to cultivate faith in the virtuous qualities of the Three Jewels derive merely from your acceptance of another person's word, and as long as you are unable to recognize any reason [that has the ability] to establish that the Three Jewels even exist, much less ascertain a reason [that has the ability] to determine that they possess this or that particular virtuous quality, you may recite earnestly, in a loud voice, and for long periods of time verses that express the act of taking refuge, and you may even—despite being unable to state any reason why—shed streams of tears that seem like rain falling from the heavens; however, this activity will provide no benefit for you beyond the mere reciting of names,[227] as it in no way fulfills the true meaning of the act of taking refuge.[228]

The use of the phrase "cognitional Teaching"[229] here is a reference to the Dharma Jewel. It is the form of the Buddha's teaching that is generated in the mind as spiritual awareness and is identified with the three trainings and the five paths. The "ultimate" Dharma Jewel[230] is those aspects of the cognitional Teaching that are achieved when a practitioner attains the transcendent path. This is the true source of refuge, as one's actual salvation comes through attaining both the Truth of the Path and the Truth of Cessation for oneself. By contrast, the "scriptural Teaching"[231] is the conventional form of the Dharma Jewel, which provides a verbal description of the ultimate Dharma Jewel and the means of attaining it, along with either of the two supreme goals of Hīnayāna nirvana or unsurpassed Buddhahood. That is to say, the scriptural Teaching is the eighty-four thousand heaps of the Buddha's spoken word that is organized into three collections known as "baskets."[232] Khedrup Je's reference to these two forms of the Teaching is meant to establish a link between the two that will lead one to generate profound reverence for the canonical scriptures as well.

In the strictest sense, "faith born of insight"[233] does not arise until after one has achieved a direct realization of ultimate truth during the Seeing Path. Nevertheless, Asaṅga also writes in his *Listeners' Stage* that an approximation of this type of faith is also present during the Preparation Path:[234]

> The "faculty of faith" and the "strength of faith" are to be regarded as the four forms of faith born of insight.
>
> Why is that?
>
> They are the causes, conditions, and primary factors for the faith born of insight that is possessed by one whose practice has reached a flawless state.[235] Therefore, on the basis of this causal relationship and by reason of the fact that [the faith born of insight] is a fruit that is governed by them, the Lord declared that [the faculty of faith and the strength of faith] should be regarded in this manner, not because that is their actual state or true character.[236]

The faculty of faith and the strength of faith are identified with a group of five virtuous mental factors that are present at different levels of the Preparation Path. At an earlier stage of this path, the five qualities of faith, effort, recollection, concentration, and wisdom are referred to as "faculties"[237] because they exercise a powerful influence toward bringing about a realization of the Truths. When these same qualities develop to the point where they can no longer be overcome by any nonvirtuous states, they are called "strengths."[238]

It is clear that Khedrup Je's reference to the faith born of insight is not meant in relation to the Seeing Path, since he is describing a type of faith that is elicited by inferential knowledge, not direct yogic perception. Of the four types of faith born of insight, only the first three actually constitute faith; the fourth is actually defined as a form of pure morality. As the original Sanskrit phrase indicates, the term translated in Tibetan as "faith" is more literally the same "clarity"[239] that describes one of the three types of faith identified in the *Summary of the Five Heaps*. In his *Commentary to the Treasury of Higher Learning*,[240] Vasubandhu states the following about these four types of "clarity of mind":

> What is the meaning of "faith born of insight"?
>
> Faith born of insight is the firm conviction[241] that is gained by having realized the [Four Noble] Truths exactly as they are. The traditional order in which they are enumerated conforms to the order in which they occur to a practitioner after he [or she] has arisen [from the meditative absorption in which the Four Truths were realized directly].
>
> How do they occur to a practitioner who has arisen [from a direct realization of the Four Truths]?

> He [or she] thinks to himself: "How marvelous! Truly, the Lord is a fully enlightened Buddha! Truly, his system of Dharma is well spoken! Truly, his Sangha of Listener Disciples is well established [in a genuine spiritual life]!" The practitioner develops these thoughts because [he or she perceives the Buddha, Dharma, and Sangha] as being like a doctor, medicine, and those who tend the sick, respectively. The fourth quality[242] is [also] referred to by the term ["faith born of insight"] because it is a purity[243] of morality that is engendered by a purity of mind—which is to say, it is the conduct of one who has developed such purity of thought or because [this purity of morality is perceived] as being a state that is free of affliction. Alternatively, [the four objects of these attitudes] are thought of as representing the guide, the path, traveling companions, and the vehicle.[244]

These excerpts from Khedrup Je's commentary to *The Extensive Treatise on Knowledge* suggest a standard for the ideal form of faith that one should seek in relation to the Three Jewels. My comments have sought to clarify how it is possible to establish a logical foundation for believing, not only in the existence of the Three Jewels, but also in their unique and unfailing capacity to provide a means of refuge from the suffering nature of samsaric existence. In the West, it is commonly held that faith cannot and does not need to be justified on the basis of reason. It is often referred to as a belief in the unknowable. Indeed, faith and reason are regarded as radically distinct, perhaps even competing, states of mind. Such views are not supported by Buddhist doctrine. In the Buddhist tradition, faith, as well as other virtuous states, can be fostered and strengthened by reason and understanding. Many techniques of Buddhist mental training appeal to reason as a means of controlling the mental afflictions, by providing a basis for recognizing their inappropriateness and harmfulness. A similar process is used for evoking such positive emotions as patience, loving-kindness, equanimity, and the like.

Numerous renowned Tibetan teachers have declared that because the Buddhist treatises on epistemology are principally a means of defending the faith from its opponents, they hold little importance for personal spiritual development. Je Tsongkapa, however, regarded the writings of Dignāga and Dharmakīrti as having a unique ability to generate powerful convictions regarding all areas of spiritual practice, including faith. He asserts this position forthrightly in his autobiographical poem *A Brief Account of My Spiritual Life:*[245]

Many in this Northern Land—both those who have
And have not studied the treatises on knowledge—
Declare with one voice that neither the *Aphorisms*[246]
Nor the *Seven-part Collection*[247] contain explanations
On the practice that leads to enlightenment.

Yet they also consider as authoritative
Mañjughoṣa's direct admonition to Dignāga
In which he urged: "You must compose this [work].
In the future, it will become like eyes for all beings."[248]

Seeing this as the height of an unreasonable position,
I undertook to scrutinize that system with special care.
Having done so, I gained a profound conviction that the meaning
Of the verse of homage from *The Compendium of Knowledge*—
[As explained] in [the chapter entitled] "Establishing the [Buddha's]
authority"[249]
Through presentations in both the original and reverse order—
Proves that Lord [Buddha] is an authoritative being
For those who seek liberation and, through that [proof],
Also [establishes] that his Teaching alone is
The place of refuge for those who desire liberation.

Through this, I also experienced exceptional joy
Upon discovering, through the path of reasoning,
That [this system] contains in a condensed form
All the key elements of the two vehicles' paths.

Reflecting on this, I find that my spiritual aims have been fulfilled.
How exceptionally kind you have been, O Treasure of Wisdom![250]

A LOGICAL JUSTIFICATION FOR THE DOCTRINE OF KARMA

The final topic in the instructions for "lesser" persons is how to cultivate the fundamental principles of morality based on the doctrine of karma. At the conclusion of the section on taking refuge, Je Tsongkapa presents the following explanation of the importance of this topic:

When you recall death as described earlier and then generate fear by reflecting on the prospect of being reborn in the lower states following your death, you may have the following thought: "Recognizing that the Three Jewels are the refuge object that saves me from this fate, once I adopt them as a refuge object and adhere to the precepts[251] associated with the act of taking refuge, what is the method by which they save me?" A verse from the *Collection of Uplifting Sayings* states:

> I have taught you the path
> That removes the pangs of craving.
> You must attain this result for yourselves;
> The Tathāgatas only point the way.[252]

As this verse suggests, Buddha is the teacher who reveals how we can secure a state of refuge and the Sangha is the body of individuals who assist us in pursuing that refuge; but the Dharma Jewel is the actual refuge, because achieving the Dharma is what frees us from the object of our fear. Moreover, the ultimate Dharma Jewel is identified as the culmination of various forms of "abandonment" and "realization" that reach such a state only after these two qualities have gone through a process of being progressively improved since the novice stage, when a practitioner undertakes to abandon any portion of his or her faults and to develop the first elements of virtuous states of mind. This is how the ultimate Dharma Jewel is achieved; it does not spring into being all at once.

At this point in the instruction, then, you should consider the Dharma to be a form of practice in which you learn the classifications of virtuous and nonvirtuous karma, together with their results, and then strive properly to cultivate virtuous deeds and avoid nonvirtuous ones. This is because, if you fail to reflect extensively on the two types of karma and their results and to develop a practice that accords with that understanding, you will not put an end to the causes that bring rebirth in the lower states and then, even though you fear being reborn in the lower states, you will be unable to free yourself from the object of that fear. Therefore, in order to save yourself from the karmic result of being born in the lower states, you must restrain your mind from pursuing nonvirtuous karma,

> and the ability to accomplish that depends on gaining a firm belief in the doctrine of karma and its results.[253]

As they are being used in this passage, the terms "abandonment"[254] and "realization"[255] refer to the Truth of Cessation and the Truth of the Path, respectively. While philosophical texts make numerous distinctions about different aspects of the Three Jewels, the general definition of the ultimate Dharma Jewel is any aspect of the Truth of Cessation or the Truth of the Path that is present in the mind of an Ārya. More specifically, the Truth of Cessation is a collection of "separation results,"[256] each of which is achieved through the action of a corresponding "noninterruption path."[257] The Truth of the Path is any form of spiritual knowledge in the mind of an Ārya that serves as the means of attaining those cessations.

Although the cessations are said to be "produced" through the action of the Truth of the Path, strictly speaking they are not themselves causally produced or "conditioned" entities.[258] Rather, they are states that, once acquired, are not capable of degenerating or being lost. Liberation from samsara takes place when a practitioner gains the cessation related to the final and most subtle form of the mental afflictions. The series of noninterruption paths, which represent one aspect of the Truth of the Path, occur only in a state of meditative absorption during the Seeing Path and the Meditation Path. The exact nature of the wisdom that is present during these noninterruption paths is explained differently in the various Buddhist philosophical schools. According to the Mādhyamika Prasaṅgika School, it is always a state in which the practitioner is absorbed in a direct realization of emptiness.

When a noninterruption path completes its action of destroying some aspect of either of the two types of obscurations, the practitioner—while still in a state of meditative absorption—achieves a particular cessation and simultaneously develops what is referred to as a "liberation path."[259] Other forms of the Truth of the Path, such as the limbs of right livelihood and right action that form part of the Eightfold Noble Path, are not states of one-pointed meditative absorption.

The above passage from the *Great Treatise* describes a beginning practitioner's spiritual training as the effort to "abandon any portion of [one's] faults and to develop the first elements of virtuous states of mind." Moreover, Je Tsongkapa underscores the significance of this practice by establishing its link with the higher goal of attaining the ultimate Dharma Jewel. This exercise of abandoning faults is closely related in meaning to the phrase "the morality of abandoning the ten nonvirtuous deeds."[260] This describes a form of training that is by no means limited to novice Buddhist practitioners, since abandoning the first seven of these ten is the foundation of both the Vinaya system of morality and the aspect of Mahāyāna ethics called the "morality of restraint."[261]

One important key in the effort to cultivate this form of discipline is represented by the two virtuous mental factors of "shame" and "abashment," both of which constitute a moral impetus or strength to restrain oneself from engaging in nonvirtuous behavior. Sthiramati describes shame in part as "the sense of dejection that is felt with regard to an objectionable act" and describes it further in terms of a thought in which a person might think, "This kind of evil deed is reprehensible from the perspective of the Dharma, because it has an undesirable maturation and because it constitutes the doing of harm to another." The phrase "an undesirable maturation" is a direct reference to the doctrine of karma in that it stems from the notion that a nonvirtuous deed has the inherent potential of ripening in the future as some form of suffering for the person who committed it.

The doctrine of karma is fundamental not only to the subject of Buddhist morality; it also supersedes the belief in a divine creator, providing an alternate explanation for the formation of the entire universe—both that of sentient beings and the physical world. As Vasubandhu notes in *The Treasury of Higher Learning:* "the manifold diversity of the world is produced by karma."[262] Although not even a Buddha can circumvent the power of karma, it is a central tenet of his followers that only a fully enlightened being has the knowledge that can perceive all its minute subtlety. This is one reason why Buddha's disciples frequently asked him to reveal the past karma that caused many of the extraordinary incidents described in canonical literature.

Although a practitioner cannot comprehend everything about the subtle workings of karma, there are many principles, narratives, and illustrative examples in Buddhist writings that can be learned and applied to one's everyday conduct as the basis for a program of ethical training. Typically, this begins with a study of the ten nonvirtuous karmic paths, which are examined at length in such writings as Vasubandhu's *Treasury of Higher Learning* and Asaṅga's *Levels of Spiritual Practice*. The early Abhidharma works and later philosophical writings also clarify and explain much of the specialized terminology relating to karma that appears in canonical literature. The early Kadampa work by Drolungpa Lodrö Jung-ne, entitled *A Detailed Explanation of the Stages of the Path for Entering the Sugata's Precious Teaching*,[263] contains extensive instructions on a wide range of practices relating to the topic of karma. A number of these points are cited in the

Great Treatise. At the end of his own presentation on this subject, Je Tsongkapa makes the following observation:

> Holding a proper view of dependent origination in terms of the two types of karma and their results is the indispensable foundation for achieving [the goals] of all the [three Buddhist] vehicles, as well as all the aims of mankind. For this reason, the instructions that appear above should be taken as only an abbreviated presentation. It is of vital importance that you also read the *Sutra on Closely Placed Recollection of the True Dharma*, the *Sutra of the Wise and Foolish*, the *Hundred Chronicles on Karma*, the *Hundred Narratives*, the stories that appear in the Vinaya collection, as well as other related scriptures, in order to develop a strong and abiding conviction [regarding this topic].[264]

While it is essential to learn the theory of karma and read a wide variety of illustrative stories from canonical literature in order to develop an effective ethical practice, it is also fundamentally important to understand that the entire system is predicated on the trustworthiness of the Buddha's word. Since only a Buddha can possess absolute certainty about the exact manner in which the principles of karma play out, one is left to ponder whether there is any way to verify the accuracy of the accounts that are recorded in scripture. The principal source for our inquiry into the validity of the Buddha's testimony is a section from Dharmakīrti's own commentary to a series of five verses from his *Extensive Treatise on Knowledge*.[265] A translation of this portion of the autocommentary along with the verses appears below. The discussion centers on an aphorism from Dignāga's *Compendium of Knowledge* that states: "An authoritative person's speech possesses the nature of inference, because of its universal non-contradictoriness."[266] This assertion can be parsed as saying in part that a Buddha's statements regarding objects that lie beyond an ordinary person's comprehension merit the epistemological status of an inference, because Buddha's speech displays an overall quality of non-contradictoriness.

Dignāga and his school of Buddhist epistemology only accept two forms of valid cognition: perception and inference. Since "non-contradictoriness"[267] is the general criterion for valid cognition and our understanding of the particulars of karma is certainly not direct, Dignāga declares that Buddha's accounts concerning the workings of karma constitute a valid source of inference regarding the subject matter that they describe. The central questions that arise from Dignāga's assertion are (1) what does it mean to say that Buddha's statements about karma are not contradictory, and (2) what is the sense in which these statements are considered a source of inference. The following excerpts from Dharmakīrti's autocommentary form one uninterrupted passage; here, however, I have inserted explanatory remarks between passages with the aim of trying to answer these two questions. The excerpt begins with the following verse:

> Because words do not possess
> A necessary concomitance with their objects,
> They cannot prove [the existence of] an object.
> Therefore, they [only] indicate the speaker's intent.[268]

> Words do not operate in exact agreement with entities, such that the nature of an object could be established through them. Because their occurrence depends upon a person's desire to speak, they have a necessary concomitance with that [intention], and it is that alone which they are able to make known. Not all beliefs of a person are in exact accord with the nature of things.[269] Nor is any entity that is not dependent [on words] able to make known any other object.

In general terms, this first verse can be understood as rejecting the notion that verbal testimony constitutes a separate form of valid cognition, as held, for instance, by the non-Buddhist Nyāya and Mīmāṃsā schools. Proponents of these systems recognize two kinds of testimony: (1) the assertions of ordinary persons who are trustworthy with regard to matters about which they are knowledgeable and (2) the infallible scriptural authority of the Vedas. Dharmakīrti's verse rejects the former kind of testimony with the argument that there is no necessary logical relation between speech and its content. He counters that only the speaker's intention can be directly inferred from the meaning of speech. Regarding the latter kind of testimony, the Nyāyikas assert that the authority of the Vedas derives from the divine creator Īśvara. The Mīmāṃsākas claim the Vedas to be eternal speech that is self-validating and was not uttered by any being. Buddhist scholars have unanimously rejected both these claims because they rest on the assumption that there can be an efficient cause that is eternal and unchanging. Dharmakīrti follows up his comments on the initial verse by voicing the hypothetical rejoinder that this verse seems to contradict Dignāga's aphorism on the nature of an authoritative person's testimony:[270]

> Well, then, how do you explain the claim that authoritative scripture is a valid source of inference, as expressed in the statement that "an authoritative person's speech possesses the nature of inference, because of its universal non-contradictoriness"?

The initial verse may also be seen as mainly refuting the position that the testimony of ordinary persons can represent a source of valid knowledge. While Buddhists also deny the validity of the Vedas as an infallible source of knowledge concerning spiritual truth, this does not mean they do not believe the Buddha represents a valid alternative. Indeed, in the next four verses and their accompanying commentary, Dharmakīrti sets out to explain the theory that underlies Dignāga's position on this topic.

> An [ordinary] person cannot establish [the inferential nature of scriptural testimony[271]] except by relying upon the authoritativeness of scripture, because he [or she] has heard both the great benefits [of virtuous actions] and [the grave consequences of having to be reborn in] the lower states that come from pursuing or avoiding certain kinds of actions whose results lie beyond ordinary perception, and because he [or she] does not see anything that contradicts the possibility that [these results] will indeed occur. Thus, the determination that it would be preferable, in the face of such a recommended course of action, to proceed accordingly is said to be one whose validity derives from [having undertaken a proper] investigation.

The person who wants to develop this type of inference correctly is characterized as being one who has a reflective nature.[272] Having heard from a teacher or read that certain actions bring favorable results in future lives while others will lead to horrible forms of ruin in the lower states, he or she is concerned about the possible consequences of failing to heed this advice. These matters that lie beyond the grasp of an ordinary person are referred to as being "completely invisible" or "extremely hidden."[273] Given that status, the practitioner is further left to ponder what grounds there might be for determining the truthfulness of such scriptural statements. Dharmakīrti suggests that if one can find nothing contradictory in what the scriptures say in general and what they say about the consequences of good and bad conduct in particular, then it would be prudent to follow their admonitions.[274] The wording of this comment is telling and provides a hint as to how this particular form of inference is meant to be understood. The following statement from Karṇakagomī's subcommentary to Dharmakīrti's autocommentary provides further clarification:

> The Master was not speaking about an actual logical validity when he described scripture as possessing the nature of inference; rather, [he was using that term] in relation to a person's [ability to decide on a proper] course of action.[275]

The epithet "Master" is a reference to Dignāga and his aforementioned aphorism on scriptural authority. Karṇakagomī explains that the type of inference that Dignāga meant was not one that derives from examining either the nature or causal interaction of entities. Instead, it should be understood as a form of inference that provides reasonable justification for choosing a proper course of conduct. In short, a reflective person should subject the Buddha's teachings to a thorough logical analysis. If this investigation uncovers no flaws, then it is reasonable to conclude that scriptural statements about karma ought to be heeded. The implication is that the comprehensive nature of this investigation permits such a conclusion to rise to the level of a valid inference. As Dharmakīrti notes in his final remark about this verse, the validity of scriptural testimony is one that is said to derive from investigation.[276] The nature of this investigation is the subject of the next three verses.

Three Necessary Qualities That Make Speech Worthy of Investigation

> And that [treatise or body of speech which is worthy of being investigated] is described as follows:
>
> Speech that is worthy of investigation
> Is consistent, has a suitable means [by which it can be
> practiced],
> And describes a [genuine] aim of mankind;
> Speech other than that is unworthy.[277]
>
> Consistent speech means [speech whose] various elements contribute to one overall coherent meaning,[278] unlike such statements as "ten pomegranates, etc.,"[279] which have no orderly arrangement at

> all. [If it is] otherwise [than consistent], it reveals the flawed nature of the speaker. Furthermore, those treatises that describe a goal which is impossible to attain, like instruction on wearing a jewel from the *nāga* Takṣaka's hood as an antidote for poison, will not be deemed worthy of investigation by anyone who seeks a meaningful result. This is also true for those [treatises that describe] a result which is not a meaningful goal of mankind, like an investigation into the nature of crow's teeth. A treatise that is not subject to these flaws—which is to say, one that is well-organized, capable of being practiced, and describes a genuine aim of mankind—is worthy of being investigated, because it would be improper to devote one's attention to any other kind of work. If, upon examination, [such a body of speech] is found not to be in disagreement with reality, one would do well to follow its injunctions.

Before describing the nature of the investigation that is to be undertaken, Dharmakīrti begins by specifying three conditions that define the kind of scriptural text that merits such scrutiny. First, it must be consistent, which is to say that its various elements are logically compatible and form part of an intelligible and coherent system. Second, it should advocate a type of practice that is capable of being carried out, since no one would be interested in a treatise that sets out an unattainable goal. Third, it should describe a genuine spiritual goal—which for Buddhists is the temporary goal of attaining rebirth in the higher states and the two ultimate goals of liberation and supreme enlightenment. Dharmakīrti's concluding remark contains a reference to the Buddhist criterion for valid cognition, which is that its object "not be in disagreement with reality."[280]

In the next verse, Dharmakīrti defines the nature of the threefold investigation that allows us to conclude that Buddha's statements regarding "extremely hidden" matters are free of contradiction[281] and, therefore, ought to be followed.

> What, then, does it mean for [such speech] not to be in disagreement with reality?
>
> The non-contradictoriness of that [speech]
> With regard to seen and unseen objects
> Is for it not to be refuted by perception
> Or either of the two types of inference.[282]

> Not to be refuted by perception means for those entities that are considered to be present to the senses to actually have such a nature—as is the case with those that are (1) blue, etc.; (2) pain and pleasure; (3) the distinguishing of signs; (4) desire, etc.; and (5) awareness. Similarly, it means for those entities that are not considered to be present to the senses to lack that nature—as is the case with sound, etc., that are believed to have the nature of satisfaction, etc., and [those entities defined as] substance, action, universal, conjunction, etc.

Investigating the Objects of Direct Experience

This passage addresses the first kind of investigation that a reflective person should undertake. Such investigation is carried out in relation to what the root-text verse refers to as "seen objects," which in this instance means the objects of direct perception that make up our everyday experience. Tibetan literature describes them as "seen objects that are directly present."[283]

The five types of entities described here as those "that are considered to be present to the senses" clearly reference the Buddhist doctrine of the five heaps. "Blue, etc." means those entities that comprise the form heap; "pain and pleasure" represent the feeling heap; "the distinguishing of signs"[284] describes the essential nature of conceptions; "desire, etc." are the collection of entities that are associated with the formations heap; and "awareness"[285] is a synonym for the Buddhist term that is usually translated as "consciousness,"[286] which is to say, the fifth and final heap.

The phrase "those entities that are not considered to be present to the senses" refers to the theoretical formulations that appear in non-Buddhist philosophical systems about the objects of direct perception. For instance, the phrase "sound, etc., that are believed to have the nature of satisfaction, etc." is a reference to the doctrine of the Sāṃkhya School that the essence of all material phenomena is a combination of three attributes. While these attributes are most commonly described by the terms "intelligibility," "activity," and "inertia,"[287] here they are alluded to with the phrase "satisfaction, etc.," which is a reference to their synonyms of "satisfaction," "dissatisfaction," and "confusion."[288] Similarly, the phrase "[those entities defined as] substance, action, universal, conjunction, etc." references terms from the Vaiśeṣika School. "Substance,"[289] "activity,"[290] and "universal"[291] represent three of the school's six basic categories.[292] "Conjunction"[293] is a particular type of quality,[294] yet another of the six categories.

Dharmakīrti suggests that this first type of investigation will lead to the following conclusions: (1) Buddha's description of the objects of direct experience in terms of the doctrine of the five heaps is accurate and (2) Buddha's criticism of other theories in relation to these same objects is also correct. The most obvious point to make about this first passage is that, in order to evaluate these claims, one must first have a correct understanding of the teaching on the five heaps, not to mention basic knowledge of non-Buddhist systems of thought. Simply put, it means that, at the very least, knowledge of the five heaps is a necessary condition for one to understand why Buddha can be considered a reliable authority on the subject of karma.

Investigating Teachings Such as the Four Noble Truths

Next, the autocommentary addresses the second kind of investigation that should be undertaken:

> Similarly, [not to be refuted by inference] means for those entities that are considered to be objects of the type of inference that does not rely on scriptural authority[295] to actually have such a nature—as is the case with [those that are explained by the teaching on] the Four Noble Truths. Similarly, it means for those entities that are not objects of [valid] inference to lack that nature—as with [the objects described by non-Buddhists as constituting] a soul, etc.

Here we are informed that the second type of investigation involves objects that are the province of inferential reasoning. The purpose of this exercise is to verify the truthfulness of Buddha's teachings on the Four Noble Truths and the erring nature of non-Buddhist teachings that assert the existence of such objects as a soul, a divine creator, and the like.

Like the five heaps, the Four Noble Truths also constitute "seen objects" even though they are not directly evident. They are capable of being "seen" with the knowledge that is gained through valid inference. However, to use the Tibetan expression, they are considered "slightly hidden"[296] objects, because they will remain beyond our grasp if we fail to apply the power of correct reasoning. Typical examples of this type of object are subtle impermanence, the nonexistence of a real personal self, and emptiness.

The entities central to the doctrine of the Four Noble Truths again are the five grasping heaps. This is made clear in the following brief description that appears in Sthiramati's *Commentary to the Treatise on the Five Heaps*:

> The Truth of Suffering is the aspect of the five grasping heaps that constitutes a result. [It is suffering] because the Āryas recognize it as being adverse and [it is a truth] because its aspects of impermanence and the rest are not erroneous.
>
> The Truth of Origination is the aspect of the five grasping heaps that constitutes a cause. [It is an origination] because it is the cause of suffering and [it is a truth] because its aspects of being a condition and the rest are not erroneous.
>
> The Truth of Cessation is the state in which suffering has been terminated. [It is a cessation] because it is a state in which suffering and its causes have been terminated and [it is a truth] because its aspects of being a state of peace and the rest are not erroneous.
>
> The Truth of the Path is the Eightfold Noble Path. [It is a path] because it brings about the cessation of suffering and [it is a truth] because its aspects of leading to deliverance and the rest are not erroneous.[297]

Each of the Four Noble Truths is explained in terms of four aspects. Those that pertain to the Truth of Suffering are impermanence, suffering, emptiness, and selflessness. They are understood as follows: (1) The five grasping heaps are impermanent[298] in that they occur only when their causes are present, and they arise and pass away from moment to moment; (2) they are characterized by suffering[299] in that their existence is controlled by karma and the mental afflictions, and the Āryas recognize them as having an adverse nature; (3) they are void[300] in that they are not governed by a self that is distinct from them; and (4) they are selfless[301] in that they do not constitute an independent self. These aspects are taught as antidotes for the four erroneous assumptions[302] that (1) what is impermanent is permanent, (2) what is unsatisfactory is a form of well being, (3) what is impure is pure, and (4) what does not constitute a self is a real self. Impermanence is the antidote for the mistaken belief that what is impermanent is permanent; suffering is the antidote for both the mistaken belief that what is unsatisfactory is a form of well being and the mistaken belief that what is impure is pure; and both emptiness and selflessness are antidotes for the mistaken belief that what does not constitute a self is a real self.

The four aspects of the Truth of Origination are that the five grasping heaps also constitute the cause, origination, source, and contributing factors for the suffering nature of samsaric existence. Impure deeds and craving are the cause[303] of the grasping heaps in that they are the root cause from which the heaps arise. This aspect is an antidote for the erroneous assumption that the heaps have no cause, which is to say that they arise at random or by chance. Impure deeds and craving also constitute the origination[304] of samsaric suffering in that they produce all the manifold forms of the five heaps and they do so repeatedly. This is an antidote for the erroneous assumption that the heaps are brought into being by a single, permanent cause, such as a divine creator. Impure deeds and craving are the source[305] from which the impure heaps arise in the sense that they generate a condition of intense suffering. This is an antidote for the erroneous assumption that causation is a process in which a pre-existent and permanent nature undergoes transformation. Craving for rebirth is the contributing factor[306] in the arising of the impure heaps. That is, the particular form of craving that a person has for rebirth becomes a determining factor in the type of suffering that is manifested in that rebirth. This is an antidote for the erroneous assumption that the world was created by the will or premeditated thought of a divine creator.

The four aspects of the Truth of Cessation are cessation, peace, goodness, and deliverance. Cessation[307] refers to liberation as the condition in which the suffering of samsaric existence has been brought to an end permanently. This is an antidote for the erroneous assumption that there is no such thing as liberation. Peace[308] refers to liberation as the state in which the torment of the mental afflictions has been completely abandoned. This is an antidote for the erroneous assumption that certain impure states of samsaric existence in which the mental afflictions have not been permanently abandoned, such as the state of composure without conception,[309] constitute liberation. Goodness[310] refers to liberation as a state of ultimate well-being. This is an antidote for the erroneous assumption that certain pleasurable states of mental composure constitute liberation. Deliverance[311] refers to liberation as a state from which one will never return to samsaric existence. This is an antidote for the erroneous assumption that the elimination of suffering is only temporary.

The four aspects of the Truth of the Path are path, rightness, a means of attainment, and the factor that leads to deliverance. The Truth of the Path is referred to as a path[312] because it leads to the cessation of suffering. This is an antidote for the erroneous assumption that there is no true path. The Truth of the Path is characterized by rightness in that it represents a system of proper conduct. This is an antidote for the erroneous assumption that something which is actually a form of suffering constitutes the true path. The Truth of the Path constitutes a means of attainment[313] in that it leads definitely to the attainment of liberation. This is an antidote for the erroneous assumption that some other flawed form of practice represents the true path. The Truth of the Path is described as a factor that leads to deliverance[314] in that it brings about permanent deliverance from samsaric existence. This is an antidote for the erroneous assumption that the path does not bring a deliverance that is irreversible in nature.

Dharmakīrti devotes a lengthy series of arguments in the second chapter of his *Extensive Treatise* to proving the validity of these sixteen aspects. While a detailed analysis of those arguments is beyond the scope of the present discussion, this is precisely the type of exercise that one must carry out to complete the second type of investigation. In addition to bringing a realization of the veracity of the teaching on the Four Noble Truths, this effort should also elicit a deep sense of awe and reverence toward the Buddha for having revealed it. This comes from the recognition that his teaching alone—among all existing spiritual systems—provides unerring insight into the nature of samsaric existence, the ultimate cause of that condition, as well as knowledge of the possibility and means by which we can escape from it. For instance, the gods are reported to have proclaimed after Buddha taught the Four Noble Truths for the first time: "While staying in the Deer Park of Rishipatana near Varanasi, the Blessed One has turned the wheel of the supreme doctrine, a wheel of doctrine that no one else in the world—no ascetic, brahmin, god, or demon, or even Brahma—could turn." Finally, it should be noted that this part of the discussion implies that a correct understanding of the Four Noble Truths is a second necessary condition for understanding why Buddha can be considered a reliable authority on the subject of karma.

Investigating Scriptural Statements on the Workings of Karma

Dharmakīrti's next passage addresses the third and final type of investigation:

> And, in the case of inferences that do depend upon scripture, [not to be refuted by inference] means, for example, not to accept that desire, etc., and those entities that arise from them constitute evil, and then teach that ritual bathing, fire offerings, and the like represent the means of abandoning it. This [characteristic], that within one's ability to make a determination, [Buddha's teachings on] a complete range of objects is free of error, is what it means [for his speech] to be in accord with reality.

This third form of investigation leads to the attainment of a second type of inference that one should apply in relation to objects that are "extremely hidden." While the ordinary person cannot verify for himself the exact nature of the consequences that follow from evil, he can examine what a religious tradition identifies as morally good and bad. In this case, evil is the mental afflictions of desire, hatred, and ignorance, as well as the physical and verbal misdeeds that are generated by them. However, unlike various non-Buddhist Indian traditions, Buddha does not assert that practices such as ritual bathing and fire offerings represent a genuine means of removing this evil. The reflective person can recognize that these external practices are not consistent with the effort to remove flaws that are essentially internal—that is, mental—in nature. Since Buddha does not teach such contradictory forms of practice, we are able to conclude that this type of inference cannot refute his speech, but it can refute the non-Buddhist treatises that urge us to engage in these and other ineffectual practices. This is the third necessary condition for understanding why Buddha can be considered a reliable authority on the subject of karma.

Dharmakīrti concludes his explanation of this verse with the observation that, on the basis of this threefold examination, a reflective person can determine that, within the limits of his intellectual capacity, every topic about which a Buddha expounds is free of error.[315] Tibetan commentaries on the subject of a Buddha's testimony describe his word as "speech that has been proven to be 'pure' (that is, without flaws) on the basis of the three types of examination."[316] This is the "universal non-contradictoriness" that, according to Dignāga, endows an authoritative person's speech with the status of valid inference. In the next verse of the root text, Dharmakīrti quotes Dignāga's aphorism and summarizes the essence of his explanation.

> An authoritative person's speech possesses the nature of
> inference,
> Because of its universal non-contradictoriness.
> This was said due to the mind's ineffectiveness,
> And pertains, as well, to the object of that [speech] which is
> beyond comprehension.[317]

> Because of the universal non-contradictoriness of an authoritative person's speech as [indicated] there [in Dignāga's aphorism] and [explained] here in the above manner, one can infer that the awareness of an entity which cannot be known by perception or

> [ordinary] inference, but which is an object of that [authoritative person's speech] which is unerring with regard to the unseen,[318] is not contradictory. By relying upon that [authoritative speech], [such an awareness] takes on the same [non-contradictoriness] as that of other kinds of [cognitive] awareness. Therefore, even though it [is an understanding that] derives from speech, unlike [ordinary] verbal knowledge it does not merely convey [the speaker's] intention. Rather, because it is free of contradiction [with regard to its extremely hidden object], it is also [a valid form of] inference.

This verse and the accompanying commentary summarize Dignāga's theory of authoritative testimony. In short, it is that an ordinary person's understanding of the extremely hidden objects described in Buddhist canonical literature can take on the status of a valid inference, based on the determination that those scriptures, taken as a whole, are unerring with regard to three types of epistemic object. This is true despite the fact that one's understanding of those extremely hidden objects is itself "ineffective"[319] in relation to them—which is to say, it is incapable of discerning them by any means other than scriptural authority. Hence, this is a type of inference that has the practical significance of permitting a reflective person to reasonably conclude that he or she ought to follow the Buddha's moral injunctions.

In the next verse, Dharmakīrti presents a different way of interpreting Dignāga's view:

> Alternatively, there is another way of explaining how an authoritative person's speech possesses the nature of inference on the strength of its non-contradictoriness.
>
> Or, through the establishment of what to abandon
> And what to acquire, along with the means [that bring them about],
> The nature of inference [can be established] toward another object
> Based upon the non-contradictoriness of the principal topic.[320]
>
> Non-contradictoriness means the absence of error in that [authoritative person's] instructions concerning what ought to be abandoned, what ought to be acquired, as well as the [respective] means that bring them about, as in the manner that the Four Noble Truths

> are explained later.[321] Because of the non-contradictoriness of these [teachings], which are both useful to [the pursuit of] mankind's aim and worthy of being cultivated, one should also accept that [Buddha's statements] with regard to other entities have the same [non-contradictory] nature and are not intended to deceive, because they are not subject to any logical fallacy and because the speaker would gain nothing by falsely teaching something that is useless.

"What ought to be abandoned"[322] refers to the Noble Truth of Suffering; "what ought to be acquired"[323] refers to the Noble Truth of Cessation; and the term "means"[324] refers to the respective causes of these two truths. The means that brings about what ought to be abandoned is the Noble Truth of Origination, and the means that brings about what ought to be acquired is the Noble Truth of the Path. This teaching is described in the verse as the "principal topic," because knowledge of it is what enables one to achieve liberation. By implication, the Buddha's instruction on karma is secondary in importance, since that mainly represents the means of attaining a favorable rebirth.

On the face of it, this verse seems to be asserting that one can infer the validity of Buddha's statements about extremely hidden objects through realizing the truthfulness of the teaching on the Four Noble Truths. However, this should not be taken as meaning that the truthfulness of what Buddha declared about the Four Noble Truths in and of itself proves the truthfulness of what Buddha said about the nature of good and bad karma and their respective results. As noted earlier, the teaching on the Four Noble Truths relates to objects that are only "slightly hidden" and its correctness can be proven on the basis of the type of inference that does not rely on scriptural authority. On the other hand, Buddha's statements about the details and long-term results of good and bad deeds relate to objects that are "extremely hidden," and as such they cannot be verified by either ordinary inference or direct perception.

How, then, can one infer the validity of Buddha's statements about extremely hidden objects through realizing the truthfulness of his teaching on the Four Noble Truths? Both Khedrup Gelek Pelsang and Gyeltsab Darma Rinchen assert that the veracity of the Four Noble Truths serves only as a "concordant example"[325] for the main argument, which is that Buddha's statements about extremely hidden objects are accurate, because they are statements that the three types of investigation have shown to be free of error. Khedrup Je formulates this argument as follows:

> The scriptural statement "From generosity [comes] wealth, from morality [the] happiness [of a favorable rebirth]" is accurate with regard to the meaning it conveys, because it is a scriptural statement that the three types of investigation have shown to be free of error, like the sacred word that teaches the Four Noble Truths.[326]

If the structure of the argument underlying this verse is precisely the same as the one that was summarized in the preceding verse, one might ask why Dharmakīrti saw a need to present it again in the root text. One possibility is that he wanted to emphasize the singular importance of the teaching on the Four Noble Truths to the argument. Knowledge of the Four Noble Truths arises from the second of the three types of investigation explained earlier. Furthermore, knowledge of Buddha's teaching on the five heaps—which is gained through the first type of investigation—is a prerequisite for carrying out a proper analysis of the Four Noble Truths. Similarly, the ability to conduct the third type of investigation presupposes knowledge of the nature and characteristics of psychological states that have a moral dimension. This knowledge, in turn, is sure to be enhanced by the understanding that is gained from the two preceding investigations. Clearly, then, a full and certain understanding of the Four Noble Truths is the pivotal element of this threefold investigation and the centerpiece of the argument that rests upon the insight that is gained from such an analysis. When viewed in this way, it is not difficult to see how knowledge of the Four Noble Truths is the principal reason for concluding that we ought to assume that Buddha's statements about karma are true. In fact, the insight that arises from this knowledge is what provides the impetus for making this unique form of inference regarding objects that are otherwise beyond our grasp.

Dharmakīrti summarizes this discussion with the following statement:

> Moreover, in the case of both [these latter two verses], it is due to the absence of [any other] resource that sacred scripture has been described as possessing the nature of an inference. Given this [system for developing a meaningful] course of action on the basis of sacred scripture, it would be best to proceed accordingly. This concludes our response [to the objection] that [authoritative scripture] cannot then be [a valid source of] inference, because [of Dharmakīrti's contention that] there is no necessary relation between words and their meaning.

This passage makes these two final points: (1) scriptural authority allows us to make decisions about adopting a prudent course of action in relation to matters that would otherwise remain hidden from us, and (2) the unique quality of truthfulness that is accorded the Buddha's speech on the basis of a threefold analysis does not contradict the general assertion that there is no necessary connection between the content of speech and objective reality.

Candrakīrti Presents a Similar Analysis

Āryadeva's *Four Hundred Verses*, a text composed some four centuries before the time of both Dignāga and Dharmakīrti, also addresses the validity of Buddha's assertions about extremely hidden objects. In his commentary on a verse from this text, the Mādhyamika Prasaṅgika scholar Candrakīrti expresses views that are quite similar to the ones we have just reviewed here. At the end of the passage presented below, Candrakīrti posits an argument that is identical to Dharmakirti's except that he cites the teaching on emptiness as a concordant example instead of the Four Noble Truths, since in his school the knowledge of this teaching is what constitutes the principal means of attaining liberation.

> Moreover, on the strength of this very explanation regarding the means of attaining "total renunciation,"[327] one can understand that Lord Buddha is a teacher of things as they truly are, in the sense that his transcendent awareness operates in an unimpeded manner with regard to absolutely everything. And by their inability to explain the means of attaining total renunciation, it is established that the *Tīrthika* extremists also have a mistaken understanding with regard to other kinds of objects. This is a point that does not require further debate.
>
> Do you not also maintain that because objects of knowledge are limitless and because those extrasensory entities that [Buddha] gave instructions about are not evident [to the ordinary person], one can only generate uncertainty about their nature and wonder, "Does this object exist as [Buddha] taught that it does, or does it have some other nature?" and that, therefore, there is no means of ascertaining the truthfulness of [Buddha's] mind [in relation to those objects]? The following verse is stated in response to such a view:

Whoever doubts what Buddha said
About objects that lie beyond one's grasp
Should come to believe this very subject
By relying upon [the teaching on] emptiness.[328]

Not all entities are realized on the basis of direct awareness; there are also entities that are understood on the basis of inference. Moreover, it is possible to make an inference about this topic, because there is an example by which it can be illustrated. Concerning this discussion, the means of attaining [complete] renunciation[329] is the fact that all entities are empty of any real essence. This [emptiness] is a reality that cannot be altered by anything. Although this subtle object is also always near at hand, it is evident to no one. Therefore, its truthfulness was proven [by Buddha] in a proper manner by refuting the belief that all entities possess a real essence. Indeed, this should be acknowledged as certain. If there is any reason for the slightest uncertainty about this topic, such that one might wonder whether it is so or otherwise, and that has not been removed by the certainty of the proofs either taught in previous chapters or those to come later, then that [reason] should be advanced. And if one cannot put forward even the slightest cause for such uncertainty, then this example should be understood as definitely proven.

You should, therefore, also be convinced, on the basis of your very own principles, that the Lord's statements in explanation of other objects that are not evident [to the ordinary person] are true as well. The argument can be stated as follows: "[The Buddha's statements regarding objects that lie beyond ordinary comprehension are true], because they were taught by the Tathāgata, just as his statements describing [entities] as empty of any real essence [are true]." Therefore, how could there be any opportunity for one to have doubt about the Buddha's statements regarding objects that lie beyond the comprehension of an ordinary person?[330]

A SPIRITUAL PRACTICE BASED ON THE DOCTRINE OF KARMA

A correct belief about karma and its results should become the foundation for a crucial form of spiritual practice. The justification for holding this belief derives from one's ability to establish that the word of Buddha is authoritative speech. That certainty is itself gained through subjecting his teachings to a threefold investigation. And this investigation involves assessing the veracity of Buddha's instruction on such topics as the five heaps, the Four Noble Truths, and emptiness, as well as verifying whether Buddha's statements about the moral significance of extremely hidden objects contain any inconsistencies.

Moreover, the first of eleven virtues described in Vasubandhu's *Summary of the Five Heaps* is faith. One of its three forms is described as the faith that believes in karma and its results. The logical justification for this belief is the one described above. This shows that the strength of one's faith in the doctrine of karma is determined ultimately by how well such essential Buddhist teachings as the five heaps, the Four Noble Truths, and emptiness are understood. It also needs to be stressed that this faith is much more than the passive acceptance of scriptural assertions about the long-term consequences of one's actions. One of its main roles is to serve as the incentive for cultivating the virtuous mental factor of mindfulness. As a verse from the *Collection of Uplifting Sayings* states:

> Mindfulness is the deathless abode;
> Heedlessness is the abode of death.
> Those who are mindful do not die;
> Heedless persons are forever dead.[331]

Śāntideva also wrote:

> This alone is my fixed concern
> At all times, both day and night:
> Nonvirtue brings certain suffering;
> How, then, can I rid myself of that?[332]

Although mindfulness[333] is also listed as one of eleven virtuous mental factors, it is not a distinct mental entity but rather a state of mind that, in Vasubandhu's words, pursues "the abandoning of nonvirtuous entities together with the cultivating of those virtuous entities that are their antidotes, on the basis of the [virtuous] mental factors ranging from nonattachment to effort."[334] Thus, the practice of mindfulness consists essentially of applying one of four virtuous minds—avoidance of attachment, avoidance of hatred, avoidance of ignorance, and effort—whenever necessary, either to counteract some nonvirtuous thought or deed, or to enhance those virtuous thoughts and activities that properly constitute the focus of one's spiritual practice. The principal reason for the need to practice mindfulness is that we have strong habitual tendencies to develop the various root and secondary mental afflictions. This is why mindfulness is also described as the "antidote to lack of mindfulness,"[335] which itself appears among the twenty secondary mental afflictions.

The ability to cultivate mindfulness effectively requires that the practitioner make use of two additional mental factors, recollection[336] and vigilance.[337] Śāntideva affirms this in the following verse:

> To those who wish to guard their minds
> I make this appeal with palms joined:
> You must use every effort to observe
> Both recollection and vigilance.[338]

This pair of mental factors figures prominently in the first two of the three Buddhist trainings, those of morality and one-pointed concentration. In the case of morality, recollection and vigilance are essential to cultivating mindfulness, and the latter is the antidote for the heedlessness or lack of mindfulness that represents one of the four "doors that lead to the occurrence of moral transgressions."[339] In the case of the Buddhist training to develop one-pointed concentration, *The Treatise That Distinguishes the Middle View from Extreme Views* lists recollection and vigilance among the eight factors that must be cultivated to overcome the five faults that prevent one from attaining quiescence.[340] In this context, recollection is described as the antidote for the fault of "losing the instruction."[341] In a more narrow sense, it represents the mental factor that keeps the mind focused on the meditation object. For its part, the principal function of vigilance is to recognize the occurrence of languor[342] and excitation,[343] the two flaws that are considered together as one of the five faults. Vigilance itself is a particular form of the mental factor wisdom. Excitation is one of the twenty secondary mental afflictions. Although languor is not itself included among these secondary mental afflictions, its cause, torpor,[344] does appear there. It is explained as a loss of clarity in relation to the meditation object. The Indian master Bhavya states in his *Essence of the Middle Way:*

> Fasten the wayward elephant-like mind
> With recollection's rope to the post of the [meditation] object;

Then gradually bring it under control
Using the hook of wisdom.[345]

Recollection is not a mental factor that is intrinsically virtuous; yet it is central to all aspects of Buddhist spiritual practice. Separately from the effort to pursue one-pointedness of mind, the purpose of cultivating recollection and vigilance at this point is to assist in accomplishing the two goals of mindfulness: (1) protecting the mind from engaging in nonvirtuous deeds and (2) cultivating virtuous mental states and deeds.

The mental factor of recollection is *not* meant simply as the quality by which one remembers past events and conversations, or recalls the location of misplaced objects. Rather, it is the faculty by which an understanding of some form of practice or instruction relating to spiritual training is retained in the mind. And, if such a mental object should inadvertently escape attention, it is the faculty by which one returns it to the forefront of awareness. Vasubandhu describes it as "the avoidance of inattentiveness toward a familiar object." Recollection can be exercised in the course of ordinary activities just as much as when a practitioner is sitting in meditation. In the context of pursuing mindfulness, it is certainly applied in common everyday situations, particularly in interactions with other persons.

For its part, vigilance itself is not found in Vasubandhu's work among the mental factors; however, its opposite—lack of vigilance—does appear among the secondary mental afflictions. Nevertheless, the positive quality of vigilance is a form of wisdom that is meant to be exercised both in a range of ordinary activities and while practicing meditation.[346] A verse from *Engaging in Bodhisattva Activities* describes it as follows:

In short, the essential nature
Of vigilance is simply this:
To examine again and again
The state of your body and mind.[347]

Vigilance does not itself directly counteract any of the root or secondary mental afflictions. Its role is to observe both the mind and the physical surroundings in order to avert potential obstacles and, with regard to mindfulness, to recognize any improper motivations or mental attitudes as soon as they appear. Ideally, a person who exercises vigilance effectively will become aware of any of the root or secondary mental afflictions at the first hint of their occurrence, well before they have had the opportunity to enter the mind in full force, as that is the most opportune time to thwart them. Moreover, the ability to develop a proper degree of vigilance is dependent on the cultivation of recollection. Again, Śāntideva states:

> The time at which vigilance arrives
> And, once come, does not depart again
> Is when recollection, in order to guard
> The mind, remains fixed at its door.[348]

A crucial element in the practice of mindfulness is the psychological mechanism that allows us both to overcome nonvirtuous entities and to develop virtuous ones. This ability depends ultimately on the innate tendency to avoid what is perceived as harmful and to pursue what is considered beneficial. As discussed earlier, all the mental afflictions are activated by the mistaken belief in a real self. For example, any entity that is perceived to enhance the well-being of such a self will immediately cause us to develop desire for it and anything that is thought to pose a threat to the well-being of the self will automatically give rise to aversion or animosity. Indeed, this is how all the mental afflictions gain a foothold in the mind.

In practicing mindfulness, this basic impulse of attraction and aversion is put to use in a conceptual framework that is defined, not by the mistaken belief regarding the self, but rather by a set of spiritual values and principles. In this context it becomes the psychological force by which we subdue the mental afflictions that might otherwise overwhelm us, as well as the inspiration that enables us to evoke and nurture virtuous mental states. The central principle in this process is, of course, the doctrine of karma. This belief allows us to regard nonvirtuous thoughts and actions as profoundly harmful in that they are capable of inflicting much more severe and long-lasting suffering than any physical or mental pain we might have to endure in our present existence. A strong conviction regarding the unfavorable consequences of the mental afflictions gives us the necessary impetus to expel them from the mind. By directing our attention to those undesirable qualities, we are able to awaken the feeling that they are indeed harmful, which makes us want to avoid any contact with them and to deny them the opportunity of gaining entry in the mind. As Śāntideva writes in *Engaging in Bodhisattva Activities:*

> Even if all the gods and men
> Were to become my enemies,

They still could not hurl me
Into the fires of Avīci.[349]

Yet the mighty foe of the afflictions
Can hurl me instantly into a place
That if it were to touch even Mount Meru
Would not leave even ashes behind.[350]

The following verses from the *Ornament of Mahāyāna Sūtras* also describe many of the disadvantages associated with the mental afflictions:

The mental afflictions destroy you,
They destroy beings, and they destroy morality.
They bring dejection, material loss, loss of protection,
As well as the Master's reproach.

You become subject to conflict and disrepute.
In the future you are reborn in inopportune states.
Losing what you've attained and not yet attained,
You will undergo great mental suffering.[351]

Buddhist literature contains numerous examples of instruction in which the mental afflictions are described with such negative imagery as poison, enemies, and thieves. Virtuous mental states are just as often described with metaphors such as treasure, medicine, protector, and the like. Thus, the exercise of reflecting on the benefits of virtuous mental states represents the means by which we can awaken and develop them further. Systematic study of the descriptions of the mind and the mental states like those that appear in Sthiramati's commentary to Vasubandhu's root text on the five heaps also contributes greatly to one's ability to cultivate mindfulness. Not only does it heighten our awareness of how the mind functions and provide insight into what motivates our thoughts and deeds, it can also greatly enhance our ethical practice. A number of Tibetan scholars have written commentaries in a genre known as "mind and mental factors."[352] These works address the subject matter that largely makes up the latter four of the five heaps. One of the most popular examples of this literature in the Gelukpa tradition is a text composed by Tsechok Ling Yongzin Yeshe Gyeltsen,[353] an important eighteenth-century scholar who served as tutor to the eighth Dalai Lama. Entitled *A Necklace for Those of Clear Mind: An Elucidation of Mind and Mental*

Factors,[354] it draws on the same kind of explanations as are found in Vasubandhu's and Sthiramati's texts. The author closes his work with the following remarks:

> Therefore, it is a principal element of all virtuous activities and a point of paramount importance that you examine your mind repeatedly and continually—both during formal meditation periods and during the times in between—and apply an antidote for any mental affliction that may arise.
>
> Similarly, regarding the virtuous mental states, you should recall the appropriate methods for developing the ones that pertain to each and every kind of virtuous activity, beginning with the topic of how to serve a spiritual teacher. Then, while applying recollection and vigilance repeatedly, exert yourself in every way possible to generate [for the first time] those virtuous states that you have not generated before and to develop more fully those that you have [previously generated].[355]

Throughout this work, Yongzin Yeshe Gyeltsen refers to Je Tsongkapa's *Great Treatise* to illustrate how knowledge of the mental states can enhance one's practice of the Lamrim teachings.

In reviewing this portion of the Lamrim teaching, I have addressed several of the important philosophical issues that have a strong connection with the various topics of practice. I have attempted to show that knowledge of such fundamental Buddhist teachings as the five heaps and the Four Noble Truths are essential to gaining a correct understanding of the arguments in support of past and future lives, why the Three Jewels constitute an infallible source of refuge, and the logical basis for accepting the doctrine of karma.

The instruction that is presented in traditional Lamrim commentaries does not address this material in any detail. Even Je Tsongkapa's *Great Treatise* only refers in the briefest manner to Vasubandhu's *Summary of the Five Heaps* towards the end of the instruction for practitioners of middling capacity. In one instance he notes:

> I have explained these ten mental afflictions according to the descriptions that are found in *The Compendium of Higher Learning*, *The Levels of Spiritual Practice*, and the commentary to *A Summary of the Five Heaps*.[356]

A few pages later Je Tsongkapa quotes the following statement by the Kadampa [Gönbawa] Wangchuk Gyeltsen that describes in practical terms what we need to know about the mental afflictions:

> In order to abandon the mental afflictions, you must learn their disadvantages, essential qualities, and antidotes, as well as the causes from which they arise. Once you have learned those disadvantages, you must consider [the mental afflictions] to be harmful and regard them as your enemy. If you don't learn their disadvantages, you won't view them as an enemy. Therefore, reflect on [those disadvantages] as they are described in *The Ornament of the Mahāyāna Sutras* and *Engaging in Bodhisattva Activities*. . . . To learn the essential qualities of the mental afflictions, you must listen to teachings on the Abhidharma. At a minimum, you must receive instruction on *A Summary of the Five Heaps*. Once you have learned how to recognize the root and secondary mental afflictions, whenever desire, hatred, or any of the other mental afflictions enters your mind, you must be able to tell yourself, "This [mental factor] is definitely that [mental affliction]. It is now active [in my mind]." Then, as you become aware of their presence, you should fight [to overcome] them.[357]

Nowhere in this first division of the Lamrim instruction is the correct view concerning the self addressed in any direct manner. Indeed, it is possible to take refuge in the Three Jewels and cultivate the ethics of avoiding misdeeds and pursuing virtue without undertaking any investigation of the ultimate nature of the self. One might respond that, given the graded nature of the Lamrim instructions, it is not appropriate at this point in the teaching to begin to explain such a difficult and complex topic. While this is true, it is also the case that if the teaching on selflessness is overlooked entirely or not pursued in a sufficiently thorough manner, this can eventually undermine the value of all one's spiritual efforts.

The mistaken belief regarding the self is the very source of all the mental afflictions. As long as we have not taken any meaningful steps to correct this erring mind, we will always be vulnerable whenever we find ourselves in situations that hold some risk of causing the mental afflictions to arise. Even an individual who has had some exposure to the teaching on selflessness and who professes to espouse such a view may fail to recognize the degree to which the mistaken belief in a real self is ingrained in the psyche. As a result, even our efforts at study and practice can end up lending support to the mental afflictions. Je Tsongkapa makes this point in the introductory section of his *Instruction Manual on the Middle View*:

> Because all the suffering of the lower states and samsara that we currently experience is at its essence caused by grasping at a self,[358] all the suffering of the lower realms [in particular] and of samsara [as a whole] will be brought to an end by abandoning this [mistaken view of] grasping at a self. On the other hand, as long as we have failed to abandon grasping at a self, we will have to undergo all manner of suffering like the continuous flow of a river, because grasping at a self forms part of the essence of all the causes and conditions that produce all our suffering. For example, as long as the great outer ocean exists, all the [rivers and] streams will continue to flow [as well].
>
> In that case, what is the means of abandoning grasping at a self? It is abandoned by the wisdom that realizes selflessness. Can it be abandoned by any other virtuous activities? In certain situations, even those [ostensibly virtuous] activities can cause the mental afflictions that are derivatives of grasping at a self—such as desire, hatred, jealousy, and the like—to arise individually or in combination.
>
> For example, while the qualities of learning and contemplation can make you a great scholar, this can lead to pride as you reflect, "I am a scholar of great learning." Other mental afflictions such as jealousy, contentiousness, contempt, and all manner of disdain toward others can also arise on the basis of this scholarship. In addition to this, some persons may pursue the causes of quiescence while staying in a secluded retreat. Whether they make only modest progress or achieve great success, their experience can cause them to develop pride, which may then induce them to disparage those holy beings who are not dwelling in a secluded retreat but who may well be wise and virtuous. They can also develop jealousy and other mental afflictions.[359]

Near the end of the instruction that is held in common with "lesser" persons, Je Tsongkapa describes the type of spiritual outlook that is the immediate goal for this portion of the teaching:

> This is the measure for recognizing whether you have developed that attitude:[360] Previously, you had a natural longing for this life, while your concern for future lives was merely a verbal understanding [of what that attitude is supposed to be like]. When [these two viewpoints] change their respective positions and your concern for future lives has become paramount while your interest in this life is only incidental, then you have developed [the proper attitude]. Nevertheless, [the concern for future lives] still needs to be made firm; therefore, even after achieving it, you should continue to cultivate it diligently.[361]

The goal of developing a concern for future lives is deceptively simple. However, there are several essential concepts that present a significant challenge, especially for Westerners. First of all, the notion of past and future lives is widely questioned if not simply rejected out of hand in modern Western culture. For this same reason and others, the doctrine of karma also represents a topic that easily engenders great uncertainty. Although the ability to shift one's attention to the period following this life can be gained without having to learn much at all about the five heaps, the Four Noble Truths, and emptiness, I have sought to point out some of the pitfalls that remain if a practitioner fails to achieve some degree of knowledge about these three crucial topics. Indeed, as the passage just cited suggests, we must continue to strengthen our concern for future lives through ongoing reflection. Since the kinds of philosophical knowledge discussed above are directly relevant to the range of topics that represent the focus of this concern, clearly they can only help to bring greater firmness to it. Moreover, the fundamental Buddhist practices of taking refuge and avoiding nonvirtuous deeds are certainly not to be ignored simply because one's attention has turned to more "advanced" topics. Indeed, these later topics should also become the means of refining and deepening our understanding of the Three Jewels and the trustworthiness of the teachings on karma.

Renunciation, the Four Noble Truths, and Closely Placed Recollection

3

WHILE IT IS crucial to practice the fundamental Buddhist instructions identified with "lesser" persons, this effort by itself only provides a temporary respite from the imminent danger of being reborn in the lower states. Even if we succeed in attaining a favorable rebirth after this human existence, it is inevitable that we will eventually have to endure the terrible suffering of the lower states if we to fail to pursue additional spiritual knowledge. As Śāntideva states in a verse from *Engaging in Bodhisattva Activities:*

> Having come to the happy states again and again
> Where they enjoyed themselves over and over,
> Those who delight in pleasure fall to the lower states when they die,
> And there the pain is long-lasting and severe.[362]

The poet Candragomī also writes in his *Letter to a Disciple:*

> One who, seated on the ever-turning wheel of samsara,
> Considers it pleasurable to be whirling to and fro
> Is certain to remain a helpless being that roams successively
> and hundreds of times
> To all the pleasant and unpleasant states of existence.[363]

Therefore, the main purpose of the next division of the instruction is to engender an understanding of how the transitory well-being of the higher states is unreliable and does not represent genuine happiness. In short, we must come to recognize all samsaric existence as intensely unsatisfactory. As Āryadeva observes in his *Four Hundred Verses:*

Even the celestial realms cause fear in the wise
That is equal to what they feel toward the hells.
It is hard to find any [samsaric] existence
That does not cause them fear.[364]

RENUNCIATION

To some extent, this portion of the instruction continues to rely on principles that appeal to a common-sense view of experience. However, a number of fundamental and deeply ingrained beliefs that are simply assumed to be true by those who view life from a largely untutored perspective must ultimately be challenged. Such a critical analysis requires that we develop an understanding of the doctrines of the five heaps and the Four Noble Truths, as they are means of gaining deeper insight into the nature of samsaric existence.

A principal goal of the instructions that are identified with "middling" practitioners is to enable us to develop a spiritual attitude that is commonly rendered in English as "renunciation." The Sanskrit and Tibetan equivalents of this term literally mean "deliverance,"[365] a synonym for liberation or nirvana. In traditional exegesis, this type of usage is described as one in which the cause is figuratively referred to by a term that stands for the result.[366] In other words, the attitude is called "deliverance" because it is a mind that seeks to achieve the goal of deliverance from samsara. In fact, that is precisely how renunciation is described in Buddhist literature.[367] In relation to this attitude, Je Tsongkapa writes:

> The ability to develop the desire to achieve the liberation in which [all] the suffering of the grasping heaps has been [permanently] quelled depends upon perceiving the defects of the grasping heaps that possess a suffering nature. Therefore, if you fail to develop an awareness that wishes to abandon [samsaric] existence through having meditated on its faults, you will not be able to engender the wish to attain the state in which that suffering has been terminated. As the text *Four Hundred Verses* states:
>
> How could one who lacks aversion for this [samsara]
> Become devoted to the peace [of nirvana]?
> Moreover, the difficulty of departing from this [world of] being
> Resembles [the difficulty of] leaving one's home.[368]

The term "aversion"[369] refers to a state of mind that is central to the process of developing renunciation. The Tibetan equivalent, *skyo ba*, can be somewhat misleading, as its meaning in ordinary usage is that of "sadness," which is too passive for this particular context. The original Sanskrit, *udvegaḥ*, suggests more a sense of intense agitation, distress, anxiety, and fear. Thus, properly understood, it represents the antithesis of desire for and attachment to samsaric existence. It also acts as the antidote for complacency and lack of concern about our everyday condition.

While cultivating an aversion for all of samsaric existence is a necessary precondition for developing the wish to seek liberation, it should not be mistaken for the attitude of renunciation itself. Nevertheless, because we have habitually regarded, throughout our numberless past lives, all forms of samsaric well-being as pleasurable and ascribed the quality of attractiveness to those circumstances, one of the main challenges we face in our effort to develop renunciation is that of reversing this inclination. The Lamrim instruction teaches that its antidote is to meditate on samsara's faults.[370] As Je Tsongkapa writes, the need for doing so is also why, among the Four Noble Truths, the Truth of Suffering was taught first:

> Unless those who are to be trained[371] are first able to develop an unerring aspiration for liberation, the root cause [for pursuing this goal] will remain severed. How, then, could they be led to liberation? Thus, those followers [whose minds] are obscured by the darkness of ignorance and who, because of the error that regards what is unsatisfactory as a state of well-being, have deceived themselves into thinking that the prosperity of samsara is pleasurable must initially be persuaded to develop aversion. As the text *Four Hundred Verses* states:
>
> > This ocean of suffering
> > Has no limit whatsoever.
> > Fool, you who are mired here,
> > Why are you not terrified?[372]
>
> This is accomplished by teaching many forms of suffering so that followers will understand that this [prosperity of samsara] is not truly pleasurable, but rather a form of suffering. This is also why the Truth of Suffering was taught first.[373]

The ability to develop genuine renunciation—which is to say, the natural, spontaneous, and sincere aspiration to achieve liberation—requires an understanding of all of the Four Noble Truths. While acknowledging the importance of the entire teaching, Je Tsongkapa's Lamrim writings place more emphasis on the first two Truths, suffering and origination. As already noted, the Truth of Suffering represents the means of generating aversion toward all of samsara, which is a prerequisite for developing a genuine desire to attain liberation. For its part, the Truth of Origination not only identifies the causes of samsara, but also points to the possibility of ending suffering when it is understood that those causes can be eliminated. In addition, knowledge of the Truth of Origination helps to insure that our spiritual efforts are more fruitful, in that a better understanding of the path's obstacles makes it less likely that we will engage in misguided activities.

A BRIEF ACCOUNT OF THE FOUR NOBLE TRUTHS

Sthiramati states that one of the main purposes of Vasubandhu's *Summary of the Five Heaps* is to enable those with busy lives to gain a concise overview of the voluminous subject matter contained in such major works as Asaṅga's *Levels of Spiritual Practice.*[374] In other words, Vasubandhu's *Summary* represents a brief introduction to the body of Buddhist philosophical literature known as the Abhidharma or "Higher Learning." In a broader sense, one could also say that both Vasubandhu's root text and Sthiramati's commentary provide a beginning student with the conceptual framework that is needed to properly understand the doctrine of the Four Noble Truths. This is true despite the fact that the root text makes only a passing reference to the Truths and Sthiramati's commentary gives no more than a few brief descriptions of them, of which the principal one is made in connection with his discussion of faith.

The five heaps are the principal subject matter of both works, and, as noted, Sthiramati defines the Noble Truth of Suffering as "the aspect of the five grasping heaps that constitutes a result," and the Noble Truth of Origination as "the aspect of the five grasping heaps that constitutes a cause." While the Noble Truth of the Path is also included among the five heaps, unlike the first two Truths, it does not form part of the five *grasping* heaps, as they represent the samsaric aspect of existence. To use the technical Buddhist term, the entities that make up the first two Truths are characterized as being "related to the outflows."[375] By contrast, the Noble Truth of the Path consists of those conditioned entities that are unrelated to or free of the outflows.[376] Since the five heaps are coextensive with conditioned entities,[377] the Truth of the Path can be identified with the five pure heaps—which means principally, though not exclusively, untainted wisdom. Thus, it corresponds to the ultimate sense of the term "Higher Learning" or Abhidharma. As Vasubandhu describes in his *Commentary to the Treasury of Higher Learning:*

> What does the term "Higher Learning" mean?
>
>> Higher Learning is untainted wisdom together with its attendants.
>
> Here "wisdom" is the discrimination of entities. "Untainted" means to be unrelated to the outflows. "Together with its attendants"[378] means together with its followers. Thus, "Higher Learning" is explained as meaning the collection of five heaps that are unrelated to the outflows. This, then, is Higher Learning in its ultimate sense.[379]

Finally, the Noble Truth of Cessation is not found among the five heaps at all, because the latter include only conditioned entities and this Truth is one of several types of unconditioned entity. This means that the Noble Truth of Cessation is not a causally produced entity; rather, it is a state that, once brought into being, continues to exist unchanged. This Truth is found both among the twelve bases and the eighteen constituents, where it is classified within the entity basis and entity constituent, respectively. The technical term for the Noble Truth of Cessation is "analytic cessation,"[380] which is further described as a collection of "separation results."[381] They are only results in a nominal sense, because, as just noted, they are not impermanent entities that are directly produced by causes. Again, the *Commentary to the Treasury of Higher Learning* explains:

>> The analytic cessation is a separation.
>
> The analytic cessation is a [state of] separation from those entities that are related to the outflows. Analysis is the analyzing that is done in relation to the Noble Truths of suffering and the rest—which is to say, it is a particular form of wisdom. Thus, an analytic cessation is a cessation that is achieved by that [analysis]. [The original

Sanskrit expression is a compound that] is formed by an ellipsis of intervening words, as in the expression "oxcart."[382]

Is there only one analytic cessation for all the entities that are related to the outflows?

No.

What then?

> They are multiple.

There are as many separations as there are entities that constitute a form of possession. Otherwise, it would follow incorrectly that, when one has brought about the cessation of those mental afflictions that are abandoned by the seeing of suffering, one will have brought about the cessation of all the mental afflictions. And, if that were so, there would be no need to meditate on the remaining antidotes.[383]

The theory of the mental afflictions and the process by which they are abandoned form a complex subject in the Abhidharma literature. All Buddhist schools recognize that there are ten root mental afflictions. These are differentiated by their relation to each of the Four Noble Truths and the fact that different forms of them operate in each of the three realms.[384] Some of the root mental afflictions, such as doubt and wrong view, are abandoned completely by the Seeing Path.[385] Others, such as desire, hatred, ignorance, and pride, also have "innate" forms that can only be abandoned by further practice on what is termed the Meditation Path. The system presented in Vasubandhu's *Treasury of Higher Learning* describes, in all, ninety-eight forms of mental afflictions. The Mahāyāna tradition recognizes a slightly larger number, and adds a second type of obstacle called "obscurations to objects of knowledge,"[386] which principally hinders one from attaining the supreme enlightenment of a Buddha rather than simply liberation from samsara. Nevertheless, the removal of each form of both types of obstacle involves the attainment of a distinct, corresponding analytic cessation.

In the opening section of his commentary, Sthiramati notes that "the heaps are exactly five in number, neither more nor less, because they were taught as the entities that constitute the basis for grasping an 'I' and a 'mine.'" Since the direct aim of the teaching on the Four Noble Truths is to counteract the four errors, and especially the erroneous belief that regards what is not a real self as constituting a real self, the topic of the five heaps provides the conceptual framework for undertaking and pursuing that goal. The five heaps represent the vocabulary for the ideas that allow one to immerse oneself in the domain of Buddhist philosophical doctrine.

For example, all the fifty-one mental factors are properly understood in terms of their relationship to either the process by which samsara is perpetuated or that by which one gains freedom from it. While Vasubandhu only describes their "essential characteristics" in his root text, Sthiramati includes their "actions"[387] in his commentary. The actions of positive mental factors are the functions that they fulfill in relation to one's spiritual endeavors. For example, "the action of aspiration[388] is that it "serves as a support for generating effort"; that of conviction[389] is "[to endow an individual with] the quality of being incapable of being led astray, because the person who values conviction cannot be persuaded by adherents of another philosophical system to give up [his or her] own beliefs"; the action of concentration[390] is "to provide support for knowledge"; that of shame[391] is "to provide the support [that allows you] to restrain yourself from committing misdeeds." Similarly, the actions of the root and secondary mental afflictions are cast in language that conveys how they obstruct the practitioner's spiritual development: the action of desire[392] is "to give rise to suffering"; the action of the view that grasps at an extreme[393] is "to obstruct the deliverance [that is gained] through the middle way"; the action of deceitfulness[394] is "to give support to wrong livelihood"; the action of guile[395] is "to obstruct [an individual] from receiving correct [spiritual] instruction"; the action of distraction[396] is "to obstruct [the attainment of] freedom from attachment"; and the action of lack of vigilance[397] is "to give support to [the committing of] moral transgressions."

The student who wants to delve more deeply into the central Buddhist teaching of the Four Noble Truths must replace the vocabulary of the ordinary, secular world with the terminology of the Abhidharma literature in general, and this begins with the topic of the five heaps. In doing so, the student is introduced to explanations that will enable him or her to begin questioning a number of beliefs and attitudes that govern the ordinary perspective of everyday existence. In their place, one must begin to examine and identify the elements of experience using the ideas and meanings that are conveyed through the specialized language of Buddhist doctrine.

THE THREE STATES OF SUFFERING

Je Tsongkapa explains several classifications of suffering in his *Great Treatise*. The first is an eightfold formulation that is found in sutras describing the very first discourse that the Buddha gave following his enlightenment:

> Further, O mendicants, this verily is the Noble Truth of Suffering. Birth is suffering; old age is suffering; disease is suffering; death is suffering; meeting with disagreeable things is suffering; separation from agreeable things is suffering; not acquiring what is desired and sought after is also suffering. In short, the five grasping heaps are suffering.

Except for the last example, all the instances of suffering mentioned here describe experiences that are certainly familiar to everyone, regardless of their knowledge of the technical terminology of Buddhist doctrine. However, even the term "birth" needs to be understood in a manner that is not the everyday notion that most Westerners have. Buddhist literature mentions four types: womb birth, egg birth, birth from moisture and heat,[398] and spontaneous birth.[399] In cases where there is development of an embryo, the term "birth" is understood to include the entire period ranging from conception,[400] through the time spent in the womb or egg, and even the period immediately following emergence from the womb or egg. This passage from Asaṅga's *Levels of Spiritual Practice* describes how conception occurs in the case of womb birth:

> Through the power of karma, an intermediate state being only perceives sentient beings of the same class as the one into which it is about to be reborn. Thus, it develops a desire to see and interact with such beings. This is what causes it to approach the place where it will take birth. As the intermediate state being draws near, it mistakenly perceives what is actually the semen and egg of a couple who engaged in sexual intercourse, as the couple themselves. This perception causes the intermediate state being to become sexually aroused. If it is to be reborn as a female, it will generate desire to have intercourse with the male that it sees. If it is to be reborn as a male, it generates desire toward the female. As it approaches the pair, an intermediate state being that is to be born as a female wants the female figure to depart. Similarly, an intermediate state being that is to be born as a male wants the male figure to depart. Following this, the intermediate state being that is to be born as a female perceives itself alone with the male figure, and the one that is to be born as a male perceives itself alone with the female

> figure. Then, as it draws closer still, it perceives itself in the presence of just the male or female sexual organ. Angered by this, the intermediate state being dies and is immediately reborn in the next life.[401]

Meditation on the suffering of birth includes reflecting on the unpleasant experiences that one must undergo from the time of conception until just after emerging from the womb. While this is an essential form of practice, it only represents suffering in the common, everyday sense of the word. The technical term for this type of experience is "the suffering of suffering."[402] In his *Listeners' Level*, Asaṅga explains why this form of suffering is preeminent in the eightfold formulation of suffering quoted above:

> [The following should be understood in relation to the statement] "In short, the five grasping heaps are suffering." While the [first seven] examples of birth and the rest only illustrate the suffering of suffering, in this [last] statement the remaining forms—namely, the suffering of change and the suffering of conditioned existence—also are explained by [making reference to] the suffering of the five heaps. That is, the five grasping heaps that include the three kinds of feeling[403] represent the vessel in which the [seven types of] suffering of suffering that were described occur. However, it should further be recognized that the [two kinds of suffering] that were not [explicitly] mentioned—namely, the suffering of change and the suffering of conditioned existence—are present in the [heaps] as well.
>
> Why, then, was the suffering of suffering alone mentioned explicitly by the Lord, while the suffering of change and the suffering of conditioned existence [were only mentioned] in an indirect manner?
>
> Since the awareness of suffering that is developed in relation to the suffering of suffering is the same for both Āryas and immature beings,[404] the suffering of suffering was mentioned first in order to instill aversion in those who have not yet developed wisdom. Thus, when instructed in this manner, those who are to be trained will easily devote themselves to practicing the Truths.[405]

Birth and the remainder of the first seven forms of suffering mentioned above can also be understood in a more sophisticated manner. For instance,

Asaṅga presents this fivefold interpretation of the suffering of birth in his *Collection of Determinations:*

> How is birth suffering?
>
> [Birth is suffering] in five ways: (1) it is accompanied by suffering; (2) it is accompanied by a state of indisposition; (3) it is a source of suffering; (4) it is a source of the mental afflictions; and (5) it possesses the quality of causing us to undergo an unwanted separation.[406]

The first of these five is the common-sense meaning of suffering that was mentioned above. For example, birth brings intense suffering when one is reborn in the hells or as a tortured spirit. In addition, the very nature of womb birth and egg birth involves great discomfort. In the *Compendium of Higher Learning*, Asaṅga describes the period in the womb as "the suffering of compression,"[407] a reference to the oppressive nature of being confined in such a cramped space where one is surrounded by foul substances.

The four remaining aspects of suffering are explained as follows. To say that samsaric rebirth is "accompanied by a state of indisposition"[408] means that the grasping heaps of all the three realms' beings come into existence possessing a quality that naturally facilitates the arising of the mental afflictions. This condition impedes our efforts to develop virtuous mental states and contributes to our remaining under the control of the mental afflictions.

Birth is a "source of suffering" in the sense that it inevitably leads to old age, disease, and the rest. It is a "source of the mental afflictions" in that, following birth, an undisciplined person will naturally tend to develop attachment, aversion, and bewilderment toward those objects that are conducive to these three root mental afflictions. As a result, one will experience both physical and mental agitation and suffering, and remain in a discontented state.[409] To say that birth "possesses the quality of causing us to undergo an unwanted separation" is an allusion to the fact that everyone must ultimately die.[410] "Unwanted separation" refers in particular to the loss of such cherished objects as one's wealth, family, friends, and even one's own body. Moreover, the apprehension we feel toward death only adds to the discomfort of the actual physical experience.

Of these five explanations, the second comes closest in meaning to the most subtle form of samsaric suffering, which is referred to as the suffering of conditioned existence.[411] This aspect of suffering is typically explained in connection with the threefold classification of (1) the suffering of suffering, (2) the suffering of change, and (3) the suffering of conditioned existence. Asaṅga alludes to all three in his remarks about the last of the eight types of samsaric suffering mentioned in the sutra passage quoted earlier:

> The suffering that is referred to in the statement "In short, the five grasping heaps are suffering" should also be understood in five ways: (1) [the five grasping heaps] are the vessel for the suffering that will be produced; (2) they are the vessel for the suffering that is based on having been produced; (3) they are the vessel for the suffering of suffering; (4) they are the vessel for the suffering of change; and (5) they possess the suffering of conditioned existence as [part of] their essential nature.[412]

Je Tsongkapa explains the phrase "[the five grasping heaps] are the vessel for the suffering that will be produced"[413] as meaning that once we take on the grasping heaps of this life, they become the cause that brings about suffering in our future lives through continuing to generate mental afflictions and karma. Similarly, he describes the phrase "they are the vessel for the suffering that is based on having been produced" as meaning that once the heaps have come into being, they become the basis for experiencing the suffering of old age and the rest in the current life. The remaining three phrases make direct reference to the three types of suffering.

The three types of suffering have a close correlation with the three types of experience that make up the feeling heap, which is the second of the five grasping heaps. The suffering of suffering is described in relation to unpleasant experiences; the suffering of change in relation to pleasant experiences; and the suffering of conditioned existence in relation to experiences that are neither pleasant nor unpleasant. However, the three types of suffering do not refer just to these three experiences; their meaning also extends to the other four heaps that accompany those experiences. Thus, it includes the forms of consciousness and mental factors that accompany those three kinds of feeling, as well as the internal faculties and external objects that cause them to occur. Vasubandhu describes this in his *Commentary to the Treasury of Higher Learning*:

> When only a portion of feelings has the nature of suffering, how is it that all impure conditioned entities are said to constitute suffering?

> Impure entities that are attractive, unattractive,
> And different from those [two] are without exception
> [Forms of] suffering, because they are subject,
> As appropriate, to the three states of suffering.[414]

There are three states of suffering: the suffering of suffering, the suffering of change, and the suffering of conditioned existence. On the basis of these [three], all impure conditioned entities are, in the appropriate manner and without exception, characterized by suffering.

Regarding this, those [impure conditioned entities] that are attractive [are characterized by suffering] in terms of the suffering of change; those that are unattractive are [so characterized] in terms of the suffering of suffering; and those that are different from those two are [also characterized as suffering] in terms of the suffering of conditioned existence.

What, then, are [the impure conditioned entities] that are attractive; what are those that are unattractive; and what are those that are neither?

The three types of feeling, as well as those [other] conditioned entities that, on the strength of those feelings, are experienced as pleasant, unpleasant, or neither pleasant nor unpleasant, receive the designation of being attractive, unattractive, and different from those two, respectively. A pleasant feeling is a state of suffering in that it undergoes change. As the sutras declare, "A pleasant feeling is pleasant when it arises and pleasant while it lasts, but unpleasant when it undergoes change."[415] An unpleasant [feeling] is a state of suffering by the very nature of its unpleasantness. Again the sutras declare, "An unpleasant feeling is unpleasant when it arises and unpleasant while it lasts." A feeling that is neither pleasant nor unpleasant is a state of suffering by virtue of being a conditioned entity. The sutras further declare, "That which is impermanent is suffering, because it is produced by cooperating causes." Just as with [the three types of] feeling, those conditioned entities that are experienced [as pleasant, etc.] should also be understood [as constituting one of the three states of suffering] in the same way.[416]

While each of the three types of impure conditioned entities—attractive, unattractive, and those that are neither attractive nor unattractive—is identified with one of the three states of suffering, Yaśomitra notes in his subcommentary on the above passage that although attractive entities are uniquely characterized by the suffering of change, they are also forms of the suffering of conditioned existence. Similarly, unattractive entities are forms of the suffering of conditioned existence in addition to the suffering of suffering. Only those entities that are neither attractive nor unattractive are characterized by the suffering of conditioned existence alone. No doubt this is why the common Tibetan phrase for the third type of suffering is the "all-pervasive suffering of conditioned existence."[417] Asaṅga expresses this point by referring to all conditioned existence with the simile of a painful boil:

> How, then, should the embodied form of all beings that occupy the three realms be viewed?
>
> [It should be viewed] like a painful boil, because it is accompanied by a state of indisposition.
>
> How should the occurrence of a pleasant feeling in an embodied form be viewed?
>
> Like the application of [a substance that produces] a cool sensation in [the area of] a painful boil.
>
> How should the occurrence of an unpleasant feeling in an embodied form be viewed?
>
> Like the application of a caustic substance to that painful boil.
>
> How should the occurrence of a feeling that is neither pleasant nor unpleasant in an embodied form be viewed?
>
> Like the condition of pain that is naturally present in a painful boil itself, apart from any cool or caustic sensation [that might be applied to it].
>
> Therefore, the Lord declared that pleasant feelings are suffering in that they represent the suffering of change; unpleasant ones are suffering in that they represent the suffering of suffering; and those feelings that are neither pleasant nor unpleasant are suffering in that they represent the suffering of conditioned existence.[418]

THE SUFFERING OF CHANGE

In terms of practice, one begins to develop aversion for all of samsaric existence by reflecting on the suffering of suffering, as illustrated by the conditions that beings in the three lower states must endure, as well as the birth, old age, sickness, and death, etc., that humans experience. Reflecting on the suffering of change involves a more refined understanding, as it requires us to recognize pleasant feelings, such as those experienced by humans and gods, as unsatisfactory. Yaśomitra refers to the aim of the instruction that explains this type of suffering as that of "discrediting"[419] the attractiveness of pleasant feelings by pointing out that although they are pleasant when they arise and for as long as they continue to exist, they become a form of suffering when they undergo change—which is to say, when they come to an end. In short, this teaching counteracts our habitual tendency to regard pleasant experiences favorably by drawing attention to their transience. The cultivation of such an attitude seeks to overcome our attachment to ordinary pleasures as part of the effort to develop renunciation for all of samsaric existence. Incidentally, this type of reflection also frees us from the distress and anguish that is triggered when we are faced with the impending loss of some ostensible form of happiness.

In his *Listeners' Level*, Asaṅga adds another dimension to what we should understand as the suffering of change. This is one that is not usually described in Tibetan commentaries. In his description of the three states of suffering in the *Listeners' Level*, Asaṅga begins with the suffering of suffering, and states that it is exemplified by the seven forms of unpleasant feeling that begin with birth and end with the failure to acquire what is desired, together with the "seats"[420] of those unpleasant experiences. Following this, he delineates the suffering of change as comprising three categories of entities. The first of these corresponds to the description that Vasubandhu gave in the passage quoted above. The remaining two categories, however, identify two forms of the mental afflictions. One is the mental afflictions that occur in relation to unpleasant feelings and the other is the mental afflictions that occur in relation to pleasant ones. Here is the description in Asaṅga's own words:

> The suffering of change refers to (1) the conditions that are the opposite of those [just-mentioned unpleasant experiences]—that is to say, youth as opposed to old age, health as opposed to disease, continued life as opposed to death, meeting with agreeable things as opposed to meeting with disagreeable things, separation from disagreeable things as opposed to separation from agreeable things, and acquiring what is desired as opposed to failing to acquire it; (2) the mental afflictions that occur in relation to unpleasant

> feelings, together with the "seats"[421] [of those mental afflictions]; and (3) the mental afflictions that occur both in relation to those conditions of health, etc., that are representative of pleasant experiences and in relation to the [pleasant] feelings that arise from those [experiences].[422]

Following this, Asaṅga explains why these three categories of entities are called the suffering of change. What he says about the first category is virtually identical to the explanation that was cited earlier:

> A pleasant feeling together with its seat, by virtue of its transience, is subject to transformation. Thus, it is classified as suffering on the strength of its changing into something different.[423]

Then he addresses the reason for designating the mental afflictions as forms of the suffering of change. The somewhat less conventional nature of this description is suggested by the manner in which it appeals to scriptural authority:

> Furthermore, the mental afflictions, which are active everywhere [throughout the three realms], represent suffering by virtue of the inveterate manner in which they disturb the mind.[424] The [adverse] change [that they bring about] is one that pertains to sentient entities; hence [the mental afflictions] are called the suffering of change.
>
> As the Lord declared: "[Whatever monk,] ... with a mind that is overcome and altered [by desire], takes hold of a woman's hand, or ..." and so on.[425] [The Lord] also declared: "The person overcome by desire for sense pleasures experiences the mental states of suffering and unhappiness that are caused by, and arise from, the perturbation of desire for sensory pleasures ...." He made similar statements in relation to persons overcome by the perturbations of malice, torpor, sleep, excitation, regret, and doubt. On the basis of these credible and supremely trustworthy scriptural passages, both the sense of a state of suffering and that of change are seen to apply to the mental afflictions. Therefore, the mental afflictions are referred to as the suffering of change. This constitutes a presentation of the suffering of change.[426]

In his *Treasury of Higher Learning*, Vasubandhu explains the three types of suffering according to the realist viewpoint of the Abhidharma School. With regard to the suffering of change in particular, this school maintains that pleasant feelings are, in fact, genuinely pleasurable in nature and fundamentally different in kind from those feelings that are unpleasant, as well as those that are neither pleasant nor unpleasant. As to how pleasurable feelings should be regarded as a form of suffering, Vasubandhu states the following:

> Whatever feeling has an essential characteristic that is agreeable[427] in nature can never also take on one that is disagreeable in nature. It is through some other aspect that the Āryas discredit those [pleasant feelings], so that they will take on a disagreeable quality. For example, they will regard them as the abode of heedlessness,[428] as requiring great exertion to acquire, as undergoing change, and as impermanent.[429]

Vasubandhu also describes a more radical interpretation of the suffering of change, which he argues strongly against.[430] This view asserts that "there are no pleasant feelings; all [feelings] are just suffering." Thus, what ordinary beings mistakenly perceive as pleasant feelings are actually only less intense forms of suffering. Vasubandhu states the purported justification for the view in the following manner:

> [Pleasant feelings do not exist] because the causes of pleasant feelings do not have a fixed nature. Those very same conditions that are believed to be causes of pleasant feelings—such as drink, food, coolness, and warmth—can become causes of suffering when they are indulged in excessively or at an inappropriate time. It is not reasonable that increasing the cause of a pleasant feeling or applying the same [cause of a pleasant feeling] on a different occasion should give rise to an unpleasant feeling. Therefore, they must be causes of suffering from the very outset, rather than causes of a pleasant feeling. Moreover, at a later time, that suffering does increase and become apparent. This can also be described in a similar manner with regard to the particular modes of physical behavior.[431]
>
> [Pleasant feelings also do not exist] because the idea of a pleasant feeling arises in a situation where an unpleasant feeling has been assuaged or in relation to an alternate form of suffering. There is no

experience of a pleasant feeling whatsoever until someone has been overcome by some other form of suffering that originated from conditions such as hunger, thirst, heat, exhaustion, or the desire for sensory pleasure. Therefore, the ignorant develop the notion of a pleasant feeling in relation to what is nothing more than the abatement of suffering, rather than something that is truly a pleasant feeling. Foolish persons also develop the notion of a pleasant feeling in relation to an alternate form of suffering, for instance when they shift a heavy object from one shoulder to another. Therefore, there are no pleasant feelings.[432]

The main thesis of this view concerning the nature of pleasant feelings represents the position of the Mādhyamika School founded by the great Mahāyāna philosopher, Nāgārjuna, who states in his *Jewel Garland:*

Even a wheel-wielding monarch
Who rules the earth's four continents
Is known to have but two pleasures,
Those of the body and those of the mind.

Pleasant feelings of the body
Are just the abatement of pain;
Mental [pleasures] consist of conception
And are mere creations of thought.

The entirety of the world's pleasures
Are just the abatement of pain
Or mere creations of thought;
Thus, in reality, they lack substance.[433]

Nāgārjuna's foremost disciple, Āryadeva, devotes the second chapter of his *Four Hundred Verses* to correcting the error that regards what is unsatisfactory as a state of well-being. Here is one of the verses from that chapter, together with Candrakīrti's commentary on it:

At this point, some say: "Persons who seek comfort regard traveling on foot as a source of discomfort, so they ride a horse, an elephant, or in a carriage. If there were no pleasure in doing so, they would not make use of these vehicles. For this reason, [genuine forms of] pleasure do exist." To this it is replied:

> Persons do not ever experience
> Pleasure in a vehicle and the like.
> If something did not begin initially,
> How could it increase in the end?[434]

There is no [genuine] pleasure [experienced] in relation to a vehicle and the like. If [genuine] pleasure did occur in such experiences, there would be no discomfort in the end.[435] However, in a situation where suffering is perceived [to be present] at the end, there must have been a beginning to that suffering from the very outset. If there were no minute suffering present at the very beginning [of the experience], then it would not occur at some later time in a stronger form. Since suffering alone occurs at both the beginning and the end [of these experiences] and no [real] pleasure is found there [at all], there is no [real] pleasure to be found in [making use of] a vehicle and the like, just as with the foolish one who filled himself with half the cream.[436] Just as a foolish person considered drinking continually the remaining amount of cream as a way of dispelling his hunger, those who are unintelligent [only] regard [riding] in a vehicle, eating, and drinking, and the like, as well as the physical behavior of lying down and the rest, to become an unpleasant experience after an extended period. The following can be said about this:

> If a vehicle and the like
> Provided the slightest genuine pleasure,
> No suffering would occur in the end.
> A real thing would not perish.[437]

Je Tsongkapa endorses this view in his *Great Treatise* and presents it in connection with a passage from a sutra that declares all the four types of physical behavior to be nothing but forms of suffering. He concludes by quoting the following verse from Āryadeva's *Four Hundred Verses*:

> A growing pain does not
> Become reversed in the way

That a growing pleasure
Is seen to become reversed.[438]

In the Lamrim work *Liberation in Our Hands*, Kyabje Pabongka Rinpoche explains this verse in the following manner:

> Therefore, all the experiences that we normally think of as unpleasant make up the suffering of suffering, while those that we mistakenly believe are truly pleasant make up the suffering of change. A sign that the latter experiences are not truly pleasurable is the fact that if they go on for too long, they eventually bring on suffering again. The reason we wrongly believe the suffering of change to be pleasurable is that it occurs at a time when one painful experience is gradually disappearing and another one is gradually beginning.
>
> For instance, if we stay in the shade too long, we begin to feel cold. When we move into the sunlight, at first we experience a sensation that seems pleasurable. But it isn't truly pleasurable. If it were, the pleasure we feel by sitting in the sun should get stronger as time goes on, just as a painful experience increases the longer it lasts. However, this is not what happens. After we have been in the sun for a while, this experience also becomes unpleasant, and so we decide to go back into the shade again. The reason we don't notice any suffering when we first go into the sun is because, in the beginning, it is small and only grows a little at a time.
>
> Another example is what happens if we walk a long distance. After we have walked a while, we get tired and sit down to rest. When we do, the rest seems pleasurable at first, because the more intense discomfort of standing up is gradually disappearing while the discomfort of sitting down is only beginning. It isn't that there is no suffering present when we first sit down to rest; it's just that the suffering that occurs in the act of sitting down has not yet become apparent.
>
> After we have sat for some time, the suffering of that experience does become evident. So we get up and say, "It's time to start walking again." This time, the suffering that developed from sitting for so long is the greater pain that disappears slowly, while the suffering of standing up becomes the lesser pain that is not evident right away.[439]

Candrakīrti's position is that, from the perspective of ultimate truth, both pleasant and unpleasant feelings lack any independent reality. However, from the perspective of relative truth, there are only unpleasant feelings; those that are considered pleasurable exist only in a fictitious sense. It is Candrakīrti's view that Buddha acknowledged the three types of feelings—that is, pleasant, unpleasant, and neutral ones—only to comply with the view of ordinary beings.[440] For instance, Candrakīrti notes, "Likewise, ordinary beings who are devoid of learning consider this and that abatement of suffering as a pleasurable experience, due to their erroneous perceptions."[441] In the very next folio, he again remarks: "The concept of a pleasurable experience comes about through taking an erroneous perception to be valid cognition."[442] Finally, in his commentary to Nāgārjuna's *Sixty Verses on Reasoning*, he states unambiguously:

> Regarding perceptions, they are of two kinds: those that are erring and those that are unerring. Of these, erring [perceptions] are the apprehension of pleasure and the like, because entities do not possess such a nature even conventionally. Unerring ones are [the apprehension] of suffering and the like, because entities do possess such a nature conventionally.[443]

The central element of this view is that ordinary beings mistakenly perceive themselves to have pleasurable experiences based upon their inability to recognize that entities are not substantially real. This fundamental error leads to another mistaken apprehension that certain experiences have a truly favorable nature, which forms the basis for recognizing them as pleasurable. The attachment that arises in response to these illusory experiences causes beings to engage in the kinds of activities that only serve to perpetuate their samsaric existence. Moreover, while Buddha taught the four doctrines of impermanence, impurity, suffering, and selflessness to counteract the four mistaken beliefs that the five heaps are permanent, pure, pleasurable, and constitute a self, Candrakīrti maintains that these four teachings do not have the capacity to permanently eradicate the mental afflictions. Their purpose is to engender in beings an aversion for samsaric existence by drawing attention to its unsatisfactoriness. The following passage both summarizes his view on the nature of pleasurable experiences and describes his assessment of Vasubandhu's criticism of the belief that they do not exist in reality:

Therefore, the physical and mental pleasures that are found in the realms of gods, humans, demi-gods, *kinnaras*, *siddhas*, *uragas*, and *vidyādharas*[444] exist only on the basis of the [presumed] validity of those beings' perceptions. [However, those pleasures] lack the essence that is attributed to them by foolish ordinary beings whose mind's eye has been blinded by the darkness of ignorance. Their existence is one that is fabricated merely by false and mistaken beliefs and their [perceived] essential nature is nonexistent. Those feelings are like the physical and mental pleasures that are experienced during a dream state in relation to imaginary objects. For this reason, how could there be real entities in the form of pleasurable feelings in the three realms? As it was said:

> Whoever holds that entities [truly] arise
> Becomes subject to nihilism and the like,
> As well as the contradictions that the world
> Both does and does not have a limit.[445]

If a real substance were to disappear immediately following its appearance, that would amount to its annihilation. That is like saying a sprout could arise from a seed that has been burned by fire. Therefore, it should be a settled understanding that those inner and outer entities that arise from causes and conditions are void of any truly existent nature and lack any real substance, and that pleasurable experiences come about through the continuous play of the net of false conceptual thought.

Having written the verse: "Samsaric existence is the same as / A fire-brand wheel, an emanation, a dream, / An illusion, a moon in water, fog, / An interior echo, a mirage, a cloud,"[446] how could the venerable Master Āryadeva be someone who professes that entities have real essences, such that Master Vasubandhu would say of him: "The one who discredits pleasurable feelings should then be asked...," and so forth? These assertions, which are based on a doctrine that entities have real natures, result from having failed to accept the nondual teaching that seeks to refute any belief in being or non-being. As such, they are extremely ill-considered, because they represent a perspective that does not understand the most profound and extensive reality perceived by nondual awareness.[447]

The justification for this interpretation of the suffering of change ultimately relies upon the Mahāyāna doctrine of two truths; however, it is beyond the scope of this essay to take up that topic here. My main purpose has been to point out the genuine disparity between Buddhist realists and followers of the Mādhyamika School. In many ways, Mahāyāna philosophy should be seen as a critical interpretation of the early Abhidharma realist tradition. Thus, anyone who would hope to comprehend the arguments of Nāgārjuna and his followers must first have a clear grasp of such fundamental Buddhist concepts as the doctrine of the five heaps. We will revisit the role of such topics in gaining a genuine understanding of Mahāyāna philosophy in the next chapter. For now, we simply note Candrakīrti's admonition:

> There is no means of arriving at Peace for those
> Who are outside the venerable Master Nāgārjuna's path;
> For they have fallen from conventional and ultimate truth,
> And liberation is not possible if one deviates from them.[448]

THE SUFFERING OF CONDITIONED EXISTENCE

The third state of suffering is the most difficult for ordinary individuals to recognize because, to appreciate its meaning correctly, one must gain an understanding of subtle impermanence. Nevertheless, the benefit of doing so is profound and takes one a long way toward the goal of developing genuine renunciation. The difficulty that it presents for beginners, as well as its effect on those who have acquired a more refined understanding, is expressed in the following verses:

> Just as an eyelash is unrecognized by humans
> When situated in the palm of the hand
> But that very object causes displeasure and pain
> If it should become lodged in the eye,
>
> The immature, like the palm of the hand,
> Do not perceive the eyelash of the suffering
> Of conditioned existence; but for the wise,
> Who resemble the eye, it causes deep agitation.[449]

Nevertheless, Dharmakīrti notes in his *Extensive Treatise on Knowledge* that "[Lord Buddha] had the suffering of conditioned existence in mind /

[when he] said that one should meditate upon suffering."[450] In the passage presented below, Khedrup Gelek Pelsang explains the significance of these lines to mean that, while meditation on suffering by itself does not directly free us from samsara, it is an essential practice in that it ripens the mind so that one can successfully develop the true antidote to samsaric existence—the wisdom that realizes the nonexistence of a real personal self. Furthermore, of the various forms of suffering that Buddha taught, the most important one for developing renunciation toward all of samsaric existence is the suffering of conditioned existence:

> Concerning this, there are two paths: one is the path that ripens [the mind] and the other is the path that brings deliverance [from samsara]. Of these, the path that ripens us so that we may attain liberation includes such practices as meditating on the impermanence and suffering of the impure heaps.
>
> Moreover, the order for meditating on [the topics that make up] the ripening path is as follows: Initially, one should meditate upon the qualities of birth, sickness, old age, death, and so forth, that pertain to these very heaps. [However,] this represents [only] a coarse form of impermanence, which is to say [one that recognizes that the heaps] are subject to change. When you have meditated on these points and experienced an attitude of [deep] dissatisfaction [in relation to the heaps], then you should cultivate an understanding that their nature is also circumscribed both by subtle impermanence and the condition of being subject to karma and the mental afflictions. In the case of the former quality, this means more specifically that, with each passing moment, [the heaps] are as inconstant as the [ever-changing] waves [that undulate] upon a body of water.
>
> After having meditated on these two qualities long enough for his [or her] understanding to develop to a sufficient degree, the practitioner will abandon any sense that the heaps possessing these two qualities might be satisfactory in the sense of being an object that one might take comfort in or rely upon. Thus, once you determine the heaps to be unsatisfactory and unreliable, and develop a genuine feeling of wanting to free yourself from them, even the ease associated with the meditative states of the two higher realms[451] will be seen as resembling a fire pit in that they possess these two qualities [of impermanence and suffering]. Ultimately, nothing will

remain of the mind that delights in samsara beyond the words that were once used to describe it.[452]

Therefore, in order to develop the mind that genuinely wishes to become free from samsara as a whole, it is absolutely necessary to meditate both on subtle impermanence and the suffering of conditioned existence. If your meditation is limited to the suffering of suffering, you will only be able to generate aversion for such things as the suffering of the lower states. While this will allow you to develop the basic practice of avoiding nonvirtuous deeds and cultivating virtuous ones in order to achieve the status of a human or divine existence in a future life, you cannot possibly develop aversion for the happiness of a divine rebirth in which the overt suffering of the lower states has been [temporarily] quelled. This is why [the root text of Dharmakīrti's *Extensive Treatise on Knowledge*] states that "[Lord Buddha] had the suffering of conditioned existence in mind / [when he] said that one should meditate upon suffering."[453]

While this passage does affirm the need to meditate on the suffering of conditioned existence and also indicates that subtle impermanence plays an integral role in the process of doing so, it does not clarify in any detailed manner what the nature of this form of suffering is or how one should go about developing a realization of it. How the suffering of conditioned existence should be understood is addressed in the following passage from Asaṅga's *Listeners' Level:*

As for the suffering of conditioned existence, it is present in every form of the five grasping heaps. Briefly, this is what the suffering of conditioned existence refers to: Excluding those forms of the heaps that represent the suffering of suffering and the suffering of change—with the latter including mental afflictions and pleasant feelings together with their seats—it is all those remaining forms of the heaps that are accompanied by feelings that are neither unpleasant nor pleasant, those that arise from [the heaps that were just described], those that constitute the conditions which cause [the just-mentioned heaps] to arise, and those that constitute the vessel in which [the heaps] that have arisen continue to exist. Those heaps that are impermanent in that they arise and pass away, that are accompanied by grasping,[454] that are closely connected with the

> three types of feeling, that are accompanied by a state of indisposition,[455] that constitute a state in which one's welfare is not secure,[456] that are not free from the suffering of suffering and the suffering of change, and that are not under one's control are referred to as a state of suffering in the sense of the suffering of conditioned existence. This constitutes a presentation of the suffering of conditioned existence.[457]

This passage begins by noting that, while the suffering of conditioned existence is present in every form of samsaric existence, it is to be distinguished from the two other states of suffering that have already been discussed—that is, the suffering of suffering and the suffering of change. Just as those two forms of suffering are generally associated with painful and pleasurable experiences, respectively, the suffering of conditioned experience is related to "all those remaining forms of the five heaps that are accompanied by feelings that are neither unpleasant nor pleasant." This suggests that understanding the suffering of conditioned existence involves recognizing a manner in which experiences that are ordinarily considered neutral—that is, neither overtly pleasurable nor painful—have some deeper level of unsatisfactoriness.

Asaṅga's description continues by saying that the suffering of conditioned existence also includes "those [heaps] that arise from [the heaps that are accompanied by feelings that are neither unpleasant nor pleasant]." This phrase seems to be designed to indicate the transitoriness of the grasping heaps, as well as the fact that succeeding moments form part of a continuum that is directly and causally linked with those moments that came before.

The next phrase—"those [heaps] that constitute the conditions which cause [the previously mentioned heaps] to arise"—is a reference to the overall causal process by which the five heaps come into being. Buddhist literature describes four "conditions": the causal condition, the homogeneous immediate condition, the objective condition, and the governing condition.[458] These terms are said to encompass all aspects of causality and, although they are not interpreted in an identical manner by all Buddhist philosophical schools, there is general agreement about their signification. Buddhist theory of causality is much too broad a topic to be addressed in detail here. The most relevant elements that relate to the present discussion are the ones embodied in the doctrine of the twelve limbs of dependent origination.

The last phrase that is intended to identify what entities constitute the suffering of conditioned existence refers to "the heaps that constitute the vessel in which those [heaps that make up animate beings] . . . continue to exist." The term "vessel"[459] here means the inanimate physical world in which sentient beings reside. Thus, the external samsaric physical world, in that it forms part of the five grasping heaps, also represents an aspect of the Noble Truth of Suffering. As Asaṅga states:

> What is the Truth of Suffering?
>
> It is to be understood in terms of the living beings that take birth and in terms of the abode of those beings that take birth.
>
> . . . What is the abode of those beings that take birth?
>
> It is the [physical] world that is a vessel [in which animate sentient beings reside].
>
> . . . Every form of the world of living beings and the world that is [their] vessel—both of which are produced by karma and the mental afflictions and are governed by karma and the mental afflictions—is called the Truth of Suffering.[460]

In the passage describing the suffering of condition existence cited above, Asaṅga lists the following seven characteristics to indicate what the nature of this type of unsatisfactoriness is like: (1) the impermanence of arising and passing away, (2) being related to the four kinds of grasping, (3) being closely connected with the three types of feeling, (4) being accompanied by a state of indisposition, (5) constituting a state in which one's welfare is not secure, (6) remaining bound to the other two forms of suffering, and (7) existing in a state that is beyond one's control.

Of these seven, we have already addressed the four kinds of grasping, the meaning of the term "state of indisposition," and how the other two forms of suffering relate to pleasant and unpleasant feelings. The three remaining characteristics of impermanence, a state of insecurity, and a state that is not under our control are explained in detail in the final section of *Listeners' Level*, as part of a comprehensive description of how to meditate on each of the sixteen aspects of the Four Noble Truths. We will consider the portion that deals with the four aspects of the Noble Truth of Suffering, as this is where the import of the suffering of conditioned existence is most clearly delineated.

The Four Aspects of the Noble Truth of Suffering

Asaṅga's discussion begins by stating that the meditation practitioner[461] will become established in the four aspects of the Noble Truth of Suffering by examining them on the basis of ten points. These points are prefaced by a presentation of several scriptural passages in which Lord Buddha declares that both the world of living beings and that of the physical cosmos is impermanent. This is meant to instill conviction in the practitioner regarding the doctrine of impermanence that is based upon faith in the trustworthiness of the Buddha's word.

Five forms of impermanence

The first five of the ten points relate to impermanence, which is itself the first of the four aspects of the Noble Truth of Suffering. For the first of these five points, called "the impermanence of change,"[462] the practitioner is directed to reflect upon the impermanence of conditioned entities that is evidenced by observable change. This involves reflecting in a comprehensive and systematic manner on the various forms and causes of change that inner and outer objects can be seen to undergo.

As one might expect, the term "inner objects" applies to sentient beings; however, the term that the text uses to refer to them is the technical expression "six bases."[463] Vasubandhu's *Summary of the Five Heaps* notes that the term "basis" is meant to designate those entities that are "the sources for the appearance of consciousness."[464] There are two sets of bases: the six outer ones are the categories of objects that are perceived by each of the six forms of consciousness, and the six inner ones are the faculties through which these individual forms of consciousness arise. In this case, the six bases are the six inner bases of the eye, ear, nose, tongue, body, and mind. The mind basis, in particular, is synonymous with the consciousness heap.

Inner objects, which include both oneself and others, are meant to be examined in relation to fifteen categories and eight causes of change. These include reflecting on the way in which the physical body changes as it develops from childhood through the different stages of life, how an individual's complexion, physique, and health fluctuates over time, as well as how a person's appearance is altered by changes in climate and season, physical exertion, and injury, etc. The practitioner should also be mindful of the different pleasurable, painful, and neutral feelings that he or she experiences, as well as how fleeting and temporary they are. One should take note of how the root and secondary mental afflictions variously enter and disappear from the mind. This exercise culminates with observing how all living beings eventually die, and their corpses gradually decompose until finally even their very bones disintegrate and completely disappear. Here is Asaṅga's description of how to reflect on the impermanence of change in relation to the tenth category of inner object:

> How does one examine the impermanence of change that is caused by contact?
>
> As [the practitioner] who has met with a [particular form of] contact[465] that will produce a pleasurable experience comes to experience the pleasurable feeling that has arisen on the basis of a [form of] contact that produces a pleasurable experience, he [or she] should fully discern for himself [or herself] this pleasurable state. Just as [the practitioner] does with states that contain a pleasurable feeling, he [or she] should also [fully discern] those states that contain a painful feeling or one that is neither pleasurable nor painful. The [practitioner] should perceive the manner in which each of these [various] feelings that appear successively is recent, not old, transitory, temporary, momentary, and subject to change. Having perceived this, he [or she] should reflect, "How remarkable is the impermanence of these conditioned entities!"[466]

Outer objects are similarly examined in terms of sixteen categories that range from the surrounding physical environment—both the natural world of forests, mountains, and bodies of water, and man-made elements such as buildings, fields, and places of commerce and industry—to all manner of personal objects, such as food, vehicles for travel, clothing, jewelry, tools and other paraphernalia that are used in daily life. The practitioner reflects on the manner in which each of these types of object undergoes changes that include being newly created, varying with the fluctuation of season and climate, being ravaged by wind, fire or flood, etc., and simply undergoing gradual deterioration. Each meditation on both inner and outer objects concludes with the observation: "How remarkable is the impermanence of these conditioned entities!"

Subtle impermanence

The second of the five forms of impermanence is called "the impermanence of perishability."[467] In this exercise, the practitioner relies upon inference to develop a conviction with regard to subtle impermanence. Asaṅga expresses the main features of this doctrine in the following words:

> Having examined in this way the impermanence of change using a means of reflection that is based upon direct observation, [the practitioner] does not recognize that the existence and presence of physical conditioned entities is characterized by a state of disintegration in which those entities arise and pass away each moment. Concerning this matter, he [or she] should make an inference that is based upon the reflection that relies on direct observation. And he [or she] should form this inference in the following manner.
>
> The change that these conditioned entities undergo over time is reasonable only if they are subject to a form of disintegration in which they arise and pass away with each moment; this phenomenon is not reasonable if entities remained in an unchanging state. Therefore, while momentary conditioned entities come into being when certain specific conditions are present, those entities that have arisen disintegrate of their own accord and independently of some cause [that would be necessary to bring about their] destruction.
>
> Moreover, the eight causes of change[468] initiate the arising of an alteration and serve as causes for the arising of a modification [in the continuum of entities]; however, they are not causes of their destruction. Why is that? It is due to the [momentary] destruction of conditioned entities, along with the causes of their destruction, that the occurrence of dissimilarity is perceived[469]; however, [this momentary destruction] does not represent a complete and total cessation of existence.
>
> Moreover, with regard to situations in which there seems to be a complete and total cessation of conditioned entities, such as the complete and total disappearance that ultimately occurs when [conditioned entities in liquid form] are boiled [continuously], or the circumstances in which those [conditioned entities] that make up the physical world are consumed by fire [at the end of a great kalpa] such that not even smoke or ashes can be perceived to remain, their ultimate complete and total annihilation is a case where the successive causes [necessary for their continued appearance] have come to an end; it is not the case that [their destruction] is caused by fire [for instance]. Therefore, the nature of the eight causes of change is as was described above, while the [momentary] destruction [of

> conditioned entities] is a condition that they undergo of their own accord. In this way, using a form of reflection that is based on inference, the practitioner should gain a conviction regarding the state of disintegration in which conditioned entities arise and pass away each moment.[470]

The topic of subtle impermanence is not one that is closely examined in the literature of the Lamrim tradition. It has also been my experience that Tibetan lamas typically make only passing reference to this doctrine in public discourses. It is routinely noted that the unschooled devotee cannot be expected to gain a genuine understanding of this difficult topic. Practitioners are instead urged to focus on the rough form of impermanence that is embodied in their impending mortality. Nevertheless, as one might expect, the doctrine of subtle impermanence is addressed in Buddhist philosophical literature, and those monk scholars who do study these works benefit from the opportunity to consider the arguments in support of this singularly important topic. The following paragraphs outline the central elements of this doctrine as it has been approached by two eminent Indian Buddhist scholars.

Dharmakīrti argues in his *Extensive Treatise on Knowledge* that the quality of being perishable is something that exists inherently in all causally produced entities at the very moment that they come into being. Because no external cause is required to occur at some later time in order to bring about their destruction, all causally produced entities without exception perish in the very next moment immediately following their appearance. As he states in his autocommentary to the first chapter of his work:

> Now then, how is it to be determined that a produced entity necessarily is impermanent, such that you would describe it that way?
>
> The reason is as follows:
>
> Because destruction is uncaused
> And connected with the essential nature.[471]
>
> Perishable entities do not depend on a [separate] cause for that nature,[472] because they come into being as perishable entities on the basis of their own cause. Therefore, anything that is a produced entity is perishable by its very nature.[473]

Shortly after this, the author notes that this quality can be observed in certain circumstances. Tibetan commentaries suggest that this is a reference to such phenomena as an instantaneous flash of lightning. From such examples we should infer that all causally produced entities, including those whose immediate perishability cannot be directly perceived, also undergo destruction with each passing moment, because they are alike with regard to this fundamental nature.

Some individuals do not believe that Candrakīrti espoused the doctrine of subtle impermanence. However, the following passage clearly indicates that he did, although only from the perspective of conventional truth. In this statement, he describes an empirical basis for this view and also identifies two of the classic reasons that support this fundamental Buddhist tenet:

> It is not exceedingly difficult to recognize the momentary perishability of the mind, because of the manner in which it swiftly changes objects. For example, if one recites the letters [of the Sanskrit alphabet[474]] in quick succession, beginning with [the vowel] *a*, etc., it can be understood that, just as [the sound of] each letter is distinct in time and form, the states of awareness that perceive [each letter] are also distinct in time and form. Thus, the momentariness of the mind can be established on the basis of this distinctness of time and form.
>
> An instant is considered to be the smallest unit of time. Sixty-five instants make up the duration of a healthy person's finger snap.[475] Consciousness is momentary in this sense of an instant. Just as consciousness is momentary, all [other] conditioned entities have the same momentary nature as the mind, because nothing obstructs the perishing of all conditioned entities as soon as they appear and because the impermanence [of entities] depends only upon [their] arising.[476]

After having determined the manner in which all conditioned entities are subject to subtle impermanence, Asaṅga observes in his *Listeners' Level* that the activity of inferential reflection should also include consideration of the great diversity of beings: some are graceful in form while others are unattractive; some are born into families of high position, others into families of a lowly status; some are wealthy and others poor; some enjoy great distinction while others are of little renown; some are long-lived, others short-lived; the word of some is highly trusted and that of others not at all; some have a sharp intellect and others are dull-witted. We should recognize that this diversity in the human condition is determined by the variety of good and bad karma that beings perform and accumulate, not by the will of any divine creator. This exercise is meant to produce, on the basis of inferential reflection, a conviction regarding the manner in which conditioned entities that occur in one life exert an influence on those that appear in other lives.[477]

The final three forms of impermanence that are to be contemplated represent exercises in which the practitioner considers how his or her own personal circumstances do not remain in a fixed, unchanging state. For the first of these, called "the impermanence of separation,"[478] one considers, for example, how an individual who may be enjoying personal freedom and independence at one time can later become subject to the influence and control of others. Likewise, one's property and wealth can be lost, stolen, or confiscated.

For the fourth aspect of impermanence, called "the impermanence that is the ultimate nature of things,"[479] one should reflect, "Although I may not be experiencing the impermanence of change and separation at this time, it is the inevitable nature of these conditioned entities[480] that, at some time in the future, I will have to undergo them." The last form of impermanence is called "the impermanence that is present."[481] For this, one should reflect on the impermanence of change, perishability, and separation that one is currently experiencing.

If one studies the nature and order of these five categories of impermanence, it becomes clear that the process is meant to initially evoke a vivid awareness of the transitoriness of every aspect of the world as a whole, and then to bring that understanding directly to one's own individual circumstances. The effect of this practice is to awaken a sense of concern, discontent, and urgency about the uncertainty and instability of one's circumstances.

Three forms of suffering

The next three of the ten points that collectively address the Noble Truth of Suffering are devoted to the three states of suffering: the suffering of suffering, the suffering of change, and the suffering of conditioned existence. Indeed, the understanding of impermanence that is produced by contemplating the first five points plays an important role in preparing the practitioner to contemplate the suffering nature of the five impure heaps in a more profound manner. Asaṅga describes the logic of this transition as follows:

> The [practitioner] who has attained a conviction regarding the five types of impermanence that relate to inner and outer conditioned entities, through having reflected on them extensively and appropriately on the basis of these five aspects and in a manner that relies on a form of contemplation that establishes their correctness, should then apply himself [or herself] to the aspect of suffering. This is done by thinking to oneself as follows: "It is right for these conditioned entities that are characterized by impermanence to possess the quality of being born."[482] Regarding these conditioned entities that possess the quality of being born, birth is suffering. Just as with birth, so too should it be understood that old age, disease, death, meeting with disagreeable things, separation from agreeable things, and the failure to achieve what is desired [are forms of suffering]. This, then, is how the practitioner applies himself to the aspect of suffering on the basis of the aspect of impermanence.[483]

The first two of the three points that relate to the aspect of suffering are called "the aspect of fetters and bondage"[484] and "the aspect of being undesirable,"[485] respectively. The first of these aspects alludes to the potential harm that accompanies the suffering of change, in that the impure heaps which are associated with pleasurable feelings represent, in Asaṅga's words, "the basis for developing the fetter of craving, and the fetter of craving, in turn, is the basis for developing the bondage of birth, old age, disease, death, grief, wailing, pain, sadness, and agitation, as well as the bondage of desire, hatred, and ignorance." For their part, the heaps that are associated with painful feelings represent the aspect of being undesirable in that they constitute the suffering of suffering. It should further be noted that, at this point, the practitioner's understanding of these two forms of suffering is heightened by the fact that it is also informed by an understanding of subtle impermanence.

The third point that relates to the aspect of suffering is called "the aspect [of being a state] in which one's welfare is not secure."[486] Asaṅga also used this expression in his earlier description of the suffering of conditioned existence. It is meant to be identified with the nature of the five impure heaps that are associated with feelings that are neither painful nor pleasurable. This is how the contemplation of this point is described:

> Based on the fact that [the five grasping heaps] represent a state in which one's welfare is not secure, [the practitioner] applies himself to the [Noble Truth of Suffering's] aspect of suffering in relation to the heaps that are associated with feelings that are neither painful nor pleasurable. Specifically, those heaps [are a state in which one's welfare is not secure because they] are related to the outflows; they are connected with [the four forms of] grasping; they are accompanied by a state of indisposition[487]; they possess the seeds of the suffering of suffering and the suffering of change, and, [therefore, they] are not free from [these two types of suffering]; they are impermanent; and they possess the quality of undergoing cessation [from moment to moment].[488]

In fact, Asaṅga repeats here a number of the same expressions that he used in his earlier description of this form of suffering. The principal difference is that here they are being presented in the wake of a systematic series of reflections on several forms of impermanence that culminate with subtle impermanence. Knowledge of subtle impermanence imparts a unique appreciation of the five impure heaps in which the practitioner realizes that, as they arise and pass away from moment to moment, their character is largely determined by the propensities of our past mental afflictions, that these propensities urge us to react in a way that only causes us to further strengthen the seeds of the mental afflictions, and that these seeds have a deep-seated capacity to impede us from developing such spiritual qualities as the one-pointedness of mind and the discriminative insight that are necessary to realize the true nature of the five heaps. The overall character of this aesthetic experience creates a profound sense of helplessness that represents a realization of the suffering of conditioned existence. This is the reason for calling this point "a state in which one's welfare is not secure."

Such an understanding will have varying degrees of authenticity depending on whether it is based upon wisdom derived from listening, contemplation, or meditation. Because wisdom derived from listening does not rise above the level of correct belief, the extent of its impact on an individual, both spiritually and aesthetically, is likely to be somewhat limited. In the verse that was quoted earlier, this kind of sensibility is compared to the effect that an eyelash will have on an individual when it is situated in the palm of the hand.

In contrast to this type of understanding, wisdom derived from contemplation represents correct inferential knowledge,[489] which does exert a profound spiritual influence on a practitioner. All the meditation topics in the first two divisions of the Lamrim teaching are intended to evoke this type of realization. Indeed, genuine renunciation is a form of experiential awareness that is based upon correct inferential knowledge. Moreover, if one develops an understanding of the suffering of conditional existence that represents this type of wisdom, it will take on a sensitivity that resembles the impact created by an eyelash that has become lodged in the eye. In the Hīnayāna system, the attainment of renunciation marks the point at which a practitioner enters the path to liberation. This initial stage is called the Accumulation Path,[490] and represents the first of five paths that culminate with the attainment of the status of an Arhat.

The Accumulation Path involves pursuing a range of virtues[491] as well as cultivating the three trainings, in order to further develop one's knowledge of the Four Noble Truths. For a practitioner to achieve wisdom derived from meditation, he or she must first cultivate the form of one-pointed concentration that is called quiescence, using the conceptual understanding of the suffering of conditioned existence—or any of the other aspects of the Four Noble Truths—as his or her meditation object. After having achieved quiescence in relation to this object, one then begins to analyze the same object with the form of discriminative wisdom that is called insight meditation. The practitioner begins to develop wisdom derived from meditation from the point at which he or she is able to cultivate these two types of practice in tandem, in a manner called "the practice that unites quiescence and insight." This also marks the attainment of the second of the five paths, called the Preparation Path.[492] The cultivation of this type of wisdom culminates in the transcendent realization known as direct yogic perception,[493] which marks the attainment of the Seeing Path and the point at which one becomes an Ārya.

Understanding suffering is a prerequisite for understanding selflessness

The final two points of Asaṅga's discussion on the Noble Truth of Suffering relate to the aspects of emptiness and selflessness. An understanding of these aspects is gained through reflection on the two points called "the aspect of nondiscernment"[494] and "the aspect of a lack of self-determination,"[495] respectively. Here is how the author describes the nature of these two aspects:

> [The practitioner] has the following thoughts: "I discern merely a faculty, merely an object, merely an experience that [the faculty and object] cause to arise, and merely a mind. The notions of an 'I' and

a 'mine' are mere names, mere impressions, mere figures of speech. There is nothing beyond that, nothing more than that. The objects that exist in this manner are merely the heaps. No permanence, durability, constancy, or quality of 'being owned'[496] can be found among these heaps. Nor can any self or sentient being be found [among the heaps] that is born, ages, and dies, or who, having performed deeds here and there, experiences the ripening of their fruit. Therefore, these conditioned entities are empty and devoid of a self." In this way, [the practitioner] arrives at an understanding of the aspect of emptiness on the basis of the point called "nondiscernment."

[The practitioner then also] has the following thoughts: "These conditioned entities that are endowed with their own unique defining attributes,[497] as well as the attribute of impermanence[498] and the attribute of suffering, lack the quality of self-determination[499] in that they are subject to dependent origination, and those entities that lack self-determination are void of a self." In this way, [the practitioner] arrives at an understanding of the aspect of selflessness on the basis of the point called "lack of self-determination."[500]

While no special emphasis was placed on the close epistemic relationship that exists among the four aspects of the first of the Four Truths, Asaṅga's presentation does make it clear that such a relationship exists and that one's practice must follow the course dictated by that logic. Thus, knowledge of subtle impermanence is a necessary condition for gaining an awareness of the most important form of samsaric suffering—the suffering of conditioned existence. Similarly, a proper understanding of the suffering of conditioned existence represents the means to gaining insight into the final two aspects of emptiness and selflessness. The nature of this relationship also reveals the justification for the traditional order of their presentation. Dharmakīrti affirms this point in his *Extensive Treatise on Knowledge*:

For this very reason, [Buddha] taught suffering through
impermanence,
And selflessness through suffering.[501]

Genuine Renunciation

It is also important to point out that all four of the aspects of the Noble Truth of Suffering must be understood in order to gain complete and genuine renunciation. This claim is derived largely from the presentation of the Four Noble Truths that appears in Dharmakīrti's *Extensive Treatise on Knowledge.* Je Tsongkapa seems to have emphasized this in oral lectures that he delivered to his followers. It is recorded by Gyeltsab Je in a compilation of notes from Je Tsongkapa's teachings on epistemology.[502] Gyeltsab Je describes the following passage as explaining "the manner in which the aspiration to achieve liberation cannot be developed in its complete form if one fails to achieve a realization of all four aspects of [the Noble Truth of] Suffering":

> Although you will develop a desire to free yourself from samsara as a result of having realized the suffering nature [of the heaps], you will not be able to stop the craving[503] of not wanting to be separated from the heaps unless you realize [their] impermanence. However, once you realize [the impermanence of the heaps] you will recognize the certainty of having to be separated from them, and this will stop the craving of not wanting to be separated from them. Moreover, by failing to realize selflessness, you will automatically elicit a form of craving in which you have a special attachment to the faculties, etc., that are [mistakenly] perceived as belonging to the self. Therefore, even though it will seem that, as a result of having realized impermanence and suffering, you have developed an attitude that wishes to become free of the heaps in general, your belief in a real personal self will definitely bring forth a mind that has a special attachment for certain particular impure [conditioned entities] that are [wrongly perceived as] the means of producing happiness for the self. Therefore, the effect of realizing the impermanence of the heaps is to generate the understanding that you are certain to be separated from them. Similarly, the realization of the suffering nature [of the heaps] will produce the wish to become free of them. However, to develop the attitude that wishes to achieve liberation in its complete form, you must realize [the aspect of] the selflessness [of the five impure heaps].[504]

This does not mean that we only need to examine the Noble Truth of Suffering to understand both the unsatisfactoriness of samsara and the means of freeing ourselves from it. However, it does suggest that all the other forms of meditation that relate to the remaining aspects of the Four Noble Truths are subordinate to the main goal of developing the wisdom that realizes the nonexistence of a real personal self. As Dharmakīrti declares:

> For liberation occurs through the view [that perceives] emptiness
> And [all] remaining forms of meditation have that as their aim.[505]

Mahayanists Must Also Develop Renunciation

Finally, although the Mahayanist does not pursue his or her own liberation exclusively as an ultimate goal, it is still essential for the so-called "great" person to develop genuine renunciation and, therefore, to achieve wisdom derived from contemplation in relation to the four aspects of the Noble Truth of Suffering. The most essential Mahāyāna practice is to develop and sustain *bodhicitta*, or "enlightenment mind," which is both the doorway to and mainstay of the path to supreme Buddhahood. The compassion underlying enlightenment mind urges Bodhisattvas to forego eliminating their own suffering and to deliberately remain in samsara in order to ripen beings spiritually and develop themselves further toward the ultimate goal of supreme enlightenment. This might lead some might to think that, if a person devoted to the Mahāyāna path were to cultivate aversion for samsara too strongly, it would cause him or her to abandon pursuing the welfare of others in favor of the peace of liberation. Je Tsongkapa unequivocally rejects this notion in his *Great Treatise:*

> This is a great error that stems from a perverted understanding of the [Mahāyāna] sutras' meaning. Passages indicating that "[a Bodhisattva] should not feel aversion toward samsara" do not mean that [a Mahayanist] should not develop antipathy toward the suffering of birth, old age, disease, and death that beings who wander in samsara experience because of the power of karma and the mental afflictions. Rather, the point that [such passages] are expressing is this: When Bodhisattvas don the armor that is needed to cultivate Bodhisattva activities on behalf of beings for as long as samsara exists, they should not become upset or disheartened even if, with each passing moment, they should have to endure all the combined physical and mental suffering that all sentient beings experience. Thus, they should not feel aversion toward a samsara in which they must generate a form of effort that is willing to undertake the extensive activities [of the Mahāyāna path].
>
> ... The same sutra[506] also states that, when Bodhisattvas strive on behalf of sentient beings, their happiness will increase in direct proportion to the amount of effort that they exert. Thus, the expression

> that "[Bodhisattvas] should not feel aversion for samsaric existence" can [also] be taken to mean that [Bodhisattvas] should not be averse to acting on behalf of sentient beings while in samsara; indeed they should take pleasure in doing so.
>
> Anyone who wanders in samsara under the power of karma and the mental afflictions will be tormented by many forms of suffering and, for that reason, will remain unable to accomplish his [or her] own welfare, much less that of others. Because this [samsaric] condition is the source of all misfortune, [the Mahayanist] should feel much greater aversion toward it and have a much greater desire to end it than even a Hinayanist does. On the other hand, [the Mahayanist] should also feel a sense of delight about being reborn in samsara through the power of his compassion, prayers, and the like; hence, these two situations are not at all alike.
>
> If an individual who professes the view described above without making this distinction should also have taken the Bodhisattva vows, [Asaṅga] states in his *Bodhisattvas' Level* that such a person will commit an afflicted form of one of the [secondary Bodhisattva] misdeeds.[507] However, out of concern that the discussion might become too lengthy, I will not write anything further about this point here.
>
> Therefore, it is truly wondrous that even though [Bodhisattvas] develop great aversion for samsara after perceiving all of its faults, they do not abandon samsara because their minds are governed by great compassion. On the other hand, how could the wise be pleased with those who profess that they have refused to abandon samsara out of concern for others, when they have not reduced in the slightest degree their own craving for the pleasures of samsaric existence and they view [those pleasures] as if they were [the attributes of] some celestial mansion?[508]

Thus, all Buddhists—Hinayanist and Mahayanist alike—should seek the understanding that will enable them to avoid being subject to the four mistaken beliefs that regard what is impure as pure, what is impermanent as permanent, what is unsatisfactory (i.e., suffering) as a state of well-being, and what is not a real self as constituting a real self. The ability to cultivate the antidotes to these mistaken beliefs is the best means of overcoming the habitual tendency to develop any of the mental afflictions and to inadvertently commit misdeeds and moral transgressions. The next topic will be to examine one of the main practices that enable us to cultivate the antidotes to the four mistaken beliefs and, in so doing, to develop an understanding that conforms to the teaching on the Four Noble Truths.

THE FOUR CLOSELY PLACED RECOLLECTIONS

How does an understanding of the five heaps contribute to our ability to practice the instruction for "middling" persons? The main purpose of this portion of the Lamrim instruction is to enable the practitioner to develop renunciation and begin to understand the nature of the three trainings that lead to liberation. The four mistaken beliefs represent the very antithesis of this aim, as they are largely responsible for perpetuating the turmoil of samsaric existence. More specifically, these four beliefs serve as the underpinning for the way in which the ordinary secular person perceives and interprets his or her world. Even the individual who subscribes to the Buddhist doctrines of samsaric suffering and selflessness does not easily recognize the degree to which these four mistaken beliefs can continue to influence the manner in which he or she interprets his or her daily experience. The notions of self, pleasure, physical beauty, as well as the appearance that objects continue to exist through time, are so much a part of the ordinary way of interpreting our experience that they cannot be reversed simply by espousing the belief that they are flawed and professing to identify with the principles of Buddhist doctrine that repudiate them. Because they are deeply ingrained in the way individuals habitually think, perceive the circumstances of their existence, and form their view of the world, the influence of the four mistaken beliefs on our minds cannot be overcome without pursuing a rigorous and disciplined form of mental training. One model for such a course of training is the thirty-seven "factors conducive to enlightenment."[509] This collection of practices is arranged into seven groups, the first of which is known as "the four closely placed recollections."[510]

In his subcommentary on the *Treatise That Distinguishes the Middle Way from Extreme Views*, Sthiramati makes the following general observations about the role and significance of the four closely placed recollections:

> Because immature beings do not understand the good qualities of nirvana or the defects of samsara, they remain attached to the notion that conditioned entities are satisfactory, pure, permanent, and constitute a self. As a result, they delight in the enjoyment of samsaric existence and are frightened by the idea of nirvana. Moreover,

> this lack of knowledge regarding good qualities and defects, along with the attachment to the notions of satisfactoriness, etc., can be removed through gaining an awareness of the [Four Noble] Truths. Therefore, meditation on the closely placed recollections is mentioned first [among the thirty-seven factors conducive to enlightenment] in order to bring [the practitioner to] an understanding of the Four Truths so that [he or she] may develop an aversion for samsara and take up the pursuit of nirvana.[511]

This brief passage captures the essence of why it is important to study the two texts translated here in Part Two. In short, the ability to put the four closely placed recollections into practice begins with understanding the Buddhist doctrine that conditioned existence in general and that of individual sentient beings in particular is defined by and limited to the five heaps. In the course of examining the heaps from the perspective of these four recollections, one is able not only to recognize the role that the four mistaken views play in our habitual thinking, but also to counteract them by replacing them with an understanding of the central Buddhist doctrine of the Four Noble Truths. This involves nothing less than learning and integrating into one's belief system a new way of interpreting our everyday experience and defining the nature of our very being. We turn now to a consideration of what this process involves.

Each of the seven groups of practice that make up the thirty-seven factors conducive to enlightenment is referred to by a specific descriptive phrase in the classic Indian Buddhist treatises. The four closely placed recollections, in particular, are known as "the path that examines objects."[512] Jinaputra's commentary to the *Compendium of Higher Learning* states that this is "because [the four closely placed recollections represent a path] that examines the objects of the body, feelings, mind, and entities at the outset, on the basis of the aspects of being unattractive, etc."[513] This does not mean that the four closely placed recollections are only practiced for a limited period at the beginning of the path, and that they are then abandoned when no longer necessary. They are, in fact, practiced throughout the course of both the Hīnayāna and the Mahāyāna paths.

Three Levels of Meditation Practitioner

Both Asaṅga and Vasubandhu describe three types of meditation practitioner: (1) a novice, (2) one whose investigations are completed, (3) one who has gone beyond applying a form of attention. This formulation reportedly appears in the early Sanskrit Abhidharma work, the *Great Treatise on Alternative Explanations*.[514] Following Asaṅga's description, the novice[515] is either a meditation practitioner who is pursuing but has not yet achieved one-pointedness of mind, or someone who, motivated by the desire to become free of the mental afflictions, has begun cultivating the first of seven forms of attention called "that which repeatedly analyzes properties."[516] In either case, this first type of practitioner is one who has not yet achieved the Preparation Path. The second type of practitioner, referred to as "one whose investigations are completed,"[517] is someone who has carried out all the reflective examination that is necessary for cultivating the next five of the seven forms of attention. This individual is further identified as someone who has reached the Preparation Path but not yet achieved the Seeing Path. The third type of meditation practitioner, described as "one who has gone beyond applying a form of attention,"[518] is someone who has reached the Seeing Path, which is to say that he or she has achieved a direct realization of the Four Noble Truths and attained the status of an Ārya. Such an individual is said to have "gone beyond applying a form of attention" because he or she has surpassed all the preliminary forms of mental application and reached a state in which one is no longer dependent on others for gaining a true understanding of the Buddha's teaching and also is not susceptible to the risk of being led away from the true path.

Most of the discussion presented here relates to the novice practitioner. From that perspective, the main reason that the four closely placed recollections are cultivated at the outset of the path is that they are the principal means of overcoming the four mistaken beliefs.

The Purpose for Practicing Closely Placed Recollection

Asaṅga offers four explanations of why Lord Buddha formulated the practice of the four closely placed recollections. Here is the first one:

> Regarding this [topic], the Lord [Buddha] formulated the four closely placed recollections as an antidote for the four errors. Closely placed recollection of the body was formulated as the antidote for the error that regards what is impure as pure.[519] For example, with regard to meditation on closely placed recollection of the body, the Lord taught the four types of charnel ground[520] that possess the quality of unattractiveness. When [a practitioner]

> repeatedly brings to mind this object, the error that regards what is impure as pure is abandoned.
>
> Closely placed recollection of feelings was formulated as an antidote for the error that regards what is unsatisfactory as a state of well-being. When [a practitioner] abides in a state of watching feelings as feelings, he [or she] will correctly realize [the meaning of the phrase] "anything whatsoever that is experienced here is a state of suffering."[521] In this way, [the practitioner's] error that regards what is unsatisfactory as a state of well-being is abandoned.
>
> Closely placed recollection of the mind was formulated as an antidote for the error that regards what is impermanent as permanent. When [the practitioner] recognizes within the different states of his [or her] mind—such as those that are associated with desire and the like[522]—that all those [states of mind] which occur during the day and night are so numerous, varied, and diverse because they disappear with each passing instant, moment, and brief period, then the error that regards what is impermanent as permanent is abandoned.
>
> Closely placed recollection of entities was formulated as an antidote for the error that regards what is not a [real] self as constituting a [real] self. [The practitioner] sees a self in relation to the heaps because of the presence of such afflicted entities as the [mistaken] view that believes in a [real] self and the absence of such virtuous entities as the [correct] view that recognizes there is no real self. Thus, when he [or she] considers entities in relation to their general and unique attributes and perceives them as they truly are, the error that regards what is not a [real] self as constituting a [real] self is abandoned.[523]

Asaṅga describes a second interpretation based on the observation that most human beings fail to recognize that they are made up of nothing more than the five heaps. This error causes them to develop these mistaken views: (1) the body is the seat in which a real self resides; (2) pleasant and unpleasant feelings are experiences that a real self undergoes; (3) the mind constitutes a real self; and (4) the various mental factors are the entities that cause a real self either to remain afflicted or to become spiritually purified. Each of the four closely placed recollections was formulated to remove one of these forms of ignorance and to develop the understanding that the individual consists solely of the five heaps. Closely placed recollection of the body brings about a correct understanding of the form heap; closely placed recollection of feelings brings about a correct understanding of the feeling heap; closely placed recollection of the mind brings about a correct understanding of the consciousness heap; and closely placed recollection of [mental] entities brings about a correct understanding of the remaining two heaps of conception and the formations.

In a third interpretation, Asaṅga describes how the four closely placed recollections represent a means of better understanding the process by which deeds are carried out. This is explained in relation to these four points: (1) the body is the object in relation to which deeds are carried out; (2) feelings are the object that constitutes the aim or purpose for which deeds are carried out; (3) the mind is the agent that carries out deeds; and (4) entities (i.e., the mental formations) are the means or the motivating force by which deeds are carried out. By cultivating the four closely placed recollections, a practitioner will develop a better understanding of the process by which misdeeds occur so that they can be avoided, as well as a better understanding of what constitutes the essence of virtuous mental states so that they can be more easily developed. In an important sense, this interpretation describes how the main practice identified with "lesser" persons—that of avoiding nonvirtuous deeds and cultivating virtuous ones—can be pursued in a more refined and effective manner.

Finally, a fourth interpretation states that practicing the four closely placed recollections enables one to better understand both the process by which one continues to be afflicted by the samsaric condition and the process by which one can purify oneself in order to escape from it. This explanation consists of the following four points: (1) the body is the object in relation to which both affliction and purification occur; (2) feelings are the objects for the sake of which affliction and purification occur; (3) the mind is the object that continues to be afflicted or can gradually undergo purification; and (4) [mental] entities are the means by which both affliction and purification occur. Thus, by cultivating the four closely placed recollections, a practitioner will better understand the samsaric condition so that he or she can avoid perpetuating it. In addition, cultivating the four closely placed recollections enables the practitioner to pursue more effectively the three trainings that will bring about spiritual purification. This interpretation has a close correlation with the Lamrim practices associated with "middling" persons.

In short, all four of these explanations indicate how this practice serves the dual purpose of (1) correcting both a flawed view of one's being and the mistaken conduct that flows from such a view, and (2) replacing those erroneous thoughts and deeds with a correct understanding of both the nature of samsaric existence and the process by which that condition can be brought to an end.

Practicing the Four Closely Place Recollections Brings an Understanding of the Four Noble Truths

The following verse from the *Treatise That Distinguishes the Middle Way from Extreme Views* describes how practicing the four closely placed recollections leads to a correct understanding of the Four Noble Truths:

> Through indisposition, through being craving's cause,
> Through being the object, and through removing ignorance—
> The aim of meditating on the closely placed recollections
> Is to bring an understanding of the Four Truths.[524]

Vasubandhu's commentary on the initial phrase "through indisposition" states:

> Indisposition[525] becomes evident through the body. By examining [the body] one arrives at an understanding of the Truth of Suffering, because the main characteristic [of the Truth of Suffering] is that conditioned entities possess the nature of being a state of indisposition. That is, indisposition means the suffering of conditioned existence, and it is on the basis of this [quality] that Āryas perceive all impure entities as having a suffering nature.[526]

Sthiramati glosses the indisposition that is made evident through the body as referring in particular to the resistance that the body poses in the face of our daily efforts.[527] This interpretation suggests a form of meditation on the nature of the body that leads to a realization of the suffering of conditioned existence. Clearly, this is a different form of practice from the meditation on unattractiveness mentioned above that is meant to overcome the mistaken belief that the body is pure. Various Mahāyāna sutras that describe how to cultivate closely placed recollection of the body also reveal that the range of meditations can be quite diverse. We will have more to say about this later.[528]

The focal point for initially developing an understanding of the suffering of conditioned existence is those feelings that are neither pleasurable nor painful. In the present context, one is assumed to have already developed a general understanding of this most subtle type of suffering. By cultivating it in relation to the form heap, the practitioner will deepen his or her knowledge of the Noble Truth of Suffering. Thus, rather than counteracting a mistaken view, this form of meditation represents meditating in a manner that accords with a correct understanding of the body.

The phrase "through being craving's cause" refers to the objects that are the focus of the second closely placed recollection. Regarding them, Vasubandhu explains:

> Feelings are the cause of craving. By examining them, one arrives at an understanding of the Truth of Origination.[529]

Sthiramati points out that the term "feelings" here refers to those that arise from contact that is accompanied by ignorance,[530] since the pure feelings that are "unrelated to the outflows"[531] do not give rise to craving. Pleasurable feelings are a cause for the craving that wants to meet with pleasure again and the craving that does not want to be separated from it when it is being experienced. Painful feelings are a cause for the craving that does not want to meet with suffering initially and the craving that wants to be separated from it when it is being experienced. Those states of composure above the third level of the form realm are all associated only with feelings that are neither painful nor pleasurable. Such neutral feelings can generate the craving for the enjoyment associated with those meditative states, as well as the craving that wants to meet with those experiences in the future and that does not want to be separated from them when they are occurring. A sutra passage also states: "The individual who comes into contact with a painful feeling generates desire for sensory pleasure." This is meant to indicate that painful feelings can also give rise to craving for pleasure in the sense that pleasure represents a state that provides relief from pain.

Sthiramati glosses the phrase "by examining them" to mean that the meditation practitioner should carefully and comprehensively scrutinize feelings in terms of their essential nature, cause, result, impermanence, and form of suffering. Similarly, he interprets the phrase "one arrives at an understanding of the Truth of Origination" to mean that one will realize the manner in which they are the main factor that gives rise to craving. As the Sutras declare:

> What is the Noble Truth of the Origin of Suffering? It is craving for rebirth, [the craving] that accompanies desire for pleasure, and [the craving] that takes delight continually here and there. That is to say, it is craving for pleasure, craving for existence, and craving for extinction.[532]

Dharmakīrti describes craving for existence[533] as the desire for samsaric existence; moreover, he identifies this as the most potent and necessary cause for the continued occurrence of rebirth. Craving for pleasure[534] is the desire to acquire the kinds of happiness that are experienced in the desire realm. Similarly, craving for extinction[535] is the desire to become free of pain. Even though the sutra mentions all three types of craving as representing the essence of the Truth of Origination, craving for existence is viewed as the primary form of desire, because it sets in motion the other two:

> Moreover, because this desire for existence
> Activates beings' desire to obtain happiness
> And to avoid suffering, the two cravings
> For pleasure and extinction are also understood.[536]

The Lamrim literature explains the causes of samsaric existence in terms of two main factors: karma and *all* the mental afflictions taken collectively—not just desire. Moreover, the root cause of all the mental afflictions is universally recognized by all Buddhist schools as being the perishable collection view. Why, then, did Buddha single out desire and limit his instruction to that mental affliction when he taught the essence of the Truth of Origination? Dharmakīrti offers this explanation:

> Though it is also a cause, ignorance was not mentioned;
> Craving alone was declared [to be the Truth of Origination],
> Because it propels the continuum toward [continued] existence
> And because it is [the] immediate [cause]. Karma, too, [was not
>   included,]
> Because, even when present, [rebirth] may not occur.[537]

Thus, although ignorance is the underlying root cause of samsaric existence, craving for continued existence represents the immediate cause in that it is most directly responsible for bringing about rebirth. In addition, while karma plays a role in determining and manifesting what form a samsaric being's rebirth will take, that potential cannot be activated without the presence of desire. In light of these distinctions, we should recognize that it is our undisciplined and misguided reaction to ordinary samsaric feelings that triggers the three types of craving that were just described. Therefore, when we reflect on the manner in which the three types of feelings arise and recognize the role that they play in evoking one of the three forms of craving, this will engender a clearer understanding of the Truth of Origination.

With regard to the phrase "through being the object," Vasubandhu states:

> Mind is the object of the false belief in a self. By examining [the mind], one arrives at an understanding of the Truth of Cessation, because that overcomes the fear that the self will be annihilated.[538]

Sthiramati explains Vasubandhu's remarks in the following manner. Because there is no partless, permanent, and independent self, the object of the erring belief in a real self is actually the mind itself.[539] By examining the mind in relation to the qualities of impermanence and the rest,[540] the practitioner will both abandon the false belief in a real self and develop an awareness of the mind's suffering nature. In so doing, one loses any fear that the self will be annihilated upon the attainment of nirvana. Instead, one recognizes that nirvana represents only the extinction of the suffering of samsaric existence. Through gaining this knowledge, one arrives at an understanding of the Truth of Cessation in the sense of recognizing that it represents a state of peace.[541] This is a reference to the fact that the belief in a substantially real self is the source of all the mental afflictions. Since practicing the third closely placed recollection counteracts this erring belief, it contributes to an understanding that the ultimate form of the Truth of Cessation—that is, nirvana—represents a state in which the torment of the mental afflictions has been permanently extinguished.

With regard to the phrase that relates to the fourth closely placed recollection, Vasubandhu states:

> By examining [mental] entities, one is able to remove confusion concerning those entities that contribute to defilement and those that bring purification. Through this, [the practitioner] arrives at an understanding of the Truth of the Path.[542]

Sthiramati glosses "the entities that contribute to defilement"[543] as the root and secondary mental afflictions, and "those that bring purification"[544] as the virtuous practices that counteract the mental afflictions, such as meditation on unattractiveness and loving-kindness. Both of these groups of entities are included within the formations heap. Through understanding that the mental afflictions are the obstacles that create our suffering and the virtuous mental factors serve as their antidotes, the practitioner's attention becomes oriented in the direction of the path that leads to the abandonment of all samsaric misfortune. This is the sense in which closely placed recollection of entities brings one to an understanding of the Truth of the Path.

The Essential Nature of Closely Placed Recollection

Asaṅga's account of the four closely placed recollections is organized around several key expressions that occur in the canonical passages where the practices are described. While the thirty-seven factors conducive to enlightenment appear in both Mahāyāna and Hīnayāna literature, here we will consider mainly those aspects of the practice that are common to both vehicles. There are, however, only a few sutras in the Tibetan Kangyur collection[545] that represent canonical texts from the Hīnayāna tradition, and, to my knowledge, none of them addresses the four closely placed recollections in any comprehensive manner. Moreover, virtually none of the Sanskrit sutras from the Hīnayāna *āgama* collections is extant in complete form. Nevertheless, the four closely placed recollections are described at some length in both the one-hundred-thousand-line and the twenty-five-thousand-line versions of the *Perfection of Wisdom* sutras. Both texts address this topic in the opening portion of the ninth chapter. The only difference between these descriptions and the Hīnayāna versions is that in this quintessential Mahāyāna discourse the Bodhisattva is said not to "form any deliberative thoughts" in relation to the body, etc., and to practice the closely placed recollections "without apprehending [the body, etc., as real]."

The following formula is the opening statement that appears in the *Twenty-five-Thousand-Line Perfection of Wisdom Sutra*. The same language is then repeated, substituting "feelings," "the mind," and "entities" for "the body":

> Moreover, O Subhūti, the Great Vehicle of the Bodhisattva, the Great Being, includes, specifically, the four closely placed

> recollections. What are the four? They are closely placed recollection of the body, closely placed recollection of feelings, closely placed recollection of the mind, and closely placed recollection of entities.
>
> Regarding that, what is closely placed recollection of the body? Here, O Subhūti, the Bodhisattva, the Great Being, dwells watching the body in relation to an inner body. Moreover, he [or she] does not form deliberative thoughts associated with the body, on account of his [or her] not apprehending [any object that constitutes a real body]. He [or she] is ardent, vigilant, and possessed of recollection, having dispelled all longing for and dejection toward the world.
>
> He [or she] dwells watching the body in relation to an outer body. Moreover, he [or she] does not form deliberative thoughts associated with the body, on account of his [or her] not apprehending [any object that constitutes a real body]. He [or she] is ardent, vigilant, and possessed of recollection, having dispelled all longing for and dejection toward the world.
>
> He [or she] dwells watching the body in relation to a body that is both inner and outer. Moreover, he [or she] does not form deliberative thoughts associated with the body, on account of his [or her] not apprehending [any object that constitutes a real body]. He [or she] is ardent, vigilant, and is possessed of recollection, having dispelled all longing for and dejection toward the world.[546]

In *Listeners' Level,* Asaṅga organizes his discussion of closely placed recollection around four topics. The first one consists of identifying the range of objects that make up the body, feelings, mind, and entities. The remaining three clarify what is meant by the terms "watching," "recollection," and "closely placed recollection." We begin with the latter three elements.

With regard to the exercise of "watching"[547] the body, etc., Asaṅga describes this as being of three types in that it can be cultivated with any of the three types of wisdom—wisdom derived from listening, wisdom derived from reflection, and wisdom derived from meditation. With these different levels of wisdom, a practitioner is described as being able to variously scrutinize, judge, gain insight into, and observe all forms of the body, etc., accurately and in every respect.[548]

Asaṅga describes "recollection" as follows:

> The term "recollection" here refers to [recollection of] those dharma instructions pertaining to the body,[549] as well as the meanings of those very dharma instructions, that, having been established in the mind, are kept clearly present there through reflection and meditation. It is also the mind's avoidance of inattentiveness while those expressions and meanings are being kept clearly present there.[550]

The only difference between this description of recollection and the one that appears in Sthiramati's *Commentary* is that the latter is more generic, while here Asaṅga is describing it in the context of practicing closely placed recollection. The function of recollection is that of keeping clearly present in the mind the words and meanings of the dharma instruction, which in this case consists largely of the five heaps and the Four Noble Truths. The "action" of recollection—that is, its primary function—is to prevent distraction. It should also be noted that one of the secondary mental afflictions represents the antithesis of recollection, namely "clouded recollection."[551]

Asaṅga describes the essence of the practice itself as follows:

> The close placement of recollection is when recollection has been closely placed so that one can determine such things as, "Are [all] the dharma [instructions] well retained in my [mind], or not?" "Have they been well considered in every way by wisdom, or not?" "Has liberation been properly attained in relation to everything, or not?"[552]

This description makes reference to three levels of practice, in the order that they are developed. In the first level, recollection combines with the wisdom derived from listening to cause the meaning of the instruction to be "well retained"[553] in the mind. In the second level, recollection combines with the wisdom derived from reflection to cause the meaning to be "well considered."[554] In the final level of practice, recollection combines with the wisdom derived from meditation to cause liberation to be "properly attained."[555] Liberation can be thought of in terms of both the mundane and the transcendent paths, although the liberation that is gained through the latter path, of course, represents the ultimate aim.

He adds that close placement of recollection has three principal aims: (1) preserving recollection,[556] (2) preventing objects from afflicting [the mind],[557] and (3) fixing [the mind] upon a [meditation] object.[558] The method of pursuing the first two of these aims is discussed at length early on in *Listeners' Level* within the topic known as "restraint of the faculties."[559] Briefly, recollection is preserved by applying oneself to, and cultivating both diligently and at appropriate times, the activities of listening, reflection, and meditation, in order to maintain a proper state of recollection in relation to the practice. Similarly, the effort to prevent objects from afflicting the mind is accomplished through cultivating a state of equanimity that will enable the practitioner to keep any of the nonvirtuous mental factors from entering the mind. Asaṅga's description of both these activities is essentially a finely calibrated analysis of how to cultivate the mindfulness that was described earlier in relation to the instructions for a "lesser" person.[560]

The third aim, that of fixing the mind upon a meditation object, refers to the practices of quiescence and insight. These two forms of meditation will be addressed below in the context of the four categories of objects that represent the focus of closely placed recollection.

Asaṅga closes his discussion of the four closely placed recollections in *Listeners' Level* with the following summary:

> What is the meaning of the expression "closely placed recollection"?
>
> Closely placed recollection refers both to that toward which recollection is closely placed and that by which recollection is closely placed. "That toward which recollection is closely placed" means the meditation object in relation to which closely placed recollection is practiced. "That by which recollection is closely placed" means the wisdom and recollection that are conducive to one-pointed concentration in relation to that [meditation object]. The latter [description] constitutes the essential form of closely placed recollection. Those other entities that are forms of consciousness and secondary mental factors, and that accompany that [wisdom and recollection], are the concomitants of closely placed recollection.
>
> In addition, closely placed recollection refers to those pure and impure virtuous paths that arise in relation to the body, feelings, the mind, and entities. These [paths] can consist of [wisdom] derived from listening, reflection, or meditation. Those that are derived from listening and reflection are impure; those that are derived from meditation can be pure as well as impure.[561]

The First Object of Closely Placed Recollection: the Body

With regard to the body as an object, Asaṅga identifies thirty-five types of physical object, both animate and inanimate, that are encountered in everyday experience and toward which one should develop a proper understanding and then cultivate an appropriate form of closely placed recollection. This list includes pairs of objects that are opposites or closely related, as well as groups that represent different types of sentient being, gender, interpersonal relationship, quality, or stage of life.

The complete list is as follows: (1) [a body] that is inner and (2) one that is outer; (3) [a body] that possesses faculties and (4) one that does not; (5) [a body] that is considered a sentient being and (6) one that is not considered a sentient being; (7) [a body] that is associated with indisposition and (8) one that is associated with agility; (9) the body that is made up of the [primary] elements and (10) the body that is made up of the secondary elements; (11) the body as name and (12) the body as form; (13) [the body] of a hell being, (14) a hungry ghost, (15) an animal, (16) a human being, or (17) a [worldly] god; (18) [a body] that possesses consciousness and (19) one that does not; (20) an internal body and (21) an external body; (22) [a body] that is in an altered state and (23) one that is not; (24) the body of a female, (25) a male, or (26) a sexually deficient person; (27) the body of a friend, (28) an adversary, or (29) one who is neither friend nor foe; (30) an inferior body, (31) a body of middling quality, or (32) an excellent body; (33) the body of a child, (34) that of a young adult, or (35) that of an elderly person.[562]

All of the closely placed recollections can be practiced both as meditation exercises carried out while seated on a cushion and as forms of mental training that are cultivated while engaging in ordinary activities. In the latter case, closely placed recollection is observed within the broader practice of cultivating vigilance. Here is a description from the *Twenty-five-Thousand-Line Perfection of Wisdom Sutra* as to how that should be done:

> How does the Bodhisattva, the Great Being, dwell watching the body in relation to the inner body? O Subhūti, as the Bodhisattva, the Great Being, walks, he [or she] realizes "I am walking." When standing, he [or she] realizes, "I am standing." When sitting, he [or she] realizes, "I am sitting." When lying down, he [or she] realizes,

> "I am lying down." However his [or her] body may be situated—whether in an excellent state or one that is not excellent—he [or she] realizes that it is situated in that manner . . . .
>
> Furthermore, Subhūti, . . . [the Bodhisattva, the Great Being,] maintains vigilance when he [or she] goes out [from his residence] or returns; he [or she] maintains vigilance when gazing without forethought or gazing intentionally; he [or she] maintains vigilance when drawing back or extending [a foot, arm, hand, or other appendage]; he [or she] maintains vigilance when taking hold of his [or her] cloak, robe, or alms bowl; he [or she] maintains vigilance in relation to that which is eaten, chewed, drunk, or savored; he [or she] maintains vigilance when sleeping or dispelling drowsiness; he [or she] maintains vigilance when going, coming, standing, sitting, reclining, remaining wakeful, speaking, remaining silent, or retiring in order to practice meditation. O Subhūti, thus does the Bodhisattva, the Great Being, who is practicing the Perfection of Wisdom, dwell watching the body in relation to the inner body. Moreover, he [or she] does not form deliberative thoughts associated with the body, on account of his [or her] not apprehending [any object that constitutes a real body]. He [or she] is ardent, vigilant, and possessed of recollection, having dispelled all longing for and dejection toward the world.[563]

The first paragraph describes a form of mental training in which the practitioner essentially remains alert and circumspect with regard to his or her body while engaging in any of the four forms of physical conduct. The second paragraph, however, describes closely placed recollection of the body as maintaining vigilance in relation to a range of specific activities. Several are further examples of ordinary behavior, although speaking, of course, could refer to teaching spiritual doctrine to others. Moreover, the last example—that of "retiring in order to practice meditation"[564]—obviously refers to more formal methods of meditation practice. Asaṅga addresses all of these activities in some detail in the second chapter of his *Listeners' Level.*[565] In addition to remaining alert, the practice of vigilance also includes remembering what is morally proper and improper in relation to a particular activity and comporting oneself accordingly.

Prerequisites for Meditation

Before pursuing formal types of meditation practice, there are several preliminary attributes that the novice should seek to develop. Vasubandhu makes reference to several of these in the following lines from his *Treasury of Higher Learning*:

> A virtuous person, possessed of learning and reflection,
> Is qualified to apply himself [or herself] to meditation.[566]

"A virtuous person" refers to someone who has properly cultivated the Buddhist training of morality. This form of spiritual training is considered the foundation for the latter two trainings in that the ability to overcome inner mental distraction depends on our having successfully brought under control the rough mental afflictions that cause us to engage in nonvirtuous deeds. To be "possessed of learning and reflection" means to have received and developed a clear understanding of the instructions necessary to pursue a structured program of meditation practice.

In the very next verse of the root text, Vasubandhu also notes that a successful practice can only be achieved "by those who possess the two seclusions":[567] (1) the physical isolation of dwelling in solitude and (2) the mental isolation of abandoning nonvirtuous thoughts.[568] In addition, practitioners are advised to maintain the two qualities of "having few wants"[569] and "being satisfied with what one has."[570] A similar discussion of these preliminary qualities is presented in Je Tsongkapa's *Great Treatise*, where they are referred to as "the requisites for [attaining] quiescence."[571] Lord Atiśa also alludes to their importance in the following verse from his *Lamp of the Path to Enlightenment*:

> Despite having meditated with great effort,
> One who is deficient in the conditions for quiescence
> Will not achieve a one-pointed mind
> Even after a thousand years.[572]

The practices of quiescence and insight constitute the heart of the latter two of the three Buddhist trainings—one-pointed concentration and wisdom. Initially, the practitioner cultivates quiescence, followed by advanced forms of insight meditation as well as a technique in which quiescence and insight are "united"[573]—which is to say they are practiced in combination.

To fully understand the practice of the four closely placed recollections, it is necessary to at least touch on some elements of the two Buddhist trainings of one-pointed concentration and wisdom. As a frequently quoted statement from the sutras declares, "The person whose mind is composed realizes things as they truly are."[574] Śāntideva also affirms the need to achieve quiescence before cultivating insight meditation:

> Realizing that insight well yoked to quiescence
> Brings destruction of the mental afflictions,
> One should pursue quiescence first,
> By engaging in detachment toward the world.[575]

A Series of Personality Types

Two of the most basic forms of practicing closely placed recollection of the body are to cultivate mindfulness of one's breath and to meditate on the body's unattractiveness. In *The Treasury of Higher Learning*, Vasubandhu's discussion of the four closely placed recollections is preceded by a discussion of these two practices, which are referred to as the means of entry into the domain of meditative practice:

> Entry into [meditation] is [achieved] through [cultivating]
> The unattractive and recollection of the breath.[576]

Vasubandhu further portrays these two exercises as having the capacity to culminate in the attainment of quiescence. He also briefly touches on a topic that relates to the Buddhist theory of personality types, saying that these meditations are meant for "those in whom desire and discursive thoughts are exceedingly strong."[577]

At various places in *Listeners' Level*, Asaṅga discusses a range of issues that relate to different kinds of personality types. One classification of seven types is based on the degree to which an individual may be susceptible to any of five mental afflictions. They are described as (1) one who has a strong tendency to develop desire[578]; (2) one who has a strong tendency to develop hatred; (3) one who has a strong tendency to develop ignorance; (4) one who has a strong tendency to develop pride; (5) one who has a strong tendency to develop discursive thoughts; (6) one who is equally [but only moderately] disposed [to all the mental afflictions]; and (7) one whose mental afflictions are weak. The first five types are said to be individuals who, because they indulged in one of the five named mental afflictions extensively and habitually in past lives, will develop that fault in an intense and long-lasting form whenever they encounter objects that have the potential to evoke it.

The sixth type of person—who is equally [but only moderately] disposed [to all the mental afflictions][579]—is described as an individual who did not indulge in any of the five mental afflictions extensively and habitually in previous lives. However, in those previous lives this type of person also did not reflect correctly on the disadvantages of the mental afflictions or attempt to reduce them. As a result, while this individual does not develop desire or any of the other mental afflictions in an intense and long-lasting form, he or she still does manifest them whenever objects that have the potential to evoke them are present.

The last type of person—one whose mental afflictions are weak[580]—is an individual who did not indulge in any of the mental afflictions extensively and habitually in previous lives, and who also did reflect correctly on their disadvantages and succeeded in reducing them. As a result, this type of individual will only develop a weak form of desire, etc., even when objects that have a very great potential to evoke those particular mental afflictions are present. Moreover, he or she will not develop the mental afflictions at all in relation to objects that only have a moderate or slight potential to evoke them.

Among four categories of meditation object that are discussed in *Listeners' Level*, one is called "the object that purifies an unfavorable mental trait."[581] This category identifies the meditation object that is essential for each of the five types of person who are particularly susceptible to developing one of the five mental afflictions just mentioned. The meditation object for those who are highly prone to develop desire is unattractiveness; the one for those who are highly prone to develop anger is loving-kindness; the one for those who are highly prone to develop ignorance is dependent origination; the one for those who are highly prone to develop pride is the diversity of the constituents[582]; and the one for those who are highly prone to develop discursive thoughts is to cultivate mindfulness of one's breath.

Later on in the text, Asaṅga makes an important point concerning the ability of these five types of practitioner to develop one-pointed concentration and, ultimately, quiescence. Near the end of the second chapter, he declares in a direct and unambiguous manner that individuals who are prone to one of the five mental flaws *must* first purify themselves of that obstacle before seeking to develop mental stability. At the same time, he notes that this requirement does not apply to the latter two of the seven types of person. A significant portion of his analysis of the process for achieving mental stability and quiescence is devoted to this initial stage of meditative practice in which these unfavorable mental traits must be overcome. Here is his assertion:

> Those [five types of individual] who are highly prone to develop desire, hatred, ignorance, pride, and discursive thoughts must at the very outset purify themselves of their unfavorable mental trait on the basis of the type of meditation object that purifies those who are highly prone to a particular mental affliction. Following that, they will [be able to] attain mental stability.[583] The [appropriate meditation] object for these individuals is absolutely fixed and [these practitioners] must apply themselves using their specific [meditation] object.
>
> On the other hand, the person who is equally [but only moderately] disposed [to all the mental afflictions] may take up whatever meditation object [he or she] prefers. That [type of person] applies [himself or herself] to that [meditation object] solely for the sake of [developing] mental stability, not for the sake of purifying some unfavorable mental trait. As with the person who is equally [but only moderately] disposed [to all the mental afflictions], the same is true for a person whose mental afflictions are weak.[584]

Cultivating Mindfulness of One's Breath

The practice of being mindful of one's breath is described as follows in the *Twenty-five-Thousand-Line Perfection of Wisdom Sutra:*

> Furthermore, Subhūti, the Bodhisattva, the Great Being, one who is engaged in the practice of Perfection of Wisdom, maintains recollection when he [or she] breathes in, and knows this [action] as it truly is, thinking, "I maintain recollection as I breathe in." He [or she] maintains recollection when he [or she] breathes out and knows this as it truly is, thinking, "I maintain recollection as I breathe out."
>
> When he [or she] breathes in a long breath, he [or she] knows this as it truly is and thinks, "I breathe in a long breath." When

he [or she] breathes out a long breath, he [or she] knows this as it truly is and thinks, "I breathe out a long breath." When he [or she] breathes in a short breath, he [or she] knows this as it truly is and thinks, "I breathe in a short breath." When he [or she] breathes out a short breath, he [or she] knows this as it truly is and thinks, "I breathe out a short breath."

For example, Subhūti, when a potter or a potter's apprentice causes the [pottery] wheel to turn and makes a long spinning rotation, he [or she] knows this as it truly is and thinks, "I make a long spinning rotation." When he [or she] makes a short spinning rotation, he [or she] knows this as it truly is and thinks, "I make a short spinning rotation." O Subhūti, thus does the Bodhisattva, the Great Being, who is engaged in the practice of Perfection of Wisdom, maintain recollection when he [or she] breathes in, and knows this action as it truly is, thinking, "I maintain recollection as I breathe in." He [or she] maintains recollection when he [or she] breathes out and knows this as it truly is, thinking, "I maintain recollection as I breathe out."

When he [or she] breathes in a long breath, he [or she] knows this as it truly is and thinks, "I breathe in a long breath." When he [or she] breathes out a long breath, he [or she] knows this as it truly is and thinks, "I breathe out a long breath." When he [or she] breathes in a short breath, he [or she] knows this as it truly is and thinks, "I breathe in a short breath." When he [or she] breathes out a short breath, he [or she] knows this as it truly is and thinks, "I breathe out a short breath." O Subhūti, thus does the Bodhisattva, the Great Being, who is practicing Perfection of Wisdom, dwell watching the body in relation to the inner body. Moreover, he [or she] does not form deliberative thoughts associated with the body, on account of his [or her] not apprehending [any object that constitutes a real body]. He [or she] is ardent, vigilant, and possessed of recollection, having dispelled all longing for and dejection toward the world.[585]

Meditating on the Body's Unattractiveness

In his *Listeners' Level*, Asaṅga identifies five different kinds of desire for which there are six types of unattractiveness to be meditated upon as their antidotes.[586] Of the five kinds of desire, the first two are the main ones that a beginning practitioner seeks to overcome by cultivating closely placed recollection of the body. They are (1) inward sensual longing and desire for sense objects and (2) outward sexual longing and desire for sense objects. The antidote for both of these forms of desire involves meditating on "the unattractiveness of impurities," which has two forms, inner impurities and outer impurities.

Inner impurities

The first type of desire, "inward sensual longing and desire for sense objects," arises in relation to one's own body, primarily because the sense faculties that reside in the coarse physical body are the medium through which sensory pleasures are enjoyed. The nature and extent of attachment toward one's own body is complex, deep-seated, and multifaceted. Meditation on inner impurities is meant to serve as an antidote for this form of attachment, and consists of reflecting on the impure substances that make up the physical body. Here is how this practice is described in the *Twenty-five-Thousand-Line Perfection of Wisdom Sutra*:[587]

> Furthermore, Subhūti, the Bodhisattva, the Great Being, who is engaged in the practice of Perfection of Wisdom, examines this very body as it truly is, from the soles of the feet up and the tips of the hair down, bounded [on the outside] by nails, body hair, and skin, and filled [on the inside] with many kinds of impurities. He [or she] observes this body as it truly is and that in it there are the following: (1) hair of the head, (2) hair of the body, (3) fingernails and toenails, (4) teeth, (5) skin, (6) skin irritations,[588] (7) flesh, (8) tendons, (9) blood, (10) bones, (11) marrow, (12) heart, (13) kidneys, (14) liver, (15) lungs, (16) spleen, (17) large intestine, (18) small intestine, (19) mesentery,[589] (20) stomach, (21) urine, (22) feces, (23) tears, (24) sweat, (25) fat, (26) saliva, (27) nasal mucus, (28) pus, (29) bile, (30) phlegm, (31) watery body fluid, (32) oily body fluid (?), (33) impurities, (34) brain matter, (35) cerebral membrane, (36) mucous discharge of the eye, and (37) ear secretions.[590]
>
> For example, Subhūti, if a person with seeing eyes were to open a farmer's sack filled with different kinds of grain, such as sesame, mustard seed, lentils, mung beans, barley, wheat, and rice, he [or she] would know, "This is sesame," "This is mustard seed," "This is lentils," "This is mung beans," "This is barley," "This is wheat," and "This is rice." Likewise, Subhūti, a Bodhisattva, a Great Being,

> examines this very body as it truly is, from the soles of the feet up and the tips of the hair down, bounded [on the outside] by nails, body hair, and skin, and filled [on the inside] with many kinds of impurities. He [or she] observes this body as it truly and that in it there are the following: (1) hair of the head, (2) hair of the body, (3) fingernails and toenails, (4) teeth, (5) skin, (6) skin irritations, (7) flesh, (8) tendons, (9) blood, (10) bones, (11) marrow, (12) heart, (13) kidneys, (14) liver, (15) lungs, (16) spleen, (17) large intestine, (18) small intestine, (19) mesentery, (20) stomach, (21) urine, (22) feces, (23) tears, (24) sweat, (25) fat, (26) saliva, (27) nasal mucus, (28) pus, (29) bile, (30) phlegm, (31) watery body fluid, (32) oily body fluid (?), (33) impurities, (34) brain matter, (35) cerebral membrane, (36) mucous discharge of the eye, and (37) ear secretions. O Subhūti, this is how the Bodhisattva, the Great Being, who is practicing the Perfection of Wisdom, dwells watching the body in relation to the inner body. Moreover, he [or she] does not form deliberative thoughts associated with the body, on account of his [or her] not apprehending [any object that constitutes a real body]. He [or she] is ardent, vigilant, and possessed of recollection, having dispelled all longing for and dejection toward the world.[591]

Outer impurities

The second type of desire, outward sexual longing and desire for sense objects, arises in relation to other beings' bodies and produces the urge to pursue some form of sexual gratification. Both Vasubandhu's *Treasury of Higher Learning* and Asaṅga's *Listeners' Level* identify this type of desire as occurring in relation to four types of object: (1) shapes, (2) colors, (3) tangible objects, and (4) ornaments.[592]

Several commentaries to Vasubandhu's *Treasury of Higher Learning* quote the following sutra verses in relation to this form of closely placed recollection of the body:

> If he [or she] wants to overcome desire,
> The novice *bhikṣu* [or *bhikṣuṇī*] who is still in training
> And whose mind is not yet fully developed
> Should proceed to a charnel ground.
>
> Once there, he [or she] should gaze at a blue corpse;
> After that, he [or she] should gaze at a putrid one.

> After that, he [or she] should gaze at a swollen one,
> As well as a skeleton of [mere] bones.[593]

In the *Compendium of Higher Learning*, Asaṅga interprets the phrase "watching the body in relation to a body" to mean "perceiving the sameness that exists between one's actual physical body and a conceptual image of that body."[594] One example of this would be to make the determination that the body is impermanent by reflecting on the appearance of corpses in various stages of decay. The purpose of forming such a judgment is to help urge ourselves not to become attached to our body or the ephemeral pleasures of this life. Asaṅga's interpretation is clearly illustrated in the following passage from the *Sutra on the Perfection of Wisdom*:

> Furthermore, Subhūti, when the Bodhisattva, the Great Being, who is engaged in the practice of Perfection of Wisdom, has gone to a charnel ground and sees many different kinds of corpses that have been discarded in that charnel ground, abandoned in that place for dead bodies, which have been dead for one, two, three, four, or five days, which are swollen, dark blue, putrid, worm-infested, partially eaten, or dismembered, he [or she] should compare his [or her] own body with them in the following way: "This body [of mine] also has the same quality. It is of the same nature, and it has not gone beyond that condition." O Subhūti, this is how the Bodhisattva, the Great Being, who is engaged in the practice of Perfection of Wisdom, dwells watching the body in relation to an outer body. Moreover, he [or she] does not form deliberative thoughts associated with the body, on account of his [or her] not apprehending [any object that constitutes a real body]. He [or she] is ardent, vigilant, and possessed of recollection, having dispelled all longing for and dejection toward the world.[595]

Meditation on the Body's Essential Nature

The *Twenty-five-Thousand-Line Perfection of Wisdom Sutra* describes one additional form of closely placed recollection of the body:

> Furthermore, Subhūti, the Bodhisattva, the Great Being, who is engaged in the practice of Perfection of Wisdom, examines this very body as it truly is, in relation to its constituent elements. [In so

doing, he or she observes,] "In this body, there is an earth element, a water element, a fire element, and an air element."

For example, Subhūti, consider how a skillful cow-butcher or cow-butcher's apprentice might slaughter a cow with a sharp knife. After slaughtering it, he [or she] might then divide it into four quarters. Then, after dividing it into four quarters, while either standing or sitting, he [or she] might examine it. In just this way, the Bodhisattva, the Great Being, who is engaged in the practice of Perfection of Wisdom, also examines this very body as it truly is, in relation to its constituent elements. [In so doing, he or she observes,] "In this body [of mine], there is an earth element, a water element, a fire element, and an air element." O Subhūti, this is how the Bodhisattva, the Great Being, who is engaged in the practice of Perfection of Wisdom, dwells watching the body in relation to an inner body. Moreover, he [or she] does not form deliberative thoughts associated with the body, on account of his [or her] not apprehending [any object that constitutes a real body]. He [or she] is ardent, vigilant, and possessed of recollection, having dispelled all longing for and dejection toward the world.[596]

In saying that the Bodhisattva "examines this very body as it truly is," the passage indicates that he or she should recognize that it is made up of the four elements of earth, water, fire, and air. This form of practice involves understanding not only the essential nature of each of the body's four elements, which are identified in Vasubandhu's *Summary of the Five Heaps* as "hardness," "fluidity," "heat," and "lightness and motility,"[597] but also their individual actions of "supporting," "cohesion," "maturation," and "expansion."[598] It also refers to the nature of the relationship between the four great elements and the derivative form of the five sense objects and the five sense faculties. In other words, we should meditate on the body as it is described in texts that explain, among the five heaps, the form heap in particular.

Asaṅga also mentions in his *Listeners' Level*[599] that a practitioner should recognize and reflect upon the predominance of the earth element in the first twenty-one of the thirty-six objects that are present in the body, and the predominance of the water element in the remaining fifteen objects.[600] Examples of the predominance of the fire element can be observed in the digestion of food and fevers. Similarly, he lists the following fourteen types of wind element that should be identified: (1) upward-moving wind, (2) downward-moving wind, (3) wind resting in the side, (4) wind resting in the belly, (5) wind resting in the back, (6) wind that produces a hard swelling in the abdomen, (7) wind that produces a swelling [of the spleen or causes gout (?)], (8) wind that produces razor-like pain, (9) wind that produces pain like a pinprick, (10) wind that produces a pain like a knife-cut, (11) wind that produces a sharp needle-like pain, (12) inhalation of the breath, (13) exhalation of the breath, and (14) wind associated with movement of the limbs and appendages.

Finally, as the practitioner develops a more intimate understanding of his or her physical body, this awareness can become the basis for reflecting on the body's general attributes of being impermanent, having a suffering nature, and lacking a controlling self. In short, this last passage from the *Twenty-five-Thousand-Line Perfection of Wisdom Sutra* indicates how to meditate on closely placed recollection of the body in a manner that conforms with the Noble Truth of Suffering.

ACHIEVING QUIESCENCE

Any of the forms of meditation associated with the four closely placed recollections can serve as the basis for cultivating the type of one-pointed concentration known as "quiescence." Je Tsongkapa's *Great Treatise* contains a detailed presentation of how to cultivate quiescence that is based on a range of Buddhist works, including *The Treatise That Distinguishes the Middle Way from Extreme Views*, *The Ornament of Mahāyāna Sutras*, Asaṅga's *Listeners' Level*, and Kamalaśīla's trilogy entitled *The Stages of Meditation*.

Quiescence is a state of meditative composure that must be achieved before one can develop the higher forms of insight meditation. The entire system that explains its method of cultivation is too complex to be presented here. However, the essence of this process involves developing nine levels of mental stability by cultivating eight factors that bring about the abandonment of five faults. This is described in the following verse from *The Treatise That Distinguishes the Middle Way from Extreme Views:*

> The fitness of [mental] stability that occurs then
> For the sake of prosperity in all the [spiritual] aims
> Results from the cultivation of eight factors
> And the abandonment of five faults.[601]

The term "fitness"[602] here refers to the essential characteristic of the particular forms of mental and physical agility that define the attainment of quiescence. This agility[603] is the eighth of eleven virtuous mental factors presented in Vasubandhu's *Summary*. Its significance is largely associated with the cultivation of quiescence and insight. The next verse from *The Treatise That Distinguishes the Middle Way from Extreme Views* identifies the five faults:

> Laziness, forgetting the instruction,
> Languor and excitation, lack of application,
> And, likewise, application—
> These are regarded as the five faults.[604]

"Laziness" here means the disinclination to pursue the developing of quiescence. "Forgetting the instruction" refers principally to the fault of allowing the meditation object to escape from one's attention. "Languor and excitation," which taken together constitute a single fault, are the main obstacles to one-pointed concentration. Languor is a lack of clarity that occurs when the mind relaxes its grip on the meditation object. Sthiramati describes excitation as "a form of desire that causes a lack of calmness in the mind through recalling previous [experiences] that are consistent with desire, such as [occasions of] laughter, amusement, and the like."[605] "Lack of application" is the failure to generate the antidote to languor and excitation when either of them occurs. The last fault, "application," is the failure to allow the mind to remain in a state of equanimity when the obstacles are no longer active.

There are four factors that counteract the fault of laziness: faith, aspiration, effort, and agility. Each of the four remaining faults has one factor that serves as its antidote. They are (1) the recollection that enables you to keep from losing hold of the meditation object; (2) the vigilance that becomes aware of languor or excitation as soon as either one arises; (3) the volition that applies the antidote to languor or excitation in whatever manner is appropriate; and (4) the equanimity that effortlessly maintains an evenness of mind when languor and excitation no longer occur.

Cultivation of these eight factors gradually brings the attainment of nine states of mental stability. Learning how to do this correctly and in sufficient detail is something that should be pursued under the guidance of a meditation teacher. Nevertheless, a concise summary of these levels can be found in Pabongka Rinpoche's *Liberation in Our Hands*.[606] They are called (1) placement, (2) continued placement, (3) renewed placement, (4) close placement, (5) subduing, (6) pacification, (7) heightened pacification, (8) one-pointedness, and (9) equipoise.[607] The main characteristic of each of the nine is briefly indicated in the following verses from *The Ornament of Mahāyāna Sutras:*

> Having fixed the mind on an object,
> He [or she] should not let that momentum slip away.
> Having quickly become aware of distraction,
> He [or she] should return [the mind] to that [object] once again.
>
> More and more, the intelligent one
> Should concentrate the mind inward.
> Then he [or she] should also gladden the mind
> Toward meditative composure by seeing its virtues.
>
> He [or she] should quell displeasure toward it
> By seeing the faults of distraction.
> Likewise, he [or she] should quell the arising
> Of such states as yearning and dejection.
>
> After that, the ascetic should attain a natural flowing
> In the mind that is accomplished by application [of an antidote];
> [And], after repeated practice of that, [he or she should attain
> A natural flowing] that is free of application.[608]

The first of these verses identifies the initial three levels. In the level called "placement," the practitioner begins to fix the mind on a suitable meditation object, but is not able to keep it there for any length of time. During the second level, "continued placement," the practitioner is periodically able to preserve the "momentum" of placing the mind on its object, even if only for a short period. The main characteristic of the third level, called "renewed placement," is that one becomes more adept at returning the mind to the meditation object whenever it slips away.

The second verse addresses the next two levels. On the fourth level, "close placement," a strengthened recollection enables the practitioner to keep the mind's attention focused inward. As a result, a higher degree of concentration begins to develop gradually. During the level of "subduing," one needs to "gladden" or invigorate the mind by recalling the benefits of one-pointed concentration in order to counteract the inclination to generate more subtle forms of languor and excitation.

The next two levels are identified in the third verse. During "pacification," the main obstacle is subtle excitation, which is controlled by reflecting on its disadvantages and developing a strong form of vigilance. "Heightened pacification" marks the level on which the practitioner continues to reject all forms of the secondary mental afflictions whenever they occur.

The last verse describes the final two levels. "One-pointedness" marks the stage at which the practitioner only needs to apply a small amount of effort in order to maintain uninterrupted one-pointed concentration. The expression "natural flowing" refers to the condition in which the attention is able to be conveyed to the meditation object without the arising of any obstruction. As this practice is further cultivated, the meditator finally develops the ability to maintain such a state of one-pointed concentration without the need to apply any effort. This marks the attainment of the ninth level, called "equipoise." Even though this form of concentration is flawless, it still does not represent quiescence. In the following passage from *Liberation in Our Hands*, Pabongka Rinpoche describes how that state is achieved:

> After the ninth level of mental stability has been achieved, it is possible to maintain, effortlessly and for long periods of time, a type of one-pointed concentration that is free of any subtle languor or subtle excitation. However, while this state has certain qualities that are similar to those of quiescence, it is not actual quiescence. In order to achieve genuine quiescence, you must continue to practice one-pointed concentration until you gain the extraordinary ease and joy of physical and mental agility.
>
> Of these two types of agility, mental agility arises first. And of the two types of ease, the ease of physical agility arises first. When the wind element associated with indisposition[609] of the body ceases to be active, a pronounced feeling of ease is experienced. In addition, a special kind of heaviness is felt inside the top of the head. This latter sensation is similar to what it feels like when you press your warm hands on your newly shaven head. Right after this, you develop a unique mental agility because you are no longer subject to the indisposition that previously kept your mind in an afflicted state and prevented you from directing your mind at will to a virtuous object.
>
> This mental agility causes your body to become filled with a type of wind element that brings great suppleness and eliminates all physical indisposition. It also produces a physical agility that makes

your body feel as light as cotton and allows you to apply yourself physically to any virtuous activity without hesitation. This physical agility is followed by an intense and extremely pleasurable bodily sensation that is known as the ease of physical agility.

As you continue to practice one-pointed concentration, your mental agility will cause you to develop a feeling of extreme joy and rapture; this is the ease of mental agility. When this happens, you lose all awareness of any other objects including your own body. It is as if they have all dissolved into the meditation object. The joy is so overwhelming that you feel as though you won't be able to keep your mind fixed on the meditation object.

After a short while, the extreme joy brought on by this mental agility subsides and your mental agility acquires an especially strong steadiness that enhances one-pointed concentration and keeps the mind fixed unshakably on its meditation object. The arising of this agility marks the attainment of quiescence—a state of one-pointed concentration that precedes the first meditative absorption level of the form realm and is known as the all-powerful.[610] It is called "all-powerful" because it is a path that is essential to the attainment of many mundane and transcendent realizations.[611]

The Second Object of Closely Placed Recollection: Feelings

Vasubandhu's *Summary of the Five Heaps* states that feelings are classified according to three types of experience: (1) that which is pleasant, (2) that which is unpleasant, and (3) that which is neither pleasant nor unpleasant. As noted earlier, these three types of feeling have an important and direct correlation with the explanation of the three types of suffering. Thus, one of the main forms of practicing closely placed recollection of feelings is for the practitioner to reflect on and recognize the meaning of the three types of suffering in relation to the range of experiences that make up his or her own feeling heap. This exercise corresponds to Asaṅga's remark that "closely placed recollection of feelings was formulated as an antidote for the error that regards what is unsatisfactory as a state of well-being." Asaṅga further notes that such a practice will enable one to "correctly realize [the meaning of the phrase] 'anything whatsoever that is experienced here is a state of suffering.'"

In his *Commentary* to Vasubandhu's root text, Sthiramati introduces several additional classifications of feelings. Without mentioning the phrase directly, he describes in a very brief manner what canonical literature refers to as "the six collections of feelings."[612] This expression differentiates the three types of feeling in terms of whether they arise through contact with the eye, ear, nose, tongue, body, or mind faculty. A second classification combines these same six categories into two: "corporeal"[613] and "mental."[614] The former includes all the feelings that arise through contact with any of the five sense faculties. These feelings are said to be corporeal because the faculties from which they arise reside within the body and are composed of physical atoms. By contrast, the three types of feeling that arise through contact with the mind faculty are said to be mental because that faculty is exclusively mental in nature.

When a practitioner reflects introspectively in order to isolate each of these eighteen types of feeling and to identify the faculty through which it arises, this constitutes a form of closely placed recollection that examines feelings in terms of both their essential nature[615] and their cause. This type of exercise can also form the basis for overcoming the mistaken notion that feelings are experienced by a real personal self. One should recall, for example, Asaṅga's earlier description of how to reflect on the two points called "nondiscernment" and "lack of self-determination" that were part of the discussion on the Truth of Suffering.[616]

Sthiramati's final point about the feeling heap involves four somewhat technical expressions. He introduces them by saying that "each experience can also be classified into two pairs of categories that describe them either as obstacles or as antidotes."[617] The four types are (1) feelings that are associated with corporeal desire[618]; (2) feelings that are free of corporeal desire[619]; (3) feelings that are related to greed[620]; and (4) feelings that are related to departure.[621]

Asaṅga identifies these same four categories in his *Listeners' Level* as the last group of objects to be contemplated when practicing closely placed recollection of feelings. He adds that each category includes all three of the basic types of feeling, noting that there are (1) pleasant feelings associated with corporeal desire, (2) unpleasant feelings associated with corporeal desire, and (3) feelings associated with corporeal desire that are neither pleasant nor unpleasant. A similar distinction applies to each of the other three categories. Several lines later, Asaṅga offers this description of the nature of these types of feeling:

> A feeling that is free of corporeal desire is one that is derived from penetrating insight[622] and is consistent with nirvana; it is conducive to absolute fulfillment, absolute purity, and absolute completion of a spiritual life. A feeling that is associated with corporeal desire is one that is connected with [any of] the [three] realms and with [samsaric] existence.
>
> A feeling that is related to departure is one that is associated with either the form or the formless realm, or that is consistent with absence of attachment. A feeling that is related to greed is one that is associated with [the] desire [realm] and is not consistent with absence of attachment.[623]

Gyeltsab Darma Rinchen states in his commentary to Asaṅga's *Compendium of Higher Learning* that the first pair of terms relates to the transcendent path[624] while the second pair relates to the mundane path.[625] As Sthiramati notes, "the expressions 'related to greed' and 'related to departure' are defined in terms of their connection with the process of freeing oneself from attachment [to the desire realm, for example] through the mundane path." Thus, "feelings that are related to greed" are any of the three kinds of experience that either provoke further desire for sensory pleasures and the like, or that arise as a result of our having indulged the desire to enjoy sensory pleasures and the like. Thus, one form of closely placed recollection of feelings would consist of developing greater awareness of this connection between feelings and desire, and of trying to counteract it.

The feelings associated with our effort to counteract the tendency to remain under the control of our attachment to sensory pleasure represent the elements of the category of feelings that are said to be "related to departure." The culmination of this process is the detachment that is achieved through cultivating the insight meditation of the mundane path. The nature of those feelings as well as the specific form of detachment associated with them is identified below in the descriptions of the four meditative absorptions and the four formless states of composure.

The pair of categories known as "feelings associated with corporeal desire" and "feelings that are free of corporeal desire" are related to the transcendent path in that they are defined by whether or not the practitioner has attained a direct realization of the absence of any real personal self. As long as this realization has not been achieved and an individual's understanding remains subject to the "perishable collection view,"[626] his or her feelings will automatically be associated with and influenced by craving for continued samsaric existence, which Sthiramati describes as "craving for one's individual existence."[627] Only the transcendent path has the ability to irreversibly overcome this form of desire. Thus, the antithesis of this category, "feelings that are free of corporeal desire," only occur after one has reached the Seeing Path and developed the pure feelings that are described as being "unrelated to the outflows." Cultivating an awareness of this aspect of one's feeling heap represents the most profound form of closely placed recollection of feelings.

THE MUNDANE PATH

We conclude our review of this second form of closely placed recollection with an overview of the mundane and the transcendent paths. These terms reflect the Buddhist view that there are two principal methods of abandoning the mental afflictions.

The mundane path is a form of insight meditation in which a lower level of consciousness is regarded as coarse and a higher level as tranquil.[628] This coarseness is described in brief as being twofold: (1) the condition of dwelling in a state of great unsatisfactoriness and lack of tranquility and (2) the condition of dwelling in a state where one's lifespan is shorter. Asaṅga explains this form of meditation in terms of progressively cultivating these seven forms of attention:[629] (1) that which repeatedly analyzes properties,[630] (2) that which is accompanied by conviction,[631] (3) that which brings separation,[632] (4) that which promotes delight,[633] (5) that which examines,[634] (6) that which completes the practice,[635] and (7) the fruit of having completed the practice.[636]

A detailed account of how these seven forms of attention are cultivated can be found in *Listeners' Level.* This forms the basis for Je Tsongkapa's discussion in his *Great Treatise.* Here is the abridged description of them that Jinaputra presents in his commentary to Asaṅga's *Compendium of Higher Learning:*

> How, then, does the practitioner who is pursuing the first meditative absorption develop the seven forms of attention?
>
> The attention known as "that which repeatedly analyzes properties" is a mental application present in a level of mental composure[637] that clearly recognizes both the properties of coarseness [associated with the desire realm], through perceiving the disadvantages, etc.,[638] of sensory pleasures, and the properties of tranquility associated with the first meditative absorption, because [those disadvantages]

are absent [there]. This [form of attention] is also understood to be one in which a combination of [the wisdom derived from] listening and [the wisdom derived from] reflection are present.

Following that, after [the practitioner] has developed beyond [the activities of] listening and reflection, he [or she] exclusively practices a form of meditation in which both quiescence and insight are cultivated using the marks of those properties of coarseness and tranquility as a meditation object. In doing so, close attention is directed toward the previously investigated coarseness and tranquility again and again. This is referred to as the [the form of attention] "that is accompanied by conviction."

The form of attention that, through repeated practice of that [second form of attention], initially develops an "abandoning path"[639] is [known as] "that which brings separation" because it brings about the abandonment of the [three] great forms of the mental afflictions and the removal of the indisposition that is related [to those mental afflictions].

Following that, the practitioner generates delight for abandoning [the mental afflictions] and perceives the benefits of abandoning [them]. Having attained a limited form of the joy and ease that is born from separation,[640] he [or she] periodically becomes greatly exhilarated by a mental application characterized by a deep serenity that has the express purpose of removing torpor, drowsiness, or excitation. This [form of attention] is referred to as "that which promotes delight."

Because [the practitioner] who is fully absorbed in this manner[641] is firmly established in a virtuous sphere of thought, the perturbations of the desire realm's mental afflictions become inactive. Therefore, in order to determine whether they have been [completely] abandoned or not, he makes an investigation by means of a form of attention that brings to mind the marks of attractive objects that are conducive to the arising of those [perturbations]. [This investigation constitutes the essence of] the form of attention referred to as "that which examines."[642]

As [the practitioner] continues to meditate with this investigative antidote in a systematic manner for the purpose of achieving detachment from all the mental afflictions that are operative in the desire realm, [he or she develops] the corrective form of attention

> that brings to a conclusion the path that leads to the first meditative absorption, and which, therefore, is known as "that which completes the practice."
>
> Immediately following that, one attains the main level of the first meditative absorption, [which is the form of attention referred to as] "the fruit of having completed the practice."
>
> [The form of attention] that repeatedly analyzes properties [first] brings about a comprehensive understanding of what is to be abandoned and what is to be attained, and then directs the mind toward their respective abandonment and attainment. Following that, [the form of attention] that applies conviction takes up the correct practice. [The form of attention] that brings separation abandons the great forms of the mental afflictions. [The form of attention] that promotes delight abandons the middling forms of the mental afflictions. [The form of attention] that engages in an examination places the mind in a state that is free of the exaggerated pride[643] that believes [the goal] has been attained. [The form of attention] that completes the practice abandons the small forms of the mental afflictions. [The form of attention that is] the fruit of having completed the practice experiences the fruit of having meditated effectively on those [preceding six] forms of attention.
>
> In a manner that conforms to each specific instance, it should be understood that a description similar to the one that explains the seven forms of attention that bring about the attainment of the first meditative absorption applies to all the other meditative levels up to the Sphere in Which There Is Neither Conception nor Absence of Conception.[644]

In short, a practitioner achieves the first meditative absorption of the form realm by gradually overcoming all attachment toward the sensory pleasures of the desire realm. A similar effort is carried out in order to achieve the remaining three meditative states of the form realm, as well as the four absorptions of the formless realm. This type of practice is nominally described as resulting in "freedom from attachment"[645] toward any of eight[646] levels of samsaric existence. However, it is only a temporary suspension of those mental afflictions in that their overt form is prevented from arising through the power of one-pointed concentration. Asaṅga describes this as a "suppression"[647] of the mental afflictions:

> What is cessation in the conventional sense? It is a cessation that is achieved through suppressing the seeds [of the mental afflictions] by means of the mundane paths.[648]

Though not unique to Buddhism, this type of meditation is certainly made use of by Buddhist practitioners. For instance, the Hīnayāna path is described as bringing the attainment of four fruits of asceticism:[649] (1) Stream Enterer, (2) Once Returner, (3) Nonreturner, and (4) Arhat. While each of these fruits is achieved exclusively through a form of the transcendent path, a practitioner can gain them by different routes, so to speak. For instance, individuals who have not abandoned the mental afflictions of the desire realm through the mundane path will only achieve the fruit of a Stream Enterer when they attain the Seeing Path. However, some practitioners gain freedom from attachment toward most of the desire realm or freedom from attachment toward the entire desire realm through the mundane path before they attain the transcendent path for the first time. This allows the latter two types of individuals immediately to become a Once Returner and a Nonreturner, respectively. Asaṅga describes this in his *Compendium of Higher Learning*:

> What is a Stream Enterer?
>
> It is a person who has reached the sixteenth moment of the Seeing Path. The Seeing Path is entry into the complete certainty of ultimate correctness.[650] It is also the clear realization of [the true nature of] entities.[651]
>
> A person who has not [previously] achieved freedom from attachment toward the [five] sense objects[652] becomes a Stream Enterer upon attaining entry into the complete certainty of ultimate correctness. A person who has achieved freedom from attachment toward most [of the desire realm] becomes a Once Returner upon attaining entry into the complete certainty of ultimate correctness. A person who has achieved [complete] freedom from attachment toward the [five] sense objects becomes a Nonreturner upon attaining entry into the complete certainty of ultimate correctness.[653]

Thus, the term "departure" in the phrase "feelings that are related to departure" should be understood to mean principally the "freedom from attachment" for the five sense objects of the desire realm, or a freedom from attachment relating to all the other states of the form and formless realms excluding the Peak of Existence. Secondarily, "departure" also refers to the mundane path that brings about the attainment of any of these states. The feelings that are related to departure are those that accompany that state or are conducive to its attainment. Yaśomitra gives three examples of this type of mental feeling:

> Some [persons] develop a happiness of mind when they think, "I shall attain departure." Some develop unhappiness of mind when they think, "I failed to exert myself for the sake of departure." Through careful analytic reflection, some develop equanimity toward [the sense objects of] visible form and the rest.[654]

"Happiness of mind,"[655] "unhappiness of mind"[656] and "equanimity"[657] are synonyms for the three main types of feeling that can accompany mind consciousness—that is, a pleasant feeling, an unpleasant feeling, and a feeling that is neither pleasant nor unpleasant. All three of the examples mentioned here can be understood as describing a specific feeling that is conducive to developing, in particular, the first meditative absorption of the form realm and, thereafter, the other higher forms of the mundane path as well.

Happiness of mind, for instance, describes the feeling that accompanies the faith and aspiration necessary to develop the initial determination to pursue any of the eight principal states of mental composure. Similarly, the unhappiness that stems from recognizing one has not made sufficient effort is a feeling associated with a virtuous form of regret. This reaction is a positive one in that it will help renew one's resolve to continue practicing. Finally, the equanimity that arises from having cultivated analytic reflection should be understood as referring to a feeling that is neither pleasant nor unpleasant, and therefore is to be distinguished from the equanimity that is one of the four immeasurables as well as the equanimity that is one of the eleven virtuous mental formations.[658] More specifically, the equanimity that arises from analytic reflection describes the effect of having cultivated the insight meditation of the mundane path. This form of wisdom gradually overcomes attachment toward the five sense objects of the desire realm. Thus, in this example, equanimity describes the neutral mental feeling that is generated in that process. With the experience gained through study and reflection, as well as through formal efforts to achieve one-pointed concentration, one can discover numerous other forms of virtuous mental feelings that, in Asaṅga's words, are "consistent with absence of attachment."

Developing such an awareness of "feelings that are related to departure" constitutes an important aspect of closely placed recollection of feelings.

The First Meditative Absorption

The quintessential examples of "feelings that are related to departure" are the feelings that accompany the actual levels of mental composure achieved through the mundane path. These forms of one-pointed concentration include mainly the four meditative absorptions of the form realm and the four states of composure of the formless realm. Asaṅga glosses the term "meditative absorption" in the following manner:

> The term "meditative absorption" refers to [a state in which the mind] meditates correctly on an object and recollection holds fast [to an object] one-pointedly.[659]

The sutras describe each of the four meditative absorptions with a formulaic statement. Asaṅga glosses each expression that appears in these statements in his *Listeners' Level*. The canonical description of the first meditative absorption is as follows:

> Separated from the objects of desire, separated from evil and nonvirtuous qualities, [the practitioner] achieves and then remains in the first meditative absorption, which is characterized by the joy and ease that are born of separation and is accompanied by deliberation and reflection.[660]

Commentarial literature defines the meditative absorptions in terms of their main components or limbs.[661] The first meditative absorption consists of these five limbs: (1) deliberation, (2) reflection, (3) joy, (4) ease, and (5) one-pointedness of mind. Of these, deliberation and reflection are corrective limbs, in that they enable the practitioner to abandon the faults of the desire realm, including desire for sensory pleasures, malice,[662] harmfulness,[663] and [nonvirtuous] deliberative thoughts. Joy and pleasure are beneficial limbs, because the practitioner experiences the joy and ease that arise through having attained separation from the coarseness of the desire realm. One-pointedness of mind is the supporting limb in that the power of concentration enables the other limbs to take effect.

Joy[664] is a pleasant mental feeling also described as mental well-being or happiness of mind.[665] There is some disagreement in the commentarial literature regarding the limb called "ease."[666] Je Tsongkapa explains that, according to the philosophical tradition associated with Asaṅga's *Compendium of Higher Learning*, joy and ease refer to separate elements of one and the same pleasant feeling that accompanies the primary mind consciousness. It is called "joy" in that it is a mental feeling and "ease" in that it also benefits the sense faculties and the coarse physical body in which those faculties reside. However, *The Treasury of Higher Learning* states that, according to Vaibhāṣika School, the "ease" of both the first and second meditative absorptions does not refer to a feeling at all, but rather to the mental factor called "agility."[667] Following the first interpretation, the joy and ease of the first meditative absorption represent feelings that are related to departure in that they are associated with a state of separation from the unhappiness of the desire realm.

The Second Meditative Absorption

The canonical description of the second meditative absorption states:

> Through having quelled deliberation and reflection, through [having attained] inner tranquility, and through [having reached] a state in which there is uniform attention of the mind, [the practitioner] achieves and then remains in the second meditative absorption, which is characterized by the joy and ease that are born of concentration and is free of deliberation and reflection.[668]

Vasubandhu describes the "inner tranquility" mentioned here as a kind of faith:

> Through having attained the second meditative absorption, there arises in [the practitioner] a [strong sense of] confidence[669] toward the condition of having escaped from [the relative coarseness of a lower] state of mental composure. That is referred to here as "inner tranquility."[670]

In contrast with this, Asaṅga's *Collection of Determinations* identifies the essence of inner tranquility as [a combination of] recollection, vigilance, and [the] equanimity [that is a mental formation].[671]

Asaṅga also describes the third characteristic, "through [having reached] a state in which there is uniform attention of the mind," as follows:

> Through repeated cultivation of meditation, [the practitioner's] one-pointed concentration that is free of both deliberation and reflection transcends the state in which it is [occasionally] broken and interrupted by a form of one-pointed concentration that includes deliberation and reflection, and reaches a state in which it is no longer broken or interrupted [by such one-pointed concentration].[672]

The second meditative absorption is described as being made up of these four limbs: (1) inner tranquility, (2) joy, (3) ease, and (4) one-pointedness of mind. "Inner tranquility" is the corrective limb because it removes the unsettling effect that deliberation and reflection continue to have upon the mind after the first meditative absorption has been achieved. The descriptions of the remaining three limbs are similar to those that were given for the first meditative absorption. The main difference is that here joy, ease, and one-pointed concentration have a greater depth and strength due to the absence of deliberation, reflection, and the mental afflictions that are specific to the first meditative absorption. The joy and ease of the second meditative absorption again represent feelings related to departure. The departure of this level constitutes separation from the discomfort caused by the indisposition that is present in the first meditative absorption.

The Third Meditative Absorption

The canonical description of the third meditative absorption states:

> Free of attachment to joy, [the practitioner] abides possessed of equanimity, recollection, and vigilance. He [or she] is also caused to experience pleasure with the body. [In this way,] he [or she] achieves and then remains in the third meditative absorption, [a state] in which joy is absent and about which the Āryas declare, "Possessed of recollection and equanimity, he [or she] dwells in [a state of] pleasure."[673]

The third meditative absorption is made up of five limbs: (1) recollection, (2) vigilance, (3) equanimity, (4) pleasure, and (5) one-pointedness of mind. The principal obstacles to attainment of the third meditative absorption are joy and the mental afflictions that pertain to the second meditative absorption. Joy, in particular, has an exciting effect upon the mind that prevents the practitioner from maintaining a state of continuous equanimity.[674] This equanimity is developed through cultivating recollection and vigilance. Hence, these three mental factors represent the corrective limbs of the third meditative absorption.

Asaṅga describes the fourth limb, called "pleasure," in the following manner:

> At that time, [the practitioner] is caused to experience with his physical and his mental body both a pleasant feeling and a pleasurable form of agility. Below the third meditative absorption, there exists neither such a form of pleasure nor uninterrupted equanimity. And while [uninterrupted] equanimity is possessed above the third meditative absorption, no pleasure exists there. Thus, because pleasure and equanimity do not exist together below this [level] and pleasure is not found above it, while this [level]—that is to say, the third meditative absorption—does support [both of these qualities], the Āryas declare in relation to a person who is abiding in such a state of attainment, "Possessed of recollection and equanimity, he dwells in [a state of] pleasure."[675]

The pleasure of the third meditative absorption is a feeling related to departure in that the third meditative absorption is a state in which joy—also called happiness of mind[676]—has been transcended.

The Fourth Meditative Absorption

The canonical description of the fourth meditative absorption states:

> With the abandonment of pleasure as well as the earlier abandonment of discomfort, and with the disappearance of both happiness and unhappiness of mind, [the practitioner] achieves and then remains in the fourth meditative absorption, which is characterized by the absence of any pleasant or unpleasant feeling, as well as by the purity of equanimity and recollection.[677]

The fourth meditative absorption is made up of four limbs: (1) purity of equanimity, (2) purity of recollection, (3) a feeling that is neither pleasant nor unpleasant, and (4) one-pointedness of mind. The purity of the first two limbs stems from having overcome any and all movement or instability of the mind that is caused by the principal flaws associated with the first three meditative absorptions—that is, deliberation, reflection, joy, and the inhalation and exhalation of the breath. The third limb—a feeling that is neither pleasant nor unpleasant—refers to the fact that in the fourth meditative absorption there are no pleasant or unpleasant physical or mental feelings. This limb also represents a feeling related to departure in that the fourth meditative absorption constitutes a state of separation from the pleasant feelings of the third meditative absorption.

The Formless States of Composure

The following passage presents language found in the sutras describing all four of the states of mental composure that are associated with the formless realm:

> Through having completely transcended conceptions of form, through the disappearance of conceptions of resistance, and through not attending to conceptions of the multiplicity [of physical things], [the practitioner] develops a perception of unlimited space. By doing so, he [or she] achieves and then remains in the Sphere of Unlimited Space.[678]
>
> Having completely transcended the Sphere of Unlimited Space, [the practitioner] develops a perception of unlimited consciousness. By doing so, he [or she] achieves and then remains in the Sphere of Unlimited Consciousness.[679]
>
> Having completely transcended the Sphere of Unlimited Consciousness, [the practitioner] develops a perception that nothing at all exists. By doing so, he [or she] achieves and then remains in the Sphere of Nothingness.[680]
>
> Having completely transcended the Sphere of Nothingness, [the practitioner] achieves and then remains in the Sphere in Which There Is Neither Conception nor Absence of Conception.[681]

Unlike the meditative absorptions of the form realm, these states of composure are not differentiated on the basis of limbs.

THE TRANSCENDENT PATH

In *Listeners' Level*, Asaṅga introduces his discussion of the transcendent path with the following statement:

> Now, [the practitioner] who is desirous of proceeding by means of the transcendent path should progressively develop, in relation to the Four Noble Truths, the seven forms of attention, beginning with that which repeatedly analyzes properties, etc., and ending with the fruit of having completed the practice, until he [or she] has attained the status of an Arhat.[682]

The form of attention that repeatedly analyzes properties

The first form of attention consists of learning and reflecting on the meaning of the sixteen aspects of the Four Noble Truths. Asaṅga presents an extensive account of the four aspects of the Noble Truth of Suffering on the basis of ten points. These points were discussed earlier in relation to the topic of the suffering of conditioned existence.[683] Following this, he also presents an explanation of the four aspects that relate to each of the remaining three Truths. He closes this discussion by saying: "This [analysis of the sixteen aspects by the practitioner] is referred to as 'the form of attention that repeatedly analyzes properties internally and individually with regard to the Four Noble Truths.'" The practitioner not only analyzes his own five heaps that exist in the desire realm; he or she must also recognize through inference that the heaps that occur in the form and formless realms, which are not directly evident, must also exhibit the same nature as those of his or her own actual heaps. As was stated in the case of the mundane path, this first form of attention of the transcendent path is also one in which the practitioner practices a combination of the wisdom derived from listening and the wisdom derived from reflection.

The form of attention that is accompanied by conviction

The second form of attention is achieved when the practitioner's analysis results in a sure and definite certainty[684] concerning the Four Noble Truths on the basis of their sixteen aspects, which is to say that he or she gains a realization of the full extent of their range as well as the true nature of their being.[685] Having transcended the form of attention in which the main practice comprises a combination of listening wisdom and reflective wisdom, one begins to cultivate this thoroughgoing comprehension by applying a form of conviction that exclusively cultivates the type of wisdom that is derived from meditation. In short, it is a stage in which the practitioner remains absorbed in a state of meditative composure with the Four Noble Truths as his or her meditation object.

Asaṅga notes that continuous practice of this form of attention brings about an "awareness of boundlessness"[686] in relation to the Truths of suffering and origination. This is an understanding that recognizes with deep conviction the limitless nature of such conditions as impermanence, suffering, selflessness, affliction, misdeeds, going to the lower states, the loss of prosperity, old age, sickness, death, sorrow, lamentation and the rest. The boundlessness of this awareness refers to the recognition that there will be no end or limit to these conditions, unless one is able to terminate the samsaric condition of continuous death and rebirth.

Despite the aversion and fear evoked by the understanding developed toward the first two of the Four Noble Truths, there remains in the practitioner's mind an innate disinclination toward the peacefulness represented by nirvana. Asaṅga attributes this resistance to the habitual and deep-rooted preoccupation that one has had toward sensory pleasures throughout beginningless time; however, he identifies its ultimate source as a coarse form of egoistic pride[687] that, in the present context, is referred to as an "obstruction to spiritual realization."[688] While absorbed in the current form of attention, the practitioner periodically manifests this pride through a variety of thoughts, such as these: "I exist as one who wanders in samsara"; "I exist as one who shall [for some time continue to] wander in samsara"; "I exist as one who shall attain nirvana [at some time in the future]"; "I exist as one who cultivates virtuous qualities, so that I may achieve complete nirvana"; "I exist as one who [correctly] perceives suffering as suffering, origination as origination, and cessation as cessation"; "I exist as one who perceives the path as the path"; "I exist as one who perceives the empty as being empty, that which is not to be desired as not worthy of being desired, and the signless as being free of signs";[689] and "These are my [virtuous] attributes." These are the causes and conditions that keep the practitioner's mind from surging toward nirvana, even when his or her intense resolve is directed toward that goal.

Realizing the obstructive nature of this egoistic pride, the practitioner rejects the form of attention that permits the mind to follow its natural inclination and undertakes to examine the Truths anew with a more disciplined form of attention. This leads to the recognition that, as each instance of consciousness arises and then disappears, its perishing nature is perceived with the succeeding instance of consciousness, and, in this manner, the mind forms an uninterrupted series.

The practitioner then directs his or her attention to the mind as the meditation object and grasps it firmly with the mind, in order to prevent that obstructive form of egoistic pride from having any opportunity to reappear. As one continues to meditate in this manner, the various aspects of the Four Noble Truths are perceived successively while observing the nature of the mind continuum. By means of this exercise, the practitioner is said to become "well established in the Noble Truths."[690] As this understanding is cultivated continuously, the practitioner develops an awareness in which the apprehending mind is recognized as having the very same nature as the meditation object that is being apprehended.[691] With the arising of this awareness, the egoistic pride that obstructs the mind from engaging nirvana with delight is abandoned, in the sense that it no longer becomes active. This awareness is further described as being "accompanied by a weak form of forbearance."[692] This represents the first of the four main levels of the Preparation Path. It is called "heat," because at this level one experiences the first sign of the eventual transcendent path whose fire will consume the kindling of the mental afflictions. This is followed by a moderate form of forbearance, called "the summits,"[693] because it represents the highest point at which one's virtue roots remain unsteady—which means that there is still a possibility of either falling back or developing further. The third level is called "forbearance,"[694] because one accepts the Truths in a strong manner and because there is no longer any possibility of suffering a downfall.

This progressive spiritual development is accomplished by a form of exertion in which the practitioner continuously analyzes and examines the nature of the mind continuum. Eventually, he or she is able to establish himself or herself in a nondiscriminating state of mind[695] that does not recognize the need for any mental exertion. At that point, the practitioner experiences a sensation in which the mind seems to have ceased functioning, although it has not done so. The mind also seems to lack any object, although it is not devoid of an object; and the mind seems as if it might disappear into a state of peace, although it does not actually disappear. Although the meditator has not yet actually reached the direct realization of the Seeing Path, he or she is on the verge of doing so. Thus, he or she is not far from achieving entry into the complete certainty of ultimate correctness.[696] The fourth and final level of the Preparation Path, which is called "the supreme mundane entities,"[697] is the last phase of this nondiscriminating state of mind. Immediately following this, the practitioner initiates a new mental exertion in relation to the Truths that he or she has previously analyzed. It is called "the supreme mundane entities" because, subsequent to this, the practitioner will develop a transcendent mind for the first time. Thus, it represents the final boundary or limit of mundane conditioned entities. This entire range of practice comprises the stage in which the form of attention is one that is accompanied by conviction.

The form of attention that brings separation

Following the stage of the supreme worldly entities, the practitioner initiates yet another mental exertion with regard to the previously examined Truths. As soon as this exertion is made, there arises a certain knowledge that is a direct perception of the true nature of the Four Noble Truths. It arises sequentially and in the same order as that in which the Truths were previously examined, both with regard to those forms of entities that occur in the desire realm and those of the higher two realms. The arising of these realizations brings about the destruction of the mental afflictions of the three realms that are abandoned by the Seeing Path. This stage of the path represents the form of attention that brings separation. The Abhidharma literature in general and Asaṅga's writings in particular have much to say about the nature of the mental afflictions as well as how and when they are abandoned; however, it would be too much of a digression to consider those details further here.

As noted earlier, Asaṅga describes feelings that are free of corporeal desire as those that are "derived from penetrating insight." The phrase "penetrating insight" is a synonym for the Seeing Path. Therefore, the qualities associated with this type of feeling are not achieved until the practitioner reaches the status of an Ārya. By extension, it also follows that all the feelings of an ordinary person, who still possesses the seeds of all the three realms' mental afflictions, represent feelings that are associated with corporeal desire.

The form of attention that examines

The next three forms of attention are all cultivated during the Meditation Path. During this stage of the path, the practitioner sets about abandoning all the remaining "innate" forms of the mental afflictions. Asaṅga describes this process in *Listeners' Level* as consisting of eight activities and eleven types of meditation.[698] Although they are not identified by number or addressed in exactly the same manner, Asaṅga also discusses these activities and forms of meditation in the second chapter of his *Compendium of Higher Learning*, as part of the presentation on the Noble Truth of the Path.

With regard to the form of attention that examines, Asaṅga states:

> The entire Meditation Path is characterized by the fact that, whatever [level of the] path has been reached and is being cultivated, the form of attention that examines is continually applied to investigate what [obstacles] have been abandoned and what [obstacles] have yet to be abandoned.[699]

The form of attention that promotes delight

With regard to this form of attention, Asaṅga states:

> As [the practitioner] engages in meditation [during this portion of the path], the form of attention that promotes delight consists of (1) periodically investigating what [obstacles] have or have not been abandoned, (2) periodically instilling aversion in the mind toward those entities for which one should feel aversion, and (3) periodically instilling great delight toward those entities for which one should feel great delight.[700]

The form of attention that completes the practice

Asaṅga continues:

> As a consequence of cultivating, meditating upon, and repeatedly practicing the form of attention that promotes delight, there [eventually] arises the final stage of training, called "the diamond-like concentration,"[701] whose purpose is to abandon all the remaining forms of the mental afflictions that are abandoned by the Meditation Path.[702]

The form of attention that is the fruit of having completed the practice

After several pages of remarks, Asaṅga concludes:

> This diamond-like concentration represents the form of attention that completes the practice.[703]

Asaṅga closes the work *Listeners' Level* with this statement:

> Moreover, the form of attention that is the fruit of having completed the practice is the attention that embodies the paramount

fruit of the Arhat's state. On the basis of the transcendent path and through employing these seven forms of attention, [a practitioner] achieves the state of absolute completion.[704]

The Third Object of Closely Placed Recollection: the Mind

Asaṅga lists twenty types of mind that make up the range of objects that relate to the third form of closely placed recollection. These are divided into two categories: the first six are states of mind that can occur while one is moving about,[705] and the next fourteen occur while one is engaged in meditative practice.[706]

Those that relate to occasions when one is moving about are (1) a mind that is associated with desire, (2) a mind that is free of desire, (3) a mind that is associated with hatred, (4) a mind that is free of hatred, (5) a mind that is associated with ignorance, and (6) a mind that is free of ignorance. Clearly, the purpose of this distinction is to emphasize the need for the practitioner to prevent objects from afflicting his or her mind. The principal exercise for accomplishing this is to cultivate the activity called "restraint of the faculties." As mentioned earlier,[707] this involves developing and maintaining a state of equanimity that enables the practitioner to prevent any of the root and secondary mental afflictions from entering his or her mind. Here is Asaṅga's description of the qualities that are central to this exercise:

> How does [the practitioner] become one who has developed well-guarded recollection?[708]
>
> With the specific aim here of keeping the doors of the senses restrained, [the practitioner] completes the activities of taking up learning, reflection, or repeated meditation. On the strength of this learning, reflection, and meditation, one becomes endowed with recollection. In order to avoid becoming inattentive with regard to this very recollection that one has developed, or damaging it, or having it completely disappear, [the practitioner] periodically applies himself [or herself] to the cultivation of that same learning, reflection, or meditation. He [or she] does not relax this exercise or allow it to be abandoned. In this way, through the periodic exercise of learning, reflection, and meditation, there is accomplished a preservation of the recollection that has been attained through

learning and reflection. And thus, one develops a recollection that is well guarded.

How does [the practitioner] become one who has developed diligent recollection?[709]

[The practitioner does so by becoming] one who perpetually and zealously engages in that very recollection. In this context, perpetual engagement is referred to as "continual engagement" and zealous engagement is referred to as "attentive engagement." In this way, [the practitioner] who continually and attentively engages in [recollection] is said to be one who has developed diligent recollection.

To the extent that [the practitioner] develops well-guarded recollection, he [or she] will not become inattentive regarding that form of recollection. To the extent that [the practitioner] develops diligent recollection, he [or she] will become endowed with the strength to maintain a recollection that is unclouded. With this strength, [the practitioner] gains the power and ability to maintain control over visible forms, sounds, smells, tastes, tangible objects, and objects of the mind.

How does one develop a mind that is protected by means of recollection?[710]

Eye consciousness arises in dependence on the eye and visible forms. Immediately following the occurrence of this eye consciousness, there arises a mind consciousness that engages in deliberative thoughts. This deliberative mind consciousness generates desire toward those visible forms that have an attractive nature and generates aversion toward those visible objects that have an unattractive nature. On the strength of the very recollection [that was just described], [the practitioner] protects himself [or herself] from those improper deliberative thoughts that generate an afflicted state of mind to insure that he [or she] does not give rise to any of the mental afflictions.

Similarly, [all the other forms of consciousness up to] mind consciousness arise in dependence on the ear, nose, tongue, body, and mind, as well as [sounds, smells, tastes, tangible objects, and] objects of the mind. Similarly, [the remaining forms of consciousness, including] that mind consciousness, are accompanied by improper deliberative thoughts that cause [various] mental afflictions to be generated. This occurs when [these improper deliberative thoughts] generate

> desire toward those objects that have an attractive nature and generate aversion toward those that have an unattractive nature.
>
> Therefore, [on the strength of the very recollection that was just described, the practitioner] protects his [or her] mind from those improper deliberative thoughts that generate an afflicted state of mind [in order to insure that he or she does not give rise to any of the mental afflictions]. In this way, one develops a mind that is protected by means of recollection.
>
> How does one become settled into a balanced state?[711]
>
> A "balanced state" refers to a form of equanimity that is either virtuous or [morally] indeterminate. Having protected his [or her] mind from those improper deliberative thoughts that generate mental afflictions, [the practitioner] settles himself [or herself] into a state of equanimity that is either virtuous or [morally] indeterminate. This is referred to as "being settled into a balanced state," and this is how one becomes settled into a balanced state.
>
> How does one guard the mind from those improper deliberative thoughts that generate the mental afflictions?
>
> This is accomplished by not being one who grasps at signs[712] or one who grasps at secondary marks[713] in relation to those objects of sight, hearing, smell, taste, touch, and the mind, such that they might cause evil and nonvirtuous entities to flow subsequently into the mind. If, however, due to inattentive recollection or an abundance of mental afflictions, the activities of grasping at signs and grasping at secondary marks should occur despite one's effort to avoid them, and this results in one being taken over by evil and nonvirtuous entities such that they do flow subsequently into one's mind, one should strive to put a stop to them. Through these two forms [of practice], one guards the mind from those improper deliberative thoughts that generate the mental afflictions.[714]

The fourteen remaining states of mind consist of seven pairs that relate to aspects of meditation practice. Asaṅga provides the following brief description of these states:

> Regarding [the fourteen states of mind that relate to contemplative practice], (1) a contracted mind[715] is one that, by means of a form of quiescence, has been fastened inwardly to a meditation object; (2) a distracted mind[716] is one that has become dispersed outwardly

> toward the five sense objects; (3) a languid mind[717] is one that is accompanied by torpor and drowsiness; (4) a retained mind[718] is one that has been invigorated by means of an object that instills clarity; (5) an excited mind[719] is one that, because of having been overly invigorated, has become perturbed by excitation[720]; (6) an unexcited mind[721] is one in which equanimity is achieved when efforts are being made either to invigorate [the mind] or draw it inward; (7) a pacified mind[722] is one that has been freed of the hindrances[723]; (8) an unpacified mind[724] is one that has not been freed [of the hindrances]; (9) a composed mind[725] is one that, through having been freed of the hindrances, has entered any of the main levels of meditative absorption; (10) an uncomposed mind[726] is one that has not entered [any of the main levels of meditative absorption]; (11) a well-cultivated mind[727] is one that, through having developed a familiarity with one-pointed concentration over a long period of time, has acquired the ability to enter a state of composure quickly, effortlessly, and whenever desired; (12) a mind that has not been well cultivated[728] should be understood as being the opposite of that [previous] mind; (13) a thoroughly liberated mind[729] is one that has been completely and absolutely liberated; (14) a mind that is not thoroughly liberated[730] is one that has not been completely and absolutely liberated.[731]

Of these fourteen states, Asaṅga further identifies the first eight as "contemplative mental states that relate to the stage of purifying oneself of the hindrances,"[732] and the last six as "contemplative mental states that relate to purification of the mental afflictions."[733] Put differently, the first eight states have a direct correlation with the effort to develop quiescence through overcoming the five hindrances to meditative composure, and the last six have a direct correlation with developing and perfecting the practice of insight through either the mundane or the transcendent paths, in order to bring about the permanent abandonment of the mental afflictions.

The Fourth Object of Closely Placed Recollection: Entities

Asaṅga's list of objects that are the focus for closely placed recollection of entities is directly related to the twenty states of mind that were identified in the previous form of this practice. The only difference is that here the individual mental factors and states that are associated with the preceding twenty types of mind are presented in isolation from consciousness. Thus, Asaṅga lists these objects in the following manner:

> What are entities? They are (1) desire, (2) the subdual of desire, (3) hatred, (4) the subdual of hatred, (5) ignorance, (6) the subdual of ignorance, (7) contraction, (8) distraction, (9) languor,[734] (10) retention,[735] (11) excitation,[736] (12) absence of excitation, (13) pacification, (14) absence of pacification, (15) the state of being well composed, (16) the state of not being well composed, (17) the state of having cultivated the path well, (18) the state of not having cultivated the path well, (19) the state of having cultivated liberation well, and (20) the state of not having cultivated liberation well. These twenty entities should be understood as a presentation of the negative qualities that relate to the process of affliction and the positive ones that relate to the process of purification.[737]

In short, these twenty entities represent the mental factors and states that obstruct or promote the pursuit of quiescence and insight. Asaṅga does not explain them further, since they can be understood by referring to the descriptions of the twenty states of mind that represent the objects for the practice of closely placed recollection of the mind.

As for the practice of closely placed recollection of entities, it is described initially as consisting mainly of recognizing any of the five hindrances when they occur, understanding the causes that will engender them, and cultivating their antidotes as needed. Paraphrasing canonical literature, Asaṅga describes this process as follows:

> Whenever a hindrance is present internally, [the practitioner] knows this, [realizing to himself or herself,] "A hindrance is present in me." Whenever a hindrance is not present, [the practitioner] knows this, [realizing to himself or herself,] "A hindrance is not present in me." [The practitioner] also realizes both the manner in which a hindrance that has not arisen could arise and the manner in which one that has arisen can be removed.[738]

Similarly, an understanding of how the twelve inner and outer bases[739] have the potential to generate a variety of mental afflictions is also part of this form of closely placed recollection. More specifically, this is described as developing an awareness of how each pair of inner and outer factors that cause the six types of consciousness to arise may evoke any of a group of nine fetters, and applying the appropriate antidote when needed. The nine fetters[740] are (1) attachment, (2) hatred, (3) pride, (4) ignorance, (5) views, (6) supreme considerations, (7) doubt, (8) jealousy, and (9) stinginess. Asaṅga provides the following brief description of this aspect of the practice:

> Whenever [any of the fetters ranging from] a fetter related to the eye up to a fetter related to the mind is present, [the practitioner] knows this, [realizing to himself or herself,] "[A fetter ranging from those related to the eye, etc.] up to a fetter related to the mind is present in me." Whenever [a fetter ranging from those related to the eye, etc.] up to a fetter related to the mind is not present, [the practitioner] knows this, [realizing to himself or herself,] "[A fetter ranging from those related to the eye, etc.] up to a fetter related to the mind is not present in me." [The practitioner] also realizes both the manner in which [a fetter ranging from those related to the eye, etc.] up to a fetter related to the mind that has not arisen could arise and the manner in which one that has arisen can be made to cease.[741]

The final point that Asaṅga makes with regard to closely placed recollection of entities concerns how the culmination of this practice ultimately leads to a state of transcendent realization. This is suggested in a reference to another group of the thirty-seven factors conductive to enlightenment called "the seven limbs of enlightenment."[742]

> Whenever the enlightenment limb of recollection is present internally, [the practitioner] knows this, [realizing to himself or herself,] "The enlightenment limb of recollection is present in me." Whenever it is not present, [the practitioner] knows this, [realizing to himself or herself,] "It is not present in me." [The practitioner] also realizes both the manner in which the enlightenment limb of recollection that has not arisen can be made to arise and the manner in which that which has arisen can be maintained, how one can avoid being inattentive regarding it, as well as how one's meditation on it

> can be accomplished and brought to a state in which it is further developed, increased, and expanded. As with the inner presence of the enlightenment limb of recollection, the same should be understood for the enlightenment limbs of discrimination of entities, joy, effort, agility, concentration, and equanimity.[743]

Asaṅga's discussion of the fourth closely placed recollection concludes with this observation:

> The overall subject of closely placed recollection of entities consists of this thorough knowledge of impure afflicted entities from the perspective of their essential nature, causes, disadvantages, and antidotes.[744]

In short, when the practitioner of the Listeners' Vehicle succeeds in overcoming the hindrances and achieves quiescence, he or she continues to meditate on the nature of the five heaps and the Four Noble Truths within the structure of the transcendent path in order to achieve, successively, the Preparation Path, the Seeing Path, the Meditation Path, and ultimately the fruit of becoming an Arhat. While the Mahāyāna practitioner does not seek to attain the goal of a Hīnayāna Arhat, it is important to recognize that a Bodhisattva does need to practice and be well versed in the forms of spiritual training taught in the Hīnayāna scriptures. As Je Tsongkapa explains in his *Great Treatise:*

> The aim of the Bodhisattvas is to accomplish the welfare of the world. Moreover, since they must look after and instruct those beings who are associated with all three types of spiritual lineage,[745] they must also train themselves in each of those respective paths; because, if they themselves lack an accurate understanding [of those paths], they cannot possibly teach them to others. This is indicated in the *Commentary on Bodhicitta*, which states:
>
> > Desirous of instilling in others
> > The same knowledge as that
> > Which they themselves have gained,
> > The wise strive continually and without error.[746]
>
> The *Extensive Treatise on Knowledge* also states:

> Without knowing the aim and its cause,
> It is difficult to explain them.[747]

Likewise, the Invincible One[748] declares in the following line of verse that knowledge of the paths associated with all three vehicles is the means by which Bodhisattvas can accomplish their aim:

> . . . which, through the Knowledge of the path, accomplishes the aim of the world for those who aid beings.[749]

It is also stated in the *Mother of the Conquerors*:[750]

> The Bodhisattva, [the Great Being,] should generate all the paths and cognize all the paths. Moreover, he [or she] should perfect these paths—which include the Listeners' path, the Solitary Realizers' path, and the path to Buddhahood. [The Bodhisattva] should also carry out, by means of these [paths], the activities of the path that are to be carried out . . .[751]

> Therefore, to assert that one should not train oneself in the Hīnayāna collection of scriptures because one is a Mahayanist is an argument in which the reason supports the opposite of what is being claimed. The pursuit of the Mahāyāna path includes two aspects: a common path and an uncommon path. Since the common path is that which is found in the Hīnayāna collection of scriptures, how could that be something that one should discard? Thus, except for a few unique elements such as the aspiration to achieve the happiness of [Hīnayāna] Peace for oneself alone, all the practices found there must also be practiced by Mahayanists. This is the reason that all three vehicles are taught at length in the very extensive collection of Bodhisattva scriptures.[752]

The first point that Je Tsongkapa stresses in this passage is the fact that a Mahayanist must be proficient in the Hīnayāna path so that he or she can teach beings of that spiritual lineage the practices that must be cultivated in order to pursue and attain the goal of personal liberation. However, a person who possesses the Mahāyāna spiritual lineage must also develop the fundamental knowledges that are common to all the Buddhist vehicles in order to further his or her own spiritual development. This includes, in particular, the attitude of renunciation and knowledge of the insubstantiality of the person. We have already examined the manner in which an understanding of the five heaps is essential to developing a more refined understanding of these two topics. In the final chapter of this study we will address how these fundamental teachings are also critical to a practitioner's ability to generate the kind of spiritual knowledge that is unique to the Mahāyāna path.

Mahāyāna Practice 4

Every element of the Lamrim instructions is meant to be understood in terms of how it contributes to the pursuit of the Mahāyāna path and its ultimate goal. As such, the teachings that are described as being for "lesser" or "middling" persons represent forms of spiritual training that are necessary preparations for the main practice of developing enlightenment mind and cultivating all the Bodhisattva activities in general, especially the profound view that realizes the insubstantiality of all entities. As for the main practice, Nāgārjuna identifies the following three as central in his *Jewel Garland*:

> If you and this world desire
> To attain unsurpassed enlightenment,
>
> Its roots are an enlightenment mind
> As firm as the great king of mountains,
> Compassion that reaches every quarter,
> And the wisdom that avoids the two [extremes].[753]

Among the three, Je Tsongkapa initially places greatest emphasis on enlightenment mind in his *Great Treatise*, devoting a section of his work to a topic that is entitled "Establishing that enlightenment mind is the sole entrance to the Mahāyāna."[754] Here, we will begin our discussion of Mahāyāna practice by exploring the relationship between compassion and enlightenment mind.

In his introduction to one of the two main bodies of instruction for developing enlightenment mind, Je Tsongkapa refers to compassion as "the root of the Mahāyāna path." This expression is meant to indicate that great compassion is essential for maintaining enlightenment mind at all stages of the path. At the outset, it is the impulse that motivates one to pursue supreme enlightenment for the sake of all beings. Throughout the path, it is the attitude that sustains one in the daunting task of perfecting the vast Bodhisattva activities. Even after having attained supreme enlightenment, compassion is the force that continues to generate a Buddha's pure activities for as long as samsara exists. As Candrakīrti states in his *Introduction to the Middle Way:*

> Because compassion is viewed as the seed of the Conquerors' excellent harvest,
> The water that makes it grow, and the fruition [that ensures]
> It will continue to be enjoyed for a long time,
> I praise compassion at the beginning.[755]

The most common Sanskrit word for compassion is *karuṇā*. A classic Sanskrit "etymology," or literal interpretation, of this term describes it as an attitude that "prevents [one from remaining at] ease."[756] In other words, it is a mental state that causes you to feel discomfort at seeing others suffer. Sthiramati notes in his *Commentary* that, although compassion is identified with the virtuous mental factor called "avoidance of harm,"[757] its essence is the root of virtue called "avoidance of hatred."[758] Moreover, even though loving-kindness and compassion are both recognized as forms of this mental factor, they are distinguished by the manner in which they engage their objects. In the case of loving-kindness, one first recognizes any of various kinds of spiritual well-being that sentient beings lack, and then generates the desire that they acquire such happiness. By contrast, compassion is preceded by an awareness of the suffering that sentient beings undergo, and then is generated by developing the desire that they should become free of that misfortune.

GREAT COMPASSION

The form of compassion that must be cultivated in order to generate genuine enlightenment mind is significantly different from the compassion that is practiced in the Hīnayāna tradition—for instance, as one of four "immeasurables."[759] This distinction is clarified in monastic texts by observing that Hinayanists develop a more passive form of compassion, one that merely "wishes that beings might become free of suffering,"[760] while Mahayanists must develop a much stronger form that "seeks to save beings."[761] This latter form of compassion is the basis for what is called the "extraordinary intention"[762] in the Sevenfold Instruction of Cause and Effect, one of two teachings on how to develop enlightenment mind that are presented in Je Tsongkapa's *Great Treatise*. Although this term can refer to any kind of strongly held aim, it is frequently used in Mahāyāna literature to describe a Bodhisattva's resolute conviction to pursue the ultimate goal of saving others. For example, Asaṅga's *Bodhisattvas' Level* includes a chapter entitled "extraordinary intention," in which fifteen forms of such an attitude are described. However, in the context of the instruction for how to initially generate enlightenment mind, "extraordinary intention" should be understood as a sense of duty and personal responsibility that is motivated by "great compassion." The person who possesses this form of obligation feels the urgent need to free all beings from every form of suffering that they experience and provide them with every form of well-being, rather than merely wishing that this might occur. This attitude immediately precedes generating enlightenment mind itself.

There are three types of compassion that Bodhisattvas cultivate: (1) the compassion that apprehends a sentient being; (2) the compassion that apprehends entities; and (3) non-apprehending compassion.[763] Je Tsongkapa stresses that all three of these forms of compassion have the same aspect[764]—that is, they all constitute a desire that beings become free of suffering. They are distinguished by the manner in which the beings that form the object of that attitude are recognized.

More specifically, "the compassion that apprehends entities" is defined as being preceded by the realization that sentient beings are nominally ascribed on the basis of a collection of impermanent entities (i.e., the five heaps) and that these heaps are void of a substantially real self that is able to subsist independently.[765] After recognizing beings as having such a nature, one generates the desire that they become free of suffering. Similarly, "non-apprehending compassion" is preceded by the realization that sentient beings (as well as their heaps) have no self-existent essence.[766] Maintaining the awareness that sentient beings have such a nature, one generates the desire that they become free of suffering. In order to generate "the compassion that apprehends sentient beings," one does not initially need to identify beings as being characterized in either of these special ways. Instead, the practitioner simply reflects in an ordinary, common-sense manner on the variety of samsaric suffering that sentient beings are observed to undergo and then generates the desire that they become free of that suffering. Candrakīrti refers to all three in the opening verses of his *Introduction to the Middle Way.* In discussing them, Je Tsongkapa makes the following general observation:

> Regardless of which of the three objects these three types of compassion apprehend, they [all] have the [same] aspect of seeking to save all sentient beings from every form of suffering; therefore, they are vastly different in nature from the compassion [that is practiced by] Listeners and Solitary Realizers.[767]

The following statement, which appears in Kamalaśīla's first of three works entitled *Stages of Meditation,* is identified as the classic description of great compassion:

> When compassion occurs spontaneously toward all sentient beings equally and in a form that wishes to remove their suffering as if they were your own dear ailing children, then it has become fully developed and takes on the name "great compassion."[768]

A key point to understand in relation to this type of compassion is what it takes for us to properly appreciate the suffering that beings undergo. Renunciation is developed by reflecting on the suffering that we ourselves must continue to undergo in the lower states in particular and in samsara as a whole, unless we are able to successfully traverse the path that leads to liberation. We have already noted how an understanding of the five heaps and the Four Noble Truths can enhance the attainment of this attitude in a genuine form. Equally important, however, is the recognition that, in order to generate the enlightenment mind that is the mainstay of the Mahāyāna path, we must cultivate in a sincere and effective manner the virtues of loving-kindness and compassion toward all sentient beings. This effort essentially consists of shifting the focus of our understanding of the nature of spiritual well-being and samsaric suffering from ourselves and directing it toward all sentient beings. Moreover, the ability to do this effectively depends entirely on the depth of understanding that we gain regarding these conditions as they relate to each of us individually. In other words, if our awareness of the nature of our own samsaric suffering is superficial and incomplete, then we cannot possibly develop the kind of loving-kindness and compassion that is necessary to generate a genuine form of enlightenment mind.

In the following verse, Candrakīrti compares samsaric beings who wrongly believe in the existence of a real self to the buckets of a wheel device[769] that is used to raise water from a well to irrigate a field, and praises the compassion that Bodhisattvas cultivate toward such helpless beings. This verse is identified as representing the type of compassion that apprehends sentient beings in a common-sense manner:

> I bow to the compassion that is felt toward beings
> Who, after first becoming attached to the self as an "I,"
> Generate desire for entities they regard as "mine,"
> And who are as powerless as a revolving water wheel.[770]

In his autocommentary, Candrakīrti describes six ways in which the samsaric existence of beings resembles different parts of this machine: (1) like the clay buckets that are fastened to the wheel, samsaric beings are tightly bound by the ropes of karma and the mental afflictions; (2) like the oxen or other animals that drive the wheel with its buckets, samsaric beings are propelled by the motivating force of their own undisciplined minds; (3) like the buckets, beings revolve continuously in the deep well of samsara that reaches from the Peak of Existence down to the lowest hell, called Avīci; (4) like the rising and falling buckets, beings descend to the lower realms of samsara effortlessly due to their bad deeds but are drawn up to higher levels only when the effort necessary to accomplish good deeds has been exerted; (5) just as the water wheel turns continuously without beginning, middle, or end, samsaric beings continuously manifest the three aspects of afflicted samsaric existence: the mental afflictions, karma, and birth[771]; and (6) just as each day some of the water wheel's clay buckets are damaged or broken, beings are continually battered by the three forms of suffering. Through contemplating the helplessness of this samsaric condition, Bodhisattvas develop the form of compassion that is described above as "apprehending a sentient being." However, as Je Tsongkapa notes in the following statement, before one can develop this compassion, one must first have contemplated the same kind of suffering in relation to oneself:

> Regarding this [analogy], you must first reflect on the manner in which you yourself wander in samsara, in order to evoke a [genuine] awareness [of your own samsaric suffering]. Otherwise, without having [previously] developed [such an awareness] to any degree at all [in relation to himself or herself], a beginning practitioner who tries to contemplate this [topic] in relation to other sentient beings will not be able to develop the sense that their

> suffering is unbearable. Therefore, as described in the commentary to [Āryadeva's] *Four Hundred Verses*, you must first contemplate [samsaric suffering] in relation to yourself. Following that, you can meditate upon it in relation to others.[772]

In a remark that also bears directly on this point, Lord Atiśa is said to have observed disparagingly: "Tibet knows Bodhisattvas that don't know how to cultivate loving-kindness and compassion."[773] In saying this, he meant that although Tibetans of that time aspired to be Mahāyāna practitioners, most did not understand how to practice loving-kindness and compassion in the manner necessary to develop genuine enlightenment mind. When he was asked, "How, then, should one practice?" he replied, "You must train yourself from the beginning in a step-by-step manner."[774]

THE INSUBSTANTIALITY OF ENTITIES

The insubstantiality of entities is not found among the five heaps because this term refers to an unconditioned entity, and the heaps are made up exclusively of conditioned entities. All unconditioned entities, including the insubstantiality of entities, are classified within both the twelve bases and the eighteen constituents. Among the bases, they are included in the "entity basis"[775] and, among the constituents, the "entity constituent."[776] Vasubandhu refers to the insubstantiality of entities in his *Summary of the Five Heaps* as "suchness,"[777] which he describes as "the true nature of entities and the insubstantiality of entities." This unconditioned entity has a variety of synonyms, including "ultimate truth,"[778] "emptiness,"[779] "reality,"[780] "summit of reality,"[781] and "sphere of reality,"[782] to mention a few.

Mahāyāna Philosophical Schools

The nature of the entity that all these synonyms refer to is largely the province of Mahāyāna philosophical literature. It is what is realized by "the wisdom that doesn't rely upon the two [extremes]," which Nāgārjuna identified as the last of the three necessary causes for pursuing unsurpassed enlightenment. The insubstantiality of entities is not mentioned in Vasubandhu's *Treasury of Higher Learning*, because that work presents mainly the views of the Kashmir Vaibhāṣikas, a Buddhist Hīnayāna school that arose out of the early Abhidharma tradition. Vasubandhu's *Summary of the Five*

Heaps, however, is a literary work associated with the Mahāyāna Mind Only School, which is traditionally regarded as having been founded by his elder brother, Asaṅga. In fact, the *Summary* does not set out primarily to identify the principal tenets of the Mind Only School. Rather, it presents a concise account of the subject matter that is shared by all Buddhist philosophical traditions.

Aside from the present topic of "suchness" or the insubstantiality of entities, the only other elements of Mind Only doctrine that appear explicitly in this work are the "storehouse consciousness,"[783] and the related "afflicted mind,"[784] both of which are addressed within in the context of the consciousness heap. A somewhat less obvious element of Asaṅga's views is evident in the fact that Vasubandhu classifies the fifty-one mental factors using the same categories that appear in Asaṅga's *Levels of Spiritual Practice*. For instance, the category known as "the five universal mental factors"[785] represents the group of mental factors that accompanies every moment of the storehouse consciousness. Beyond this, there is little in either Vasubandhu's root text or Sthiramati's commentary that one could characterize as representing a unique tenet of the Mind Only School. Moreover, Vasubandhu's *Summary* makes no reference whatsoever to such central Mahāyāna topics as enlightenment mind and the six perfections, and Sthiramati's *Commentary* only does so in a cursory manner.

Within his exposition of Vasubandhu's root text, Sthiramati does present a series of arguments that are meant to show that one could not formulate a coherent account of how samsaric existence is both set in motion and brought to an end without including reference to the storehouse consciousness. These arguments are mainly directed against Buddhist realist schools, which do not accept the existence of such a form of consciousness. As relates to the "insubstantiality of entities," Sthiramati simply offers a literal interpretation of what the term means and then observes: "If we were to examine this topic further, there would be much to say. [However,] in order to avoid excessive length, I will let this suffice and continue with the subject at hand."[786]

It is difficult to ascertain whether there was ever a distinct Tibetan tradition that espoused the views of Asaṅga's Mind Only School. The scholar Yeshe De, who was active around the end of the eighth and the beginning of the ninth centuries, translated both Vasubandhu's *Summary* and Sthiramati's *Commentary* and is also listed among the translators of a great many of this school's major works. The Indian scholar Śāntarakṣita and his disciple

Kamalaśīla, who were proponents of the Mādhyamika School, both visited Tibet around this time. Śāntarakṣita, also known as the "Bodhisattva Abbot,"[787] is credited with having ordained the first group of Tibetan monks sometime in the latter half of the eighth century. His disciple Kamalaśīla came to Tibet toward the end of the eighth century and engaged in a famous debate with proponents of Ch'an meditation. It is reasonable to assume that the views of these two Indian teachers exerted an influence upon certain elements of the Tibetan Buddhist community of that time. Yeshe De wrote a summary of Mahāyāna Buddhist doctrine entitled *Distinctions of Views*, which he describes in the opening lines as follows:

> [The following text] is a brief review that was written in order to fix in my mind [a number of] topics that I have learned from teachers and that also appear both in the sutra scriptures and in commentaries. These include a variety of [Buddhist] philosophical views, such as those of scholars who postulate the existence of an external world, as well as [important doctrines], such as those of the three vehicles and [a Buddha's] three bodies.[788]

In fact, Yeshe De discusses the views of three Mahāyāna philosophical systems in this work. One is the Mādhyamika School as explained by Bhavya, who accepts that the external world exists conventionally. A second is the Mādhyamika School as explained by Śāntarakṣita and Kamalaśīla, who follow Asaṅga's Mind Only doctrine that there is no real external world. However, they do so only from the perspective of conventional truth, as they also affirm that, from the perspective of ultimate truth, consciousness is not real. Third is the Mind Only school of Asaṅga and Vasubandhu, who deny that the external world is real but assert that consciousness is real and exists in an ultimate sense. Nevertheless, Yeshe De does not express an opinion that favors or criticizes any of these systems.

Atiśa, who introduced the Lamrim tradition to Tibet in the middle of the eleventh century, espoused the Mādhyamika School as explained by the Indian scholar Candrakīrti. He declares this in his *Introduction to the Two Truths*:

> How can emptiness be realized?
> Nāgārjuna, who was prophesied by the Tathāgata
> And who perceived the truth of ultimate reality,
> Had a disciple named Candrakīrti.

The truth of ultimate reality can be realized
Through instruction handed down by him.[789]

Nevertheless, the writings of Asaṅga also play an important role in the Lamrim tradition, particularly in relation to the instruction on the Bodhisattva practices. Asaṅga's *Levels of Spiritual Practice* is an indispensable source for a great many topics in this body of teachings. In the present study, I have referred extensively to the section of that work entitled *Listeners' Level*. The Mahāyāna portion of Asaṅga's work, entitled *Bodhisattvas' Level*, is even more important to the Lamrim tradition, as evidenced by the fact that the early Kadampa tradition counted this text among its "six major treatises."[790]

Lord Atiśa is said to have received instructions from one hundred and fifty-two spiritual teachers. Despite his philosophical preference for the Mādhyamika School, the teacher he regarded most highly was the one known as Suvarnadvīpa Guru.[791] Though an adherent of Asaṅga's Mind Only School, Atiśa revered him for the effective manner in which he taught the instructions on generating enlightenment mind.

The Two Truths

While the topic of the insubstantiality of entities represents the effort to clarify and establish with certainty the nature of the Mahāyāna doctrine of ultimate truth, it is a fundamental error to view this as the categorical and wholesale rejection of those entities that are referred to as "conventional truth" or "relative truth." It is more accurate to characterize Mahāyāna philosophy as exposing inconsistencies in the attempts by Buddhist realist schools to formulate Buddha's teaching on the Four Noble Truths in terms of physical and mental entities that have the status of real substances. Thus, Nāgārjuna's criticism of the entities described in Abhidharma literature is not that they have no validity whatsoever, but rather that it is wrong to believe that they have real essences. In the Gelukpa literature, this is sometimes described in terms of a distinction between existence and real existence, as well as between lack of inherent existence and nonexistence. That is to say, the five heaps do exist, but not by way of having a real or independent essence. Similarly, when one denies that the five heaps exist inherently, this should not be interpreted as meaning they are nonexistent. These distinctions lie at the heart of the effort to develop a correct understanding of the insubstantiality of entities. The process of developing that understanding cannot be undertaken without learning the doctrine of two truths. As Nāgārjuna states in his *Root Treatise on the Middle Way*:

> The Buddhas' Dharma instruction
> Is based upon these two truths:
> Worldly conventional truth
> And truth in an ultimate sense.
>
> Those who do not understand
> The distinction between these two truths
> Do not understand the profound reality
> Contained in the Buddhas' teaching.
>
> Without relying upon convention,
> The ultimate cannot be taught.
> Without understanding the ultimate,
> Nirvana cannot be achieved.
>
> An improper view of emptiness
> Destroys a person of weak intellect,
> Like a serpent wrongly held
> Or a spell wrongly performed.[792]

While much can be extrapolated from these verses, I would like to consider the lines that state: "without relying upon convention, the ultimate cannot be taught." In his commentary on the root text, Candrakīrti first raises a hypothetical objection and then responds to it:

> If the ultimate is what has the nature of being free of elaboration,[793] then let that alone [be taught]; what purpose is there in those other teachings [concerning entities] that are not the ultimate—such as the heaps, the constituents, the bases, the [Four] Noble Truths, and dependent origination? That which is not [ultimate] reality is to be abandoned. What purpose is there in teaching what is to be abandoned?
>
> Although what you say is true, without accepting worldly convention—which is characterized by expressions, objects of expression (i.e., "meanings"), knowledge, objects of knowledge, etc.—it

> would not be possible to teach the ultimate. And if [the ultimate] is not explained, it cannot be understood. Without having understood the ultimate, it is not possible to achieve nirvana.[794]

Candrakīrti seems to agree with the suggestion that everything other than ultimate truth is to be abandoned in some sense. I interpret this as an acknowledgment that everything that constitutes conventional truth is false because, while it appears to exist independently to a dualistic mind, proper analysis reveals this to be an illusion. Nāgārjuna alludes to this point in his *Sixty Verses of Reasoning*:

> Since the Buddhas declared
> That nirvana is the sole truth,
> What wise person would surmise
> That all else is not false?[795]

How, then, are we to understand the manner in which Candrakīrti "accepts" conventional entities? In the context of rejecting the Mind Only School's view that causally dependent entities have a real essence, he makes the following observations in his *Commentary to the Introduction to the Middle Way*:

> Of your own accord and appealing [only] to your philosophical system, you assert [the existence of] a dependent essence that an Ārya perceives with his [or her transcendent] wisdom; but we do not explain the conventional in that manner.
>
> What then?
>
> Though [conventional truth] does not exist [in reality], [its existence] is accepted by the ordinary world. Therefore, we assert only a mode of being that is held to exist by the ordinary world; for to express oneself in that manner is the means by which it can be refuted. As the Lord [Buddha] declared, "The world quarrels with me. I do not quarrel with the world. Whatever the world believes to exist, I too believe to exist. Whatever the world does not believe to exist, I too do not believe to exist."
>
> . . . Therefore, we accept the conventional [only] insofar as it is something that is dependent upon others, not in any independent sense.[796]

This description implies that one needs to rely upon a coherent conceptual model of ordinary experience in order to reveal the logical inconsistencies in dualistic language and thought. That model is represented by none other than the teachings on the five heaps, the Four Noble Truths, the Three Jewels, karma and its results, etc. The Mādhyamika School's critical analysis of ordinary experience does not, however, set out to completely reject the validity of these topics; more properly, it seeks to reveal that the entities that are represented in these doctrines do not possess a real, independent mode of existence. In the following verse, Nāgārjuna suggests that only a proper understanding of ultimate truth allows us to preserve a coherent account of Buddha's teaching on the Four Noble Truths:

> Everything is acceptable to the one
> For whom emptiness is acceptable;
> Nothing is acceptable to the one
> For whom emptiness is unacceptable.[797]

Candrakīrti explains this verse in part as follows:

> To the one for whom the proposition that all entities are void of a real essence is acceptable, for that person everything that was described [previously][798] is acceptable.
>
> How is that so?
>
> Because dependent origination is what we assert emptiness to mean; therefore, for whomever this emptiness is acceptable, for that person dependent origination is acceptable. For whomever dependent origination is acceptable, for that person the Four Noble Truths are acceptable.
>
> How is that so?
>
> It is because that which arises dependently constitutes suffering; not that which does not arise dependently. And that [dependently arisen suffering] is empty, because it lacks any real essence. Once the existence of suffering is established, the origination of suffering, the cessation of suffering, and the path leading to the cessation of suffering become acceptable. Therefore, the realization of suffering, the abandonment of its origination, the actualization of its cessation, and the cultivation of the path [that leads to its cessation also] become acceptable.
>
> And once the realization of the [Noble] Truth of Suffering, etc.,

has been established, the [four] fruits [of the path] become acceptable. Once the existence of the fruits has been established, the beings that abide in the fruits become acceptable. Once the beings that abide in the fruits become acceptable, those that are pursuing the fruits become acceptable. Once the existence of both those that strive after and those that abide in the fruits has been established, the Sangha becomes acceptable. Once the authenticity of the Four Noble Truths has been established, the Holy Dharma becomes acceptable. Once the existence of both the Sangha and the Dharma has been established, the Buddha becomes acceptable. And therefore, the Three Jewels become acceptable. The distinct realizations that relate to all the mundane and transcendent entities become acceptable. In addition, the spiritual and that which opposes the spiritual; the results of [the spiritual and that which opposes the spiritual]—namely, the happy and unhappy states of existence; indeed all worldly conventions become acceptable.[799]

In short, the Mādhyamika theory of ultimate truth is not one that completely discards such teachings as the five heaps, the Four Noble Truths, the Three Jewels, or virtuous and nonvirtuous karma and their results; rather, it assigns them the status of relative truth. The task of identifying the precise nature of ultimate truth and of explaining the degree of falsity present in conventional truth lies at the heart of Mahāyāna Buddhist philosophy. Moreover, one cannot rely only on canonical scripture to resolve these issues, as Je Tsongkapa notes in the opening passage from his *Essence of Eloquence:*

As a verse from the *Sutra of Questions Posed by Rāṣṭrapāla* declares:

The world is forced to wander by failing to know
This empty, tranquil, and unoriginated nature.
The Compassionate One enables beings to understand it
Through hundreds of expedient means and reasons.[800]

Seeing that the suchness of entities is extremely difficult to realize and that one cannot become liberated from samsara without realizing it, the Compassionate Master [Buddha Śākyamuni] caused it to be understood using many different forms of reasoning and expedient means. Therefore, those who possess intelligence must apply themselves to the methods by which the nature of that reality can be understood. Moreover, that depends upon being able to distinguish between the Conqueror's scriptures whose meaning requires interpretation[801] and those that are of definitive meaning.[802]

The ability to distinguish between these two types of scripture cannot be accomplished merely on the basis of passages that state, "This is a meaning that requires interpretation and that is the definitive meaning." Otherwise, there would be no purpose for the great philosophical champions[803] to compose commentaries on the [Buddha's] intent that seek to differentiate between those scriptures that require interpretation and those that are of definitive meaning. It is also the case that canonical scriptures themselves present a variety of incompatible explanations regarding what requires interpretation and what is of definitive meaning. And if one cannot accept the general premise that a passage is true simply because it states, "This is such and so," then it must also be true in the more specific context of qualified and definitive scriptures that one cannot prove something simply because a passage states, "This is such and so."

Therefore, we must seek to understand the [Buddha's] genuine intent by relying upon explanations that have been made by the great philosophical champions who were prophesied as being able to distinguish between qualified and definitive scriptures. Moreover, we should do so because those explanations are well founded upon reasons that both disprove any interpretations that explain the meaning of a definitive scripture in some manner other [than what it explicitly states] and that also establish why the meaning [of a definitive scripture] should be accepted as being just what [that scripture] declares to be true. Ultimately, then, we must distinguish between [the two types of scripture] on the basis of flawless reasoning, because it would be wrong to hold a teacher as a valid authority if one has accepted a philosophical system that is based on mistaken reasoning and because the ultimate reality of entities is something that is supported by sound reasoning. Realizing the importance of this point, [the Buddha] declared:

> O Bhikṣus, just as gold is [accepted as genuine]
> After burning, cutting, and rubbing,

> The wise should accept my speech
> Only after examining it, not [merely] out of respect.[804]

At several places in his commentary to Nāgārjuna's *Root Treatise on the Middle Way*, Candrakīrti describes different levels of disciples and the need for Buddha to posit teachings that are appropriate to their particular states of mind. He notes that inferior disciples are materialists and other like-minded persons who do not believe in past and future lives or the efficacy of good and bad deeds. Thus, Buddha posited to them a provisional "self" or being that exists in past and future lives and that is the agent of good and bad karma, in order to stop them from continually engaging in nonvirtuous activities. Candrakīrti identifies middling disciples as those beings who avoid nonvirtuous deeds and are able to engage in virtuous acts, but who are also bound firmly to belief in a real self. Because this belief will not allow them to escape from samsara, he likens them to birds that are tethered to a very long and sturdy string that prevents them from flying away completely. He then states:

> The Lord Buddhas, who are desirous of aiding their disciples,[805] also taught these middling followers the doctrine known as "the absence of a self," in order to loosen their attachment to the view of the perishable collection and to engender in them the aspiration for nirvana.[806]

Finally, superior disciples are characterized as those who have overcome attachment for a self and have matured to the point of possessing the capacity to grasp the most profound teaching of emptiness. To them, Buddha taught the doctrine of ultimate truth in which neither a self nor the absence of a self is posited. Candrakīrti concludes this discussion with the following words:

> Since the Dharma instruction of the Lord Buddhas has been set forth to [variously posit] a self, [posit] the absence of a self, and then refute the existence of both, based on the distinctness in attitudes exhibited by those beings who are inferior, middling, and superior followers, therefore scripture does not invalidate [the views expressed by] proponents of the Mādhyamika School. For this very reason the venerable Āryadeva said:

> First is the stopping of nonvirtue;
> In between is the stopping of the self;
> Last is the stopping of everything.
> Wise is the one who understands this.[807]

Likewise, the venerable Master [Nāgārjuna] declared:

> Like a grammarian who also instructs
> [Beginning students how] to recite the alphabet,
> Buddha taught Dharma in a similar way,
> According to the capacity of his followers.
>
> To some he taught Dharma
> To turn [beings] away from evil;
> To some [he taught it] so that [they] would pursue virtue.
> To some [he taught Dharma] that relies on duality;
>
> To some [he taught] the profound that does not rely
> On duality and terrifies those who are timid;
> To some [he taught an instruction] whose essence is emptiness
> And compassion, and which brings enlightenment.[808]

Candrakīrti's formulation of three types of disciples closely parallels the Lamrim tradition's three "persons." With regard to the doctrine of "no self" that Candrakīrti states was taught to middling disciples, this should be understood as a reference to the teaching on the Four Noble Truths. And when he remarks that this instruction was given to "loosen their attachment to the perishable collection view," he is also implying that by itself the teaching on the Four Noble Truths can only suppress the belief in a real self but not completely eradicate it, because it is limited to the relative truth nature of entities. It is a unique tenet of such Indian Mādhyamika scholars as Buddhapālita, Candrakīrti, Śāntideva, and Atiśa that the mental afflictions can only be eliminated by achieving a direct realization of ultimate truth, and then continuing to meditate on this realization until the innate form of belief in real essences has been completely destroyed. Put another way, the proponents of this school maintain that one cannot achieve a complete realization of the insubstantiality of the person without also realizing the insubstantiality of entities. Since Candrakīrti believes that followers of the Hīnayāna path do achieve nirvana, it follows that he must believe they achieve a realization of the insubstantiality of entities. He states this quite explicitly in his *Commentary to the Introduction to the Middle Way*:

> It can be clearly determined on the basis of this scriptural passage[809] that the Listener and Solitary Realizer disciples also possess the knowledge that all entities lack a real essence. Otherwise, the Bodhisattva who has generated the first level of [ultimate enlightenment] mind would surpass those [Hīnayāna Arhats] on the strength of his [or her] intellect as well,[810] because [Hīnayāna Arhats] would then lack the realization that entities do not possess any real essence, as is the case with those who have [only] attained freedom of attachment through the mundane path. And like the [non-Buddhist] extremists, these [Hīnayāna Arhats] would not have abandoned any of the "attachments"[811] that operate in the three realms. Moreover, by virtue of being subject to a mistaken belief in that they [incorrectly] apprehend [physical] form and the rest [of the five heaps] to possess an inherent nature, they also would not achieve realization of the insubstantiality of the person.[812]

While Candrakīrti argues that understanding the teaching on the Four Noble Truths alone is not sufficient to eliminate the mental afflictions, he does believe that it is a necessary prerequisite for developing a correct understanding of ultimate truth. The second reason that Candrakīrti gave for this instruction is that it will "engender in [middling followers] the aspiration for nirvana." This aspiration is developed initially through learning the relative truth nature of samsaric existence, as embodied in the teaching on the Four Noble Truths, and through cultivating the antidotes to the four mistaken beliefs. For instance, it was mentioned earlier[813] that unless one first develops aversion for samsara through meditating on its defects, one cannot generate an aspiration to achieve the peace that comes with achieving liberation from samsara. Similarly, cultivating the four closely placed recollections is the means for overcoming the habitual attachment to samsaric existence that is fed especially by the misguided notions that conditioned entities are satisfactory, pure, permanent, and constitute a self.

The need to develop an aspiration for nirvana also relates to Nāgārjuna's assertion that ultimate truth cannot be taught independently of the instructions on conventional truth. A systematic process of spiritual training is necessary to prepare the individual for cultivating the understanding that all the phenomena of ordinary experience are ultimately empty of any real or inherent essence. This preliminary instruction is not merely intellectual in nature. To become a suitable vessel one must develop oneself spiritually through ripening one's virtue roots. This training can be greatly enhanced by learning the instruction on such conventional truth doctrines as the five heaps and the Four Noble Truths.

It is also true that having an understanding of these preliminary teachings does not necessarily qualify one to hear about ultimate truth. The two principal concerns are that a listener might reject teachings on emptiness because of his or her inability to give up attachment to realism; or one might wrongly understand the teaching on emptiness to be advocating nihilism. Therefore, it is considered a root transgression of the Mahāyāna vows to teach emptiness to those individuals whose minds have not been properly trained. In his *Compendium of Training*,[814] Śāntideva quotes the *Ākāśagarbha Sūtra* as listing this misdeed as the first among eight root transgressions that are associated with novice Mahāyāna practitioners. Śāntideva also composed a series of verses that summarize the root transgressions in the tradition of Mahāyāna ethics that he followed. These verses include the following lines: "Describing emptiness to beings / Who have not prepared their minds."[815] Addressing this same point, Āryadeva states:

> One who desires virtue should not
> Speak about emptiness at all times.
> Can medicine not become poison
> If applied at the wrong time?[816]

Candrakīrti glosses the phrase "one who desires virtue" to mean "a compassionate [Mahāyāna practitioner] who wishes to gain virtue [in order to further his or her own spiritual development] and to benefit other beings." The first eight chapters of Āryadeva's *Four Hundred Verses* are considered the preliminary instruction for a disciple who wishes to learn the profound topic of emptiness. Of these eight chapters, the first four in particular present instructions that counteract the four mistaken beliefs. The final eight chapters of the work are devoted to an explanation of ultimate truth.

In the next section, we will address a form of the Perfection of Wisdom in which knowledge of emptiness is combined with both an understanding of the Four Noble Truths' sixteen aspects and the great compassion of conventional enlightenment mind. By doing so, the Mahāyāna practitioner is able to strike a balance between aversion for samsara and the willingness to pursue the welfare of sentient beings.

THE PERFECTION OF WISDOM KNOWN AS "KNOWLEDGE OF ENTITIES"

In several of its opening verses, the *Ornament of Realizations* describes the entire Perfection of Wisdom teaching as comprising eight subjects:

> The Perfection of Wisdom is fully expressed
> On the basis of eight subjects.
> The knowledge of all modes, knowledge of the path,
> And the knowledge of all [entities]; following them,
>
> The realization of all modes, attainment of the summit,
> The successive [realization], the realization of
> A single moment, and the dharma body—
> These are its eight aspects.[817]

Of these eight, Haribhadra describes the three knowledges that form the first three topics in the following passage:

> The knowledge of all modes is explained first, in the form of a presentation of the result, so that the Bodhisattva who is desirous of achieving Buddhahood might fully comprehend [the nature of] all the modes [of supreme enlightenment, which include the ten topics of] generating [enlightenment] mind and the rest. Knowledge of the path is explained next, because that [knowledge of all modes] cannot be gained without fully comprehending the knowledge of [all] the paths that relate to the Listeners, and the rest. The knowledge of all [entities] is explained immediately after, because that [knowledge of the path] too cannot be gained without fully comprehending the knowledge of all entities.[818]

As noted above,[819] a Bodhisattva needs to practice and be well versed in the forms of spiritual training taught in the Hīnayāna scriptures. Haribhadra reaffirms that point here when he says that a Bodhisattva must fully comprehend the knowledge of all entities in order to perfect his understanding of the knowledge of the path. What follows is an attempt to clarify the manner in which the Mahāyāna practitioner is meant to cultivate this "knowledge of all entities."[820]

Following the verses cited above, the *Ornament of Realizations* goes on to state in the next thirteen verses that these eight principal subjects of the Perfection of Wisdom teachings themselves comprise seventy topics. One of the texts that Gelukpa monasteries use to study the *Ornament of Realizations* is actually referred to by the generic name *Seventy Topics.*[821] Its purpose is to provide definitions for these seventy topics and to identify where the forms of knowledge that relate to them fit in the overall structure of the Mahāyāna path. The exact language of these definitions varies slightly in the separate versions that different colleges use; however, the general sense conveyed by them is largely the same. The definition of the knowledge of all entities that follows is taken from a fairly modern text[822] used by the Mey College of Sera Monastery. It was compiled by the scholar Jampel Gendun Gyatso, who drew mainly from the writings of Khedrup Tenba Dargye,[823] the principal author of the manuals used by this college. The description found there states:

> The definition of the knowledge of entities is a form of knowledge possessed by an Ārya that is either a Hīnayāna Ārya's knowledge or a form of knowledge possessed by an Ārya that represents the class of realizations pursued in the Hīnayāna path. There are two main types: the favorable and the adverse forms of knowledge of entities. Its range extends from the Seeing Path in the Listeners' Vehicle up to and including Buddhahood.[824]

The definition itself indicates a number of points. Because it is an Ārya's knowledge, only someone who has attained the wisdom that directly perceives the insubstantiality of the person can possess it in its true form. The term Ārya, however, applies not only to those practitioners who have reached either the Seeing Path or the Meditation Path of one of the three vehicles but also to a Buddha. To say that it is "a class of realizations" indicates that this knowledge can be represented by an awareness of any of the Four Noble Truths' sixteen aspects of impermanence and the rest. Unlike Candrakīrti's Mādhyamika Prasaṅgika School, Haribhadra's Yogācāra Mādhyamika Svatantrika School[825] considers all sixteen of these forms of awareness as realizations of a relative truth entity, including the direct perception of the insubstantiality of the person.

The unfavorable form of the knowledge of entities[826] is that Hīnayāna Ārya's knowledge which is not supported by extraordinary wisdom and means. The favorable form of the knowledge of entities[827] is that which is possessed by Bodhisattva Āryas and Buddhas, and this form is supported by extraordinary wisdom and means. "Extraordinary wisdom" is the wisdom that has realized ultimate truth or emptiness directly. "Extraordinary means" refers principally to the great compassion that seeks to benefit all sentient beings. This favorable form of the knowledge of entities is described in the opening verse of the *Ornament of Realizations'* third chapter:

> Perfection of Wisdom is understood
> As not abiding in the near shore,
> Nor in the far shore, nor in between the two,
> Through realizing the sameness of the [three] times.[828]

The term "Perfection of Wisdom" as it is being used here refers to the knowledge of entities. The "near shore" is the extreme of samsaric existence[829]; the "far shore" is the extreme of Hīnayāna nirvana's passive tranquility.[830] Not abiding "in between the two" means that while the Bodhisattva does cultivate a path that lies between these two extremes in a conventional sense, this path does not constitute a middle way that exists inherently. The extreme of samsaric existence is overcome by developing the wisdom that recognizes the disadvantages of samsara and perceives the insubstantiality of the person; the extreme of Hīnayāna nirvana is overcome by generating and maintaining great compassion; and the third extreme is avoided by developing the wisdom that directly perceives all conditioned entities of the three times as void of any real essence. Those practitioners who believe conditioned entities to be real and who lack the great compassion that underlies enlightenment mind remain "far" from this Perfection of Wisdom, while Bodhisattva Āryas and fully enlightened Buddhas are said to be "near" to it, because they possess both great compassion and a direct realization of emptiness. In his gloss of Haribhadra's remarks on the above verse, Gyeltsab Darma Rinchen presents the following explanation:

> Consider the form of Perfection of Wisdom that is the knowledge of entities. It is regarded as being "near" to the minds of the Buddhas and [Ārya] Bodhisattvas, because they directly perceive the sameness of [all conditioned] entities of the three times, which is that they lack the nature of arising in a truly existent manner.
>
> Because this aspect of the path form of Perfection of Wisdom[831] contains numerous elements, including the wisdom that realizes impermanence and the rest [of the Four Noble Truths' sixteen aspects], great compassion, and the realization of emptiness, the

specific effects [of these three types of mind in particular] may be described as follows.

Consider the Bodhisattva's wisdom that directly perceives impermanence and the rest. It prevents the extreme of samsaric existence that is referred to as the "near shore," and that also represents [a form of] the eternalistic extreme in that it causes beings to be reborn continuously by the power of karma and the mental afflictions, because it destroys the root of samsaric existence.

Consider the Bodhisattva's great compassion. It prevents the extreme of [Hīnayāna] nirvana that is referred to as the "far shore," and that also represents [a form of] the nihilistic extreme in that it causes samsaric birth to be terminated, because through its power [the Bodhisattva] is reborn in samsara again and again, and thus it is the path that brings about the attainment of "non-abiding" nirvana.[832]

In sum, consider the form of Perfection of Wisdom that is the knowledge of entities. It does not abide in [either of] the [two] extremes of [samsaric] existence and [the] passivity [of Hīnayāna nirvana], nor does it abide in an ultimate sense in some state that lies between those two [extremes], because it prevents the [two] extremes of existence and passivity that relate to the realm of conventional truth, and because it does not abide in between those two [extremes] in an ultimate sense since it also realizes that both [samsaric] existence and [the] passivity [of Hīnayāna nirvana] do not truly exist.[833]

Haribhadra notes that while the above verse does not refer explicitly to the manner in which the Hīnayāna realists practice the knowledge of entities, their view can be inferred. In essence, it is that Hīnayāna practitioners are "far" from knowing true Perfection of Wisdom, because they perceive entities as real and they lack great compassion. As a result of their limited understanding, they should be recognized as "abiding" in both the extreme of samsaric existence and the extreme of Hīnayāna nirvana. The way in which they "abide" in these two extremes is not simply the opposite of the way in which Mahayanists avoid them. Clearly, the Hīnayāna Ārya does both perceive the defects of samsara and realize the insubstantiality of the person. It is the ordinary person or non-Ārya who still believes in the existence of a real personal self and therefore remains attached to samsaric existence in that most basic sense. Just as he did with the Mahāyāna Āryas' antidote to the two extremes, Gyeltsab Je explains the manner in which Hīnayāna Āryas abide in the two extremes in terms of conventional truth. He identifies lack of compassion as the cause of their "abiding" in the samsaric extreme and lack of far-reaching wisdom as the cause of their "abiding" in the extreme of passivity.

> Consider the Listener Āryas and others, such as the Solitary Realizer [Āryas]. They abide in a manner that is "far" from genuine Perfection of Wisdom, because, due to their adherence to the belief that the two extremes of existence and passivity are truly existent, they fail to realize the sameness of the three times.
>
> Listeners and Solitary Realizers practice a form of the knowledge of entities that is incomplete and limited to their [respective] levels of understanding. Consider the Listener [Āryas] who abide in this imitation of Perfection of Wisdom. They abide in the extreme of samsara, because they regard the "substantial existence"[834] that is rebirth in samsara as something to be categorically abandoned. We reaffirm that this proposition is true, because [Listener Āryas] wish to put a stop not only to the samsaric rebirth that is caused by [impure] karma and the mental afflictions but also to the rebirth that is brought about by the power of compassion and prayer; therefore, they lack the compassion that is the [Bodhisattva's] cause for taking rebirth.
>
> It should also be understood that [Listener Āryas] abide in the extreme of [Hīnayāna] nirvana, because they perceive the "insubstantial nonexistence"[835] that is the complete termination of all rebirth in samsara as a goal that ought to be pursued. We reaffirm that this proposition is true, because [Listener Āryas] do wish to achieve the termination of rebirth in samsara and because they also lack the wisdom that not only stops the samsaric rebirth that is caused by karma and mental afflictions but also understands that [continually] taking birth in samsara [by the power of compassion and prayer] also represents the means of pursuing [the nonabiding] nirvana [of a fully enlightened Buddha].[836]

By reflecting on this topic of the *Perfection of Wisdom Sutras*, one can recognize that it directly addresses how a practitioner should combine what Je Tsongkapa calls the three principal elements of the path: (1) renunciation, (2) enlightenment mind, and (3) the correct view that realizes emptiness. By learning and meditating on the sixteen aspects of the Four Noble Truths, one can develop the renunciation that wishes to escape the unsatisfactoriness of samsaric existence. Knowledge of the insubstantiality of the person, in particular, counteracts the karma and mental afflictions that generate ordinary samsaric rebirth. Through developing and maintaining great compassion and enlightenment mind, knowledge of the Four Noble Truths does not lead the practitioner to pursue his or her own liberation exclusively as the ultimate goal. More specifically, the power of prayer that is motivated by great compassion replaces the impure causes of samsaric rebirth and enables a Bodhisattva to be reborn in the most favorable circumstances for continuing to practice the Mahāyāna path. Finally, the correct view that realizes the emptiness of the five heaps allows a practitioner to cultivate the path in a manner that remains untainted by the defects of samsara and to continue collecting the wisdom accumulation that culminates in the attainment of a Buddha's wisdom body.

THE FOUR CLOSELY PLACED RECOLLECTIONS IN THE MAHĀYĀNA TRADITION

Practice of the four closely placed recollections as taught in the Mahāyāna tradition differs from the account that was presented in the previous chapter, where we examined how this leads to an understanding of the Four Noble Truths. The following passage is from Vasubandhu's commentary to several verses from the *Ornament of Mahāyāna Sutras*:

> Three verses present distinctions relating to the closely placed recollections:
>
> > Because the meditation of the wise[837]
> > On closely placed recollection
> > Is unequalled in fourteen aspects,
> > It is superior to that of others.[838]
>
> What are the fourteen [aspects]?
>
> > It is superior in its source,
> > Antidote, entry, as well as
> > In its object, attention,
> > And what it gains,

In its conformity, compliance,
As well as in its knowledge,
Rebirth, magnitude, preeminence,
Meditation, and attainment.[839]

The Bodhisattvas' meditation on the closely placed recollections is superior in terms of these fourteen aspects.

(1) How is it [superior] in terms of its source?

[The Bodhisattvas' meditation on the closely placed recollections is superior because] it arises through relying upon the wisdom derived from listening, reflection, and meditation [that is cultivated] in relation to the Mahāyāna [teachings].

(2) How is it [superior] in terms of being an antidote?

[The Bodhisattvas' meditation on the closely placed recollections is superior] because, through developing [an understanding of] the insubstantiality of entities in relation to the body, etc., it is also an antidote for [the belief that] the conceptions of impurity, suffering, impermanence, and selflessness—which themselves are the antidotes for the four mistaken notions]—[have as their objects a real body, real feelings, a real mind, and real entities].

(3) How is it [superior] in terms of being a means of entry?

[It is superior] because, on the basis of the four closely placed recollections, [Bodhisattvas] are able to cause both themselves and others to arrive at an understanding of the [Four Noble] Truths of suffering, origination, cessation, and the path, in their respective order, as explained in the *Treatise That Distinguishes the Middle Way from Extreme Views*.[840]

(4) How is it [superior] in terms of its object?

[The Bodhisattvas' meditation on the closely placed recollections is superior] because it focuses on the bodies, etc., of all sentient beings.[841]

(5) How is it [superior] in terms of its form of attention?

[The Bodhisattvas' meditation on the closely placed recollections is superior] because it does not apprehend the body, etc., [as real].

(6) How is it [superior] in terms of what it gains?

[The Bodhisattvas' meditation on the closely placed recollections is superior] because it seeks to achieve neither separation from the body, etc., nor lack of separation from them.

(7) How is it [superior] in terms of conformity?

[The Bodhisattvas' meditation on the closely placed recollections is superior] because, through being in conformity with the perfections, it serves as a remedy to the obstacles that oppose them.

(8) How is it [superior] in terms of compliance?

[The Bodhisattvas' meditation on the closely placed recollections is superior] because, in order to comply both with mundane beings and with the Listeners and Solitary Realizers, [Bodhisattvas] meditate on the form of closely placed recollection that those beings practice, so that they can teach it to them.

(9) How is it [superior] in terms of knowledge?

[The Bodhisattvas' meditation on the closely placed recollections is superior] because, through realizing the illusoriness of the body, its unreal nature becomes evident to them; through realizing the dreamlike quality of feelings, they experience them as false; because they realize the mind's primordial luminosity to be like space; and because they realize entities to be adventitious, like the dust, smoke, clouds, or mist that occasionally obscure the sky.

(10) How is it [superior] in terms of rebirth?

[It is superior] because, when [Bodhisattvas] knowingly take birth in samsara, they do so in the form of beings like a wheel-wielding monarch who possesses the prosperity of an extraordinary body, etc., but this [prosperity] does not cause their minds to become afflicted.

(11) How is it [superior] in terms of its magnitude?

[It is superior] because, due to the naturally sharp faculties [of Bodhisattvas], even when they meditate on the closely placed recollections only to a slight degree, [their meditation] is much greater in its force than that of other practitioners.

(12) How is it [superior] in terms of its preeminence?

[It is superior] because, those [Bodhisattvas] who have perfected the practice are able to meditate [on the closely placed recollections] effortlessly both in a "mixed" and a "closely mixed" manner.

(13) How is it [superior] in terms of meditation?

[It is superior] because, due to their having been cultivated so completely, even when [a Bodhisattva] enters the nirvana without remainder, [that meditation] does not come to an end.

(14) How is it [superior] in terms of its attainment?

[It is superior] because it brings attainment of the ten [Ārya Bodhisattva] levels and Buddhahood [rather than the four fruits of the Hīnayāna path].[842]

With regard to the second point, that the Bodhisattva's practice is a superior form of antidote, and the fifth point, that the Bodhisattva's form of attention does not apprehend the body, etc., as real, these are references to the fact that the Mahāyāna form of meditation includes cultivating the awareness of the insubstantiality of entities. This is touched on in the *Perfection of Wisdom Sutra*, in passages like the following:

> Regarding that, what is closely placed recollection of the body? Here, O Subhūti, the Bodhisattva, the Great Being, dwells watching the body in relation to an inner body. Moreover, he does not form deliberative thoughts associated with the body, on account of his not apprehending [any object that constitutes a real body].[843]

Similarly, the *Dharma Recitation Sutra* states:

> While examining the question, "What is this [object] that is here [referred to as] a body?" [the Bodhisattva practitioner] has the following thought: "This body is the same as space." Then [the practitioner] closely establishes [his or her] recollection in relation to the space-like body. He [or she] perceives this entire [body] as space [in that it lacks any real essence]. In order to achieve complete knowledge of the body, [the practitioner's] recollection no longer extends toward anything, nor withdraws from anything, nor reestablishes itself on anything.[844]

Sthiramati's subcommentary on the above three verses from the *Ornament of Mahāyāna Sutras* is extremely helpful in interpreting some of the more obscure points. For example, the quality of being superior in terms of what it gains[845] should be understood as making the same point that was described earlier in relation to the form of Perfection of Wisdom called "knowledge of entities." That point is that Mahāyāna practice should avoid falling into either of the two extremes of samsara or Hīnayāna nirvana. Sthiramati's explanation states the following:

> How is [the Bodhisattvas' meditation on the closely placed recollections] superior [to that of the followers of the Listeners' Vehicle] in terms of what it gains?
>
> While Listeners and others meditate [on the four closely placed recollections] in order to achieve separation[846] from their body and feelings, etc., Bodhisattvas neither meditate to achieve separation

nor do they meditate to achieve lack of separation; therefore, their practice is superior in terms of what it gains.

How is it that they do not seek to achieve separation?

They do not seek to be separated from a Tathāgata's three bodies. Rather, they meditate in order to achieve them; therefore, they do not seek to achieve separation.

How is it that they do not seek to achieve lack of separation?

They do not seek to achieve lack of separation in that they do meditate to separate themselves from a body, etc., that is generated by karma and the mental afflictions.

Put differently, they do not seek to achieve separation from this body in that they wish to attain the three bodies [of a Buddha]. They also do not seek to achieve lack of separation [from it] in the sense that the aim to attain [a Buddha's] three bodies is pursued on the basis of this body. Hence, they also do seek to achieve [a form of] separation, because they will forever remain in samsara like an ordinary person if they remain attached to this body that is produced by karma and the mental afflictions and is an [insubstantial] "mass of foam"[847] whose nature is suffering.[848] As the *Sutra of Teachings by [the Bodhisattva] Akṣayamati* declares in part: "[the Bodhisattva] examines the past of the body, the future of the body" . . . up to "[the Bodhisattva reflects,] 'I shall not take hold of this body as my own; rather, I shall attain the true value of ultimate enlightenment by means of this worthless body. What is that true value? I shall achieve the body of a Tathāgata, the dharma body (i.e., *dharmakāya*), the adamantine body, the indestructible body, the eternal body, the body that surpasses all the three realms. Although my body possesses many faults, I shall attain the body of a Tathāgata that is free of all faults.' Perceiving the benefits [of Buddhahood] and with the power of reflective analysis, he sacrifices the body that is composed of the [four] great elements."[849]

Here is Sthiramati's description of how the Bodhisattvas' meditation on the four closely placed recollections is in conformity[850] with the six perfections:

How is it superior in terms of the aspect of conformity?

The Bodhisattvas' meditations on closely placed recollection of the body, etc., are in conformity with the six perfections because

> [the closely placed recollections] serve as antidotes that abandon the stinginess, etc., that represent the [specific] obstacles to the six perfections.
>
> How is this so?
>
> When [a practitioner] realizes that his [or her] body and feelings, etc., are void and false, like a magical illusion or a mirage, then he [or she] will not generate desire for inner and outer entities. Through being free of desire, [the practitioner] gives away inner and outer objects, thereby coming into conformity with generosity. One who is able to give away inner and outer objects will come to be in conformity with morality by taking it up. Those who observe morality will be in conformity with patience, because they will be able to carry out the patience that does not respond to physical blows with physical blows and does not respond to abusive speech with abusive speech.[851] Those who observe patience will come to be in conformity with effort, because they are able to maintain the effort that does not give up virtuous activities even when heat or cold are being experienced. Those who observe effort will come to be in conformity with concentration and wisdom, because they will realize the impermanence and emptiness of the body, etc., and be able to meditate [on those understandings] one-pointedly.[852]

The preeminence[853] of the Bodhisattvas' meditation on closely placed recollection refers to a sympathetic power and sensitivity that is achieved when the practitioner has reached the eighth Ārya Bodhisattva level. Again, Sthiramati describes this in the following manner:

> How is [the Bodhisattvas' meditation on the closely placed recollections] superior in terms of the aspect of preeminence?
>
> On the eighth [Ārya Bodhisattva] level, [a practitioner's] meditation on the four closely placed recollections becomes fully accomplished. Because [the practitioner] can cultivate [the recollections] effortlessly and spontaneously, his [or her] meditation is superior in terms of the aspect of preeminence, which means that it can be practiced in a manner that is mixed and closely mixed.[854]
>
> Regarding this, when a Bodhisattva who has reached the eighth level meditates on the four closely placed recollections, others will meditate on them as well. This is called a "mixed" practice. When others meditate on them, [that Bodhisattva] himself [or herself]

> also will meditate on them. This called a "closely mixed" practice.
>
> Alternatively, [the practice of closely placed recollection] during the first moment that a Bodhisattva of the seventh level has reached the eighth level is called "mixed." During the period following that, from the second moment until [the Bodhisattva] reaches the ninth level, it is called "closely mixed."[855]

The following passage from the *Sutra Requested by [the Bodhisattva] Ratnacūḍa* reveals how a Mahāyāna practitioner should also incorporate great compassion into closely placed recollection:

> About this, O son of good family, the Bodhisattva who is cultivating closely placed recollection in terms of watching feelings in relation to feelings develops great compassion toward those beings who are experiencing pleasurable feelings. He [or she] also trains himself [or herself] by thinking, "Happiness is where there are no [impure samsaric] feelings." The [Bodhisattva] meditates on feelings in relation to feelings in order to get rid of the [impure] feelings that all sentient beings experience. He [or she] also dons the armor [that is required] to put a stop to the [impure] feelings of sentient beings, but does not seek to put a stop to his [or her] own feelings. Rather, no matter what feeling he [or she] experiences, [the Bodhisattva] experiences them all in a manner that is embraced by great compassion.
>
> Whenever [the Bodhisattva] experiences a pleasurable feeling, he [or she] develops great compassion toward those beings who give expression to desire, and also abandons his [or her] own mental affliction of desire. Whenever [the Bodhisattva] experiences a painful feeling, he [or she] develops great compassion toward those beings who give expression to hatred, and also abandons his [or her] own mental affliction of hatred. Whenever [the Bodhisattva] experiences a feeling that is neither painful nor pleasurable, he [or she] develops great compassion toward those beings who give expression to ignorance, and also abandons his [or her] own mental affliction of ignorance.[856]

Similar instructions are expressed in the following passage from the *Sutra of Teachings by [the Bodhisattva] Akṣayamati*:

> [The Bodhisattva] who comes in contact with a painful feeling generates great compassion toward all sentient beings who have been born in the lower realms or into [any of the] inopportune states,[857] and he [or she] does not cling to the mental affliction of aversion. . . . He [or she] dons the armor [that is required] to gain complete knowledge of all sentient beings' feelings and thinks to himself [or herself], "These beings do not correctly realize the [means of obtaining] deliverance from [impure samsaric] feelings. Because they are unaware of [the means of obtaining] deliverance, they generate desire whenever they come in contact with a pleasurable feeling; they generate aversion whenever they come in contact with a painful feeling; and they generate ignorance whenever they come in contact with a feeling that is neither painful nor pleasurable. With a feeling that is accompanied by wisdom and knowledge, and with an accumulation of virtue roots that is embraced by great compassion and a skillful means that has put a stop to [impure afflicted] feelings, I shall teach dharma to sentient beings in order to remove all their [impure samsaric] feelings."[858]

In this final chapter, we have sought to establish how an understanding of the five heaps contributes to a practitioner's ability to develop what Nāgārjuna identified as the three "roots" of the Mahāyāna path: great compassion, enlightenment mind, and nondual wisdom. In the case of compassion, we noted how a beginning practitioner must first reflect on his or her own suffering before trying to engender the kind of empathy that cannot bear the suffering of others. This premise links one back to the discussion of the Noble Truth of Suffering in Chapter Three, and thus also to the doctrine of the five heaps. As for the topic of nondual wisdom, my aim was to show that the doctrine of emptiness presupposes an understanding of such formulations as the five heaps, twelve bases, eighteen constituents, Four Noble Truths, and twelve limbs of dependent origination. Without such a foundation, one is simply not equipped to appreciate the type of critical analysis that lies at the heart of the teachings on emptiness.

SUMMARY

Three basic points summarize the main arguments of this study. First, most "ordinary" individuals, using that term in the technical Buddhist sense, unwittingly labor under the influence of the four mistaken beliefs regarding the impurity, impermanence, suffering, and selflessness of the five impure grasping heaps. Unless the nature and extent of this fourfold error is examined, understood, and gradually overcome, one cannot make significant progress in the effort to bring about spiritual transformation. Secondly, as Kamalasīla notes, the ability to pursue the temporary Buddhist goal of rebirth in the higher states and the ultimate goals of liberation and Buddhahood depends on being able to reverse these mistaken beliefs through gaining three fundamental knowledges: (1) the worldly correct view that properly understands the relationship between karma and its results; (2) the unerring realization of the insubstantiality of the person; and (3) the unerring realization of the insubstantiality of entities. Of these, the teachings that lead to the realization of the insubstantiality of the person in particular are the most effective means of overcoming the four mistaken beliefs. Finally, while the Mahāyāna instruction known as the Stages of the Path is a comprehensive system of practice that is designed to enable a practitioner to achieve all three of these knowledges, one's effort to pursue this instruction is greatly enhanced by learning the Buddha's teaching on the five heaps and incorporating that understanding into one's practice. If this is done properly and effectively, the blessings of the Buddha's teaching are sure to be deep and long-lasting.

Part Two: *Translations*

TRANSLATOR'S NOTE

The two English translations that follow were prepared mainly on the basis of various Tibetan editions of the texts. A few passages from Vasubandhu's *Summary of the Five Heaps* are cited in the Sanskrit text of Yaśomitra's *Subcommentary to the Treasury of Higher Learning* (S: *Sphuṭārthābhidharmakośavyākhyā*). A number of sections from Sthiramati's commentary to the *Summary of the Five Heaps* also occur verbatim in the Sanskrit text of his *Commentary on the Thirty Verses* (S: *Triṃśikābhāṣyam*). It is clear as well that in a number of instances Sthiramati drew material from Vasubandhu's *Commentary on the Treasury of Higher Learning* (S: *Abhidharmakośabhāṣyam*), Asaṅga's *Compendium of Higher Learning* (S: *Abhidharmasamuccayaḥ*), and Jinaputra's *Commentary on the Compendium of Higher Learning* (S: *Abhidharmasamuccayabhāṣyam*). The subject matter presented in the two translations corresponds broadly to the material found in the first chapter of Asaṅga's *Compendium of Higher Learning.*

For Vasubandhu's *Summary of the Five Heaps*, a total of four Tibetan editions were compared. Variant readings can be found in the footnotes to the Tibetan text that is presented in the appendix. For Sthiramati's commentary, the main Tibetan source was the version found in the Derge (T: *sDe dge*) edition of the Tengyur collection. A number of minor errors that occur in this edition were identified on the basis of an early Tibetan handwritten manuscript. This latter text was made available in a digital format by the Tibetan Buddhist Resource Center, which is based in New York City. It was created from a microfilm version that is in the Beijing Nationalities Library. In those instances where conjectural Sanskrit terms or phrases appear in notes, the convention is followed of placing an asterisk at the beginning of the entry.

A Summary of the Five Heaps *by Master Vasubandhu* 1

Obeisance to Mañjuśrī in his form as a divine youth.

THE FIVE HEAPS

THERE ARE five heaps: form, feeling, conception, formations, and consciousness.

The Form Heap

What is form?

It is all form whatsoever that is included in the four great elements and that is derived from the four great elements.

What are the four great elements?

The earth constituent, the water constituent, the fire constituent, and the air constituent.

What is the earth constituent?

Hardness.

What is the water constituent?

Fluidity.

What is the fire constituent?

Heat.

What is the air constituent?

Lightness and motility.

What is derivative form?

The eye faculty, the ear faculty, the nose faculty, the tongue faculty, the body faculty, [visible] form, sound, smell, taste, a portion of tangible objects, and noninformative [form].

Regarding them, what is the eye faculty?

Clear form that has color as its object.

What is the ear faculty?

Clear form that has sound as its object.

What is the nose faculty?

Clear form that has smells as its object.

What is the tongue faculty?

Clear form that has tastes as its object.

What is the body faculty?

Clear form that has tangible entities as its object.

What is [visible] form?

The object of the eye, which is color, shape, and informative [form].

What is sound?

The object of the ear, and it is caused by great elements that are [either] retained, unretained, or both.

What is smell?

The object of the nose, which is pleasant smells, unpleasant smells, or those that are other than that.

What is taste?

The object of the tongue, which is sweet, sour, salty, pungent, bitter, or astringent.

What is a portion of tangible objects?

Those objects of the body excluding the great elements—namely, smoothness, roughness, heaviness, lightness, cold, hunger, and thirst.

What is noninformative [form]?

It is form that is derived either from informative form or one-pointed concentration; and it is both not capable of being indicated and does not possess resistance.

The Feeling Heap

What is feeling?

The three types of experience: pleasant, unpleasant, and neither pleasant nor unpleasant. A pleasant experience is one that you desire to be united with again when it ceases. An unpleasant experience is one that you desire to be separated from when it arises. An experience that is neither pleasant nor unpleasant is one for which you develop neither of those desires when it occurs.

The Conception Heap

What is conception?

The grasping of an object's sign, which is of three types: limited, great, and immeasurable.

The Formations Heap

What are the formations?

The mental factors other than feeling and conception, and the entities that do not accompany consciousness.

What are the mental factors?

Those entities that are concomitants of consciousness.

What are they?

Contact, attention, feeling, conception, volition, aspiration, conviction, recollection, concentration, wisdom, faith, shame, abashment, the root virtue that is avoidance of attachment, the root virtue that is avoidance of hatred, the root virtue that is avoidance of ignorance, effort, agility, mindfulness, equanimity, avoidance of harm, desire, hatred, pride, ignorance, views, doubt, anger, resentment, dissembling, spite, envy, stinginess, deceitfulness, guile, conceit, harmfulness, shamelessness, absence of abashment, torpor, excitation, lack of faith, laziness, lack of mindfulness, clouded recollection, distraction, lack of vigilance, regret, sleep, deliberation, and reflection.

Among these, five are universal, five are limited to a particular object, eleven are virtues, six are [root] mental afflictions, the remaining ones are secondary mental afflictions, and four can also vary.

The Three Remaining Universal Mental Factors

What is contact?

The determination that occurs upon the convergence of three.

What is attention?

The bending of the mind.

What is volition?

It is the shaping of consciousness in relation to that which is good, bad, or neither; and it is activity of the mind.

The Five Mental Factors That Have Specific Objects

What is aspiration?

The desire for an object that has been thought about.

What is conviction?

The certitude that an object about which a determination has been made exists in just that manner.

What is recollection?

The avoidance of inattentiveness toward a familiar object; a state of mental discourse.

What is concentration?

One-pointedness of mind toward an object that is being closely examined.

What is wisdom?

Discrimination with respect to that same object, whether it is generated correctly, incorrectly, or otherwise.

The Eleven Virtuous Mental Factors

What is faith?

Belief, aspiration, or clarity of mind toward karma and its results, the [Four Noble] Truths, and the [Three] Jewels.

What is shame?

Embarrassment about objectionable acts for reasons relating to oneself or the Dharma.

What is abashment?

Embarrassment about objectionable acts for reasons relating to the world.

What is avoidance of attachment?

The antidote to attachment—[that is to say,] dissatisfaction and freedom from acquisitiveness.

What is avoidance of hatred?

The antidote to hatred—[that is to say,] loving-kindness.

What is avoidance of ignorance?

The antidote to ignorance—[that is to say,] the correct understanding of things as they truly are.

What is effort?

The antidote to laziness—[that is to say,] exertion of the mind toward virtue.

What is agility?

The antidote to indisposition—[that is to say,] fitness of body and mind.

What is mindfulness?

The antidote to lack of mindfulness—[that is to say,] the abandoning of nonvirtuous entities together with the cultivating of those virtuous entities that are their antidotes, on the basis of the mental factors ranging from avoidance of attachment to effort.

What is equanimity?

Evenness of mind, inactivity of mind, and effortlessness of mind that is gained on the basis of those very same mental factors ranging from avoidance of attachment to effort. It is that [mental factor] which, having dispelled afflicted entities, remains in a state of constant adherence to those that are free from affliction.

What is avoidance of harm?

The antidote to harmfulness—[that is to say,] compassion.

The Root Mental Afflictions

What is desire?

Strong affection for, and attachment to, the five grasping heaps.

What is hatred?

Animosity toward sentient beings.

What is pride?

There are seven types of pride: [ordinary] pride, extraordinary pride, extreme pride, egoistic pride, exaggerated pride, pride of inferiority, and wrong pride.

What is [ordinary] pride?

The swelling up of the mind in which you think of someone who is inferior to you, "I am better [than him or her]," or of someone who is your equal, "I am [his or her] equal."

What is extraordinary pride?

The swelling up of the mind in which you think of someone who is your equal, "I am better [than him or her]," or of someone who is superior to you, "I am [his or her] equal."

What is extreme pride?

The swelling up of the mind in which you think of someone who is superior to you, "I am better [than him or her]."

What is egoistic pride?

The swelling up of the mind that originates from the mistaken notion that the five grasping heaps constitute an "I" and a "mine."

What is exaggerated pride?

The swelling up of the mind in which you think toward higher special attainments that you have not achieved, "I have achieved them."

What is pride of inferiority?

The swelling up of the mind in which you think of someone who is very much superior to you, "I am only slightly inferior to him."

What is wrong pride?

The swelling up of the mind in which you think, "I possess good qualities," when you are not someone who possesses good qualities.

What is ignorance?

Absence of knowledge with regard to karma and its results, the [Four Noble] Truths, and the [Three] Jewels; moreover, it is innate and contrived.

The desire, hatred, and ignorance that occur in the desire realm are the three roots of nonvirtue—that is, the root of nonvirtue that is attachment, the root of nonvirtue that is hatred, and the root of nonvirtue that is ignorance.

What are views?

There are five views: the perishable collection view, the view that grasps an extreme, wrong view, the consideration that views are supreme, and the consideration that morality and asceticism are supreme.

What is the perishable collection view?

The afflicted wisdom that regards the five grasping heaps as "I" and "mine."

What is the view that grasps an extreme?

The afflicted wisdom that, in relation to that very [view], regards [its object] as undergoing extinction or as existing permanently.

What is wrong view?

The afflicted wisdom that denies causes, results, and actions, and rejects entities that exist.

What is the consideration that views are supreme?

The afflicted wisdom that regards those very three views and their basis, the heaps, as foremost, superior, most excellent, and the highest.

What is the consideration that morality and asceticism are supreme?

The afflicted wisdom that regards morality, asceticism, and their basis, the heaps, as purifying, liberating, and conducive to deliverance.

What is doubt?

Ambivalence about the [four Noble] Truths and so forth.

Of these [root] mental afflictions, the latter three views and doubt [only have forms that] are contrived; the remaining ones [have forms that] are innate as well as [forms that are] contrived.

The Twenty Secondary Mental Afflictions

What is anger?

Animosity of the mind toward a current source of harm that has become evident.

What is resentment?

Adherence to enmity.

What is dissembling?
Concealment of objectionable acts.

What is spite?
Acrimony [expressed] through heated words.

What is envy?
The complete vexation of mind at another's success.

What is stinginess?
The acquisitiveness of mind that opposes generosity.

What is deceitfulness?
The displaying of something that is untrue [in order to] deceive others.

What is guile?
A deviousness of mind that adopts a means of concealing one's faults.

What is conceit?
[It is] the delight of someone who is infatuated with [his or her] own well-being and [a state in which] the mind is overwhelmed.

What is harmfulness?
[The impulse to do] injury to sentient beings.

What is shamelessness?
Lack of embarrassment about objectionable acts for reasons relating to oneself.

What is absence of abashment?
Lack of embarrassment about objectionable acts for reasons relating to others.

What is torpor?
[It is] unfitness and immobility of the mind.

What is excitation?
Lack of calmness in the mind.

What is lack of faith?
[It is] the lack of belief and lack of clarity of mind toward karma and its results, the [Four Noble] Truths, and the [Three] Jewels; and the antithesis of faith.

What is laziness?

[It is] the mind's lack of exertion toward virtue; and the antithesis of effort.

What is lack of mindfulness?

Those forms of desire, hatred, ignorance, and laziness that do not protect the mind from the mental afflictions and do not cultivate virtue.

What is clouded recollection?

[It is] afflicted recollection; and a lack of clarity with regard to virtue.

What is distraction?

Those forms of desire, hatred, and ignorance that cause the mind to flow outward to the five sense objects.

What is lack of vigilance?

[It is] wisdom that is concomitant with a mental affliction and [the mental factor] that causes one to engage in activities of body, speech, or mind inattentively.

The Four Variable Mental Factors

What is regret?

The mind's sense of remorse.

What is sleep?

The uncontrolled contraction of the mind's activity.

What is deliberation?

It is a form of mental discourse that investigates; and a particular type of wisdom and volition that is a coarseness of mind.

What is reflection?

It is a form of mental discourse that examines [an object] closely. It is like [the previous mental factor, except that it is] a fineness of mind.

The Formations That Do Not Accompany Consciousness

What are the formations that do not accompany consciousness?

They are [entities] that are nominally ascribed to a particular state of form, consciousness, or the mental factors. They are not [entities that are] ascribed to [form, consciousness, or the mental factors] themselves or to something distinct from them.

What, then, are they?

Acquirement, the state of composure without conception, the state of composure that is a cessation, the quality of having no conception, the faculty of a life force, class affiliation, birth, aging, duration, impermanence, the collection of names, the collection of assertions, the collection of syllables, the state of an ordinary being, as well as those [other entities] that are of the same kind.

What is acquirement?

[It is] obtainment and possession; moreover, according to circumstances, it is applied to [the states of] a seed, mastery, and actualization.

What is the state of composure without conception?

[It is] the cessation of inconstant minds and mental factors that is preceded by a form of attention that conceives of deliverance; and it is achieved by someone who has overcome desire for Complete Virtue but not for the level above it.

What is the state of composure that is a cessation?

[It is] the cessation of inconstant minds and mental factors, as well as a portion of the constant minds, that is preceded by a form of attention that conceives of abiding [in a state of ease]; and it is achieved by someone who has overcome desire for the Sphere of Nothingness and who has set out to rise above the Peak of Existence.

What is [the quality of] having no conception?

[It is] a result of the state of composure without conception; and the cessation of inconstant minds and mental factors of a being who has been born among the deities who lack conception.

What is the faculty of a life force?

[It is] the fixed period of time for the continued existence of the formations [that occur] within [various] class affiliates [of different sentient beings] that is projected by past karma.

What is class affiliation?

The similarity in the composition of beings.

What is birth?

The origination of previously nonexistent formations in relation to a class affiliate.

What is aging?
The modification of their continuum in relation to that.

What is duration?
The uninterrupted succession of their continuum in relation to that.

What is impermanence?
The destruction of their continuum in relation to that.

What is the collection of names?
The expressions [that describe] the essences of entities.

What is the collection of assertions?
The expressions [that describe] the distinguishing characteristics of entities.

What is the collection of syllables?
[It is the collection of] phonemes, because they are what allow both of them to become manifest. They are also the [basic] sounds [of spoken language], because meanings are communicated on the basis of names and assertions. Moreover, they are [called] "phonemes" because they cannot be replaced by any alternative form.

What is the state of an ordinary being?
The condition of not having achieved the qualities of an Ārya.

This group of entities constitutes the formations heap.

The Consciousness Heap

What is consciousness?
It is awareness of an object. It is also [referred to as] thought and mind, because it is diverse and because mind serves as its support.

Primarily, thought is the storehouse consciousness, because that is where the seeds of all the formations are collected. Moreover, [the storehouse consciousness] does not have a discernible object or aspect; it is of a single type; and it occurs continuously—because, after coming out of the state of composure that is a cessation, the state of composure without conception, and the state [of being born as a worldly god] that has no conception, the active forms of consciousness, which are referred to as "awareness of objects," arise again. It exists because of the occurrence of different aspects in relation to the objective condition, [because of] their occurrence after having been interrupted, and [because] samsara is both set in motion and brought to an end.

That very [consciousness] is [called] the "storehouse consciousness," because of its quality of being the storehouse for the seeds of all [afflicted entities], its quality of being the storehouse and cause of [a sentient being's] individual existence,[1] and its quality of residing in [a sentient being's] body. It is also [called] the "acquiring consciousness," because it takes on [a sentient being's] embodied existence.

Primarily, mind is what apprehends the storehouse consciousness as its object. It is a consciousness that is always accompanied by bewilderment toward a self, the view that believes in a self, pride toward a self, and attachment toward a self, and so on. It is of one type and it occurs continually, except when [one becomes] an Arhat, [when one has generated] the Ārya path, and [when one is absorbed in] the state of composure that is a cessation.

Why are they called "heaps"?

Because they are aggregates in the sense of the quality of being collections of form, etc., that are distinct in terms of time, continuum, type, being, and region.

THE TWELVE BASES

There are twelve bases: the eye basis, the form basis, the ear basis, the sound basis, the nose basis, the smell basis, the tongue basis, the taste basis, the body basis, the basis of tangible objects, the mind basis, and the entity basis.

The bases of the eye, etc., and those of form, sound, smell, and taste are explained in the same manner as before.

The basis of tangible objects is [made up of] the four great elements and those entities that were described as a portion of tangible objects.

The mind basis is [made up of] the consciousness heap.

The entity basis is [made up of] feelings, conceptions, the formations, noninformative form, and unconditioned entities.

What are unconditioned entities?

Space, the nonanalytic cessation, the analytic cessation, and suchness.

Regarding these, what is space?

A place for form.

What is the nonanalytic cessation?

It is the cessation that is not a separation; and it is the permanent nonarising of the heaps that is unrelated to an antidote to the mental afflictions.

What is the analytic cessation?

It is the cessation that is a separation; and it is the permanent nonarising of the heaps that is related to an antidote to the mental afflictions.

What is suchness?

It is the [true] nature of entities and the insubstantiality of entities.

Why are they called "bases"?

Because they are the sources for the appearance of consciousness.

THE EIGHTEEN CONSTITUENTS

There are eighteen constituents: the eye constituent, the form constituent, the eye-consciousness constituent, the ear constituent, the sound constituent, the ear-consciousness constituent, the nose constituent, the smell constituent, the nose-consciousness constituent, the tongue constituent, the taste constituent, the tongue-consciousness constituent, the body constituent, tangible-object constituent, the body-consciousness constituent, the mind constituent, the entity constituent, and the mind-consciousness constituent.

The [description of the five] constituents of the eye, etc., and the [five] constituents of form, etc., is the same as [that which was made] for the [ten corresponding] bases.

The six consciousness constituents are the forms of awareness that are based upon the eye, etc., and have form, etc., as their objects.

The mind constituent is made up of those very six consciousness constituents in the moment immediately following their cessation, in order to indicate a basis for the sixth consciousness. In this manner, it is established that there are eighteen constituents.

The form heap corresponds to ten bases and a portion of the entity basis, as well as ten constituents and a portion of the entity constituent. The consciousness heap corresponds to the mind basis and to the seven mental constituents. The other three heaps, together with a portion of the form heap and unconditioned entities, correspond to the entity basis and the entity constituent.

Why are they called "constituents"?

Because they do not act upon anything and because they retain their unique essential characteristics.

Why were the heaps and the rest taught?

As antidotes, respectively, for three types of belief in a self. The three types of belief in a self are belief in a unity, belief in an experiencer, and belief in an agent.

FURTHER CLASSIFICATIONS

How many of the eighteen constituents are material?

Those [constituents] whose nature [it] is [to be included in] the form heap.

How many are not material?

The remaining ones.

How many are capable of being indicated?

Only the form constituent, which is an object that is capable of being indicated.

How many are not capable of being indicated?

The remaining ones.

How many possess resistance?

The ten [constituents] that are material—[which is to say,] those that occupy a place where something can strike against them.

How many lack resistance?

The remaining ones.

How many are related to the outflows?

Fifteen [constituents] and a portion of the final three, because they are the direct fields of experience that give rise to the mental afflictions.

How many are free of the outflows?

A portion of the final three.

How many are related to desire?

All of them.

How many are related to form?

Fourteen [constituents]—all those except for smells, tastes, and the nose and tongue forms of consciousness.

How many are related to the formless?

The final three.

How many are unrelated?

A portion of three.

How many are contained within the heaps?

All those except for the unconditioned.

How many are contained within the grasping heaps?

Those that are related to the outflows.

How many are virtuous, how many are nonvirtuous, and how many are indeterminate?

Ten are of [all] three types—[namely,] the seven mental constituents, as well as the form, sound, and entity constituents. The remaining ones are indeterminate.

How many are inner?

Twelve—all those except for the form, sound, smell, taste, tangible object, and entity constituents.

How many are outer?

Six—[that is,] those that were excluded.

How many have apprehended objects?

The seven mental constituents and a portion of the entity constituent—[namely,] those that are mental factors.

How many do not have apprehended objects?

The remaining ten and a portion of the entity constituent.

How many are associated with concepts?

The mind constituent, the mind consciousness constituent, and part of the entity constituent.

How many are not associated with concepts?

The remaining ones.

How many are retained?

Five of the inner [constituents] and a portion of four [outer ones]—[namely,] the form, smell, taste, and tangible-object [constituents].

How many are unretained?

The remaining nine [constituents] and a portion of [the previous] four.

How many have a shared [action]?

The five inner ones that are material, because they have the same object as their respective forms of consciousness.

How many resemble those [that have a shared action]?

The very same entities when they are divorced from their respective forms of consciousness, because they are similar to those of the same type.

This concludes the treatise entitled *A Summary of the Five Heaps* that was composed by Master Vasubandhu. It was translated [into Tibetan], revised, and set in its final form by the learned Indian teachers Jinamitra, Śīlendrabodhi, and Dānaśīla, and by the great Tibetan translator Venerable Yeshe De, and others.

A Detailed Commentary on the Summary of the Five Heaps *by Master Sthiramati* 2

Homage to all Buddhas and Bodhisattvas.

INTRODUCTION

WHY WOULD SOMEONE compose a summary[2] of the five heaps and other similar topics?

[It is done] to make known the general and specific characteristics of entities.

Since the characteristics of entities have already been examined in such treatises as the *Levels of Spiritual Practice*,[3] is it not meaningless to undertake an examination of them again?

It is not meaningless, because the purpose of this work is to instruct those who are quick learners.[4] And since a quick learner is someone who can understand all aspects of a subject completely with only a brief indication of its meaning, such individuals prefer only a brief presentation of a particular subject, not an extensive explanation. Therefore, this summary has been composed to benefit those who prefer concise explanations.

An alternative explanation of why it is not meaningless to compose this summary is the following. Because householders are involved in a great many activities, they are unable to apply themselves to the study of a large work.[5] In addition, those homeless ascetics[6] who are engaged in some form of meditative practice would become distracted if they were to devote themselves to the study of an [excessively] large work. Thus, it is to enable these two types of individuals to comprehend the characteristics of entities that they are explained briefly in this summary.

Yet another explanation is that by learning a brief presentation of the characteristics of entities you become able to comprehend more extensive explanations without having to exert great effort. Thus, the Master[7] composed this summary as a means of enabling someone to take up the study of such large works as the *Levels of Spiritual Practice*.

What would you be unable to accomplish without knowledge of the characteristics of entities and which thus prompted the Master to devote himself to presenting an explanation of those characteristics?

His purpose was to enable others to fix their minds one-pointedly and to respond skillfully to questions posed by those who investigate rigorously subjects of philosophical discourse. That is to say, you will become free of doubt through mastering the characteristics of entities. Only then, and not otherwise, will you be able to fix your mind one-pointedly on a suitable object. Moreover, through discerning the characteristics of entities you will develop superior wisdom, which in turn brings lack of fear.[8] Only when you gain such fearlessness, and not otherwise, will you be able to respond fully to questions posed by those who investigate subjects of philosophical discourse.

THE NUMBER AND ORDER OF THE HEAPS

The phrase in the root text that "there are five heaps" establishes their number in order to prevent the notion that there might be either more or fewer than this. The use of the term "heaps" in an unqualified manner encompasses both those that are impure and those that are pure.[9]

The heaps are exactly five in number, neither more nor less, because they were taught as the entities that constitute the basis for grasping an "I" and a "mine." Most immature beings[10] grasp their own consciousness as an "I," and the remaining heaps as "mine."[11]

Thus, when the inner and outer form[12] that represent an agent and an object, respectively, are perceived as being related to an "I," this is what constitutes grasping the form heap as "mine."

When one thinks, "I am experiencing the feelings that are the ripening of virtuous and nonvirtuous karma," that is what constitutes grasping the feeling heap as "mine." Regarding this, pleasurable experiences are [generally regarded as] the ripening of virtuous karma, painful ones as the ripening of nonvirtuous karma, and those that are neither pleasurable nor painful as the ripening of both kinds of karma. However, only the neutral sensations that accompany the storehouse consciousness[13] are truly a karmic ripening, because only the storehouse consciousness is a genuine ripening of virtuous and nonvirtuous karma. Because pleasurable and painful feelings are derived from such actual karmic ripenings, they are ripenings only in a figurative sense.

The conception heap is grasped as "mine" when, while one is apprehending an "I," [this mental factor] identifies[14] the things that are seen, heard, considered, and perceived.

The formations heap is grasped as "mine" when the mind that is believed to constitute an "I" engages in virtuous and nonvirtuous activities by means of the formations.[15] Thus, the heaps are exactly five in number.

What is the reason for the order of the heaps?

The order conforms to their relative coarseness. Form is the most coarse of all the heaps, because (1) it possesses resistance,[16] (2) it [includes those entities that are] the supports[17] for the five collections of [sensory] consciousness, and (3) it is the object of the six forms of consciousness. Therefore, it is mentioned first.

Feelings are more coarse in their appearance[18] than the other three remaining heaps. Like conception and the rest [of the heaps that are essentially mental in nature], feelings do not have any physical location. However, because of the coarseness of their appearance, it can still be said that a location is discerned in relation to them—as when one says, "[I experience] a feeling in my hand," or "[I experience] a feeling in my head." However, no such statements can be made in relation to conception and the other [mental entities]. Therefore, feelings are mentioned next after form.

Conceptions are easy to recognize because their essential nature is that of grasping a sign.[19] Therefore, they are coarser than the other two remaining heaps.

Formations are also somewhat easy to discern, because their essential nature is that of forming [an intention].[20] For this reason, they are coarser than consciousness.

Consciousness is mentioned last because it is the most subtle[21] of all the heaps.

THE FORM HEAP

Is the expression "form heap" a *samānādhikaraṇa* compound or a *tatpuruṣa* compound?[22]

It is not a *samānādhikaraṇa* compound, because a heap is not a real substance. The term *skandha*[23] is synonymous with an ordinary heap.[24] Therefore, the [five] *skandhas* are only nominally existent, like a heap [of grain]. Therefore, the expression "form heap" is not a *samānādhikaraṇa* compound.

It is not a *tatpuruṣa* compound either. If the two members were distinct entities, there could be a relation between them, as in the phrase, "Devadatta's uncle."[25] The grammatical case that is implied in the compound "form heap" is the genitive, and it is meant to convey the sense of a relation between the members. Thus, a heap should be something that is distinct from form. However, because something that is nominally existent cannot be described as either identical with or distinct from the object that it is dependent upon, you also cannot hold [that this is a *tatpuruṣa* compound].

The alleged error does not apply. Compounds where the sixth [grammatical case][26] is implied are seen to occur even when the relation is not between distinct entities or where the members cannot be described as either identical or distinct from one another. This occurs, for example, in such phrases as "a body made of form"[27] and "[the condition of] form [that it] has not existed before."[28]

[In the first example,] the quality of being made of form is not distinct from the body itself. [In the second example,] the condition of never having existed before is not a substance; therefore, it cannot be described as being either identical with or distinct from form.

A [necessary] cause for positing identity or difference [between two things] is that they must be real. Because [this condition] has no real essential nature, its existence depends upon the perception of some other substance. Anything that is held in the mind or described in words on the basis of something else is nominally existent, because it has no essential nature that is distinct from that entity upon which it is dependent. [In short,] that which is not real is said to be nominally existent.

Therefore, even though something cannot be described as either identical with or distinct from that upon which it is dependent, that does not mean there can be no genitive relation. We may conclude, then, that the expression "form heap" is a genitive *tatpuruṣa* compound.

The Four Elements

Regarding the passage, "What is form? It is . . . the four great elements and [that which] is derived from the four great elements," [a hypothetical opponent might state that] it is inconsistent for the question to be worded, "What is form?"

It is not inconsistent, because the heaps are lacking in substance. Thus, if one refers to [a heap's] essential nature, that cannot be defined. However, one can define the entities with which that [nominally existent object] is related; therefore, the question is worded "What is form?" and not "What is the form heap?"

The phrase, "the four great elements . . .," and so forth is made to present a classification of form in terms of those types that represent a cause and those that represent a result. That is to say, the four great elements collectively are the cause of all derivative form[29] and all derivative form is a result of all [four] of the great elements.

The greatness of the elements is due to their magnitude,[30] in that they constitute the substratum for all derivative form. Alternatively, the greatness [of the four elements] is because hardness and the rest[31] are present in all aggregate instances of [visible] form and the rest, or because [the elements] play a large role in the composition [of all form].

The elements are called *bhūtāni*[32] in the sense that, when the various types of derivative form are produced, they come into being[33] with an appearance that is largely determined by this or that element. Alternatively, the elements are called *bhūtāni* because there has never been a time in beginningless samsara when they did not exist by the power of all sentient beings' karma.[34]

No other entities [besides these four] possess the nature of being elements. Their names are well known, as evidenced in phrases such as "lying on the surface of the earth."[35] The elements are exactly four in number, because no more [than that number] is needed and because [form] could not exist if there were any less [than that number].

Space Is Not an Element

The actions of the elements are wholly described by [the properties of] supporting,[36] cohesion,[37] maturation,[38] and expansion,[39] [respectively]. Because their actions are fully exhausted by these properties and they do not possess any other actions, the elements are exactly four in number.

Like [the actions of] supporting and the rest, isn't the action of space that of giving way?[40] And since space performs that action, would it not, then, like earth and the rest also be a great element?

That is not the case.

Why?

Space is nothing but the mere absence of any form that possesses [the quality of] resistance. An object that possesses resistance can move from a particular location and [thus] give way so that another entity that possesses resistance can take its place. Space, however, does not perform any such action. That is, unlike form, space cannot leave a particular location and thus [perform the action] that is referred to as "giving way." Form that possesses resistance prevents another form from arising in its place; however, space does not carry out any such action. Therefore, when the presence of some object does not make room for anything else and its absence does make room for something else, this means that the departure of some object from a particular place is what constitutes the action of giving way. Moreover, this is not something that space does. Therefore, unlike earth and the rest, space is not a great element.

The Relation Between the Great Elements and Derivative Form

The expression "[form] that is derived from the four [great] elements" is meant to indicate that the term "form" refers to two types: the form that is represented by the four great elements and the form that is derived from the four great elements. This is because the [four great] elements are closely tied to derivative form by virtue of five kinds of causal relation: (1) generating, (2) dependence, (3) foundation, (4) supporting, and (5) strengthening. The expression "derived from"[41] has the meaning of a cause, as in the phrase, "fire is derived from fuel." Thus, it should be understood that [in the present context] this expression indicates that [the four great elements] are the cause of [derivative form].

[The great elements] are the generating cause[42] [of derivative form], because [derivative form] cannot occur if [the great elements] are absent. [The great elements] are a dependence cause,[43] because whatever modification [the great elements] undergo, the derivative form that is dependent on the elements undergoes a similar modification. [The great elements] are a foundation cause,[44] because when the elements arise as a uniform continuum, derivative form continues to exist uninterruptedly as well. [The great elements] are a supporting cause[45] in that, by their power, derivative form does not cease to exist. They are a strengthening cause[46] in that when the elements become strengthened, the derivative form that is dependent on them becomes strengthened as well.

The Term "Constituent" as Relates to the Four Elements

With regard to the explanations of the expressions "earth constituent" and the rest, [the four elements of] earth and the rest are constituents[47] in that they [each individually] hold an essential attribute and they [collectively] hold [all] derivative form. The phrase "earth and the rest" is used here to distinguish the elements individually—that is, one from the other—as well as to distinguish them collectively from other classifications of the constituents,[48] such as the eye constituent, etc.

The term "constituent" also distinguishes the meaning of the elements from the mundane notions of earth, and the rest. Earth and the rest are to be understood in two ways, according to the way they are known in the ordinary world and [how they are understood] in philosophical treatises. In the ordinary world, that which has the nature of color and shape is referred to as earth.[49] Therefore, that sense is not the earth constituent. The descriptions [of the elements that are found] in the philosophical treatises are of those entities that have the nature of hardness and the rest. Therefore, the latter explanations represent the true meaning of the constituents.

The Essential Nature of the Elements

Just as with the elements, the nature of the constituents will remain unknown until they have been explained. Therefore, the questions "What is the earth constituent?" and the rest are posed in the root text. The term "hardness"[50] means simply that which is hard; it has no other signification. The terms "hard," "solid,"[51] and "rigid"[52] are synonyms.

Regarding the passage that identifies [the essential nature] of water as "fluidity,"[53] a fluid is something that exerts cohesion[54] and causes things to become moist.

[The essential nature of] the fire constituent is heat[55]—which is to say, that [property] which has the ability to burn.

Regarding the description of the air constituent as "lightness and motility,"[56] if the air constituent were said to consist [only] of lightness, it would wrongly follow that a derivative form is a [primary] element.[57] [On the other hand,] if the air constituent were said to consist [only] of motility, one would be referring to its action, not its essential nature. Therefore, to distinguish the air constituent both from a derivative form and from its own action, it is described with the phrase, "lightness and motility." Motility is the cause that makes an entity's continuum appear in a different place.

How is it understood that the constituents of earth, water, fire, and air, as well as derivative form, do not occur separately from one another? This is made evident by the actions [of the elements] and it is the reason that their actions are described as supporting, cohesion, maturation, and expansion.

Although one cannot directly perceive the essential natures of all [four of] the elements in such objects as a stone, how can one infer their presence through their actions? For instance, the simultaneous occurrence of water, fire, and air in combination with the earth constituent in [solid] objects like a rock is apparent from the presence of the qualities of cohesiveness, dryness, and the capacity to be moved. The simultaneous occurrence of earth, fire, and air in combination with the water constituent in bodies of water is apparent from their ability to support objects such as wood, the development of a lotus blossom,[58] and the water's [ability to] move. The simultaneous occurrence of earth, water, and air in combination with the fire constituent in a burning fire is apparent from the ability of the flames to hold objects aloft, as well as the cohesiveness of the flames and their movement. The simultaneous occurrence of earth, water, and fire in combination with the air constituent in wind is apparent from its ability to hold objects aloft, avoid becoming dispersed, and dry clothing and other objects.

The Difference Between Action and Essential Nature

What is the difference between the action and the essential nature [of each of the four elements]? The actions of the constituents are set forth in relation to the performance of some activity. Thus, the action of the earth constituent is described as "supporting" in that it holds up substances that can be supported. The action of the water constituent is the cohesion that it exerts in relation to entities that are capable of being held together. The action of the fire constituent is to bring about the maturation of those entities capable of being ripened or developed. The action of the air constituent is the expansion that occurs in relation to objects capable of growth and development, such as a fetus during the various embryonic stages known as *kalalam*,[59] etc., and a plant during the stages of a sprout, etc. Moreover, expansion should be understood as meaning both growth and movement.[60]

The essential nature[61] of [each of] the constituents is a quality that is independent of all other entities. This is the difference between the actions [of the four elements] and their essential natures.

This concludes the explanation of both the general and individual terms that describe the elements and their essential natures.

Derivative Form

The topic that is to be explained after the elements is derivative form. Because their variety and essential natures are not known, the root text asks, "What is derivative form?" The meaning of this question is to ask how many kinds of derivative form there are and what their essential natures are.

The Five Sense Faculties

[If you were to ask,] "What is the nature of the eye faculty?" its nature is indicated by the statement, "clear form that has color as its object." It should be understood that this statement is made in connection with form that is derived from the four great elements, because that is the current topic.

Color is the four [main] types of yellow and the rest.

[The eye faculty] is the unique cause for [the action of] looking at colors and for the [particular type of] consciousness that perceives colors. Therefore, the phrase, "[an entity] that has color as its object,"[62] means that color is the object of this [faculty].

The meaning of the term "clear"[63] here is as follows. Just as the reflection of a [visible] form[64] appears [on the surface of] a clear mirror or a container of clear water in dependence on that [visible] form, the various [sense] perceptions of [visible] form, sound, and so forth arise in dependence on those [visible] forms, sounds, etc., and through [the medium of] the five [faculties] of the eye and the rest that have the nature of clear form.

In the present context, each of the sense faculties of the eye and so forth should be distinguished from the other sense faculties, from those kinds of clear form that are [external] objects,[65] from the mind faculty,[66] and from faith. [For the eye faculty in particular,] it must be described both as "[an entity] that has color as its object" and as a "clear form," because the latter phrase alone does not distinguish the eye from other kinds of clear form, while the former phrase does not distinguish it from other entities that can have color as their object. Thus, the phrase, "[an entity] that has color as its object," distinguishes [the eye] from the ear and the other sense faculties, as well as from other objects that have the nature of clear form, since the ear, etc., and other clear objects may be clear, but they do not have color as their object. Asserting that [the eye faculty] has the nature of clear form distinguishes it from the mind faculty, since the mind faculty can have color as its object, but it does not have the nature of clear form. Asserting that [the eye faculty] is form distinguishes it from the type of faith that has the nature of clarity,[67] since faith can have both the nature of clarity and color as its object. This is one reason for declaring [the eye faculty] to be form. That is, if the eye faculty were described only as "the clarity that has color as its object," that would incorrectly apply to faith as well. Therefore, [the eye faculty] is asserted to be form, since faith does not have the nature of form.

The eye and the rest are called faculties because they are powerful.[68] That is to say, they exercise power over a particular group of things. Thus, the meaning of the term "faculty" is that of having power.[69]

The Five Sense Objects

Visible Form

Just as [the root text] distinguishes the internal faculties[70] of the eye, etc., from one another on the basis of their different objects by saying, "What is the eye faculty? Clear form that has color as its object. What is the ear faculty? Clear form that has sound as its object..." and so forth, it also distinguishes the [external] objects of [visible] form, etc., on the basis of the different faculties of the eye, etc., by saying that [visible] form is exclusively the object of the eye [faculty] and not of the ear [or any other sense faculty], because the objects of those [other faculties] are classified as sound, etc. The mind faculty is neither included nor excluded from the discussion here, because it does not form part of the current topic.[71] This is the manner in which [visible] form and the rest [of the five external objects] are distinguished from one another. Since [visible] form alone and no other [type of form] constitutes the object of the eye faculty, [all] the different kinds of object that the eye faculty [perceives], such as blue, yellow and so on, can be indicated without qualification as representing [visible] form.

If [visible] form is distinguished by virtue of being exclusively the object of the eye faculty, why does [the root text] specify "color, shape, and informative [form]?"

By explaining the different categories of [visible] form to those who have doubt, crror, or lack of knowledge about this classification, one is able to remove their doubt, error, or lack of knowledge.[72]

Color is of four types: blue, yellow, red, and white.

Why are cloud, smoke, dust, mist, shadow, sunshine, light, darkness, openings, and the sky not mentioned?[73]

They are not mentioned here as distinct types of [visible] form in the way that color and shape are [for the following reason]. [This group of entities comprising] cloud, and the rest, can occur either as well-defined objects[74] or as objects that are not well-defined. Those that are well defined [objects] are included in the category of shape; those that are not well-defined objects represent types of color. Therefore, they cannot be classified in a manner that is distinct from the two categories of color and shape. That is why they are not mentioned separately.

Within that group, an opening[75] is an area [of space] that is free of any obstructing tangible object.

The sky[76] is the upper expanse that appears blue.

Shape

Shapes are long, short, square, round, high, low, even, and uneven.

What is shape?

Was it not just said [that shape is made up of] long and the rest?

[The nature of] those very things is [precisely] what is not understood.

That entity in relation to which the idea of being long and the rest occurs is what constitutes a long shape, etc.

In that case, shape does not exist apart from color.

Why?

Because the notion of being long occurs when a large amount of color, etc., extends in one direction; the notion of short occurs when only a small amount of color, etc., is so arranged; the notion of a square occurs when it is arranged equally in four directions; the notion of round occurs when it is arranged equally on all sides; the notion of high occurs when it is arranged predominantly in the center; the notion of low occurs when there is only a small amount in the center; the notion of being even occurs when it is arranged in one plane; and the notion of uneven occurs when it is arranged on different planes.

How do you know that shape is nothing more than the notion of being long, etc., that arises in relation to a particular arrangement of a preponderance of color, etc., and that it is not a distinct entity?

[This view is known] because the notion of long, etc., can also arise on the basis of touch.

It is unacceptable for the object of one faculty to generate the notion of that object through a different [faculty], since that would lead to the consequence that it would be meaningless to have multiple faculties.

The mind that perceives shapes is an inferential awareness[77] and not a sense consciousness, as in the case of knowing the color of a flower from its smell.

Because the sense of touch does not determine shape in the same way that smell enables one to ascertain a flower's color, this example is not analogous.[78] Therefore, since the awareness of a shape such as long, etc., can occur through two faculties, as it does in the case of a pot,[79] shape is not an entity that is distinct from color.

It is also the case that, since atomic particles[80] have no parts, there are no separate natures of longness, etc., that could be distinct from one another. Therefore, there are no atomic particles that have a nature of being long, etc., as there are with atomic particles for the qualities of being blue, etc. For that reason, it is unacceptable that there could be entities such as a long shape, etc., that refer to a mass of atomic particles having the nature of a shape, since there are no atomic particles that have the nature of being a shape.

Shape is not a uniform substance, because it has aspects of a near side, a center, and a far side. Those [aspects] do not form an indivisible whole. They are distinct [as objects of] direct perception [that can be perceived] simultaneously; they are distinct [as objects that] do not exist "face to face"[81]; and they are distinct [in the sense of being objects] that are related [to one another]. Therefore, they are unquestionably distinct. Alternatively, if it were accepted that they are not distinct, the unwanted consequence would follow that, as related elements of a specific [shape], they would not occupy separate spatial locations. Therefore, a shape such as long, etc., is not a real substance, but rather something that is nominally ascribed to a color, etc., that is situated in such and such a particular manner.

Bodily informative form

Now then, what is this entity called "informative [form]"?[82]

It is a body shape that arises from a mind that [consciously] holds that [configuration of the body in the mind][83] and that is dependent on the body's four great elements. It is called "informative" because it makes known the mind that caused it to arise. In this instance, only [the body shape] that arises from a mind that [consciously] holds that [body shape in the mind] is informative form; not [a body shape] that may have arisen from a mind that [consciously] holds some different object [in the mind]. This excludes the shape of [a person's] lips during speech and the like, which are not instances [of a shape] that arises from a mind that [consciously] holds that [configuration of the body in the mind],[84] as well as [a shape] that is produced by [the power of] prayer.[85] The latter instance is [a shape] that arises from a prayerful mind [that occurred while the Master[86] was still a Bodhisattva]; other instances [of shapes that are not bodily informative form] can also arise from a mind that represents the cause of a [karmic] ripening.[87] Therefore, [these examples] are not considered to represent [bodily] informative form.

If the shape that is called informative were a unity that extended throughout a person's body, it would have to be present everywhere in the body and, therefore, it could be apprehended in each of the various limbs as well. Alternatively, if it were composed of parts, then it could not be a unity. Such a view of shape would also contradict the doctrine that ten of the bases are made up of aggregations of atomic particles. Therefore, shape is not a separate substance, and it is also not the essential nature of [bodily] informative form.

If [bodily] informative form is not a shape that is distinct from the body, then what is it?

[Bodily informative form] is caused by a volition that [consciously] holds that [configuration of the body in the mind] and it, in turn, is the entity that causes the continuum of the body to arise uninterruptedly in separate places. [This explanation is correct,] because the characteristic of being caused by volition establishes that the wind constituent is what causes the continuum of the body to arise in separate places.

The quality of causing the body to arise in separate places is informative because it makes known the volition that is its cause. While that quality does not itself have either a virtuous or a nonvirtuous nature, it is produced by a volition that can be either virtuous or nonvirtuous. Therefore, [bodily informative form] is also designated as being either virtuous or nonvirtuous in the sense that a result can be figuratively assigned a quality that pertains to its cause.

This description of [visible] form is organized according to essential nature, position, and characteristic action. The entities that are classified according to the essential nature [of visible form] are the four colors of blue and the rest, because they represent its essential nature. The entities that are classified according to position are the eight types of shape—that is, long and the rest, because they are essentially color that is situated in some particular manner. The entity that is classified according to characteristic action is [bodily] informative form, because it has the nature of causing movement of the body.

If your view is that the [true] objects of the eye [and the other sense faculties] are real entities and that shapes and [bodily] informative form are not [true] objects of the eye because they only exist nominally, how do you explain the description [in the root text] that [visible] form is the object of the eye?

In order to comply with [the view of] the [ordinary] world, we hold that a color possessing the characteristic of a particular shape is the object of the eye. That is, the eye grasps a color that is also characterized by having a particular shape. [The eye] does not grasp either color or shape alone, because eye consciousness arises in the form of an awareness that perceives a color characterized by any of various shapes such as long, etc. Therefore, [both] color and shape are recognized in [the view of] the ordinary world as objects of the eye. In a similar manner, [bodily] informative form is also recognized as an object of the eye because it supports the continuum of the body in the sense of being the quality that causes [the body] to arise in separate locations.

In an ultimate sense, color is not the object of the eye just as shape is not, because atomic particles are unreal just as shape is unreal and because there are no external entities that are [real] objects of [the five forms of sense] consciousness. Therefore, it should be understood that the Master has presented this topic in accordance with the views of both the ordinary world and the treatises.[88]

Sound

Because the presentation of sound follows that of [visible] form [in the root text], it is proper that we should undertake to explain sound right after we have concluded our explanation of [visible form]. In response to the question, "What is sound?" [the root text] declares [in part], "The object of the ear." [This part of the description] indicates that sound is exclusively the object of the ear [faculty] and not that of any other faculty. Thus, while the quality of being a type of derivative form does not differentiate [sound from any of the other sense objects], [saying that it is the object of the ear] does indicate how it is distinct from [visible] form and [the objects of the other sense faculties].

Moreover, stating that sound alone is the object of the ear [faculty] merely indicates that the various distinct types of sound make up the sound basis,[89] without specifying what any of those distinct types of sound are. To indicate their variety, the root text [also] states that [sound] "is caused by great elements that are [either] retained, unretained, or both."

The term "retained"[90] refers to entities that make up a [sentient being's] body; hence, retained entities are those that the mind and mental factors take hold of in the manner of a support.[91] Those entities that are the opposite of this are unretained. [Sound] has [the great elements] as its cause in the sense that [sound] arises from the great elements, and it can be generated [variously] by great elements that are retained, [by great elements that are] unretained, and [by great elements that are] both [retained and unretained].

With regard to these [three varieties], [examples of sound] caused by great elements that are retained are the sound of [a person clapping his or her] hands [together], speech, and the like. [Examples of sound] caused by great elements that are unretained are the sound of the wind, a forest tree, flowing water, and the like. [Examples of sound] caused by great elements that are both [retained and unretained] are the sound of a drum,[92] etc.

Smells

[The response to] the question, "What is smell?" [should be taken to mean] that [smell] is exclusively the object of the nose [faculty] and that the nose [faculty] has no other object except smell, as was explained before.[93]

A "moderate" smell[94] is one that neither benefits nor harms the great elements of the [nose] faculty.

Smells can be natural, compounded, or developmental.[95] [Examples of] natural smells are those of sandalwood, saffron, and the like. [Examples of] compounded smells are those of [a variety of substances that are combined together in] an incense preparation, and the like. [Examples of] developmental smells are those of a mango that has become ripe, and the like.

Tastes

[The response to] the question, "What is taste?" should be explained in detail in the same manner as before. [That is, it should be taken to mean] that [taste] is exclusively the object of the tongue [faculty] and that the tongue [faculty] has no other object except taste.

Six different types are mentioned in the root text, because these are the ones that have distinct natures. [These six] can be further classified in an unlimited manner, based on the various ways in which they can be combined together.

A Portion of Tangible Objects

Because the current subject is derivative form, the topic that is presented after taste [in the root text] is the portion of tangible objects that is derivative form. With the aim of describing that topic, the root text asks, "What is a portion of tangible objects?"

There are two types of tangible objects: the [four great] elements and the [tangible] form that is derived from them. The elements have already been presented [in the root text] and explained [in this commentary]. Therefore, since the present topic is derivative form, when it is asked, "What is a portion of tangible objects?" the question should be understood in connection with derivative form.

The phrase "objects of the body" means [that tangible objects are] exclusively objects of the body [faculty] and not those of the eye or any of the other faculties. This indicates that [tangible objects] are distinct from [visible] form, sounds, and other [sense objects].

The phrases "[tangible objects are] exclusively objects of the body" and "[the body faculty has] no other object except tangible objects" indicate that although the primary elements[96] and secondary elements[97] are different from one another, they are alike in that both are tangible objects. Because the primary elements are also objects of the body, the phrase "objects of the body" without any qualification would wrongly suggest that the primary elements are derivative form. Therefore, the root text adds, "excluding the great elements."

To indicate more specifically the portion of tangible objects that are derivative form, the root text declares, "smoothness, roughness . . . ," and the rest.

If smoothness and the rest are said to be tangible objects because they come in contact with the body faculty, wouldn't that also make the body faculty a tangible object, since that with which those objects come into contact also definitely comes into contact with them?

[The body faculty] is not something that comes into contact with anything at all. If every part of the body faculty comes into contact with an object, then all [sentient beings'] bodies[98] could only be the size of a single atomic particle. On the other hand, if only a portion [of the body faculty] comes in contact with an object, then atomic particles would possess parts and that would undermine the notion of what an atomic particle is.[99] Therefore, when a [tangible] object and a [body] faculty come into being with no empty space between them, that entity which [body] consciousness depends upon to perceive a [tangible] object is described as making contact with the object. [At the same time,] the [tangible] object does not represent the basis that consciousness depends upon [in order to arise]. Therefore, the body faculty is understood to come into contact only with the elements and not the [visible] form, etc., which abide in the elements, because body consciousness does not perceive them.

When [attributes such as] the color of a flower and the like are damaged, it is the result of damage done to the seat in which [those attributes] reside; it is not because the body [faculty] comes in contact with [those attributes of] the color, etc.

If the body [faculty] does not [in reality] make contact with the seat of [such attributes as] color, etc., either, how could [the seat of those attributes] become damaged?

This point needs to be considered further. Therefore, the present discussion should be understood as conforming to the manner of discourse in the ordinary world and should not be taken in the sense of the way things truly are.

Smoothness is softness and the absence of roughness—that is to say, a sensation that is easily endured. Smoothness is simply the quality of being smooth.

The term "roughness" should be understood in the manner that an object having this quality is described as being rough, like a yak hair whisk.

To be rough is to have a texture that is strong. Roughness is the very quality of being rough—that is to say, a harsh, coarse, and uneven texture.

Heaviness means to have weight. Heaviness is the quality of being heavy. It is what causes a scale to go lower when objects are being weighed.

Lightness is what fails to lower a scale when objects are being weighed. It is what makes even something large easy to lift. It is what causes the tip of a scale to remain in a low position.

Cold is that which, when felt, brings about a desire for warmth.

Isn't it so that when it is cold in summer and autumn you do not desire warmth?

Because the desire for warmth does not occur in any other situation, cold is defined as [a sensation that] causes the desire for warmth. Moreover, even the result[100] of that [tangible object] is understood by philosophers [as having the nature of a cold sensation], because it is the same class of entity [as the tangible object that causes the desire for warmth].

Hunger is that which causes the desire for food.

Thirst is that which causes the desire for drink.

If you object that a mental entity is not the object of the body faculty, hunger and thirst are described using the convention in which a cause is figuratively designated by the name of its result. A predominance of the wind constituent is what causes [the sensation of] hunger. Thus, the occurrence of a particular type of tangible object is what causes hunger, and that is what is referred to as "hunger." Similarly, a predominance of the fire constituent is called "thirst," because it is the cause of thirst.

The types of tangible object that are mentioned elsewhere[101]—such as fainting, strength, weakness, and the rest—are not mentioned separately in the root text because they can be subsumed among the ones that are found there. Fainting is not distinct from smoothness. Strength is not separate from roughness and heaviness. Similarly, the remainder of those other tangible objects can be subsumed among the ones found in the root text.

Smoothness and the rest can also be distinguished on the basis of [the elements that constitute their] specific substratum. Smoothness occurs where there is a predominance of the water and fire constituents; roughness where there is a predominance of the earth and wind constituents; heaviness where there is a predominance of the earth and water constituents; and lightness where there is a predominance of the fire and wind constituents. This is the reason for the greater heaviness of a dead person's body. Cold occurs where there is a predominance of the water constituent; hunger where there is a predominance of the wind constituent; and thirst where there is a predominance of the fire element. This principle of [identifying] the specific substratum can also be applied in the appropriate manner to explain the differences among the other types of [tangible objects that constitute] derivative form. Only a portion [of the examples] have been explained here, in order to avoid making the text excessively long.

Noninformative Form

Within the form heap [as a whole] and, [more specifically] among [the various types of] derivative form, the only entity that remains to be explained is noninformative [form]. The root text introduces this topic by asking, "What is noninformative [form]?" And then it is described with the response, "It is form that is derived either from informative [form] or one-pointed concentration; and it is both not capable of being indicated[102] and does not possess resistance."

Concerning this description, there are two types of informative form: bodily informative form and verbal informative form. Each of these can be of three distinct types: virtuous, nonvirtuous, and indeterminate.[103]

Noninformative form is also classified into three types: that which occurs in the desire realm, that which occurs in the form realm, and that which is pure.[104] Of these, the noninformative form that occurs in the desire realm can arise from virtuous informative form and from nonvirtuous informative form—that is to say, from the discipline[105] of individual liberation, the Bodhisattva discipline, negative discipline,[106] and that which is different from those [three].

Of these, the discipline of individual liberation[107] includes four entities: the fully ordained monk, the novice monk, the layperson, and the one-day fasting vow. When one distinguishes between a fully ordained monk and a fully ordained nun, and so forth, these [four entities] nominally comprise eight different types.[108]

The discipline of individual liberation consists of turning away from every manner of harm to others, as well as the causes of such harm.

The Bodhisattva discipline consists of having undertaken to benefit others in every way through body, speech, and mind, and to do so without concern for one's own life or body.

Negative discipline consists of having undertaken, without reservation,[109] to do harm to others.

Undertaking to benefit or harm others in a limited manner does not constitute either discipline or negative discipline.

Noninformative form that occurs in the form realm and noninformative form that is pure both arise from one-pointed concentration. They are called, respectively, discipline arising from meditative absorption and pure discipline.

The discipline that arises from meditative absorption occurs in conjunction with the impure one-pointed concentration of the four meditative absorptions, as well as those [forms of one-pointed concentration] that are called "all-powerful," and "superior meditative absorption."[110]

Pure discipline[111] is a quality that arises in conjunction with pure one-pointed concentration.

[Noninformative form] is derivative form because it arises in dependence on, and remains in a state of conformity with, the primary elements.

"Indication"[112] means [to point out] by saying, "This [entity] is here; that [entity] is over there." This particular type of form is not capable of being indicated because it does not possess that quality.

Resistance[113] means the quality by which one entity opposes the arising of another object in the space that it occupies. Since noninformative form does not occupy any space, it is not possible for it to exhibit this quality; therefore, it does not possess resistance.

All form can be classified into three categories: (1) that which is both capable of being indicated and also possesses resistance; (2) that which is not capable of being indicated but does possess resistance; and (3) that which is neither capable of being indicated nor possesses resistance. The object of the eye faculty is form that is both capable of being indicated and also possesses resistance. The five sense faculties of the eye, etc., and four of the five sense objects—namely, sound, smell, taste, and tangible objects—are form that is not capable of being indicated but does possess resistance. The form that is included in the entity basis[114] is neither capable of being indicated nor possesses resistance.

That latter type of form is made up of five types: (1) compact,[115] (2) open,[116] (3) undertaken,[117] (4) contrived,[118] and (5) supernatural.[119]

The root text holds that the form heap is made up of only eleven entities. Thus, only "undertaken form"[120] is described there with the phrase, "[it is] both not capable of being indicated and does not possess resistance." [The root text] does not mention the other [four types of form that are included in the entity basis].

Why are those [other types] not mentioned?

Compact form refers to atomic particles, which do not exist apart from the colors of blue and the rest. That is to say, among the various colors of blue, etc., what appears as color is nothing other than [atomic particles].

Open form also refers to atomic particles because they are intangible in the sense that they do not obstruct anything.

Since [atomic particles] have the nature of color and color is included [in the root text], it was unnecessary to mention atomic particles separately.

Contrived form is a type of form that is a [mental] image,[121] like that of a skeleton.

Supernatural form is the form that is manifested in the states of mental composure known as the "deliverances."[122] This type of form is not included in the root text, because it has the nature of a mental construct[123]; thus, it does not exist apart from the consciousness that has taken on the aspect of that kind of form and is manifesting such an appearance.

The [form that is a mental] image is also just a consciousness in which a [mental] object is being perceived. Thus, the [mental] image does not exist apart from the consciousness nor is the consciousness anything distinct from the [mental] image.

For these reasons, only "undertaken form" is referred to in the root text, not any of the other [four] kinds. Nevertheless, how could someone like me fully comprehend the reasoning of a person of such great intellectual prowess? Therefore, the Master [Vasubandhu's] intent must be further investigated to understand [with certainty] why he did not explain the other kinds of form.

Noninformative form is described as follows.[124] It is a continuum of derivative form that can be either virtuous or nonvirtuous. It can arise from informative form as well as from one-pointed concentration. It exists whether the mind is distracted or not, even during states in which there is no thought. It continues to exist as long as the cause of its abandonment has not come into being. It is noninformative because, although it is both form and performs an action, unlike informative form it does not make known to others the mind that produced it.

Noninformative form does not exist as the followers of the Vaibhāṣika School claim it does, just as informative form does not, because [their views] are not supported by valid reason. However, this does not mean that the discipline of individual liberation and the other [examples of noninformative form] do not exist.

Initially, an individual who participates in the ordination ritual generates a volition that promises to observe [all the precepts]. That volition in which one resolves to restrain oneself from committing a range of physical and verbal misdeeds plants a seed in the storehouse consciousness[125] that will generate a similar kind of self-restraint in the future. Following that, the individual recalls that he or she has accepted the commitment to abandon taking of life and other misdeeds. The embarrassment[126] [about wrongdoing] that is maintained in the wake of such recollection is what insures that one's [moral] training does not become damaged. Thus, the mental act of accepting [a particular body of moral precepts] together with its continuum is what is meant by the term "discipline."

Similarly, once a practitioner achieves any of the meditative absorptions or [a direct realization of] the [transcendent] path, even in the absence of any [real] noninformative form, his [or her] mind takes on a condition such that after arising [from those meditative states] he [or she] does not engage in wrong speech and other misdeeds and he [or she] does engage in right speech and the rest. Thus, both the discipline associated with the Eightfold Noble Path and that which arises from the meditative absorptions are established through the convention of figuratively ascribing the name of a result to the cause.[127]

As for negative discipline, in the case of those who are born into families where killing is a means of livelihood, it is the volition in which an individual makes the determination to engage in that activity. For those who are not born into such families, [negative discipline] is the volition in which the individual agrees to take up that kind of activity. The negative discipline does not disappear even when that volition is not present [in a manner that one is consciously aware of it], because the individual has not renounced the intention to do harm to sentient beings. Thus, the volition in which an individual engages in an activity with the intention of doing harm to sentient beings or the volition in which an individual agrees to take up such an activity is what is meant by the term "negative discipline."

The phrase in the root text that noninformative form is "derived either from informative form or one-pointed concentration" is easy to understand and therefore does not need to be explained.

The volition that generates discipline and negative discipline is virtuous and nonvirtuous, respectively, by its very nature. Its continuum is either virtuous or nonvirtuous both because it is projected by a virtuous or a nonvirtuous volition and because it is the result of a virtuous or nonvirtuous volition.

The discipline that arises from meditative absorption and pure discipline are both virtuous because they are caused by meditative absorption and the pure path.

Right speech and the rest are virtuous because they are results [of a virtuous cause]. Bodily form and verbal form are objects; therefore, they are [virtuous] in the sense that the subject is referred to by the object.[128]

The phrase that noninformative form is "both not capable of being indicated and does not possess resistance" is [also] easily understood and therefore does not need to be explained.

Why is this [collection of entities] that ends with the noninformative called "the form heap"?

Because it displays [the quality of] form.[129]

The Lord [Buddha] declared in detail: "Because [the elements that comprise it] exhibit and display the nature of form, O monks, that is why it is called the 'grasping heap of form.' What does it mean to exhibit the nature of form? For instance, an object that can be touched with the hand exhibits the nature of form."[130]

Another sutra declares, "Form is [an object] that exhibits [the nature of] form in that it can be touched with the hand, etc."

What is [this quality] by which form exhibits the nature of form?

It is the quality by which an object that is touched with the hand, etc., can be made to arise in a place that is different from the one it previously occupied. This description is made in the sense of the continuum [of form]. It does not apply to a [single] moment [of form], because a moment only has a state of arising and passing away; there is no [period during which it] continues to exist.

THE FEELING HEAP

The next subject for discussion following that of the form heap is the feeling heap. Therefore, after having concluded [the presentation of the form heap, the root text] introduces the next topic by asking, "What is feeling?" and then describes it with the response, "The three types of experience."

Experience[131] is experiential awareness. Its nature is to make directly evident the qualitative essence of an object that is either pleasurable, painful, or neither of those two. Alternatively, an experience is that which experiences the qualitative essence of an object that is either pleasurable, painful, or neither of those two.

The entity that has this essential nature is further classified as being of three types, [which the root text describes as] "pleasant, unpleasant, and neither pleasant nor unpleasant."

How is it known that there is a third type of experience—namely, [a feeling that is] neither pleasant nor unpleasant?

It is known through scripture and reasoning. The phrase "three types of feeling" appears in the sutras. There are also statements in the sutras that include such language as "having abandoned both pleasant and unpleasant [feelings] . . . [the practitioner experiences a feeling that is] neither pleasant nor unpleasant . . . ."

The reasoning is that no mind ever arises without [being accompanied by] a feeling and we do perceive states of mind that lack [the quality of being accompanied by] either a pleasant or an unpleasant feeling.

Master Saṃghabhadra states that "feeling is the experiencing of contact."[132] Thus, [according to him,] feeling is the experiencing of a desirable contact, an undesirable contact, or a contact that is different from those two. As the sutras state, "A pleasant feeling arises in dependence on a contact that will bring about a pleasant experience." The reason for specifying that [feeling is the experiencing of contact] is that [contact] generates feelings that are pleasant, etc. Furthermore, if feeling is [described as] the experiencing of an object, what distinguishes it from those [other mental entities] that [all grasp] the same object [as feeling]? Therefore, feeling should be defined as the experiencing of contact.

In that case, just as with feeling, the essential natures of conception, conviction, recollection, wisdom, etc., also should not be described on the basis of the object that they grasp. On the other hand, if you hold that conception and the rest *can* be distinguished on the basis of their [essential characteristic of] apprehending a mark, etc., [despite the fact that they all hold] the same object, why do you not also maintain that [the essential nature of] feeling is that of experiencing an object?

Since [you hold that] it is not possible [to explain feeling as the experiencing of] the object that it holds, do you maintain that the phrase "experiencing contact" should be explained as meaning that [feeling] accompanies [contact] or that [contact] represents the cause [of feeling]? [Feeling] cannot be explained [as the experiencing of contact] in the sense that it accompanies contact, because all the mental factors without exception [share the characteristic of] accompanying contact. Nor can [feeling] be explained [as experiencing contact in the sense that] contact is its cause, because contact is also without exception the cause of all the mental factors. Both in [the discourse of] the ordinary world and in [the more precise language of] the [philosophical] treatises the term "experience" is recognized as meaning that which makes something directly evident[133]; it is not understood in terms of being either a result or a cause.[134]

Some [scholars] believe the following. [Feeling is experience] in the sense of being [the entity] that experiences the various ripening results of virtuous and nonvirtuous deeds. Thus, pleasant experiences are the ripening results of virtuous deeds, unpleasant experiences are the ripening results of nonvirtuous deeds, and those experiences that are neither pleasant nor unpleasant are the ripening results of both. [However,] regarding this explanation, the storehouse consciousness alone is the ripening of virtuous and nonvirtuous deeds. In an ultimate sense, only the neutral feelings that accompany [the storehouse consciousness] are the ripening of virtuous and nonvirtuous deeds. Pleasant and unpleasant feelings are only figuratively referred to as a ripening, because they are derived from the [actual] karmic ripening.[135]

If [the root text] describes a pleasant feeling as "[one that you desire to be united with again] when it ceases," what about the description that appears in [Vasubandhu's commentary on] dependent origination, which states, "A pleasant feeling is one that you desire not to be separated from when it arises?"[136]

The two descriptions are not incompatible because, in fact, each one implies the other. That is, the statement [describing a pleasant feeling as] "one that you desire not to be separated from when it arises" implicitly indicates that you will desire to be united with it again when it ceases. [Similarly,] the statement, "[A pleasant feeling is] one that you desire to be united with again when it ceases," also implies that you will desire not to be separated from it when it arises.

Well then, consider those ascetics who develop the fetter of desire despite not wanting to, and who subsequently experience a pleasant feeling as a result of that desire. Would they not develop the desire to be separated from that pleasant feeling when it arises and desire not to be joined with it again when it ceases?

Such a reaction is due to the corrupting nature of that feeling; it does not arise from the fact that it is pleasant. Those practitioners regard that kind of pleasant feeling as an obstacle to morality and one-pointed concentration. Therefore, even though such individuals do not develop either of the two kinds of desire that are used to describe the nature of a pleasant feeling, that example does not contravene the original explanation.[137]

Concerning the statement that "an unpleasant experience is one that you desire to be separated from when it arises," [it can also be understood to mean] one that you do not desire to be united with again when it ceases. "Separation" here means [the desire for that feeling] not to continue. The term "desire" means to long for, or to wish for, something.

[As the root texts states,] "An experience that is neither pleasant nor unpleasant is one for which you develop neither of those desires when it occurs."

An experience is pleasant because it enhances the body and mind and has a favorable nature; this is the sense in which it is described [in the root text] as one that you desire to be united with again when it ceases.

An experience is unpleasant because it diminishes the body and mind and has a disagreeable nature; this is the sense in which it is described [in the root text] as one that you desire to be separated from when it arises.

There is also a type of experience in which neither of these characteristics is present—namely, one that is neither pleasant nor unpleasant, like a deed that is neither white nor black. Because it is neither beneficial nor harmful, it is [a type of feeling] for which you develop neither of those desires when it occurs.

Each of these three experiences is also classified as being of six types when distinguished according to their basis,[138] which is to say those that arise from contact with the eye, ear, nose, tongue, body, and mind.

They can also be combined into two groups, according to whether the basis upon which they depend is corporeal or mental. Because the faculties of the eye, ear, nose, and tongue do not exist apart from the body, because they have resistance, and because they are aggregates,[139] they are included within the body and are described as "corporeal." Therefore, the experiences that arise from contact with the eye, ear, nose, tongue, and body are said to be corporeal. Experiences that arise from contact with the mind are described as "mental," because they depend upon a basis that is exclusively mental in nature.

Each experience can also be classified into two pairs of categories that describe them either as obstacles[140] or as antidotes.[141] These are called "associated with corporeal desire" or "free of corporeal desire," as well as "related to greed" or "related to departure."[142]

Corporeal desire[143] is craving for one's individual existence.[144] "Individual existence" refers to the inner grasping heaps.[145] Craving [for one's individual existence] engages [the inner heaps] in a manner that resembles the way in which [a parent] embraces a cherished only child and does not wish to be separated from it. This [form of craving] represents corporal desire. The expression "associated with corporeal desire"[146] means to be accompanied by that attitude. The expression "free from corporeal desire"[147] means not to be accompanied by that craving or to be conducive to a state of separation from it.

Greed[148] is the continuous and repeated manifestation of desire for attractive visible form or any of the other four sense objects. This desire is characterized by anticipation of, devotion to, and yearning for those objects. In short, greed is devotion to and yearning for the sense objects. The expression "related to greed"[149] means either to be dependent on that [greed] or for that greed to be dependent on it.

"Departure" means either absence of attachment[150] for the sense objects or the path leading to that state. The expression "related to departure"[151] means either to be dependent on that [absence of attachment] or for that absence of attachment to be dependent on it.

Thus, the two expressions "associated with corporeal desire" and "free of corporeal desire" are defined as the state of being an obstacle and an antidote, respectively, in connection with the process of freeing oneself from attachment to the perishable collection [through the transcendent path]. Similarly, the expressions "related to greed" and "related to departure" are defined [as the state of being an obstacle and an antidote, respectively,] in connection with the process of freeing oneself from attachment for [various levels of samsara] through the mundane path.

Why does [the root text] only present feelings in terms of their essential nature and not any of the other classifications, such as the different kinds of support [through which they can arise], etc., as are found in other works?

The classifications of feelings according to the different kinds of support, etc., are not presented here because [Vasubandhu's root text] is intended to be an abbreviated presentation and because [the feelings described in] those separate classifications are not different [in kind] from [the three main types that are identified in the classification according to] their essential nature.

THE CONCEPTION HEAP

The next subject for discussion after the feeling heap is the conception heap. Therefore, [the root text] asks, "What is conception," and indicates [its essential nature] with the response, "The grasping of an object's sign."

"Object" means a mental object. "Sign" means that quality of the object that serves as the cause for determining that it is blue or yellow, etc. Thus, to grasp a [particular object's] sign means to make the determination, "This is blue," or "This is yellow," and the like.[152]

In that case, since the specific conception that accompanies eye consciousness or any of the other [forms of sense consciousness] is aconceptual,[153] it must not have the essential nature of grasping an object's sign.

Those [conceptions that accompany sensory consciousness] should definitely be understood as having the essential nature of grasping a sign; however, they are not able to form a judgment[154] because of their dullness.[155] Otherwise, one would not be able make such later [conceptual] determinations as "This is blue," or "This is yellow," since no specific characteristic would previously have been distinguished.[156]

While [all] conceptions have the same essential nature, they are [also] distinguished in relation to their basis and their object. In terms of their basis, they comprise "the six collections of conceptions,"[157] ranging from the conception that arises from contact with the eye up to the conception that arises from contact with the mind.

In terms of their object,[158] there are (1) [conceptions whose objects are] accompanied by signs,[159] (2) [conceptions whose objects are] signless,[160] (3) [conceptions whose objects are] limited,[161] (4) [conceptions whose objects are] great,[162] (5) [conceptions whose objects are] immeasurable,[163] and (6) [conceptions associated with] the Sphere of Nothingness.[164]

In this context, a sign is [a quality] that is ascribed to an object's essential nature on the basis of words. An entity's essence that is accompanied by such a sign is referred to as "that which is accompanied by a sign." The conception that recognizes that an object's ascribed nature is referred to by this or that name is [a conception] whose object is accompanied by a sign.

"Signless" means that which is not associated with any ascribed sign. This [quality] can refer to an object's essence, nirvana, and the Peak of Existence.[165] The three [types of conception that have these objects] are called "signless" because [in the first instance] no sign is ascribed to the object, [in the second instance] no signs of form or feeling are present, and [in the third instance] it is an indistinct state of mind.

A person who has not learned the relationship between words and objects only develops a conception in relation to the essence of an object; he [or she] does not recognize [an instance of form] as something that is called "form," [for instance].[166] Therefore, [the conception] that recognizes such an object is [a conception] whose object lacks a sign.

The sphere of nirvana is a state in which all signs of causally conditioned entities[167] have disappeared. Therefore, the conception accompanying the one-pointed concentration that grasps that object is said to be [a conception] whose object lacks a sign.

The Peak of Existence is signless in the sense that it is an indistinct state of mind. Therefore, the conception of a person who has entered that state of composure is said to be [a conception] whose object lacks a sign, in the sense that it does not form [a clear] sign with respect to its object. In this instance, the conception that is present during this state of mind has an indistinct sign. Therefore, it is called signless in the same manner that a thin woman is described as "[one who] has no belly." It should not be considered signless in the sense that no sign whatsoever is present. Otherwise, it would follow incorrectly that it is not a conception, since the [complete] absence of a sign would mean that the action of grasping a sign does not occur.

A limited [conception] is one that occurs in the desire realm, because that realm is inferior.

A great [conception] is one that occurs in the form realm, because that realm is superior.

An immeasurable [conception] is one that occurs in the spheres of Unlimited Space[168] and Unlimited Consciousness,[169] because [the conceptions that occur there] are boundless.

[A conception associated with] the Sphere of Nothingness is [one that grasps the idea of] nothingness, in the sense that it has no object whatsoever.[170]

Thus, [the conceptions] whose objects occur in the desire realm, etc., are described as a "limited conception," etc.

THE FORMATIONS HEAP

The formations heap is the next subject for discussion after the conception heap. Therefore, to introduce the next topic [the root text] asks, "What are the formations?" and indicates what they are with the response, "The mental factors other than feeling and conception, and the entities that do not accompany consciousness."

All the entities that are included in the heaps of form and the rest are formations in the sense that they are produced by the convergence and combination of conditional factors.[171] In the present context, however, formations are viewed only as those entities that are included in the formations heap. The formations that are included in the form, feeling, and conception heaps have already been explained; those that are included in the consciousness heap will be discussed later.

Of these [formations], the two of feeling and conception are not different from contact, attention, and the rest in the sense that they are also mental factors.[172] However, the phrase "mental factors other than feeling and conception" indicates that while feeling and conception are mental factors, because those two are classified in [their own separate] heaps they are not included in the formations heap.

Feeling is a state of [direct] acquaintance [with an object].[173] Thus, feeling experiences the ripening result of virtuous and nonvirtuous deeds. Conception is the entity that applies expressions [to things].[174] It grasps the signs of entities that are seen, heard, discerned, and known and then applies such everyday expressions to them as "I saw such and such," "I heard such and such," "I discerned such and such," and "I realized such and such." Therefore, feeling and conception in particular are assigned separate heaps, while the other mental factors are not.[175]

If your view is that all the mental factors other than feeling and conception—ranging from contact up to reflection—and those formations that do not accompany consciousness—that is, acquirement and the rest—are included in the formations heap, that contradicts the sutras, because the sutras state, "What is the formations heap? It is the six collections of volition."[176]

[Our position] does not contradict the sutras, because the intent of that statement is to indicate the preeminent importance of volition. The essence of volition is to shape the mind and this is of preeminent importance. Since attention and the other [entities included in the formations heap] conform to volition, it alone was described as constituting the formations heap, for [volition] is the entity that causes the mind to engage in what is virtuous, nonvirtuous, or neutral, as well as what is a source of happiness or suffering.

Because the [individual] mental factors, like the [the meaning of the term] "formations," are also not familiar, [the root text] asks what they are and responds with the statement, "Those entities that are concomitants of consciousness."

Since [the entities that are indicated by that phrase] are not familiar either, [the root text] asks what they are and then responds with the full list that begins "contact, attention," and so on. These mental factors ranging from contact to reflection are concomitants of consciousness because they conform to consciousness and operate in conjunction with it in terms of five kinds of sameness—namely, sameness of basis, object, aspect, time, and substance.[177]

While all the mental factors can be concomitant with consciousness, it does not follow that all of them accompany all instances of consciousness. To dispel this [misconception, the root text states,] "Among these, five are universal, five are limited to a particular object, eleven are virtues, six are [root] mental afflictions, the remaining ones are secondary mental afflictions, and [the final] four" of regret and so on "can also vary."

Among [all] these [mental factors], the first five—contact, attention, feeling, conception, and volition—are universal. These five entities are called "universal"[178] because they accompany all states of consciousness. Thus, they can be concomitant with the virtuous minds of the three realms, with pure states of mind, with nonvirtuous minds of the form realm, as well as with afflicted and neutral minds of the three realms.

All instances of mind necessarily include the convergence of three elements. The convergence of three elements is a property that is necessarily connected with contact. Therefore, contact is a universal mental factor. The mind could not engage any object if it were not "bent" [i.e., turned] in some direction; hence, attention is also a universal mental factor. Feeling and conception are also universal factors, because no mind can function without experiencing something or in the absence of the grasping of a sign. Since volition is activity of the mind, it too must accompany all instances of mind. Therefore, these [five entities] are universal mental factors.

[The root text] states that "five are limited to a particular object."[179] They are limited to a particular object because they only occur in relation to certain objects and not toward all objects. The [five] are aspiration, conviction, recollection, concentration, and wisdom.

[The root text] states that "eleven are virtues." These are [the eleven] that begin with faith and end with avoidance of harm. They are virtues either because they are antidotes to lack of faith and the like or because they occur in concomitance with any of the roots of virtue.[180] The minds with which they are concomitant are also virtuous.

[The root text] states that "six are [root] mental afflictions." They are desire, hatred, pride, ignorance, views, and doubt. They are mental afflictions because they cause the mind to become agitated.

[The root text] states that "the remaining ones are secondary mental afflictions." These are [the twenty mental factors] ranging from anger to lack of vigilance.

[The root text] states that the [last] four [mental factors] of regret and so on "can also vary."

Although [the root text] makes the unqualified statement that "the remaining ones are secondary mental afflictions," this refers only to the group of twenty that ends with lack of vigilance.[181] They are called "secondary mental afflictions" because they are related to the mental afflictions, they cause the mind to become disturbed, and they closely resemble the mental afflictions.[182]

"The four of regret and the rest" means regret, sleep, deliberation, and reflection. To say that they "can also vary" means that they are not only secondary mental afflictions; they can also be virtuous or [morally] indeterminate.[183]

The sum total of these mental factors is fifty-one.

The Individual Mental Factors Explained

Because the nature of these various mental factors is unfamiliar, [the root text] introduces each of them by asking, "What is contact?" "What is attention?" and so on. Because [the root text] intends to present a brief account of this material, it only presents the essential characteristic of each mental factor; it does not describe their actions, which can be found elsewhere.[184] I shall explain the action of the mental factors as well, so that [the mental factors] may be better understood. In keeping with the presentation [that is in the root text], the commentary will first explain the essential nature of each mental factor.[185] Additional points will then also be discussed as [deemed] appropriate for each of the individual mental factors.

The Three Remaining Universal Mental Factors[186]

Contact

[The root text] describes contact with the phrase, "the determination that occurs upon the convergence of three." In the present context, "three" means the three of faculty, object, and consciousness. Their "convergence" means their collective occurrence in terms of being related to one another by cause and effect.[187]

When this occurs, the faculty present at that moment takes on a modification that is consistent with [the arising of] a particular type of feeling—namely, one that is pleasant, unpleasant, or neutral. By conforming to that modification of the faculty, contact is described as determining the aspect of the object that is to be experienced as pleasant, unpleasant, or neutral.

Moreover, the "modification"[188] of the faculty means that quality by which it becomes the cause of a pleasant, unpleasant, or neutral feeling. By taking on a character that conforms to that modification, contact is said to make contact with the faculty. Alternatively, this is said to describe the process by which contact undergoes contact with the faculty.

Its action is to serve as the support for feelings.[189] As the sutras state, "A pleasant feeling arises in dependence on a contact that will bring about a pleasant experience."

Attention

[The root text] asks, "What is attention?" and then responds, "The bending of the mind." Bending[190] is that which causes something to bend. Bending of the mind is the condition by which the mind is directed toward an object.

Its action is to cause the mind to keep hold of an object.[191] Causing the mind to keep hold of an object means to repeatedly turn the mind toward it. Moreover, this description of its action is made in the sense of a particular kind of attention—namely, one that causes the continuum of the mind to remain fixed upon an object. It is not meant in terms of individual moments of the mind.[192] This point is illustrated by the expression "one who has attained attention has attained one-pointed concentration." The phrase "one who has attained attention" means [a meditation practitioner] who has attained an extraordinary kind of attention. Otherwise, since every moment of consciousness includes the mental factor of attention, it would follow incorrectly that all sentient beings have attained attention.

Volition

[The root text] asks, "What is volition?" and then responds, "It is the shaping of consciousness in relation to that which is good, bad, or neither; and it is activity of the mind."

"Good" refers to virtuous entities, "bad" to nonvirtuous ones, and "neither" to those that are morally indeterminate. Alternatively, "good" means those entities that are beneficial, "bad" means those that are harmful, and "neither" means those that are different from the preceding two.

"The shaping of consciousness"[193] means [the activity of] setting the mind in motion; it is that entity whose presence causes the mind to flow toward an object, like the movement of iron filings that is caused by a magnet.

As a verse describes:

> Volition is the action of the mind
> That causes the inactive mind,
> Which exists but an instant,
> To appear to be active.

If volition is described as "the shaping of consciousness," why is it also said to be "activity of the mind"[194]?

Since all the mental factors [help to] shape the mind, volition is described as activity of the mind in order to distinguish it from the other mental factors. Thus, the additional qualification is to suggest that volition alone is the entity that causes the mind to flow outward.

The action [of volition] is revealed by the description that it is the "shaping of consciousness in relation to that which is good, bad, or neither."[195] Its essential nature is indicated by the phrase, "It is activity of the mind."

The Five Mental Factors That Have Specific Objects

Aspiration

[The root text] asks, "What is aspiration?" and then responds, "The desire for an object that has been thought about."

The reason for saying that the object must be one that "has been thought about" is to make clear that no aspiration can develop toward something that has not been thought about. Thus, it indicates the quality that aspiration [only] occurs in relation to a particular kind of object.

An entity that has been thought about is one that has been considered as a possible object for such actions as seeing, hearing, and the like. Thus, [aspiration is] a desire for and an eagerness to see, hear, etc., some particular thing.

If the essence of aspiration is desire, what is the difference between craving[196] and aspiration?

The difference is that the essential characteristic of craving is intense attachment,[197] while that of aspiration is [a kind of] desire [that wishes for something].

The action [of aspiration] is that it serves as a support for generating effort.[198]

Conviction

In response to the question, "What is conviction?" [the root text] declares, "The certitude that an object about which a determination has been made exists in just that manner."

The object is described as one "about which a determination has been made" in order to make clear that not all things can become the object of conviction. That is, if no determination has been reached about an object, it is not possible to [have a sense of] certitude [that it exists] in just that manner.

A determination[199] is the freedom from doubt about an object that is gained through reasoning or trustworthy scripture. It is the strong adherence by the mind to a determination that has been made about some aspect of an object, such as its impermanence or its suffering [nature]. Conviction is the [sense of] certitude that [some particular object exists] in that [very] manner and not any other.

Its action is [to endow an individual with] the quality of being incapable of being led astray,[200] because the person who values conviction cannot be persuaded by adherents of another philosophical system to give up [his or her] own beliefs.

Recollection

In response to the question, "What is recollection?" the root text declares, "The avoidance of inattentiveness toward a familiar object; a mental discourse."

The term "familiar"[201] indicates that there can be no recollection of an object that is unfamiliar. A familiar object is one that was previously experienced.

"Avoidance of inattentiveness"[202] means the quality that enables you to keep from losing hold of a mental object. It [also] means to recall again and again as a mental object some entity that was previously understood.[203]

The phrase "a state of [mental] discourse" means that [recollection] resembles [verbal] discourse. A state of discourse is simply the activity of discourse. When there is discourse with a [particular] mental object, the mind will not be distracted to a different mental object or a different aspect [of the same object]. Therefore, the action [of recollection] is to prevent distraction.[204]

Concentration

In response to the question, "What is concentration?" [the root text] declares, "One-pointedness of mind toward an object that is being closely examined." [The description of the object as one] "that is being closely examined"[205] indicates [that concentration] will not [be achieved] otherwise. Thus, concentration is also being presented as a mental factor that has a specific object.

The phrase "an object that is being closely examined" refers to [those objects that are closely examined] with regard to having good qualities or bad qualities.

"One-pointedness of mind" means the state of holding a single object in the mind. Thus the single point [referred to in the term "one-pointedness"] is the mental object.

The action of concentration is to provide support for knowledge,[206] [as the scriptures state,] "Because complete and true knowledge occurs when the mind is well composed."[207]

The objects that receive close examination are the Four [Noble] Truths. The Truth of Cessation is examined with regard to its aspects of being a state of peace,[208] and the rest; and the Truth of the Path is examined with regard to its aspects of leading to deliverance,[209] and the rest. Thus, the Truth of Cessation and the Truth of the Path represent objects that have good qualities.

The Truth of Suffering is examined with regard to its aspects of impermanence,[210] and the rest; and the Truth of Origination is examined with regard to its aspects of being a cause[211] [of the five grasping heaps], and the rest. The Truth of Suffering and the Truth of Origination represent objects that have bad qualities.

Similarly, in relation to the nine levels,[212] the lower ones are regarded as having bad qualities and the higher ones as having good qualities.

The topic of what objects receive close examination can also be explained in a suitable manner with regard to the unique and general characteristics of various other types of meditation objects.

Wisdom

In response to the question, "What is wisdom?" [the root text] declares, "Discrimination with respect to that same object, whether it is generated correctly, incorrectly, or otherwise."

The phrase "That same object" means the very same "object that is closely examined." Thus, wisdom is also being indicated as having a specific object, as was the case with concentration.

Discrimination[213] is that which discriminates. It is an awareness that makes distinctions,[214] correctly or incorrectly, with regard to entities whose general and specific characteristics have the appearance of being mixed together.

"Correct" means proper; and it refers to trustworthy scripture, inference, or direct perception. The discrimination that is produced in any of these three ways is "generated correctly." Furthermore, it can be derived from listening, reflection, or meditation. The realization that is gained on the authority of trustworthy scripture is wisdom derived from listening. The realization that arises from the contemplation of reasons is wisdom derived from reflection. The realization that arises from one-pointed concentration is wisdom derived from meditation.

"Incorrect" refers to scripture that is not trustworthy, to faulty inference, and to one-pointed concentration that is wrongly directed. [The discrimination] that is produced from any of these incorrect means is [discrimination] that has been "generated incorrectly." The discrimination that followers of the Saṃkhya, Vaiśeṣika, and other such schools derive from listening and reflection is incorrectly generated, because it is based on untrustworthy scripture and bad reasoning. The discrimination of those who have attained absence of attachment,[215] but who are proponents of eternalism or nihilism, or who adhere to a particular form of eternalism, is incorrectly generated, because it results from one-pointed concentration that is wrongly directed.

The discrimination that is gained from birth or that is related to knowledge of worldly affairs is neither correctly generated nor incorrectly generated.

The action of wisdom is to remove doubt,[216] because the removal of doubt occurs when a person gains certainty in relation to entities by applying to them wisdom's discriminative power.[217]

The Eleven Virtues

Faith

In response to the question, "What is faith?" [the root text] declares, "Belief, clarity of mind, or aspiration toward karma and its results, the [Four Noble] Truths, and the [Three] Jewels."

There are three kinds of karma: good, bad, and unvarying. Of these, bad [karma] is associated with the desire realm exclusively, because it occurs in conjunction with nonvirtuous states of mind. Good [karma] also is associated with the desire realm exclusively, because the manner of its ripening is not fixed. Unvarying [karma] is that which is constant in relation to its ripening.

The ripening of bad karma is that ripening of the desire realm which is disagreeable. The ripening of good karma is that ripening of the desire realm which is agreeable. The ripening of unvarying karma is that ripening of the form and formless realms which is agreeable.

The faith that believes in the two kinds of karma and their results is the belief[218] that there is such a thing as virtuous and nonvirtuous karma, and that their results are agreeable and disagreeable, respectively. Moreover, this belief holds that those two results are caused by virtuous and nonvirtuous karma, and they are not governed by Iśvara or any other supposed entity of that kind. Thus, the faith that believes in two kinds of karma and their results is the belief that the unerring nature of karma and its results is that the two kinds of karmic ripenings are governed by a relation of cause and effect.

The [Four Noble] Truths are those of suffering, origination, cessation, and the path. The Truth of Suffering is the aspect of the five grasping heaps that constitutes a result. [It is suffering] because the Aryas recognize it as being adverse and [it is a truth] because its aspects of impermanence and the rest are not mistaken.

The Truth of Origination is the aspect of the five grasping heaps that constitutes a cause. [It is an origination] because it is the cause of suffering and [it is a truth] because its aspects of being a condition and the rest are not erroneous.

The Truth of Cessation is the state in which suffering has been terminated. [It is a cessation] because it is a state in which suffering and its causes have been terminated and [it is a truth] because its aspects of being a state of peace and the rest are not erroneous.

The Truth of the Path is the Eightfold Noble Path. [It is a path] because it leads to the cessation of suffering and [it is a truth] because its aspects of leading to deliverance, and the rest, are not erroneous.

Faith toward the two truths of suffering and origination is the belief that both suffering and the origination of suffering exist. Faith toward the two truths of cessation and the path is the aspiration[219] in which it is believed, "I can achieve cessation" and "I can develop the path."

The Jewels are three in number: Buddha, Dharma, and Sangha. They are characterized as jewels because they resemble [ordinary] jewels by their rarity and great value as well as their ability to engender joy, provide benefit, and counteract the harm of spirits and other beings.

The rarity of the Buddha Jewel is illustrated by the fact that Bodhisattvas, who are indifferent to both their life and body because they have no attachment to samsara or wealth, must devote themselves uninterruptedly to the task of accumulating the requisites for enlightenment over three [vast intervals of time, each of which comprises a] "countless" number of kalpas,[220] in order to achieve the goal of Buddhahood. Thus, the appearance of a Buddha is described as being as rare as that of the *uḍumbara* flower.[221] Since the appearance of the Dharma Jewel and Sangha Jewel is dependent on that of the Buddha, they too should be understood as rare.

The great value of the Buddha Jewel stems from the fact that those who have achieved the state that is the fulfillment of all one's aims[222] do so by means of the two accumulations of merit and wisdom. The merit accumulation[223] is made up of the perfections of generosity, morality, and patience. The wisdom accumulation[224] is made up of the perfections of wisdom and meditative absorption. Because the perfection of effort forms part of [both] the merit and the wisdom accumulations, it is included in both accumulations. The Dharma Jewel is of great value because it is achieved by giving up [attachment for] all conditioned entities. The Sangha Jewel is of great value because it is superior to the acquisition of any samsaric gain and it is achieved through the two accumulations of merit and wisdom.

The Three Jewels are said to engender joy because they are a cause of joy—which is to say that they bring joy to those who see, hear, or recollect them.

The Three Jewels provide benefit in that they are beneficial to those who carry out the activities of approaching, serving, seeking, and gaining full knowledge with regard to them. This is described in the following lines:

> Approaching you brings fortune;
> Honoring [you] brings happiness;
> Seeking [you] out brings wisdom;
> Full knowledge [of you] brings purity.[225]

The quelling of harm caused by evil spirits as well as other beings is described in the following passage from a sutra: "O monks, when you are staying in a forest . . . that fear, apprehension, or terror will disappear."[226] Similar remarks also are made in relation to recollection of the Dharma Jewel and recollection of the Sangha Jewel.

A Buddha is one who has achieved the transcendent state in which one's knowledge has the power to move freely and without obstruction in relation to all objects of knowledge, and [the transcendent state] in which the seeds of all impure entities have been eliminated and the seeds of all pure entities have been fully developed. Because a Buddha possesses unlimited power, he can accomplish the interests of all sentient beings effortlessly, like a wish-granting gem.

The Dharma is threefold: the Dharma of instruction, which includes the scriptural divisions of the sutra, mixed verse and prose, and the rest[227]; the Dharma of practice, which is the Eightfold Noble Path along with its retinue; and the ultimate Dharma, which is nirvana. The latter also has two aspects: the nirvana in which the support of the heaps still remains[228] and the nirvana in which the support of the heaps does not remain.[229] The nirvana in which the mental afflictions have been terminated is [the aspect of nirvana] in which the support of the heaps still remains. The nirvana in which, following the end of the present rebirth, no future rebirth occurs is [the aspect of nirvana] in which the support of the heaps does not remain.

The Sangha is made up of eight types of person, four of whom are striving after a fruit and four of whom are abiding in a fruit.[230] They are referred to as a Sangha because they cannot be divided from one another or from the Master [Buddha Śākyamuni].

Faith in the Lord Buddha is the clarity of mind that is demonstrated by a bristling of the body hair or the flowing of tears and is felt toward that object which has perfected all virtuous qualities and completely removed all faults.

Faith in the Dharma is clarity of mind toward [that state which is] the termination of suffering and its cause,[231] as well as that which directly brings the attainment [of that state][232] or that which elucidates [either of those two].[233]

Faith in the Sangha is clarity of mind toward those who have escaped from the mire of samsara and those who are traversing the path that will free them from the mire of samsara.

[To summarize,] there are three types of faith: the type that believes in entities that do exist and are either possessed of good qualities or bad qualities; the type that is clarity of mind toward entities that do exist and are possessed of good qualities; and the type that desires to achieve or develop those entities possessed of good qualities that are capable of being achieved or developed.

Since the latter type is a form of desire, would it not then be either craving or aspiration?

It is not either one. It is not craving, because it has a virtuous entity as its object. Nor is it aspiration, because aspiration must be preceded by faith.

The type of faith that is called clarity of mind is a quality that opposes turbidity of mind. Therefore, if the mind is accompanied by it, the turbidity of the [root] mental afflictions and the secondary mental afflictions will not arise. It is called "clarity of mind" because the presence of faith causes the mind to become clear and bright. This clarity [of mind] is a mental factor that resembles the [special] jewel that can cause water to become clear. It is described as clarity of mind to indicate that it does not have the nature of clear form,[234] since it is not form. Its action is to serve as a support for aspiration.[235]

Shame

In response to the question, "What is shame?" [the root text] declares, "Embarrassment about objectionable acts for reasons relating to oneself or the Dharma."

Whatever thing or person affects whether someone engages in or refrains from an activity is said to relate to that activity, which is to say that it influences it.

An objectionable act[236] is one that is evil, because it is reproached by those who are wise and because it has an undesirable maturation.

Embarrassment[237] is the sense of dejection that is felt with regard an objectionable act—whether it was committed or not—for reasons relating to oneself or the Dharma. Because of such things as one's family standing or knowledge, a person who knows that it is wrong to commit evil deeds might think, "How could one such as I commit this kind of evil deed, now or in the future!" or [this person] might think, "This kind of evil deed is reprehensible from the perspective of the Dharma, because it has an undesirable maturation and because it constitutes the doing of harm to another." Thus, shame is the embarrassment that is felt toward an objectionable act out of regard for oneself or the Dharma, as illustrated in the situations just described. Its action is to provide the support [that allows you] to restrain yourself from committing misdeeds.[238]

Abashment

In response to the question, "What is abashment?" [the root text] declares, "Embarrassment about objectionable acts for reasons relating to the world."

For such reasons as fear of disrepute, a person might feel embarrassment about an objectionable act and think, "This act is despised in the world. I would be despised if it became known that I had done such an act." This type of embarrassment also has the action of providing the support [that allows you] to restrain yourself from committing misdeeds.

Shame can bring restraint even after you have committed a misdeed, because it can compel you to stop doing misdeeds. Therefore, shame and abashment have the action of supporting restraint even after you have committed a misdeed, because they can compel you to stop doing misdeeds. Abashment also restrains you from doing misdeeds when you have not committed them. Therefore, [shame and abashment] both have this supporting action as well; indeed, they are conditions that necessarily precede restraint.

Avoidance of Attachment

With regard to [the root text's] question, "What is avoidance of attachment?" the expression "avoidance of attachment"[239] can be applied to three types of entity: the nonexistence of attachment; something that is distinct from attachment; and an antidote to attachment. To indicate that in the present context the term applies to an antidote to attachment and not to its nonexistence or something distinct from it, the response in the root text states that it is "the antidote to desire." This description applies in a similar way to avoidance of hatred and avoidance of ignorance.

The phrase "dissatisfaction and freedom from acquisitiveness"[240] makes known its essential nature. Attachment is an attraction to and desire for samsaric existence and the things that sustain samsaric existence.[241] Avoidance of attachment is the antidote for that [attraction and desire]. That is, it is the lack of desire and disgust for samsaric existence and the things that sustain samsaric existence. "Dissatisfaction" is an aversion for samsaric existence and the things that sustain it, [a feeling] that derives from having developed a thorough knowledge of their disadvantages. "Freedom from acquisitiveness" is freedom from attachment for both samsaric existence and the things that sustain it.

Alternatively, the term "dissatisfaction" is expressed to indicate a particular form of freedom from acquisitiveness. In that case, avoidance of attachment refers to the form of freedom from acquisitiveness that is an aversion for samsaric existence and the things that sustain it.

Its action is to provide support for the avoidance of misdeeds.[242]

Avoidance of Hatred

In response to the question, "What is avoidance of hatred?" [the root text] declares, "The antidote to hatred—[that is to say,] loving-kindness."

Hatred is animosity[243] toward beings, suffering, and those entities that cause suffering. The antidote to that is the avoidance of animosity. Because there are other antidotes to hatred, it is described here specifically as loving-kindness. Thus, avoidance of hatred should be understood as being that antidote to hatred which has the nature of loving-kindness; it should not be recognized as being anything other than that. Its action is to provide support for the avoidance of misdeeds.

Avoidance of Ignorance

In response to the question, "What is avoidance of ignorance?" [the root text] declares, "The antidote to ignorance—[that is to say,] the correct understanding of things as they truly are."

All virtuous entities are antidotes to afflicted entities in that they oppose their arising. Therefore, the root text states that [avoidance of ignorance] is "the correct understanding of things as they truly are." [That is to say,] it is the unerring comprehension of things as they truly are.

That comprehension is distinguished as being of two types: knowledge and consideration. Knowledge[244] is of four types, as distinguished by its causes of maturation, scripture, reflection, and realization.[245] Consideration[246] is wisdom together with firmness. "Firmness"[247] is a term that can refer to wisdom, effort, and one-pointed concentration. Since it is not possible for two forms of wisdom to accompany one another, "consideration" refers to wisdom that is accompanied by effort or one-pointed concentration. It means the strength that enables you not to give way to the mental afflictions even when their seeds have not yet been eradicated or destroyed.

Here, then, is the meaning of the description [that appears in the root text]: avoidance of ignorance is a particular form of discernment that has the nature of either knowledge or consideration of the way things truly are. Thus, the action [of avoidance of ignorance] is to provide support for the avoidance of misdeeds.

Effort

In response to the question, "What is effort?" [the root text] declares, "The antidote to laziness—[that is to say,] the exertion of the mind toward virtue." With regard to this [description], laziness is inferior endeavor. That is to say, it is to engage in idleness, which is a lack of exertion toward both virtuous and nonvirtuous objects. Effort is the antidote to this [laziness]. To exclude the possibility that effort might apply to the same two [types of object] that idleness does, [the root text further] states that effort is "the exertion of the mind toward virtue"; it is not exertion toward an afflicted object. Because exertion toward an afflicted object is contemptible, it is [considered a form of] laziness.[248]

One might ask, "What need is there to make an exertion toward an afflicted object, since one's continuous and repeated practice of such activities would lead one to engage in them effortlessly?" While that is true for the most part, there are nevertheless some instances where those activities require exertion.

Moreover, depending upon the qualities that accompany it, effort can be described as "armor-like," "endeavoring," "dauntless," "unrelenting," and "unquenchable."[249] Effort is the exertion of the mind toward a variety of other virtuous objects as well. Its action is to accomplish and complete [all practices] that are virtuous in nature.[250] To "accomplish" [a virtuous practice] refers to [the effort that is applied in order] to enter the main stage [of a particular spiritual level]. To "complete" [a virtuous practice] refers to [the effort that] perfects the spiritual exercises[251] [that pertain to a particular level].

Agility

In response to the question, "What is agility?" [the root text] declares, "The antidote to indisposition—[that is to say,] fitness of body and mind."

Indisposition[252] is a condition of the body and mind. [Indisposition] of the body is a state of unfitness while [indisposition] of the mind is the seeds of afflicted entities.[253] Agility is an antidote to indisposition in the sense that it is present when the other has disappeared.

The essential characteristic of agility is fitness[254] of body and mind. Regarding that, fitness of the body is that condition of the body which enables it to engage in activities readily. Fitness of the mind is a distinct mental factor that serves as a cause for bringing delight and facility to a mind that is accompanied by right attention.[255] It is called "fitness of the mind" because the mind that possesses this mental factor is able to engage an object in an unhindered manner.

Agility of the body, further, should be understood as a particular tangible object of the body that is elicited by joy, since a sutra declares, "A joyful mind puts the body at rest."[256] Although agility of the body is not a mental factor, since the present subject is the mental factors the term should be understood here as it is explained in the context of the enlightenment limb of agility.[257] Alternatively, because fitness of body brings about fitness of mind, agility of body is mentioned here as fitness of body even though it is not a mental factor.

The action [of agility] is to eliminate all the obscurations of the mental afflictions and the rest, in the sense that it has the power to bring about a transformation of one's being.[258]

Mindfulness

In response to the question, "What is mindfulness?" [the root text] declares, "The antidote to lack of mindfulness—[that is to say,] the abandoning of nonvirtuous entities together with the cultivating of those virtuous entities that are their antidotes, on the basis of those mental factors ranging from avoidance of attachment to effort."

Lack of mindfulness is [a state] that fails to protect the mind from the mental afflictions and diminishes virtuous entities. [By contrast,] mindfulness abandons the mental afflictions and cultivates the entities that are their antidotes. Therefore, mindfulness is described as the antidote to lack of mindfulness.

The phrase "ranging from avoidance of attachment to effort" refers to [the four mental factors of] avoidance of attachment, avoidance of hatred, avoidance of ignorance, and effort.

The phrase "the abandoning of nonvirtuous entities . . . on the basis of" [those mental factors] ranging from avoidance of attachment, and so on, up to effort means to do so in dependence on and in reliance on them. This indicates that all those mental factors of avoidance of attachment and the rest can [in the appropriate circumstances] constitute mindfulness.

The expression "nonvirtuous entities" should be understood to mean the mental afflictions and those objects that support the mental afflictions. To "abandon" the mental afflictions means to overcome them, to destroy them, and to completely eradicate them.[259] The objects of the mental afflictions are abandoned by rejecting them.

The phrase "their antidotes" means the antidotes to those nonvirtuous entities. It refers to both impure and pure virtuous entities. To "cultivate" those virtuous entities means to practice them and to bring them into being repeatedly.

Thus, mindfulness is the term that is nominally ascribed to [the three roots of virtue of] avoidance of attachment and the rest, together with effort, because it is on the basis of these [four] mental factors that nonvirtuous entities are abandoned and virtuous ones are cultivated. This explanation indicates that mindfulness is a case in which a term is ascribed to those entities that constitute its basis and its cause.

Its action is to culminate all mundane and transcendent excellence.[260] "Mundane excellence" means to attain a superior state in samsaric existence and superior forms of those qualities that sustain samsaric existence.[261] "Transcendent excellence" means to attain the enlightenment of the Listeners' Vehicle or that of any of the other vehicles.

Equanimity

In response to the question, "What is equanimity?" [the root text] declares [in part], ". . . on the basis of those very same mental factors ranging from avoidance of attachment to effort." Thus, the explanation [of this phrase] that was given with regard to mindfulness applies here as well.

The three expressions "evenness of mind . . ." and so on illustrate equanimity in a beginning, middle, and final stage. Languor and excitation are uneven states of mind. The initial stage in which they are absent is called "evenness of mind."[262] Following that, there occurs a stage of "inactivity"[263] in which the mind engaged in meditative absorption is able to function appropriately and evenly without the need to take any action or exert any effort. [However,] during this period there is still some concern that languor or excitation might occur, because the practitioner has not been meditating very long. The period following this is one in which there is no concern that either of those two [faults] might occur, because the practitioner's meditation has reached a degree of excellence and he [or she] has greatly distanced himself [or herself] from those obstacles. At this point, the practitioner is able to remain in a state of "effortlessness"[264] in that he [or she] does not need to make any exertion in relation to the causes that constitute the antidotes to languor and excitation.

In the phrase, "that [mental factor] which, having dispelled afflicted entities . . . ," "that which" refers to equanimity. "Afflicted entities" means those that are related to desire and the other [mental afflictions]. To "dispel" those [afflicted entities] means to prevent them from arising again. Because equanimity is incompatible with an afflicted state of mind, it is certain that it will not give desire and the other mental afflictions an opportunity to arise. That is why it is said to "dispel" afflicted entities.

Accordingly, because abiding in an afflicted [state of mind] is incompatible with equanimity, to abide in equanimity means to abide in an unafflicted state of mind. For that very reason, the action of equanimity is to provide support for preventing the occurrence of any afflicted [entities].[265]

Avoidance of Harm

In response to the question, "What is avoidance of harm?" [the root text] declares, "The antidote to harmfulness—[that is to say,] compassion."

Avoidance of harm refers to [the mental state] that [causes one to] avoid hurting or doing injury to sentient beings, by such acts as killing or binding them.[266]

The antidote to harmfulness is identified as compassion,[267] which is interpreted literally as meaning "that which prevents ease."[268] "Ease"[269] is a term that means happiness. Thus, compassion means that which keeps one from being happy in the sense that a compassionate person is made unhappy by the suffering of others.

This [mental factor], like mindfulness, exists only nominally. It is ascribed to a form of avoidance of hatred; therefore it is not [a distinct,] substantially real [entity].

The action [of avoidance of harm] is to prevent the inflicting of injury.[270]

This concludes the explanation of the eleven virtuous mental factors.

The Six Root Mental Afflictions

The next topic for discussion is the six [root] mental afflictions.

Desire

In response to the question, "What is desire?" [the root text] declares, "Strong affection for, and attachment to, the five grasping heaps."

Impure form, feeling, conception, formations, and consciousness are the five grasping heaps of form, feeling, conception, formations, and consciousness. The grasping heap of form is the form that is found in [the first] two of the [three] realms. The four grasping heaps of feelings and the rest are the feelings, etc., that are found in all three realms. Craving[271] is referred to as "grasping" either because it causes a being to take birth in [any of] the three levels of [samsaric] existence or because it takes hold of the karma that brings rebirth.

The term "grasping heaps" is interpreted as meaning either that the impure heaps originate from grasping, or that they are governed by grasping, or that grasping arises from them.[272]

Affection[273] is similar to [the physical property of] viscosity.[274] Just as sesame oil or any other oily substance that comes in contact with, and penetrates into, cloth or some other absorbent material is difficult to remove, even though great effort is made to do so, desire also is a kind of affection that adheres to the objects that it comes in contact with and is very difficult to separate from them.

Attachment[275] has the very same nature [as affection]. Or else, the purpose of the term "attachment" is to clarify that affection, as it is being used here, does not mean the stickiness that is the tangible object of the same name.

The action of desire is to give rise to suffering.[276] The term "suffering" as it is being used here refers to the five heaps of the three realms, in that they represent, according to circumstances, any of the three types of suffering.[277]

Moreover, that suffering is produced by the power of craving for the desire, form, and formless [realms]. This is the reason that the action of desire is explained as being to give rise to suffering.

Hatred

In response to the question, "What is hatred?" [the root text] declares, "Animosity toward sentient beings."

Animosity[278] is a harshness of mind toward sentient beings that, if you are overcome by it, will cause you to consider engaging in such wrongful conduct as killing or binding sentient beings.[279]

Its action is to support [both] remaining in a discontented state and engaging in misdeeds.[280] A contented state[281] means a state of happiness; to remain in that state means to remain contented. To remain discontented means not to remain in a contented state—that is to say, it means to remain in an unsatisfactory state. A person who is feeling animosity will necessarily have a tormented mind, because [he or she] is subjecting [himself or herself] to mental distress. Because the body is influenced by the mind, [his or her] body will become distressed as well. [He or she] will also remain discontented in the sense that all [his or her] activities will be accompanied by unhappiness and failure. A person with a hostile mind is never far from every sort of misdeed. For these reasons, the action of hatred is described as being to support [both] remaining in a discontented state and engaging in misdeeds.

Pride

In response to the question, "What is pride?" [the root text begins by] responding, "There are seven types of pride." Concerning this, all pride occurs on the basis of the perishable collection view.[282] Its essential characteristic is a swelling up of the mind.[283] That is to say, after incorrectly ascribing the nature of an "I" and a "mine" to the five heaps, the mind forms the notions "I am this" and "this is mine." Then, on the basis of various characteristics, the mind elevates that self and considers it to be superior to others.

Its action is to give support to both disrespectfulness and the engendering of suffering.[284] Disrespectfulness is a haughtiness of mind and irreverence of body and speech toward those deserving of veneration and those endowed with good qualities. The phrase "the engendering of suffering" should be understood here as meaning to bring about rebirth.

While pride does not vary in that its essential nature is a swelling up of the mind, it is distinguished as being of seven types on the basis of the causes that produce that swelling up of the mind. [These seven are the ones identified in the root text as] pride, extraordinary pride, and so on.[285]

Ordinary pride

[Ordinary] pride is the swelling up of the mind in which you think of someone who is inferior to you in [his or her] social class, knowledge, or wealth, etc., "I am better [than him or her] because of my social class, knowledge, or wealth, etc." It is also the swelling up of the mind in which you think of someone who is similar to you in [his or her] social class, etc., "I am [his or her] equal."

Extraordinary pride

Extraordinary pride is the swelling up of the mind in which you think of someone who is your equal in [his or her] social class, knowledge, or wealth, etc., "I am better [than him or her] because of my [greater] generosity, morality, or courage." It is also the swelling up of the mind in which you think of someone who is superior to you in [his or her] social class, knowledge, or wealth, etc., "I am [his or her] equal."

Extreme pride

Extreme pride is the swelling up of the mind in which you think of someone who is superior to you in [his or her] social class, knowledge, or wealth, etc., "I am better [than him or her] in social class, knowledge, or wealth, etc."

Egoistic pride

The root text describes egoistic pride as occurring in relation to the grasping heaps. The term "grasping"[286] refers to aspiration and desire. Aspiration[287] means desire for a future existence. Desire[288] is attachment. Thus, you grasp at a future existence in the sense of longing for it, and you grasp at your present heaps in the sense that your desire for them makes you not want to give them up. Therefore, these two attitudes are called "grasping." The heaps that are associated with them are the grasping heaps.

Egoistic pride, then, is the swelling up of the mind that originates from the mistaken notion that the five grasping heaps—which are devoid of a self and do not belong to a self—constitute a self and belong to a self.

Exaggerated pride

In response to the question, "What is exaggerated pride?" [the root text] declares, "The swelling up of the mind in which you think toward a higher special attainment that you have not achieved, 'I have achieved it.'"

Regarding that description, [ordinary] human qualities are desire, hatred, ignorance, and the like, as well as the karma of body, speech, and mind that they produce. Their antidotes are [such qualities as] the meditative absorptions,[289] the states of mental composure,[290] and the like. These latter [states of one-pointed concentration] are referred to as "higher special [qualities]" in comparison to [ordinary] human qualities. Their "attainment" means their acquisition. Thus, exaggerated pride is the swelling up of the mind that occurs when you think, in relation to a higher special attainment that can be acquired but is not in your possession, "I have achieved that extraordinary higher attainment."

Pride of inferiority

Pride of inferiority is the swelling up of the mind in which you think of someone who is very much superior to you in [his or her] social class, knowledge, or wealth, etc., "I am only slightly inferior [to him or her] in [my] social class, etc."

Now then, those situations in which you think of someone who is your equal, "I am [his or her] equal," or of someone who is your equal, "I am better [than him or her]," or of someone who is superior to you, "I am better [than him or her]," can properly constitute pride, because they are circumstances in which a swelling up of the mind might well occur. But how could a situation in which you view yourself as inferior be one in which a swelling up of the mind might occur such that it could [rightly] be called pride?

In this instance, the person regards himself [or herself] as only slightly inferior to someone who is very much superior to him [or her]; he [or she] does not view himself [or herself] as inferior to a very great degree. Therefore, it does indeed represent a situation in which a swelling up of the mind can occur. Moreover, it is also possible for someone to think much of himself [or herself] when in the company of excellent persons that he [or she] regards highly, even though he [or she] is inferior to them.[291]

Wrong pride

In response to the question, "What is wrong pride?" [the root text] declares, "The swelling up of the mind in which you think, 'I possess good qualities,' when you are not someone who possesses good qualities."

Good qualities are generosity, morality, patience, and the rest. The person who lacks such qualities is "not someone who possesses good qualities." Alternatively, immorality and the like are not good qualities, and the person who possesses such bad qualities is "not someone who possesses good qualities." Therefore, when a person thinks to himself, "I possess good qualities," and believes that he possesses good qualities even though he lacks morality and the rest, this is called "wrong pride," because it is [an attitude] that is based on what is unreal.

Ignorance

In response to the question, "What is ignorance?" [the root text] declares, "Absence of knowledge with regard to karma and its results, the [Four Noble] Truths, and the [Three] Jewels; moreover, it is innate and contrived."

"Innate"[292] ignorance is that which is not commingled with—that is, not concomitant with—other mental afflictions. "Contrived"[293] ignorance is that which is concomitant with such mental afflictions as doubt, wrong view, and the view that one's conduct and asceticism are supreme.

The "absence of knowledge with regard to karma" that is an innate form of ignorance is the absence of knowledge that good, bad, and unvarying karma do in fact exist. It is a lack of awareness and a lack of understanding.

[The following are examples of "absence of knowledge with regard to karma" that are] contrived [forms of ignorance]: (1) [the ignorance that is] concomitant with uncertainty and is uncertain about the existence of good, bad, and unvarying karma; (2) [the ignorance that is] concomitant with wrong view and denies that good, bad, and unvarying karma exist; and (3) [the ignorance of] those who conceive of what is virtuous as nonvirtuous and engage in such practices as animal sacrifice and suicide by fire, as well as [the ignorance of] those who conceive of what is nonvirtuous as virtuous and engage in such practices as animal sacrifice and suicide by fire.[294]

The action [of ignorance] is to provide support for the arising of wrong determinations, doubt, and states of affliction with regard to entities.[295]

The Five Views

Wisdom that has the nature of a judgment is called a "view."[296] Thus, since the unwanted consequence would follow that the worldly correct view and the like[297] would be included among the [afflicted] views, the root text states that "there are five views" in order to indicate that the term is being used here to refer to the five [afflicted] views that are known as "the perishable collection view," and the rest. Moreover, while they do not differ in that they are all afflicted in nature, they are identified as the "perishable collection view" and so on, in order indicate that they differ in terms of having different objects and different ways of holding their object.

The perishable collection view

To be "perishable"[298] means to undergo destruction.[299] To be a "collection"[300] means to be an assemblage of things.[301]

This view that is described as occurring in relation to a multitude of perishable entities indicates by its very name that there is neither [a real self that can be viewed as] an "I" nor [any entities that are] "mine" [in the sense that they pertain to such a self]. Those who profess a doctrine of a real self believe that the self is both permanent and a unity. Because the object of this [view] is [described as being] impermanent and multiple, it makes clear that its object is not such a self.

With regard to the description of the perishable collection view that it "[regards] the five grasping heaps as . . ." and so on, the sutras state the following: "Whatever ascetics or brahmins perceive an 'I' or a 'mine,' all of them perceive nothing but these five grasping heaps." [In relation to this,] those [who adhere to a real self] ascribe the existence of the self either in terms of its essential nature or in terms of its results.

The Sāṃkhyas consider the self to have the essential nature of a "knowing existent." Moreover, because they are not skilled in the classifications of consciousness and mental factors, they declare the collection of consciousness and mental factors as a whole to be this knowing existent. Hence, they recognize four heaps as constituting the self and the form heap as belonging to that self. [Moreover, a person's] ordinary understanding cannot describe or recognize this separate knowing existent, which is distinct from the operation of intellect.[302]

Certain Nirgranthas[303] also declare that the self has the essential nature of knowing. Their understanding of the self and what belongs to the self should be viewed in the same way as the previous description.

The Vaiśeṣikas and others describe the self in terms of its results. That is, [they regard it as] that entity which [carries out the mental actions] ranging from seeing up to thinking; similarly, it is the agent that experiences, conceptualizes, recalls, forms volitions, and cognizes.

Proponents of these views [must then] hold the extreme notion that such things as the eye [and the other sense faculties as well as mind] constitute a self, since there is nothing other than the eye that constitutes an agent that sees. [The activities of] seeing, etc., are identified as eye consciousness and the other [forms of consciousness]. The eye can be described as that which sees, because it is the unique cause of that action. It is like the expression "the bell makes a sound," [which is appropriate] because [the bell] is the unique cause of sound.

Well then, what do you say of the statement that, "Although the eye sees a form, the mind is neither pleased nor displeased?"

Regarding that, the [nominal] self is ascribed to the collection [of the heaps] or its continuum and that alone is said to see forms with the eye. It is nothing but the appearance of form[304] [in the mind] that one describes as seeing form. Thus, when there is [an appearance of form in the mind], that is what it means to see form, and when there is not, that is what it means to not see form. The same explanation applies to the actions of hearing and the rest.

Regarding the range of notions suggesting that [the self] is an experiencing agent that experiences a feeling, a conceptualizing agent that develops a conception, a cognizing agent that generates a consciousness, because we reject that there is any cognizing agent apart from consciousness itself, we declare that the mere entity[305] itself is the agent. We give the same explanation for feelings and the rest. Alternatively, as indicated just before, [consciousness itself] is explained as the agent [of perception] in the sense that it gives rise to the appearance of an object.

Because all phenomena are momentary, they do not continue to exist [for the length of time it would take] to carry out an activity[306]; therefore, the only activity [that they carry out] is [for them] to come into being.[307]

[Non-Buddhist philosophers argue:] There cannot be an action without an agent.

[The Buddhist response:] If phenomena do not undergo destruction as soon as they come into being, they will not perish at a later time since their destruction does not have any [external] cause.[308] This is because nothing arises at a later time that has the distinct nature of [the action of] destruction or that of a destroying agent.

If you [non-Buddhists] propose that destruction has a [separate] cause, do you consider it to be a destroying agent or some other [entity that represents the] cause of destruction? In the former case, it follows that entities would either perish as soon as they come into being or they would never perish. Something independent that lacks [the quality of] being a cause of something at an earlier time will not acquire [the quality of] being the cause of that thing later, because it never possessed that distinct nature. In the latter case as well, there could be no certainty that the cause [of an entity's] destruction would [ever] occur.

[If you non-Buddhists suggest that] just as results [must have a cause], it is certain that destruction also has a cause, that is not the case. Results each have their own distinct mode of being. Therefore, it is not inconsistent that the causes [of each] of those [results] would also necessarily have a distinct capacity [for generating a specific result]. However, [the quality of] destruction[309] has no distinct essential nature of its own since it is not asserted to be a real entity. Who, then, could establish the certainty [of every destruction having its own distinct cause]? Therefore, it should be understood either that everything is the cause of all destruction, or destruction does not have [its own separate] cause.

Furthermore, if destruction were something that existed prior to its cause, then there would be no purpose for that cause of destruction. It would also follow absurdly that, since all entities [begin to] arise at the same time that they are undergoing destruction, entities would come into being after they had already perished. On the other hand, if destruction did not exist prior to its cause, then it would follow absurdly that, as with real entities, you could say that unreal things also [have the property known as] "prior nonexistence."[310] Because anything that [has the property of] "prior nonexistence" must be a real entity, it must also be something that [has the property of] "nonexistence by destruction."[311] In that case, there would be no distinction between being real and unreal, and, therefore, either everything would have the nature of being real or everything would have the nature of being unreal.

Moreover, if [the quality of] "nonexistence by destruction" can undergo nonexistence by destruction yet again, then those things that become nonexistent by destruction would do so endlessly and the same would be true of their causes. If that were denied, then since both [forms of nonexistence] lack any distinct essential nature of their own, you should also not maintain that an entity becomes nonexistent by destruction.

Moreover, do you consider an action[312] to exist separately from an entity or not to exist separately from [an entity]? If you hold that it does not exist separately [from an entity], then [the logical relationship between it and] its agent and object would not be proper. If you hold that [an entity] performs an action after it has come into being, then that [entity] would [never] take on that nature. It is improper for something that arises without a particular quality to take on that nature [after it has arisen]. [Moreover,] it is improper for something that is devoid of an action to be an agent.

In the absence of an action—that is, when there is no [entity] that possesses an action—how could [anything] take on the nature of being either the agent of some action or [its] object? Since it is never seen [that something] both lacks and possesses an action simultaneously, you must accept that the former [state of lacking an action] undergoes destruction, followed by the arising of the succeeding [state of possessing an action].

Furthermore, if something has not yet come into being, it would also not be proper for the nature of an agent or the nature of an action to exist. And since neither [agent nor action] exists, nothing at all exists. In addition to that, since one [state of the entity] lacks an action while the other possesses one, [the status of being] an agent is not [established].[313] And if there is no agent, there cannot be any action. Since entities must then undergo destruction on their own, you [non-Buddhists] should accept that [entities] are momentary.

[The non-Buddhist argues:] An action does not exist apart from an agent and an object; rather, agents give rise to actions and the object is what is produced by the action.[314] It is also improper for there to be an agent or an object without an action. [Therefore,] in that circumstance,[315] there must be a separate action as well.

[The Buddhist replies: But then] that [action too] must have another [agent]; therefore, action and agent will become subject to an infinite regression. On the other hand, if [you non-Buddhists claim that an agent] carries out an action independently of any other action, why do you not [also] accept that a substance lacking a separate action can carry out [an action]? What is accomplished by postulating a separate action that is not seen to have its own essential nature or capacity?

Moreover, if [you non-Buddhists accept that] agents are able to carry out an action, but that substances are not, then it would be possible for an action to possess both [the property of] "prior nonexistence" and [that of] "nonexistence by destruction," and a substance would not possess either of them. [And, in that case,] you would have to accept either that all substances exist eternally or that they could never exist at all.

Moreover, if actions existed separately from agents, [the agents] would not be capable of producing anything. In that case, actions would occur endlessly and nothing would be produced. [In that case,] because there is no production, then there could not be any actions either—which is to say, without the existence of any production, there cannot be any action.

Here is yet another point. If the goer were distinct from the act of going, then the goer could never reach a different place because [he or she] would not be able to move from [his or her] previous location. Similarly, if rice were distinct from [the action of] cooking, [the state of being cooked] would not become evident[316] because the rice would not be able to change from its former state [of being uncooked].

Now then, you [non-Buddhists] might assert that since an action is the cause of change in its substratum,[317] the [Buddhist argument] fails to refute that [an entity is capable of] changing from its previous state. However, the term "change"[318] means to take on a particular essential nature that is different from that which existed previously. And that cannot take place without the occurrence of some transformation.[319] Therefore, since a former [state] and a succeeding [state] cannot exist at the same time, you [non-Buddhists] must accept [the absurd proposition] that there can be such a thing as an earlier destruction and a subsequent arising that do not take place at different times. But in that case, since the substratum of the action is not present and does not continue to exist, how could [the action] be the cause of some change?

Therefore, there are only the five grasping heaps that undergo destruction as soon as they come into being and they are not associated with any unchanging "internally active" person.[320] [It is these five heaps alone that] grasp a different set of heaps that never existed before as constituting a self or as belonging to a self, and then, following that [mistaken belief, such a self] is [further] considered to be permanent, an agent, and an experiencing subject. However, these [five heaps] neither constitute a self nor belong to a self.

[The wording of] the statement [in the root text] that [the perishable collection view "regards the five grasping heaps] as 'I' and 'mine'" is meant to exclude the view that grasps an extreme.[321]

To say that this view "regards"[322] the heaps in that way means that it is a form of discriminating awareness.

The phrase "afflicted wisdom"[323] suggests that, if [this view] were not a confused state, it would not conceive of something that is not a self as being a self. Thus, the term "afflicted" means that [this form of discriminating awareness] is accompanied by ignorance and is erroneous.[324]

[Only] those [heaps] that make up one's own continuum can be regarded as [constituting an] "I."[325] Those [heaps] that make up the continua of other [sentient beings] and those [heaps] that are "unretained"[326] are regarded as "mine." Likewise, when [an individual] regards a portion of [his or her] own continuum as "I," others regard [that same entity or entities] as "mine."

The action of this [view] is to provide support for all [mistaken] views.[327]

The view that grasps an extreme

The phrase [in the root text] "in relation to that very [view]" refers to the perishable collection view. Because this [view] occurs on the strength of the perishable collection view, it is governed by the perishable collection view.

The phrase [that this view regards its object] "as undergoing extinction or as existing permanently" means that [this view regards] the very same entity that the perishable collection apprehends as an "I" as existing permanently—that is, as being eternal. [To regard the self as] "undergoing extinction" here means [to believe that it] perishes and does not undergo rebirth.

The phrase "afflicted wisdom that . . . regards . . ." should be described in the same way as [was explained] previously.[328]

The action of this [view] is to obstruct the deliverance [that is gained] through the middle way.[329] "Middle way" means the knowledge of dependent origination that shuns grasping at extinction and permanence.

Wrong view

Regarding the description that [this view] "denies causes, results, and actions,[330] and rejects entities that exist," it is meant in terms of those causes, etc., that are distinguished by their preeminent importance; it should not be taken as referring to all causes, etc.

Its action is to completely destroy the roots of virtue and to support the continued strength of the roots of nonvirtue.[331]

The consideration that views are supreme

Regarding the question [in the root text] "What is the consideration that views are supreme?" this term means a belief that holds one's own views and other [entities] to be the best.

"Those very three views" means the perishable collection view, the view that grasps an extreme, and wrong view. These [three views] are known as "the main body for those who hold views," which is to say they form the basis for the arising of [other] views.

With regard to the phrase that this view [also] regards "their basis, the heaps, . . . as foremost, superior, most excellent, and the highest,"[332] the terms "foremost," etc., are all similar in meaning; however, each successive term is expressed in order to clarify the one that preceded it.

The action of this view is to support continued attachment to bad views.[333] Attachment for that which has the characteristic of an [afflicted] view means to regard [such a view] as having a superior nature. Because [this attitude] keeps you from abandoning [such views], [the consideration that views are supreme] is described as supporting all inferior views.

The consideration that morality and asceticism are supreme

Concerning the phrase [that this view occurs in relation to] "morality, asceticism, and their basis, the heaps," "morality" is that which abandons bad conduct; "asceticism" refers to spiritual observances associated with outer appearance, conduct, and activities of body and speech.[334] Those heaps upon which morality and asceticism are based constitute the "basis" for morality and asceticism. The consideration that morality and asceticism are supreme is [a view] that is preceded by the belief that inferior views are superior; it then holds [flawed] morality and asceticism to be supreme. This is why the consideration that views are supreme is presented before the consideration that morality and asceticism are supreme.

This view regards morality and asceticism as "purifying" in that it believes they remove and purify you of the stain of evil deeds. It regards them as "liberating" in that it believes they liberate you from the fetters of the mental afflictions. It regards them as "conducive to deliverance" in that it believes they bring about your departure from samsara. "Conducive to deliverance" is an expression that means the path to liberation. A belief that "regards" things a certain way is a judgment. The consideration that morality and asceticism are supreme is a discriminating awareness[335] that believes morality and asceticism are of surpassing importance, and the like. It is "afflicted" because it apprehends its object in an incorrect manner. Its action is to support fruitless exertion.[336]

Doubt

In response to the question, "What is doubt?" [the root text] declares, "Ambivalence about the [Four Noble] Truths and so forth." The phrase "and so forth" includes karma and its results, and the Three Jewels.

"Ambivalence"[337] is the uncertainty about whether something is or is not the case. This mental factor should be considered to have a nature that is distinct from wisdom. Its action is to support the failure to pursue those entities that are virtuous in nature.[338]

Contrived versus Innate Mental Afflictions

How many of the mental afflictions of desire and the rest [only have forms that] are contrived? How many [have forms that] are innate as well as [forms that are] contrived?[339]

If [the root text] merely said "the three views," that could be misconstrued as referring to the first three [views]; therefore, they are further identified as "the latter [ones]." The three [latter views] are wrong view, the consideration that views are supreme, and the consideration that morality and asceticism are supreme. It is not merely these mental afflictions that [only have forms that] are contrived; doubt also only has a contrived form.

The phrase "the remaining ones [have forms that] are innate as well as [forms that are] contrived" means that the [the six remaining mental afflictions] are of both types.

What are "the remaining ones"?

They are desire, hatred, ignorance, pride, the perishable collection view, and the view that grasps an extreme.

This concludes the explanation of the [root] mental afflictions.

The Twenty Secondary Mental Afflictions

The secondary mental afflictions[340] need to be presented, so they will now be explained.

Anger

The term "current" means an object that exists at the present time, not one of the past or the future. "A source of harm that has become evident" means [an object] that has been perceived to be harmful. This part of the description indicates the object of anger.

Anger occurs only toward an object that is a source of harm in the present moment and not otherwise. The phrase "animosity of the mind" indicates both the essential nature of this mental factor and the fact that it is associated with consciousness. Given that its nature is animosity,[341] anger is not distinct from [the root mental affliction of] hatred; however, because the term is ascribed to a certain type of hatred that occurs in a particular circumstance, it is a form of hatred.

Thus, anger is ascribed to the animosity of the mind that occurs in relation to a source of harm that is actually present. Its object can be a sentient being or something that is inanimate. Its action is to give support to such conduct as inflicting punishment and the like.[342]

Resentment

Resentment [is a mental factor that arises] in the wake of anger. It is the unwillingness to relinquish, and the continuous occurrence of, rancor and enmity that stems from thinking, "This [person] harmed me in such and such a way."

Its action is to provide support for remaining in a state of impatience.[343] "Impatience" means the unwillingness to tolerate a wrong that was done [to you] and the desire to do something harmful in return.

Like anger, this term also is ascribed to a form of hatred that occurs in a particular circumstance; therefore, it should be understood to be [a mental factor that is only] nominally existent.

Dissembling

Dissembling is a form of ignorance in which you conceal objectionable acts [that you committed]; [for instance,] when someone who wishes to be helpful and is not motivated by such [attitudes] as desire, hatred, or fear, asks at an appropriate time, "Did you do this?"[344] Dissembling is a form of ignorance because it [is a mental state that] takes the form of concealing objectionable acts.

Its action is to provide support for regret and for remaining in a discontented state.[345] It is natural that someone who conceals [his or her] misdeeds will give rise to regret. And, because regret unavoidably causes mental distress, [the person who engages in dissembling] will remain in a discontented state.

Spite

"Heated words" means exceedingly harsh speech [that is expressed] in the most hurtful way possible. To be spiteful means to have an acrimonious nature; the quality itself is acrimony.[346] Thus, spite is described as "acrimony [expressed] through heated words"[347] in the sense [of being a mental factor] that seeks to hurt others by means of heated words.

The essential nature of this [mental factor] is an animosity of the mind that is preceded by anger and resentment. Therefore, it is a form of hatred and does not constitute a separate [mental] substance.[348]

Its actions are to engender verbal misconduct and [to cause others] to remain in a discontented state.[349] [The latter is] due to the fact that it is difficult to associate with a person who possesses this [mental factor].

Envy

Envy, which is a form of hatred, is the complete vexation of mind that occurs at the perception of [another person's] excellent qualities, such as those of gain, honor, fame, family lineage, morality, learning, and the like. "Complete vexation" is a vexation that fills one's mind[350] entirely.

Its action is to cause one to become dejected and to remain in discontented state.[351]

Stinginess

Generosity is the [mental factor] that causes [a person] to give an object that [he or she] possesses—whether of a material or spiritual nature, or a skill—from a desire to honor or benefit someone, regardless of whether [the individual] seeks that object. Because generosity does not occur when [stinginess] is present, [the root text states that it] "opposes [generosity]."

Stinginess is a form of desire that is possessed by a person who is attached to gain and honor. The phrase "acquisitiveness of mind" means an unwillingness to part with objects that represent a means of subsistence.

Its action is to provide support for the avoidance of simplicity.[352] [The explanation of this action should be understood as follows:] Avoidance of simplicity is the accumulation of objects that are not required for one's subsistence, due to stinginess.

Deceitfulness

In response to the question, "What is deceitfulness?" [the root text] states, "The displaying of something that is untrue [in order to] deceive others." It is the misrepresentation of a matter relating to such things as morality and the like, by a person who is strongly attached to gain and honor, and whose intention is to deceive others.

This term is ascribed to a combination of desire and ignorance, because it refers to [the intention to] present false qualities due to [the influence of] both desire and ignorance. Therefore, like [the secondary mental affliction] anger, it exists only nominally and not as a [distinct] real entity. Its action is to give support to wrong livelihood.[353]

Guile

In response to the question, "What is guile?" [the root text] states, "A deviousness of mind that adopts a means of concealing one's faults." With regard to this [description, the phrase] "a means of concealing one's faults" is [the attempt] to keep others from knowing [one's faults]. This, further, [may be accomplished when] a person, by distorting facts,[354] misleads or obfuscates.

Therefore, guile is distinct from dissembling. The latter involves a direct [act of] concealment; the former is the adoption of an [indirect] means of concealing one's faults, which represents a cause [of dissembling].

The phrase "deviousness of mind" means dishonesty—a quality that, if present in the mind, prevents one from following the right path.

Moreover, [prompted] by both desire and ignorance, and by a strong attachment to gain and honor, this [mental factor] sets about to conceal one's faults and to keep others from becoming aware of them. [Thus, the term "guile"] is ascribed to this [particular] combination [of desire and ignorance].

Its action is to obstruct [an individual] from receiving correct [spiritual] instruction.[355] Correct [spiritual] instruction is that which, once obtained, [leads to] proper attention.[356] [Thus, this mental factor also] acts as an obstacle to [the attainment of] that [proper attention].

Conceit

In response to the question, "What is conceit?" the root text states, "[It is] the delight of someone who is infatuated with [his or her] own well-being and [a state in which] the mind is overwhelmed."

[One's] "own well-being" refers to a preeminence of such things as family, health, [attractive] physical form, youthfulness, strength, influence, intelligence, or learning.

"Delight" is a particular type of joy.

"[A state in which] the mind is overwhelmed"[357] [also] indicates [the nature of] this joy. It is a form of joy that causes the mind to lose its composure and come under the control of that [feeling]. Thus, because the mind is overwhelmed in this way, it is described as a state in which the mind is overwhelmed. In short, conceit refers to a form of attachment[358] that is accompanied by a particular type of delight.

Its action is to give support to all the root and secondary mental afflictions.[359]

Harmfulness

Harmfulness is the [impulse to do] harm to sentient beings by [any of] a variety of methods, such as killing, binding, beating, or threatening. [It is described as "the impulse to do] injury to sentient beings" in the sense that sentient beings are injured on the basis of this [mental factor. That is,] it causes them to undergo physical pain and mental suffering through [such acts as] killing and binding, etc.

This [mental factor] is a form of hatred that consists of lack of sympathy, compassion, and pity. These three terms, lack of sympathy, etc., should be understood as referring, respectively, to doing such acts as killing, etc., oneself, causing others to do them, and rejoicing when you see or hear that others have done them. Alternatively, each succeeding term clarifies the one before it. In short, harmfulness refers to a form of hatred that is a harshness of mind toward sentient beings.

Its action is to cause injury to sentient beings.[360]

Shamelessness

Shamelessness is the quality that causes [a person] who possesses it to be called shameless. It [is the mental factor that] constitutes the antithesis of shame. Shamelessness is the lack of embarrassment about objectionable [behavior], even though [a person] recognizes, "It is wrong for me [to do] this act."

Absence of Abashment

Abashment is the quality that causes someone to feel abashed. The opposite of that is absence of abashment.[361]

The action of these two [mental factors, shamelessness and absence of abashment,] is to facilitate all the root and secondary mental afflictions.[362] These two terms are [nominally] ascribed to those aspects of desire, hatred, and ignorance that serve as causes for engendering wrongful activities. Since desire and hatred cannot occur simultaneously, [this description refers to] those circumstances in which [any of these three mental afflictions] is able to occur in this manner. As such, [shamelessness and absence of abashment] are not independent [mental factors].

Torpor

In response to the question, "What is torpor?" [the root text] states, "[It is] unfitness and immobility of the mind."

The term "immobility" describes [this mental factor] in an alternative manner [from that of "unfitness of mind"]. Immobility is the state of being immobile. It is a quality that when present in the mind causes it to become dull[363] and motionless—that is to say, unable to perceive an object.

Its action is also to facilitate all the root and secondary mental afflictions.

Because [this term] is ascribed to a form of ignorance, it is [a mental factor that is] only nominally existent and does not exist as [distinct] substance.

Excitation

In response to the question, "What is excitation?" [the root text] states, "Lack of calmness in the mind."

Calmness is [a state of] quiescence.[364] Lack of calmness is a quality that is in opposition to [quiescence]. Moreover, this [mental factor] is a form of desire that causes a lack of calmness in the mind through recalling previous [experiences] that are consistent with desire, such as [occasions of] laughter, amusement, and the like.

The action [of this mental factor] is to obstruct quiescence.[365]

Lack of Faith

With regard to the phrase "the antithesis of faith," faith is the belief in entities that do exist, the clarity of mind toward virtuous entities, and the desire to achieve those virtuous entities that are capable of being achieved.[366] Lack of faith is the opposite of these [attitudes].

The action [of this mental factor] is to support laziness,[367] in the sense that a person who lacks faith does not aspire to pursue [entities that are virtuous in nature].

Laziness

Laziness is a form of ignorance that, because of resorting to such comforts as sleep, resting on one's side, and reclining, results in the mind's lack of exertion toward virtuous activities of body, speech, and mind. "Laziness" [literally means] that which sinks into what is contemptible.[368]

Concerning the phrase "the antithesis of effort," effort is the exertion of the mind in the pursuit of entities that are virtuous in nature. Since laziness is the antithesis of [effort], its action is to obstruct the pursuit of entities that are virtuous in nature.[369]

Lack of Mindfulness

Lack of mindfulness is ascribed to [particular forms of] the desire, hatred, and ignorance that have already been explained. Its action is to support the strengthening of nonvirtue and the decrease of virtue.[370]

Clouded Recollection

With regard to the phrase "afflicted recollection," the term "afflicted" means [a form of recollection that is] concomitant with a mental affliction.

Concerning the phrase "a lack of clarity with regard to virtue," [this means that] the recollection that is concomitant with a mental affliction does not have a different object from [the one that is being held by] the mental affliction. Therefore, the mind is not able to develop clarity with regard to a virtuous object.[371]

Its action is to provide support for distraction.[372]

Distraction

"Distraction" [literally means] that which casts the mind about in a variety of ways.[373] It is [those forms of] desire, hatred, or ignorance that cause the mind to be directed outward, away from the object of one-pointed concentration. The secondary mental affliction of distraction is ascribed to [any form of] these [three root mental afflictions] that functions in this manner.

Its action is to obstruct [the attainment of] freedom from attachment.[374]

Lack of Vigilance

In response to the question, "What is lack of vigilance?" [the root text] states, "[It is] wisdom that is concomitant with a mental affliction." [The root text] also describes [this mental factor] as one "that causes [a person] to engage in activities of body, speech, or mind inattentively," when going out, returning, and so on.[375]

Its action is to give support to [the committing of] moral transgressions,[376] because it causes one to fail to determine what ought to be done and what ought not to be done.

The Four Variable Mental Factors

Regret

In response to the question, "What is regret?" [the root text] states, "The mind's sense of remorse."

A bad deed is one that is contemptible; [thus,] *kaukṛtyam* means the state of having acted badly. However, in the present context *kaukṛtyam* means the mental distress that is felt toward the object of one's wrongdoing, because the current topic is that of the mental factors.[377]

[Nonvirtuous] regret is a form of ignorance that is the mind's sense of remorse. [Regret, in general,] can occur in relation to something virtuous, nonvirtuous, or indeterminate; something that was done or not done; something done willingly or unwillingly; something that was proper or improper; and something done at an opportune time or at an inopportune time. Its action is to obstruct mental stability.[378]

Something that was done willingly means an action that was preceded by a pleased state of mind. Something that was done unwillingly means an action that someone else forced you to do—that is, an action that was done while overcome by mental distress. An opportune time means one during which an action need not be avoided. An inopportune time is one that falls outside that period. A proper act is one that is fitting to be done. An improper act is one that is not fitting to be done. All of these alternatives can be of three types: virtuous, nonvirtuous, and indeterminate. In the present case, the type of regret that is being considered is only that which is a form of ignorance and [therefore] constitutes one of the secondary mental afflictions.

Sleep

In response to the question, "What is sleep?" [the root text] states, "The uncontrolled contraction of the mind's activity."

"Activity" here means the engaging of an object [by the mind]. Sleep is the state that gives rise to the mind's loss of control over that [activity]. Alternatively, the mind's inability to maintain its hold on the body is the mind's loss of control over its activity; and sleep is the state that gives rise to that [condition].

On one hand, "contraction of the mind" refers to the condition that results from the loss of control over the mind's activity. On the other, "loss of control over the mind's activity" describes a condition that is due to the contraction of the mind. "Contraction of the mind" means the suspension of its activity through the "doors" of the [sense] faculties of the eye, etc.

Moreover, sleep can be virtuous, nonvirtuous, or indeterminate. [Nonvirtuous sleep, in particular, is described as] a form of ignorance that arises on the basis of such causes as physical weakness, fatigue, heaviness of the body, and the bringing to mind of an image of darkness.

Its action is to provide support for letting [an opportunity to complete] an activity that ought to be done slip by.[379] In the present instance, the description of sleep is limited to the type that is a form of ignorance and, therefore, is nonvirtuous.

Deliberation

In response to the question, "What is deliberation?" [the root text] states, "a form of mental discourse that investigates; a particular type of wisdom and volition."

"[A state of mind] that investigates" means a type of [mental] inquiry that sets about trying to determine, "What is this [object]?"

"Mental discourse" is a discourse that takes place in the mind. It is called "discourse" because it resembles [ordinary] discourse. Discourse is verbal discussion about any substantive matter.

Regarding the phrase "a particular type of volition and wisdom," the nature of volition is to cause the mind to be put in motion, while wisdom is a type of mental factor that distinguishes those things that are virtuous from those that are detrimental. Because the mind can be set in motion on the strength of [either of] these [qualities], deliberation is sometimes ascribed to a situation in which the mind is [operating in combination] with volition, and sometimes to one in which the mind [is operating in combination] with wisdom. [These two are] occasions in which reasoning is absent and present, respectively. Alternatively, deliberation is ascribed to volition and wisdom when they are operating in combination, because the mind can be activated in that manner [as well]. This method [of explanation] should be regarded as applying to reflection as well.

The phrase "a coarseness of mind" means a roughness, because [this mental factor] investigates only the [overall nature of an] object.

Reflection

In response to the question, "What is reflection?" [the root text] states in part, "a form of mental discourse that examines [an object] closely." "To examine closely" means a type of mental inquiry that determines about something that was previously identified, "The nature of this object is such and such."

Regarding the phrase "it is like [the previous mental factor, except that it is] a fineness of mind," "like [the previous mental factor]" means that it is [also] a particular type of wisdom and volition. It is a "fineness of mind" in the sense that it "examines [an object] closely."

The action of these two [mental factors] is to give support both to remaining in a contented state and to remaining in a discontented state.[380] They are distinguished on the basis of having been characterized as a coarseness and a fineness [in the way that they examine an object of thought].

With regard to the description of the formations heap as [being made up of] the mental factors other than feeling and conception, and the formations that do not accompany consciousness, this concludes the explanation of [the portion of the formations heap that consists of] mental factors.

The Formations That Do Not Accompany Consciousness

Now the formations that do not accompany consciousness need to be explained. Therefore, in relation to that, [the root text] asks, "What are the formations that do not accompany consciousness?" In keeping with this question, [the root text] makes the following general statement: "They are [entities] that are nominally ascribed to a particular state of form, consciousness, or the mental factors. They are not [entities that are] ascribed to [form, consciousness, or the mental factors] themselves or to something distinct from them."[381] It can be understood that this refers to the formations that are not associated with consciousness, because that is the topic at hand.

These [entities] are nominally existent because the terms that designate them indicate particular states[382] of form, etc.—which is to say, their essential natures do not exist apart from a particular state of form, etc. Therefore, since [each of these states] has a basis[383] to which it is related, the existence [of each of the formations that do not accompany consciousness] is ascribed to the state [of the basis to which it is related] and not to [the basis] itself or to something [real that is] distinct from [the basis]. Otherwise, it would follow that the state and the entity possessing that state[384] must either be one and the same or completely distinct from one another. It would also follow that the entity possessing a [particular] state would have a permanent result.[385]

Having presented that general explanation, [the root text] asks, "What, then, are they?" from a desire to make known the specific forms of these entities. It then indicates their specific forms by presenting the list [of fourteen entities] that is made up of [those entities called] "acquirement," "the state of composure without conception," and so on.

The phrase "those [other entities] that are of the same kind" means those [other entities] that have the same nature—which is to say, any other entities [whose existence] is [nominally] ascribed to a state of form, consciousness, or the mental factors, and which should be understood as being formations that do not accompany consciousness. If you ask what these [other entities] are, they include progression, specificity of natural law, congruity, swiftness, sequence, time, place, number, completeness, and the like.[386]

Now, in order to specify the essential nature of "completeness" and the rest, [the root text] successively asks, "What is acquirement?" and so on, and then responds [to each question] with the statements "obtainment and possession" and so on.

Acquirement

"Obtainment"[387] is the initial acquiring of that which had not been acquired previously. "Possession"[388] is the second moment of the obtainments and thereafter. [The acquirement] that comes after [an initial obtainment] is called "possession." Thus, [the root text] indicates that the term "acquirement"[389] applies equally to obtainment and to possession.

This acquirement is classified as being of three types: a seed, mastery, and actualization.

The circumstances that are implicit in the phrase "according to circumstances" are as follows: From the first moment of acquirement until the point of achieving mastery is called the stage of a seed. Thus, seed refers both to obtainments and possessions, whereas mastery and actualization are exclusively stages of possession.

What does seed mean?

"Seed" is a particular capacity or cause that generates the same kind of entities in the mind at some future time as those virtuous, nonvirtuous, or indeterminate ones that were previously gained. Because an object is dependent on its seed once it has been obtained, even though the object has not yet been actualized, that which constitutes its seed is referred to as its "acquirement."

"Mastery"[390] is the stage in which a continuing result is produced on the basis of that condition.

"Actualization"[391] is the period in which the result of that acquirement has been achieved.

The State of Composure Without Conception

It is called "the state of composure without conception"[392] in the sense that it is a state of composure that lacks conception or in the sense that it is the state of composure possessed by beings that lack conception.[393]

[The phrase in the root text that describes the person who develops this state of composure as] "someone who has overcome desire for Complete Virtue" means an individual who has overcome desire for the third meditative absorption. The third meditative absorption consists of three levels: Limited Virtue, Immeasurable Virtue, and Complete Virtue. Regarding them, whoever overcomes desire for the level known as Complete Virtue[394] has overcome desire for the [entire] third meditative absorption.

"Not for the level above it" means [the level] that is above the third meditative absorption—[which is to say,] the fourth meditative absorption. Thus, [the phrase indicates that] the individual [being described here] has not overcome desire for the fourth meditative absorption.

The phrase "preceded by . . . that conceives of deliverance" means that the person who [seeks to enter this state of composure] initially develops a form of attention that conceives of deliverance.[395] That is to say, those who enter the state of composure without conception are individuals who regard the state of having no conception as constituting liberation or [who regard] the state of composure [without conception] as constituting the path that leads to liberation. Therefore, the phrase "conceives of deliverance" means either [to develop] the conception that [the state of having no conception] constitutes liberation or [to develop] the conception that [the state of composure without conception] constitutes the path to liberation.

It is held that the phrase "preceded by a form of attention that conceives of deliverance" refers to a form [of reflection] that strongly discredits [conceptions].[396] Therefore, even though the mind and mental factors have [actually] been suspended, [the practitioner] who generates the state of composure that lacks conception is described as "entering" a state in which conception is absent. That is to say, it is a state in which the mind and all mental factors are suspended, and one that is gained through discrediting conception in particular.

With regard to the phrase "the cessation of inconstant minds and mental factors," the term "inconstant" refers to the active forms of consciousness,[397] which is to say, the collection of the six forms of consciousness together with their associated mental factors. They are "inconstant" because they are never present in unconscious states and because they are not always present in conscious states.[398] The "constant" states of awareness are the storehouse consciousness and the afflicted mind, along with [the mental factors] that are associated with them. [They are considered constant] because they are always present, except for (1) when [a practitioner who has attained] the transcendent path enters a state of composure with regard to the [Four Noble] Truths, (2) when [a practitioner] has entered the state of composure that is a cessation, and (3) when [a practitioner] has reached the stage that is beyond training.[399] Because [the storehouse consciousness and the afflicted mind, along with the mental factors that are associated with them] are present at all times other than these three occasions,] the term "inconstant" is specified here [to identify the minds and mental factors that are suspended in the state of composure without conception].

[The phrase in the root text that states, "It is] the cessation . . ." refers to [a condition] that is brought about by a composed mind. It is a cessation because this [condition] causes [the active forms of consciousness and their concomitant mental factors] to be suspended.[400] [Therefore, this term] refers to the particular condition of a being's physical basis[401] that obstructs the occurrence of inconstant minds and mental factors for a certain period of time. This indicates that the state of composure without conception is [nominally] ascribed to a particular condition of a person's physical basis.

[This condition] is said to be [one that is] "brought about by a composed mind" because a composed mind generates a [condition in the] body that opposes the arising of further moments of consciousness in the period of time that immediately follows it.

The State of Composure That Is a Cessation

Concerning the phrase [in the root text that describes this state of composure as being achieved by] "someone who has overcome desire for the Sphere of Nothingness and who has set out to rise above the Peak of Existence," [the latter part of this description—that is,] "someone who has set out to rise above the Peak of Existence"—[is meant to exclude ordinary beings,] because, while there are ordinary beings who have overcome desire for the Sphere of Nothingness, there aren't any who have set out to rise above the Peak of Existence.[402] Moreover, there are certain [practitioners] who have set out to rise above the Peak of Existence but who have not yet overcome desire for the Sphere of Nothingness. These can be individuals who are "abiding in a [particular] fruit [of asceticism]," as well as individuals who are "striving after a [particular] fruit [of asceticism]."[403] [To exclude these types of Ārya practitioners as well, the root text] states [that the person who enters this state of composure is] "someone who has overcome desire for the Sphere of Nothingness."[404] [The reason that the root text] does not describe [this person] as "someone who has not overcome desire for a higher level" is because an Arhat who has [completely and permanently] overcome desire for the Peak of Existence also enters the state of composure that is a cessation.

[In short, the reason for] stating both "someone who has overcome desire for the Sphere of Nothingness" and "[someone] who has set out to rise above the Peak of Existence" is to indicate that a Nonreturner Ārya or an Arhat [can] enter this state of composure, but an ordinary person cannot. An ordinary person does not set out to rise above the Peak of Existence, because the mundane path is not [able to serve as] an antidote for [attachment to] the Peak of Existence. However, the transcendent Seeing Path *is* an antidote for [attachment to] the Peak of Existence. Therefore, only an Ārya can set out to rise above the Peak of Existence, because [such a practitioner] overcomes [his or her] attachment [for that level] through abandoning the mental afflictions to be abandoned by the Seeing Path and the mental afflictions to be abandoned by the Meditation Path.[405]

Regarding the phrase that [this state of mental composure is] "preceded by a form of attention that conceives of abiding [in a state of ease],"[406] unlike the state of composure without conception, the state of composure that is a cessation is not entered after having developed a form of attention that conceives of deliverance; rather, it is entered after having developed a form of attention that conceives of [this mental absorption as] abiding [in a state of ease].

The state of composure that is a cessation is a state that exists within the Peak of Existence. Āryas do not enter it with the conception that it represents deliverance from samsaric existence; rather, because they are weary of [samsaric] feelings and conceptions and [these mental factors] are absent in this state of composure, they develop the conception [that it represents a state] of abiding in [a state of] peace.[407]

The "conception of abiding" means the conception [that this mental absorption is] a state of well-being.[408] It is [a form of] "abiding" in that it [is a mental absorption that] causes one to abide [in a state of ease][409]—that is to say, it means that one abides [in such a state] for a certain period of time. Thus, the phrase "preceded by a form of attention that conceives of abiding" refers to a form of attention that formulates the conception, "I shall abide in a special state of composure that approximates nirvana." This [mental absorption] that exists within the Peak of Existence is extremely subtle,[410] because the state of composure that is a cessation is generated in the moment immediately following [attainment of the general state of the Peak of Existence].

The adjective "inconstant" [that modifies "minds and mental factors" in the root text] refers to the six, four, and one active forms of consciousness [along with their mental concomitants] that operate in the desire, form, and formless realms, respectively, and that are suspended by the individual who enters the state of composure that is a cessation.

Regarding the phrase "as well as a portion of the constant minds," the adjective "constant" [that modifies "minds" in the root text] also includes the "maturation consciousness"[411]; therefore, [the root text] indicates that [only] a portion [of the constant minds is suspended during this state of composure]. While the afflicted mind is not active during the state of composure that is a cessation or when a practitioner has reached the stage that is beyond training, it is considered a constant mind because it is present during all impure states of awareness.[412]

[The phrase in the root text that states, "It is] the cessation . . ." refers to [a condition] that is brought about by active forms of consciousness. It [is a condition that] obstructs the seeds of the [six] active forms of consciousness and the [form of] consciousness known as the afflicted mind, both of which are [contained] in the maturation consciousness. It is a cessation because this [condition] causes the active forms of consciousness and the afflicted mind to become inactive and remain suspended for a certain period of time. Therefore, the expression "state of composure that is a cessation" is [nominally] ascribed to that condition in which [certain] seeds [contained] in the storehouse consciousness have been impaired [temporarily] by a composed mind.

The Quality of Having No Conception

In response to the question, "What is [the quality of] having no conception?" [the root text] states, "[It is] a result of the state of composure without conception; and the cessation of inconstant minds and mental factors of a being who has been born among the deities who lack conception." Regarding this description, [the beings referred to here as] "deities" are the ones called Those of Great Fruit. They inhabit a region that lies within the third level of the fourth meditative absorption.[413] The realm of the deities who lack conception lies in the higher reaches of that region, which resembles the upper story of a mansion. To be born there is the maturation result of having generated the state of composure without conception.[414]

The phrase "the cessation of inconstant minds and mental factors" identifies the essential nature [of this quality]. The inconstant minds and mental factors of a being who is born in this realm oppose the seeds of the same kind of minds and mental factors [that are situated] in their seat.[415] This causes [the mind and mental factors of this worldly deity] to become progressively ever more subtle until, finally, they are so subtle that the seeds [of those minds that are situated] in their seat are no longer able to generate further [active] states of consciousness, because they have been impaired. During this period of time, inconstant minds and mental factors do not arise from the seat [that is their source]. Thus, [the quality of] having no conception is [an entity that is] nominally ascribed to the period of time during which the seeds [of inconstant minds and mental factors] remain impaired. [In other words, this entity is] a state in which [the seeds of active forms of consciousness] remain [impaired] for a [fixed] duration.[416] It is a cessation because it causes [inconstant minds and mental factors] to remain suspended.

The Faculty of a Life Force

In response to the question, "What is the faculty of a life force?" [the root text] states, "[It is] the fixed period of time for the continued existence of the formations [that occur] in relation to [various] class affiliates [of different sentient beings] that is projected by past karma."

"Life force"[417] is that which keeps [a sentient being] alive. It is a faculty in that it has the power to cause [the formations of a particular sentient being] to continue to exist within a particular "class affiliate."[418]

"Class"[419] refers to a collection [of entities] that relate to a [particular] sentient being. "Affiliate"[420] means [an entity] that has an equal share in something[421]—that is to say, a similarity. [Thus,] "class affiliate" means something that has an affiliation with a class [by virtue of a shared similarity]. Regarding the phrase "within [various] class affiliates," [this refers to] those [class affiliates] that occur in different states of existence[422] and that are made different by different karma. [In general,] the term "class affiliate" refers to the continuum of heaps that occurs within a particular [sentient being's] single birth.[423] [A class affiliate] that is "projected by past karma" means one that is produced by virtuous, nonvirtuous, or invariable karma that was accumulated in the past.

With regard to the phrase "the fixed period of time for the continued existence [of the formations] . . . ," the term "continued existence"[424] refers to the succession of formations that occur within one uninterrupted class affiliate. The "fixed period of time"[425] of such a continued existence means the span of time—whether a hundred or a thousand years—during which [a series of formations] will remain in existence in relation to a [single] class affiliate. Therefore, that fixed period of time during which [a continuum of heaps] will continue to exist describes [the meaning of] a life span.[426] The seat [of that life span] is those stable formations that are governed by the storehouse consciousness and that possess a particular efficacy[427] projected by karma accumulated in the past.

Class Affiliation

In response to the question, "What is class affiliation?"[428] [the root text] states, "The similarity in the composition of sentient beings." The term "sentient beings" refers to gods and humans, etc.—that is, the five types of migrating beings.[429] "The composition of sentient beings"[430] is that which is recognized as constituting their individual being—which is to say, it is [the totality of] their four or five grasping heaps.[431] "Similarity" means commonality. Thus, [the description of this entity] can be [further] indicated as follows: Among the various sentient beings that are distinguished by type, realm, physical form, etc., there exist [various kinds of] commonality in the makeup or composition of these sentient beings that are distinguished by type, realm, physical form, etc., and it is to this [nominally existent entity] that the term "class affiliation" is ascribed.

Birth

In response to the question, "What is birth?" [the root text] states, "The origination of previously nonexistent formations in relation to a class affiliate."[432] The term "class affiliate" [is included] in this description to indicate that birth does not refer to the origination of formations in an unqualified sense; rather, it refers only to the origination of previously nonexistent formations that make up a class affiliate.[433] Therefore, the reason [for including the term "class affiliate" here] is to indicate that [the characteristic of birth] does not apply to all formations.

The phrase "the origination of previously nonexistent [formations]"[434] is meant to reject the position of those who believe (1) that birth is a distinct substance associated with entities that have not yet arisen and have not yet disappeared and (2) that time is [logically] established on the basis of the activities [of birth etc].[435] Thus, the condition that constitutes the origination of [a series of] formations that did not previously exist is called their "birth." It is not a separate entity nor is the existence of the three times established by the [collective] actions [of birth and the rest].

Aging

In response to the question, "What is aging?" [the root text] states, "The modification of their continuum in relation to that." Regarding this description, the phrase "their [continuum] in relation to that"[436] refers to those formations that make up a class affiliate. The phrase "modification of [their] continuum" refers to [the continuum of formations] that exists between the birth state and the death state. The continuous series of causally related formations that occurs during that period is referred to as a "continuum."[437]

The condition by which [this continuum] undergoes change is its "modification."[438] For example, it is the transformation that occurs when the [fetal] stage [known as] *kalalam* changes into *arbudam*,[439] and, similarly, it is the transformation from the stage of youthfulness to that of old age. "Modification" also refers to the changes that occur within the succession of individual moments that make up [each of] the [various] stages of *kalalam* and the rest. Thus, [this description indicates that] "aging" is a term that is [nominally] ascribed to the modification of [such a] continuum. It does not refer to [a condition that applies to] a single moment [of this continuum], and it is not a distinct [real] entity.

Duration

In response to the question, "What is duration?" [the root text] states, "the uninterrupted succession of their continuum in relation to that." The phrase "in relation to that" refers to [the formations that occur within] a single class affiliate. Thus, [this description indicates that] "duration" is a term that is [nominally] ascribed to the uninterrupted succession of a continuum of formations that lasts until death. It does not refer to [a condition] that occurs in relation to a single moment [of this continuum], and it is not a distinct [real] entity.

Impermanence

In response to the question, "What is impermanence?" [the root text] states, "The destruction of their continuum in relation to that."

With regard to this [description], the phrase "their [continuum] in relation to that" means that "impermanence" is a term that is [nominally] ascribed to the destruction of a continuum of formations within a single class affiliate. [This description] also indicates that the term does not refers to [a condition] that occurs within a single moment [of this continuum] and it is not a distinct [real] entity. The phrase "destruction of a continuum" here should be understood as meaning death.

If it is also certainly true that outer form possesses [the characteristics of] birth, aging, duration, and impermanence, why then are birth and the rest only described in relation to a continuum of formations [that exists] within a class affiliate, and not in relation to outer form?

It is because those characteristics of conditioned entities that Lord [Buddha] described as "birth," "aging," "duration," and "impermanence" were meant only in relation to formations that are recognized as [comprising] sentient beings; they were not meant in relation to outer formations.

If the characteristics of birth and the rest apply equally to both types of formations, why did the Lord [only] describe them in relation to those formations that are retained?[440]

It is because outer form is characterized by appearance and disappearance, whereas inner formations are characterized by birth and the rest. That is, the established terms of everyday usage for the birth and destruction of external form are "appearance" and "disappearance."[441] For this reason, the Lord also described [outer form] with the same terms and not those of birth and the rest, in order to conform to everyday usage. Inner formations, however, are characterized by [using such terms as] birth, aging, etc., as when it is said [of someone] that [he or she] was born, aged, continued to exist, and passed away. Thus, it is explained that Lord [Buddha] also used the terms "birth," etc., to describe the arising, etc., [of inner formations,] in order to conform to [the expressions that are used by] the world [at large].

The Collection of Names

In response to the question, "What is the collection of names?" [the root text] states, "The expressions [that describe] the essences of entities."

A name[442] is what turns the mind toward a word[443] and the entity that is signified [by that word].[444] That is, it is a combination of syllables[445] that gives expression to objects. Thus, the term "collection of names" refers to the aggregate of names, each of which is made up of a combination of syllables.

Because the essences of dharmas are ineffable, [the word] "expression"[446] [as it is being used here] means a form of speech that [refers to an essence that] has been [artificially] ascribed. An essence is a unique characteristic.[447] Thus, the term "name" means a word that indicates the essential nature of an entity, even though [the ultimate nature of] that [essence] is incapable of being expressed. Examples are [the words] "eye," "ear," "[visible] form," "sound" and the like.

The Collection of Assertions

In response to the question, "What is the collection of assertions?" the root text states, "The expressions [that describe] the distinguishing characteristics[448] of entities." The word "assertion"[449] [as it is being used here] means that which causes the meaning of a distinguishing characteristic to be understood. Thus, [the Sanskrit word *padam* as it is being used here] is different from both that of a name and that of the word *padam* [as it is used] in the [everyday] world.[450]

The essence of a name and an assertion are the same in that both are combinations of syllables. However, they are distinguished by the fact that the meanings [of these two terms] are different. A name is an expression [that describes] the essence of an entity. The essence [of something] is the subject[451] [about which attributes or characteristics can be predicated]; therefore, the statement "expressions [that describe] the essences [of entities]" was mentioned first.[452]

Distinguishing characteristics are [attributes] such as impermanence and the like. They [indicate] distinctions that can have the nature of a positive or a negative [meaning], as well as other [propositions] that are inconclusive in nature. Examples include [such statements as] "All formations are impermanent," "All entities are devoid of a self," and "Nirvana is peace."

Thus, a name merely states the essence of an entity, while an assertion states the distinguishing characteristics [that pertain to] an entity's essence. The remainder [of this discussion on the collection of assertions] should be understood in the same manner as the explanation that was given for names.[453]

The Collection of Syllables

In response to the question, "What is the collection of syllables?" the root text states [in part], "[It is the collection of] phonemes, because they are what allow both of them to become manifest." [Thus,] syllables are what allow [both names and assertions] to become expressed.[454] The aggregate of syllables is called "the collection of syllables." The word "collection" indicates that [this aggregate] includes all the syllables.

By itself, the word "them" in the description only indicates a reference to something that was stated previously. And if the word "both" appeared alone, you could not discern what it referred to. This is why the [the root text] states, "both of them"—that is, in order to indicate that syllables are what allow the names and assertions that were just explained to become manifest.

How do syllables allow names and assertions to become manifest?

The terms "name" and "assertion" are nominally ascribed to those combinations of syllables that [form] the expressions [that describe] the essential nature and distinguishing characteristics of things. This is the manner in which syllables allow names and assertions to become manifest.

Syllables [by themselves] do not have the nature of informative speech. Nevertheless, it is commonly accepted in the everyday world that syllables and the rest[455] are the [basic] sounds [of spoken language]. Hence, they are [also referred to in the root text as] "the [basic] sounds [of spoken language],"[456] because they are the means of communicating meanings in that they are the basis for names and assertions. [Syllables] are the basis for [names and assertions], because names and assertions are ascribed in relation to them; and, thus, they serve as the basis through which meanings are expressed.

The root text states, "Moreover, [syllables] are [called] 'phonemes,'[457] because they cannot be replaced by any alternative form." For instance the word "eye"[458] can be replaced with synonyms such as "guide"[459] and the like, which is to say one and the same object can be made known by a variety of equivalent terms. However, there is no alternative for the phoneme *a* that is different from it and by which it can be made known.

This entire subject can be summarized as follows: there are essences, attributes, and the expressions for them. They are all designated within these [three] topics. In this way, the meaning of the collections of names, expressions and syllables has been established.[460] It should be understood that [the explanations of] the other formations that do not accompany consciousness are also established in relation to [some specific] purpose, as is the case with the collections of assertions and syllables.

The State of an Ordinary Being

In response to the question, "What is the state of an ordinary being?" the root text states, "The condition of not having achieved the qualities of an Ārya." The state of an ordinary being[461] is the quality by virtue of which an individual is called an "ordinary being."

Āryas are those beings who have reached [a state] that is far removed from evil, nonvirtuous entities.[462] They are of two types: those who are [still undergoing] training and those who are beyond [the need for any further] training. The qualities that [Āryas] possess are those of the Seeing Path, the Meditation Path, and the Path that is Beyond Training.[463] [The condition of] not having achieved [any of] these qualities is the state of an ordinary being. Not to have achieved the qualities of an Ārya means not to have developed them. Thus, the continuum of a sentient being who has not developed the qualities of an Ārya is called an "ordinary being." Likewise, [the continuum of a sentient being] who has developed the qualities of an Ārya is called an "Ārya."

Progression

What is progression?

The term "progression"[464] refers to an unbroken succession of causes and effects; it does not apply to a single moment or to a series that has become interrupted.

Specificity of Natural Law

What is specificity of natural law?

Specificity of natural law[465] is defined as the diversity of cause and effect. Moreover, the phrase "diversity of cause and effect" refers to such things as the connection between good conduct and its desirable consequences, bad conduct and its undesirable consequences, and so forth. That is to say, it is the fixed connection between the various different kinds of results and their respective causes.

Congruity

What is congruity?

Congruity[466] is the quality that is ascribed to the conformity that exists between cause and effect. For example, because of the appropriateness and conformity that exists between generosity and abundance of wealth, the [karmic] result of generosity is [to experience] an abundance of wealth.

Swiftness

What is swiftness?

Swiftness[467] is the quality that is ascribed to the rapid appearance of causes and effects.

Sequence

What is sequence?

Sequence[468] is the quality that is ascribed to the regular manner in which causes and effects appear one after the other—which is to say, the manner in which they do not occur at the same time.

Time

What is time?

Time[469] is the quality that is ascribed in relation to the continuous occurrence of causes and effects. With regard to this occurrence of causes and effects, the past is ascribed to [the state in which] causes and effects have ceased subsequent to their arising; the future is ascribed to [the state in which] they have not yet arisen; and the present is ascribed to [the state in which] they have arisen but not yet ceased.

Place

What is place?

Place[470] is the quality that is ascribed to the presence of causes and effects in all the ten directions of east, south, west, north, below, above, and the rest. [In other words,] place is ascribed to the extension of causes and effects in some direction. It should be understood that [in the present context] "causes and effects" is limited to [those entities that have the nature of] form, since those that lack form are incapable of extending in some direction.

Number

What is number?

Number[471] is the quality that is ascribed to the separateness of each and every [individual entity that is included] among the formations. The term "separateness" [as it is being used here] is meant to indicate that it would be logically impossible to formulate a count of two [or three, etc.,] in relation to something that had the nature of an inseparable unity.

Completeness

What is completeness?

Completeness[472] refers to the convergence of [all] the causes and conditions [that are necessary for the occurrence of some event].[473]

It should be understood that [all] these formations that are not associated with consciousness are nominally existent, because they are ascribed to a particular state of some entity or entities. This concludes the explanation of the formations heap.

THE CONSCIOUSNESS HEAP

Following the formations heap, the consciousness heap is to be explained. Therefore, in response to the question, "What is consciousness?" [the root text] states [in part], "Knowledge of an object." Object[474] means an object of mind and the mental factors. It is of six types, ranging from visible objects to entities.[475] Awareness[476] is synonymous with perception, cognition, and apprehension. This description refers to the six active forms of consciousness—that is, those that range from eye consciousness to mind consciousness. Eye consciousness is the recurrent awareness[477] of [visible] objects on the basis of the eye faculty. This explanation is similar for the other [five] forms of consciousness up to mind consciousness, which is described as the recurrent awareness of all entities on the basis of the mind faculty.

After explaining the essence of consciousness, [the root text] declares, "It is also [referred to as] thought and mind" in order to indicate its synonyms. Thus, consciousness is also called "thought" and "mind."

To explain the meanings of these synonyms, [the root text] then states, "because it is diverse and because mind serves as its support." The term "thought"[478] literally means that which is diverse.[479] The term "mind" means that which serves as the support for the very next moment of thought.[480]

Thus, the six active forms of consciousness have the nature of recurrent apprehension of objects. These six forms of consciousness of the eye and the rest are called "diverse" because the recurrent apprehension of objects has many different forms. This is why, when a consciousness arises on the basis of a particular faculty, [the consciousness] is said to know the object, not the faculty.

The six forms of consciousness of the eye and the rest that have just ceased serve as the basis for the arising of the very next moment of [mind] consciousness.[481] This is why the consciousness that represents the basis for the very next moment of awareness is called "mind."

[The literal explanation of the term] "thought" as being "that which is diverse" is meant in the sense of [the various] types of consciousness, not in the sense of individual moments [of consciousness]. The momentary aspect [of consciousness] is one that ascertains a specific object; therefore, this is not what is being described as diverse, because that [diversity] does not represent the true meaning of thought.

The Storehouse Consciousness

[The root text] states, "Primarily, thought is the storehouse consciousness."[482] In order to indicate the reason for this statement, [the root text] explains, "because that is where the seeds of all the formations are collected." In this sense, thought is what collects the seeds of all the formations [with] each [passing] moment. This is the true meaning of thought. The collection of these seeds means either the repeated strengthening of the seeds of the formations or the continuous preservation of their existence.

The term "formations" here means those [conditioned] entities that are impure.[483] Moreover, these [entities] arise from the four types of conditions.[484] The causal condition[485] is the imprints [of the formations] that reside in the storehouse consciousness. "Imprint"[486] means the strengthened state of the seeds [of the formations] that is brought about by their repeated occurrence. The governing condition[487] is the faculties of the eye, etc. The homogeneous immediate condition[488] is the consciousness that has just ceased. The objective condition[489] is visible form, etc. As the sutras declare, "When the eye is not damaged and [visible] forms are present, and when the type of attention that produces this consciousness has been developed, the eye consciousness that arises from these [conditions] will come into being." With appropriate changes, a similar description can be given for ear consciousness and the [other] remaining [active] forms of consciousness. The causal condition is not mentioned [in this sutra passage] because it is always present and because it is difficult to recognize.

Following that, there arises an investigating form of mind consciousness.[490] Following this investigating consciousness, there arises a mind consciousness that makes a determination. Following the determining stage of mind consciousness, there arises a mind consciousness that gives further consideration. At this point, the awareness begins to take on a nature that is either afflicted or leads to purification, depending on the type of object. During this stage, the [mental] formation of volition—which can have either a virtuous, nonvirtuous, or invariable nature—begins to form specific intentions. When these intentions cease, they strengthen "maturation imprints"[491] and "consequence imprints"[492] within the storehouse consciousness. On the basis of consequence imprints, new formations arise that are virtuous, nonvirtuous, or invariable. On the basis of maturation imprints, new instances of the storehouse consciousness arise from [prior states of] the storehouse consciousness and they become manifest as karmic maturations within [subsequent,] distinct class affiliates.[493] This describes the process that occurs for all impure phenomena that are either nonvirtuous or virtuous. Indeterminate phenomena strengthen only "consequence imprints." They do not strengthen "maturation imprints," because they do not bring about any [karmic] maturations.

Thus, the storehouse consciousness is twofold. In relation to consequence imprints, it is both a cause and a result. More specifically, all formations are able to generate the seeds of their own future existence.[494] Therefore, because [the formations] constitute a causal state that is able to produce a storehouse consciousness of a specific nature, the storehouse consciousness is a result of formations. But since all the formations arise from the storehouse consciousness that receives their seeds, [the storehouse consciousness] constitutes a cause of all the formations [as well].

When considered in relation to maturation imprints, the storehouse consciousness is only a result of virtuous and nonvirtuous formations; it does not [also] serve as their cause. In this context, cause means [that virtuous and nonvirtuous formations are] the cause of a "maturation consciousness"[495] within subsequent class affiliates, on the basis of maturation imprints.

The active forms of consciousness perceive [visible] form, sound, etc., [as their objects], and they take on the aspect of their unique and general characteristics. Therefore, they do have objects that are discernible and aspects that are discernible.[496] However, [the root text] states that the storehouse consciousness "does not have a discernible object or aspect."[497] This is because its object and internal form are not capable of being discerned.

Why?

It is because the storehouse consciousness operates in relation to two objects: (1) internally it perceives the condition of grasping and (2) externally it perceives the [physical] world. However, it does not do so in such a way that [allows] the form [of these two types of awareness] to be discernible.[498] "Inner grasping"[499] refers to the imprints of the mistaken belief that those entities which are [in fact only] mental constructs[500] [are independent and real substances], as well as the form that makes up the sense faculties together with their seats.[501] These two objects are very subtle; therefore, they cannot be perceived even by those [beings] who are knowledgeable about [the nature of] the world. This is why [the root text states that the storehouse consciousness] "does not have a discernible object or aspect." [This statement] does not mean that it has no objects of any kind.

The active forms of consciousness can have a nature that is virtuous, nonvirtuous, or indeterminate. However, [the root text states that] the storehouse consciousness "is of a single type."[502] That is, it does not have a nature that is virtuous or nonvirtuous, because it is not accompanied by entities that are virtuous or nonvirtuous. Its only concomitants are the five universal mental factors: attention, contact, feeling, conception, and volition. The storehouse consciousness, together with its concomitants, is caused to arise by previous karmic formations. Therefore, its type is [exclusively] that of an indeterminate entity, because its nature is solely that of a [karmic] maturation.

With regard to the phrase "it occurs continuously,"[503] the storehouse consciousness arises without a moment's interruption, from the point of reentering[504] [a birth state at the conception of] a new class affiliate until the occurrence of death. Unlike the active forms of consciousness, it does not occasionally cease to operate. For instance, the arising of eye consciousness is [at times] followed by ear consciousness or any of the other remaining [active] forms of consciousness; [while at other times] the arising of ear consciousness is followed by eye consciousness or any of the other remaining [active] forms of consciousness. The same [description] applies for nose consciousness and the other remaining [active] forms of consciousness. Similarly, virtuous states of mind are [at times] followed by nonvirtuous ones, nonvirtuous states of mind by virtuous ones, and both virtuous and nonvirtuous states of mind by indeterminate ones. States of mind that pertain to the lower realm are [at times] followed by those of the middling realm[505]; those that pertain to the middling realm are [at times] followed by those of the superior realm[506]; those that pertain to the superior realm are [at times] followed by those that pertain to the inferior realm; and those that pertain to the inferior realm are [at times] followed by those of the middling realm, etc. Thus, these states of mind [other than the storehouse consciousness] that arise until the occurrence of death are not of one and the same nature.

Scriptural Sources

What evidence is there for the existence of this storehouse consciousness that is distinct from the six active forms of consciousness?

Evidence of its existence is based on scriptural authority and reasoning. The scriptural authority is the following. The Blessed One declared in a verse from an Abhidharma scripture:

> It is the element that has existed since beginningless time
> And the place where all entities dwell together.

All the states of transmigration and the attainment
Of nirvana as well occur because of its existence.[507]

A verse from the *Saṃdhinirmocana Sutra* also declares:

The acquiring consciousness[508] is subtle and profound;
It flows like a river[509] and contains the seeds of all things.
I did not reveal it to immature beings, so that
They would not conceive of it as a self.[510]

The Active Forms of Consciousness Arise Again Following Unconscious States of Composure

[The root text] states the following as a logical justification [for the existence of the storehouse consciousness]: "... because, after coming out of the state of composure that is a cessation, the state of composure without conception, and the state [of being born as a worldly god] that has no conception, the active forms of consciousness, which are referred to as 'awareness of objects,' arise again." [The implicit assertion that] completes this statement is, "[Therefore] the storehouse consciousness is an entity distinct from the active forms of consciousness."

When a person is absorbed in either the state of composure that is a cessation or the state of composure without conception, or when someone is born as [a worldly god] that has no conception, the active forms of consciousness are completely suspended. And, if the storehouse consciousness did not exist, the active forms of consciousness would not arise again when a person comes out of [either of those two states of composure or that state of samsaric existence]. [The active forms of consciousness] would not arise again from those states of mental composure, because a lengthy period of time goes by during which they do not occur and their cessation constitutes a state of nonexistence. It is unreasonable for anything that is nonexistent to be a cause or a result, just as primordial matter or a self [are nonexistent and, therefore, cannot serve as a cause for anything].[511]

There are those who believe the following:[512] Entities do not inherently possess the qualities of arising or destruction. The future, present, and past are established on the basis of the actions[513] of entities. Thus, the future is the state in which [an entity] does not carry out its action, the present is the state in which it does carry out its action, and the past is the state in which an action has terminated.

If that were true, it would have to be accepted that an entity is distinct from its action; because [proponents of this view] believe that an entity exists during both the past and the future, even though its action does not. However, in that case it would be the action [of an entity] and not the entity itself that undergoes both arising—in the sense of appearing after not having existed—and destruction—in the sense of disappearing after having existed. This would mean that [the five heaps of] form, feeling, conception, formations, and consciousness do not undergo arising and destruction, because [these entities] would possess their essential natures at all times and, therefore, they would neither arise nor undergo destruction. This would further entail that the heaps of form and the rest resemble the cessations and are not impermanent. As a result of that, they would not be characterized by suffering, since the sutras declare, "That which is impermanent is suffering." Thus, it would be a form of error to think that the heaps are characterized by impermanence and suffering.

It is unreasonable [to maintain] that an erroneous belief could bring about the abandonment of the mental afflictions, as with the erroneous belief that regards what is impermanent as permanent and [the erroneous belief that regards] what is unsatisfactory as a state of well-being. Moreover, since actions are what possess the qualities of arising and destruction, they must be conditioned entities. But since actions are not included in the [five] heaps of form, etc., [proponents of this view] would have to accept that there is a sixth heap. This amounts to a denial that the [five] grasping heaps subsume all impure entities and the [five] heaps in general subsume all conditioned entities!

Others declare the following: "Action" means to retain a result—which is to say, it is the quality by which an entity takes on the nature of being a cause. Thus, the state of being a cause is determined by the quality of retaining some particular entity as its result. Since the very quality of retaining a result is what constitutes the causal nature of entities, this means that entities are not distinct from their actions. Therefore, the errors mentioned above do not apply.

That is precisely what the expression "not distinct" means. In other words, [this expression] indicates the following: The action is not distinct from the entity—thus, the entity itself is the action. Similarly, the entity is not distinct from the action—and this means that the action itself is the entity. However, in that case, entities would not exist in either the past or the future, just as actions do not. Therefore, [proponents of this view] have abandoned [their] doctrine that the past and the future exist [in the form of real entities]. Alternatively, they must accept that an action also exists in the three times, just as the essence of an entity does, since the action is not distinct from an entity. But in that case, their explanation of the three times on the basis of actions is untenable.

According to the view that the present is [the state in which an entity] carries out an action, [the entity that performs the action] must be one thing and [the action] that it carries out another. [But if the entity and the action are not distinct, the action] would already have been completed [when the entity is present to carry out the action]. Therefore, [the entity] could not be the agent that carries out [the action]. That is, [the action] that is to be carried out must be something that has not yet been completed; it cannot be something that has already been completed. Therefore, since the entity and the action cannot both be completed and not yet completed, it is evident that they must be distinct. Therefore, the error that was posited earlier still stands.

Furthermore, if the entity and the action are not distinct, then the relationship between cause and effect would no longer exist. That is, since the existence of the result would already be established from the beginning, as it is with the cause, what action is there for the cause to carry out with respect to a result that would validate it as being a cause? [On the other hand,] if no action is carried out, what [entity] is there that one could refer to as a cause? Moreover, if that [entity] does not produce a result, how could one establish anything as being its result?

[It might be argued that] the mutual actions [of entities] themselves constitute the state of a cause and a result; [the state of being a cause and a result] is not something that pertains to entities. That is, when [one] action is present, then another action comes into being; if [the first action] is not present, then a second one will not occur. [The nature of cause and effect] is not something that occurs in relation to an entity's essential nature. Moreover, the essence of an entity does not arise from that [same] entity's essence, because it always exists.

The view that is commonly accepted in the everyday world is the following: A cause is that [entity] whose presence is [necessarily] followed by the appearance of some other [entity]; and whose absence precludes its appearance. That subsequent entity is its result. Thus, the view that the essence of an entity is neither a result nor a cause is at odds with both the everyday world and the philosophical treatises.

Another group [of scholars] asserts that the action cannot be described as either identical with or distinct from the entity.

Why can [the action] not be described as identical [with the entity]?

Because [the action] is not an entity's essential nature.

Why can [the action] not be described as distinct [from the entity]?

Although an entity's essential nature also is not the essence of [the action], this does not justify asserting that they are distinct [in the sense of distinct real entities].

In that case, something that is neither the essential nature of one entity nor the essential nature of anything else must be nonexistent, like the horn of a rabbit, because it has no essential nature of any kind. How could something that is nonexistent be the basis for defining the nature of the three times? Accordingly, the view that the three times can be established on the basis of an action is completely invalid. Therefore, it should be agreed that the future is that state in which entities have not yet arisen, the past is that state in which entities have ceased to exist, and the present is that state in which they have arisen but not yet ceased. It should not be held that the future is that state in which [an entity] does not carry out its action, the present is that state in which it does carry out its action, and the past is the state in which an action has terminated.

Still others[514] believe that the form that makes up the faculties[515] can serve as the seed from which thought [arises] and vice versa. Therefore, thought can arise from the form that constitutes the faculties when someone arises from the state of composure that is a cessation or the state of composure without conception, or when someone departs from the state of having been born among those [worldly deities] that have no conception. For example, this is like the situation in which the form that constitutes the faculties, after having ceased for a very long time, arises from the mind of someone who has passed away from the formless realm. Hence, [the proponents of this view] conclude: What need is there for positing a storehouse consciousness in order to explain this [situation]?

According to this [view], every sentient being must have two [separate] mind continua. One is derived from the form that constitutes the faculties and the other arises from consciousness. Furthermore, a being of the formless realm who has entered the state of composure that is a cessation would not be able to come out of that state, because there is no form in that level of existence. Therefore, this notion is unacceptable, because it leads to the absurd conclusion that such a person has entered nirvana.

Our view is that causes possess only the qualities of (1) existence, (2) motionlessness, (3) impermanence, and (4) efficacy; and [anything that possesses] the opposite [of these qualities] is not [a cause]. The Blessed One expressed this by declaring: "Thus, when this is present, that comes into being; from the arising of that, this arises. That is to say, conditioned by ignorance are the formations . . . ." Therefore, causes are neither permanent nor nonexistent; and they neither exert an action nor lack efficacy.[516]

The storehouse consciousness contains the seeds of all conditioned entities and it arises continuously up to the moment of death. When someone arises from a state [of composure] in which the active forms of consciousness are suspended, those [active forms of consciousness] begin to arise again on the basis of the storehouse consciousness. It is also declared in the sutras that the consciousness of one who has entered the state of composure that is a cessation "does not depart from the body." During this state of composure, there is no other form of consciousness that could be described as remaining within the body except the storehouse consciousness.

Why is that?

If you maintain that the consciousness that still functions when someone has entered the state of composure that is a cessation is a consciousness other than the storehouse consciousness, then you would have to accept that the two mental factors of conception and feeling are also present, because the sutras declare that "contact is the convergence of three, and feeling, conception, and volition arise together with contact." And if conception and feeling are present, it would not be the case that conception and feeling had ceased [being active].

Moreover, you cannot argue that this objection does not hold, because the sutra phrase "conditioned by feeling is craving" does not mean that all feelings serve as the condition that generates craving, and therefore not all contact necessarily serves as the condition that generates conception and feeling. While other sutras add the qualification that "craving arises on the basis of feelings that are produced by [the form of] contact that is accompanied by ignorance," there is no such qualification made with regard to contact as relates to [the arising of] conception and feelings.[517] Therefore, the two situations are not analogous. Consequently, it must be accepted that when someone comes out of the state of composure that is a cessation, the state of composure without conception, or the state [of having been born as a worldly god] that has no conception, the [six] active forms of consciousness begin to function again on the basis of the storehouse consciousness that possesses all the seeds [of conditioned entities] and exists during all circumstances.

The Active Forms of Consciousness Have Different Aspects

It should also be understood that the storehouse consciousness exists separately from the active forms of consciousness "[because] of the occurrence of different aspects in relation to the objective condition." The term "because"[518] that occurs at the end [of this sentence] should be understood as applying here as well.

"Objective condition"[519] refers to the [visible] form, etc., that are the objects of the five forms of [sense] consciousness of the eye and the rest, and to all entities that are the objects of mind consciousness.

"Different aspect" means that the aspect of [perceiving] a [visible] object, etc., is different from that of [perceiving] sound, etc. Similarly, it means that the aspect of [perceiving] sound, etc., is a different aspect from that of [perceiving visible] form, etc.; and that [the aspect of perceiving] a yellow [visible] form, etc., is a different aspect from that of [perceiving] a blue [visible form], etc. [These different aspects can be] described further at great length to illustrate all [the possible ways that they can vary].

The quality of occurring in a different aspect is something that pertains to certain types of consciousness. Thus, it is those [particular] forms of consciousness that are said to occur in different aspects. Because this condition exists, [the root text] refers to it as "the occurrence of different aspects."[520]

The condition of occurring in different aspects in a manner that is caused by, and takes place in relation to, the objective condition is what is meant by the phrase "the occurrence of different aspects in relation to the objective condition." When you add the term "because" to this phrase, it provides a reason for understanding why the storehouse consciousness exists separately from the active forms of consciousness.

Regarding this topic, [the various active] forms of consciousness are distinct from one another because they take on the varied appearance of their distinct objects; they are not distinguished on the basis of having different homogeneous immediate conditions or different governing conditions.[521] This is why [the root text] states, "[because] of the occurrence of different aspects in relation to the objective condition." Just as the occurrence of different aspects is not unrelated to the objective condition, it is also not unrelated to the causal condition. That entity which possesses the seeds [for the arising] of [multiple] other objects represents a universal condition. But the active forms of consciousness cannot mutually serve as one another's seeds, since they occur in [widely varying] gradations, such as those forms that are virtuous, nonvirtuous, indeterminate; those that pertain to the lesser, intermediate, and superior realms; those that are mundane and transcendent; as well as those that are related to the outflows and those that are free of the outflows.[522]

Nor can we see how the imprints of those very [active forms of consciousness] could become implanted [in the absence of a storehouse consciousness]. They also could not be implanted in relation to some different object existing at a different time, nor could they be implanted without some kind of connection [to another object]. However, we do observe that oils can be impregnated with the fragrance of flowers and the like when those [separate entities] arise and disappear together.

Therefore, [the following explanation] should definitely be accepted [as correct]: The active forms of consciousness arise and pass away in dependence on the "consciousness that is produced by maturation imprints"[523] and they exist simultaneously with it. This maturation consciousness is recognized as having the capacity to generate results[524] [of the active forms of consciousness] that are similar in nature [to their prior occurrences]. That capacity is referred to as an "imprint." Therefore, the maturation consciousness is [the entity that is] impregnated [with imprints created] by instances of the active forms of consciousness that occur at different times and in a variety of aspects. And it is from [this maturation consciousness] that the active forms of consciousness—which occur in relation to a [specific] object and in a variety of virtuous, nonvirtuous, and other aspects—arise. Consequently, it is established that there must exist a maturation consciousness that is different in nature from the active forms of consciousness and that [this consciousness] contains the seeds of all conditioned entities.

The Active Forms of Consciousness Arise Again After Unconscious States

[The root text] states that it can [also] be understood that there is a storehouse consciousness that is different from the active forms of consciousness "because of the occurrence [of the active forms of consciousness] after [their] having been interrupted." During such unconscious states as sleep and fainting, the active states of consciousness cease to function. Therefore, in the absence of a storehouse consciousness, it would not be possible for someone to awaken from such states as sleep or fainting and have their active forms of consciousness begin to function once again. The same kind of analysis should be applied here as was described in the case of the [conscious] mind [that arises again] when someone arises from the state of composure that is a cessation.

How Samsara Is Set in Motion

[Another justification for the storehouse consciousness is] "because samsara is both set in motion and brought to an end." [This means] one can know there is a storehouse consciousness that is different from the active forms of consciousness, because there are causes that set samsara in motion and bring it to an end.

"Samsara" refers to the arising of the grasping heaps within the uninterrupted continuum of a class affiliate that does not stand still for even an instant. For [samsara] to be "set in motion"[525] means [for the grasping heaps] to reenter [a birth state at the conception of] another class affiliate. For samsara to be "brought to an end"[526] refers to the states that are called "the nirvana in which the support of the heaps still remains" and "the nirvana in which the support of the heaps does not remain."[527] Regarding these concepts, it is not possible to explain how samsara is set in motion if you do not accept that there is a storehouse consciousness, because [in the absence of the storehouse consciousness] there is no way that consciousness could be conditioned by the formations.[528]

If you do not accept the existence of the storehouse consciousness, does the limb that states "consciousness is conditioned by formations" refer to the [mind] consciousness that occurs at [the moment of] reentry [into a new rebirth at conception]?[529] Or does [the phrase] mean that the collection of the six [active] forms of consciousness that have been impregnated by [the imprints of] the formations arise through having been conditioned by the formations?[530]

[If you claim the first alternative to be true,] then the consciousness that occurs at [the moment of] reentry [into a new rebirth] could not be conditioned by formations that were accumulated in a previous life, because a long period of time has passed since those formations underwent cessation. An entity that has undergone cessation no longer exists, and a nonexistent entity cannot be a conditioning factor.

If you maintain that [an entity that] has undergone cessation cannot be a conditioning factor, it would follow that no maturation would be produced by a deed carried out in the present, which [subjects you to the error that] karma has no result.[531]

That is not the case, because the state of being impregnated [by the imprint of a deed] continues to exist. The imprint that is produced by a deed is the unique transformation of [a prior] deed that has the capacity to produce a maturation. [This imprint] exists in the mind continuum. Therefore, it is not the case that a deed does not produce a result, nor [are we subject to the error that] a maturation arises from a deed that underwent cessation [at some time in the past and, therefore, no longer exists].[532]

[Moreover,] during [the first moment of] reentry [into a new rebirth at conception], name and form are also present; [therefore,] that [moment] is not a state in which consciousness alone exists. What reasoning is there [to support the notion] that consciousness alone is conditioned by the formations, and that name and form are not? Therefore, [according to the proponents of the Vaibhāṣika School, the language of dependent origination should be revised to assert] "name and form are conditioned by the formations" rather than "[name and form are conditioned] by consciousness." What is [the nature of] that separate [limb] described with the phrase "name and form are conditioned by consciousness"?

[The limb that states "name and form are conditioned by consciousness"] refers to the moments that follow the first instant of rebirth at conception.

What distinguishes the nature [of the name and form that exist during those subsequent moments] from that of the name and form that exist at [the moment of] reentry, such that [one would be justified in identifying] only the succeeding moments of name and form as being conditioned by consciousness? Why would the preceding moment [of name and form] be conditioned by the formations, but not the succeeding moments? Therefore, [if you claim that the consciousness being referred to in the phrase "consciousness is conditioned by the formations" is the consciousness that exists at the first moment of conception,] you must accept that name and form are conditioned by the formations [because they are also present at conception]. What need is there to posit an additional limb that accounts for consciousness at [the moment of] reentry? Consequently, it is not correct [to assert] that [the consciousness that is] conditioned by the formations is the consciousness that exists at [the moment of] reentry.

[The explanation that is] free of error is the following: The formations are conditioned by ignorance, and the [storehouse] consciousness that is impregnated by their [imprints] is [the form of consciousness] that is conditioned by the formations. The state of reentry [into a new rebirth at conception] that is conditioned by that [storehouse consciousness] is the very [aspect of] name and form [that is conditioned by consciousness].

The explanation that the collection of six [active] forms of consciousness that have been impregnated by [the imprints of] the formations is the meaning of the limb "consciousness is conditioned by the formations" is also badly formulated.[533]

Why?

[The active forms of] consciousness could not cause the maturation imprints and consequence imprints to be produced within them, because it is contradictory for [an agent] to act upon itself. Nor could [the imprints] be produced in the next moment [of consciousness], because that [next moment of consciousness] has not yet arisen at the time [that the formation is created]. Anything that is not present is nonexistent. [The impregnation of the karmic imprints] also could not occur when [the succeeding moment of] consciousness has arisen, because in that [succeeding] moment [the preceding moment of consciousness] has undergone cessation.

[Furthermore, according to the proponents of the Sautrāntika School,] it is not possible to establish the existence of the limb "name and form is conditioned by consciousness," because during such unconscious states as sleep and the like, there is not any form of consciousness present that could be impregnated by [the imprints of] the formations. In the absence of that limb, it would also not be possible to establish the existence of the six bases.[534] Similarly, it would not be possible to establish the existence [of all the remaining limbs] up to that of old age and death. Therefore, [this view of the nature of consciousness] is incompatible with the process by which samsara is set in motion.

How Samsara Is Brought to an End

If there were no storehouse consciousness, the process by which samsara is brought to an end also could not be properly explained. The causes of samsara are karma and the mental afflictions. And, of the two, the mental afflictions are the principal factor. That is, it is only through the power of the mental afflictions that karma is able to project a rebirth; it cannot do so otherwise. Thus, the karma [accumulated] by those who have [directly] perceived the [Four Noble] Truths does not project a rebirth, because [those individuals] no longer possess the mental afflictions that are abandoned by the Seeing Path.[535] Similarly, karma that [has the power] to project a rebirth will not produce a rebirth if the mental afflictions no longer exist. Thus, even though those individuals who have freed themselves of all attachment to the three realms still possess [the seeds of] karma that can generate rebirth, [that karma] is unable to bring about any new rebirth because those beings have abandoned all the mental afflictions. Therefore, they do not generate any rebirth. In this way, because they are the principal factor, the mental afflictions are the root of the process by which samsara is set in motion. For this reason, samsara can be brought to an end only when they have been abandoned, and not otherwise.

However, in the absence of the storehouse consciousness, it would not be possible to abandon the mental afflictions. It must be either the active forms of the mental afflictions that are abandoned or their seeds. If you maintain that their active forms are what is abandoned, that view is not accepted, because the path that abandons the mental afflictions cannot exist at a time when the mental afflictions are present in their active form.[536]

It would also not be possible to abandon the mental afflictions in the form of their seeds [if there were no storehouse consciousness], because you do not accept that anything other than the antidote is present in that situation where the seeds of the mental afflictions would have to be present so that an antidote could abandon them.[537] If you maintain that the state of mind that is the antidote exists in combination with the seeds of the mental afflictions, the fact that that mind is combined with the seeds of the mental afflictions makes it improper for it to constitute their antidote. And, it is not possible for those who have not abandoned the seeds of the mental afflictions to bring an end to samsara.

Therefore, you must accept that the storehouse consciousness is the entity that is impregnated by the imprints of the [root] mental afflictions and secondary mental afflictions in such a way that causes their seeds to be strengthened, and that [the active forms of] these [root and secondary mental afflictions] accompany the [six active] forms of consciousness other than the storehouse consciousness. Moreover, [these imprints] continue to exist as an [ever-changing, impermanent] continuum [within the storehouse consciousness]. And, whenever they become sufficiently strong to exercise their function, the root and secondary mental afflictions are caused to arise from that very [storehouse consciousness].

A path that exists simultaneously with [these seeds of the mental afflictions] and is the antidote to the mental afflictions can remove those seeds that reside in the storehouse consciousness. When they have been removed [in their entirety], the mental afflictions are no longer able to arise from their [former] source and [the practitioner] achieves the state of nirvana in which the support of the heaps still remains. When that [final] rebirth that was projected by previously collected karma comes to an end, there will be no further reunion with a rebirth, at which point [the practitioner] achieves the state of nirvana in which the support of the heaps does not remain. Even though [that person] still possesses [the seeds of projecting] karma, they are unable to bring about a [new] rebirth, because once the mental afflictions have been abandoned the efficient cause [that is necessary for rebirth to occur] no longer exists.

Thus, with the existence of the storehouse consciousness, both the continuation of samsara and its termination can be properly explained, and not otherwise. Therefore, you must accept that the storehouse consciousness exists.

The Meaning of "Storehouse Consciousness"

Why is this [form of consciousness] called the "storehouse consciousness"? [The root text] states that it is the storehouse consciousness "[because of] its quality of being the storehouse for the seeds of all [afflicted entities]." The expression "because of" that appears after the final [interpretation] applies equally to all [three interpretations of this term].

When the *tā*[538] suffix is attached to the word "storehouse consciousness," that denotes the state of being the storehouse consciousness. That state constitutes the basis for applying the term "storehouse consciousness." It is consciousness because it [is an entity that] knows distinctly. This explanation refers to the bare entity[539] as the agent in order to indicate that there is no other knowing agent.

The phrase "storehouse for all the seeds" means the place for storing the seeds of all afflicted entities. Storehouse is a synonym for a storage place.[540]

Alternatively, [this consciousness] is a storehouse because all entities "reside" in it—that is, [they] are located in it—in the sense that they are its result. Or, it is [a storehouse], because [the storehouse consciousness] "resides" in all entities—that is, it is located [in them]—in the sense of being their cause.[541]

[The root text also] states, "[That very consciousness is called the 'storehouse consciousness' because of . . .] its quality of being the storehouse and cause of [a sentient being's] individual existence." The phrase "individual existence"[542] [here] means name and form. [A sentient being's] individual existence "resides" [in the storehouse consciousness] in the sense that it arises by the power of [the storehouse consciousness].[543] To have that nature is what it means [to say that the storehouse consciousness possesses] "the quality of being a storehouse."

[The root text also describes the storehouse consciousness as being] the "cause of [a sentient being's] individual existence," because a [sentient being's] individual existence comes about when the seeds [of an individual's five heaps, which are located in the storehouse consciousness,] are activated maintained that this very [storehouse consciousness is what] "retains"[553] [a particular samsaric existence] until [the occurrence of] death. The [five sensory forms of] consciousness of the eye, etc., do not [acquire samsaric existence], nor does the mind consciousness that arises after that [first moment of conception], because [the six forms of active consciousness] are conditioned and caused by [the various faculties of] the eye, etc. Regarding this [point], mind consciousness is not caused by the [karmic] formations, because it can be virtuous or nonvirtuous in nature. That entity which is caused by the [karmic] formations can only have an indeterminate nature, because it is a maturation.[554] Moreover, unlike the eye and the rest, a maturation does not undergo reentry [into a new rebirth] after having ceased functioning for a period of time. And no other consciousness besides the storehouse consciousness can be seen to exhibit the nature of being a maturation that is always, perpetually, and exclusively indeterminate.

Furthermore, [each of the active forms of consciousness that make up] the six collections of consciousness arises on the basis of a specific region [of the body], and also comes into being after having ceased for a period of time. Therefore, it is not acceptable that they could "retain" the totality of one's physical being. A consciousness can be said to retain [only] that portion of the body from which it arises. It cannot retain any of the remaining portions [of the body], because [those remaining portions of the body] are not associated with that consciousness. Since eye consciousness and the other [active] forms of consciousness arise again and again after having undergone periods in which they did not function, the error occurs that these forms of consciousness acquire those regions again and again. Therefore, it is the storehouse consciousness alone that acquires [a sentient being's] individual existence from the [first] moment of reentry [at conception] until the time of its death, and this [form of acquisition] occurs in relation to the entire body. Therefore, [the storehouse consciousness] is [also] called the "acquiring consciousness," because it alone [is the form of consciousness that] takes on [a sentient being's] individual existence from the [first] moment of reentry [at conception and continues to retain it without interruption] until [the occurrence of] death.

The Afflicted Mind

[The root text] states, "Primarily, mind is what apprehends the storehouse consciousness as its object." The afflicted mind[555] at all times apprehends the storehouse consciousness as a self, because it is accompanied by [these and take birth [as a new class affiliate]. Therefore, the existence of the stor house consciousness should be accepted because it is the storehouse an cause of [a sentient being's] individual existence.

Other [editions] have this variant reading: "[It is called the 'storehous consciousness'] because of its quality of being the storehouse and cause o belief in a self."[544] [To explain that reading,] "belief in a self" is the [mis taken] belief that occurs when the storehouse consciousness is [wrongly apprehended as constituting a self. Thus, the storehouse consciousness is th "storehouse of belief in a self,"[545] because the belief in a self "resides"[546] in [th storehouse consciousness] in the sense of holding it as an object. Or els [the storehouse consciousness] is a storehouse because it "resides" in beli in a self, in the sense of being its cause. The remainder of the explanation[5 is the same as was described earlier.

[Finally, the root text also] states [this interpretation]: ". . . and [that ver consciousness is called the 'storehouse consciousness' because of] its qual ity of residing in [a sentient being's] body." The word "and" indicates tha [this interpretation] is [also] to be included [along with the previous two] "Body"[548] here refers to the [coarse] physical body along with the [five sense faculties. The storehouse consciousness extends throughout the entire phys ical body. Therefore, it resides or abides in the body in the sense that it oper ates in combination with the [entire] body. This condition is described a "the quality of residing in [a sentient being's] body." Therefore, the qual ity of residing in [a sentient being's] individual existence should [also] b understood as a reason for [calling this form of consciousness] the "store house consciousness."

The Meaning of "Acquiring Consciousness"

This [consciousness] is not only referred to as the "storehouse consciousness" [the root text adds], "It is also [called] the 'acquiring consciousness.'"

Why is [this consciousness also] called the "acquiring consciousness"?[549]

[The root text states as the reason,] "because it takes on [a sentient being's] embodied existence." Thus, [the storehouse consciousness] is [also] calle the "acquiring consciousness" because it is what takes on [a sentient being's] embodied existence.[550] This establishes that the mind is what takes on [a sentient being's] embodied existence, not a self. Moreover, the cause from which [a new samsaric existence] arises is a previous [karmic] formation[551] and [a new samsaric] existence is "acquired" when the mind loses conscious-ness after entering into the [united] semen and egg [of one's parents].[552] It is four mental factors that grasp the storehouse consciousness in the form of] (1) bewilderment toward a self, (2) the view that believes in a self, (3) pride toward a self, and (4) attachment toward a self. Moreover, this [form of consciousness] is [called] "mind" because its nature is that of a perpetual state of reflective thought.[556] This is the true sense of the term "mind."

The state of any instance of the six collections of consciousness [that are made up] of eye [consciousness], etc., in the moment immediately following its cessation is [also] referred to as "mind" in order to establish a basis[557] for mind consciousness, [which is also referred to as] the sixth [form of consciousness].[558] [This past state of the six active forms of consciousness is] not [referred to as "mind"] because it is a form of self-reflective thought. Therefore, this usage is not the true sense of the term "mind."

[The afflicted mind] is always accompanied by these four mental afflictions: bewilderment toward a self, the view that believes in a self, pride toward a self, and attachment toward a self. "Bewilderment toward a self"[559] indicates that the afflicted mind is not associated with a general form of ignorance; rather it is the specific ignorance that is bewilderment toward a self. A similar description applies to the other mental afflictions.[560] The expression "and so on" means that the afflicted mind is also associated with the five universal mental factors of contact, attention, and the rest. [The root text] also refers to [the afflicted mind] as a [form of] "consciousness" to specify its essential nature, because [that nature] is not widely known and to indicate that it is associated with [a range of] mental factors.

The phrase "It is of one type" means that it is only an afflicted type of entity and not one that is virtuous or indeterminate, because it is always accompanied by the four mental afflictions of bewilderment toward a self and so on.[561]

The phrase "it occurs continually" means that it arises uninterruptedly.

As an exception to this general statement, [the root text] states, "except when [one becomes] an Arhat, [when one has generated] the Ārya path, and [when one is absorbed in] the state of composure that is a cessation." [The afflicted mind] no longer arises when one becomes an Arhat, because an Arhat is someone who has abandoned all the afflicted entities of the three realms. It also does not arise when [one has generated] the Ārya path, because [transcendent] knowledge of the ultimate object is completely incompatible with the occurrence of belief in a self. Following that [period during which one has generated the Ārya path], the afflicted mind arises again from the storehouse consciousness, because during the time that [one is still undergoing spiritual] training, it has not yet been abandoned. [The afflicted mind] also does not arise when [one is absorbed in] the state of composure that is a cessation, because that state of composure is much more tranquil than the state of composure without conception.[562] For this reason, it should be understood that the afflicted mind does not occur [in these three instances].

It should be understood that this [discussion] has presented the topic of mind in relation to the literal meaning of the term, its object, the mental factors that accompany it, and the periods when it occurs.

What Does the Term "Heap" Mean?

In response to the question, "Why are they called 'heaps'?" [the root text] states, "Because they are aggregates."[563] Thus, the term "heap" is considered to mean an aggregate. As such, the form heap is the form aggregate. Similarly, the same is true for the other heaps, up to the consciousness heap being the consciousness aggregate.

Thus, it is taught in the sutras that form and the rest comprise heaps because they are collections of form, etc., that are distinct in terms of time, continuum, types, being, and region. The [sutras] declare, "Whatever form there is of the past, future, or present, outer or inner, coarse or subtle, inferior or excellent, whatever is far or near, all of that collected together as one is considered the form heap." The same is said for the other entities up to consciousness.

That [form, etc.] which is differentiated as being of the past, future, and present is distinct in terms of time.

"Inner or outer" [form, etc.] refers to that which relates to distinct continua. That is to say, inner [form, etc.] is that which is included within your own continuum. Outer [form, etc.] is that which is other than [the form included in] your own [continuum].

"Coarse or subtle" describes distinct types of entities. The coarseness and subtleness of form is relative. Or, coarse form is that which possesses resistance[564]; subtle form is that which lacks resistance. In the case of feeling, conception, the formations, and consciousness, that which arises in dependence on the five sense faculties is coarse; that which arises in dependence on mind is subtle.

"Inferior and excellent" is differentiated on the basis of beings. That is, those [entities] that pertain to an inferior being are inferior; those that pertain to excellent beings are excellent.

"Whatever is far or near" is differentiated on the basis of region. Feeling and the rest are near or far on the strength of their source.[565]

"Form, etc." means form, feeling, conception, formations, and consciousness.

Regarding the phrase "in the sense of the quality of being a collection," a collection is the group that is obtained by combining together all the form, feeling, conception, formations, and consciousness that is distinct in terms of time, continuum, type, being, and region. That quality is "the quality of being a collection."

Thus, it should be understood that the meaning of "heap" is explained in the sutras as the aggregate of those entities that is obtained when they have been collected together. This is described in the sutras with the phrase "[whatever] form . . . of the past . . . all of that collected together as one is considered the form heap." This presentation should be made in the same way for the other conditioned entities ranging up to consciousness. This concludes the explanation of the five heaps and the meaning of the term "heap."

THE TWELVE BASES

All conditioned entities are included within the five heaps; however, it is taught that all entities—both those that are conditioned and those that are unconditioned—are included [both] within the twelve bases and within the eighteen constituents. Thus, after explaining the five heaps, the bases need to be presented. It should, then, be asked, How many bases are there and what is the meaning of the term "basis"? In response to this question, [the root text begins by] saying, "There are twelve bases."

What are they?

[The root text identifies them as] ranging from the "eye basis and form basis" up to the "mind basis and entity basis."

The Five Inner Bases of the Eye and the Rest

The phrase [in the root text that states], "The bases of the eye, etc., . . . are explained in the same manner as before" means that the essential natures of the [five inner] bases of the eye, etc., are to be explained here in the same manner that the essential natures of the eye, etc., were presented in the separate explanations of [the entities that comprise] the form heap. In that part [of the root text], the eye faculty was explained as [form] "that is derived from the four great elements" and as "clear form that has color as its object." Similarly, [the remaining four sense faculties were also described as being form] that has sound, smells, tastes, and tangible entities as their objects, respectively. Thus, [those sense faculties of] the ear and the rest also have an essential nature that consists of clear form.

The Four Outer Bases of Visible Form and the Rest

The phrase "are explained in the same manner as before" also applies to the [four outer] bases of form, sound, smells, and tastes. Previously, [visible form was described as] "the object of the eye, which is color, shape, and informative form." Sound [was described as] "the object of the ear," and as [a type of derivative form that is] "caused by the four great elements that are [either] retained, unretained, or both." The rest [that is, the two sense objects—smells and tastes—were also] described [in a similar manner].

The Basis of Tangible Objects

[The root text describes] the basis of tangible objects as [being made up of] "the [four] great elements and those [entities] that were described as a portion of tangible objects." The [entities] that are grouped together with the [four] great elements are [the list of seven tangible objects that consists of] smoothness and the rest.

The Mind Basis

Concerning the description, "The mind basis is [made up of] the consciousness heap," the consciousness heap includes the eight forms of consciousness—namely, the six active forms of consciousness, the storehouse consciousness, and the afflicted mind. [Thus,] in the formulation of the bases, the term "mind basis" refers to the consciousness heap.

The Entity Basis

The entity basis is [made up] of eight types [of entity]: the feeling, conception, and formation heaps, noninformative form, and the four types of unconditioned entities.

The Four Types of Unconditioned Entities

Of these, the feeling, conception, and formation heaps, as well as noninformative form, were explained in the separate explanations of [the entities that comprise] the [five] heaps; however, the unconditioned entities have not been explained. Therefore, desiring to present their classification, [the root text] asks, "What are unconditioned entities?"

The essential nature of an unconditioned entity is that it does not depend on causes and conditions. [The root text] presents their classification as [consisting of] "space, the nonanalytic cessation, the analytic cessation, and suchness."

Space

[The root text] asks, "What is space?" in order to make known the essential nature of space. It then describes its essential nature with the phrase, "A place for form." Descriptions are also given in a similar manner for the nonanalytic cessation and the rest.

"Place"[566] describes a region where [the type of] form that possesses resistance is not obstructed. Therefore, the term "space" refers to [a region that] gives way to physical entities.

The Nonanalytic Cessation

The nonanalytic cessation is mentioned next after space [among the four types of unconditioned entities]; therefore, after space has been explained, [the root text] asks, "What is the nonanalytic cessation?" from a desire to make known the essential nature of the nonanalytic cessation. Analysis, correct notion, investigation, and discernment all have the same meaning.[567] The prefix *prati*[568] [in *pratisaṃkhyā*—the Sanskrit for "analytic"]—indicates repetitive action. Thus, the term "analytic" refers to the repetitive analysis that is carried out in relation to the [Four] Noble Truths of Suffering, etc. This [term] describes a particular form of wisdom.

"Nonanalytic" refers to that which does not constitute repetitive analysis.

What, then, is it?

An insufficiency of [necessary] conditions.[569] That is, the nonanalytic cessation is the condition by which future entities are permanently obstructed from arising due to an insufficiency of [necessary] conditions.

The [complete] statement, "It is the cessation that is not a separation . . . ," is the response to the question, ["What is the nonanalytic cessation?"] Just as the term "cessation" is used in relation to the nonanalytic cessation, it is also used to refer to [various other things, such as] a state that is produced by repeated analysis, a state of composure, an absence of arising, and impermanence. Therefore, in order to differentiate this cessation from the analytic cessation [in particular], the root text states that [the nonanalytic cessation] "is not a separation."[570]

This phrase "not a separation" should be understood as follows: It is a general principle that the existence of a seed insures [the possibility] that certain entities can arise [in the future]. Therefore, [the meaning of a seed] is established as [the possibility] that certain entities will be encountered in the future. [One kind of] cessation [is the state that occurs when] the antidote to [certain future entities] removes their seeds from their resting place, thus bringing about a permanent nonarising [of those entities].[571] Therefore, [the present explanation] indicates that, although the nonanalytic cessation does not result from the premeditated [i.e., intentional] removal of the seeds [of certain future entities], it does represent a state that is the permanent nonarising of future entities due to the insufficiency of [necessary] conditions.

Even though an Arhat possesses the seeds of virtuous and indeterminate heaps that are associated with further samsaric rebirths, he [or she] has attained the state of their permanent nonarising. Therefore, one might think that this state also constitutes a nonanalytic cessation. In order to [counter this mistaken notion, the root text] states, "it is the permanent nonarising of the heaps that is unrelated to an antidote to the mental afflictions." This statement [can be explained] as follows: Although [an Arhat] possesses the seeds of virtuous and indeterminate heaps, [this state of being an Arhat] is not attained without [having developed] the antidote to [all] the mental afflictions; therefore, it constitutes an analytic cessation and not a nonanalytic cessation. Accordingly, this [part of the statement][572] indicates that both the state of nirvana in which the support of the heaps still remains and the state of nirvana in which the support of the heaps does not remain constitute an analytic cessation. The phrase "antidote to the mental afflictions" is understood here as referring to the pure path.[573]

The term "permanent" in the expression "permanent nonarising" is meant to distinguish this cessation from the cessation that follows the arising of entities and the cessation that is a state of composure. Both of these latter types of cessation are states in which entities do not arise; however, they are not permanent because mind and the mental factors can arise again in the future.

The term "nonarising" distinguishes this cessation from the cessation that is impermanence. The cessation of impermanence occurs in relation to [entities] that exist in the present; however, the term "nonarising" refers to future [entities] that do not exist in the present. For instance, when an eye consciousness is occupied with [the perception of] one particular visible object, the collections of five forms of sense consciousness are unable to arise in relation to any other visible object or any of the other [four] sense objects that have gone into the past, because no [homogeneous] immediate condition[574] can occur in relation to [entities] of the present and no objective condition[575] can occur in relation to [entities] of the past. Therefore, a nonanalytic cessation exists with regard to those particular entities.[576]

The Analytic Cessation

With regard to the question, "What is the analytic cessation?" analysis is a form of tranquil consideration and a particular type of wisdom—namely, that of the noninterruption path.[577] The analytic cessation is a cessation that is achieved by [this type of] analysis. [Thus, this term is] a [type of] compound in which the intervening words have been left out.

If [the analytic cessation] were merely described as "a cessation," it would follow incorrectly that [the term "analytic cessation"] applied to all the [varieties of] cessation; therefore it is further described [as a cessation] "that is a separation."[578] In so doing, [the analytic cessation] is distinguished from the other four types of cessation, because none of them is a separation.

The phrase "permanent nonarising of the heaps that is related to an antidote to the mental afflictions" refers specifically to this separation.

When this body comes into existence, it is accompanied by all the seeds of the mental afflictions that are related to the three realms. Then, when a particular moment of the path that is an antidote for a certain portion of the mental afflictions arises, the body that exists at that moment becomes a condition that is incompatible with the occurrence of succeeding moments of the body that will continue to possess the seeds of those particular mental afflictions that are being abandoned by that [moment of the path]. [Thus, the body that exists at that moment of the path] becomes incapable of generating succeeding moments of the body [that will continue to possess the seeds of those particular mental afflictions that are being abandoned by that moment of the path], because it has taken on that [quality of being an] incompatible condition. However, [that moment of the body] only takes on the nature of being a cause for the termination of the seeds that are abandoned by that [moment of the path], because it still possesses [other] conditions that are compatible with the occurrence of those [seeds of other mental afflictions that are not abandoned by that moment of the path]. That moment of the path should also be described [in the same way]. That is, it becomes a condition that is incompatible with the occurrence of succeeding moments [of a being's continuum] that will continue to possess the seeds of those particular mental afflictions that are being abandoned by that [moment of the path. However,] it is [still] compatible with [the occurrence of succeeding moments of a being's continuum that will continue to possess the seeds of] other [mental afflictions].[579]

Likewise, when the antidote to the smallest of the small of those mental afflictions associated with the Peak of Existence that are abandoned by the Meditation Path arises, that moment of the body takes on the nature of being a cause for the termination of all the seeds of the three realms' mental afflictions that are abandoned by the paths of Seeing and Meditation during all subsequent moments [of the body]. In addition to those mental afflictions whose seeds have been removed in the sense that the body no longer can give rise to [any of the mental afflictions], all the entities that accompany [the mental afflictions] have also been rendered permanently unable to arise by the [very same] antidotes to the mental afflictions. This is [the sort of] analytic cessation [that the root text describes as] a "separation."

Suchness

[In the root text,] suchness is mentioned after the analytic cessation. Therefore, following the explanation of the latter, it is asked, "What is suchness?" wishing to make known its essential nature. Then suchness is explained with the response, "It is the [true] nature of entities and the insubstantiality of entities."

"Suchness" [literally] means a nature that does not become anything else.[580] The term "entities" [in this description] refers to [the five heaps of] form, feeling, conception, formations, and consciousness. Their "[true] nature"[581] is their [genuine] mode of being—that is to say, it is their nature as it truly is and their ultimate mode of being.

Because entities also have such natures as the resultant quality of impermanence and the like, [the root text] adds the qualifying phrase "the insubstantiality of entities."[582] Entities do not truly possess that essence which is the object of [ordinary] mind and speech. Because they do not have that nature and they lack any such substance, they are insubstantial. That state is their insubstantiality. It is the emptiness[583] [of entities] that is characterized by their absence of any [mentally] contrived nature. If we were to examine this topic further, there would be much to say. [However,] in order to avoid excessive length, I will let this suffice and continue with the subject at hand.

What Does the Term "Basis" Mean?

With regard to the question, "Why are they called 'bases'?" the term "basis" occurs equally in relation to those entities of the eye, etc., that have distinct essential natures; therefore, it must be applied to them in some general sense that they [all] have in common. Since that is not understood, [the root text] asks, "Why are they called 'bases'?"

With regard to the response, "Because they are the sources for the appearance of consciousness,"[584] "appearance" means arising. Consciousness takes on existence through its arising.

"Source for the appearance of consciousness" means its cause. The "source for the appearance" [of something] means its productive cause[585] and efficient cause.[586] Thus, they are called "bases" because they are the causes for the arising of consciousness.

How is this made evident? It can be made evident through the literal explanation of the term. They are "bases" because they extend—that is, expand—the appearance of mind and the mental factors.[587] This means that they continually cause them to come into being. [This can be described as follows:] "eye and [visible] form are the source for the appearance of eye consciousness together with its associated mental factors." A similar description applies for the other [forms of consciousness], up to "mind and entities are the source for the appearance of mind consciousness together with its associated mental factors."

THE EIGHTEEN CONSTITUENTS

Following the description of the bases, the classification and essential nature of the constituents needs to be presented. Therefore, in order to indicate their classification, [the root text] declares, "There are eighteen constituents." In order to indicate them individually, [the root text] declares, "the eye constituent, the form constituent, the eye-consciousness constituent," and so on, up to "the mind constituent, the entity constituent, and the mind-consciousness constituent."

Concerning this [classification of the constituents], the classification of the heaps described the five faculties of the eye, ear, nose, tongue, and body, and their five objects of [visible] form, sound, smells, tastes, and tangible objects. In the presentation of the bases, those very same five faculties are identified as the eye basis, etc., and the [five] objects of [visible] form and the rest are identified as the form basis, etc. The presentation of the constituents also identifies these very [same ten groups of] entities as [the ten constituents] that range from the eye constituent to the body constituent, and range from the form constituent to the tangible-object constituent. Therefore, [the root text] states, "The [description of the five] constituents of the eye, etc., and the [five] constituents of form, etc., is the same as [that which was made] for the [ten corresponding] bases."

The entity constituent is described in the same way that the entity basis was said to consist of the three heaps of feeling, etc., noninformative form, and the four types of unconditioned entities.

In the presentation of the bases, the mind basis is [described as being made up of] the consciousness heap. In the presentation of the constituents, however, the mind constituent is not [described] in the same way as the mind basis. When the [entities that make up the] mind basis [are identified] in the presentation of the constituents, they [are described as] the seven mental constituents.[588] Therefore, [the root text] declares, "The six consciousness constituents are . . . ."

The phrase "based upon the eye, etc." means that [the six consciousness constituents] are based upon [the faculties of] the eye, ear, nose, tongue, body, and mind. The phrase "have form, etc., as their objects" means that [the six consciousness constituents] have form, sound, smells, tastes, tangible objects, and entities as their objects. The phrase "forms of awareness" means forms of consciousness. Thus, the eye consciousness that is based upon the eye and has form as its object is the eye-consciousness constituent. Similarly, those forms of consciousness that are based upon the ear, nose, tongue, body, and mind, and have as their objects sound, smells, tastes, tangible objects, and entities, in that order, are the ear-, nose-, tongue-, body-, and mind-consciousness constituents.

The mind constituent is not distinct from the six forms of consciousness.

[Rather,] those very six consciousness constituents in the moment immediately following their cessation are called "the mind constituent."

In that case, since the mind constituent and the six consciousness constituents are each subsumed in the other category, is it not the case that there are more properly either seventeen constituents or twelve constituents?

No, [because] as the root text states, "[The mind constituent is formulated] in order to indicate a basis[589] for the sixth consciousness. In this manner, it is established that there are eighteen constituents." The phrase "in this manner" refers to the manner in which this is described in the preceding portion [of the root text].

Correspondences Among the Heaps, Bases, and Constituents

With regard to the phrase "the form heap," the form heap is described as [comprising] eleven entities. Regarding them, the five sense faculties of the eye, etc., and the five sense objects of [visible] form, etc., correspond to ten bases in the formulation of the bases, and they correspond to ten constituents in the formulation of the constituents. [The phrases] "a portion of the entity basis" and "a portion of the entity constituent" [both] refer to noninformative form.

With regard to the statement, "The consciousness heap corresponds to the mind basis and to the seven mental constituents," [the seven mental constituents are] those that range from the eye-consciousness constituent up to the mind constituent.

The "other three heaps" are those other than the form heap and the consciousness heap—which is to say, the feeling heap, the conception heap, and the formations heap. "A portion of the form heap" refers to noninformative form. These aspects of the heaps, together with the unconditioned entities of space and the rest, correspond to the entity basis and the entity constituent.

What Does the Term "Constituent" Mean?

Concerning the question, "Why are they called 'constituents'?" the same observation that was made in relation the bases should be stated again here.[590]

Regarding the phrase, "Because they do not carry out any action[591] and they retain their unique essential characteristics,"[592] it was explained previously that momentary entities cannot be active agents.

Why the Heaps, Bases, and Constituents Were Taught

Those entities that were explained as constituting the heaps were also taught within [the formulations of] the bases and constituents. Therefore, [the root text] asks, "Why were the heaps and the rest taught?" Everything that the Buddhas, the Blessed Ones, taught is meaningful in that it benefits sentient beings and serves as an antidote for the mental afflictions. Because the purpose for teaching the entities that were described here in a variety of different ways is unclear, [the root text] asks, "Why were the heaps and the rest taught?" in order to state that purpose. And therefore, [the root text responds to that question by] declaring, "As antidotes for three types of belief in a self."

Because it is not known what the three types of belief in a self are and what topic was taught as an antidote for [each of] them, [the root text] states that the heaps and the rest were taught as antidotes "respectively" for three types of belief in a self, which are (1) belief in a unity,[593] (2) belief in an experiencer,[594] and (3) belief in an agent.[595] The correspondence is that the heaps were taught as an antidote for the belief in a unity; the bases were taught as an antidote for the belief in an entity that experiences; and the constituents were taught as an antidote for the belief in an agent.

Belief in a Unity

All proponents of a doctrine that asserts the existence of a [real] self hold that the very same entity that sees also hears, smells, tastes, and touches; and that it also forms volitions, conceptualizes, and cognizes. However, within one's being there is nothing at all that exists apart from the five heaps and has the nature of a unity, because no such nature or effect of that nature can be ascertained.

There is no seeing agent apart from the eyes. The phrase "the two eyes see" indicates that they are the unique cause and seat for [eye] consciousness, and therefore can be designated as the agent that sees. A similar description can be made for each of the other sense organs of the ear, etc. Likewise, feelings are the agent that experiences in that their essential nature is that of experiencing. Conceptions are the agent that conceptualizes in that their essential nature is that of grasping an object's sign. A similar description is to be made universally. Therefore, because the individual existence[596] of sentient beings is made up of the heaps, their essential nature consists of a multiplicity of entities. Regarding this, there is no unity that exists apart from the five heaps. Thus, when the belief in a unity is reversed through teaching the heaps, the belief in a real self that is premised on the belief in a unity will also be reversed. Therefore, the heaps are taught as an antidote for the belief in a real self that is logically predicated on the belief in a unity. The phrase "belief in a unity" can be explained as referring to belief in a real self by figuratively applying the term for a result to its cause.

Belief in an Experiencer

All those who profess belief in an experiencer describe the self as the entity that experiences the favorable and unfavorable results of virtuous and nonvirtuous deeds that are distinguished in terms of pleasurable and painful feelings, and the entity that experiences such objects as forms, sounds, and the like. Thus, the bases were taught as an antidote for this form of belief in a self.

The act of experiencing the results of virtuous and nonvirtuous deeds, and experiencing such objects as forms, sounds, and the like, is perception.[597] The entity that carries out that action is what experiences the results of deeds and [experiences] form, etc. It is the bases alone, and nothing else, that carry out the six types of perception. Therefore, the eye, etc., and form, etc., are called the bases because they are the sources for the appearance of consciousness. Thus, there is nothing at all apart from the eyes, etc., that experiences the results of deeds and objects; and hence the explanation of the bases constitutes the antidote for the belief in an experiencer.

Belief in an Agent

The belief in an agent refers to an entity that carries out such actions as those that bind one to virtuous and nonvirtuous deeds, as well as those that shake off[598] [that bondage]. The constituents were taught as an antidote for this form of belief in a self. Thus, the constituents are [those entities] that do not carry out any action and [those entities] that retain their unique essential characteristics. This means that the mere existence of a cause brings about the arising of its result, and the existence of the result is due entirely to its dependence on a cause. It was already explained earlier that there is no action that exists separately from the essential natures of causes and effects. Without the existence of actions, how could there be an agent? Therefore, the constituents were taught as an antidote for the belief in an agent.

FURTHER CLASSIFICATIONS OF THE CONSTITUENTS

Those entities that were explained as constituting the heaps, bases, and constituents in order to benefit [beings] by such classifications are now to be considered in a variety of further aspects. These aspects are to be considered in relation to the constituents rather than the heaps and the bases, because form and mind were differentiated in greater detail within that system of classification, making it easier to comprehend such distinctions as being related to the outflows, etc.

How Many Are Material?

Therefore, [the root text words the questions in the form,] "How many of the constituents are material?" etc.

Form is that which exhibits form. Because these [entities][599] have that [nature], they are [said to be] material.[600] Alternatively, these [entities] are material because each in its particular manner is either the form that constitutes a basis or the form that is dependent [on that basis].[601] Moreover, this explanation does not also incorrectly apply to eye consciousness and the rest,[602] because while the [six] faculties of the eye, etc., are [referred to as] the basis[603] [for the arising of their respective forms of consciousness], they are not the vessel[604] for [each of] those forms of consciousness.

[The root text responds to the above question by saying,] "Those [constituents] whose nature [it] is [to be included in] the form heap." This statement refers to ten constituents, those ranging from the eye constituent to the body constituent, as well as those ranging from the form constituent to the tangible-object constituent. Even though it is acknowledged that non-informative [form] does exhibit [the quality of] form, it does not follow that the entity constituent is material, (1) because [the entity constituent] does not contain [any form] that constitutes a basis or that is dependent on a basis,[605] (2) because it does contain entities that lack the quality of exhibiting form,[606] and (3) because [the entity constituent as a whole] does not exhibit form even though it contains entities that are included in the form heap.[607]

How Many Are Not Material?

[In response to the question, "How many are not material[608]?" [the root text] states, "The remaining ones." The constituents that are not material are the ones that were not included among those that are material. These consist of eight [constituents]—that is, the seven mental constituents and the entity constituent.

How Many Are Capable of Being Indicated?

[When the root text asks,] "How many are capable of being indicated?" this is meant in terms of the constituents, since that is the topic under consideration. In response to this question, [the root text] declares [in part], "Only the form constituent." "Indication"[609] is the quality by which an object can be pointed out [with such language as] "This [entity] is here; that [entity] is there." An object that has this characteristic is described as capable of being indicated,[610] as with the term "capable of apprehending [an object].[611]"

In order to further explain this phrase "capable of being indicated," the root text adds, "which is an object that is capable of being indicated." The phrase "which is an object that is capable of being indicated" means the quality by which an object can be pointed out as being present in this or that location.

How Many Are Not Capable of Being Indicated?

Since only the form constituent is identified as capable of being indicated, it can be determined that the remaining seventeen constituents are "not capable of being indicated."

How Many Possess Resistance?

[When the root test asks,] "How many possess resistance?" it should be understood that all the questions refer to the eighteen constituents, since that is the topic under consideration. The response states that it is those [ten constituents] that are "material," in order to exclude those that are not material. Since the entity constituent also includes noninformative form, they are identified as "ten," in order to indicate which type of form is considered to be material. Moreover, these are the five material constituents of the eye faculty, etc., and the five material constituents that are their objects.

Resistance means opposition. Entities that have that quality are said to "possess resistance."[612] There are three types of opposition: (1) object-opposition,[613] (2) apprehension-opposition,[614] and (3) obstruction-opposition.[615] To indicate that in this instance the quality of possessing resistance is held to be obstruction-opposition, [the root text] states, "those that occupy a place where something can strike against them." Obstruction-opposition is the quality by which one entity opposes the arising of another object in the space that it occupies. Thus, both the entity that prevents something else from arising in the space that it occupies and the location where that obstruction occurs indicate the meaning of possessing resistance [as the term is being used here]. These ten material constituents make up the entities that possess resistance because they obstruct and oppose one another in the sense of preventing anything else from arising in the place that each one individually occupies.

How Many Lack Resistance?

It can be determined that the remaining [constituents]—that is, the seven mental constituents and the entity constituent—are the ones that lack resistance.

How Many Are Related to the Outflows?

[When the root text asks,] "How many are related to the outflows?" the topic at hand is that of the constituents. With regard to the response "fifteen [constituents] and a portion of the final three," the fifteen are the five constituents of the eye faculty, etc., the five constituents that comprise the [sense] objects of form, etc., and the five constituents that comprise eye consciousness, etc. These [fifteen] constituents in their entirety are related to the outflows.

[The constituents are also classified in groups of three. Therefore, if one simply said "three" instead of "the final three"] this could also be taken to mean the first [group of] three [constituents]—that is, the eye constituent, the form constituent, and the eye-consciousness constituent. This is why [the root text] states the [adjective] "final." The "final three" [constituents] are the mind constituent, the entity constituent, and the mind-consciousness constituent. A "portion" of them means that only part of them is related to the outflows. Unlike the eye and the rest, not all [the entities contained in] these three [final] constituents are related to the outflows. Among the entities [contained in those final three constituents], those that are distinct in nature from the Truth of the Path and unconditioned entities are the ones that are related to the outflows.

Related to the outflows[616] means to be associated with them; therefore, the root text states that "they give rise to the mental afflictions." That is to say, these entities are declared to be related to the outflows because the mental afflictions arise from them.

Since the [sensory] forms of consciousness of the eye, etc., are aconceptual, how is it that they generate the mental afflictions in relation to form, etc.?

The mental afflictions are not said to arise in relation to form, etc., in the sense that they [directly] accompany the [sensory] forms of consciousness of the eye, etc. However, the phrase "because they are the direct fields of experience"[617] means that the mental afflictions *are* generated in relation to form, etc. This can be understood in the following manner. Eye consciousness arises on the basis of the eye [faculty] and in relation to [visible] form. Mind consciousness then conceptualizes about those forms that were experienced by eye consciousness. The mental afflictions, in turn, arise on the basis of that conceptualization. A similar description should be made for the remaining [constituents].

How Many Are Free of the Outflows?

[In response to the question,] "How many are free of the outflows?" [the root text] states, "A portion of the final three." This means [a portion] of the mind, entity, and mind-consciousness constituents. The Truth of the Path and those entities that are unconditioned make up [the group that is] free of the outflows.

How Many Are Related to Desire?

The question, "How many are related to desire?" is made in reference to the eighteen constituents. The five [sense] objects of [visible] form, etc., are called "desires"[618] because they are objects of desire, and the desire realm should be understood as the realm in which these [entities] are cherished. Alternatively, the phrase "related to desire" should be understood as a literary device that is intended to convey the question, "How many are related to the desire realm?" without directly stating the word "realm."

To be related to the desire realm means to be contained within it—which should be understood as meaning "to have the nature of [being included in] the desire realm." Thus, all [of the constituents] that give rise to craving for the sense objects [should be understood as being] contained within the desire realm; and they are the six constituents that are faculties, the six constituents that are objects, and the six constituents that are forms of consciousness.

How Many Are Related to Form?

[In response to the question,] "How many are related to form?" [the root text] states, "Fourteen [constituents]." The fourteen constituents that [contain entities that are] related to the form realm are the constituents of the eye, ear, nose, tongue, body, and mind faculties, as well as four constituents that are objects and four constituents that are the forms of consciousness that perceive those objects.

Why are there no smells, tastes, or the two forms of consciousness that perceive those [two sense] objects in the form realm?

Smells and tastes are exclusively associated with food that is taken in morsels[619]; they do not have the nature of the food of volition or [the food of] contact. Furthermore, those who have freed themselves of desire for food taken in morsels are reborn in the form realm. When beings overcome desire for a [particular type of] object, that object will not be present in the place where they are reborn. For example, when beings who have overcome desire [for the desire and form realms] are reborn in the formless realm, [none of the five forms of sense consciousness are present there] because [the sense faculties of] the eye, etc., [are absent]. Similarly, [when beings who have overcome desire for food taken in morsels are reborn in the form realm] the [two] forms of consciousness that perceive smells and tastes are also not present there because their objects are absent.

How Many Are Related to the Formless?

[In response to the question,] "How many are related to the formless?" the root text states, "The final three." These are the mind constituent, the entity constituent, and the mind-consciousness constituent. The beings who are born in the formless realm are those who have freed themselves of desire for form. Therefore, the ten constituents that have the nature of form[620] and the five consciousness constituents that are based on them and take hold of them as objects do not exist there.

How Many Are Unrelated?

[In response to the question,] "How many are unrelated?" [the root text] states, "A portion of three." They are the entities that are not objects of the craving that occurs in the desire, form, and formless realms. They are referred to as "unrelated" because they are unrelated to any of the three realms. They are the entities that make up the Truth of the Path as well as those that have an unconditioned nature, which are found in the mind, entity, and mind-consciousness constituents, and which are unrelated to the outflows.

How Many Are Virtuous, How Many Are Nonvirtuous, and How Many Are Indeterminate?

The question, "How many are virtuous, how many are nonvirtuous, and how many are indeterminate?" is made in reference to the eighteen constituents, since that is the present topic.

The virtuous[621] are those who have overcome the contemptible, which means they have gone beyond it.[622] Alternatively, *kuśaḥ* is a synonym for wisdom. The syllable *la* means "to take." Thus, virtues are those entities that are taken up by wisdom; or the virtuous ones are those who take up wisdom.[623] Another interpretation is that *kuśa* grass is that which has a vile character in that it cuts and pierces. The syllable *la* means to gather. Thus, any individual that gathers *kuśa* grass without being cut or pierced is called a skillful (i.e., virtuous) person. Similarly, any action worthy of being praised to others is called a virtue. The opposite of these descriptions explains the meaning of nonvirtue. An indeterminate[624] entity is one that was not declared to have either a virtuous or a nonvirtuous nature.

Regarding the phrase "Ten are of [all] three types," this means that they can be virtuous, nonvirtuous, or indeterminate. Since it is not clearly understood which ones among the eighteen constituents are the ten that are meant, [the root text] adds, "[namely,] the seven mental constituents, as well as the form, sound, and entity constituents." Regarding this statement, the seven mental constituents can be either virtuous or nonvirtuous only in the sense of being concomitant with entities of those two types; they are not either virtuous or nonvirtuous by their very nature. Thus, they are virtuous or nonvirtuous on the strength of being concomitant with either the roots of virtue or the roots of nonvirtue. Accordingly, any of the seven mental constituents that are associated with avoidance of attachment, avoidance of hatred, or avoidance of ignorance are virtuous; those that are associated with attachment, hatred, or ignorance, are nonvirtuous. All other instances are indeterminate.

Those instances of the form and sound constituents that are bodily or verbal informative form can be virtuous or nonvirtuous on the strength of having been generated by either a virtuous or a nonvirtuous mind. All other instances are indeterminate.

Those entities within the entity constituent that have the nature of avoidance of attachment, etc., or that are concomitant with them or that are generated by them, as well as the analytic cessation and suchness, are virtuous. Those that have the nature of attachment, etc., or that are concomitant with them or that are generated by them, are nonvirtuous. All other instances are indeterminate.

Eight constituents are indeterminate: smells, tastes, and tangible objects, as well as the five of the eye, etc. These are exclusively indeterminate, because (1) they are neither virtuous nor nonvirtuous in an ultimate sense, (2) they are neither virtuous nor nonvirtuous by their nature, (3) they are neither virtuous nor nonvirtuous on the strength of being concomitant with the roots of virtue or the roots of nonvirtue, and (4) they are neither virtuous nor nonvirtuous on the strength of being generated by the roots of virtue or the roots of nonvirtue.[625]

How Many Are Inner?

The question, "How many are inner?" is meant in terms of the eighteen constituents. Concerning the response, "Twelve," since it is not understood which twelve, [the root text] adds, "all those except the form, sound, smell, taste, tangible-object, and entity constituents." Thus, the remaining twelve constituents—those six that are faculties and those six that are forms of consciousness—are inner entities.

How Many Are Outer?

[When the root text asks,] in relation to the constituents, "How many are outer?" and then states, "Six," it also adds, "[that is,] those that were excluded," since it is not clear which ones are meant. Thus, it should be understood that these six are outer entities.

Which are the ones that were excluded?

The form, sound, smell, taste, tangible-object, and entity constituents.

That which relates to oneself is said to be "inner." Inner entities are those that only belong to oneself.

If there is no [real] self, how can there be either an "inner" or an "outer," just as there could be no training related to morality if there were no morality?

The mind is figuratively called the self, because it forms the basis for self-awareness.[626] The basis of self-awareness is what those who posit a [real] self call the "self." That is, [they explain that] self-awareness perceives either attributes of the self or the self itself. However, [in reality] self-awareness is based upon [perception of] the mind, since there is no self that exists apart from that. The mind is referred to as the self because egoistic pride is generated in relation to it. Since mind is the basis or support for the mental factors, mind alone is figuratively referred to as the self.

What is the basis of this opinion that the self refers to the mind?

The Lord declared, "For it is by a well-subdued self / That a wise man attains heaven."[627] Elsewhere, he also stated that the mind is what ought to be subdued: "Excellent is the subduing of the mind/ A subdued mind brings happiness."[628] Thus, since Buddha declared that mind is what needs to be tamed and that a well-subdued mind brings happiness, it is apparent that the lines "For it is by a well-subdued self / That a wise man attains heaven" should be understood as referring to the mind.

Therefore, because of the close relationship of the eye, etc., with the mind in the sense of being its support, the constituents of the eye, etc., are considered inner entities. The constituents of form, etc., are outer entities because they have the nature of objects.

In that case, the six consciousness constituents would not be inner entities, because, as long as they have not taken on the property of being the mind constituent, they would not be a support for the mind.

When they are [supports for the mind] they are just that; they do not take on a different nature.[629]

How Many Have Apprehended Objects?

In response to the question, "How many have apprehended objects[630]?" the root text states, "Seven," which is meant in terms of the constituents, as that is the current topic. Because it is not understood which ones those seven are, the root text adds, "mental constituents."

Does this exhaust all the constituents that apprehend objects?

No. As the root text states, "and a portion of the entity constituent" [have apprehended objects]. The term "and" indicates inclusion, which is to say that the seven mental constituents, as well as a portion the entity constituent, are entities that apprehend objects. They are described as "having apprehended objects" because objects are apprehended by them. "Object,"[631] "field of experience,"[632] and "apprehended object"[633] are equivalent terms.

The seven mental constituents are those of the eye, ear, nose, tongue, body, mind, and mind consciousness. "A portion of the entity constituent" means those entities that are mental factors.

How Many Do Not Have Apprehended Objects?

[In response to the question,] "How many do not have apprehended objects?" [the root text] states, "The remaining [ones]," which are "ten" in number. These are the five constituents of the eye, etc., that are faculties and the five constituents of form, etc., that are objects. The phrase "a portion of the entity constituent" here means those entities that are not mental factors.

How Many Are Associated with Concepts?

The question, "How many are associated with concepts?" is meant in terms of the eighteen constituents. The response, "The mind constituent, the mind-consciousness constituent, and a part of the entity constituent," identifies the constituents that can be concomitant [with concepts]. That is, they can be concomitant with two kinds of concepts, those that are investigative and those that are recollective. Only [the mind consciousness and mental factors that are concomitant with these two types of concepts] are conceptual [in nature]; [all] the other [entities contained in these three constituents and all the entities contained in the remaining fifteen constituents] are not, because they are not concomitant with these two [types of concepts]. The phrase "a part of the entity constituent" means those that are mental concomitants; no other [entities that are included in that constituent] can be associated with concepts.

A recollective concept[634] refers to recollection itself, in the sense of those forms of recollection that do not lose hold of an object that the mind has experienced. An investigative concept[635] is either the wisdom or volition that investigates those entities of the three times that are not directly evident to the senses in a manner that makes such determinations as, "This object is like this; it is not like that."

As the *Compendium of Higher Learning* states,[636] "What is a recollective concept? It is [a concept] that generates a formation in relation to a former experience.[637] What is an investigative concept? It is the investigative reflection that occurs with respect to 'hidden' entities of the past, future, and present."

[On the basis of this explanation] it is established that all the remaining constituents are not associated with concepts. Moreover, those constituents that are not associated with concepts are the remaining fifteen constituents and a portion of the entity constituent.

How Many Are Retained?

In response to the question, "How many" of the eighteen constituents "are retained?" [the root text] states [in part], "Five of the inner [constituents]." Those are the constituents of the eye, ear, nose, tongue, and body. They have the exclusive nature of being retained.

Was it not explained elsewhere[638] that they are of two types?

They were so explained. In particular, those of the past and the future were said to be unretained. Those entities are nonexistent; and that which is nonexistent cannot be said to be either retained or unretained.

Those faculties of the present are retained because they exist and they are retained by mind and the mental factors. Therefore, the [five] faculties of the eye, etc., are never unretained.

Is it the faculties of the eye, etc., alone that are retained?

No, "A portion of four [outer ones]" [also has the quality of being retained]. Because it will be wondered which ones the four are, [the root text] states, "[namely,] the form, smell, taste, and tangible-object [constituents]." Those instances of the form, smell, taste, and tangible-object constituents that do not exist separately from the faculties are retained in the same manner that the faculties are. The other instances of those constituents are unretained—such as those that form the parts of the hair of the head, body hair, nails, and teeth that lie beyond the roots, those that are present in feces, urine, phlegm, nasal mucus, blood, etc., as well as those that are present in earth, water, etc.

What is the meaning of being retained?

It refers to that which is held onto by the mind and mental factors in the manner of a support, such that they [i.e., the mind and the retained entities] are mutually affected by what is beneficial or harmful to one another. It is that which the ordinary world describes as being alive.[639]

How Many Are Unretained?

[In response to the question] "How many are unretained?" [the root text] states, "The remaining nine [constituents] and a portion of [the previous] four." The remaining [constituents] are those other than the ones that were just discussed. Thus, they are the seven mental constituents, the entity constituent, and the sound constituent. "A portion of [the previous] four" means a portion of the form, smell, taste, and tangible-object constituents. Moreover, they are [the instances of] these four constituents that were excluded from the category of those that do not exist separately from the faculties,[640] as well as those that lie beyond the roots of the hair of the head, body hair, etc.

How Many Have a Shared Action?

Regarding the question, "How many have a shared [action]?"[641] this is meant in reference to the eighteen constituents, as that is the current topic. Concerning the phrase "The five inner ones that are material," since twelve constituents were mentioned as being inner, it would not be known how many of them were meant; therefore, [the root text] indicates that it is "five." By stating that they are the ones that are "material," it is understood that they are the constituents of the eye, ear, nose, tongue, and body.

Because it is not known what entities are the ones with which [the five inner material constituents share [an action], or the manner in which they share it, the root text states, "Because they have the same object as their respective forms of consciousness." The eye's respective form of consciousness is eye consciousness. That respective consciousness and the eye have [visible] form as the same object. Both [visible form and the eye] are alike in that they share [the quality of contributing to] the arising of eye consciousness.

"Because they have the same [object]" is meant to ascertain the sense of the term. That is to say, the eye shares its object of [visible] form [with eye consciousness]. Similarly, the ear, etc., can be described as sharing their objects [with their corresponding forms of consciousness]. Thus, [the five sense faculties of] the eye, etc., are said to "have a shared [action]" when they serve as the basis for their respective forms of consciousness.

How Many Resemble Those That Have a Shared Action?

In response to the question, "How many resemble those [that have a shared action]?" the root text identifies [the entities that are said to] resemble those [that have a shared action] as "those very same entities" of the eye, etc., "when they are divorced from their respective forms of consciousness."

Why are they said to "resemble those [that have a shared action]"[642]?

The root text states that it is "because they are similar to those of the same type." Those instances of the eye, etc., in which [the sense faculties] are divorced from their respective forms of consciousness are referred to as [the entities that] "resemble those [that have a shared action]," because they resemble the eye, etc., that have a shared [action] in the sense that they form part of the same class [of entities].

Because these [entities of the eye, etc.] are unique [to a particular sentient being], whenever they [take on the quality of] having a shared [action] or [the quality of] resembling those [that have a shared action] in relation to one [sentient being], they possess that same quality in relation to all sentient beings. Therefore, [the qualities of] having a shared [action] and of resembling those [that have a shared action] as it relates to [the sense faculties] is fixed.[643] [However,] because [visible] form, etc., can [either] have a shared [action] or resemble those [that have a shared action] in relation to different sentient beings, and because [consciousness] has no action other than perception, the other [constituents][644] are not described as "having a shared [action]" or as "resembling those [that have a shared action]."

This concludes *A Detailed Commentary on the Summary of the Five Heaps*, composed by Master Sthiramati. It was translated [into Tibetan], revised, and recorded in its final form by the learned Indian teachers[645] Jinamitra, Śīlendrabodhi, and Dānaśīla, the great Tibetan Translator[646] Venerable Yeshe De, and others.

Appendix 1: The Tibetan Translation of Vasubandhu's *Summary of the Five Heaps*

The following text was prepared by comparing the versions that appear in these four Tibetan Tengyur collections: (1) Derge (T: *sDe dge*); (2) Chone (T: *Co ne*); (3) Narthang (T: *sNar thang*); and (4) Peking. Variant readings, obvious misspellings, and inadvertent errors appear in footnotes with the initials of the edition in which they occur.

༄༅། །རྒྱ་གར་སྐད་དུ། པཉྩ་སྐནྡྷ་པྲ་ཀ་ར་ཎ། བོད་སྐད་དུ། ཕུང་པོ་ལྔའི་རབ་ཏུ་བྱེད་པ། འཇམ་དཔལ་གཞོན་ནུར་གྱུར་པ་ལ་ཕྱག་འཚལ་ལོ། །ཕུང་པོ་ལྔ་ནི་གཟུགས་ཀྱི་ཕུང་པོ་དང་། ཚོར་བའི་ཕུང་པོ་དང་། འདུ་ཤེས་ཀྱི་ཕུང་པོ་དང་། འདུ་བྱེད་ཀྱི་ཕུང་པོ་དང་། རྣམ་པར་ཤེས་པའི་ཕུང་པོའོ། །གཟུགས་གང་ཞེ་ན། གཟུགས་གང་ཅི་ཡང་རུང་སྟེ། དེ་དག་ཐམས་ཅད་འབྱུང་བ་ཆེན་པོ[1]་བཞི་དག་དང་། འབྱུང་བ་ཆེན་པོ་བཞི་དག་རྒྱུར་བྱས་པའོ། །འབྱུང་བ་ཆེན་པོ་བཞི་དག་གང་ཞེ་ན། སའི་ཁམས་དང་། ཆུའི་ཁམས་དང་། མེའི་ཁམས་དང་། རླུང་གི་ཁམས་སོ། །དེ་ལ་སའི་ཁམས་གང་ཞེ་ན། སྲ་བ་ཉིད་དོ། །ཆུའི་ཁམས་གང་ཞེ་ན། གཤེར་བ་ཉིད་དོ། །མེའི་ཁམས་གང་ཞེ་ན། ཚ་བ་ཉིད་དོ། །རླུང་གི་ཁམས་གང་ཞེ་ན། ཡང་ཞིང་གཡོ་བ་ཉིད་དོ། །རྒྱུར་བྱས་པའི་གཟུགས་གང་ཞེ་ན། མིག་གི་དབང་པོ་དང་། རྣ་བའི་དབང་པོ་དང་། སྣའི་དབང་པོ་དང་། ལྕེའི་དབང་པོ་དང་། ལུས་ཀྱི་དབང་པོ་དང་། གཟུགས་དང་། སྒྲ་དང་། དྲི་དང་། རོ་དང་། རེག་བྱའི་ཕྱོགས་གཅིག་དང་། རྣམ་པར་རིག་བྱེད་མ་

1 D, C པོའི་

ཡིན་པའོ[2]། །དེ་ལ་མིག་གི་དབང་པོ་གང་ཞེ་ན། ཡུལ་ཁ་དོག་གཟུགས་དང་བའོ།
།རྣ་བའི་དབང་པོ་གང་ཞེ་ན། ཡུལ་སྒྲ་གཟུགས་དང་བའོ། །སྣའི་དབང་པོ་གང་ཞེ་ན།
ཡུལ་དྲི་གཟུགས་དང་བའོ། །ལྗེའི་དབང་པོ་གང་ཞེ་ན། ཡུལ་རོ་གཟུགས་དང་བའོ[3]།
།ལུས་ཀྱི་དབང་པོ་གང་ཞེ་ན། ཡུལ་རེག་བྱ་གཟུགས་དང་བའོ། །གཟུགས་གང་ཞེ་ན།
མིག་གི་ཡུལ་ཏེ། ཁ་དོག་དང་། དབྱིབས་དང་། རྣམ་པར་རིག་བྱེད་དོ།། སྒྲ་གང་
ཞེ་ན། རྣ་བའི་ཡུལ་ཏེ། ཟིན་པ་དང་མ་ཟིན་པ་དང་གཉི་གའི་སྟེ། འབྱུང་བ་ཆེན་པོ་
བཞིའི་རྒྱུ་ལས་བྱུང་བའོ།། དྲི་གང་ཞེ་ན། སྣའི་ཡུལ་ཏེ། དྲི་ཞིམ་པ་དང་། དྲི་ང་བ་
དང་། དེ་ལས་གཞན་པའོ། །རོ་གང་ཞེ་ན། ལྗེའི་ཡུལ་ཏེ། མངར་བ་དང་། སྐྱུར་
བ་དང་། ལན་ཚྭ་དང་། ཚ་བ་དང་། ཁ་བ་དང་། བསྐ་བ་ཞེས་བྱའོ། །རེག་
བྱའི་ཕྱོགས་གཅིག་གང་ཞེ་ན། ལུས་ཀྱི་ཡུལ་ཏེ། འབྱུང་བ་ཆེན་པོ་རྣམས་བཞག་སྟེ།
འཇམ་པ་ཉིད་དང་། རྩུབ་པ་ཉིད་དང་། ལྗི་བ་ཉིད་དང་། ཡང་བ་ཉིད་དང་། གྲང་བ་
ཉིད་དང་། བཀྲེས་པ་ཉིད་དང་། སྐོམ་པའོ། །རྣམ་པར་རིག་བྱེད་མ་ཡིན་པ་གང་ཞེ
ན། རྣམ་པར་རིག་བྱེད་དང་། ཏིང་ངེ་འཛིན་ལས་བྱུང་བའི་གཟུགས་ཏེ། བསྟན་དུ་
མེད་ལ་ཐོགས་པ་མེད་པའོ། །ཚོར་བ་གང་ཞེ་ན། མྱོང་བ་རྣམ་པ་གསུམ་སྟེ། བདེ་བ་
དང་། སྡུག་བསྔལ་བ་དང་། སྡུག་བསྔལ་བ་[4]ཡང་མ་ཡིན་བདེ་བ་ཡང་མ་ཡིན་པ་སྟེ[5]།
བདེ་བ་ནི་[6]གང་འགགས་ན་ཕྲད་པར་འདོད་པའོ། །སྡུག་བསྔལ་ནི་གང་བྱུང་ན་བྲལ་
བར་འདོད་པའོ། །བདེ་བ་ཡང་མ་ཡིན་སྡུག་བསྔལ་བ་ཡང་མ་ཡིན་པ་ནི་གང་བྱུང་ན་
གཉིས་ཀར་འདོད་པར་མི་འགྱུར་བའོ། །འདུ་ཤེས་གང་ཞེ་ན། ཡུལ་ལ་མཚན་མར་
འཛིན་པའོ། །དེ་ནི་རྣམ་པ་གསུམ་སྟེ། ཆུང་ངུ་དང་། རྒྱ་ཆེན་པོར་གྱུར་པ་དང་།
ཚད་མེད་པའོ། །འདུ་བྱེད་རྣམས་གང་ཞེ་ན། ཚོར་བ་དང་འདུ་ཤེས་ལས་གཞན་པ་
སེམས་ལས་བྱུང་བའི་ཆོས་རྣམས་དང་། སེམས་དང་ལྡན་པ་མ་ཡིན་པ་རྣམས་སོ།
།དེ་ལ་སེམས་ལས་བྱུང་བའི་ཆོས་རྣམས་ཀྱང་གང་ཞེ་ན། ཆོས་གང་དག་སེམས་དང་

2 N པའི་

3 N བའི་

4 D, C སྡུག་བསྔལ་

5 N, P དེ་

6 D, C དེ་ in place of ནི་

མཆུངས་པར་ལྡན་པ་རྣམས་སོ། །དེ་དག་ཀྱང་གང་ཞེ་ན། རེག་པ་དང་།ཡིད་ལ་བྱེད་པ་དང་། ཚོར་བ་དང་། འདུ་ཤེས་དང་། སེམས་པ་དང་། འདུན་པ་དང་། མོས་པ་དང་། དྲན་པ་དང་། ཏིང་ངེ་འཛིན་དང་། ཤེས་རབ་དང་། དད་པ་དང་། ངོ་ཚ་ཤེས་པ་དང་། ཁྲེལ་ཡོད་པ་དང་། མ་ཆགས་པའི་དགེ་བའི་རྩ་བ་དང་། ཞེ་སྡང་མེད་པའི་དགེ་བའི་རྩ་བ་དང་། གཏི་མུག་མེད་པའི་དགེ་བའི་རྩ་བ་དང་། བརྩོན་འགྲུས་དང་། ཤིན་ཏུ་སྦྱངས་པ་དང་། བག་ཡོད་པ་དང་། བཏང་སྙོམས་དང་། རྣམ་པར་མི་འཚེ་བ་དང་། འདོད་ཆགས་དང་། ཁོང་ཁྲོ་བ་དང་། ང་རྒྱལ་དང་། མ་རིག་པ་དང་། ལྟ་བ་དང་། ཐེ་ཚོམ་དང་། ཁྲོ་བ་དང་། ཁོན་དུ་འཛིན་པ་དང་། འཆབ་པ་དང་། འཚིག་པ་དང་། ཕྲག་དོག་དང་། སེར་སྣ་དང་། སྒྱུ་དང་། གཡོ་དང་། རྒྱགས་པ་དང་། རྣམ་པར་འཚེ་བ་དང་། ངོ་ཚ་མེད་པ་དང་། ཁྲེལ་མེད་པ་དང་། རྨུགས་པ་དང་། རྒོད་པ་དང་། མ་དད་པ་དང་། ལེ་ལོ་དང་། བག་མེད་པ་དང་ །བརྗེད་ངས་པ་དང་། རྣམ་པར་གཡེང་[7]བ་དང་། ཤེས་བཞིན་མ་ཡིན་པ་དང་། འགྱོད་པ་དང་། གཉིད་དང་། རྟོག་པ་དང་། དཔྱོད་པའོ།། དེ་རྣམས་ལས་ལྔ་ནི་ཀུན་ཏུ་འགྲོ་བའོ། །ལྔ་ནི་ཡུལ་སོ་སོར་ངེས་པའོ། །བཅུ་གཅིག་ནི་དགེ་བའོ། །དྲུག་ནི་ཉོན་མོངས་པའོ། །ལྷག་མ་རྣམས་ནི་ཉེ་བའི་ཉོན་མོངས་པའོ། །བཞི་ནི་གཞན་དུ་ཡང་འགྱུར་བའོ། །རེག་པ་གང་ཞེ་ན། གསུམ་འདུས་ནས་ཡོངས་སུ་གཅོད་པའོ། །ཡིད་ལ་བྱེད་པ་གང་ཞེ་ན། སེམས་ཀྱི[8]འཇུག་པའོ། །སེམས་པ་གང་ཞེ་ན། ཡོན་ཏན་དང་། ཉེས་པ་དང་། གཉི་ག་མ་ཡིན་པ་ལ་སེམས་མངོན་པར་འདུ་བྱེད་པ་ཡིད་ཀྱི་ལས་སོ། །འདུན་པ་གང་ཞེ་ན། བསམ་པའི་དངོས་པོ་ལ་འདོད་པའོ། །མོས་པ་གང་ཞེ་ན། ངེས་པའི་དངོས་པོ་ལ་དེ་བཞིན་དུ་ངེས་པར་འཛིན་པའོ།། དྲན་པ་གང་ཞེ་ན། འདྲིས་པའི་དངོས་པོ་ཉིད་མ་བརྗེད་པ་སྟེ། སེམས་ཀྱི་མངོན་པར་བརྗོད་པ་ཉིད་དོ། །ཏིང་ངེ་འཛིན་གང་ཞེ་ན། བརྟག་[9]པའི་དངོས་པོ་ལ་སེམས་རྩེ་གཅིག་པ་ཉིད་དོ།

7 D, C གཡེངས་

8 N, P ཀྱིས་

9 N, P བརྟགས་

།ཞེས་རབ་གང་ཞེ་ན། དེ་དག་ཉིད་ལ་རབ་ཏུ་རྣམ་པར་འབྱེད་པ་སྟེ། རིགས་[10]པ་དང་། རིགས་པ་མ་ཡིན་པས་བསྐྱེད་པ་དང་། གཞན་པའོ། །དད་པ་གང་ཞེ་ན། ལས་དང་འབྲས་བུ་དང་། བདེན་པ་དང་། དཀོན་མཆོག་ལ་མངོན་པར་ཡིད་ཆེས་པ་དང་། འདོད་པ་དང་། སེམས་དང་བའོ། །ངོ་ཚ་ཤེས་པ་གང་ཞེ་ན། བདག་གམ་ཆོས་ཀྱི་དབང་དུ་བྱས་ཏེ[11]། ཁ་ན་མ་ཐོ་བས་འཛེམ་པའོ། །ཁྲེལ་ཡོད་པ་གང་ཞེ་ན། འཇིག་རྟེན་གྱི་དབང་དུ་བྱས་ཏེ། ཁ་ན་མ་ཐོ་བས་[12]འཛེམ་པའོ། །མ་ཆགས་པ་གང་ཞེ་ན། ཆགས་པའི་གཉེན་པོ་སྟེ། ཡིད་བྱུང་ཞིང་མི་ལེན་པའོ། །ཞེ་སྡང་མེད་པ་གང་ཞེ་ན། ཞེ་སྡང་གི་གཉེན་པོ་སྟེ། བྱམས་པའོ། །གཏི་མུག་མེད་པ་གང་ཞེ་ན། གཏི་མུག་གི་གཉེན་པོ་སྟེ[13]། ཡང་དག་པ་ལ་ཡང་དག་པར་རྟོགས་པའོ། །བརྩོན་འགྲུས་གང་ཞེ་ན། ལེ་ལོའི་གཉེན་པོ་སྟེ། དགེ་བ་ལ་སེམས་མངོན་པར་སྤྲོ་བའོ། །ཤིན་ཏུ་སྦྱངས་པ་གང་ཞེ་ན། གནས་ངན་ལེན་གྱི་[14]གཉེན་པོ་སྟེ། ལུས་དང་སེམས་ལས་སུ་རུང་བ་ཉིད་དོ། །བག་ཡོད་པ་གང་ཞེ་ན། བག་མེད་པའི་གཉེན་པོ་སྟེ། མ་ཆགས་པ་ནས་བརྩོན་འགྲུས་ཀྱི་བར་དེ་དག་ལ་གནས་ནས་མི་དགེ་བའི་ཆོས་སྤོང་ཞིང་། དེའི་གཉེན་པོ་དགེ་བའི་ཆོས་རྣམས་བསྒོམ་པའོ། །བཏང་སྙོམས་གང་ཞེ་ན། མ་ཆགས་པ་ནས་བརྩོན་འགྲུས་ཀྱི་བར་དེ་དག་ཉིད་ལ་གནས་ཤིང་སེམས་མཉམ་པ་ཉིད་དང་། སེམས་རྣལ་དུ་འདུག་པ་དང་། སེམས་ལྷུན་གྱིས་གྲུབ་པ་ཡང་ཐོབ་པ་སྟེ། གང་གིས་[15]ཉོན་མོངས་པ་ཅན་གྱི་[16]ཆོས་རྣམས་བསལ་ནས་ཉོན་མོངས་པ་ཅན་མེད་པར་གནས་པ་ཉིད་དོ། །རྣམ་པར་མི་འཚེ་བ་གང་ཞེ་ན། རྣམ་པར་འཚེ་བའི་གཉེན་པོ་སྟེ། སྙིང་རྗེ་བའོ། །འདོད་ཆགས་གང་ཞེ་ན། ཉེ་བར་ལེན་པའི་ཕུང་པོ་ལྔ་[17]ལ་མངོན་པར་ཞེན་པ་དང་། ལྷག་

10 N, P རིག་
11 D, C སྟེ་
12 N, P insert གཞན་ལ་
13 N, P drop སྟེ་
14 N, P གྱིས་
15 D, C གི་
16 N, P གྱིས་
17 N, P drop ལྔ་

པར་ཆགས་པའོ། །ཁོང་ཁྲོ་བ་གང་ཞེ་ན། སེམས་ཅན་རྣམས་ལ་ཀུན་ནས་མནར་སེམས་པའོ། །ང་རྒྱལ་གང་ཞེ་ན། ང་རྒྱལ་རྣམ་པ་བདུན་ཏེ[18]། ང་རྒྱལ་དང་། ཆེ་བའི་ང་རྒྱལ་དང་། ང་རྒྱལ་ལས་ཀྱང་ང་རྒྱལ་དང་། ངའོ་སྙམ་པའི་ང་རྒྱལ་དང་། མངོན་པའི་ང་རྒྱལ་དང་། ཅུང་ཟད་སྙམ་པའི་ང་རྒྱལ་དང་། ལོག་པའི་ང་རྒྱལ་ལོ། །ང་རྒྱལ་གང་ཞེ་ན། ཆུང་ངུ་བས་བདག་ཆེ་བའམ། མཚུངས་པ་དང་མཚུངས་སོ་སྙམ་དུ་སེམས་ཁེངས་པ་གང་ཡིན་པའོ། །ཆེ་བའི་ང་རྒྱལ་གང་ཞེ་ན། མཚུངས་པ་བས་བདག་ཆེ་བའམ། ཆེ་བ་དང་མཚུངས་སོ་སྙམ་དུ་སེམས་ཁེངས་པ་གང་ཡིན་པའོ། །ང་རྒྱལ་ལས་ཀྱང་ང་རྒྱལ་གང་ཞེ་ན།ཆེ་བ[19]བས་བདག་ཆེའོ་སྙམ་དུ་སེམས་ཁེངས་པ་གང་ཡིན་པའོ། །ངའོ་སྙམ་པའི་ང་རྒྱལ་གང་ཞེ་ན། ཉེ་བར་ལེན་པའི་ཕུང་པོ་ལྔ་པོ་རྣམས་ལ་བདག་གམ་བདག་གིར་ལྟ་བའི་སེམས་ཁེངས་པ་གང་ཡིན་པའོ། །མངོན་པའི་ང་རྒྱལ་གང་ཞེ་ན། གོང་མའི་ཁྱད་པར་ཐོབ་པར་བྱ་བ[20]མ་ཐོབ་པར་བདག་གིས་ཐོབ་བོ་སྙམ་དུ་སེམས་ཁེངས་པ་གང་ཡིན་པའོ། །ཅུང་ཟད་སྙམ་པའི་ང་རྒྱལ་གང་ཞེ་ན། ཁྱད་པར[21]ཆེས་འཕགས་པ་བས་བདག་ཅུང་ཟད་ཆུང་ངོ་སྙམ་དུ་སེམས་ཁེངས་པ་གང་ཡིན་པའོ། །ལོག་པའི་ང་རྒྱལ་གང་ཞེ་ན། ཡོན་ཏན་མ་ཡིན་པ་དང་ལྡན་པ་ལ་བདག་ཡོན་ཏན་དང་ལྡན་ནོ་སྙམ་དུ་སེམས་ཁེངས་པ་གང་ཡིན་པའོ། །མ་རིག་པ་གང་ཞེ་ན། ལས་དང་འབྲས་བུ་དང་། བདེན་པ་དང་། དཀོན་མཆོག་རྣམས་མི་ཤེས་པ་སྟེ[22]། དེ་ཡང་ལྷན་ཅིག་སྐྱེས་པ་དང་། ཀུན་ཏུ་བརྟགས་པའོ། །འདོད་པ་ན་སྤྱོད་པའི་འདོད་ཆགས་དང་། ཁོང་ཁྲོ་བ་དང་། འདོད་པ་ན་སྤྱོད་པའི་མ་རིག་པ་དེ་དག་ནི་མི་དགེ་བའི་རྩ་བ་གསུམ་སྟེ། ཆགས་པ་དང་ཞེ་སྡང་དང་གཏི་མུག[23]མི་དགེ་བའི་རྩ་བའོ། །ལྟ་བ་གང་ཞེ་ན། ལྟ་བ་ལྔ་སྟེ། འཇིག[24]ཚོགས་ལ་ལྟ་བ་དང་། མཐར་འཛིན་པར་ལྟ་

18 D, C སྟེ་

19 N, P drop བ་

20 N, P བའི་

21 N, P drop པར་

22 N, P དེ་

23 N, P insert གི་

24 N, P འཇིགས་

བ་དང་། ལོག་པར་ལྟ་བ་དང་། ལྟ་བ་མཆོག་ཏུ་འཛིན་པ་དང་། ཚུལ་ཁྲིམས་དང་། བརྟུལ་ཞུགས་མཆོག་ཏུ་འཛིན་པའོ།། འཇིག་[25]ཚོགས་ལ་ལྟ་བ་གང་ཞེ་ན། ཉེ་བར་ལེན་པའི་ཕུང་པོ་ལྔ་རྣམས་ལ་བདག་གམ་བདག་གིར་ལྟ་བའི་ཤེས་རབ་ཉོན་མོངས་པ་ཅན་གང་ཡིན་པའོ། །མཐར་འཛིན་པར་ལྟ་བ་གང་ཞེ་ན། དེ་ཉིད་ཀྱི་དབང་དུ་བྱས་ཏེ། རྟག་པའམ་ཆད་པར་ལྟ་བའི་ཤེས་རབ་ཉོན་མོངས་པ་ཅན་གང་ཡིན་པའོ། །ལོག་པར་ལྟ་བ་གང་ཞེ་ན། རྒྱུའམ་འབྲས་བུའམ། བྱེད་པ་ལ་སྐུར་བ་འདེབས་པ་དང་། ཡོད་པའི་དངོས་པོ་ལ་འཇིག་[26]པའི་ཤེས་རབ་ཉོན་མོངས་པ་ཅན་གང་ཡིན་པའོ། །ལྟ་བ་མཆོག་ཏུ་འཛིན་པ་གང་ཞེ་ན། ལྟ་བ་རྣམ་པ་གསུམ་པོ་དེ་དག་ཉིད་དང་། དེའི་གནས་ཕུང་པོ་རྣམས་ལ་མཆོག་དང་། གཙོ་བོ་དང་། ཁྱད་པར་དུ་འཕགས་པ་དང་། དམ་པར་ལྟ་བའི་ཤེས་རབ་ཉོན་མོངས་པ་ཅན་གང་ཡིན་པའོ། །ཚུལ་ཁྲིམས་དང་བརྟུལ་ཞུགས་མཆོག་ཏུ་འཛིན་པ་གང་ཞེ་ན། ཚུལ་ཁྲིམས་དང་བརྟུལ་ཞུགས་དང་། དེའི་གནས་ཕུང་པོ་རྣམས་ལ་དག་པ་དང་། གྲོལ་བ་དང་། ངེས་པར་འབྱིན་པར་ལྟ་བའི་ཤེས་རབ་ཉོན་མོངས་པ་ཅན་གང་ཡིན་པའོ། །ཐེ་ཚོམ་གང་ཞེ་ན། བདེན་པ་ལ་སོགས་པ་ལ་གང་ཡིད་གཉིས་ཟ་བའོ། །ཉོན་མོངས་པ་དེ་དག་ལས་ལྟ་བ་འོག་མ་གསུམ་དང་། ཐེ་ཚོམ་ནི་ཀུན་ཏུ་བརྟགས་པའོ། །ལྷག་མ་ནི་ལྷན་ཅིག་སྐྱེས་པ་དང་ཀུན་ཏུ་བརྟགས་པའོ།། ཁྲོ་བ་གང་ཞེ་ན། འཕྲལ་དུ་གནོད་པ་བྱེད་པ་ལ་གནས་ཏེ། གང་སེམས་ཀྱི་ཀུན་ནས་མནར་སེམས་པའོ། །ཁོན་དུ་འཛིན་པ་གང་ཞེ་ན། མདུད་པར་འཛིན་པའོ། །འཆབ་པ་གང་ཞེ་ན། བདག་གི་ཁ་ན་མ་ཐོ་བ་མཁྲུད་པའོ། །འཚིག་པ་གང་ཞེ་ན། ཚིག་བརླང་པོས་ཞེར་འདེབས་པ་ཉིད་དོ། །ཕྲག་དོག་གང་ཞེ་ན། གཞན་གྱི་ཕུན་སུམ་ཚོགས་པ་ལ་སེམས་ཁོང་ནས་འཁྲུག་[27]པའོ། །སེར་སྣ་གང་ཞེ་ན། སྦྱིན་པ་དང་མི་མཐུན་པའི་སེམས་ཀྱིས་[28]ཀུན་ཏུ་འཛིན་པའོ། །སྒྱུ་གང་ཞེ་ན། གཞན་སླུ་[29]བ་ཡང་དག་པ་མ་ཡིན་པའི་དོན་སྟོན་པའོ།། གཡོ་གང་ཞེ་ན། བདག་གི་ཉེས་པ་བཅབ་

25 N, P འཇིགས་

26 N, P འཇིགས་

27 N, P འཁྲུགས་

28 N, P ཀྱི་

29 N, P བསླུ་

པའི་ཐབས་གཟུང་སྟེ་སེམས་གྱ་གྱུ་བའོ། །རྒྱུགས་པ་གང་ཞེ་ན། བདག་གི་ཕུན་སུམ་ཚོགས་པ་ལ་ཆགས་པའི་རབ་ཏུ་དགའ་བ་སྟེ[30]། སེམས་ཡོངས་སུ་འཛིན་པའོ། །རྣམ་པར་འཚེ་བ་གང་ཞེ་ན། སེམས་ཅན་རྣམས་ལ་རྣམ་པར་ཐོ་འཚམས་པའོ[31]། །ངོ་ཚ་མེད་པ་གང་ཞེ་ན། ཁ་ན་མ་ཐོ་བས་བདག་ལ་མི་འཛེམ་[32]པའོ། །ཁྲེལ་མེད་པ་གང་ཞེ་ན། ཁ་ན་མ་ཐོ་བས་གཞན་ལ་མི་འཛེམ་[33]པའོ། །རྨུགས་པ་གང་ཞེ་ན། སེམས་ལས་སུ་མི་རུང་བ་སྟེ། བློང་[34]བ་ཉིད་དོ། །རྒོད་པ་གང་ཞེ་ན། སེམས་རྣམ་པར་མ་ཞི་བའོ། །མ་དད་པ་གང་ཞེ་ན། ལས་དང་འབྲས་བུ་དང་། བདེན་པ་དང་། དཀོན་མཆོག་རྣམས་ལ་ཡིད་མི་ཆེས་པ་དང་། སེམས་མ་དད་པ་སྟེ། དད་པའི་མི་མཐུན་པའི་ཕྱོགས་སོ། །ལེ་ལོ་གང་ཞེ་ན། དགེ་བ་ལ་སེམས་མངོན་པར་སྤྲོ་བ་མེད་པ་སྟེ། བརྩོན་འགྲུས་ཀྱི་མི་མཐུན་པའི་ཕྱོགས་སོ། །བག་མེད་པ་གང་ཞེ་ན། ཆགས་པ་དང་། ཞེ་སྡང་དང་། གཏི་མུག་དང་། ལེ་ལོ་གང་ཡིན་པ་དག་གིས་ཉོན་མོངས་པ་ལས་སེམས་མི་སྲུང་བ་དང་དགེ་བ་མི་བསྒོམ་[35]པའོ། །བརྗེད་ངས་པ་གང་ཞེ་ན། དྲན་པ་ཉོན་མོངས་པ་ཅན་[36]ཏེ། དགེ་བ་ལ་མི་གསལ་[37]བའོ། །རྣམ་པར་གཡེང་བ་གང་ཞེ་ན། འདོད་ཆགས་དང་ཞེ་སྡང་དང་གཏི་མུག་གི་ཆ་ཤས་ཀྱི་[38]འདོད་པའི་ཡོན་ཏན་ལྔ་པོ་དག་[39]ལ་གང་སེམས་རྣམ་པར་འཕྲོ་བའོ། །ཤེས་བཞིན་མ་ཡིན་པ་གང་ཞེ་ན། ཉོན་མོངས་པ་དང་མཚུངས་པར་ལྡན་པའི་ཤེས་རབ་སྟེ། དེས་ལུས་དང་ངག་དང་ཡིད་ཀྱི་སྤྱོད་པ་ལ་མི་ཤེས་བཞིན་དུ་འཇུག་པའོ། །འགྱོད་པ་གང་ཞེ་ན། ཡིད་ལ་གཅགས་

30 D, C, N, P དེ་. Revision based on language found in translations of Indian commentaries.

31 N, P མཐོ་མཚམས་པའོ་

32 N, P འཛེམས་

33 N, P འཛེམས་

34 D, C བླང་

35 N, P སྒོམ་

36 D, C, N, P ཉོན་མོངས་ཅན་. Revision based on language found in Indian commentaries.

37 N, P བསལ་

38 D, C ཀྱིས་

39 N, P drop དག་

པའོ། །གཉིད་གང་ཞེ་ན། འཇུག་པ་རང་དབང་མེད་པར་སེམས་སྡུད་པའོ། །རྟོག་པ་གང་ཞེ་ན། ཀུན་ཏུ་ཚོལ་[40]བའི་ཡིད་ཀྱིས་བརྗོད་པ་སྟེ། སེམས་པ་དང་ཤེས་རབ་ཀྱི་བྱེ་བྲག་གང་སེམས་རྩིང་བའོ[41]།།དཔྱོད་[42]པ་གང་ཞེ་ན། སོ་སོར་རྟོག་པའི་ཡིད་ཀྱིས་བརྗོད་པ་སྟེ། དེ་བཞིན་དུ་གང་སེམས་ཞིབ་པའོ། །སེམས་དང་མི་ལྡན་པའི་འདུ་བྱེད་རྣམས་གང་ཞེ་ན། གང་དག་གཟུགས་དང་སེམས་དང་[43]སེམས་ལས་བྱུང་བའི་གནས་སྐབས་ལ་གདགས་པ་སྟེ། དེ་ཉིད་དང་གཞན་དུ་མི་གདགས་སོ། །དེ་དག་ཀྱང་གང་ཞེ་ན། ཐོབ་པ་དང་། འདུ་ཤེས་མེད་པའི་སྙོམས་པར་འཇུག་པ་དང་། འགོག་པའི་སྙོམས་པར་འཇུག་པ་དང་། འདུ་ཤེས་མེད་པ་[44]དང་། སྲོག་གི་དབང་པོ་དང་། རིས་[45]མཐུན་པ་དང་། སྐྱེ་བ་དང་། རྒ་བ་[46]དང་། གནས་པ་དང་། མི་རྟག་པ་ཉིད་དང་། མིང་གི་ཚོགས་དང་། ཚིག་གི་ཚོགས་དང་། ཡི་གེའི་ཚོགས་དང་། སོ་སོའི་སྐྱེ་བོ་ཉིད་དང་། དེ་ལྟ་བུའི་ཆ་དང་མཐུན་པ་དག་གོ །དེ་ལ་ཐོབ་པ་གང་ཞེ་ན། རྙེད་པ་དང་ལྡན་པའོ། །དེ་ཡང་ས་བོན་དང་། དབང་དང་། མངོན་དུ་གྱུར་པ་དང་ཅི་རིགས་སུ་སྦྱར་རོ། །འདུ་ཤེས་མེད་པའི་སྙོམས་པར་འཇུག་པ་གང་ཞེ་ན། དགེ་རྒྱས་ཀྱི་འདོད་ཆགས་དང་བྲལ་ལ།གོང་མའི་མ་ཡིན་པ་འབྱུང་བའི་འདུ་ཤེས་སྟོན་[47]དུ་བཏང་བའི་[48]ཡིད་ལ་བྱེད་པས་སེམས་དང་སེམས་ལས་བྱུང་བའི་ཆོས་བརྟན་པ་མ་ཡིན་པ་རྣམས་འགོག་པ་གང་ཡིན་པའོ། །འགོག་པའི་སྙོམས་པར་འཇུག་པ་གང་ཞེ་ན། ཅི་ཡང་མེད་པའི་སྐྱེ་མཆེད་ཀྱི་འདོད་ཆགས་དང་བྲལ་ལ། སྲིད་པའི་རྩེ་མོ་ལས་གྱེན་དུ་བསྐྱོད་པའི་གནས་

40 N, P འཚོལ་

41 D, C པའོ་

42 N, P སྤྱོད་

43 D, C drop སེམས་དང་

44 N, P insert a second པ་

45 C རུས་

46 D, C, N, and P all do not include རྒ་བ་ in this list, although it does appear among the individual explanations. It is restored on the basis of the list quoted in Guṇaprabha's commentary on the root text.

47 D, C, N, and P all read མངོན་ in place of སྟོན་. However, Indian commentaries and extant Sanskrit passages from other works confirm the revision.

48 D, C unnecessarily insert འདུ་ཤེས་ a second time here.

པར་འདུ་ཤེས་སྟོན་[49]དུ་བཏང་བའི་ཡིད་ལ་བྱེད་པས། སེམས་དང་སེམས་ལས་བྱུང་བའི་ཆོས་བརྟན་པ་མ་ཡིན་པ་རྣམས་དང་། བརྟན་[50]པ་རྣམས་ལས་ཀྱང་ཁ་ཅིག་འགོག་པ་གང་ཡིན་པའོ།། འདུ་ཤེས་མེད་པ་གང་ཞེ་ན། འདུ་ཤེས་མེད་པའི་སྙོམས་པར་འཇུག་པའི་འབྲས་བུ་སྟེ།[51] འདུ་ཤེས་མེད་པའི་སེམས་ཅན་གྱི་ཁྲོད་ཀྱི་ལྷ་རྣམས་ཀྱི་ནང་དུ་བསྐྱེད་པའི་སེམས་དང་། སེམས་ལས་བྱུང་བའི་ཆོས་བརྟན་[52]པ་མ་ཡིན་པ་རྣམས་གང་[53]འགོག་པའོ། །སྲོག་གི་དབང་པོ་གང་ཞེ་ན། རིས་མཐུན་པ་རྣམས་སུ་སྔོན་གྱི་ལས་ཀྱིས་འཕངས་པས། གང་འདུ་བྱེད་རྣམས་ཀྱི་གནས་པའི་དུས་ངེས་པའོ།། རིས་མཐུན་པ་གང་ཞེ་ན། གང་སེམས་ཅན་རྣམས་ཀྱི་ལུས་འདྲ་བའོ།། སྐྱེ་བ་གང་ཞེ་ན། རིས་མཐུན་པར་འདུ་བྱེད་རྣམས་མ་བྱུང་བ་ལས་བྱུང་[54]བ་གང་ཡིན་པའོ། །རྒ་བ་གང་ཞེ་ན། དེ་ལྟར་[55]དེ་དག་གི་རྒྱུན་གཞན་དུ་འགྱུར་བའོ། །གནས་པ་གང་ཞེ་ན། དེ་ལྟར་དེ་དག་གི་རྒྱུན་རྒྱུད་ཆགས་པའོ། །མི་རྟག་པ་[56]ཉིད་གང་ཞེ་ན། དེ་ལྟར་དེ་དག་གི་རྒྱུན་ཆད་པའོ། ། མིང་གི་ཚོགས་གང་ཞེ་ན། ཆོས་རྣམས་ཀྱི་ངོ་བོ་ཉིད་ཀྱི་[57]ཚིག་བླ་དགས་སོ། །ཚིག་གི་ཚོགས་གང་ཞེ་ན། ཆོས་རྣམས་ཀྱི་ཁྱད་པར་གྱི་ཚིག་བླ་དགས་སོ། །ཡི་གེའི་ཚོགས་གང་ཞེ་ན། ཡི་གེ་[58]རྣམས་ཏེ། དེ་གཉིས་ཀ་གསལ་[59]བར་བྱེད་པའི་ཕྱིར་རོ། །བརྗོད་པ་ཡང་དེ་དག་ཡིན་ཏེ། མིང་དང་ཚིག་ལ་བརྟེན་[60]ནས་དོན་བརྗོད་པའི་ཕྱིར་རོ། །ཡི་གེ་ཡང་རྣམ་གྲངས་གཞན་དུ་མི་འགྱུར་བའི་ཕྱིར་རོ། །སོ་

49 N, P མངོན་

50 D, C བསྟན་

51 N, P drop this entire opening phrase up to འབྲས་བུ་སྟེ།

52 D, C བསྟན་

53 D, C, N, and P all read དང་ instead of གང་. Revision is based on Indian commentaries.

54 N འབྱུང་

55 N, P ལྟོ་

56 N, P drop པ་

57 P གྲི་

58 D, C གེའི་

59 N, P བསལ་

60 N, P རྟེན་

སོའི་སྐྱེ་བོ་ཉིད་གང་ཞེ་ན། འཕགས་པའི་ཆོས་རྣམས་མ་ཐོབ་པའོ།། འདི་ནི་འདུ་བྱེད་ཀྱི་ཕུང་པོ་ཞེས་བྱའོ། །རྣམ་པར་ཤེས་པ་གང་ཞེ་ན། དམིགས་པ་རྣམ་པར་རིག་པའོ། །སེམས་དང་ཡིད་ཀྱང་དེ་ཡིན་ཏེ། སྣ་ཚོགས་པ་དང་[61]ཡིད་རྟེན་བྱེད་པའི་ཕྱིར་རོ།། དངོས་སུ་ན་སེམས་ནི་[62]ཀུན་གཞི་རྣམ་པར་ཤེས་པ་སྟེ། འདི་ལྟར་དེ་ནི་འདུ་བྱེད་ཐམས་ཅད་ཀྱི་ས་བོན་བསགས་པའོ། །དེ་ཡང་དམིགས་པ་དང་རྣམ་པ་ཡོངས་སུ་མ་ཆད་པའོ།། རིགས་གཅིག་པ་དང་། རྒྱུན་ཆགས་པར་འཇུག་པའོ།། འདི་ལྟར་འགོག་པའི་སྙོམས་པར་འཇུག་པ་དང་། འདུ་ཤེས་མེད་པའི་སྙོམས་པར་འཇུག་པ་དང་། འདུ་ཤེས་མེད་པ་པ་རྣམས་ལས་[63]ལངས་ནས་ཡང་ཡུལ་རྣམ་པར་རིག་པ་ཞེས་བྱ་བ་འཇུག་པའི་རྣམ་པར་ཤེས་པ་འབྱུང་བ་དང་། དམིགས་པའི་རྐྱེན་ལ་ལྟོས་[64]ནས་རྣམ་པ་གཞན་དུ་འཇུག་པ་ཉིད་དང་། ཆད་ནས་ཡང་འབྱུང་བ་ཉིད་དང་། འཁོར་བར་འཇུག་པ་དང་ལྡོག་པའི་ཕྱིར་རོ། །ཀུན་གཞི་རྣམ་པར་ཤེས་པ་དེ་ཉིད་ནི་ས་བོན་ཐམས་ཅད་ཀྱི་གཞི་ཉིད་དང་། ལུས་ཀྱི་ཀུན་གཞི་[65]དང་། རྒྱུ་ཉིད་དང་། ལུས་ལ་གནས་པ་ཉིད་ཀྱི་ཡང་ཕྱིར་རོ། །ལེན་པའི་རྣམ་པར་ཤེས་པ་ཡང་དེ་ཡིན་ཏེ། ལུས་ལེན་པའི་ཕྱིར་རོ། །དངོས་སུ་ན་[66]ཡིད་ནི་[67]ཀུན་གཞི་རྣམ་པར་ཤེས་པ་ལ་དམིགས་ཏེ། རྟག་ཏུ་བདག་ཏུ་རྨོངས་པ་དང་། བདག་ཏུ་ལྟ་བ་དང་། བདག་ཏུ་ང་རྒྱལ་[68]དང་། བདག་ལ་ཆགས་པ་ལ་སོགས་པ་དང་མཚུངས་པར་ལྡན་པའི་རྣམ་པར་ཤེས་པ་སྟེ། རིགས་གཅིག་པ་དང་། རྒྱུན་ཆགས་པར་འཇུག་པ་སྟེ། དགྲ་བཅོམ་པ་[69]དང་། འཕགས་པའི་ལམ་དང་། འགོག་པའི་སྙོམས་པར་འཇུག་པའི་དུས་མ་གཏོགས་སོ།།ཅིའི་ཕྱིར་ཕུང་པོ་ཞེས་

61 N, P drop དང་

62 N, P substitute ཀྱི་ for ནི་

63 D, C drop ལས་

64 N, P བལྟོས་

65 Sthiramati (see Part Two, p. 343) reports the existence of Sanskrit editions of the root text that have a variant reading here. The Tibetan equivalent of this would be བདག་ཏུ་ང་རྒྱལ་ཀྱི་གཞི་ in place of the phrase ལུས་ཀྱི་ཀུན་གཞི་.

66 D ནི་

67 D ན་

68 P ང་རྒྱལ་བ

69 C drops པ་

བྱ་ཞེ་ན། སྐྱུངས་པའི་ཕྱིར་ཏེ་དུས་དང་རྒྱུད་དང་རྣམ་པ་དང་འགྲོ[70]བ་དང་། ཡུལ་ཐ་དད་པའི་གཟུགས་ལ་སོགས་པ་མདོར་བསྡུས་པ་ཉིད་ཀྱི་ཕྱིར་རོ། །སྐྱེ་མཆེད་བཅུ་གཉིས་ནི་མིག་གི་སྐྱེ་མཆེད་དང་། གཟུགས་ཀྱི་སྐྱེ་མཆེད་དང་། རྣ་བའི་སྐྱེ་མཆེད་དང་། སྒྲའི་སྐྱེ་མཆེད་དང་། སྣའི་སྐྱེ་མཆེད་དང་། དྲིའི་སྐྱེ་མཆེད་དང་། ལྕེའི་སྐྱེ་མཆེད་དང་། རོའི་སྐྱེ་མཆེད་དང་། ལུས་ཀྱི་སྐྱེ་མཆེད་དང་། རེག་བྱའི་སྐྱེ་མཆེད་དང་། ཡིད་ཀྱི་སྐྱེ་མཆེད་དང་། ཆོས་ཀྱི་སྐྱེ་མཆེད་དོ། །མིག་ལ་སོགས་པ་དང་། གཟུགས་དང་སྒྲ་དང་དྲི་དང་རོའི་སྐྱེ་མཆེད་ལ་སོགས་པ་ཡང་སྔ་མ་བཞིན་དུ་བཤད་དོ། །རེག་བྱའི་སྐྱེ་མཆེད་ནི་འབྱུང་བ་ཆེན་པོ་བཞི་དག་དང་། གང་རེག་བྱའི་ཕྱོགས་གཅིག་བཤད་པའོ། །ཡིད་ཀྱི་སྐྱེ་མཆེད་ནི་རྣམ་པར་ཤེས་པའི་ཕུང་པོ་གང་ཡིན་པའོ། །ཆོས་ཀྱི་སྐྱེ་མཆེད་ནི་གང་ཚོར་བ་དང་། འདུ་ཤེས་དང་། འདུ་བྱེད་རྣམས་དང་།རྣམ་པར་རིག་བྱེད་མ་ཡིན་པ་དང་། འདུས་མ་བྱས་སོ། །འདུས་མ་བྱས་གང་ཞེ་ན། ནམ་མཁའ་དང་། སོ་སོར་བརྟགས་པ་མ་ཡིན་པའི་འགོག་པ་དང་། སོ་སོར་བརྟགས་པའི་འགོག་པ་དང་། དེ་བཞིན་ཉིད་དོ། །དེ་ལ་ནམ་མཁའ་གང་ཞེ་ན། གཟུགས་ཀྱི་གོ་འབྱེད་པའོ། །སོ་སོར་བརྟགས་པ་མ་ཡིན་པའི་འགོག་པ་གང་ཞེ་ན། གང་འགོག་པ་ལ་བྲལ་བ་མ་ཡིན་པ་སྟེ། དེ་ནི་ཉོན་མོངས་པའི་གཉེན་པོ་མེད་པར་ཕུང་པོ་རྣམས་གཏན་དུ་མི་སྐྱེ་བའོ།། སོ་སོར་བརྟགས་པའི་འགོག་པ་གང་ཞེ་ན། གང་འགོག་པ་དེ་ནི་བྲལ་བ་སྟེ། དེ་ནི་གང་ཉོན་མོངས་པའི་གཉེན་པོས་ཕུང་པོ་རྣམས་གཏན་དུ་མི་སྐྱེ་བའོ། །དེ་བཞིན་ཉིད་གང་ཞེ་ན། གང་ཆོས་རྣམས་ཀྱི་ཆོས་ཉིད་དང་། ཆོས་བདག་མེད་པ་ཉིད་དོ། །ཅིའི་ཕྱིར་སྐྱེ་མཆེད་ཅེས་བྱ་ཞེ་ན། རྣམ་པར་ཤེས་པ་སྐྱེ་བའི་སྒོའི་ཕྱིར་རོ། །ཁམས་བཅོ་བརྒྱད་ནི་མིག་གི་ཁམས་དང་། གཟུགས་ཀྱི་ཁམས་དང་། མིག་གི་རྣམ་པར་ཤེས་པའི་ཁམས་དང་། རྣ་བའི་ཁམས་དང་། སྒྲའི་ཁམས་དང་། རྣ་བའི་རྣམ་པར་ཤེས་པའི་ཁམས་དང་། སྣའི་ཁམས་དང་། དྲིའི་ཁམས་དང་། སྣའི་རྣམ་པར་ཤེས་པའི་ཁམས་དང་། ལྕེའི་ཁམས་དང་། རོའི་ཁམས་དང་། ལྕེའི་རྣམ་པར་ཤེས་པའི་ཁམས་དང་། ལུས་ཀྱི་ཁམས་དང་། རེག་བྱའི་ཁམས་དང་། ལུས་ཀྱི་རྣམ་པར་ཤེས་པའི་ཁམས་དང་། ཡིད་ཀྱི་ཁམས་དང་། ཆོས་ཀྱི་ཁམས་དང་།

70 D, C གྲོལ་

ཡིད་ཀྱི་རྣམ་པར་ཤེས་པའི་ཁམས་སོ། །མིག་ལ་སོགས་པའི་ཁམས་དང་། གཟུགས་ལ་སོགས་པའི་ཁམས་ནི་སྐྱེ་མཆེད་རྣམས་ཇི་ལྟ་བ་བཞིན་ནོ། །རྣམ་པར་ཤེས་པའི་ཁམས་དྲུག་པོ་དག་ནི་མིག་ལ་སོགས་པ་རྣམས་ལ་བརྟེན་[71]ཏེ། གཟུགས་ལ་སོགས་པ་ལ་དམིགས་པ་རྣམ་པར་རིག་པའོ། །ཡིད་ཀྱི་ཁམས་ནི་དེ་དག་ཉིད་འགགས་[72]མ་ཐག་པ་སྟེ། རྣམ་པར་ཤེས་པ་དྲུག་པའི་གནས་བསྟན་[73]པའི་ཕྱིར་རོ། །དེ་ལྟར་ན་ཁམས་བཅོ་བརྒྱད་དུ་རྣམ་པར་གཞག་གོ །གཟུགས་ཀྱི་ཕུང་པོ་གང་ཡིན་པ་དེ་ནི་སྐྱེ་མཆེད་དང་། ཁམས་བཅུ་དང་། ཆོས་ཀྱི་སྐྱེ་མཆེད་དང་། ཁམས་ཀྱི་ཕྱོགས་གཅིག་གོ །རྣམ་པར་ཤེས་པའི་ཕུང་པོ་གང་ཡིན་པ་དེ་ནི་ཡིད་ཀྱི་སྐྱེ་མཆེད་དང་། སེམས་ཀྱི་ཁམས་བདུན་ནོ། །གཞན་ཕུང་པོ་གསུམ་པོ་[74]གང་ཡིན་པ་དག་དང་། གཟུགས་ཀྱི་ཕུང་པོའི་ཕྱོགས་གཅིག་པོ་དེ་དང་། འདུས་མ་བྱས་དང་བཅས་པ་ནི་ཆོས་ཀྱི་སྐྱེ་མཆེད་དང་། ཆོས་ཀྱི་ཁམས་སོ། །ཅིའི་ཕྱིར་ཁམས་[75]ཞེས་[76]བྱ་ཞེ་ན། བྱེད་པ་མེད་ལ་རང་གི་མཚན་ཉིད་འཛིན་པའི་ཕྱིར་རོ། །ཅིའི་ཕྱིར་ཕུང་པོ་ལ་སོགས་པ་བཤད་ཅེ་[77]ན། བདག་ཏུ་འཛིན་པ་རྣམ་པ་གསུམ་གྱི་གཉེན་པོར་[78]གོ་རིམས་བཞིན་ནོ། །བདག་ཏུ་འཛིན་པ་རྣམ་པ་གསུམ་ནི་གཅིག་པུར་འཛིན་པ་དང་། ཟ་བར་འཛིན་པ་དང་། བྱེད་པར་འཛིན་པའོ།། ཁམས་བཅོ་བརྒྱད་ལ་གཟུགས་ཅན་དུ་ཞེ་ན། གང་དག་གཟུགས་ཀྱི་ཕུང་པོའི་ངོ་བོ་ཉིད་དོ།། གཟུགས་ཅན་མ་ཡིན་པ་དུ་ཞེ་ན། ལྷག་མ་རྣམས་སོ། །བསྟན་[79]དུ་ཡོད་པ་དུ་ཞེ་ན། གཟུགས་ཀྱི་ཁམས་གཅིག་སྟེ། ཡུལ་བསྟན་དུ་ཡོད་པའོ། །བསྟན་དུ་མེད་པ་ནི་[80]དུ་ཞེ་ན། ལྷག་མ་རྣམས་སོ། །ཐོགས་པ་དང་བཅས་པ་དུ་ཞེ་ན།

71 N རྟེན་

72 N, P འགག་

73 D, C བརྟན་

74 C པ་

75 N གཡས་. This appears to be an inadvertent corruption.

76 N, P ཤེས་

77 P ཅེས་

78 D, C པོ་

79 D, C བརྟེན་ ; N, P བརྟན་

80 N, P insert གང་ in place of ནི་

གཟུགས་ཅན་བཅུ་སྟེ། གང་ལ་གང་ཐོགས་པའོ། །ཐོགས་[81]པ་མེད་པ་དུ་ཞེ་ན། ལྷག་
མ་རྣམས་སོ། །ཟག་པ་དང་བཅས་པ་དུ་ཞེ་ན། བཅོ་ལྔ་དང་ཐ་མ་གསུམ་ཀྱི་ཆའོ།[82]
།དེ་དག་ཉོན་མོངས་པ་སྐྱེ་བའི་མངོན་སུམ་ཀྱི་སྤྱོད་ཡུལ་གྱི་ཕྱིར་རོ། །ཟག་པ་མེད་པ་དུ་
ཞེ་ན། ཐ་མ་གསུམ་གྱི་ཆའོ། །འདོད་པ་དང་རབ་ཏུ་ལྡན་པ་དུ་ཞེ་ན། ཐམས་ཅད་དོ།
།གཟུགས་དང་རབ་ཏུ་ལྡན་པ་དུ་ཞེ་ན། བཅུ་བཞི་སྟེ། དྲི་དང་། རོ་དང་། སྣ་དང་།
ལྕེའི་རྣམ་པར་ཤེས་པ་མ་གཏོགས་པའོ། །གཟུགས་མེད་པ་དང་རབ་ཏུ་ལྡན་པ་དུ་ཞེ་ན།
ཐ་མ་གསུམ་མོ། །མི་ལྡན་པ་དུ་ཞེ་ན། གསུམ་གྱི་ཆའོ། །ཕུང་པོར་བསྡུས་པ་དུ་ཞེ་ན།
འདུས་མ་བྱས་མ་གཏོགས་པའོ། །ཉེ་བར་ལེན་པའི་ཕུང་པོས་བསྡུས་པ་དུ་ཞེ་ན། གང་
ཟག་པ་དང་བཅས་པ་རྣམས་སོ། །དགེ་བ་དུ། མི་དགེ་བ་དུ། ལུང་དུ་མ་བསྟན་པ་དུ་
ཞེ་ན། བཅུ་ནི་རྣམ་པ་གསུམ་ཆར་ཏེ། སེམས་ཀྱི་ཁམས་བདུན་དང་། གཟུགས་
དང་། སྒྲ་དང་། ཆོས་ཀྱི་ཁམས་སོ། །ལྷག་མ་རྣམས་ནི་ལུང་དུ་མ་བསྟན་པའོ།
།ནང་གི་དུ་ཞེ་ན། བཅུ་གཉིས་ཏེ། གཟུགས་དང་། སྒྲ་དང་། དྲི་དང་། རོ་དང་།
རེག་བྱ་དང་། ཆོས་ཀྱི་ཁམས་མ་གཏོགས་པའོ། །ཕྱི་རོལ་གྱི་དུ་ཞེ་ན། དྲུག་སྟེ།
གང་དག་མ་གཏོགས་པ་རྣམས་སོ། །དམིགས་པ་དང་བཅས་པ་དུ་ཞེ་ན། སེམས་ཀྱི་
ཁམས་བདུན་དང་། ཆོས་ཀྱི་ཕྱོགས་གཅིག་ཀྱང་ཡིན་ཏེ། གང་སེམས་ལས་བྱུང་བའོ།
།དམིགས་པ་མེད་པ་དུ་ཞེ་ན། ལྷག་མ་བཅུ་དང་། ཆོས་ཀྱི་ཁམས་ཀྱི་ཕྱོགས་སོ།
།རྣམ་པར་རྟོག་པ་དང་བཅས་པ་དུ་ཞེ་ན། ཡིད་ཀྱི་ཁམས་དང་ཡིད་ཀྱི་རྣམ་པར་ཤེས་
པའི་ཁམས་དང་། ཆོས་ཀྱི་ཁམས་ཀྱི་ཕྱོགས་སོ། །རྟོག་པ་མེད་པ་དུ་ཞེ་ན། ལྷག་མ་
རྣམས་སོ། །ཟིན་པ་དུ་ཞེ་ན། ནང་གི་ལྔ་དང་། བཞིའི་[83]ཕྱོགས་[84]ཏེ[85]། གཟུགས་
དང་།[86]དྲི་དང་། རོ་དང་། རེག་[87]བྱ་རྣམས་ཀྱིའོ། །ཟིན་པ་མ་ཡིན་པ་དུ་ཞེ་ན། ལྷག་

81 P ཐོག་

82 N, P both incorrectly insert །མི་ལྡན་པ་དུ་ཞེ་ན། གསུམ་གྱི་ཆའོ། here and then repeat the same text again below, where it properly should appear.

83 N, P ཕྱིའི་

84 N ཕྱུགས་

85 C ཏ་

86 D, C, N, and P all incorrectly insert སྒྲ་དང་།

87 C རག་

མ་དགུ་དང་[88]བཞིའི་ཕྱོགས་སོ། །བསྟེན་[89]པ་མཚུངས་པ་དུ་ཞེ་ན། ནང་གི་གཟུགས་ཅན་ལྔ་སྟེ། རང་གི་རྣམ་པར་ཤེས་པ་དག་དང་ཡུལ་ཐུན་མོང་[90]བ་ཉིད་ཀྱི་ཕྱིར་རོ། །དེ་དག་དང་མཚུངས་པ་དུ་ཞེ་ན། དེ་དག་ཉིད་རང་གི་རྣམ་པར་ཤེས་པས་སྟོང་པ་སྟེ། རང་གི་རིགས་[91]དང་མཐུན་པའི་ཕྱིར་རོ། །ཕུང་པོ་ལྔའི་རབ་ཏུ་བྱེད་པ་སློབ་དཔོན་དབྱིག་གཉེན་གྱིས་མཛད་པ་རྫོགས་སོ།། རྒྱ་གར་གྱི་མཁན་པོ་ཛི་ན་མི་ཏྲ་དང་། ཤཱི་ལེནྡྲ་བོ་དྷི་དང་། དཱ་ན་ཤཱི་ལ་དང་། ཞུ་ཆེན་གྱི་ལོ་ཙྪ་བ་བན་དེ་ཡེ་ཤེས་སྡེ་ལ་སོགས་པས་བསྒྱུར་ཅིང་ཞུས་ཏེ། གཏན་ལ་ཕབ་པ།། །།

88 D, C, N, and P all fail to include the phrase ལྷག་མ་དགུ་དང་ , which is confirmed by the commentaries of both Sthiramati and Sa'i rtsa lag.

89 D, P བསྟན་

90 C མོངས་

91 D, P རིག་

APPENDIX 2: A Reconstruction of the Original Sanskrit Text of Vasubandhu's *Summary of the Five Heaps*

A NUMBER OF decades ago the Indian monk scholar Śāntibhikṣu Śāstri published a Sanskrit reconstruction of Vasubandhu's root text.[1] This version was consulted as the English translations of Vasubandhu's and Sthiramati's works were being prepared. After comparing that edition with passages from various Sanskrit and Tibetan Abhidharma texts, it was decided certain revisions could be proposed. I readily admit that a number of the readings that appear here are conjectural and apologize for any new errors that may have been introduced.

पञ्चस्कन्धप्रकरणम्

पञ्चस्कन्धाः। रूपस्कन्धो वेदनास्कन्धः संज्ञास्कन्धः संस्कारस्कन्धो विज्ञानस्कन्धश्च॥

रूपं कतमत्। यत् किंचिद्रूपं सर्वं तच्चत्वारि महाभूतानि चत्वारि च महाभूतान्युपादाय॥

कतमानि चत्वारि महाभूतानि। पृथिवीधातुरब्धातुस्तेजोधातुर्वायुधातुश्च॥

1 *Sārasvatī Suṣamā* (*Journal of Sampurnanand Sanskrit University*, published quarterly), 1955. A later edition was also published in Sri Lanka: *Pañcaskandhaprakaraṇa of Vasubandhu, A restitution into Sanskrit from the Tibetan Version together with an Introduction, English translation, Notes, A Tibetan-Sanskrit Vocabulary and an Index of Important Sanskrit Words*. Kelaniya, 1969. Efforts to locate a copy of this edition were unsuccessful.

तत्र पृथिवीधातुः कतमः। खरत्वम्[2] ॥
अब्धातुः कतमः। स्नेहत्वम्[3] ॥
तेजोधातुः कतमः। उष्णता॥
वायुधातुः कतमः। लघुसमुदीरणत्वम्॥
उपादायरूपं कतमत्। चक्षुरिन्द्रियं श्रोत्रेन्द्रियं घ्राणेन्द्रियं जिह्वेन्द्रियं कायेन्द्रियं रूपं शब्दो गन्धो रसः स्प्रष्टव्यैकदेशोऽविज्ञप्तिश्च॥
तत्र चक्षुरिन्द्रियं कतमत्। वर्णविषयो रूपप्रसादः॥
श्रोत्रेन्द्रियं कतमत्। शब्दविषयो रूपप्रसादः॥
घ्राणेन्द्रियं कतमत्। गन्धविषयो रूपप्रसादः॥
जिह्वेन्द्रियं कतमत्। रसविषयो रूपप्रसादः॥
कायेन्द्रियं कतमत्। स्प्रष्टव्यविषयो रूपप्रसादः॥
रूपं कतमत्। चक्षुर्विषयः। वर्णः संस्थानं विज्ञप्तिश्च॥
शब्दः कतमः। श्रोत्रविषयः। उपात्तानुपात्तोभयमहाभूतहेतुकः॥
गन्धः कतमः। घ्राणविषयः। सुगन्धो दुर्गन्धस्तदन्यश्च॥
रसः कतमः। जिह्वाविषयः। मधुर अम्लो लवणः कटुकस्तिक्तः कषायश्चेति॥
स्प्रष्टव्यैकदेशः कतमः। कायविषयः। महाभूतानि स्थापयित्वा श्लक्ष्णत्वं कर्कशत्वं गुरुत्वं लघुत्वं शीतत्वं जिघत्सा पिपासा च॥
अविज्ञप्तिः कतमा। विज्ञप्तिसमाधिसम्भूतं रूपमनिदर्शनाप्रतिघम्॥
वेदना कतमा। त्रिविधोऽनुभवः। सुखो दुःखोऽदुःखासुखश्च। सुखो यस्मिन्निरुद्धे संयोगेच्छा। दुःखो यस्मिन्नुत्पन्ने वियोगेच्छा। अदुःखासुखो यस्मिन्नुत्पन्ने नोभयेच्छा भवति॥
संज्ञा कतमा। विषयनिमित्तोद्ग्रहणम्। सा त्रिविधा परीत्ता महद्गता अप्रमाणा च॥
संस्काराः कतमे। वेदनासंज्ञाभ्यामन्ये चैतसिका धर्माश्चित्तविप्रयुक्ताश्च॥
तत्र चैतसिका धर्माश्च कतमे। ये धर्माश्चित्तसंप्रयुक्ताः॥

2 This reading is based on *AK*. *AS* has *kaṭhinatā*; *MVy* has *khakkhaṭatvam*. All three are translated into Tibetan by the same term, i.e., *sra ba nyid*.

3 *AS* has *niṣyandatā*; *MVy* has *dravatvam*. All three are rendered in Tibetan as *gzher ba nyid*.

ते पुनः कतमे। स्पर्शो मनस्कारो वेदना संज्ञा चेतना छन्दोऽधिमोक्षः स्मृतिः समाधिः प्रज्ञा श्रद्धा ह्रीरपत्राप्यमलोभःकुशलमूलमद्वेषःकुशलमूलममोहःकुशलमूलं वीर्यं प्रश्रब्धिरप्रमाद उपेक्षा अविहिंसा रागः प्रतिघो मानोऽविद्या दृष्टिर्विचिकित्सा क्रोध उपनाहो म्रक्षः प्रदाश ईर्ष्या मात्सर्यं माया शाठ्यं मदो विहिंसा आह्रीक्यमनपत्राप्यं स्त्यानमौद्धत्यमाश्रद्ध्यं कौसीद्यं प्रमादो मुषितस्मृतिता विक्षेपोऽसंप्रजन्यं कौकृत्यं मिद्धं वितर्को विचारश्च॥ एतेषां पञ्च सर्वत्रगाः। पञ्च प्रतिनियतविषयाः। एकादश कुशलाः। षट् क्लेशाः। शेषा उपक्लेशाः। चत्वारोऽन्यथापि भवन्ति॥

स्पर्शः कतमः। त्रिकसंनिपाते परिच्छेदः॥

मनस्कारः कतमः। चेतस आभोगः॥

चेतना कतमा। गुणदोषानुभयेषु चित्ताभिसंस्कारो मनस्कर्म॥

छन्दः कतमः। अभिप्रेते वस्तुन्यभिलाषः[4] ॥

अधिमोक्षः कतमः। निश्चिते वस्तुनि तथैवावधारणम्[5] ॥

स्मृतिः कतमा। संस्तुते वस्तुन्येवासंप्रमोषश्चेतसोऽभिलपनता[6] ॥

समाधिः कतमः। उपपरीक्ष्ये वस्तुनि चित्तस्यैकाग्रता[7] ॥

प्रज्ञा कतमा। तत्रैव प्रविचयो योगायोगविहितोऽन्यथा च[8] ॥

श्रद्धा कतमा। कर्मफलसत्यरत्नेष्वभिसंप्रत्ययोऽभिलाषश्चेतसः प्रसादः॥

ह्रीः कतमा। आत्मानं धर्मं वाधिपतिं कृत्वावद्येन लज्जा॥

अपत्राप्यं कतमत्। लोकमधिपतिं कृत्वावद्येन लज्जा॥

अलोभः कतमः। लोभप्रतिपक्षो निर्विदनाग्रहः॥

अद्वेषः कतमः। द्वेषप्रतिपक्षो मैत्री॥

अमोहः कतमः। मोहप्रतिपक्षो भूतसंप्रतिपत्तिः॥

वीर्यं कतमत्। कौसीद्यप्रतिपक्षः कुशले चेतसोऽभ्युत्साहः॥

प्रश्रब्धिः कतमा। दौष्ठुल्यप्रतिपक्षः कायचित्तकर्मण्यता॥

4 *AKV*, p. 187.

5 Ibid.

6 *AKV*, p. 477.

7 *AKV*, pp. 477–478.

8 *AKV*, p. 478.

अप्रमादः कतमः। प्रमादप्रतिपक्षोऽलोभाद्यावद्वीर्यं यान्निश्रित्याकुशलान्धर्मान् प्रजहाति तत्प्रतिपक्षांश्च कुशलान्धर्मान्भावयति॥

उपेक्षा कतमा। स एवालोभाद्यावद्वीर्यं यान्निश्रित्य चित्तसमतां चित्तप्रशठतां चित्तानाभोगतां च प्रतिलभते[9]। यया निर्वासितेषु क्लिष्टेषु धर्मेषु असंक्लिष्ट-विहरी भवति॥

अविहिंसा कतमा। विहिंसाप्रतिपक्षः करुणा॥

रागः कतमः। पञ्चोपादानस्कन्धेष्वभिस्नेहोऽध्यवसानम्॥

प्रतिघः कतमः। सत्त्वेष्वाघातः॥

मानः कतमः[10]। सप्त मानाः। मानोऽतिमानो मानातिमानोऽस्मिमानो-ऽभिमान ऊनमानो मिथ्यामानश्च॥

मानः कतमः। हीनाच्छ्रेयानस्मि सदृशेन सदृशोऽस्मीति वा या चित्तस्योन्नतिः॥

अतिमानः कतमः। सदृशाच्छ्रेयानस्मि श्रेयसा सदृशोऽस्मीति वा या चित्तस्यो-न्नतिः॥

मानातिमानः कतमः। श्रेयसः श्रेयानस्मि या चित्तस्योन्नतिः॥

अस्मिमानः कतमः।पञ्चोपादानस्कन्धानात्मत आत्मीयतो वा पश्यतो या चित्तस्योन्नतिः॥

अभिमानः कतमः। अप्राप्त उत्तरे विशेषाधिगमे प्राप्तो मयेति या चित्तस्योन्नतिः॥

ऊनमानः कतमः। बह्वन्तरविशिष्टादल्पान्तरहीनोऽस्मीति या चित्तस्योन्नतिः॥

मिथ्यामानः कतमः। अगुणवतो गुणवानस्मीति या चित्तस्योन्नतिः॥

अविद्या कतमा। कर्मफलसत्यरत्नेष्वज्ञानम्। सा पुनः सहजा परिकल्पिता च॥

रागः कामावचरः प्रतिघोऽविद्या कामावचरा एतानि त्रीण्यकुशलमूलानि लोभो ऽकुशलमूलं द्वेषो मोहश्च[11]॥

दृष्टिः कतमा। पञ्च दृष्टयः। सत्कायदृष्टिरन्तग्राहदृष्टिर्मिथ्यादृष्टिर्दृष्टिपरामर्शः शील-व्रतपरामर्शश्च॥

9 T: *thob pa.*

10 This description of the seven types of pride seems to be virtually identical with *AS*, p. 45.

11 Cf. *AK*, Ch. 5, v. 20 and related remarks in autocommentary. For example, *AKV* clarifies that the root of nonvirtue that is ignorance does not include that ignorance of the desire realm that is associated with either the view of the perishable collection or the view that grasps an extreme. This is because these forms of ignorance are not nonvirtues; they are obstructive-indeterminate entities (S: *nivṛtāvyākṛtaḥ*, T: *sgrib lung ma bstan*). See Part Two, note 561.

सत्कायदृष्टिः कतमा। पञ्चोपादानस्कन्धानात्मत आत्मीयतो वा पश्यतो या क्लिष्टा प्रज्ञा॥

अन्तग्राहदृष्टिः कतमा। तानेवाधिपतिं कृत्वा शाश्वतत उच्छेदतो वा पश्यतो या क्लिष्टा प्रज्ञा॥

मिथ्यादृष्टिः कतमा। हेतुं वापवदतः फलं वा क्रियां वा सद्वा वस्तु नाशयतो या क्लिष्टा प्रज्ञा॥

दृष्टिपरामर्शः कतमः। ता एव तिस्रो दृष्टीस्तदाश्रयांश्च स्कन्धानग्रतः श्रेष्ठतो विशिष्टतः परमतश्च पश्यतो या क्लिष्टा प्रज्ञा॥

शीलव्रतपरामर्शः कतमः। शीलं व्रतं तदाश्रयांश्च स्कन्धान् शुद्धितो मुक्तितो नैर्याणिकतश्च पश्यतो या क्लिष्टा प्रज्ञा॥

विचिकित्सा कतमा। सत्यादिषु या विमतिः॥

एतेषां क्लेशानाम दृष्टयो तिस्रो पश्चिमा विचिकित्सा च परिकल्पिताः। शेषाः सहजाश्च परिकल्पिताश्च॥

क्रोधः कतमः। वर्तमानमपकारमागम्य यश्चेतस आघातः॥

उपनाहः कतमः। वैरानुबन्धः॥

म्रक्षः कतमः। आत्मनोऽवद्यप्रच्छादना॥

प्रदाशः कतमः। चण्डवचोदाशिता॥

ईर्ष्या कतमा। परसंपत्तौ चेतसो व्यारोषः॥

मात्सर्यं कतमत्। दानविरोधी चेतस आग्रहः॥

माया कतमा। परवञ्चनाभूतार्थसंदर्शनता॥

शाठ्यं कतमत्। स्वदोषप्रच्छादनोपायसंगृहीतं चेतसः कौटिल्यम्॥

मदः कतमः। स्वसंपत्तौ रक्तस्योद्धर्षश्चेतसः पर्यादानम्॥

विहिंसा कतमा। सत्त्वविहेठना॥

आह्रीक्यं कतमत्। स्वयमवद्येनालज्जा॥

अनपत्राप्यं कतमत्। परतोऽवद्येनालज्जा॥

स्त्यानं कतमत्। चित्तस्याकर्मण्यता[12] स्तैमित्यम्॥

12 *AS* has *cittākarmaṇyatā*. *AKB* (p. 56) also quotes this form in a passage that is apparently from the original Sanskrit Abhidharma work *Jñānaprasthānam*. However, I follow the Sanskrit manuscript of Sthiramati's *TB* (p. 96), because he seems to follow closely the descriptions for the secondary mental afflictions that Vasubandhu presents in the *PS*. The genitive form of *citta* would also permit this term to modify both *akarmaṇyatā* and *staimityam*.

औद्धत्यं कतमत्। चित्तस्याव्युपशमः॥

आश्रद्ध्यं कतमत्। कर्मफलसत्यरत्नेष्वनभिसंप्रत्ययश्चेतसोऽप्रसादः[13]श्रद्धा-विपक्षः॥

कौसीद्यं कतमत्। कुशले चेतसोऽनभ्युत्साहो वीर्यविपक्षः॥

प्रमादः कतमः। यैर्लोभद्वेषमोहकौसीद्यैः क्लेशाच्चित्तं न रक्षति कुशलं च न भावयति॥

मुषितस्मृतिता कतमा। क्लिष्टा स्मृतिः कुशलेऽस्पष्टता॥

विक्षेपः कतमः। पञ्चसु कामगुणेषु रागद्वेषमोहांशिको यश्चेतसो विसारः॥

असंप्रजन्यं कतमत्। क्लेशसंप्रयुक्ता प्रज्ञा ययासंविदिता कायवाक्चित्तचर्या प्रवर्तते॥

कौकृत्यं कतमत्। चेतसो विप्रतिसारः॥

मिद्धं कतमत्। अस्वतन्त्रवृत्तिचेतसोऽभिसंक्षेपः॥

वितर्कः कतमः। पर्येषको मनोजल्पश्चेतनाप्रज्ञाविशेषो या चित्तस्यौधारिकता[14]॥

विचारः कतमः। प्रत्यवेक्षको मनोजल्पस्तथैव या चित्तस्य सूक्ष्मता[15]॥

चित्तविप्रयुक्ताः संस्काराः कतमे। ये रूपचित्तचैतसिकावस्थासु प्रज्ञप्यन्ते तत्त्वान्यत्वतश्च न प्रज्ञप्यन्ते॥

ते पुनः कतमे। प्राप्तिरसंज्ञिसमापत्तिर्निरोधसमापत्तिरासंज्ञिकं जीवितेन्द्रियं निकायसभागो जातिर्जरा स्थितिरनित्यता नामकायः पदकायो व्यञ्जनकायः पृथग्जनत्वमेवंजातीयकाश्च॥

प्राप्तिः कतमा। प्रतिलम्भः समन्वागमश्च। सा पुनर्बीजं वशित्वं सम्मुखीभावश्च यथायोगं योजयितव्यम्॥

असंज्ञिसमापत्तिः कतमा। शुभकृत्स्नवीतरागस्य नोर्ध्वस्य निःसरणसंज्ञापूर्वकेण मनसिकारेणास्थावराणां चित्तचैतसिकानां धर्माणां यो निरोधः॥

13 Cf. *AKB*, p. 56.

14 *AKV*, p. 89.

15 Ibid.

निरोधसमापत्तिः कतमा। आकिंचन्यायतनवीतरागस्य भवाग्रादुच्चलितस्य विहारसंज्ञापूर्वकेण[16] मनसिकारेणास्थावराणामेकत्यानां च स्थावराणां चित्तचैतसिकानां धर्माणां यो निरोधः॥

आसंज्ञिकं कतमत्। असंज्ञिसमापत्तिफलम्। असंज्ञिसत्त्वमध्येषु देवेषूपपन्नस्यास्थावराणां चित्तचैतसिकानां धर्माणां यो निरोधः॥

जीवितेन्द्रियं कतमत्। निकायसभागेषु पूर्वकर्माविद्धेन यः संस्काराणां स्थितिकालनियमः॥

निकायसभागः कतमः। यत्सत्त्वानामात्मभावसादृश्यम्॥

जातिः कतमा। निकायसभागे यः संस्काराणामभूत्वाभावः॥

जरा कतमा। तथैव तेषां प्रबन्धान्यथात्वम्॥

स्थितिः कतमा। तथैव तेषां प्रबन्धानुवृत्तिः[17]॥

अनित्यता कतमा। तथैव तेषां प्रबन्धोपरमः[18]॥

नमकायाः कतमे। धर्माणां स्वभावाधिवचनानि॥

पदकायाः कतमे। धर्माणां विशेषाधिवचनानि॥

व्यञ्जनकायाः कतमे। अक्षराणि तदुभयाभिव्यञ्जनतामुपादाय। वर्णोऽपि ते नामपदाश्रयत्वेनार्थसंवर्णतामुपादाय। अक्षरं पुनः पर्यायाक्षरणतामुपादाय॥

पृथग्जनत्वं कतमत्। आर्यधर्माणामप्रतिलाभः[19]। अयं संस्कारस्कन्ध इति॥

विज्ञानं कतमत्। आलम्बनविज्ञप्तिः। चित्तं मनोऽपि तत् चित्रतां मनःसंनिश्रयतां चोपदाय। प्राधान्येन चित्तमालयविज्ञानं। तथा हि तच्चितं सर्वसंस्कारबिजैः। तत्पुनरपरिच्छिन्नालम्बनाकारम्। एकजातीयं संतानानुवृत्तिश्च[20]। यतो निरोधसमापत्त्यसंज्ञिसमापत्त्यासंज्ञिकेभ्यो व्युत्थितस्य पुनर्विषयविज्ञप्त्याख्यं प्रवृत्तिविज्ञानमुत्पद्यते। आलम्बनप्रत्ययमपेक्ष्य प्रकारान्तरवृत्तितां छिन्नपुनरवृत्तितां

16 *PSV* (f. 227b) and *PSB* (f. 84a) support the reading that Vasubandhu dropped the initial *śānta* from the phrase *śāntavihārasaṃjñāpūrvakeṇa* that appears in *AS* (pp. 10–11). Cf. also *AKB*, p. 72.

17 T: *rgyud chags pa*. *AS* has *avipraṇāśaḥ*, but the Tibetan equivalent for that is *mi 'jig pa*.

18 T: *rgyun chad pa*. *AS* has *vināśaḥ* (T: *'jig pa*).

19 T: *ma thob pa*. Cf. also *AKB* (p. 66): *aprāptiḥ*.

20 Cf. *MVy*, 2124.

संसारप्रवृत्तिनिवृत्तितां चोपादाय। आलयविज्ञानत्वं पुनः सर्वबीजालयतामात्मभावालयनिमित्ततां[21] कायालीनतां चोपादाय। आदानविज्ञानमपि तत् कायोपादनतां चोपदाय॥

प्राधान्येन मन आलयविज्ञानालम्बनम्। सदात्ममोहात्मदृष्ट्यात्ममानात्मस्नेहादिसंप्रयुक्तं विज्ञानम्। एकजातीयं संतानानुवृत्तिश्च। अर्हत्त्वार्यमार्गनिरोधसमापत्त्यवस्थां स्थापयित्वा॥

केनार्थेन स्कन्धाः। राश्यर्थेन। अध्वसन्तानप्रकारगतिदेशभेदभिनानां रूपादीनां संक्षेपसंग्रहणतामुपादाय॥

द्वादशायतनानि। चक्षुरायतनं रूपायतनं श्रोत्रायतनं शब्दायतनं घ्राणायतनं गन्धायतनं जिह्वायतनं रसायतनं कायायतनं स्प्रष्टव्यायतनं मनआयतनं धर्मायतनं च॥

चक्षुरादीनां पूर्ववन्निर्देशो रूपशब्दगन्धरसायतनानां च ॥

स्प्रष्टव्यायतनं चत्वारि महाभूतानि यश्च स्प्रष्टव्यैकदेश उक्तः॥

मनआयतनं यो विज्ञानस्कन्धः॥

धर्मायतनं ये वेदना संज्ञा संस्कारा अविज्ञप्तिरसंस्कृतं च॥

असंस्कृतं कतमत्। आकाशमप्रतिसंख्यानिरोधः प्रतिसंख्यानिरोधस्तथता च॥

तत्राकाशं कतमत्। रूपस्यावकाशः॥

अप्रतिसंख्यानिरोधः कतमः। यो निरोधो न च विसंयोगः। स पुनर्विना क्लेशप्रतिपक्षेण स्कन्धानामत्यन्तानुत्पादः॥

प्रतिसंख्यानिरोधः कतमः। यो निरोधः स च विसंयोगः।सः पुनर्यो क्लेशप्रतिपक्षेण स्कन्धानामत्यन्तानुत्पादः॥

तथता कतमा। या धर्माणां धर्मता धर्मनैरात्म्यं॥

केनार्थेनायतनानि। विज्ञानायद्वारार्थेन॥

अष्टादश धातवः। चक्षुर्धातू रूपधातुश्चक्षुर्विज्ञानधातुः श्रोत्रधातुः शब्दधातुः श्रोत्रविज्ञानधातुर्घ्राणधातुर्गन्धधातुर्घ्राणविज्ञानधातुर्जिह्वाधातू रसधातुर्जिह्वाविज्ञानधातुः

21 Sthiramati (see Part Two, p. 343) indicates the existence of editions of the root text that have the variant reading *ātmamānālayanimittatāṃ* for this compound.

कायधातुः स्प्रष्टव्यधातुः कायविज्ञानधातुर्मनोधातुर्धर्मधातुर्मनोविज्ञानधातुश्च॥
चक्षुरादिधातवो रूपादिधातवश्च यथायतनानि॥
षड्विज्ञानधातवश्चक्षुरादिसंनिश्रिता रूपाद्यालम्बना विज्ञप्तयः॥
मनोधातुस्त एव समनन्तरनिरुद्धाः षष्ठविज्ञानाश्रयपरिदीपनार्थम्। एवमष्टादश-धातवो व्यवस्थाप्यन्ते[22]॥
यो रूपस्कन्ध स दशायतनधातवो धर्मायतनधात्वेकदेशश्च[23]। यो विज्ञानस्कन्धः स मनआयतनं सप्त चित्तधातवश्च[24]। ये चान्ये त्रयः स्कन्धा रूपस्कन्धैकदेशश्च ते सहासंस्कृतेन धर्मायतनं धर्मधातुश्च॥
केनार्थेन धातवः। निर्व्यापारस्वलक्षणधारणार्थेन॥
किमर्थं स्कन्धादिदेशना। त्रिविधात्मग्राहप्रतिपक्षेण यथाक्रमं। त्रिविधात्मग्राह एकत्वग्राहो भोक्तृत्वग्राहः कर्तृत्वग्राहश्च॥
अष्टादाशानां धातूनां कति रूपिणः। ये रूपस्कन्धस्वभावाः॥
कत्यरूपिणः। शेषाः॥
कति सनिदर्शनाः। एको रूपधातुर्देशनिदर्शनेन॥
कत्यनिदर्शनाः। शेषाः॥
कति सप्रतिघाः। दश रूपिणः। यो येन प्रतिहन्यते[25]॥
कत्यप्रतिघाः। शेषाः॥
कति सास्रवाः। पञ्चदश त्रयाणां च पश्चिमानां भागः[26]। तेषु क्लेशोत्पतितः प्रत्यक्षगोचरतामुपादाय॥
कत्यनास्रवाः। त्रयाणां पश्चिमानां भागः॥
कति कामप्रतिसंयुक्ताः। सर्वे॥

22 Cf. *AK*, ch. 1, v. 17, and related autocommentary.

23 Cf. *AS*, p. 12.

24 For both this statement and the previous one, cf. *AS*, p. 12 and *AKV*, p. 54.

25 I have taken this construction to mirror the relevant portion of the following *AKB* (p. 19; cf. also *AKV*, p. 79) passage: *yathā hasto hastenāhataḥ pratihanyata upale vā*, which is translated into Tibetan as *dper na lag pa'am rdo ba la lag pa rdugs shing thogs pa.*

26 T: *cha.*

कति रूपप्रतिसंयुक्ताः। चतुर्दश गन्धरसौ घ्राणजिह्वाविज्ञाने स्थापयित्वा[27]॥
कत्यारूप्यप्रतिसंयुक्ताः। पश्चिमास्त्रयः॥
कत्यप्रतिसंयुक्ताः[28]। त्रयाणां भागः॥
कति स्कन्धसंगृहीताः। असंस्कृतवर्ज्याः[29]॥
कत्युपादानस्कन्धसंगृहीताः। ये सास्रवाः[30]॥
कति कुशलाः कत्यकुशलाः कत्यव्याकृताः[31]। दश त्रिधाः। सप्त चित्तधातवो रूपशब्दधर्मधातवश्च। शेषा अव्याकृताः॥
कत्याध्यात्मिकाः। द्वादश रूपशब्दगन्धरसस्प्रष्टव्यधर्मधातूंस्थापयित्वा॥
कति बाह्याः। षट् ये स्थापिताः॥
कति सालम्बनाः। सप्त चित्तधातवो धर्मैकदेशोऽपि च ये चैतसिकाः[32]॥
कत्यनालम्बनाः। शेषा दश धर्मधातुप्रदेशश्च[33]॥
कति सविकल्पाः। मनोधातुर्मनोविज्ञानधातुर्धर्मधातुप्रदेशश्च॥
कत्यविकल्पाः। शेषाः॥
कत्युपात्ताः। पञ्चाध्यात्मिकाश्चतुर्णां च प्रदेशो रूपगन्धरसस्प्रष्टव्याणाम्॥
कत्यनुपात्ताः। शेषा नव चतुर्णां च प्रदेशः॥
कति सभागाः। पञ्चाध्यात्मिका रूपिणः स्वविज्ञानविषयसामान्यताम् उपादाय॥
कति तत्सभागाः। त एव स्वविज्ञानशून्याः स्वजातिसामान्यतामुपादाय॥
पञ्चस्कन्धप्रकरणमाचार्यवसुबन्धुकृतं समाप्तम्॥

27 Cf. *AK*, ch. 1, v. 30.

28 Cf. *MVy*, 398.

29 Cf. *AK*, ch. 1, v. 4, *mārgavarjitāḥ*.

30 Cf. *AK*, ch. 1, v. 8.

31 Cf. *AKB*, p. 20, introductory phrase to *AK*, ch. 1, v. 29c.

32 Cf. *AKB*, p. 23, in explanation of *AK*, ch. 1, v. 34ab.

33 Ibid.

Notes

Notes to Part One

Introduction

1 Because this expression is widely used, I will adopt it throughout this work when referring to the overall teaching of the four truths, as well as "the Noble Truth of Suffering," etc., for each of the individual truths. The term "Noble" refers to those practitioners who have attained the status of an *Ārya*, someone who has achieved the transcendent path of any of the three vehicles (see also below, Part One, note 106; and Part Two, note 111, and p. 324). Vasubandhu gives this explanation (*AKB*, p. 328): "[The four truths] are called the Āryan Truths in the sutras. What is the meaning of that [expression]? They are called the Āryan Truths in the sutras because they are true for the Āryas. Does this mean they are false for others? They are true for everyone, because they are free of error. However, the Āryas perceive them as they are; while others do not. That is why they are said to be true for the Āryas but not for those who are not Āryas, since [those who are not Āryas] perceive them erroneously." Asaṅga gives a similar description in his *ŚB* (p. 254).

2 In *'Dul ba* section of Kg., vol. 4, ff. 45b–48a. Yasha also recounts his own story in verse form to an audience of monks, cf. *Mulasarvāstivādavinayavastu*, vol. 1, pp. 114-115; the Tibetan translation is found in *'Dul ba gzhi*, vol. 2, f. 291b.

3 T: *dgra bcom pa*. This is a Buddhist term for someone who has destroyed all the mental afflictions associated with the three samsaric realms and who, therefore, will never again have to be reborn. While traditional commentaries interpret the word in a number of ways, two versions are that it means "one who has destroyed the enemy of the mental afflictions" (S: *kleśārihatatvāt*, T: *nyon mongs pa'i dgra bcom pas na*) or "one who is worthy of veneration" (*pūjārhatvāt*, T: *mchod par 'os pas na*) because, through having attained the ultimate goal of nirvana, he or she is a supreme field for the acquisition of merit.

4 "Even while ornately dressed one should practice Dharma / By being patient, subdued, disciplined, and pure in conduct. / He who puts aside violence toward all beings / Becomes a brahmin, an ascetic, and a mendicant" (S: *Alaṃkṛtaś cāpi careta dharmaṃ kṣānto dānto niyato brahmacārī / sarveṣu bhūteṣu nidhāya daṇḍaṃ sa brāhmaṇaḥ sa śramaṇaḥ sa bhikṣuḥ*. T: *rgyan gyis brgyan bzhin du ni chos spyad de / dul zhing yang*

dag sdom la tshangs spyod la / 'byung po kun la chad pa spangs pa ni / de ni bram ze dge sbyong dge slong yin). This verse also appears in the *Udānavargaḥ* (T: *Ched du brjod pa'i tshoms*), ch. 33, v. 2. In the Tibetan edition it is the opening verse of the chapter. The Tibetan version included here is the one that appears in the Vinaya passage; the verse that appears in the Tibetan translation of the *Udānavargaḥ* differs slightly.

5 *A Letter to Lama Umapa in Dokam* (T: *Bla ma dbu ma pa la mdo khams su phul ba['i springs yig]*); see Bibliography.

6 English translations of the two principal Tibetan works are listed in the "reference works" section of the Bibliography. Stefan Anacker's *Seven Works of Vasubandhu* provides additional details taken from Chinese sources.

7 T: *gzhung chen po*. In Gelukpa monasteries, these five works are the principal focus of religious study: (1) Maitreya Nātha's *Ornament of Realizations* (S: *Abhisamayālaṃkāraḥ*), (2) Dharmakīrti's *Extensive Treatise on Knowledge* (S: *Pramāṇavārttikam*), (3) Candrakīrti's *Introduction to the Middle Way* (S: *Madhyamakāvatāraḥ*), (4) Vasubandhu's *Treasury of Higher Learning* (S: *Abhidharmakośakārikā*), and (5) Guṇaprabha's *Aphorisms on the System of Moral Training* (S: *Vinayasūtram*).

Prologue

8 *AKB*, p. 14: *vedanāsvādavaśāddhi kāmān abhiṣvajante viparītasaṃjñāvaśācca dṛṣṭīr iti / saṃsārasyāpi te pradhānahetū; T: tshor ba ro myang ba'i dbang gis ni 'dod pa rnams la mngon par zhen la / 'du shes phyin ci logs gis ni lta rnams la'o // de dag ni 'khor ba'i rgyu'i gtso ba yang yin te.*

9 S: *skandhaḥ*, T: *phung po*. The term *skandhaḥ* is most commonly explained to mean an ordinary "heap" (S: *rāśiḥ*, T: *phung po*). See also Part Two, pp. 346–347, for additional interpretations of the term.

10 S: *ye kecit bhikṣavaḥ śramanā vā brāmaṇā vā ātmeti samanupaśyantaḥ samanupaśyanti sarve ta imān eva pañcopadāskandhān*; T: *dge slong dag sge sbyong ngam bram ze gang la la bdag go snyam du rjes su lta ba de dag thams cad ni nye bar len pa'i phung po lnga po 'di dag kho na la.*

11 Part Two, p. 246.

12 S: *asmimānaḥ*, T: *nga'o snyam pa'i nga rgyal*. See Part Two, pp. 293–294.

13 S: *upādānam*, T: *nye bar len pa*. See also note 454, below.

14 Part Two, p. 291.

15 Part Two, p. 291. See also related note 272, where Vasubandhu's original statement is cited.

Chapter One

16 That is, we will fail to gain anything of true spiritual value.

17 T: Sa skya paṇḍita Kun dga' rgyal mtshan. Fourth of the five patriarchs of the Sakyapa tradition (1182–1251/2).

18 *Classification of the Three Systems of Vows* (T: *sDom pa gsum gyi rab tu dbye ba*), p. 319, f. 4. T: *rta dang nor bu la sogs pa / cung zad tsam gyi nyo tshong la'ang / kun la 'dri zhing brtags nas dpyod / tshe 'di'i bya ba cung zad la'ang / de 'dra'i 'bad pa byed pa mthong / skye ba gtan gyi legs nyes ni / dam pa'i chos la rag las kyang / chos 'di khyi yi zas bzhin du / bzang ngan gang du'ang mi dpyod par / gang phrad de la gus par 'dzin.* The wording of this quote that appears in *Liberation in Our Hands* differs slightly.

19 *Liberation in Our Hands*, Part One, pp. 19–20. This work was compiled from notes taken during the course of an oral teaching on the Lamrim given by the influential Gelukpa lama Pabongka Rinpoche in 1921. See listing in Bibliography under Pha bong kha pa, *rNam grol lag bcangs.*

20 S: *Abhisamayālaṃkāraḥ*, T: *mNgon par rtogs pa'i rgyan*. This text, one of five that are collectively referred to as the "Five Maitreya Teachings" (T: *byams chos lnga*), is an analysis of the Mahāyāna path system that is taught implicitly in the Perfection of Wisdom Sutras.

21 *LC*, f. 3a.

22 The prayer, which is entitled *Opening the Door to the Supreme Path* (T: *Lam mchog sgo 'byed*), is the first item in his collection of miscellaneous works (T: *bKa' 'bum thor bu*).

23 *Liberation in Our Hands*, Part One, pp. 20–21.

24 *Jo bo rje dpal ldan mar me mdzad ye shes kyi rnam thar rgyas pa*. See listing in Bibliography under this title.

25 T: *rGya chen spyod brgyud.*

26 T: *Zab mo lta brgyud.*

27 T: *Byams chos sde lnga*. The other four besides the *The Ornament of Realizations*, which has already been mentioned, are (1) *The Ornament of the Mahāyāna Sutras* (S: *Mahāyānasūtrālaṃkāraḥ*); (2) *The Higher Science of the Mahāyāna* (S: *Mahāyānottaratantraśāstram*); (3) *The Treatise That Distinguishes the Middle View from Extreme Views* (S: *Madhyāntavibhāgakārikā*); and (4) *The Treatise That Distinguishes Phenomena and Their Ultimate Nature* (S: *Dharmadharmatāvibhāgakārikā*). According to tradition, Maitreya imparted all five works to Asaṅga after transporting him to his Tuṣita Paradise.

28 T: *Sa sde lnga*. Butön Rinchen Drup describes this formulation of Asaṅga's major writings on Buddhist doctrine in his *History of Buddhism* (Part One, pp. 54–56). The first of the five "sections" is the *Levels of Spiritual Practice* (S: *Yogācārabhūmiḥ*, T: *rNal 'byor spyod pa'i sa*), which is the principal work in the collection. It is organized in seventeen "levels," and referred to in the Tibetan tradition as the *Main Text on the Levels* (T: *Sa'i dngos gzhi*). In the Tengyur collection, this work actually appears in three parts. The first of the three, which carries the title of *Levels of Spiritual Practice*, actually contains only fifteen of the just-mentioned seventeen levels. This portion of the work is also referred to in the Tibetan tradition as *Multiple Levels* (T: *Sa mang po pa*). The remaining two levels—the thirteenth and the fifteenth—are the *Listeners' Level* (S: *Śrāvakabhūmiḥ*, T: *Nyan thos kyi sa*) and the *Bodhisattvas' Level* (S: *Bodhisattvabhūmiḥ*, T: *Byang chub sems dpa'i sa*), respectively. Extracted from the main work, they are identified as separate titles.

The remaining four of the *Five Sections* are considered supplements to the just-described work. None is extant in the original Sanskrit. They are (1) *Collection of Determinations* (S: *Viniścayasaṃgrahaṇī*, T: *rNam par gtan la dbab bsdu ba*); (2) *Collection of Topics* (S: *Vastusaṃgrahaṇī*, T: *gZhi bsdu ba*); (3) *Collection of Terms* (S: *Prayāyasaṃgrahaṇī*, T: *rNam grangs bsdu ba*); and (4) *Collection of Explanations* (S: *Vivaraṇasaṃgrahaṇī*, T: *rNam par bshad pa bsdu ba*). The first of these, *Collection of Determinations*, further elucidates the main work in seventeen levels and is an important work in its own right. *Collection of Topics* describes how the subject matter in the main treatise relates to the three divisions of the Buddhist canon—that is, Sutra, Vinaya, and Abhidharma. The final two works are much shorter—only slightly more than twenty folios each. *Collection of Terms* explains the specific sense of a variety of terminology that occurs in the literature. The final text describes the manner in which all the various topics should be explained and taught. Of the five, the seventeen-part *Levels of Spiritual Practice* and *Collection of Determinations* are the most substantive and represent major sources for much of the Tibetan commentarial literature on Mahāyāna doctrinal theory.

29 T: *Rigs pa'i tshogs drug*. They are (1) *Root Verses on the Middle Way* (S: *Mūlamadhyamakakārikā*, T: *dBu ma rtsa ba'i tshig le'ur byas pa*); (2) *Sixty Verses on Reasoning* (S: *Yuktiṣaṣṭikā*, T: *Rigs pa drug cu pa*); (3) *Seventy Verses on Emptiness* (S: *Śūnyatāsaptatiḥ*, T: *sTong pa nyid bdun cu pa*); (4) *Crushing Aphorisms* (S: *Vaidalyasūtram*, T: *Zhib mo rnam par 'thag pa*); (5) *Rebuttal of All Controversy* (S: *Vigrahavyāvartanī*, T: *rTsod pa bzlog pa*); and (6) *Establishing Ordinary Discourse* (S: *Vyavahārasiddhiḥ*, T: *Tha snyad sgrub pa*).

30 S: *Bodhicaryāvatāraḥ*, T: *Byang chub sems dpa'i spyod pa la 'jug pa*.

31 S: *Śikṣāsamuccayaḥ*, T: *bSlab pa kun las btus pa*.

32 T: *rlabs chen spyod brgyud*. The instruction of the Lojong tradition (T: *blo sbyong*) was originally considered a restricted teaching that was only given orally to a few select disciples. The Kadampa teacher Chekawa Yeshe Dorje (T: mChad ka wa Ye shes rDo rje, 1101–1175) is said to have been the first Tibetan master to teach it more openly and to a wider audience. Since that time, a number of teachings of this genre were compiled in written form. One version that is considered among the most complete forms of the teaching is called the *Seven Point Instruction on Mind Training* (T: *Blo sbyong don bdun pa*).

33 T: *bKa' gdams pa*. *bKa'* refers to the "word" or speech of the Buddha, and *gdams pa* means "instruction."

34 T: *dGe lugs pa*. Literally "follower of the virtuous tradition," this is the most common name for the school established by Je Tsongkapa Losang Drakpa (T: rJe Tsong kha pa Blo bzang grags pa, 1357–1419).

35 *Lam rim khrid chen brgyad*. Three are works by Je Tsongkapa: (1) the *Great Treatise*; (2) the *Shorter Treatise on the Stages of the Path* (T: *Byang chub lam gyi rim pa chung ba*); and (3) a short poem known variously as the *Hymn of Spiritual Experience* (T: *Nyams mgur*) and *The Essence of the Stages of the Path* (T: *Lam rim bsdus don*). Four of the five remaining texts are considerably more abbreviated than the first two of Je Tsongkapa's works; nevertheless, they are extremely influential: (1) the Third Dalai Lama's *Essence of Refined Gold* (T: *Lam rim gser zhun ma*); (2) the Fifth Dalai Lama's *Mañjughoṣa's Oral Instruction* (T: *'Jam dpal zhal lung*); (3) Panchen Losang Chökyi Gyeltsen's *Easy Path* (T: *bDe lam*); and (4) Panchen Losang Yeshe's *Quick Path* (T: *Myur lam*). The last of the eight works is an extensive poem by Dakpo Gomchen Ngawang Drakpa (T: Dwags po sgom chen Ngag dbang grags pa) entitled *Quintessence of Excellent Speech* (T: *Legs gsungs nying khu*). The author of this text was the senior disciple of Je Lodrö Tenpa (T: *rJe Blo gros bstan pa*, 1404–1478), who founded Dakpo Shedrup Ling (T: *Dwags po bshad sgrub gling*), an important Gelukpa monastery in southeastern Tibet that was known for holding regular teachings on the Lamrim instruction.

36 *Liberation in Our Hands*, Part Three, p. 148.

37 T: *thun mong lam sbyangs*. Je Tsongkapa uses this phrase in a verse from his prayer *Opening the Door to the Supreme Path:* "Once I've become a vessel trained in the common path, / Please bless me to enter with ease / The sacred door by which fortunate

beings gain access / To the adamantine vehicle, the most excellent of all vehicles" (T: *thun mong lam sbyangs snod du gyur pa na / theg pa kun gyi mchog gyur rdo rje'i theg / skal bzang skye bo'i 'jug ngogs dam pa der / bde blag nyid du 'jug par byin gyis rlobs*).

38 S: *Pāramitāyānam,* T: *Phar phyin gyi theg pa.* The word "Perfections" here is a reference to the six *pāramitā* practices that are taught in the Perfection of Wisdom Sutras. The phrase "Vehicle of the Perfections" is meant to indicate the entire non-tantric Mahāyāna tradition.

39 T: *mdo sngags zung 'brel.* The phrase appears, for instance, in the closing verses of Panchen Losang Chökyi Gyeltsen's autocommentary to his Mahāmudrā root text.

40 *Liberation in Our Hands,* Part One, p. 20. The phrase "three principal elements of the path" (T: *lam gyi gtso bo rnam gsum*) refers to renunciation, enlightenment mind, and correct view. These are the three spiritual knowledges that form the essence of the Lamrim teachings. Renunciation (S: *niḥsaraṇaḥ,* T: *nges 'byung*) is the attitude that wishes to attain complete liberation from samsara; enlightenment mind (S: *bodhicittaḥ,* T: *byang chub kyi sems*) is the unwavering aspiration to attain Buddhahood in order to liberate all beings; and correct view (S: *saṃyagdṛṣṭiḥ,* T: *yang dag pa'i lta ba*) is the wisdom that realizes all entities are void of any real essence. These three knowledges form the subject matter of a short but highly revered poem that Je Tsongkapa originally sent as a letter to his disciple Tsako Wönpo Ngawang Drakpa (T: *Tsha kho dbon po Ngag dbang grags pa,* fl. late fourteenth to early fifteenth century). Though identified as "An instruction for Tsako Wönpo Ngawang Drakpa" in the author's *Miscellaneous Writings (bKa' 'bum thor bu,* pp. 584–586), this composition is widely known by the name *Three Principal Elements of the Path.*

41 T: *chos kyi che ba bzhi.* This description was in all likelihood formulated during the time of the early Kadampas, if not before then; however, I am not aware of any specific work written before the *Great Treatise* in which it appears.

42 S: *hīnayānam,* T: *theg pa dman pa.* This tradition includes both the Listeners' Vehicle (S: *śrāvakayānam,* T: *nyan thos kyi theg pa*) and the Solitary Realizers' Vehicle (S: *pratyekabuddhayānam,* T: *rang rgyal gyi theg pa*). From the perspective of the Mahāyāna they are considered lesser because their aim is to pursue only the limited and incomplete goal of one's own liberation from samsara, rather than the ultimate goal of Buddhahood in order to save all sentient beings, including oneself.

43 This is the expression that will be used in this work for *bodhicittaḥ* (T: *byang chub kyi sems*)—the aspiration and motivation that inspires a Bodhisattva to pursue the ultimate goal of Buddhahood.

44 A traditional ritual for taking the Tantric vows includes the line: "I shall uphold the [entire] Holy Dharma—/ The outer, the secret, and that of the three vehicles" (S: *saddharmaṃ pratigṛhṇāmi bāhyaṃ guhyaṃ triyānikam*; T: *phyi dang gsang ba theg pa gsum / dam chos so sor gzung bar bgyi*). "Outer" Dharma refers to the Kriya and Cārya forms of Tantra; "secret" Dharma is that of Yoga and Anuttarayoga Tantra, and "that of the three vehicles" means the Sūtrayāna teachings of the Listener, Solitary Realizer, and Mahāyāna traditions.

45 T: Byang chub rin chen, 1005–1077. A close personal disciple of Lord Atiśa. "Neljorpa" (T: *rnal 'byor pa*) is an epithet which means "Yogi."

46 Quoted in *LC,* f. 12a. T: *gdams ngag la nang byan tshud pa ni / be'u bum lag mthil tsam la nges pa rnyed pa la mi zer gyi / gsung rab thams cad la gdams ngag tu go ba la zer.*

47 These are the two main forms of meditation that Je Tsongkapa describes in his

Lamrim texts. The essential nature of analytic meditation (T: *dpyad sgom*) is to repeatedly analyze an object using discriminative wisdom (T: *so sor rtog pa'i shes rab*). In stabilizing meditation (T: *'jog sgom*), the goal is to focus the mind on an object steadily and one-pointedly. The nature of these two types of meditation is discussed at various places throughout the *Great Treatise*. In one section, entitled "A brief discussion of how to practice meditation" (ff. 37a–52a), Je Tsongkapa asserts the following:

> Analytic meditation is needed during the practice of such topics as reverence toward your spiritual teacher; the value of leisure and fortune and the difficulty of attaining them; impermanence as represented by death; karma and its results; the faults of samsara; and enlightenment mind. This is because, when these topics are being practiced, it is necessary to generate positive mental states that are both strong and long-lasting. Otherwise, you will not be able to put an end to their opposites, such as [the negative attitude of] disrespect [for your spiritual teacher]. Furthermore, the ability to generate these [positive mental states] depends entirely on the form of meditation in which the object [being contemplated] is repeatedly analyzed using discriminative wisdom.... On other occasions, such as when you are attempting to achieve quiescence (S: *śamathaḥ*, T: *zhi gnas*), the aim is to overcome the mind's inability to remain fixed on a single object. This is accomplished by generating a state of fitness (S: *karmaṇyam*, T: *las su rung ba*) in which [the mind] can be fixed on an object one-pointedly at will. Since the activity of repeated analysis would not allow a steadiness of mind to develop, at these times stabilizing meditation must be carried out.

48 *Liberation in Our Hands*, Part One, pp. 75–76.

49 T: Po to ba Rin chen gsal, 1027–1105.

50 This is meant as a reference to all the professional crafts and trades that are typically learned with some form of personal tutelage or apprenticeship.

51 *LC*, ff. 22b–23a.

52 T: *bsTan rim chen mo*. The complete title is *bDe bar gshegs pa'i bstan pa rin po che la 'jug pa'i lam gyi rim pa rnam par bshad pa*. Drolungpa (T: Gro lung pa Blo gros 'byung gnas, born eleventh century) is recognized as having been a principal disciple of the important Tibetan translator Loden Sherab (T: Blo ldan shes rab, 1059–1109).

53 T: *skyes bu 'bring*. This phrase probably refers to the topic of the Four Noble Truths in general or the Noble Truth of Suffering as illustrating the unsatisfactoriness of samsara (T: *'khor ba'i nyes dmigs*). This method is attributed to a lineage of teachers descending from Nagtso Lotsawa Tsultrim Gyelwa (T: Nag tsho lo tsā wa Tshul khrims rgyal ba, b. 1011), who was instrumental in successfully inviting Atiśa to Tibet and, in addition to being his disciple, also served as his interpreter/translator.

54 T: *rigs*. A-me Jangchub Rinchen (T: A mes Byang chub rin chen, 1015–1077), a direct disciple of Atiśa, introduced the Lamrim teachings using this topic. It was also used by Gampopa Sönam Rinchen (T: sGam po pa bSod nams rin chen, 1079–1153) in his *Ornament of Liberation* (T: *Dam chos yid bzhin nor bu thar pa rin po che'i rgyan*). This important Kagyü teacher studied the Lamrim teachings with Gya Yöndak (T: rGya yon bdag), a disciple of A-me Jangchub Rinchen, as well as other Kadampa teachers.

55 T: *'khor ba 'jug ldog gi tshul*. This was the approach of Gönbawa Wangchuk Gyeltsen (T: dGon pa ba dBang phyug rgyal mtshan, 1016–1082) and his disciple Neusurba

Yeshe Bar (T: sNe'u zur pa Ye shes 'bar, 1042–1118). Sthiramati's *Commentary* also discusses this topic as a way of arguing for the existence of the "storehouse consciousness" (see Part Two, pp. 338–342).

56 S: *buddhānusmṛtiḥ*, T: *sangs rgyas rjes su dran pa*. This method is identified with Potowa Rinchen Sel, and is illustrated in the *Blue Manual* (T: *Be'u bum sngon po*), an important composition of one of Potowa's disciples that records his oral instruction.

57 T: *dal 'byor rnyed dka' ba*. This method was taught by the Kadampa teacher Sharwapa Yonten Drak (T: Shar ba pa Yon tan grags, aka Sha ra ba; 1070–1141), an important lineage holder of the Mahāyāna Lojong instructions.

58 T: *rten 'brel yan lag bcu gnyis*. This method is identified with Puchungwa Shönu Gyeltsen (T: Phu chung ba gzhon nu rgyal mtshan, 1031–1107), known as one of the three Kadampa Spiritual Brothers (T: *sku mched gsum*; the other two were Potowa Rinchen Sel and Chen-nga Tsultrim Bar). Je Tsongkapa makes explicit reference to this approach in his *Great Treatise* in his presentation of the teaching on dependent origination.

59 *Udānavarga*, ch. 4, v. 22. S: *subahvapīha sahitaṃ bhāṣamāṇo na tatkaro bhavati naraḥ pramattaḥ / gopaiva gāḥ saṃgaṇayaṃ pareṣāṃ na bhāgavāṃ cchrāmaṇyārthasya bhavati*. T: *gal te rigs bcas mang du smras kyang ni / bag med mi dag de ltar byed mi 'gyur / dper na phyugs rdzis gzhan gyi phyugs bgrang ltar / de dag dge sbyong skal ba thob ma yin*.

60 T: *thos pa med pa'i sgom chen ni / lag rdum brag la 'dzegs pa 'dra*.

61 S: *śrutiḥ*, T: *thos pa*. This term supports the notion that true spiritual learning is best gained, at least initially, through direct contact with a knowledgeable individual who can properly impart the genuine import of a particular teaching. However, the term encompasses more than hearing an instruction directly from a teacher; it also includes developing fuller understanding of it through further reading and study on one's own.

62 S: *saptāryadhanāni*, T: *'phags pa'i nor bdun*.

63 T: *bShes pa'i spring yig*, v. 32. T: *dad dang tshul khrims thos dang gtong ba dang / dri med ngo tsha shes dang khrel yod dang / shes rab nor bdun lags par thub pas gsungs / nor gzhan phal pa don ma mchis rtogs mdzod*. For a description of the two moral sentiments shame (S: *hrīḥ*, T: *ngo tsha shes pa*) and abashment (S: *apatrāpyam*, T: *khrel yod pa*), see Part Two, pp. 284–285.

64 S: *parikarma*, T: *yongs sbyong*.

65 S: *bāhuśrutyatṛptatā*, T: *mang du thos pas mi ngoms pa*. The *Twenty-five Thousand Line Perfection of Wisdom Sutra* (*PVS*, vol. 1, p. 363) declares: "What is the Bodhisattva Mahāsattva's insatiable desire for extensive learning? A Bodhisattva Mahāsattva's insatiable desire for extensive learning is the insatiable yearning that leads him [or her] to think, 'I shall pursue all the teachings that the Blessed Lords have ever uttered in this world or in any of the other worlds throughout the ten directions.'"

66 *Daśabhūmisūtra*, pp. 19–20.

67 T: *chos dred*. I am not aware of any Sanskrit equivalent to this expression.

68 These lines and the next verse appear in Śāntideva's *Śikṣāsamuccayaḥ*, p. 63. S: *nekṣutvace sāram ihāsti kiṃcin madhye 'sti tatsāra supremaṇīyaḥ / bhuktvā tvacaṃ neha punaḥ sa śakyaṃ labdhuṃ nareṇekṣurasaṃ pradhānam // yathā tvacaṃ tadvad avaihi bhāṣyaṃ yathā rasas tadvad ihārthacintā*. T: *bu ram shing shun snying po ci yang med / dga' bar bya ba'i ro ni nang na 'dug / shun pa zos pas mis ni bu ram ro / zhim por rnyed par nus pa ma yin no / ji ltar shun pa de bzhin smra ba ste / ro lta bu ni 'di la don sems yin*.

69 S: *naṭo yathā tiṣṭhati raṅgamadhye anyān śūrāṇa guṇān prabhāṣate / svayaṃ ca bhotī pratipattihīno bhāṣye ramantasya ime hi doṣāḥ*. T: *gar la lta ba'i khrod na 'dug pa zhig / dpa' bo gzhan gyi yon tan brjod pa bzhin / bdag nyid nan tan nyams par 'gyur ba ste / smra la dga' ba'i nyes pa 'di dag go*.

70 T: *thos grangs mang la sgom grang nyung ba chos dred kyi rgyu yin*. In his *Quick Path*, Panchen Losang Yeshe attributes this saying to the Kadampa lama Shawo Gangpa Pema Jangchub (T: Sha bo sgang pa, 1067–1131).

71 *Liberation in Our Hands,* Part One, p. 97.

72 T: *dpyad sgom*. See note 47, above.

73 S: *śrutamayīprajñā*, T: *thos byung gi shes rab*. This is a reference to the first of three levels of wisdom. The other two are wisdom derived from reflection (S: *cintamayīprajñā*, T: *bsam byung gi shes rab*) and wisdom derived from meditation (S: *bhāvanāmayīprajñā*, T: *sgom byung gi shes rab*). Wisdom derived from listening only represents correct judgment; therefore, it is not knowledge (S: *pramānam*, T: *tshad ma*) in the epistemological sense. The main purpose of analytic meditation is precisely to generate the second type of wisdom, that which is born of reflection, because this does represent knowledge—more specifically, inferential knowledge (S: *anumānam*, T: *rjes su dpag pa*). The ability to practice quiescence (S: *śamathaḥ*, T: *zhi gnas*) and insight (S: *vipaśyanā*, T: *lhag mthong*) jointly with relation to that inferential knowledge leads to the attainment of the third type of wisdom, that which is born of meditation.

74 S: *udvegaḥ*, T: *skyo ba*. That is, aversion for the defects of samsaric existence. This is the main quality that must be cultivated in order to develop renunciation.

75 T: *yid dpyod*. Traditional Tibetan surveys of Buddhist epistemology define seven types of cognitive awareness. Only two of these—inference and direct perception—represent valid knowledge. The other five, including right belief, do not.

76 The "former awareness" is the wisdom which derives from listening; the "latter" is the wisdom which derives from reflection.

77 A complete translation of this text appears in *Liberation in Our Hands*, Part Two, Appendix F, pp. 323–344. The Tibetan text is titled *Byang chub lam gyi rim par myong khrid gnad du bkar te skyong tshul gyi man ngag phal tshig dmar rjen lag len mdzub btsugs kyi tshul du bkod pa*.

78 T: *skyes bu gsum*. *The Great Treatise on the Stages of the Path* identifies Asaṅga's *Collection of Determinations* (T: *rNam par gtan la dbab pa bsdu ba*, vol. 52, ff. 161b–165a) as the principal source for this formulation of three types of person. *The Anthology of Precious Kadampa Writings* (T: *Legs par bshad pa bka' gdams rin po che'i gsung gi bces btus nor bu'i bang mdzod*, pp. 12–24) quotes Asaṅga's material extensively and provides some analysis in the form of interlinear notes.

79 *Bodhipathapradīpaḥ*, vv. 2–5: T: *chung ngu 'bring dang mchog gyur pas / skyes bu gsum du shes par bya / de dag mtshan nyid rab gsal ba'i / so so'i dbye ba bri bar bya // gang zhig thabs ni gang dag gis / 'khor ba'i bde ba tsam dag la / rang nyid don du gnyer byed pa / de ni skyes bu tha mar shes // srid pa'i bde la rgyab phyogs shing / sdig pa'i las las ldog bdag nyid / gang zhig rang zhi tsam don gnyer / skyes bu de ni 'bring zhes bya // rang rgyud gtogs pa'i sdug bsngal gyis / gang zhig gzhan gi sdug bsngal kun / yang dag zad par kun nas 'dod / skyes bu de ni mchog yin no*. Vasubandhu presents a similar description in the following verses from his *AKB* (p. 182): "A lesser person, by various means, seeks happiness for himself. / A middling person seeks only an end to suffering and not to gain happiness, for that is the source of suffering. // The highest person seeks the happiness of others through his own suffering / In addition to a total end to suffering,

because the suffering of others is a cause of suffering for him." S: *hīnaḥ prārthayate svasantatigataṃ yais tair upāyaiḥ sukham / madhyo duḥkhanivṛttim eva na sukhaṃ duḥkhāspadaṃ tad yataḥ // śreṣṭhaḥ prārthayate svasantatigatair duḥkhaiḥ pareṣāṃ sukham / duḥkhātyantanivṛttim eva ca yatas tadduḥkhaduḥkhyeva saḥ.* T: *dman pa de dang de'i thabs kyis rang gi rgyud du gtogs pa'i bde ba don du gnyer / 'bring po sdug bsngal ldog pa kho na'o bde min gang phyir de ni sdug bsngal gnas yin phyir // dam pa rang gi rgyud la yod pa'i sdug bsngal rnams kyis gzhan dag la ni bde ba dang / sdug bsngal dag gtan ldog kho na don gnyer gang phyir de yi sdug bsngal gyis de sdug bsngal phyir.*

80 S: *Tattvasaṃgrāhapañjikā*, vol. 1, p. 12; T: Tg., vol. 191 (*ze*), f. 140a–140b.

81 S: *abhyudayaḥ*, T: *mngon par mtho ba.*

82 S: *sugatiḥ*, T: *bde 'gro.*

83 S: *apāyaḥ*, T: *ngan song.*

84 S: *durgatiḥ*, T: *ngan 'gro.*

85 S: *niḥśreyasam*, T: *nges par legs pa.* The original Sanskrit more literally means "that which has no better." The Tibetan translation for this term does not clearly convey this sense. The prefix (S: *niḥ*, T: *nges par*) can have either the negative sense of "without," "free from," etc., or a strengthening sense as in "thoroughly," "very," "entirely." The Tibetan is generally understood in the latter sense; hence this term is generally rendered as something like "definite goodness." However, the Sanskrit stem *śreyasa* is derived from a comparative form that means "better" or "more auspicious." In Tibetan, there is often no distinct form of an adjective that explicitly conveys the comparative; it is understood by the context.

86 S: *jñeyāvaraṇam*, T: *shes bya'i sgrib pa.*

87 S: *jagaddhitam*, T: *'gro ba la phan pa.*

88 S: *viparyāsaḥ*, T: *phyin ci log pa.* See Part Two, note 340, for a description of seven types of error.

89 S: *ekāntaviparyastam*, T: *gcig tu phyin ci log pa.*

90 S: *saṃtīraṇam*, T: *nges par rtog pa.*

91 S: *samāropaṇam*, T: *sgro btags pa.*

92 See Vasubandhu's *Summary* (Part Two, p. 235), and Sthiramati's *Commentary* (Part Two, pp. 296–302) for a description of the five views.

93 S: *dṛṣṭiparāmarśaḥ*, T: *lta ba mchog tu 'dzin pa.* This view is described as holding that other views—particularly the perishable collection view, the view that grasps an extreme, and wrong view—as well as their basis—that is, the five grasping heaps—are excellent. When this view mistakenly regards one's impure grasping heaps as excellent in the sense of being pure it represents the error that regards what is impure as pure. When it mistakenly regards one's impure grasping heaps as excellent in the sense of constituting a state of genuine happiness, it represents the error that regards what is unsatisfactory as a state of well-being. See Part Two, pp. 301–302.

94 The view that grasps an extreme (S: *antagrāhadṛṣṭiḥ*, T: *mthar 'dzin par lta ba*) is derivative in that it arises on the strength of the perishable collection view (S: *satkāyadṛṣṭiḥ*, T: *'jig tshogs la lta ba*). The latter view occurs when an individual mistakenly believes that his or her personal being is made up of a substantially real self. The view that grasps an extreme has two forms. One extreme is the belief that the real subjective self is permanent both in the sense that it does not change and in the sense that it survives death. The other is the belief that the real self undergoes extinction upon death. The first form of this view is the one that represents the error that regards what is impermanent—namely, the five heaps—as permanent. See Part Two, p. 301.

95 Vasubandhu's *Summary of the Five Heaps* describes the perishable collection view as "the afflicted wisdom that regards the five grasping heaps as 'I' and 'mine.'" Of its two aspects, the first is the belief that one's own subjective self is a real object. This mistaken belief incorrectly identifies such a self as the entity that is referred to by one's personal name and the pronoun "I." This form of the perishable collection view is the one that corresponds to the error that regards what is not a real self as constituting a real self. The second aspect of this view is the mistaken belief that perceives any part of one's mind or body, as well as various objects that are separate from one's personal being, as either governed by or belonging to the false self. Their relation to such an ill-conceived self is referred to by the possessive pronoun "mine."

96 *MA*, ch. 6, v. 120. S: *satkāyadṛṣṭiprabhavān aśeṣān kleśāṃś ca doṣāṃś ca dhiyā vipaśyan / ātmānam asyā viṣayaṃ ca buddhvā yogī karotyātmaniṣedham eva.* T: *nyon mongs skyon rnams ma lus 'jig tshogs la / lta las byung bar blo yis mthong gyur zhing / bdag ni 'di yi yul du rtogs byas nas / rnal 'byor pa yis bdag ni 'gog par byed.*

97 *PV*, ch. 2, v. 221: S: *ātmani sati parasaṃjñā svaparavibhāgāt parigrahadveṣau / anayoḥ sampratibaddhāḥ sarva doṣāḥ prajāyante.* T: *bdag yod na ni gzhan du shes / bdag gzhan cha las 'dzin dang sdang / 'di dag dang ni yongs 'brel bas / nyes pa thams cad 'byung bar 'gyur.*

98 S: *aviparītapudgalanairātmyāvabhodaḥ*, T: *gang zag la bdag med par phyin ci ma log par rtogs pa.*

99 S: *yathāvatkarmaphalasambandhābhisampratyayaḥ*, T: *las dang 'bras bu'i 'brel ba ji lta ba bzhin du yid ches pa.*

100 S: *laukikasaṃyagdṛṣṭiḥ*, T: *'jig rten pa'i yang dag pa'i lta ba.*

101 S: *lokottarasaṃyagdṛṣṭiḥ*, T: *'jig rten las 'das pa'i yang dag pa'i lta ba.* This form of "correct view" or "right view" leads to the attainment of a transcendent path. While it can refer either to knowledge of the insubstantiality of the person or knowledge of the insubstantiality of entities, in the Gelukpa tradition—which follows the Mādhyamika Prasaṅgika School of Buddhist philosophy—it is understood as referring to an understanding of emptiness, since Candrakīrti's position is that both these forms of wisdom represent knowledge of emptiness.

102 T: *bShes pa'i spring yig*, v. 47ab. T: *gal te mtho ris thar pa mngon bzhed na / yang dag lta la goms pa nyid du mdzod.*

103 T: Red mda' ba gzhon nu blo gros, 1349–1412. This spiritual teacher was not only a mentor of Je Tsongkapa, but also of the latter's two principal disciples, Gyeltsab Je (T: rGyal tshab Dar ma rin chen, 1364–1431) and Kedrup Je (T: mKhas grub dGe legs dpal bzang, 1385–1438).

104 S: *svargaḥ*, T. *mtho ris*. The original Sanskrit literally means "the abode of light" and refers to a divine realm or "heaven." Therefore, it is traditionally understood to mean rebirth as a worldly god. In Tibetan usage, it is generally interpreted as meaning rebirth as either a worldly god or as a human.

105 T: *bshes pa'i springs yig gi 'grel pa don gsal*, ff. 31b–32a.

106 S: *pṛthagjanaḥ*, T: *so so skye bo*. This is a Buddhist term that is meant to describe anyone that has not yet become an Ārya (T: *'phags pa*). An Ārya is someone who has achieved a direct realization of either the insubstantiality of the person or the insubstantiality of entities, and thereby achieved the transcendent path of any of the three vehicles. See also Part Two, note 111, and p. 324.

107 *Liberation in Our Hands*, Part Two, pp. 230–231.

108 S: *aviparītadharmanairātmyāvabhodaḥ*, T: *chos la bdag med par phyin ci ma log par rtogs pa.*

109 In his *Overview of the Perfection of Wisdom* (T: *Phar phyin spyi don*, p. 106), Khedrup Tenba Dargye (T: mKhas grub bstan pa dar rgyas, 1493–1568), the principal author of philosophical manuals used at Sera Monastery's Mey College, defines ultimate enlightenment mind (S: *paramārthabodhicittaḥ*, T: *don dam byang chub kyi sems*) as follows: "The definition of ultimate enlightenment mind is the mind consciousness of a Mahāyāna Ārya that represents a principal form of Mahāyāna knowledge and that realizes ultimate truth in a nondual manner. Additionally, between the two categories of view and activity that make up the class of excellent mental states that are the causes of "nonabiding" nirvana [i.e., Buddhahood], it is a form of view." The same author defines conventional enlightenment mind (S: *saṃvṛtibodhicittaḥ*, T: *kun rdzob byang chub kyi sems*) as follows: "[It is] a mind consciousness that is a principal form of Mahāyāna knowledge and an awareness that is directed toward perfect enlightenment for the sake of others and is accompanied by the aspiration to attain perfect enlightenment. Additionally, it constitutes a class of minds that share the same essential characteristics as the [initial] form [of conventional enlightenment mind] that is recognized as the entrance to the Mahāyāna path. Moreover, between the two categories of view and activity, it is a form of awareness that relates to activities." The phrase "entrance to the Mahāyāna path" here means that when a practitioner develops genuine conventional enlightenment mind for the first time, that marks his or her entry into the Mahāyāna path.

110 S: *haṃsarājā*, T: *ngang pa'i rgyal po*. In Indian culture, the white goose is a symbol of purity and spirituality; the term is also used to refer to a great religious ascetic. According to traditional commentaries, "goose king" here refers to a Bodhisattva who has attained the sixth level. The "multitude of geese" represents the other Bodhisattvas that accompany him on the path to enlightenment.

111 *MA*, ch. 6, v. 226. T: *kun rdzob de nyid gshog yangs dkar po rgyas gyur pa / ngang pa'i rgyal po de ni skye bo'i ngang pa yis / mdun du bdar nas dge ba'i rlung gi shugs stobs kyis / rgyal ba'i yon tan rgya mtsho'i pha rol mchog tu 'gro.*

112 T: *'jig rten phyi mar bde ba'i thabs.*

Chapter Two

113 In the section entitled "Generating a strong conviction about the general structure of the path" (T: *lam spyi'i rnam gzhag la nges pa bskyed pa*).

114 T: *skyes bu chung 'bring dang thun mong ba'i lam yin gyi skyes bu chung 'bring gi lam dngos ma yin.*

115 These two texts are Śāntideva's *Śikṣāsamuccayaḥ* (T: *bSlab pa kun las btus pa*) and *Bodhicaryāvatāraḥ* (T: *Byang chub sems dpa'i spyod pa la 'jug pa*), respectively.

116 *LC*, f. 60b. The "seven-limb prayer" (S: *saptāṅgikā*, T: *yan lag bdun pa*) is a Mahāyāna devotional practice that consists of (1) making prostrations, (2) presenting offerings, (3) confessing one's misdeeds, (4) rejoicing at one's own and others' virtue, (5) requesting the Buddhas to turn the Dharma wheel, (6) beseeching the Buddhas not to enter nirvana, and (7) dedicating one's virtue to enlightenment.

117 *LC*, f. 61a.

118 That is, loving-kindness (S: *maitrī*, T: *byams pa*) and compassion (S: *karuṇā*, T: *snying rje*).

119 *LC*, f. 61a–61b.

120 *LC*, f. 61a.

121 S: *abhimānaḥ*, T: *mngon pa'i nga rgyal*. Vasubandhu describes this form of pride in his

Summary of the Five Heaps as follows: "What is exaggerated pride? [It is t]he swelling up of the mind in which you think toward higher special attainments that you have not achieved, 'I have achieved them.'" See also Sthiramati's comments on this form of pride, Part Two, p. 294.

122 S: *abhisampratyayaḥ*, T: *yid ches pa.*

123 S: *avabodhaḥ*, T: *rtogs pa.*

124 S: *āptānumāṇam*, T: *yid ches rjes dpag.*

125 S: *pramāṇam*, T: *tshad ma.*

126 T: *'chi ba mi rtag pa.*

127 T: *rags pa'i mi rtag pa.*

128 *LC*, f. 67b.

129 *Liberation in Our Hands*, Part Two, p. 105. The quote is from Nāgārjuna's *Letter to a Friend* (T: *bShes pa'i spring yig*), v. 29: T: *'jig rten mkhyen pa rnyed dang ma rnyed dang / bde dang mi bde snyan dang mi snyan dang / bstod smad ces bgyi 'jig rten chos brgyad po / bdag gi yid yul min par mgo snyoms mdzod.*

130 T: dGyer 'Gro ba'i mgon po. *Gyer* is the name of a clan or family lineage. *Drowey Gönbo,* or the abbreviated form *Drogön,* is an epithet which means "Lord of Beings" (S: *jagannāthaḥ*) and is considered a synonym for a Buddha. This title refers here to the Kadampa teacher Sang-gye Wöntön (T: Sangs rgyas dbon ston, 1138–1210). The verse cited here is from an unnamed work quoted in *Anthology of Precious Kadampa Writings* (T: *Legs par bshad pa bka' gdams rin po che'i gsung gi gces btus nor bu'i bang mdzod*), pp. 301–302.

131 T: *tshe 'di'i mkhas btsun sgom chen yang / tshe 'di'i mkhas lo btsun lo 'dod / mtshams bcad ya them yi ge bris / mi dang mi 'phrad sgom chen yang / tshe 'di'i sgom chen bzang lo 'dod.*

132 T: *'chi ba dran pa ma bsgoms pa'i nyes dmigs. LC*, ff. 65b–66b.

133 T: *mi 'chi ba'i phyogs 'dzin pa.* This attitude corresponds to a form of secondary mental affliction that is described in canonical literature as "the thought that avoids death" (S: *amaravitarkaḥ*, T: *mi 'chi ba'i rnam par rtog pa*). Nāgārjuna describes it in *RA* (ch. 5, v. 25): "Likewise, the thought that avoids death is / A state that is not concerned by fear of death" (S: *tathāmaravitarko yan na mṛtyubhayaśaṅkitā*; T: *de bzhin mi 'chi rtog pa gang / 'chi ba'i 'jigs pas mi dogs pa'o*).

134 See below, pp. 133–134.

135 S: *gatiḥ*, T: *'gro ba.* That is, those of the higher and lower states.

136 *LC*, ff. 75b–76a.

137 *Drop of Nourishment for Beings: A Treatise on Ethical Conduct* (T: *Lugs kyi bstan bcos skye bo gso ba'i thigs pa*), in *Thun mong ba lugs kyi bstan bcos* section of Tg., vol. 203 (*ngo*), f. 111a. T: *rab tu tsha zhing grang ba yi / dmyal ba nyi ma gcig bzhin dran.* In Bibliography, see listing under Nāgārjuna.

138 The last phrase in the verse, "love of good," is based on the Tibetan translation; the original Sanskrit states "devotion to Buddha" (alternatively, the Tibetan might be amended to read: *rgyal la dga'*). *BCA*, ch. 6, v. 21: S: *guṇo 'paraś ca duḥkhasya yat saṃvegān madacyutiḥ / saṃsāriṣu ca kāruṇyaṃ pāpād bhītir jine spṛhā*, T: *gzhan yang sdug bsngal yon tan ni / skyo bas dregs pa sel bar byed / 'khor ba pa la snying rje skye sdig la 'dzem zhing dge la dga'.*

139 *Liberation in Our Hands,* Part Two, pp. 142–143.

140 S: *bhavaḥ*, T: *srid pa.* This is the tenth limb of the twelve-part teaching on dependent origination.

141 *Liberation in Our Hands,* Part Two, pp. 337–339.

142 S: *Pramāṇavārttikam,* T: *Tshad ma rnam 'grel.* There is some disagreement over the order of the chapters in Dharmakīrti's work. Following the Tibetan tradition, the chapter entitled *Establishing the [Buddha's] Authority* (S: *pramāṇasiddhiḥ*; T: *tshad ma grub pa*) is referred to as chapter 2.

143 T: mKhas grub dge legs dpal bzang, 1385–1438. He is often referred to simply as Khedrup Je.

144 T: *tshu rol mdzes pa pa.* Another name for this school, Lokāyata (T: *'jig rten rgyang phan pa*), is the one used more commonly by Tibetans, who usually render it in the abbreviated form *rgyang phan pa.*

145 S: *mithyādṛṣṭiḥ,* T: *log par lta ba.* Neither Vasubandhu's *Summary of the Five Heaps* nor Sthiramati's commentary directly mention the denial of past or future lives in relation to wrong view; however, this belief is clearly implicit in the remarks that they do make, since the doctrine of karma is predicated on the theory of rebirth. Moreover, as the note accompanying Sthiramati's remarks points out (Part Two, note 330), the statement that wrong view "denies . . . actions" should be understood to mean in part that "the next world does not exist," which explicitly denies the existence of future lives and therefore, by extension, that of past lives as well.

146 S: *kuśalamūlāni,* T: *dge ba'i rtsa ba rnams.* Three of the eleven virtuous mental factors—avoidance of attachment, avoidance of hatred, and avoidance of ignorace—are each described as a "root of virtue." See Part Two, pp. 285–287.

147 *AS,* p. 7. Sthiramati repeats the first part of this description in his own explanation of wrong view. See Part Two, p. 301.

148 S: *aṣṭāv akṣaṇāḥ,* T: *mi khom pa brgyad.* The following verses from Nāgārjuna's *Letter to a Friend* (vv. 63–64) describe the eight inopportune states: "To be born as a person with wrong views, / An animal, a ghost, or in the hells, / In a land lacking the Conqueror's word, / As a barbarian in some remote land, / An imbecile or a mute, or a long-lived god; / These are the eight inopportune conditions. / Yet by their absence you have found leisure, / So strive now to bring an end to rebirth." (T: *log par lta ba 'dzin dang dud 'gro dang / yi dwags nyid dang dmyal bar skye ba dang / rgyal ba'i bka' med pa dang mtha' 'khob tu / kla klor skye dang glen zhing lkugs pa nyid // tshe ring lha nyid gang yang rung bar ni / skye ba zhes bgyi mi khom skyon brgyad po / de dag dang bral khom pa rnyed nas ni / skye ba bzlog pa'i slad du 'bad par mdzod.*) In his *Sutra Anthology* (T: *mDo kun las btus pa*), Nāgārjuna cites a passage from the Hīnayāna collection of sutras known as the *Numerical Scriptures* (S: *Ekottarāgamaḥ,* T: *gCig las phros pa'i lung*) that describes these eight conditions. The portion that refers to a person who holds a wrong view states: "Moreover, even though the Tathāgata has appeared in the world and taught the dharma, and even though one has been born as a human in a central land and is neither dull-witted nor deaf and dumb, . . . and one is capable of understanding the meaning of good and bad speech, [it is an inopportune condition] when a person holds a false view and perceives things wrongly, such that he [or she] does not believe in generosity, offerings, and fire sacrifices, he [or she] does not believe in results that are the ripening of deeds both good and bad, he [or she] does not believe in this life nor in future lives, nor in [the need to honor] one's father and mother, he [or she] does not believe that in this world there are ascetics and brahmins who have set out properly and are abiding properly, and he [or she] does not believe that there are Arhats who know the world and who perceive and realize both this and future lives with their supernormal wisdom."

149 Cf. *AK*, ch. 5, v. 44 and Nāgārjuna's *bShes pa'i spring yig*, v. 51. The other two obstacles are the perishable collection view and the consideration that morality and asceticism are supreme. These three are known as the "three bonds that are abandoned by the Seeing Path" (S: *darśanaheyāni trisaṃyojanāni*, T: *mthong spang kun sbyor gsum*).

150 T: *sgro 'dogs kun brtags mngon gyur*. The point of this paragraph is to explain why, even though traditional Buddhists may profess belief in the doctrine of rebirth, there is still good reason to bolster one's belief in past and future lives with valid reasoning. This argument is all the more true for contemporary Western Buddhists, given the prevailing consensus against the doctrine.

Mental afflictions are of two types: innate (S: *sahājaḥ*, T: *lhan skyes*) and [conceptually] contrived (S: *parikalpitaḥ*, T: *kun brtags*). Those that are contrived are based on mistaken reasoning. The mental afflictions are further distinguished between forms that are overt (S: *abhimukhībhūtaḥ*, T: *mngon gyur*) and forms that are latent (S: *anuśayaḥ*, T: *bag la nyal*). Overt mental afflictions are those that are actively present in the mind, such as when one has become angry. The latent form of the mental afflictions, also described as their seeds, is when they are inactive or in a dormant state. The seeds of the mental afflictions are abandoned or destroyed when a practitioner achieves a direct realization of ultimate truth or selflessness. As a result of that realization, a Truth of Cessation specific to that mental affliction is attained, which means that it can never arise again in an overt form. Only the seeds of the conceptual mental afflictions are abandoned by the Seeing Path. The seeds of the innate mental afflictions are abandoned on the Meditation Path.

151 See note 106 above for the precise meaning of "ordinary person." Here Khedrup Je is pointing out that even those who profess belief in past and future lives still have the potential to develop this form of wrong view, since they possess the seeds of this mental affliction. Such seeds are not destroyed until one reaches the Seeing Path. Moreover, prior to reaching that point, it isn't enough that the average Buddhist assumes the doctrine of rebirth to be true, since the lack of certainty that defines mere belief deprives the practitioner of any logical basis for countering the proposition that past and future lives do not exist.

152 This argument is based on the doctrine that the Seeing Path abandons only the seeds of the contrived mental afflictions (S: *parikalpitakleśabījam*, T: *nyon mongs kun brtags kyi sa bon*). It would be absurd to suggest that the lack of exposure to philosophical discourse means that the mind of an untutored person must be free of any latent form of the contrived mental afflictions.

153 T: *so so skye bo tha mal pa*. As a result of having developed one-pointed concentration, some individuals who are still "ordinary persons" (i.e., non-Āryas) can attain various kinds of supernatural knowledge (S: *abhijñā*, T: *mngon par shes pa*), including forms that represent direct knowledge of past and future lives. One, called "recollection of former states" (S: *pūrvanivāsānusmṛtijñānam*, T: *sngon gyi gnas rjes su dran pa shes pa*), is the ability to remember one's own and others' circumstances in previous lives. Another, called "knowledge of death and rebirth" (S: *cyutyutpattijñānam*, T: *'chi pho ba dang skyes ba mkhyen pa*), is the ability to know when and where sentient beings will pass away, as well as where they will be reborn. This latter quality is also referred to as the "divine eye" (S: *divyacakṣuḥ*, T: *lha'i spyan*). These attributes set apart such individuals from the more average "ordinary person" who lacks any such exceptional qualities.

154 The phrase "and other [related paths]" (T: *la sogs pa*) principally refers here to practices that are unique to the Mahāyāna path. However, as the next paragraph of Khedrup Je's text points out, the argument applies just as strongly to the instructions that are held in common with lesser persons. For example, the certainty that this life will be followed by others and that one's actions in this life will determine the nature of those rebirths clearly provides a powerful incentive for taking refuge in the Three Jewels and developing a practice that cultivates virtuous karma and avoids nonvirtuous karma. Conversely, the lack of certainty about future lives can deter one from generating a sincere motivation to pursue these fundamental practices.

155 *RG2*, f. 9a–9b.

156 *PV*, ch. 2, vv. 35–120.

157 That is, in this section of the *Pramāṇavārttikam.*

158 S: *manomatiḥ*, T: *yid blo*. This term is equivalent to the Buddhist expression that is usually rendered "mind consciousness" (S: *mano vijñānam*, T: *yid kyi rnam par shes pa*). It is used here to distinguish from those forms of awareness that arise directly from the five senses.

159 *PV*, ch. 2, v. 36. S: *prāṇāpānendriyadhiyāṃ dehād eva na kevalāt / svajātinirapekṣāṇāṃ janma janmaparigrahe*. T: *skye ba yongs su len pa na / 'byung rngub dbang po blo dag ni / rang gi rigs la ltos med can / lus nyid 'ba' zhig las skye min.*

160 S: *upādānahetuḥ*, T: *nye bar len pa'i rgyu*. This term refers to the type of causal relation that exists between a seed and the sprout that arises from it, or between a lump of clay and the pot that is formed out of it. For Buddhists, each of the five heaps makes up a continuum in which the preceding moments of the various categories of physical matter and mind constitute the material cause of the entities that arise in the subsequent moments.

161 S: *Tattvasaṃgrāhapañjikā*, vol. 2, p. 652; T: Tg., vol. 192 (*'e*), f. 191a–191b.

162 *PV*, ch. 2, v. 188: "Since [the body's] instrumentality is accepted, we agree; / However, we reject that it is the material cause" (S: *nimittopagamād iṣṭam upādānaṃ tu vāryate*; T: *rgyu mtshan khas blangs phyir na 'dod / nyer len nyid ni bsal ba yin*).

163 *PV*, ch. 2, v. 63. S: *cetaḥśarirayor evaṃ taddhetoḥ kāryajanmanaḥ / sahakārāt sahasthānam agnitāmradravatvavat*. T: *sems dang lus kyang de bzhin no / de rgyu lhan cig byed pa las / skye ba'i 'bras bu lhan cig gnas / me dang zangs ma'i zhu ba bzhin.*

164 S: *sahakārihetuḥ*, T: *lhan cig byed pa'i rgyu*. For example, a seed is the material cause of a sprout; sunlight, moisture, fertilizer, etc., are its efficient causes.

165 *PV*, ch. 2, v. 52. S: *astūpakāroko vāpi kadācic cittasaṃtateḥ / vahnyādivad ghaṭādīnāṃ vinivṛttir na tāvatā*. T: *'ga' zhig tshe na sems rgyun la / phan 'dogs byed pa'ang yin sla ste / bum sogs la ni me sogs bzhin / de tsam gyis ni ldog pa min.*

166 S: *dehātmikā dehakāryā dehasya ca guṇo matiḥ / matatrayam ihāśritya nāstyabhyāsasya sambhavaḥ*. T: *blo ni lus kyi bdag nyid dang / lus 'bras lus kyi yon tan yin / 'dir ni lugs gsum la brten te / goms pa srid pa yod ma yin* (S: *PVA*, p. 53; T: Tg., vol. 178 [*te*], f. 46b). "Repeated practice" is a reference to the cultivation of compassion and other spiritual qualities that a Bodhisattva must carry out over countless lifetimes in order to attain supreme enlightenment. By denying the doctrine of rebirth, the materialists reject the possibility of perfecting these qualities.

167 S: *sahādharādheyabhāvaḥ*, T: *dus mnyam pa'i rten dang brten pa'i dngos po.*

168 *PV*, ch. 2, vv. 74, 75. S: *buddhivyāpārabhedena nirhrāsātiśayāv api / prajñāder bhavato dehanirhrāsātiśayau vinā // idaṃ dīpaprabhādīnām āśritānāṃ na vidyate / syāt tato 'pi viśeṣo 'sya na citte 'nupakāriṇi*. T: *lus kyi phul byung 'grib med par / blo yi byed*

pa'i khyad par gyis / shes rab la sogs phul byung dang / 'grib pa dag tu 'gyur ba yin // 'di ni mar me 'od la sogs / brten pa rnams la yod ma yin / de las kyang 'di khyad 'gyur te / sems la phan 'dogs med par min. The second half of the second verse can be interpreted as follows: Even if it is acknowledged that there are situations in which such qualities as wisdom and the like are improved due to the influence the body, it is an indirect influence; that influence does not occur except through the direct agency of the mind.

169 S: *ayoniśo manaskāraḥ*, T: *tshul bzhin ma yin pa'i yid la byed pa*. Attention is the mental factor that "bends the mind" in the sense of determining what type of object is held in one's conscious awareness (see Part Two, p. 276). When the seeds of the mental afflictions are sufficiently strong, they will activate the kind of attention that is called "improper" in that it leads to overtly nonvirtuous states of mind, such as desire. Conversely, meditation and other forms of spiritual training rely on cultivating "proper" attention.

170 S: *aśubhabhāvanā*, T: *mi sdug pa sgom pa*. This practice is meant to overcome desire. See pp. 157–160, where five types of desire and six forms of unattractiveness are described.

171 See *BCA*, ch. 6, v. 21, cited above, p. 47.

172 *PV*, ch. 2, v. 76. S: *rāgādivṛddhiḥ puṣṭyādeḥ kadācit sukhaduḥkhajā / tayoś ca dhātusāmyāder antararthasya sannidheḥ*. T: *'ga' tshe chags sogs rgyas sogs kyi / 'phel ba bde sdug las skyes yin / de yang khams snyoms la sogs pa / nang gi don ni nye ba las.*

173 *PV*, ch. 2, v. 77. S: *etena samnıpatadeḥ smṛtibhraṃśādayo gaiāḥ / vikāruyati dhīr eva hyantararthaviśeṣajā*. T: *'dis ni 'dus pa la sogs pas / dran pa nyams sogs bshad pa yin / nang don khyad par las skyes pa'i / blos ni 'gyur bar byed phyir ro.*

174 S: *mohaḥ*, T: *rmongs pa*. Though the Sanskrit original often is a synonym for ignorance or confusion, in the present context it refers specifically to fainting.

175 *PV*, ch. 2, vv. 78, 79. S: *śārdūlaśoṇitādīnāṃ santānātiśaye kvacit / mohādayaḥ sambhavanti śravaṇekṣaṇato yathā // tasmāt yasyaiva saṃskāraṃ niyamenānuvartate / tan nāntarīyakaṃ cittam ataś cittasamāśritam*. T: *dper rgyud khyad par 'ga' zhig la / stag nyid dang ni khrag la sogs / thos pa dang ni mthong ba las / rmongs pa la sogs 'byung bar 'gyur // de phyir nges par gang nyid kyi / 'du byed kyis ni rjes 'jug pa'i / sems ni de med mi 'byung ba / de phyir sems la brten pa yin.*

176 S: *viśiṣto nirvarttakahetuḥ*, T: *ldog byed kyi rgyu khyad par can.*

177 S: *avyabhicāreṇa*, T: *mi 'khrul bas.*

178 S: *asmin satīdam bhavati*, T: *'di yod na 'di byung.*

179 S: *asyotpādād idam utpadyate*, T: *'di skyes pas 'di skyes.*

180 *PV*, ch. 2, v. 50. S: *sattopakāriṇī yasya nityaṃ tadanubandhataḥ / sa hetuḥ saptamī tasmād utpādād iti cocyate*. T: *rtag tu de yi rjes 'jug phyir / gang zhig yod pas phan 'dogs byed / de rgyu de phyir bdun pa dang / skyes phyir zhes ni bshad pa yin.*

181 S: *upādeyam*, T: *nye bar blang bya*. This is the future participle of the same root that forms the noun that is being translated as "material cause." In the present context one interpretation is that it refers to the succeeding mind as the result of its material cause—that is, the moment of consciousness that precedes it. The same noun that is translated as "material cause" (S: *upādānam*, T: *nye bar len pa*) also has the special Buddhist meaning of "grasping," as in the phrase "grasping heaps" (see note 13, above). In this latter sense, the term *upādeyam* can also refer to the mind of a future life as an object that is "to be grasped" or taken on through the action of desire.

182 S: *yat sarāgaṃ cittaṃ tat svopādeyacittāntarodayasamarthaṃ sarāgatvāt pūrvāvasthā-*

cittavat / sarāgaṃ ca maraṇacittam iti svabhāvahetuḥ (*Tattvasaṃgrāhapañjikā*, vol. 2, p. 652). T: *gang 'dod chags dang bcas pa'i sems yin pa de ni rang gi nye bar blang bar bya ba'i sems gzhan bskyed par nus pa yin te / chags pa dang bcas pa'i phyir sngar gyi gnas skabs kyi sems bzhin no / 'chi ba'i sems kyang 'dod chags dang bcas pa yin no zhes bya ba ni rang bzhin gyi gtan tshigs so* (Tg., vol. 192 ['*e*], f. 191b).

183 T: *'jig rten phyi mar bde ba'i thabs bsten pa.*

184 T: *rNam par gtan la dbab bsdu ba*, in *Sems tsam* section of Tg., vol. 130 (*zhi*), ff. 185a–186a.

185 T: *nang pa sang rgyas par chud pa.* In Indian and Tibetan literature, the Buddhist religion is referred to as the "inner faith" (T: *nang pa'i chos*); all other religious traditions are designated as "outer systems" (T: *phyi rol pa'i lugs*). The *Great Treatise* presents two groups of eight benefits. The first eight are taken from Asaṅga's *Collection of Determinations:* (1) you will gain extensive merit; (2) you will gain joy and great delight; (3) you will gain one-pointed concentration; (4) you will gain purity; (5) you will acquire great protection; (6) you will gain a reduction, a cessation, and a termination of all obstructions that derive from erring convictions; (7) you will be counted among those excellent spiritual beings who have entered a righteous way of life; and (8) the Master [Buddha Śākyamuni], those who follow a pure spiritual life, and the gods who have faith in the [Buddhist] Teaching will look upon you favorably and be pleased with you. The second eight are taken from personal instruction: (1) you will enter the inner faith of Buddhism, (2) you will become a vessel that is fit to receive all the [different forms of] vows, (3) the karmic obstructions that you accumulated in the past will become reduced and [ultimately] terminated, (4) you will accumulate extensive merit, (5) you will not fall into the lower states, (6) you will not be vulnerable to harm by humans or spirits, (7) you will achieve all your aims, and (8) you will quickly attain Buddhahood.

186 Similarly, one must hold that the Dharma Jewel is the actual or true refuge (T: *skyabs dngos*) and the Sangha Jewel is the community of fellow practitioners who assist one in pursuing the true refuge (T: *skyabs sgrub pa'i zla grogs*).

187 *LC*, f. 101a.

188 Depending on the practitioner's spiritual level, the fear that properly motivates one to take refuge can be of three kinds. For a practitioner of lesser capacity, it is the fear of having to experience the suffering of the lower states in one's future lives. For a middling practitioner, it is the fear of having to undergo any kind of samsaric suffering, whether in the lower or the higher states. And in the case of a Mahāyāna practitioner, it is the fear that all beings will have to continue experiencing samsara's suffering endlessly.

189 *LC*, f. 87a–87b.

190 S: *cetāsaḥ prasādaḥ*, T: *sems dang ba.* I translate the term *prasādaḥ* as "clarity" in order to be consistent with the description of the five sense faculties that also uses this term. In his commentary, Sthiramati states that Vasubandhu describes the five sense faculties as "clear form" (S: *rūpaprasādaḥ*, T: *gzugs dang ba*) in part to distinguish them from the type of faith that has the nature of clarity (see Part Two, p. 253). In the absence of this restriction, when the term is used exclusively in relation to faith, it might be rendered as "purity of mind," "revential mind," or even "serenity of mind."

191 Part Two, pp. 283–284.

192 *AKB*, p. 353 (in explanation of ch. 6, v. 29 of the root text): "The person of dull faculties who abides in those [moments of the Seeing Path] is called 'One who proceeds on

the basis of faith' (S: *śraddhānusārī*, T: *dad pas rjes su 'brang ba*). The person of sharp faculties is called 'One who proceeds on the basis of the Dharma' (S: *dharmānusārī*, T: *chos kyi rjes su 'brang ba*)."

193 *Mahāyānottaratantraśāstram*, ch. 1, vv. 4–22.

194 This is the opening verse to Dignāga's *Compendium of Knowledge* (S: *Pramāṇasamuccayaḥ*, T: *Tshad ma kun las btus pa*). S: *pramāṇabhūtāya jagaddhitaiṣiṇe praṇamya śāstre sugatāya tāyine / kutarkasambhrāntajanānukampayā pramāṇsiddhir vidhivad vidhīyate.* T: *tshad mar gyur pa 'gro la phan bzhed pa / ston pa bde gshegs skyob la phyag 'tshal nas / tshad ma sgrub phyir rang gi gzhung kun las / btus te sna tshogs 'thor rnams 'dir gcig bya.* The second half of the Sanskrit and Tibetan versions of this verse are somewhat different; however, it is the first half of the verse that we are concerned with here. The English translation of the complete verse is based on the Tibetan version.

195 S: *pramāṇabhūtaḥ*, T: *tshad mar gyur pa.*

196 S: *āśayasampad*, T: *bsam pa phun tshogs.*

197 S: *prayogasampad*, T: *sbyor ba phun tshogs.*

198 S: *jagaddhitaiṣī*, T: *'gro la phan bzhed pa.*

199 S: *śāstā*, T: *ston pa.*

200 S: *svārthasampad*, T: *rang don phun tshogs.*

201 S: *parārthasampad*, T: *gzhan don phun tshogs.*

202 S: *sugataḥ*, T: *bde bar gshegs pa.* There are a number of traditional interpretations of this epithet, all of which generally indicate that a Buddha has reached or attained a state of ultimate well-being. Dharmakīrti explains it first as describing the state in which a Buddha has attained the ultimate cessation of all obstacles and second as referring to a Buddha's ultimate knowledge.

203 S: *tāyī*, T: *skyob pa.*

204 S: *anulomaḥ*, T: *lugs 'byung.* The phrase usually means in the "natural" or "regular" order. That order is (1) the One who desires to help the world, (2) the Teacher, (3) the One who has gone well, and (4) the Savior.

205 T: *theg pa thun mong gi lam gyi rim pa.* This is a reference to the teachings of the Hīnayāna path. It is called the "common vehicle" in the sense that the Hīnayāna teachings are held in common with the Mahāyāna tradition.

206 *RG2*, ff. 2b–3a.

207 S: *triguṇaprahāṇam*, T: *spangs pa'i yon tan gsum.* This is a reference to the epithet "Sugata," which in this presentation is interpreted as the Buddha's ultimate Truth of Cessation—that is, the condition of having completely and irreversibly abandoned the two types of obscurations. The three qualities of a Buddha's Truth of Cessation are identified below.

208 In the first presentation of the epithets, the epithet "Teacher" is identified as referring to the wisdom that directly realizes the insubstantiality of the person (T: *bdag med mngon sum du rtogs pa'i shes rab*).

209 S: *jñānadharmakāyaḥ*, T: *ye shes chos sku.*

210 T: *zag bcas gnas yongs su gyur te zag med du gyur pa'i ye shes mthar thug* (*Phar phyin spyi don*, ch. 8, f. 9a).

211 *Mahāyānasūtrālaṃkāraḥ*, ch. 9, vv. 68–75. This presentation draws on the *Buddha Stage Sūtra* (T: *Sangs rgyas kyi sa'i mdo*), which describes the wisdom body in terms of four forms of transcendent awareness: (1) mirror wisdom (S: *ādarśanajñānam*, T: *me long lta bu'i ye shes*); (2) sameness wisdom (S: *samatājñānam*, T: *mnyam pa nyid*

kyi ye shes); (3) discerning wisdom (S: *pratyavekṣājñānam*, T: *so sor rtog pa'i ye shes)*; and (4) performative wisdom (S: *kṛtyānusthānajñānam*, T: *bya ba nan tan du sgrub pa'i ye shes*). See also *Liberation in Our Hands*, Part Two, Appendix E, pp. 292–293.

212 Following the *Perfection of Wisdom Sūtras*, this text identifies the wisdom body as comprising twenty-one categories of immaculate wisdom (T: *zag med ye shes kyi sde tshan nyer gcig*). For a description, see *Liberation in Our Hands*, Part Two, Appendix E, pp. 294–306.

213 S: *svabhāvakāyaḥ*, T: *ngo bo nyid sku*. Khedrup Tenba Dargye defines the essence body as "the esential body possessing two aspects of purity" (T: *dag pa gnyis ldan gyi chos nyid kyi sku, Phar phyin spyi don*, f. 7a). These two aspects are an innate purity (T: *rang bzhin rnam dag gi cha*) and an adventitious purity (T: *glo bur rnam dag gi cha*). The former is the emptiness that is the ultimate nature of a Buddha's omniscience and the latter is the condition of having completely abandoned the two types of obscurations. The epithet "Sugata" is being explained in relation to the second aspect.

214 S: *praśastam*, T: *legs pa*.

215 S: *apunarāvṛttiḥ*, T: *slar mi ldog pa*.

216 S: *aśeṣaḥ*, T: *ma lus pa*.

217 S: *saviśeṣaṇo hetuḥ*, T: *khyad par dang bcas pa'i gtan tshigs*. This language appears in Prajñākaragupta's commentary to the *Extensive Treatise* (S: p. 106; T: vol. *te*, f. 98b), supporting the interpretation that the phrase describes a particular type of reason. Both Khedrup Je and Gyeltsab Je use the phrase "special mark" (T: *rtags khyad par can*) in a way that might be interpreted as meaning principally that compassion and other spiritual qualities "possess special marks"; however, the Tibetan word *rtags* is also used as the translation for the Sanskrit *hetuḥ* when the latter term means "logical reason."

218 S: *sthirāśrayaḥ*, T: *rten brtan pa*.

219 S: *svarasavahī*, T: *rang gi ngang gis 'jug pa*.

220 S: *abhyāsaḥ*, T: *goms pa*. This term is synonymous with the noun that is typically translated as "meditation" (S: *bhāvanā*, T: *sgom pa*).

221 T: *gsal shing rig pa'i ngo bo*.

222 *PV*, ch. 2, vv. 125–127. S: *kāṣṭhapāradahemāder agnyāder iva cetasi / abhyāsajāḥ pravartante svarasena kṛpādayaḥ // tasmāt sa teṣām utpannaḥ svabhāvo jāyate guṇaḥ / taduttarottaro yatno viśeṣasya vidhāyakaḥ // yasmāc ca tulyajātīyapūrvabījapravṛddhayaḥ / kṛpādibuddhayas tāsāṃ satyabhyāse kutaḥ stithiḥ*. T: *sems la brtse sogs goms skyes pa / rang gi ngang gis 'jug 'gyur te / me la sogs pas shing dag dang / dngul chu dang ni gser sogs bzhin // de phyir de dag las skyes te / ngo bo nyid skyes yon tan yin / des na rtsol ba phyi ma dang / phyi ma khyad par byed pa yin // gang phyir rigs mthun snga ma yi / sa bon las ni 'phel ba can / brtse ba la sogs blo de dag / goms par gyur na gang la gnas*.

223 S: *vastubalapravṛttānumāṇam*, T: *dngos po stobs zhugs kyi rjes dpag*. This is the name for a syllogistic inference, as distinguished from an inference that is based on the speech of a trustworthy person (S: *aptānumāṇam*, T: *yid ches kyi rjes dpag*). For a description of the latter, see the next section, where a proof that establishes the trustworthiness of Buddha's speech is discussed.

224 S: *pramāṇam*, T: *tshad ma*.

225 T: *yid dpyod*. This is one of five cognitive states that Buddhist epistemological texts identify as failing to meet the necessary conditions of valid knowledge. Always a con-

ceptual form of thought (as opposed to direct perception), unsubstantiated belief adheres to a true object, but does so either (1) without reason, (2) based on an incorrect reason, or, (3) although based on a correct reason, without being able to generate the certainty of a valid inference. One example is a student's unsubstantiated understanding of his or her teacher's instruction. While this is referred to as "wisdom derived from listening" (S: *śrutamayīprajñā*, T: *thos byung gi shes rab*), it constitutes only correct belief, not valid inferential knowledge.

226 S: *gotram*, T: *rigs*. This term describes both an individual's innate capacity for developing spiritual awareness and the particular forms of spiritual awareness that, once developed, become the impetus for progressing toward the Hīnayāna goal of nirvana or the Mahāyāna goal of supreme Buddhahood.

227 That is, in reciting the refuge formula, you will simply be reciting the words "Buddha," "Dharma," and "Sangha"; you will not be carrying out the act of taking refuge correctly. The essence of the act is to entrust yourself to the Three Jewels, after having determined on the basis of valid reasoning that they have the power to save you from such unfortunate consequences as falling into the lower states.

228 *RG2*, ff. 6a–7a.

229 S: *adhigamadharmaḥ*, T: *rtogs pa'i chos*.

230 S: *paramārthadharmaratnam*, T: *don dam pa'i chos dkon mchog*.

231 S: *āgamadharmaḥ*, T: *lung gi chos*.

232 S: *tripiṭakam*, T: *sde snod gsum*. The three collections are (1) general discourses (S: *sūtram*, T: *mdo sde*), (2) the canonical literature that relates to the code of moral discipline (S: *vinayaḥ*, T: *'dul ba*), and (3) the teachings on "higher learning" (S: *abhidharmaḥ*, T: *mngon pa'i chos*). A second formulation classifies the Buddha's word into twelve divisions (S: *dvādaśāṅgapravacanam*, T: *gsung rab yan lag bcu gnyis*; see *AS*, p. 78).

233 S: *avetyaprasādaḥ*, T: *shes nas dad pa*. Canonical sources describe this type of faith as being of four kinds: (1) faith born of insight regarding Buddha, (2) faith born of insight regarding Dharma, (3) faith born of insight regarding the Sangha, and (4) the morality that is dear to Āryas (S: *āryakāntāni śīlāni*, T: *'phags pa dgyes pa'i tshul khrims rnams*).

234 S: *prayogamārgaḥ*, T: *sbyor lam*.

235 S: *samyaktvaniyamāvakrāntaḥ*, T: *yang dag pa'i skyon med pa la zhugs pa*. This expression refers to a practitioner who has attained the Seeing Path. See below, p. 186.

236 *ŚB*, p. 323.

237 S: *indriyāni*, T: *dbang po rnams*.

238 S: *balāni*, T: *stobs rnams*.

239 S: *prasādaḥ*, T: *dang ba*.

240 *AKB*, p. 386.

241 S: *sampratyayaḥ*, T: *yid ches pa*. This is essentially the same term that is used to describe the type of faith translated here as "belief."

242 That is, the morality that is dear to Āryas.

243 I have substituted "purity" for "clarity" here, as it is more appropriate in this context.

244 Morality is a "vehicle" in the sense of being the most fundamental of the three trainings by which one traverses the path.

245 *Rang gi rtogs pa brjod pa mdo tsam du bshad pa*, in vol. 2 of Tsongkapa's *Collected Works*, miscellaneous writings (T: *bKa' 'bum thor bu*), f. 54a.

246 T: *mDo*. This is an abbreviated reference to the title *Aphorisms on Knowledge* (T:

Pramāṇasūtram, T: *Tshad ma mdo*), which is an alternate name for Dignāga's seminal work, known more widely as *A Compendium of Knowledge* (S: *Pramāṇasamuccayaḥ*, T: *Tshad ma kun las btus pa*).

247 This collection is made up of seven works on logic and epistemology composed by Dharmakīrti.

248 According to tradition, Dignāga was on the verge of abandoning concern for others because of mistreatment he had received at the hands of a non-Buddhist opponent. At that moment, Mañjughoṣa appeared and urged him not to do so. The divine Bodhisattva also assured him that he would watch over him and prophesied that his writings would benefit beings in the future.

249 S: *Pramāṇasiddiḥ*, T: *Tshad ma grub pa*. This is the title of the second chapter of Dharmakīrti's *Extensive Treatise on Knowledge*.

250 The last two lines serve as a refrain for each section of the text. Hence, the popular title of this work is *Fulfilled Aims* (T: *mDun legs ma*). The expression "Treasure of Wisdom" is a term of address that Je Tsongkapa uses to refer to Mañjughoṣa, whom he regarded as his personal spiritual teacher.

251 T: *skyabs 'gro'i bslab bya*. This is a series of principles that the practitioner who has taken refuge in the Three Jewels is expected to follow. The sources for the ones that are presented in Je Tsongkapa's work are identified as Asaṅga's *Collection of Determinations* (T: *rNam par gtan la dbab pa bsdu ba*, f. 184a–184b) and the oral instruction of lineage teachers. See *LC*, ff. 94a–103b.

252 S: *Udānavargaḥ*, ch. 12, v. 10. S: *deśito vo mayā mārgas tṛṣṇāśalyanikṛntanaḥ / yuṣmābhir eva karaṇīyaṃ deṣṭāro hi tathāgatāḥ*. T: *sred pa'i zug rngu gcod byed lam / ngas ni khyed cag rnams la bstan / de bzhin gshegs pa ston pa ste / khyed cag rnams kyis bya dgos so*.

253 *LC*, f. 103a–103b.

254 S: *prahāṇam*, T: *spangs pa*.

255 S: *adhigamaḥ*, T: *rtogs pa*.

256 S: *visaṃyogaphalam*, T: *bral ba'i 'bras bu*.

257 S: *ānantaryamārgaḥ*, T: *bar chad med lam*.

258 S: *saṃskṛtam*, T: *'dus byas*.

259 S: *vimuktimārgaḥ*, T: *rnam grol lam*.

260 T: *mi dge bcu spong gi tshul khrims*.

261 S: *saṃvaraśīlam*, T: *sdom pa'i tshul khrims*.

262 *AK*, ch. 4, v. 1ab: S: *karmajaṃ lokavaicitryam*, T: *las las 'jig rten sna tshogs skyes*.

263 T: *bDe bar gshegs pa'i bstan pa rin po che la 'jug pa'i lam gyi rim pa rnam par bshad pa*. It is known popularly as *The Great Treatise on the Stages of the Teaching* (T: *bsTan rim chen mo*). See listing in Bibliography under (Gro lung pa) Blo gros 'byung gnas.

264 *LC*, f. 132b. The four canonical works mentioned by name here are (1) *Saddharmasmṛtyupasthānasūtram* (T: *Dam pa'i chos dran pa nye bar bzhag pa*); (2) *Damamūkasūtram* (T: *mDzangs blun zhes bya ba'i mdo*); (3) *Karmaśatakam* (T: *Las brgya tham pa*); and (4) *Avadānaśatakam* (T: *Gang po la sogs pa'i rtogs pa brjod pa brgya pa*). Of these, only the last is still available in the original Sanskrit, and only the second exists in English translation. See Bibliography for their locations in the Tibetan Kangyur collection.

265 *PV*, ch. 1, vv. 213–217.

266 *Pramāṇasamuccayaḥ*, ch. 2, v. 5. S: *āptavādāvisaṃvādasāmānyād anumānatā*, T: *yid ches tshig ni mi slu ba / spyi las rjes su dpag pa nyid*. The sense of the Sanskrit term *sāmānya* in this statement is not immediately clear. This is evidenced by the fact that

it is translated in Tibetan both as *spyi*, which means "general,"and *mtshungs*, which means "similar." As Dharmakīrti's explanation eventually shows, it should be taken in the sense that every instance of a Buddha's speech can be recognized as being free of contradiction—which is to say, unerring in every respect.

267 S: *avisaṃvādanam*, T: *mi slu ba*. See below, note 280.

268 *PV*, ch. 1, v. 213. S: *nāntarīyakatābhāvāc chabdānāṃ vastubhiḥ saha / nārthasiddhis tatas te hi vaktrabhiprāyasūcakāḥ*. T: *sgra rnams dngos dang lhan cig tu / med na mi 'byung nyid med phyir / de las don grub min de dag / smra bo'i bsam pa ston par byed.*

269 S: *yathārthabhāvin*, T: *don ji lta ba bzhin du 'gyur ba can.*

270 S: *āptavadaḥ*, T: *yid ches tshig*. The original Sanskrit compound can be interpreted in two ways: (1) trustworthy speech, or (2) speech of a trustworthy person. The Tibetan translation here seems to assume the former sense. Yet when the same term occurs later in this passage, it is translated into Tibetan as "the speech of a person who has eliminated all faults" (T: *nyes pa zad pa'i tshig*)—which is to say, the speech of an infallible authority.

271 S: *āgamasyānumānatvam*, T: *lung rjes su dpag pa nyid.*

272 S: *prekṣāvān*, T: *rtog pa dang ldan pa.*

273 Indian literature makes a distinction between two kinds of epistemic object: (1) those that are "visible" (S: *dṛṣṭaḥ*, T: *mthong ba*) and (2) those that are "invisible" (S: *adṛṣṭaḥ*, T: *ma mthong ba*). The former category includes both entities that are directly present to the senses (S: *abhimukhībhūtaḥ*, T: *mngon du gyur pa*) and entities that are not immediately evident (S: *rahogataḥ*, T: *lkog gyur*) but which can be realized on the basis of inference derived from correct reasons. The second type would include such objects as subtle impermanence, the nonexistence of a real self, and emptiness. Tibetans refer to this type of entity as "somewhat hidden" (T: *cung zad lkog gyur*). "Completely invisible" or "extremely hidden" (S: *atirahogataḥ*, T: *shin tu lkog gyur*) entities are those that cannot be known by ordinary persons except through the testimony of an authoritative person, which, for Buddhists, means a fully enlightened Buddha. This would include such things as the nature of karma and its results.

274 S: *varam eva pravṛttaḥ*, T: *'di ltar 'jug pa yin*. The Tibetan by itself is not very clear as to how it should be interpreted; however, the Sanskrit leaves little doubt as to the meaning.

275 *PVṬ*, p. 390. S: *nācāryeṇa bhāvikaṃ pramāṇyaṃ kathayatā anumānatvam āgamasyoktam api tu puruṣapravṛttim apekṣya*, T: *slob dpon gyis dngos su tshad ma nyid du brjod pas lungs rjes su dpag pa nyid du gsungs pa ni ma yin gyi / 'on kyang skyes bu'i 'jug pa la ltos nas bstan pa yin no*. The Tibetan translation is from Śākyabuddhi's commentary, which seems to be identical to Karṇakagomī's text.

276 S: *parīkṣayā pramāṇyam āha*, T: *brtags nas tshad mar gsungs.*

277 *PV*, ch. 1, v. 214. S: *saṃbaddhānuguṇopāyaṃ puruṣārthābhidāyakam / parīkṣādhikṛtaṃ vākyam ato 'nadhikṛtaṃ param*. T: *'brel ba dang ni rjes mthun thabs / skyes bu'i don ni rjod byed ngag / yongs brtags dbang du byas yin gyi / de las gzhan pa'i dbang byas min.*

278 S: *ekārthopasaṃhāropakāraḥ*, T: *don gcig tu sdud pa la phan 'dogs par byed pa.*

279 The complete statement appears twice in Patañjali's *Great Commentary* (S: *Mahābhāṣyam*, 1.1.1.3 and 1.2.45.2) to Paṇini's master work on Sanskrit grammar (S: *Aṣṭādhyāyī*). The first occurrence states the following: "Meaningless [statements are as follows]: 'Ten pomegranates, six cakes, a basin, a goat skin, a lump of flesh (a heap of straw?), following that the young girl's falseness (?), Sphaiyakṛta's dead (recumbent?) father'" (S: *anarthikāni [vākyāni] ca daśa dāḍimāni ṣaṭ apūpāḥ kuṇḍam ajājinam*

palalapiṇḍaḥ adho rukam etat kumāryāḥ sphaiyakṛtasya pitā pratiśīnaḥ iti). The purpose of the example is to show a series of expressions that have no discernible logical connection. The following Tibetan translation of the full statement is reconstructed from various citations found in several works: *se'u bcu khur ba drug snod dang / ri dwags pags pa sha'i* (also *rtsa'i*) *gong bu / de nas brdzun ma'i bu mo 'di / spha ya kṛ ta'i pha shi'o.*

280 S: *avisaṃvādanam*, T: *mi slu ba*. The original Sanskrit is a double negative. *Visaṃvādanam* literally means "that which is in disagreement"; hence, by adding the negative prefix *a*, the term becomes "that which is not in disagreement." Given the epistemological context, I have rendered the term as "not to be in disagreement with reality." To avoid this somewhat awkward phrase, I also translate the term later in this discussion variously as "to be in accord with reality," "to be free of contradiction," and, at times, for the sake of brevity, simply "to be accurate." Manorathanandī's commentary to the *Pramāṇavārttikakārikā* glosses *visaṃvādanam* as "deception" (S: *vañcanam*), which interestingly is the literal meaning of the Tibetan equivalent (T: *slu ba*) for the former term. Dharmakīrti further describes this quality as meaning that valid cognition (S: *pramāṇam*, T: *tshad ma*) correctly apprehends objects that are genuinely efficacious (S: *arthakriyāsthitiḥ*, T: *don byed par gnas pa*).

281 S: *avisaṃvādanam*, T: *mi slu ba*. See previous note.

282 *PV*, ch. 1, v. 215. S: *pratyakṣeṇānumānena dvividhenāpyabādhanam / dṛṣṭādṛṣṭārthayor asyāvisaṃvādas tadarthayoḥ*. T: *mthong dang ma mthong dngos po yi / don de dag la mngon sum dang / rjes su dpag rnam gnyis kyis kyang / gnod med 'di ni mi slu ba'o.*

283 T: *mthong ba mngon gyur.*

284 S: *nimittopalakṣaṇam*, T: *rgyu mtshan nye bar mtshon pa*. The more familiar phrase that is used to describe the essential nature of conception (S: *saṃjñā*, T: *'du shes*) is "the grasping of signs" (S: *nimittodgrahaṇam*, T: *mtshan mar 'dzin pa*); however, the sense of the phrase that Dharmakīrti uses here is unmistakably the same.

285 S: *buddhiḥ*, T: *blo.*

286 S: *vijñānam*, T: *rnam par shes pa.*

287 These are the more familiar terms for the three attributes (S: *guṇaḥ*, T: *yon tan*). Their Sanskrit and Tibetan equivalents are (1) S: *sattvaḥ*, T: *snying stobs*; (2) S: *rajas*, T: *rdul*; and (3) S: *tamas*, T: *mun pa.*

288 The Sanskrit and Tibetan equivalents for these synonyms are, in the same order, (1) S: *sukham*, T: *bde ba*; (2) S: *duḥkham*, T: *sdug bsngal*; and (3) S: *mohaḥ*, T: *gti mug.*

289 S: *dravyam*, T: *rdzas*

290 S: *karma*, T: *las.*

291 S: *sāmanyam*, T: *spyi.*

292 S: *padārthaḥ*, T: *dngos po.*

293 S: *saṃyogaḥ*, T: *ldan pa.*

294 S: *guṇaḥ*, T: *yon tan.*

295 S: *anāgamāpekṣānumānam*, T: *lung la ltos pa med pa'i rjes su dpag pa*. This is a reference to the type of inference that is based upon the objects that ordinary beings can perceive (S: *vastubalapravṛttānumānam*, T: *dngos po rtobs zhugs kyi rjes dpag*).

296 T: *cung zad lkog gyur*. They are still considered to represent "seen objects" because ordinary persons can attain knowledge of them through inference.

297 See Part Two, pp. 281–282.

298 S: *anityam*, T: *mi rtag pa.*

299 S: *duḥkham*, T: *sdug bsngal ba.*

300 S: *śūnyam*, T: *stong pa*. This is not the same "voidness" or "emptiness" that is a central concept of Mahāyāna philosophy.
301 S: *anātmam*, T: *bdag med pa*.
302 S: *vipratipattiḥ*, T: *log par zhugs pa*.
303 S: *hetuḥ*, T: *rgyu*.
304 S: *samudayaḥ*, T: *kun 'byung ba*.
305 S: *prabhavaḥ*, T: *rab skyes*.
306 S: *pratyayaḥ*, T: *rkyen*.
307 S: *nirodham*, T: *'gog pa*.
308 S: *śāntam*, T: *zhi ba*.
309 S: *asaṃjñisamāpattiḥ*, T: *'du shes med pa'i snyoms par 'jug pa*. See Part Two, pp. 314–316.
310 S: *pranītam*, T: *gya nom pa*.
311 S: *niḥsaraṇam*, T: *nges par 'byung ba*.
312 S: *mārgaḥ*, T: *lam*.
313 S: *pratipad*, T: *sgrub pa*.
314 S: *nairyāṇikaḥ*, T: *nges par 'byin pa*.
315 S: *śakyaparicchedāśeṣaviṣayaviśuddhiḥ*, T: *yongs su gcod par nus pa'i yul ma lus pa rnam par dag pa*. While the term *viśuddhiḥ* (T: *rnam par dag pa*) often means "purity," in the present context it should be understood as meaning the absence of any logical defect.
316 T: *dpyad pa gsum gyis dag pa'i lung*.
317 *PV*, ch. 1, v. 216. S: *āptvādāvisaṃvādasāmānyād anumānatā / buddher agatyābhihitā parokṣe 'py asya gocare*. T: *yid ches tshig ni mi slu ba'i / spyi las 'di yul lkog yur na'ang / go skabs med pa'i phyir blo ni / rjes su dpag pa nyid du gsungs*.
318 The compound that appears in the Sanskrit original (S: *adṛṣṭavyabhicārasya*) is somewhat problematic in that it would seem to be describing a mind that is erring or uncertain (S: *vyabhicāraḥ*, T: *'khrul pa can*). However, the Tibetan translation (*ma mthong bar 'khrul pa med pa can*) suggests the opposite: "that which is unerring with regard to the unseen." Several commentaries seem to equate the compound with an authoritative person's speech, which supports the Tibetan translation, and that is how I have interpreted it here.
319 S: *agatiḥ*, T: *go skabs med pa*. The original Sanskrit noun literally means "lack of resource" or "inability to be successful"; here it is in the instrumental case to show that it is because of the "lack of resource" or "ineffectiveness" of an unenlightened person's mind that one needs to rely on scriptural authority in relation to objects that are "extremely hidden."
320 *PV*, ch. 1, v. 217. S: *heyopādeyatattvasya sopāyasya prasiddhitaḥ / pradhānārthāvisaṃvādād anumānaṃ paratra vā*. T: *blang dang dor bya'i de nyid ni / thabs bcas rab tu nges pa yis / gtso bo'i don la mi slu'i phyir / gzhan la rjes su dpag pa yin*.
321 This is a reference to Dharmakīrti's lengthy discussion of the Four Noble Truths in chapter 2 of the *Pramāṇavārttikam* (vv. 146–279).
322 S: *heyam*, T: *dor bya*.
323 S: *upādeyam*, T: *blang bya*.
324 S: *upāyaḥ*, T: *thabs*.
325 S: *sapakṣaḥ*, T: *mthun dpe*.
326 *Collected Works*, vol. 10, ff. 155b–156a. T: *sbyin pas longs spyod khrims kyis bde zhes pa'i lung chos can / rang gi bstan bya'i don la mi slu ste / dpyad pa gsum gyis dag pa'i*

lung yin pa'i phyir / dper na bden gzhi ston pa'i gsung rab bzhin. The statement "From generosity [comes] wealth, from morality [the] happiness [of a favorable rebirth]" is a quote from Nāgārjuna's *Jewel Garland* (S: *dānād bhogaḥ sukhaṃ śīlāt*, ch. 5, v. 38). Nevertheless, its citation here is meant to represent all scriptural statements about extremely hidden objects. Gyeltsab Je's explanation of this argument is identical even though the form in which he states it is slightly different: "Any scriptural statement that the three types of investigation have shown to be free of error is always unerring with regard to its subject matter, as is the speech that teaches the Four Noble Truths. This is also the case with Buddha's assertion that the observance of morality will bring rebirth as a god." T: *dpyad pa gsum gyis dag pa'i lung yin pa de ni rang gi bstan bya la mi slu bas khyab ste / dper na / bden bzhi ston pa'i gsung bzhin / tshul khrims bsrungs pas lhar skye bar ston pa'i sangs rgyas kyi gsung yang* (*Collected Works*, vol. 6, ff. 100b–101a).

327 S: *sarvatyāgaḥ*, T: *thams cad gtong ba*. "Total renunciation" here is a synonym for nirvana.

328 *CŚ*, ch. 12, v. 5. S: *buddhokteṣu parokṣeṣu jāyate yasya saṃśayaḥ / ihaiva pratyayas tena kartavyaḥ śūnyatāṃ prati*. T: *sangs rgyas kyis gsungs lkog gyur la / gang zhig the tshom skyes 'gyur ba / de yis stong pa nyid brten te / 'di kho na nyid yid ches bya*.

329 Again, in this context, "renunciation" means liberation itself, not simply the desire to attain it.

330 *CŚṬ*, p. 494.

331 *Udānavargaḥ*, ch. 4, v. 1. S: *apramādo hy amṛtapadaṃ pramādo mṛtyunaḥ padam / apramattā na mriyante ye pramattāḥ sadā mṛtāḥ*. T: *bag yod bdud rtsi'i* (some Tibetan translations of this verse substitute *'chi med* for *bdud rtsi'i*) *gnas yin te / bag med pa ni 'chi ba'i gnas / bag yod 'chi bar mi 'gyur te / bag med pa ni rtag tu 'chi*. The term *amṛtapadaṃ* (translated here as "deathless abode") in the original Sanskrit of the verse is not easy to translate literally. The usual translation "path to deathlessness," though not literally accurate, is a reasonable interpretation. For example, Prajñāvarma's commentary explains *amṛta* ("deathless") as referring to the Noble Truth of Cessation (i.e., nirvana) and *pada* as referring to the Noble Truth of the Path. However, the root meaning of the term *pada* is "footstep." It has secondary meanings that include "mark," "sign," "position," "rank," and "abode." I translate it here as "abode" in the sense of a "manner of abiding," based on Prajñāvarma's two interpretations of the term. He writes: "*padam* (T: *gnas*) means 'the act of standing' [S: *sthānam*, T: *gzhi*; itself a term with a wide range of meanings, including "position," "place"], because one attains nirvana by standing firmly in mindfulness. Alternatively, *padam* is that by which the deathless state is attained; thus, it signifies the means of attaining nirvana." T: *de'i gnas ni bzhi* [sic; the text should read *gzhi*] *ste gang gi phyir bag yod la gnas pas mya ngan las 'das pa 'thob pa'o // yang na 'dis 'chi ba med pa rtog(s) par byed pas gnas te / mya ngan las 'das pa 'thob par byed pa'i thabs zhes bya ba'i don no*. The Sanskrit of this passage may be tentatively reconstructed as follows: *asya padaṃ hi sthānaṃ yasmāt apramādasthānena nirvāṇaṃ prāpyate / atha vā prapadyate 'nenāmṛtam iti padaṃ nirvāṇaprāpanopāyam ityarthaḥ*.

332 *BCA*, ch. 2, v. 62. S: *iyam eva tu me cintā yuktā ratriṃdivaṃ sadā / aśubhān niyataṃ duḥkhaṃ niḥsareyaṃ tataḥ katham*. T: *mi dge ba las sdug bsngal 'byung / de las ji ltar nges thar zhes / nyin mtshan rtag tu bdag gis ni / 'di nyid 'ba' zhig bsam pa'i rigs*.

333 S: *apramādaḥ*, T: *bag yod*. See Part Two, pp. 288–289.

334 Cf. Part Two, p. 233.

335 S: *pramādapratipakṣaḥ*, T: *bag med pa'i gnyen po*. In the above verse from the *Udānavargaḥ*, this mental factor is translated as "heedlessness."

336 S: *smṛtiḥ*, T: *dran pa*.

337 S: *samprajanyam*, T: *shes bzhin*.

338 *BCA*, ch. 5, v. 23. S: *cittaṃ rakṣitukāmānāṃ mayaiṣa kriyate 'ñjaliḥ /smṛtiṃ ca samprajanyaṃ ca sarvayatnena rakṣata*. T: *sems bsrung 'dod pa rnams la ni / dran pa dang ni shes bzhin dag / thams cad 'bad pas srungs shik ces / bdag ni de ltar thal mo sbyar*.

339 T: *ltung ba 'byung ba'i sgo bzhi*. The other three are (1) not knowing what the vows consist of or how to keep them; (2) having strong mental afflictions; and (3) having little or no regard for the importance of keeping the vows.

340 *MV*, ch. 4, v. 3. "Abandonment of the five faults occurs / Through cultivating the eight factors" (S: *pañcadoṣaprahāṇāṣṭasaṃskārāsevanānvāyā*, T: *nyes pa lnga spong 'du byed brgyad / bsten pa'i rgyu las byung ba'o*).

341 S: *avavādasya sammoṣaḥ*, T; *gdams ngag brjed pa*. While the Tibetan translates literally as "forgetting the instruction," the sense of the original Sanskrit is more that of "the failure to remain aware of the instruction."

342 S: *layam*, T: *bying ba*.

343 S: *auddhatyam*, T: *rgod pa*.

344 S: *styānam*, T: *rmugs pa*.

345 *Madhyamakahṛdayam*, ch. 3, v. 16. S: *nibadhyālambanastambhe smṛtirajjvā manogajam / unmārgacāriṇaṃ kuryāt prajñāṅkuśavasaṃ śanaiḥ*. T: *yid kyi glang po log 'gro ba / dmigs pa'i ka ba brtan po la / dran pa'i thag pas nges bcings nas / shes rab lcags kyus rim dbang bya*.

346 Je Tsongkapa lists the observance of vigilance (S: *saṃprajānadvihāritā*, T: *shes bzhin to spyod pa nyid*) among a group of four requisites that are necessary for one to develop quiescence (S: *śamathaḥ*, T: *zhi gnas*) and insight (S: *vipaśyanā*, T: *lhag mthog*). For a comprehensive treatment of this practice, see Asaṅga's discussion in the *Śrāvakabhūmiḥ* (Sanskrit text: pp. 121–127, a portion at the end is missing; Tibetan text: ff. 44a–52a). An abbreviated account of that presentation also appears in Je Tsongkapa's *Great Treatise*.

347 *BCA*, ch. 5, v. 108. S: *etad eva samāsena samprajanyasya lakṣaṇam / yat kāyacittāvasthāyāḥ pratyavekṣā muhur muhuḥ*. T: *lus dang sems kyi gnas skabs la / yang dang yang du brtag bya ba / 'di nyid kho na mdor na ni / shes bzhin bsrung ba'i mtshan nyid do*.

348 *BCA*, ch. 5 v. 33. S: *samprajanyaṃ tadāyāti na ca yātyāgataṃ punaḥ / smṛtir yadā manodvāre rakṣārtham avatiṣṭhate*. T: *gang tshe dran pa yid sgo nas / bsrung ba'i don du gnas gyur pa / de tshe shes bzhin 'ong gyur zhing / song ba dag kyang 'ong bar 'gyur*.

349 T: *mnar med*. This is the name of the most severe of the eight hot hells. The name literally means "Unrelenting Torment."

350 *BCA*, ch. 4, vv. 30, 31. S: *sarve devā manuṣyāś ca yadi syur mama śatravaḥ / te 'pi nāvīcikaṃ vahniṃ samudānayituṃ kṣamāḥ // meror api yadāsaṅgān na bhasmāpyupalabhyate / kṣaṇāt kṣipanti māṃ tatra balinaḥ kleśaśatravaḥ*. T: *gal te lha dang lha min rnams / thams cad bdag la dgrar langs kyang / de dag gis kyang mnar med pa'i / me nang 'khrid cing 'jug mi nus // nyon mongs stobs chen dgra 'dis ni / gang dang phrad na ri rab kyang / thal ba yang ni mi lus pa / der bdag skad cig gcig la 'dor*. Mount Meru is the mythical mountain that lies at the center of this world and is larger than all other mountains.

351 *MSA*, ch. 17, vv. 25–26. S: *kleśair hantyātmānaṃ sattvān upahanti śīlam upahanti / savilekhalābhahīno rakṣāhīnas tathā śāstrātā // sādhikaraṇo 'yaśasvī paratra saṃjāyate*

'kṣaṇeṣu sa ca / prāptāprāptavihīno manasi mahad duḥkham āpnoti. T: *nyon mongs rnams kyis bdag 'joms sems can 'joms shing tshul khrims 'joms / nyams bcas rnyed pas dman zhing srung dang de bzhin ston pas smad / rtsod bcas mi snyan de ni gzhan du mi khom rnams su skyes / thob dang ma thob nyams pas yid la sdug bsngal chen po 'thob.* Sthiramati's commentary on these verses reveals a wealth of valuable instruction. Another important source for the disadvantages (S: *adīnavaḥ,* T: *nyes dmigs*) of the mental afflictions is the first section of Asaṅga's *Levels of Spiritual Practice* (T: *rNal 'byor spyod pa'i sa*), known as the *Manifold Levels* (T: *Sa mang po pa*), *Sems tsam* section of Tg., vol. 127 (*tshi*), ff. 87b–88a.

352 S: *cittacaittāḥ*, T: *sems sems byung.*

353 T: Tshe mchog gling yongs 'dzin Ye shes rgyal mtshan, 1713–1793.

354 T: *Sems dang sems byung gi tshul gsal bar ston pa blo gsal mgul rgyan.* See listing in Bibliography under Ye shes rgyal mtshan.

355 f. 50a.

356 *LC*, f. 152b.

357 *LC*, f. 154a–154b.

358 S: *ātmagrāhaḥ*, T: *bdag tu 'dzin pa.* Depending on the philosophical school, this term can be understood in a variety of ways. Here, Je Tsongkapa is speaking from the perspective of the Mādhyamika Prasaṅgika School, which means, in particular, the views of the Indian scholar Candrakīrti. In this context, "grasping at a self" can refer both to the belief in a real, personal self (S: *pudgalātmagrahaḥ*, T: *gang zag gi bdag 'dzin*) and to the belief that physical and mental phenomena possess a real, independent essence (S: *dharmātmagrahaḥ*, T: *chos kyi bdag 'dzin*). Nevertheless, all Buddhist schools universally share the tenet that the view of the persishable collection (S: *satkāyadṛṣṭiḥ*, T: *'jig tshogs la lta ba*), which is synonymous with belief in a real personal self, is the root cause of all the mental afflictions and must be eliminated in order to achieve liberation from samsara.

359 T: *dBu ma lta ba'i khrid yig.* In *Collected Works*, vol. 15 (*ba*), ff. 3b–4a.

360 That is, the attitude that a practitioner should develop by means of this portion of the instruction.

361 *LC*, f. 132b.

Chapter Three

362 *BCA*, ch. 9, v. 157. S: *mṛtāḥ patantyapāyeṣu dīrghatīvravyatheṣu ca / āgatyāgatya sugatiṃ bhūktvā bhūktvā sukhocitāḥ.* T: *bde 'gror yang dang yang 'ongs te / bde ba mang po spyad spyad nas / shi nas ngan song sdug bsngal ni / yun ring mi bzad rnams su ltung.*

363 *Śiṣyalekhaḥ*, v. 18. S: *saṃsāracakram aniśaṃ parivartamānam āruhya yaḥ sukham avaiti vivartamānaḥ / so 'vaśyam eva vivaśaḥ śataśaḥ krameṇa sarvāḥ samāś ca visamāś ca gatīḥ prayāti.* T: *gang zhig 'khor ba'i 'khor lo rtag tu 'gyur ba yi / nang du zhugs nas bsti ba tsam la bder sems pa / de ni nges par dbang med rim gyis brgya phrag tu / 'gro ba mnyam dang mi mnyam kun tu 'khyam par 'gyur.*

364 *CŚ*, ch. 7, v. 14. S: *svargo nirayatulyo 'pi viduṣāṃ syād bhayaṃkaraḥ / sarvathā durlabhas bhavo teṣāṃ yo na bhayaṃkaraḥ.* T: *mkhas pa rnams la mtho ris kyang / dmyal ba dang mtshungs 'jigs skyed 'gyur / rnam pa kun tu de rnams la / srid gang 'jigs pa mi skyed dkon.*

365 S: *niḥsaraṇam*, T: *nges par 'byung ba.* This term is also used to describe one of the four aspects of the Truth of Cessation. See above, page 82.

366 S: *kāraṇe kāryopacāraḥ*, T: *rgyu la 'bras bu btags pa*.
367 S: **mokṣaprārthanabuddhiḥ*, T: *thar pa don gnyer gyi blo*. Literally, "the mind that seeks liberation."
368 *LC*, f. 135a–135b. The verse is *CŚ*, ch. 8, v. 12. S: *udvego yasya nāstīha bhaktis tasya kutaḥ śive / nirgamaś ca bhavād asmāt svagṛhād iva duṣkaraḥ*. T: *gang la 'dir skyo yod min pa / de la zhi gus ga la yod / rang khyim la bzhin srid pa ni / 'di nas 'byung ba'ang bya bar dka'*. The phrase "leaving one's home" here is a reference to the act of leaving behind the householder's life and going forth into the homeless state of a religious ascetic. For those who are weak-willed, it is difficult to abandon secular life even though it is empty of spiritual value. In other words, the difficulty of carrying out this act is similar to that of developing the wish to escape from samsara in its entirety.
369 S: *udvegaḥ*, T: *skyo ba*. A Tibetan alternate is *yid 'byung ba*, which is a more specialized term and therefore is less likely to be misinterpreted.
370 S: *saṃsārādīnavabhāvanā*, T: *'khor ba'i nyes dmigs sgom pa*.
371 S: *vineyāḥ*, T: *gdul bya rnams*. This noun is formed from the future participle of a root that means "to tame" or "to train." Some traditional texts indicate that the term applies to everyone, since Buddhas seek to benefit all beings. In a narrower sense, it would seem to refer more specifically to those who are willing followers.
372 *CŚ*, ch. 7, v. 1. T: *sdug bsngal rgya mtsho 'di la mtha' / rnam pa kun tu yod min na / byis khyod 'dir ni bying ba la / 'jigs pa cis na skye mi 'gyur*. The original Sanskrit of this verse is not extant.
373 *LC*, ff. 135b–136a.
374 S: *Yogācārabhūmiḥ*, T: *rNal 'byor spyod pa'i sa*. See Part Two, p. 245.
375 S: *sāsravaḥ*, T: *zag bcas*. See Part Two, note 9. *AK*, ch. 1, v. 8ab: "Those [entities that are] related to the outflows are the grasping heaps" S: *ye sāsravā upādānaskandhās te*, T: *gang dag zag bcas nyer len pa'i / phung po'ang de dag*.
376 S: *anāsravasaṃskṛtadharmāḥ*, T: *zag pa med pa'i 'dus byas kyi chos rnams*. *AK*, ch. 1, v. 5ab: "Those [entities that are] unrelated to the outflows are the Truth of the Path as well as the three types of unconditioned entities" (S: *anāsravā mārgasatyaṃ trividhaṃ cāpyasaṃskṛtam*, T: *zag med lam gyi bden pa dang / 'dus ma byas rnam gsum yang ste*).
377 *AK*, ch. 1, v. 7ab: "Moreover, conditioned entities consist of / The five heaps of form and the rest" (S: *te punaḥ saṃskṛtā dharmā rūpādiskandhapañcakam*, T: *'dus byas chos rnams de dag kyang / gzugs la sogs pa phung po lnga*).
378 Yaśomitra glosses the "attendants" as consisting of mind (i.e., the fifth heap), mental factors (these include the second, third, and fourth heaps—i.e., the five universal mental factors, as well as faith, recollection, concentration, effort, agility, equanimity, etc.), "pure" discipline (S: *anāsravasaṃvaraḥ*, T: *zag pa med pa'i sdom pa*—this entity is included in the first heap of form; see Part Two, p. 263), and various forms of the nominally existent conditioned entities that are not mental factors (these are also included in the fourth heap; see Sthiramati's *Commentary*, Part Two, pp. 312–326).
379 *AKB*, p. 2.
380 S: *pratisaṃkhyānirodhaḥ*, T: *so sor brtags pas 'gog pa*. See Part Two, p. 241 (root text) and pp. 351–352 (commentary).
381 S: *visaṃyogaphalam*, T: *bral ba'i 'bras bu*.
382 That is, its structure is similar to the compound "oxcart," which means a cart that is drawn by an ox.
383 *AKB*, pp. 3–4.

384 Buddhist doctrine divides samsara into three domains: the desire realm, the form realm, and the formless realm. The desire realm is inhabited by the beings of the three lower states—that is, hell beings, hungry spirits, and animals—as well as humans, demigods, and six types of worldly gods. The form and formless realms are inhabited by more ethereal yet still samsaric gods, who attain that form by having cultivated different kinds of one-pointed concentration in a previous existence.

385 S: *darśanamārgaḥ*, T: *mthong lam*. Buddhist doctrine sets forth three separate "vehicles" or path systems: the Listeners' Vehicle, the Solitary Realizers' Vehicle, and the Great Vehicle (i.e., the Mahāyāna). Despite the differences in the practices and results of these systems, each is made up of five paths designated by the same five terms: (1) Accumulation Path (S: *sambhāramārgaḥ*, T: *tshogs lam*), (2) Preparation Path (S: *prayogamārgaḥ*, T: *sbyor lam*), (3) Seeing Path, (4) Meditation Path (S: *bhāvanāmārgaḥ*, T: *bsgom lam*), and (5) Path Beyond Training (S: *aśaikṣamārgaḥ*, T: *mi slob lam*). The last of these actually represents the ultimate goal of each path—nirvāṇa in the case of the two Hīnayāna systems, and Buddhahood in the case of the Mahāyāna. The following description pertains to Listeners' Vehicle.

The Accumulation Path is entered at the moment of developing genuine renunciation. The Preparation Path is achieved when one gains the ability to unite the practices of quiescence and insight while meditating on the insubstantiality of the person. The Seeing Path arises with the direct realization of the insubstantiality of the person. In that moment, the seeds of all the "contrived" (S: *parikalpitam*, T: *kun brtags*) mental afflictions that arise from incorrect reasoning are irreversibly destroyed (see Part Two, p. 303, and note 339). On the subsequent Meditation Path, the direct realization of selflessness is further cultivated to eliminate all the "innate" forms (S: *sahajaḥ*, T: *lhan skyes*) of the mental afflictions. This process culminates in the attainment of liberation.

386 S: *jñeyāvaraṇam*, T: *shes bya'i sgrib pa*.

387 S: *karma*, T: *byed las*. The principal source for the descriptions of these actions is Asaṅga's *Compendium of Higher Learning* (S: *Abhidharmasamuccayaḥ*).

388 S: *chandaḥ*, T: *'dun pa*. See Part Two, pp. 277–278.

389 S: *adhimokṣaḥ*, T: *mos pa*. See Part Two, p. 278.

390 S: *samādhiḥ*, T: *ting nge 'dzin*. See Part Two, pp. 279–280.

391 S: *hrīḥ*, T: *ngo tsha shes pa*. See Part Two, pp. 284–285.

392 S: *rāgaḥ*, T: *'dod chags*. See Part Two, pp. 291–292.

393 S: *antagrāhadṛṣṭiḥ*, T: *mthar 'dzin par lta ba*. See Part Two, p. 301.

394 S: *māyā*, T: *sgyu*. See Part Two, pp. 305–306.

395 S: *śāṭhyam*, T: *g.yo*. See Part Two, p. 306.

396 S: *vikṣepaḥ*, T: *rnam par g.yeng ba*. See Part Two, p. 309.

397 S: *asaṃprajanyam*. T: *shes bzhin ma yin pa*. See Part Two, p. 309.

398 S: *saṃsvedajā yoniḥ*, T: *drod gsher las skyes pa'i skye gnas*. *AKB*, p. 118: "What is the birth state of being born from warmth and moisture? It is those beings that are born due to the warmth and moisture of the elements—for example, worms, bugs, moths and butterflies, flying insects that bite, and the like."

399 S: *upapādukajā yoniḥ*, T: *rdzus te skyes pa'i skye gnas*. *AKB*, pp. 118–119: "What is the birth state of spontaneous birth? It is those beings that are born all at once (i.e., without parents and with no gestation period), with all their faculties intact and possessing all their limbs and appendages . . . for example, gods, hell beings, intermediate state beings, and the like."

400 S: *pratisaṃdhiḥ*, T: *nying mtshams sbyor ba*. Literally "reentry," this is the moment at

which an intermediate state being becomes reborn in one of the six types of samsaric existence.

401 *YB*, p. 23.

402 S: *duḥkhaduḥkhatā*, T: *sdug bsngal gyi sdug bsngal nyid.*

403 S: *vedanā*, T: *tshor ba.* The three kinds are feeling are pleasant experiences, unpleasant experiences, and experiences that are neither pleasant nor unpleasant. See Part Two, pp. 267–271.

404 S: *bālaḥ*, T: *byis pa.* Literally "child," this term is used to describe an "ordinary person" (S: *pṛthagjanaḥ*, T: *so so skye bo*)—that is, one who has not attained the transcendent realization of an Ārya.

405 *ŚB*, pp. 255–256.

406 *VS*, f. 160a–160b. Je Tsongkapa also discusses this explanation in his *Great Treatise.*

407 *AS*, p. 37. S: *saṃbādhaduḥkham*, T: *dogs pa'i sdug bsngal.*

408 Asaṅga defines two basic types of "indisposition" (S: *dauṣṭhulyam*, T: *gnas ngan len*) in his *Collection of Determinations:* (1) that which is identified with the outflows (S: *āsravadauṣṭhulyam*, T: *zag pa'i gnas ngan len*) and (2) that which is related to the outflows (S: *sāsravadauṣṭhulyam*, T: *zag pa dang bcas pa'i gnas ngan len*). The first of these is an unfitness of body and mind that is caused by the dormant state (S: *anuśayaḥ*, T: *bag la nyal*) or seeds of the mental afflictions. It is abandoned when one destroys all the mental afflictions and attains the status of an Arhat. The second is defined as the subtle traces or imprints (S: *vāsanā*, T: *bag chags*) of the mental afflictions, which can only be abandoned by attaining the status of a fully enlightened Buddha. The first type is often defined as the main impediment to our ability to develop the mental factor called "agility" (S: *praśrabdhiḥ*, T: *shin tu sbyangs pa*), which plays a prominent role in the topic of how to develop one-pointed concentration (S: *samādhiḥ*, T: *ting nge 'dzin*) and quiescence (S: *śamathaḥ*, T: *zhi gnas*). Vasubandhu's *Summary of the Five Heaps* describes agility as "the antidote to indisposition," and Sthiramati's *Commentary* (Part Two, p. 288) provides this further clarification: "Indisposition is a condition of the body and mind. [Indisposition] of the body is a state of unfitness (S: *akarmaṇyatā*, T: *las su mi rung ba nyid*) while [indisposition] of the mind is the seeds of afflicted entities (S: *sāṃkleśikadharmāḥ*, T: *kun nas nyon mongs pa'i chos*). Agility is an antidote to indisposition in the sense that it is present when the other has disappeared."

409 S: *asparśavihāraḥ*, T: *bde ba la reg par mi gnas pa.* For a discussion of the expression "remain in a discontented state," see Sthiramati's description of the action of the root mental affliction of hatred, Part Two, p. 292.

410 This is a reference to one of the four "ends" of conditioned entities (T: *'dus byas kyi mtha' bzhi*), namely that everything that is born must ultimately die. Cf. *Udānavargaḥ*, ch. 1, v. 22: "All accumulations are lost in the end; / Everything that rises ends up falling; / All coming together ends in separation; / Every living thing in the end must die" (S: *sarve kṣayāntā nicayāḥ patanāntāḥ samucchrayāḥ / saṃyogā viprayogāntā maraṇāntaṃ hi jīvitam.* T: *bsags pa kun gyi mtha' zad cing / bslang ba'i mtha' ni 'gyel bar 'gyur / phrad pa'i mtha' ni bral ba ste / gson pa'i mtha' ni 'chi ba yin*).

411 S: *saṃskāraduḥkhatā*, T: *'du byed kyi sdug bsngal nyid.*

412 *VS*, f. 161b.

413 T: *mngon par 'grub pa'i sdug bsngal nyid kyi snod.* Among the twelve limbs of dependent origination, Asaṅga (*AS*, p. 26) refers to the eighth, ninth, and tenth limbs (i.e., craving, grasping, and being) as the "producing limbs" (S: *abhinirvartakāṅgam*, T:

mngon par 'grub par byed pa'i yan lag) and the final two (i.e., birth, and old age and death) as the "produced limbs" (S: *abhinirvṛttyaṅgam*, T: *mngon par grub pa'i yan lag*). *ASB* (p. 31) explains: "Craving, grasping, and being are the producing limbs in the sense that (1) "due to the fact that *craving* for such things as the sense objects has not been abandoned, and (2) [because of] the presence of a consciousness that is associated with the *grasping* of attachment and desire that stem from having previously engaged in various forms of both good and bad behavior in relation to the sense objects and other entities, (3) when [a sentient being] reaches the stage that [he or she] is about to die, the imprint (S: *vāsanā*, T: *bag chags*) of some particular karma that conforms to [his or her] attachment and desire takes on a potent [form of] *being* that favors the production of a result." The result that is produced is a new rebirth. With regard to the phrase "produced limbs," the same text states: "*Birth* as well as *old age and death* are the produced limbs in the sense that when a particular karmic imprint has been rendered potent in the manner [just described], [the limbs of] name and form and the rest will be produced within some 'class affiliate' [S: *nikāyasabhāgaḥ*, T: *ris mthun pa*; this is a technical term from Abhidharma literature that in the present context refers to the continuum of a particular being's heaps—see Part Two, notes 418 and 428] that is related to a separate and distinct type of being and birth state, according to the manner in which [the continuum of that being's heaps] is projected [by karma]."

414 *AK*, ch. 6, v. 3. S: *duḥkhās triduḥkhatāyogād yathāyogam aśeṣataḥ / manāpā amanāpāś ca tadanye caiva sāsravāḥ*. T: *yid 'ong yid du mi 'ong dang / de las gzhan zag bcas rnams nyid / sdug bsngal nyid gsum ldan pa'i phyir / ci rigs ma lus sdug bsngal lo.*

415 *AKV* (p. 876) glosses the suffering of change as meaning the transience of pleasant experiences and illustrates this with the verse: "Celestial beings fall to earth / Afflicted by suffering and wailing: / 'Alas, Manifold Chariots!' 'Alas, bathing tanks!' / 'Alas, Gently Flowing!' 'Alas, dear ones!'" Manifold Chariots (S: *caitrarathavanam*, T: *shing rta sna tshogs kyi tshal*) is one of four celestial gardens in the Heaven of the Thirty-three; Gently Flowing (S: *mandākinī*, T: *dal gyis 'bab pa*) is the name of a heavenly river. As the gods of this realm realize they will soon pass away, they cry out the names of those marvelous places as well as the cherished companions they must leave behind.

416 *AKB*, pp. 328–329.

417 T: *khyab pa 'du byed kyi sdug bsngal.*

418 *YB*, p. 99.

419 S: *vidūṣaṇam*, T: *rnam par sun 'byin pa.*

420 S: *sādhiṣṭhānā*, T: *rten dang bcas pa*. In this usage, the phrase is adjectival and modifies "unpleasant feeling"; thus it refers to the other elements of the five grasping heaps that accompany this feeling.

421 This is the same term that was just used in connection with unpleasant feelings. Here it is modifying "mental afflictions," and so should be understood as referring to the other elements of the five grasping heaps that accompany the mental afflictions.

422 *ŚB*, p. 256.

423 *ŚB*, p. 256.

424 S: *paryavasthānaśaḥ*, T: *kun nas dkris pa'i sgo nas*. The term that appears here is an adverbial form of one of the synonyms for the mental afflictions. The noun, which I translate as "perturbation" (S: *paryavasthānam*, T: *kun nas dkris pa*), is meant to indicate forms of the mental afflictions that continually disturb the mind. Asaṅga glosses

the noun several times. In one instance, he writes: "they are perturbations because they overcome the mind by disturbing it repeatedly" (S: *punaḥ punar udvegena cittaṃ paryavanahyantīti paryavasthānāni; AS*, p. 47). Elsewhere he states: "They are perturbations because of their continual occurrence" (S: *abhīkṣṇaṃ samudācāritvāt paryavasthānāni; YB*, p. 167). The Abhidharma literature lists eight secondary mental afflictions as the negative mental factors that are most commonly identified with the "perturbations": torpor, sleep, excitation, regret, jealousy, stinginess, shamelessness, and absence of abashment. However, use of this term is not restricted to these eight mental factors.

425 This line is from the *Prātimokṣa Sūtra* (T: *So sor thar pa'i mdo*), and forms part of the description of the second of thirteen moral offenses of a fully ordained monk that call for disciplinary action, but not permanent expulsion, from the Sangha (S: *saṃghāvaśeṣāḥ*, T: *dge 'dun lhag ma rnams*). The reason for its citation here is the occurrence of the phrase "with a mind that is overcome and altered" (S: *avatīrṇavipariṇatacittena*, T: *nyams zhing gyur ba'i sems kyis*). The word translated here as "altered" is formed from the same verbal root as the word for "change" in the phrase "the suffering of change," and its use here is to imply alteration or change of a person's mind by the mental affliction of desire. Asaṅga takes this as evidence that the manner in which the mental afflictions "alter" the mind represents a form of the suffering of change.

426 *ŚB*, pp. 256–257.

427 S: *abhipretam*, T: *'dod pa*. The Tibetan means simply that pleasant feelings are "desired"; however, the original Sanskrit is somewhat more nuanced and suggests something that the mind is "drawn to," "values highly," or "regards with approval."

428 S: *pramādapadam*, T: *bag med pa'i gnas*. *AKV* (p. 881) glosses this phrase as meaning that pleasant feelings "cause one to fall from virtue."

429 *AKB*, pp. 330–331.

430 *AKV* (p. 880) attributes this position to "Bhadanta Śrīlāta and others." In his French translation of *AKB*, La Vallée Poussin notes (vol. 4, p. 129) that this view is recorded in the *Mahāvibhāṣaśāstra*. While the history of this doctrine is not certain, it appears to have had a variety of proponents from a relatively early period.

431 S: *īryāpathāni*, T: *spyod lam*. They are traditionally described in terms of the four modes of walking, sitting, standing, and lying down. If any of them is engaged in for a prolonged period, it will lead to physical discomfort. As Yaśomitra explains (*AKV*, p. 880), the following statement could be made: "Those very same conditions that are believed to be causes of pleasant feelings—such as lying down, etc.—can become causes of suffering when they are indulged in excessively or at an inappropriate time. It is not reasonable that the prolongation of a cause of a pleasant feeling or [the cause of a pleasant feeling] that is of the same nature [as one which can produce a favorable experience] should on a different occasion give rise to an unpleasant feeling. Therefore, they must be causes of suffering from the very outset, rather than causes of a pleasant feeling. Moreover, at a later time, that suffering does increase and then it becomes apparent."

432 *AKB*, p. 330.

433 *RA*, ch. 4, vv. 46-48. S: *catur dvīpām api prāpya pṛthivīṃ cakravartinaḥ / śārīraṃ mānasaṃ caiva sukhadvayam idaṃ matam // duḥkhapratikriyāmātraṃ śārīraṃ vedanāsukham / saṃjñāmayaṃ mānasaṃ tu kevalaṃ kalpanākṛtam // duḥkhapratikriyāmātraṃ kalpanāmātram eva ca / lokasya sukhasarvasvaṃ vyartham etad ato*

'rthataḥ. T: *gling bzhi pa yi sa thob kyang / 'khor los sgyur ba'i bde ba ni / lus kyi dag dang sems kyi ste / 'di gnyis kho nar zad par 'dod // lus kyi tshor ba bde ba ni / sdug bsngal phyir na bcos pa tsam / sems kyi 'du shes rang bzhin te / rtog pas byas pa kho nar zad // 'jig rten bde ba'i bdog pa kun / sdug bsngal phyir ni bcos tsam dang / rtog pa tsam nyid yin de'i phyir / de ni don du don med do.*

434 *CŚ*, ch. 2, v. 20. T: *bzhon pa sogs la mi rnams kyi / bde ba rtag tu yod min te / dang por gang la rtsom med pa / de la mthar 'phel ga la yod.*

435 That is, after prolonged use they would not become uncomfortable. As noted later, this argument applies equally to the physical behaviors of walking, sitting, standing, and lying down, as well as the activities of eating, drinking, and the like.

436 T: *khur skya*. Literally "white drink," *MVy* gives the Sanskrit equivalent as *maṇḍaḥ*, which, according to Monier-Williams' *Sanskrit-English Dictionary* could mean such things as "scum of boiled grain," "thick part of milk or cream," or "spiritous part of wine."

437 *CŚṬ*, f. 54a. This translation is based on the Tibetan version, as the Sanskrit original of this portion of the commentary is not extant.

438 *CŚ*, ch. 2, v. 12. S: *sukhasya vardhamānasya yathā dṛṣṭo viparyayaḥ / duḥkhasya vardhamānasya tathā nāsti viparyayaḥ*. T: *'phel bzhin pa yi bde ba la / ji ltar bzlog pa mthong gyur ba / de ltar sdug bsngal 'phel bzhin la / bzlog pa yod pa ma yin no.*

439 *Liberation in Our Hands*, Part Three, pp. 39–40.

440 S: *lokānuvṛttyā*, T: *'jig rten dan mthun par.*

441 *CŚṬ*, f. 54b. T: *so so'i skye bo thos pa dang mi ldan pa yang phyin ci log pa las sdug bsngal phyir bcos pa de dang de la bde'o snyam du sems so.*

442 *CŚṬ*, f. 55a. T: *bde bar rtog pa ni phyin ci log tshad mar byas nas 'gyur ro.*

443 *YṢV*, f. 7a–7b. T: *gang la dmigs pa yod pa yang dmigs pa de ni rnam pa gnyis te / de la phyin ci log dang phyin ci ma log pa'o / de la phyin ci log ni bde ba la sogs par 'dzin pa ste / kun rdzob tu yang de'i bdag nyid du dngos po rnam par mi gnas pa'i phyir ro // phyin ci ma log pa ni sdug bsngal la sogs pa ste / dngos po kun rdzob tu de'i bdag nyid du yod pa'i phyir ro.*

444 The last four types of beings are celestial beings or powerful spirits that are represented as experiencing significant amounts of samsaric pleasure. The Tibetan equivalents are *mi'am ci*, *grub pa*, *lto phye*, and *rig pa 'dzin pa*, respectively.

445 Nāgārjuna's *Praise of the Inconceivable* (S: *Acintyastavaḥ*, T: *bSam gyis mi khyab par bstod pa*), v. 47. T: *gang gi ltar na rdzas skye ba / de la chad la sogs 'gyur zhing / 'jig rten mtha' dang ldan pa dang / mtha' dang mi ldan pa'ang de la 'gal.*

446 *CŚ*, ch. 13, v. 25. S: *alātacakranirmāṇasvapnamāyāmbucandrakaiḥ / dhūmikāntaḥpratiśrutkāmarīcyabhraiḥ samo bhavaḥ*. T: *'gal me'i 'khor lo sprul pa dang / rmi lam sgyu ma chu zla dang / khug rna nang gi brag cha dang / smig rgyu sprin dang srid pa mtshungs.*

447 *CŚṬ*, ff. 57b–58a.

448 *MA*, ch. 6, v. 79. S: *ācāryanāgārjunapādamārgād bahirgatānāṃ na śive 'styupāyaḥ / bhraṣṭā hi te saṃvṛtitattvasatyāt tadbhraṃśataś cāsti na mokṣasiddhiḥ*. T: *slob dpon klu sgrub zhabs kyi lam las ni / phyi rol gyur pa zhi ba'i thabs med do / de dag kun rdzob de nyid bden las nyams / de las nyams pas thar pa 'grub yod min.*

449 These verses, whose authorship is unknown, appear in both Vasubandhu's *AKB* (p. 329) and Candrakīrti's *PP* (p. 209). S: *ūrṇāpakṣma yathaiva hi karatalasaṃsthaṃ na vedyate puṃbhiḥ / akṣigataṃ tu tad eva hi janayatyaratiṃ ca pīḍaṃ ca // karatalasadṛśo bālo na vetti saṃskāraduḥkhatāpakṣma / akṣisadṛśas tu vidvāṃs tenaivodvejate gāḍham.*

T: *lag mthil spu nyag gcig 'dug pa / mi rnams kyis ni mi rtogs la / de nyid mig tu song na ni / mi bde ba dang gnod bskyed ltar / byis pa lag mthil 'dra ba yis / 'du byed sdug bsngal spu mi rtogs / 'phags pa mig dang 'dra ba ni / de yis shin tu yid kyang 'byung.*

450 *PV*, ch. 2, v. 253ab. S: *saṃskāraduḥkhatāṃ mātvā / kathitā duḥkhabhāvanā*, T: *'du byed sdug bsngal la dgongs nas / sdug bsngal bsgom par gsungs pa yin.*

451 The two higher realms are the form and the formless realms. There are four meditative absorptions (S: *dhyānam*, T: *bsam gtan*) associated with the form realm and four states of composure (S: *samāpattiḥ*, T: *snyoms par 'jug pa*) that occur in the formless realm. These eight, together with a meditative level known as "the state of composure that is a cessation" (S: *nirodhasamāpattiḥ*, T: *'gog pa'i snyoms par 'jug pa*; see Part Two, pp. 316–318) comprise nine meditative absorptions that are commonly described in Buddhist literature. In addition to forming a significant portion of the subject matter that relates to the second of the three Buddhist trainings, these nine meditative states are also cultivated in order to overcome mental obstacles and to gain mastery of various spiritual qualities.

452 That is to say, any feeling of attachment for samsara will have been completely overcome.

453 *RG2*, ff. 20b–21a.

454 The term "grasping" (S: *upādānam*, T: *nye bar len pa*) is also the name of the ninth limb in the twelvefold teaching on dependent origination. *The Treasury of Higher Learning* (*AK*, ch. 3, v. 23) describes the meaning of this limb as follows: "Grasping is the running about to obtain objects of enjoyment" (S: *upādānaṃ tu bhogānāṃ prāptaye paridhāvataḥ*; T: *nye bar len pa longs spyod rnams / thob par bya phyir yongs rgyug pa'i*). Chim Jampel Yang's *Ornament of Higher Learning* (T: *mNgon pa'i rgyan*; see listing in Bibliography under the name [mChims] Nam mkha' grags) further clarifies this description as referring to "the five heaps when they are engaged in such activities as farming or household work, and in particular to the form of desire that is directed toward the cause of [pleasurable] feelings and that gives rise to the karma that will produce a future birth." Traditional exegesis identifies four types of grasping: (1) desire-grasping (S: *kāmopādānam*, T: *'dod pa nye bar len pa*), (2) grasping at views (S: *dṛṣṭyupādānam*, T: *lta ba nye bar len pa*), (3) grasping at morality and austerities (S: *sīlavratopādānam*, T: *tshul khrims dang brtul zhugs nye bar len pa*), and (4) grasping at affirmation of a [real] self (S: *ātmavādopādānam*, T: *bdag tu smra ba nye bar len pa*). As stated in *The Treasury of Higher Learning*, the Vaibhāṣika School held that these four types of grasping taken collectively are synonymous and coextensive with all the mental afflictions. The Mahāyāna position is that grasping refers more narrowly only to aspiration and/or desire. Yaśomitra (*AKV*, p. 432) states that they represent aspiration (S: *chandaḥ*, T: *'dun pa*) when they occur in relation to objects that have not yet been obtained and they represent desire (S: *rāgaḥ*, T: *'dod chags*) when they occur in relation to objects that have been obtained. Asaṅga provides a concise description of them in his *Levels of Spiritual Practice* (*YB*, p. 208): "What is desire-grasping? It is the aspiration and desire that occur in relation to sense objects. What is grasping at views? It is the aspiration and desire that occur in relation to those [mistaken] views with the exception of the perishable collection view. What is grasping at morality and austerities? It is the aspiration and desire that occur in relation to erroneous morality and asceticism. What is grasping at affirmation of a [real] self? It is the aspiration and desire that occur in relation to the perishable collection view. The first type brings about suffering in the desire realm; the remaining ones do so in all three realms."

455 S: *dauṣṭhulyopagatāḥ*, T: *gnas ngan len dang ldan pa*. See note 408 above.

456 S: *ayogakṣemapatitaḥ*, *grub pa dang bde bar gtogs pa ma yin pa*. The original Sanskrit term *yogakṣemaḥ* is a compound whose two elements mean "acquisition" (S: *yogaḥ*, T: *grub*) and "secure preservation" (S: *kṣemaḥ*, T: *bde ba*), respectively. It can be construed both as a noun and an adjective. In Tibetan literature the term is used in a special epistemological sense; here it is meant to be descriptive of the peace and well-being of liberation. Its opposite, *ayogakṣema*, refers to the unsatisfactoriness of samsara.

457 *ŚB*, p. 257.

458 While the four conditions (S: *catur pratyayāḥ*, T: *rkyen bzhi*) are mentioned with frequency in Buddhist philosophical literature, they are not often explained in any detail. Two of the most extensive discussions are found in Vasubandhu's *Commentary to the Treasury of Higher Learning* (*AKB*, pp. 98–101) and Jinaputra's *Commentary to the Compendium of Higher Learning* (*ASB*, pp. 35–42).

Both Candrakīrti and Asaṅga describe the causal condition (S: *hetupratyayaḥ*, T: *rgyu'i rkyen*) as a seed that produces results. However, while Asaṅga identifies this with the storehouse consciousness (S: *ālayavijñānam*, T: *kun gzhi rnam par shes pa*), Candrakīrti does not. In the *AS*, Asaṅga provides a lengthy series of examples, which are meant to be illustrative in nature rather than providing an exhaustive account. The first of them is the collection of elements including the eye that represent the causal condition giving rise to eye consciousness. The remaining examples cover a variety of circumstances that relate both to animate beings and to the inanimate world. Jinaputra's commentary on this section of Asaṅga's work identifies which examples correspond to, and provide an illustration of, the six kinds of causes. Readers of Sanskrit and Tibetan are encouraged to examine this informative material to gain a better sense of the breadth of this topic.

Explanations of the homogeneous immediate condition (S: *samanantarapratyayaḥ*, T: *mtshungs pa de ma thag rkyen*) typically limit the meaning of this factor to the way in which each moment of consciousness and its accompanying mental factors, upon their cessation, determine the nature of those mental entities that immediately succeed them. The discussion may also include an overview of the kinds of mental states, both similar and dissimilar, that are able to occur in the wake of a range of specific mental states. Candrakīrti represents a view that extends the meaning of this condition to include entities that are not mental in nature. He states: "The [state of] cessation that occurs immediately following [the moment in which] a cause [existed] is the condition for the arising of its result. For example, the cessation that occurs immediately following [the moment in which] a seed [existed] is the condition for the emergence of a sprout" (*PP*, p. 26).

The objective condition (S: *ālambanapratyayaḥ*, T: *dmigs rkyen*) addresses the kinds of entities that constitute the objects for each of the six types of consciousness and their accompanying mental states. Asaṅga's list of categories begins with the specific objects that are limited to each of the five types of sense consciousness and ends with the unobstructed object of a being who has eliminated from his mind all the obscurations to objects of knowledge.

The governing condition (S: *adhipatipratyayaḥ*, T: *bdag po'i rkyen*) refers to a type of factor that is both dominant and necessary for the occurrence of some entity. The most commonly cited example is that the eye faculty is the governing condition for the occurrence of eye consciousness, and each of the other sense faculties is the governing condition for its respective form of sense consciousness. Similarly, samsaric virtuous and nonvirtuous karma are the governing conditions for the various types of result that they generate. Among the mental factors, two examples are (1) that attention (S: *manaskāraḥ*, T: *yid la byed pa*) is the governing condition that determines the type and form of consciousness that will occur, and (2) that contact (S: *sparśaḥ*, T: *reg pa*) is the governing condition for the type of feeling (S: *vedanā*, T: *tshor ba*) that will be experienced. Abhidharma literature also describes a series of twenty-two faculties (S: *indriyam*, T: *dbang po*). Each of these is characterized as exercising a governing influence over some state of affairs. For example, the male and female faculties (i.e., the sexual organs) are the governing condition for samsaric rebirth; the five spiritual faculties of faith, recollection, one-pointed concentration, effort, and wisdom collectively are governing conditions for achieving a temporary subjugation of the mental afflictions on the Preparation Path (S: *prayogamārgaḥ*, T: *sbyor lam*) and the three pure faculties are governing conditions that destroy the seeds of the mental afflictions. The first of the pure faculties is called "the faculty in which one reflects, 'I shall gain full knowledge of what is not yet fully known'" (S: *anājñātamājñāsyāmīndriyam*, T: *kun shes par byed pa'i dbang po*), and it is the governing condition both for abandoning the obstacles that are removed by the Seeing Path (S: *darśanamārgaḥ*, T: *mthong lam*) and for attaining the second pure faculty, which is called "the faculty of full knowledge" (S: *ājñendriyam*, S: *kun shes pa'i dbang po*). That second pure faculty is the governing condition both for abandoning the obstacles that are removed by the Meditation Path (S: *bhāvanāmārgaḥ*, T: *bsgom lam*) and for attaining the third pure faculty, which is called "the faculty of possessing full knowledge" (S: *ājñātāvīndriyam*, T: *kun shes pa dang ldan pa'i dbang po*). This third pure faculty, which is achieved when one attains the status of an Arhat, is the governing condition both for being able to abide in a state of pure well-being during one's present lifetime (S: *dṛṣṭadharmasukhavihāram*, T: *mthong ba'i chos la bde bar gnas pa*) and for attaining the nirvana without remainder at the end of one's life.

459 S: *bhājanam*, T: *snod*.

460 *AS*, pp. 36–37.

461 S: *yogācāraḥ*, T: *rnal 'byor spyod pa*. At this point in the text, the practitioner is understood to be someone who has already heard instruction in the Four Noble Truths and reflected on its meaning. He or she has also achieved some form of the one-pointed concentration known as "quiescence" (S: *śamathaḥ*, T: *zhi gnas*). This would include any of several preliminary stages that precede attainment of the first meditative absorption (S: *dhyānam*, T: *bsam gtan*), or any of the four actual meditative absorptions associated with the form realm or the four states of composure (S: *samāpattiḥ*, T: *snyoms par 'jug pa*) that occur in the formless realm. These states of one-pointed concentration are discussed below in the sections of this chapter entitled "Achieving Quiescence" and "The Mundane Path." This form of meditation on the Four Noble Truths represents "transcendent" insight practice (S: *lokottaravipaśyanā*, T: *'jig rten las 'das pa'i lhag mthong*) in that it constitutes the direct means of attaining liberation.

462 S: *vipariṇāmānityatā*, T: *rnam par 'gyur ba'i mi rtag pa nyid*. Asaṅga describes this form of impermanence as one that is directly evident (S: *pratyakṣā*, T: *mngon sum*), not beyond the range of [ordinary] perception (S: *aviparokṣā*, T: *lkog tu ma gyur pa*), and does not depend on [explanation received from] others (S: *aparapratyayā*, T: *gzhan gyi dring mi 'jog pa*).

463 S: *ṣaḍāyatanam*, T: *skye mched drug*. The phrase "six bases" also refers to the fifth of the twelve limbs that make up the doctrine of dependent origination.

464 See Part Two, p. 241.

465 S: *sparśaḥ*, T: *reg pa*. Contact is one of the five "universal" mental factors that are present in all states of consciousness. It is described as "the determination that occurs upon the convergence of three." The three are the three entities of faculty, object, and consciousness. The "determination" it makes is that of conforming to the modification undergone by the faculty in a perceptual event. In doing so, contact governs the type of feeling—pleasant, unpleasant, or neutral—that will be experienced. Thus the "action" or function of contact is that it serves as the foundation for feelings (see Part Two, p. 176). Contact also refers to the sixth of the twelve limbs of dependent origination.

466 *ŚB*, p. 480.

467 S: *vināśānityatā*, T: *'jig pa'i mi rtag pa nyid*.

468 S: *aṣṭau vipariṇāmakāraṇāni*, T: *'gyur ba'i rgyu rnam pa brgyad*. Asaṅga identifies these eight factors as the ones that are responsible for the observable change that inner and outer entities undergo: (1) the natural deterioration caused by the passage of time; (2) damage caused by contact with other physical objects; (3) use and consumption of objects; (4) change of seasons in the year; (5) burning by fire; (6) washing away by water; (7) drying up by wind; and (8) meeting with other conditions. The last item, in particular, refers to the circumstances in which the mind undergoes change.

469 In other words, the possibility of change is due precisely to the underlying condition of subtle impermanence. That is, with each passing moment the convergence of a combination of causes produces new members in a continuous series of conditioned entities. Over the course of time, the variation in these causes and conditions creates sufficient contrast or dissimilarity in the continuum that we perceive the appearance of change.

470 *ŚB*, pp. 485–486.

471 *PV*, ch. 1, v. 193cd. S: *ahetutvād vināśasya svabhāvād anubandhitā*; T: *rgyu med phyir na 'jig pa na / rang gi ngo bos rje 'brel nyid*.

472 S: *tadbhāvaḥ*, T: *de'i ngo bo*. That is, the nature or quality of being perishable (S: *vinaśvarasvabhāvaḥ*, T: *'jig pa'i rang bzhin*.

473 *PVV*, p. 98.

474 The complete Sanskrit alphabet is made up of sixteen vowels and thirty-four consonants.

475 This description of the meaning of an instant (S: *kṣaṇam*, T: *skad cig*) is found in the traditional Abhidharma literature.

476 *CŚṬ*, f. 38a.

477 S: *ānumānikena manaskāreṇa paraloke saṃskārapravṛttau niścayam pratilābhaḥ*; T: *rjes su dpag pa las byung ba'i yid la byed pa dag gis 'jig rten pha rol tu 'du byed 'jug par 'gyur ba la nges pa thob pa*.

478 S: *visaṃyogānityatā*, T: *bral ba'i mi rtag pa nyid*.

479 S: *dharmatānityatā*, T: *chos nyid kyi mi rtag pa nyid*.

480 That is, the conditioned entities that make up one's own five grasping heaps.

481 S: *saṃnihitānityatā*, T: *nye bar gyur pa'i mi rtag pa nyid*. Although the Tibetan suggests that this term means an impermanence that is "near at hand," the original Sanskrit can also describe something that is "present," and in this context that is clearly the intended sense.

482 That is, the doctrine of subtle impermanence not only means that entities do not last more than an instant, it also provides the justification for how new entities come into being.

483 *ŚB*, p. 489.

484 S: *saṃyojanabandhanākāraḥ*, T: *kun tu sbyor ba dang 'ching ba'i rnam pa.*

485 S: *aniṣṭākāraḥ*, T: *mi 'dod pa'i rnam pa.*

486 S: *ayogakṣemākāraḥ*, T: *grub pa dang bde med pa'i rnam pa.* See also note 456 above.

487 S: *dauṣṭhulyasahagatāḥ*, T: *gnas ngan len dang ldan pa.*

488 *ŚB*, p. 490.

489 S: *anumāṇam*, T: *rjes dpag tshad ma.*

490 See note 385 above. Another name for this path is "[the path] that relates to liberation" (S: *mokṣabhagīyaḥ*, T: *thar pa'i cha dang mthun pa*).

491 Asaṅga (*ŚB*, pp. 36–166) identifies and explains in extensive detail the following thirteen "requisites for enlightenment" (S: *trayodaśabodhisambhāraḥ*, T: *byang chub kyi tshogs bcu gsum*): (1) the five fortunes that relate to oneself; (2) the five fortunes that relate to others; (3) the aspiration to acquire virtuous dharma; (4) the restraint represented by morality; (5) restraint of the faculties; (6) regulating one's food; (7) striving after virtue throughout the day and during the first and last periods of the night, as well as sleeping properly during the middle period of the night; (8) cultivating vigilance; (9) relying on a spiritual teacher; (10) listening to and contemplating holy dharma; (11) being free of inner and outer obstacles; (12) cultivating generosity; and (13) acquiring the ornaments of a spiritual ascetic. Some portions of this material are missing in the Sanskrit edition; however, they are available in the Tibetan translation.

492 S: *prayogamārgaḥ*, T: *sbyor lam.* Another name for this path is "that which relates to penetrating insight" (S: *nirvedhabhagīyaḥ*, T: *nges 'byed cha mthun*). "Penetrating insight" is a reference to the direct realization of ultimate truth.

493 S: *yogapratyakṣaḥ*, T: *rnal 'byor mngon sum.*

494 S: *anupalambhākāraḥ*, T: *mi dmigs pa'i rnam pa.* What is "not discerned" is any kind of real self that exists over and above the five heaps.

495 S: *asvatantrākāraḥ*, T: *rang dbang med pa'i rnam pa.*

496 S: *svabhūtaḥ*, T: *bdag por gyur pa.* That is, the heaps do not "belong" to a self in the sense that they are subject to the will or control of a self.

497 S: *svalakṣaṇam*, T: *rang gi mtshan nyid.* In Abhidharma, this refers to the essential defining quality of a conditioned entity. For example, the unique attribute of form is that of being susceptible to harm or damage (S: *rūpaṇam*, T: *gzugs su rung ba*); that of feeling is to experience (S: *anubhāvaḥ*, T: *nyams su myong ba*; see Part Two, p. 267); that of conception is to grasp a sign (S: *nimittodgrahaṇam*, T: *mtshan mar 'dzin pa*; see Part Two, p. 271); that of the mental formations is to shape the mind in a particular way (S: *abhisaṃskāraṇam*, T: *mngon par 'du byed pa*; this attribute pertains specifically to the mental factor of volition—see Part Two, p. 277); and that of consciousness is to know an object (S: *ālambanavijñāptiḥ*, T: *yul rnam par rig pa*; see Part Two, p. 327).

498 The Tibetan text reads "general attributes" for "attribute of impermanence." The general attributes of conditioned entities are those of arising, abiding, and perishing.

499 S: *asvatantram*, T: *rang dbang med pa.*

500 *ŚB*, pp. 490–492.

501 *PV*, ch. 2, v. 254cd. S: *anityāt prāha tenaiva duḥkhaṃ duḥkhān nirātmatām*; T: *de phyir mi rtag las sdug bsngal / sdug bsngal las ni bdag med gsungs.*

502 This work appears both in the collected writings of Je Tsongkapa (Toh. # 5400) and

the collected writings of his disciple Gyeltsab Darma Rinchen (Toh. # 5438). The passage presented here is also repeated almost verbatim in Khedrup Je's overview of the writings of Dharmakīrti, *Removing the Darkness of Incomprehension: An Ornament to the Collection of Seven Works on Knowledge* (T: *Tshad ma sde bdun gyi rgyan yid kyi mun sel*), IN *Collected Works*, vol. 10 (*tha*), f. 111a–111b.

503 S: *tṛṣṇā*, T: *sred pa*. Craving is a synonym for the root mental affliction of desire.

504 *Notes from Teachings on Pramāṇa That the Lord of Dharma Gyeltsab Je Heard Directly from Je Tsongkapa* (T: *rGyal tshab chos rjes rje'i drung du gsan pa'i tshad ma'i brjed byang chen mo*). In the *Collected Works* of Je Tsongkapa, vol. 14 (*pha*), ff. 8b–9a.

505 *PV*, ch. 2, v. 254ab. S: *muktis tu śūnyatādṛṣṭes tadārthās śeṣabhāvanāḥ*; T: *stong nyid lta bas grol 'gyur gyi / sgom pa lhag ma de don yin.* In this context, the phrase "view that perceives emptiness" should be understood to mean the wisdom in which the five impure heaps are realized to be void of a real self that is either identical with, or distinct from, them; it does not refer to the Mahāyāna understanding that all entities are void of any real or independent essence.

506 *The Sutra That Reveals the Inconceivable Mystery of the Tathāgatas* (T: *De bzhin gshegs pa'i gsang ba bsam gyis mi khyab pa bstan pa'i mdo*).

507 This is the fourteenth of forty-six secondary Bodhisattva transgressions that Asaṅga identifies in the morality chapter of his *Bodhisattvas' Level*. It corresponds to the line from Candragomī's *Twenty Verses on the Bodhisattva Vow* that describes this misdeed as "regarding samsara as the one [true] path" (T: *'khor ba gcig pu bgrod par sems*—the Sanskrit original of this phrase may tentatively be reconstructed as *saṃsāraikāyanacintā*). Here is Asaṅga's complete description of the transgression (*BB*, p. 116): "Moreover, any Bodhisattva who holds the following view or professes it [to others] becomes an offender and a transgressor who has incurred an afflicted offense: 'The Bodhisattva should not abide with an attitude that delights in nirvana; rather, he [or she] should abide with an attitude that is turned away from nirvana. He [or she] should not fear the root or secondary mental afflictions, and he [or she] should not be devoted exclusively to separating [his or her] mind from them; for the Bodhisattva pursues enlightenment while remaining in samsara for three spans of time that are each made up of a countless number of kalpas.' Why is this [an offense]? The Bodhisattva should maintain great delight toward nirvana and develop aversion for the root and secondary mental afflictions that is a trillion times greater than the delight that a Listener Disciple feels toward nirvana and the aversion that he [or she] feels toward the root and secondary mental afflictions. This is because the Listener Disciple is [merely] devoted to the pursuit of his [or her] own welfare, but a Bodhisattva is devoted to the welfare of all sentient beings. Thus, [a Bodhisattva] must attain a state of self-discipline in which [his or her] mind remains so free of afflictions that, even though he [or she] is not an Arhat, he [or she] can interact with entities that have the potential to cause the outflows to arise in such a manner that the unafflicted state of mind he [or she] possesses is even superior to that of an Arhat."

508 *LC*, ff. 168b–169b.

509 S: *bodhipakṣyadharmāḥ*, T: *byang chub kyi phyogs dang mthun pa'i chos rnams.*

510 S: *catvāri smṛtyupasthānāni*, T: *dran pa nye bar bzhag pa bzhi.*

511 *MVṬ*, pp. 125–126.

512 *AS*, p. 71. S: *vastuparīkṣamārgaḥ*, T: *dngos po yongs su rtog pa'i lam.*

513 *ASB*, pp. 83–84. S: *āditas tenāśubhādibhir ākāraiḥ kāyavedanācittadharmavastuparīkṣaṇāt*; T: *des thog ma nyid du mi gtsang ba la sogs pa'i rnam pa rnam kyis lus dang / tshor ba dang / sems dang / chos kyis dngos po la yongs so rtog pa'i phyir ro.* The most

basic meditations are that the body is examined in relation to its unattractiveness (S: *aśubhaḥ*, T: *mi sdug pa*); feelings are examined in relation to their suffering nature; the mind is examined in relation to its impermanence; and entities (S: *dharmāḥ*, T: *chos rnams*) are examined in relation to their not being related to a real personal self. However, each of the four objects is also meditated upon in a variety of other ways.

514 S: *Mahāvibhāṣāśāstram*, T: *Bye brag tu bshad pa'i bstan bcos chen mo.* A compendium of Abhidharma thought that contains presentations of the range of views that were prevalent in the Sanskrit Sarvāstivāda tradition. The work is said to have been compiled in the second century at the time of a Buddhist council convened in Kashmir under the sponsorship of King Kaniṣka. The original Sanskrit text did not survive nor is there a Tibetan translation. Several works with this name are contained in the Chinese scriptural collections.

515 S: *ādikarmikaḥ*, T: *las dang po pa.*

516 S: *lakṣaṇapratisaṃvedīmanaskāraḥ*, T: *mtshan nyid so sor rig pa yid la byed pa.* See below, pp. 169–171 for a description of all seven forms of mental application as they relate to cultivation of the mundane path, and pp. 179–184 for a description of the same seven in relation to the transcendent path.

517 S: *kṛtaparicayaḥ*, T: *yongs su sbyang ba byas pa.*

518 S: *atikrāntamanaskāraḥ*, T: *yid la byed pa las 'das pa.*

519 In this context, being pure or clean (S: *śuciḥ*, T; *gtsang ba*) is synonymous with being attractive, in the sense of being an object that has the potential to generate desire. The meditation topic of unattractiveness (S: *aśubhatā*, T: *mi sdug pa nyid*) is presented as an antidote to desire. For a description of several types of desire and the forms of unattractiveness that represent their specific antidote, see note 586 below and the related discussion in the text.

520 S: *catasraḥ śivapathikāḥ*, T: *dur khrod rnam pa bzhi.* The four charnel grounds are identified earlier in the *ŚB*, in connection with the practice of meditating on corpses in various stages of decay as an antidote to sexual desire (pp. 205–206; comparison with the Tibetan translation suggests that the Sanskrit version available to me is incomplete). This is only one form of the broader practice called meditation on unattractiveness (S: *aśubhabhāvanā*, T: *mi sdug pa sgom pa*) that will be discussed later when the first closely placed recollection is examined in greater detail. The four charnel grounds represent specific objects of meditation for four types of sexual desire. The first type of charnel ground is one in which the practitioner sees corpses of humans that have been dead for one, two, three, or up to seven days, and which have been partially eaten by crows, osprey, vultures, dogs, and jackals. The range of corpses found in such a cemetery are called (1) "blue" (S: *vinīlakam*, T: *rnam par sngos pa*), which is a corpse whose skin has become discolored from decay; (2) "putrid" (S: *vipūyakam*, T: *rnam par rnags pa*), which is one that oozes pus from various places; (3) "worm-infested" (S: *vipaḍumakam* or *vidhūtakam*, T: *rnam par 'bus gzhig pa*), which is one whose inner parts have been hollowed out by various burrowing worms; (4) "swollen" (S: *vyādhmātakam*, T: *rnam par bam pa*), which is one whose shape is in a ruined condition; and (5) "gnawed" (S: *vikhāditakam*, T: *rnam par zos pa*), which is one that has been chewed here and there by various animals. Upon seeing these corpses, the practitioner should compare his own body to those that are situated here and there, and reflect, "My own body, too, shall become like this. It presently has [the capacity to] become like this; it is not beyond this nature." The second type of charnel ground is one in which there are corpses whose skin is gone, revealing skeletons whose bones

are held together by tendons and which still have some flesh and blood attached. This type of corpse is called "red" (S: *vilohitakam*, T: *rnam par dmar ba*). The third type of charnel ground is one in which there are found heaps of bones and skeletons. The fourth type of charnel ground is one that contains the scattered bones of persons that have been dead for one, two, or even seven years. Some of these bones are white as a conch shell; others have turned gray like the color of a pigeon; still others are crumbling to dust.

521 S: *yat kiṃcit veditam idam atra duḥkhasya*; T: *gang cung zad cig tshor yang rung ste / de dag de la sdug bsngal ba yin no*. This phrase is from the sutras and was uttered by Buddha.

522 See below, pp. 184–187, for a description of the twenty states of mind that constitute the objects of this form of closely placed recollection.

523 *ŚB*, pp. 303–304.

524 *MV*, ch. 4, v. 1. S: *dauṣṭhulyāt tarṣahetutvād vastutvād avimohataḥ / catus satyāvatārāya smṛtyupasthānabhāvanā*. T: *gnas ngan len phyir sred rgyu'i phyir / gzhi yi phyir dang ma rmongs phyir / bden pa bzhi la 'jug bya bas / dran pa nye bar bzhag pa bsgom*.

525 See above, note 408. The five impure heaps are described as being "accompanied by a state of indisposition" in the two passages from Asaṅga's *ŚB* that describe the suffering of conditioned existence (see pp. 122–123 and p. 132). Here this quality is associated especially with the impediment to spiritual training that stems from the physical body.

526 *MVṬ*, p. 125.

527 *MVṬ*, p. 126. S: *pratidinam abhisaṃskriyamāṇo vikriyata eva kāya iti*; T: *nyin gcig bzhin mngon par 'dus byas kyang lus 'gyur ba nyid pas*. As described earlier, there is also a mental form of indisposition. Both are understood to be created by the seeds of the mental afflictions.

528 See below, pp. 216–223.

529 *MVṬ*, p. 125.

530 S: *avidyāsaṃsparśajā*, T: *ma rig pa'i 'dus te reg pa las byung ba*.

531 S: *anāsravā*, T: *zag pa med pa*. This adjective applies to feelings that accompany a mind that has achieved the transcendent path. In a looser sense, such feelings can be described as "pure."

532 S: *tatra katamat samudayāryasatyaṃ / yeyaṃ tṛṣṇā paunarbhavikī nandarāgasahagatā tatra tatrābhinandinī / yad uta kāmatṛṣṇā bhavatṛṣṇā vibhavatṛṣṇā ca*. T: *de la kun 'byung 'phags pa'i bden gang zhe na / gang 'di sred pa yang 'byung ba can dga' ba'i 'dod chags dang bcas pa de dang de la mngon par dga' ba'i ngang tshul can / 'di sta te / 'dod pa'i sred pa dang / srid pa'i sred pa dang / 'jig pa'i sred pa'o*. This is a version of the canonical description of the Noble Truth of Origination.

533 S: *bhavatṛṣṇā*, T: *srid pa'i sred pa*.

534 S: *kāmatṛṣṇā*, T: *'dod pa'i sred pa*.

535 S: *vibhavatṛṣṇā*, T: *'jig pa'i sred pa*.

536 *PV*, ch. 2, v. 185. S: *sā bhavecchāptyanāptīcchoḥ pravṛttiḥ sukhaduḥkhayoḥ / yato 'pi prāṇinaḥ kāmavibhavecche ca te mate*. T: *de ni srid 'dod gang phyir yang / srog chags bde sdug thob pa dang / 'dor 'dod 'jug pa de dag ni / 'dod dang 'jig sred yin par 'dod*.

537 *PV*, ch. 2, vv. 189d–190. S: *kāraṇatve 'pi noditam // ajñānam uktā tṛṣṇaiva santānapreraṇād bhave / ānantaryāc ca karmāpi sati tasmin asambhavāt*. T: *mi shes srid pa'i rgyu yin yang / ma brjod sred pa nyid bshad pa / rgyun ni 'phen par byed phyir dang / de ma thag phyir las kyang min / de yod na yod med phyir ro*.

538 *MVṬ*, p. 125.

539 This represents the common explanation that the object of the perishable collection view is either the five heaps taken as a whole or mind consciousness alone. However, proponents of the Mādhyamika Prasaṅgika School give a more radical interpretation of both what constitutes the object of the perishable collection view and how one should understand the meaning of the doctrine that there is no real, personal self (S: *pudgalanairātmyam*, T: *gang zag gi bdag med*). Regarding the former, scholars such as Candrakīrti argue that the object of the perishable collection view is the nominally existent self, not mind consciousness or the five heaps taken collectively. Thus, although this conventionally existent self is designated in dependence on the five heaps (S: *skandhān upādāya prajñaptiḥ*, T: *phung po la brten nas btags pa*), it is not to be identified with any individual aspect of the heaps or their totality. In contrast with all other Buddhist philosophical schools, the Prasaṅgikas also equate the insubstantiality of the person with the emptiness of that nominal self, which is to say that it has no valid, independent basis whatsoever.

540 The other qualities would be the remaining three aspects of the Noble Truth of Suffering—that is, suffering, emptiness, and selflessness. See the earlier discussion of Asaṅga's presentation of the ten points that are meditated upon in relation to the Truth of Suffering, pp. 125–134.

541 S: *śāntam*, T: *zhi ba*. This represents the second of the four aspects of the Truth of Cessation. It is interpreted as meaning that nirvana is characterized by peace because it is a state in which all the mental afflictions have been completely and permanently quelled. The other three are that nirvana is a cessation (S: *nirodham*, T: *'gog pa*) because it represents a state in which all samsaric suffering has been terminated; it is characterized by excellence (S: *praṇītam*, T: *gya nom pa*) because it is an unsurpassed state of liberation; and it is a state of deliverance (S: *niḥsaraṇam*, T: *nges par 'byung ba*) because one who attains it will never return to samsaric existence.

542 *MVṬ*, p. 125.

543 S: *sāṃkleśikadharmāḥ*, T: *kun nas nyon mongs pa'i chos*.

544 S: *vyavadānikadharmāḥ*, T: *rnam par byang ba'i chos*.

545 T: *bka' 'gyur*. This term is the name for the collection of Buddhist sutras and tantras that have been translated into Tibetan. Literally, it means "translation of the (Buddha's) word." Aside from the vinaya (T: *'dul ba*) section of the Kangyur collection, only one other section, variously called "discourses" (S: *sutrāntaḥ*, T: *mdo sde*) or "miscellaneous discourses" (T: *mdo mang*) in the different Tibetan editions, contains what would be identified as non-Mahāyāna texts. Some are extracts from larger works. One very large sutra that takes up nearly four volumes is entitled *Closely Placed Recollection of the True Dharma*; see also Je Tsongkapa's reference to this work above, p. 74. While this sutra does contain language that addresses the four closely placed recollections, it is more widely known for its descriptions of a great variety of good and bad karma, and the nature of their results.

546 *PVS*, vol. 1, p. 342.

547 S: *anupaśyanā*, T: *rjes su lta ba*.

548 *ŚB*, p. 292.

549 This description would, of course, apply in a similar manner to the recollection that can be maintained in relation to the other three objects—feelings, the mind, and entities.

550 *ŚB*, pp. 292–293.

551 S: *muṣitasmṛtitā*, T: *brjed ngas*. See Part Two, p. 309.

552 *ŚB*, p. 293.

553 S: *sūdgṛhītaḥ*, T: *legs par zin pa*. Literally "well taken up," the main verbal root also means "to recall."

554 S: *sūpalakṣitaḥ*, T: *legs par brtags pa*.

555 S: *susaṃsparśitaḥ*, T: *legs par reg par byas pa*. Literally, "cause (liberation) to be well touched."

556 S: *smṛtyā rakṣā*, T: *dran pa kun tu bsrung ba*.

557 S: *viṣayāsaṃkleśaḥ*, T: *yul gyi kun nas nyong mongs pa med pa*.

558 S: *ālambanopanibandhaḥ*, T: *dmigs pa la nye bar gtod pa*.

559 S: *indriyasamvaraḥ*, T: *dbang po'i sdom pa*. This is one of the thirteen requisites for enlightenment (see note 491).

560 See pp. 89–98.

561 *ŚB*, pp. 306–307. The terms "pure" and "impure" here are the technical terms that more literally are rendered as "free of the outflows" (S: *anāsravaḥ*, T: *zag pa med pa*) and "related to the outflows" (S: *sāsravaḥ*, T: *zag pa dang bcas pa*). See Part Two, note 9.

562 Among these, the "primary elements" in item 9 refer to the four great elements (S: *catvāri mahābhūtāni*, T: *'byung ba chen po bzhi*) of earth, water, fire and air (see Part Two, pp. 248–252); and the "secondary elements" in item 10 refer to "derivative form" (S: *upādāya rūpam*, T: *rgyur byas pa'i gzugs*; Part Two, pp. 252–267). The body as name (S: *nāma*, T: *ming*) in item 11 is probably a reference to the four nonphysical heaps that are referred to as "name" in the compound "name and form" (S: *nāmarūpaḥ*, T: *ming dang gzugs*).

A body that is in an altered state (S: *vipariṇataḥ*, T: *yongs su gyur pa*) likely refers to the kind of change that was discussed earlier in relation to the suffering of change (see above, pp. 125–126). For sentient beings, this would mean the manner in which a person's physical appearance can be altered by such circumstances as climate or season, physical exertion, injury, and the like. For inanimate objects, this would mean the manner in which the physical environment can be affected by changes in season, or be altered by wind, fire, and flood. This could also refer to the gradual deterioration of man-made objects.

A sexually deficient person (S: *ṣaṇḍhaḥ*, item 26) is meant here in the general sense of a person who is "neither male nor female." Buddhist Vinaya and Abhidharma literature describes two categories of persons who are afflicted by a range of sexual abnormalities. A *ṣaṇḍhaḥ* (T: *za ma*) is a person who "lacks a sexual faculty," which means that one is incapable of performing sexually at all. This could refer to someone with a congenital abnormality, a castrated person, or someone suffering complete impotency brought on by disease, injury, or some other cause. A *paṇḍakaḥ* (T: *ma ning*) is a man or woman who has a sexual faculty, but one that is deficient. Examples include a person who experiences sexual arousal only intermittently or who may sometimes feel the sexual arousal of a male and sometimes that of a female. It can also refer to an individual who experiences sexual arousal only if physically overpowered by another person, or only if he or she sees the sexual organ of another person or sees other persons engaging in sexual acts. A third category of sexual abnormality is a hermaphrodite (S: *ubhayavyañjanaḥ*, T: *mtshan gnyis pa*)—that is, a person who possesses the physical attributes of both male and female reproductive organs.

563 *PVS*, vol. 1, pp. 342–343.

564 S: *pratisaṃlayanam*, T: *nang du yang dag 'jog.*

565 He discusses them within the topic of "cultivating vigilance" (S: *saṃprajānadvihāritā*, T: *shes bzhin du spyod pa nyid*); see also note 346, above.

566 *AK*, ch. 6, v. 5ab. S: *vṛttasthaḥ śrutacintavān bhāvanāyāṃ prayujyate*; T: *tshul gnas thos dang bsam ldan pas / bsgom pa la ni rab tu sbyor.*

567 S: *vyapakarṣadvayavataḥ*, T: *bsrings gnyis ldan.*

568 S: *akuśalavitarkaḥ*, T: *mi dge ba'i rnam par rtog pa.*

569 S: *alpecchā*, T: *'dod pa chung ba.* Vasubandhu (*AKB*, p. 335) defines "having few wants" as the quality of not developing desire when one does not obtain material things of excellent quality or in great abundance.

570 S: *santuṣṭiḥ*, T: *chog shes ba.* This is defined (*AKB*, p. 335) as the quality of not becoming unhappy when the material things that one does obtain are not of excellent quality or in great abundance.

571 S: *śamathasambhāraḥ* T: *zhi gnas kyi tshogs.* The presentation that appears in the *Great Treatise* (*LC*, ff. 314a–315a) is based mainly on a passage from the second of Kamalaśīla's trilogy of works entitled *Stages of Meditation* (S: *Dvitīyabhavanakramaḥ*, T: *sGom rim bar pa*). The topic is explained in terms of the following six qualities: (1) residing in a favorable place; (2) having few wants; (3) being satisfied with what one has; (4) avoiding involvement in many activities; (5) having a pure moral practice; and (6) overcoming thoughts about sense objects and the like. See also the Lamrim Chenmo Translation Committee's English version, *The Great Treatise on the Stages of the Path to Enlightement,* vol. 3, pp. 28–30.

572 *Bodhipathapradīpaḥ*, v. 39. T: *zhi gnas yan lag rnam nyams pas / rab tu 'bad de bsgoms byas kyang / lo ni stong phrag dag gis kyang / ting 'dzin 'grub par mi 'gyur ro.*

573 S: *yuganaddhaḥ*, T: *zung du 'brel ba.*

574 S: *samāhitacitto yathābhūtaṃ prajānāti*, T: *sems mnyam par gzhag na yang dag par ji lta ba bzhin rab tu shes par 'gyur ro.*

575 BCA, ch. 8, v. 4. S: *śamathena vipaśyanāsuyuktaḥ kurute kleśavināśam ityavetya / śamathaḥ prathamaṃ gaveṣaṇīyaḥ sa ca loke nirapekṣayābhiratyā.* T: *zhi gnas rab tu ldan pa'i lhag mthong gis / nyon mongs rnam par 'joms par shes byas nas / thog mar zhi gnas btsal bya de yang ni / 'jig rten chags pa med la mngon dgas 'grub.*

576 *AK*, ch. 6, v. 9ab. S: *tatrāvatāro 'śubhayā cānāpānasmṛtena ca*; T: *de la 'jug pa mi sdug dang / dbugs rngub 'byung ba dran pa yis.*

577 *AK*, ch. 6, v. 9c. S: *adhirāgavitarkāṇām*, T: *'dod chags rnam rtog lhag rnams so.*

578 S: *rāgacaritaḥ*, T: *'dod chags spyad pa.* The names of the next four types of person are formed by substituting the corresponding mental affliction.

579 S: *samabhāgacaritaḥ*, T: *cha mnyam par spyad pa.*

580 S: *mandarajaskaḥ*, T: *nyon mongs pa chung ba'i rang bzhin can.*

581 S: *caritaviśodhanālambanam*, T: *spyad pa rnam par sbyong ba'i dmigs pa.* This is not a literal translation of the phrase. The term *carita* (T: *spyad pa*) usually means "conduct" or "behavior"; however, the sense here is that of a strong tendency to manifest a particular mental affliction. This category of meditation object is meant to "purify" or overcome such a tendency.

582 S: *dhātuprabhedaḥ*, T: *khams kyi rab tu dbye ba.* Buddhist literature contains a number of classifications that relate to the term "constituent" (S: *dhātuḥ*, T: *khams*). The most basic formulation is that of the eighteen constituents that appears in Vasubandhu's root text. However, the one that is being referred to here describes the individual as comprising these six constituents: (1) the earth element, (2) the water element,

(3) the fire element, (4) the air element, (5) space, and (6) consciousness. The four physical elements, in particular, are differentiated in terms of both inner and outer forms. The description of the inner earth and water elements corresponds exactly to the thirty-six components of the body that are listed below in note 590. The constituents of space and consciousness are contemplated as elements within the makeup of the practitioner. After listing the range of items that are to be reflected upon for this practice, Asaṅga concludes this section by saying (*ŚB*, p. 218): "When a person who is highly prone to develop pride contemplates this [formulation on the] diversity of the constituents, he [or she] will give up the notion that [his or her] body consists of a [single undifferentiated] mass and gain an awareness of its unattractiveness. This will prevent him [or her] from becoming swollen up [with a sense of self-importance and superiority] and diminish [his or her] pride. Thus, [meditation on this topic] purifies the mind [of the person] who is prone [to develop the mental affliction of pride]."

583 S: *cittasthitiḥ*, *sems gnas pa*. This term literally means "a state in which the mind remains stationary or fixed." It is a reference to the nine stages of mental stability that culminate in the attainment of quiescence. See below, pp. 163–166.

584 *ŚB*, p. 334. Put differently, neither of the last two of these seven types of person needs to cultivate a particular meditation object in order to become purified of some unfavorable mental trait that, if not overcome, will prevent him or her from developing one-pointed concentration. These two types of person are free to make use of any suitable meditation object from the outset and to apply themselves directly to the goal of developing one-pointed concentration, without first having to purify themselves of one of the five specific obstacles.

585 *PVS*, vol. 1, pp. 343–344.

586 The five kinds of desire are (1) inward sensual longing and desire for sense objects (S: *adhyātmaṃ kāmeṣu kāmacchandaḥ kāmarāgaḥ*, T: *nang gi 'dod pa rnams kyi 'dod pa la 'dun pa'i 'dod chags*); (2) outward sexual longing and desire for sense objects (S: *bahirdhā kāmeṣu maithunachando maithunarāgaḥ*, T: *phyi rol gyi 'dod pa rnams kyi 'dod pa la 'dun pa'i 'dod chags*); (3) longing and desire for a region (S: *viṣayachando viṣayarāgaḥ*, T: *yul la 'dun pa yul gyi 'dod chags*); (4) longing and desire for form (S: *rūpachando rūparāgaḥ*, T: *gzugs la 'dun pa gzugs kyi 'dod chags*); and (5) longing and desire for the perishable collection (S: *satkāyachandaḥ satkāyarāgaḥ*, T: *'jig tshogs la 'dun pa 'jig tshogs kyi chags pa*). Of these five, the first two kinds of desire are addressed below in the main body of the text. The third form of desire is attachment to what is wrongly perceived to be an attractive region in the desire realm; the fourth is attachment to the form realm; and the fifth is attachment to the formless realm in particular, but also to all three realms as a whole.

The first of the six types of unattractiveness is called "the unattractiveness of impurities" (S: *pratyaśubhatā*, T: *mi gtsang ba'i mi sdug pa nyid*). This is the antidote for the first two kinds of desire. It is discussed below in the main body of the text. The remaining five types of unattractiveness constitute the antidotes for the latter three forms of desire. They are (1) the unattractiveness of suffering (S: *duḥkhāśubhatā*, T: *sdug bsngal gyi mi sdug pa nyid*); (2) the unattractiveness of being inferior (S: *avarāśubhatā*, T: *ngan pa'i mi sdug pa nyid*); (3) relative unattractiveness (S: *āpekṣikī aśubhatā*, T: *ltos pa'i mi sdug pa nyid*); (4) the unattractiveness of the mental afflictions (S: *kleśāśubhatā*, T: *nyon mongs pa'i mi sdug pa nyid*); and (5) the unattractiveness of being perishable (S: *prabhaṅgurāśubhatā*, T: *rab tu 'jig pa'i mi sdug ba nyid*).

"The unattractiveness of suffering" refers to all forms of painful physical and mental feelings. "The unattractiveness of being inferior" refers to the understanding that the desire realm is the most inferior and misery-filled plane of existence. Meditating on these two forms of unattractiveness is the antidote for "longing and desire for a region." "Relative unattractiveness" refers to the understanding that while certain things are perceived as attractive, even they can take on an unattractive appearance when compared to other things that are much more attractive. For example, in comparison to the various levels of the formless realm, the form realm will appear unattractive. Similarly, in comparison to the state of nirvana in which the collection of perishable heaps has been terminated, even the Peak of Existence (S: *bhavāgraḥ*, T: *srid pa'i rtse mo*; i.e., the highest level of the formless realm) will appear unattractive. This third form of unattractiveness represents a specific antidote for "longing and desire for form." "The unattractiveness of the mental afflictions" refers to all the mental fetters and their seeds that occur throughout the three realms. "The unattractiveness of being perishable" refers to the impermanence, instability, untrustworthiness, and changeable nature of the five grasping heaps. These latter two forms of unattractiveness are identified as the antidote for "longing and desire for the perishable assemblage," which is to say attachment to any form of the grasping heaps within the three realms of samsaric existence.

587 In the Tibetan canon, there are two versions of the *Twenty-five-Thousand-Line Perfection of Wisdom Sutra*. One is found in the Kangyur and the other in the Tengyur. The latter is a slightly reworked version of the original sutra that identifies a correspondence between the sutra passages and the topics of the *Abhisamayālaṃkāraḥ* treatise. Sanskrit versions of the latter edition are also extant. The list of elements of the body presented here is the one found in the edition of the sutra that is contained in the Tibetan Kangyur collection. The Sanskrit list, which corresponds to the Tengyur version, contains one more item than the list in the Tibetan Kangyur edition. After item 28, it adds *lohitam* (T: *khrag rul*), which literally means "red [substance]"; the Tibetan translation of the term suggests it refers to a diseased form of blood.

588 T: *glog pa*. Both the twenty-five-thousand-line and the one-hundred-thousand-line Tibetan Kangyur versions have this term, which is the Tibetan equivalent for *rajaḥ*. The two Sanskrit editions I consulted have *carma* ("hide"); the Tibetan translation has *skyi*, which also means "hide." It is not clear how this differs from item 5, "skin" (S: *tvac*, T: *pags pa*), unless it also has a specialized meaning of "skin irritation."

589 S: *antraguṇaḥ*, T: *gnye ma*. Modern Tibetan medical texts identify this Tibetan term with the sigmoid colon, but that does not seem to have been the sense of this early usage.

590 The list of body elements found in Asaṅga's *Listeners' Level* (*ŚB*, p. 203) is somewhat different from either version of the *Perfection of Wisdom Sutra*. Asaṅga's list seems to be the one most often referenced in Tibetan commentarial literature. It includes the following thirty-six items: (1) hair of the head, (2) hair of the body, (3) fingernails and toenails, (4) teeth, (5) skin irritations and sores, (6) impurities, (7) skin, (8) flesh, (9) bones, (10) tendons, (11) tubular vessels (S: *sirā*, T: *rtsa*; for example, nerves and blood and lymph vessels), (12) kidneys, (13) heart, (14) spleen (S: *plīhakam*; the Tibetan text incorrectly has *mchin pa*, which is "liver"), (15) lungs, (16) small intestine, (17) mesentery, (18) stomach (S: *āmāśayaḥ*, T: *pho ba*; literally, "vessel for 'raw'—i.e., undigested—food"), (19) large intestine (S: *pakvāśayaḥ*, T: *long ka*; literally, "vessel for 'cooked'—i.e., digested—food"), (20) liver (S: *yakṛt*; the Tibetan text incorrectly has *mcher pa*, which is "spleen"), (21) feces, (22) tears, (23) sweat, (24)

saliva, (25) nasal mucus, (26) oily body fluid, (27) watery body fluid, (28) bone marrow, (29) fat, (30) bile, (31) phlegm, (32) pus, (33) blood, (34) brain matter, (35) cerebral membrane, and (36) urine. This list is almost identical in terminology, order, and number to the ones found in the Mūlasarvāstivāda *Vinayavastu* (vol. 2, p. 109) and the *Ratnamegha Sutra* (quoted in Śāntideva's *Śikṣāsamuccayaḥ*, pp. 115–116). The only differences are that the *Vinayavastu* does not contain "brain matter" (S: *mastakam*, T: *klad pa*) and "cerebral membrane" (S: *mastakaluṅgam*, T: *klad rgyas*), and both the *Vinayavastu* and the *Ratnamegha Sutra* include the term "urinary bladder" (S: *audaryakam*, T: *lgang pa*; cf. *MVy* entry 4028) between "large intestine" and "liver." In all three of these texts, the terms for "spleen" and "liver" seem to have been mistakenly inverted (*MVy* entries 4020 and 4021 also reproduce this error).

591 *PVS*, vol. 1, pp. 344–345.

592 S: *upacāraḥ*, T: *nye bar spyod pa*, sometimes also rendered in Tibetan as *bsnyen bkur*.

593 *AKV*, p. 896. S: *yo bhaven navako bhikṣuḥ śaikṣo 'samprāptamānasaḥ / gacched asau śivapathikāṃ hantuṃ rāgaṃ yadīcchati // tato vinīlakaṃ paśyet tataḥ paśyed vipūyakam / tato vyādhmātakaṃ paśyed asthiśaṅkalikām api*. T: *dge slong slob pa gzhon pa'i rabs / sems ma byung ba gang zhig ni / gal te 'dod chags 'joms 'dod na / des ni dur khrod 'gro bar gyis // de nas rnam par bsngos la ltos / de nas rnam par rnags la ltos / de nas rnam par bam rus pa'i / rus gong la sogs blta bar gyis.*

594 *AS*, p. 72. S: *kāye kāyānupaśyanā katamā / yā vikalpapratibimbakāyena prakṛtibimbakāyasya samatāpaśyanā*. T: *lus la lus kyi rjes su lta ba gang zhe na / rnam par rtog pa'i gzugs brnyan gyi lus dang / rang bzhin gyi gzugs kyi lus la mnyam pa nyid du lta ba gang yin pa'o*. The conceptual image of the body is one in which a practitioner imagines his or her own body as being identical in nature to the corpses that are directly observed in a cemetery. Jinaputra (*ASB*, p. 85) glosses this description as follows: "The phrase 'watching the body in relation to the body' means to observe the similarity that one body bears to another body, because [the practitioner] accurately determines the conformity that exists between [his or her] actual physical body and what is perceived about a conceptual image of that body."

595 *PVS*, vol. 1, p. 345.

596 *PVS*, vol. 1, p. 344.

597 See Part Two, p. 229.

598 See Part Two, pp. 251–252.

599 *ŚB*, pp. 212–216.

600 Asaṅga's list of the thirty-six objects present in the body is presented in note 590, above.

601 *MV*, ch. 4, v. 3. S: *karmaṇyatā sthites tatra sarvārthānāṃ samṛddhaye / pañcadoṣaprahāṇāṣṭasaṃkārāsevānvayā*. T: *der gnas las su rung ba nyid / don rnams thams cad 'byor bar 'gyur / nyes pa lnga spong 'du byed brgyad / bsten pa'i rgyu le byung ba'o.*

602 S: *karmaṇyatā*, T: *las su rung ba nyid*

603 S: *prasrabdhiḥ*, T: *shin tu sbyangs pa*. See Part Two, p. 288.

604 *MV*, ch. 4, v. 4. S: *kausīdyam avavādasya sammoṣo laya uddhavaḥ / asaṃskāro 'tha saṃskāraḥ pañca doṣā ime matāḥ*. T: *le lo dang ni gdams ngag rnams / brjed dang bying dang rgod pa dang / 'du mi byed and 'du byed de / 'di dag nyes pa lngar 'dod do.*

605 See Part Two, p. 322.

606 *Liberation in Our Hands*, Part Three, pp. 256–259.

607 In the same order, the Tibetan and Sanskrit equivalents are: (1) S: *sthāpanā*, T: *'jog pa*; (2) S: *saṃsthāpanā*, T: *rgyun du 'jog pa*; (3) S: *avasthāpanā*, T: *glan te 'jog*

pa; (4) *upasthāpanā*, T: *nye bar 'jog pa*; (5) S: *damanam*, T: *dul bar byed pa*; (6) S: *śamanam*, T: *zhi bar byed pa*; (7) S: *vyupaśamanam*, T: *rnam par zhi bar byed pa*; (8) S: *ekotīkaraṇam*, T: *rtse gcig tu byed pa*; and (9) S: *samādhānam*, T: *mnyam par 'jog pa.*

608 *MSA*, ch. 14, vv. 11–14. S: *nibadhyālambane cittaṃ tatpravedhaṃ na vikṣipet / avagamyāśu vikṣepaṃ tasmin pratiharet punaḥ // pratyātmaṃ saṃkṣipec cittam uparyupari buddhimān / tataś ca ramayec cittaṃ samādhau guṇadarśanāt // aratiṃ śamayet tasmin vikṣepadoṣadarśanāt / abhidhyādaurmanasyādīn vyutthitān śamayet tathā // tataś ca sābhisaṃskārāṃ citte svarasavāhitām / labhetānabhisaṃskārāṃ tadabhyāsāt punar yatiḥ.* T: *dmigs pa la ni sems gtad nas / de'i rgyun rnam par gyeng mi bya / rnam gyeng myur du rtogs byas nas / de la slar ni glan par bya // blo ldan gong nas gong du yang / sems ni nang du bsdu bar bya / de nas yon tan mthong ba'i phyir / ting nge 'dzin la sems gdul lo* (also *dga' bar 'gyur*) *// rnam gyeng nyes pa mthong ba'i phyir / de la mi dga' zhi bar bya / brnab sems yid mi bde la sogs / langs pa de bzhin zhi bar bya // de nas sdom brtson can gyis ni / sems la mngon par 'du byed bcas / rang gi ngang gis 'byung ba 'thob / de goms pa las 'du mi byed.*

609 See note 408.

610 S: *anāgamyam*, T: *mi lcogs pa med pa.*

611 *Liberation in Our Hands*, Part Three, pp. 262–263.

612 S: *ṣaḍvedanākāyāḥ*, T: *tshor ba'i tshogs drug.*

613 S: *kāyikī vedanā*, T: *lus kyi tshor ba.*

614 S: *caitasikī vedanā*, T: *sems kyi tshor ba.*

615 S: *svalakṣaṇam*, T: *rang gi mtshan nyid.*

616 See pp. 133–134.

617 See Part Two, p. 270.

618 S: *sāmiṣavedanā*, T: *zang zing dang bcas pa'i tshor ba.*

619 S: *nirāmiṣavedanā*, T: *zang zing med pa'i tshor ba.*

620 S: *gredhāśritavedanā*, T: *zhen pa brten pa'i tshor ba.* "Greed" here refers primarily to desire for the sense objects.

621 S: *naiṣkramyāśritavedanā*, T: *mngon par 'byung ba brten pa'i tshor ba.*

622 S: *nairvedhikī*, T: *nges par 'byed pa las byung ba.* "Penetrating insight" (S: *nirvedhaḥ*, T: *nges par 'byed pa*) is a synonym for the Seeing Path. It refers to the wisdom that directly perceives the true nature of the Four Noble Truths. The phrase "derived from penetrating insight" indicates that the primary form of this type of feeling occurs within the "pure" five heaps.

623 *ŚB*, p. 296.

624 S: *lokottaramārgaḥ*, T: *'jig rten las 'das pa'i lam.*

625 S: *laukikamārgaḥ*, T: *'jig rten pa'i lam.*

626 S: *satkāyadṛṣṭiḥ*, T: *'jig tshogs la lta ba.* See Part Two, pp. 296–301.

627 See Part Two, p. 270.

628 For example, the coarseness (S: *audārikam*, T: *rags pa*) of the desire realm refers to the many forms of adversity, misfortune, distress, and trouble that occur because of our desire and longing for the pleasure associated with the five sense objects. The relative tranquility (S: *śāntam*, T: *zhi ba*) of the first meditative absorption of the form realm refers to the absence of this coarseness in that state.

629 S: *saptamanaskarāḥ*, T: *yid la byed pa bdun.* See earlier reference to these seven on p. 140. Asaṅga also describes the insight meditation of the transcendent path in terms of another set of seven forms of mental application that have the same names. Despite the identical terminology, the nature of the two paths and their results is fundamentally different.

630 S: *lakṣaṇapratisaṃvedī*, T: *mtshan nyid so sor rig pa.*
631 S: *ādhimokṣikaḥ*, T: *mos pa las byung ba.*
632 S: *prāvivekyaḥ*, T: *rab tu dben pa.*
633 S: *ratisaṃgrāhakaḥ*, T: *dga' ba sdud pa.*
634 S: *mīmāṃsāmanaskāraḥ*, T: *spyod pa'i yid la byed pa.*
635 S: *prayoganiṣṭhaḥ*, T: *sbyor ba mthar thug pa*
636 S: *prayoganiṣṭhāphalaḥ*, T: *sbyor ba mthar thug pa'i 'bras bu.*
637 S: *samāhitabhūmikaḥ*, T: *mnyam par bzhag pa'i sa pa.* This adjective indicates that the practitioner is pursuing the first meditative absorption after having achieved quiescence.
638 This is a reference to the first of six categories that Asaṅga identifies for considering the coarseness of the desire realm.
639 S: *prahāṇamārgaḥ*, T: *spong ba'i lam.* The mental afflictions associated with the desire realm and each level of both the form and formless realms consist of nine forms. Each set of nine mental afflictions is further classified into three groups of three: three "great" forms, three "middling" forms, and three "small" forms. The great forms of the mental afflictions are the ones that are most coarse and, therefore, are eliminated first. Because the antidote to the three "great" forms of the desire realm's mental afflictions arises during this mental application, it is described as "developing an abandoning path."
640 See description of the first meditative absorption below, pp. 174–175. As Jinaputra notes later, this mental application removes the middling forms of the desire realm's mental afflictions.
641 That is, as described in the fourth mental application.
642 Asaṅga adds that this experimentation reveals that the mind still wants to enjoy sensory pleasures and lacks any inclination to turn away from them or to regard them adversely. Realizing that this means complete detachment from the desire realm has not been achieved, the practitioner renews his dedication to the goal of abandoning the remainder of the desire realm's mental afflictions.
643 S: *abhimānaḥ*, T: *mngon pa'i nga rgyal.* See Part Two, p. 294.
644 *ASB*, p. 80.
645 S: *vairāgyam*, T: *'dod chags dang bral ba.* The term should be understood as describing a condition that results from overcoming attachment for some level of samsaric existence. Here it is the result achieved through the mundane path. The transcendent path also brings about freedom from attachment that is synonymous with the Truth of Cessation.
646 There are nine principal levels of existence in samsara: the desire realm, the four levels of the form realm, and the four levels of the formless realm. It is possible to achieve freedom from attachment toward the first eight through the mundane path; however, only the transcendent path can free one from desire for the fourth and highest level of the formless realm, which is known both as "the peak of samsaric existence" (S: *bhavāgraḥ*, T: *srid pa'i rtse mo*) and "the Sphere in Which There Is Neither Conception nor Absence of Conception" (S: *naiva saṃjñā nāsaṃjñāyatanam*, T: *'du shes med 'du shes med min gyi skye mched*).
647 S: *nigrahaḥ*, T: *nyams smad pa.*
648 *AS*, p. 63.
649 S: *catasra śrāmaṇyaphalāni*, T: *dge sbyong gi tshul gyi 'bras bu bzhi.* While scriptures often describe Buddha as referring to his followers with the general term "ascetic" (S: *śramaṇaḥ*, T: *dge sbyong*), in certain contexts the term takes on a much

more specialized meaning. For instance, the *AKB* (p. 369) states: "Asceticism (S: *śrāmaṇyam*, T: *dge sbyong gyi tshul*) refers to the path that is free of the outflows (S: *anāsravo mārgaḥ*, T: *zag pa med pa'i lam*; i.e., the transcendent path), for it is by means of this [path] that one becomes a [true] ascetic in the sense of having [permanently] quelled [at least a portion of] the mental afflictions. As it is declared in a sutra: 'One is called an ascetic because he [or she] has quelled many kinds of evil and nonvirtuous entities...' and so on up to '[he or she has quelled many kinds of entities] that bring about old age and death.' Because an ordinary person (i.e., a non-Ārya) has not completely quelled [any of the mental afflictions], such an individual is not an ascetic in the ultimate sense."

650 S: *samyaktvaniyāmāvakrāntiḥ*, T: *yang dag pa nyid du nges par gyur pa la zhugs pa*. *AKB* (pp. 157, 350) states that "ultimate correctness" (S: *samyaktvam*, T: *yang dag pa nyid*) refers to nirvana, noting that a sutra declares: "the complete abandonment of desire, the complete abandonment of hatred, the complete abandonment of ignorance, and the complete abandonment of all the mental afflictions is called 'ultimate correctness.'" Attainment of the Seeing Path is described as "entry into the complete certainty of ultimate correctness" because the person who develops this transcendent path is certain of achieving nirvana. The phrase is also written in a shortened form: *niyāmāvakrāntiḥ* or the variant *nyāmāvakrāntiḥ*. The latter form, in particular, is translated into Tibetan as *skyon med pa la 'jug pa*, which means literally "entry into flawlessness," despite the fact that both terms refer to the same state. Sthiramati glosses both readings in *MVṬ* (pp. 198–199). For the second spelling, he gives the following interpretation: "Because it is the very first arising of the Ārya path that has not existed before this time, it is entry into flawlessness. A fault or a disease is called a "flaw" (S: *āmaḥ*, T: *skyon*). A state where that is absent is called "flawlessness" (S: *nyāmaḥ*, T: *skyon med pa*), like a place that is free of wind—that is to say, it is a level that is free of the outflows."

651 S: *dharmābhisamayaḥ*, T: *chos mngon par rtogs pa*.

652 Freedom from attachment toward the sense objects is achieved by attaining the first meditative absorption of the form realm. This is synonymous with the first level of "departure." Cf. Asaṅga's description that "a feeling that is related to departure is one that is associated with either the form or the formless realm, or that is consistent with absence of desire."

653 *AS*, pp. 88–89.

654 *AKV*, p. 139.

655 S: *saumanasyam*, T: *yid bde ba*.

656 S: *daurmanasyam*, T: *yid me bde ba*.

657 S: *upekṣā*, T: *btang snyoms*.

658 The equanimity associated with the four immeasurables is a state of mind in which one avoids the impartial extremes of attachment toward friends and aversion toward adversaries. The equanimity that is one of the eleven virtuous mental factors is an evenness of mind essential to developing one-pointed concentration (see Part Two, pp. 289–290).

659 *ŚB*, p. 450. S: *samyagālambanopanidhyānād ekāgrasmṛtyupanibandhād dhyānam*. T: *bsam gtan zhes bya ba ni dmigs pa la yang dag par nye bar gtod pa dang dran pa rtse gcig tu nye bar gtod pa'i phyir bsam gtan zhes bya'o*.

660 S: *viviktaṃ kāmair viviktaṃ pāpakair akuśalair dharmaiḥ savitarkaṃ savicāraṃ vivekajaṃ prītisukhaṃ prathamaṃ dhyānam upasampadya viharati*. T: *'dod pa dag las*

dben pa nyid sdig pa mi dge ba'i chos rnams las dben pa / rtog pa dang bcas pa dpyod pa dang bcas pa / dben pa las skyes pa'i dga' ba dang bde ba can bsam gtan dang po bsgrubs te gnas so.

661 S: *aṅgam*, T: *yan lag.*

662 S: *vyāpadaḥ*, T: *gnod sems.* This is the eighth of the ten nonvirtuous karmic paths. Its two main forms are described as the desire to inflict harm on another person or the wish that someone might meet with misfortune.

663 S: *vimhiṃsā*, T: *rnam par 'tshe ba.* One of the twenty secondary mental afflictions; see Part Two, p. 307.

664 S: *prītiḥ*, T: *dga' ba.*

665 S: *saumanasyam*, T: *yid bde ba.*

666 S: *sukham*, T: *bde ba.*

667 S: *praśrabdhiḥ*, T: *shin tu sbyangs pa.* See Part Two, p. 288.

668 S: *vitarkavicārāṇāṃ vyupaśamād adhyātmasamprasādāc cetasa ekotībhāvād avitarkam avicāraṃ samādhijaṃ prītisukhaṃ dvitīyaṃ dhyānam upasampadya viharati.* T: *rtog pa dang dpyod pa dang bral zhing nang rab tu dang ste / sems kyi rgyud gcig tu gyur pas / rtog pa med pa dang / dpyod pa med pa / ting nge 'dzin las skyes pa'i dga ba dang / bde ba can bsam gtan gnyis pa bsgrubs te gnas so.*

669 S: *sampratyayaḥ*, T: *yid ches pa.* This term represents one of three main kinds of faith described both in Vasubandhu's *Summary of the Five Heaps* and in Sthiramati's *Commentary* on that root text. There it is translated as "belief."

670 *AKB*, p. 440. S: *tasya hi dvitīyadhyānalābhāt samāhitabhūminiḥsaraṇe saṃpratyaya utpadyate / so 'tra adhyātmasamprasāda iti.* T: *de ni bsam gtan gnyis pa thob pa'i phyir mnyam par bzhag pa'i sa las nges par 'byung ba la yid ches pa skyes ste / de ni 'dir nang rab tu dang ba zhes bya'o.*

671 *VS*, f. 177a–177b. T: *de la nang yongs su dang ba'i chos kyi ngo bo nyid gang zhe na / smras pa / dran pa dang / shes bzhin dang / btang snyoms kyi ngo bo nyid yin no.* Tentative Sanskrit reconstruction: *tatra adhyātmasamprasādasya dharmasya svabhāvaḥ katamaḥ / āha smṛteś ca samprajanyasya ca upekṣāyāś ca svabhāvaḥ.*

672 *ŚB*, 451. S: *bhāvanābhyasāt tasyaivāvitarkāvicārāsya samādheḥ vitarkavicārasya samādheḥ savicchidrasāntarām avasthām atikramya niśchidranirāntarām avasthāṃ prāpnoti.* T: *sems kyi rgyud gcig tu gyur pas zhes bya ba ni / des bsgoms pa yongs su goms par bya ba'i phyir / rtog pa dang dpyod pa med pa'i ting nge 'dzin de nyid la rtog pa dang dpyod pas bar du gcod cing skabs su 'chad pa'i gnas skabs las yang dag par 'das te bar du gcod pa med pa dang / skabs su 'chad pa med pa'i gnas skabs thob pas na / de'i phyir sems kyi rgyud gcig tu gyur pas zhes bya ba gsungs so.*

673 S: *prīter virāgād upekṣako viharati smṛtaḥ saṃprajānan sukhaṃ ca kāyena pratisaṃvedayati yat tad āryā ācakṣate upekṣakaḥ smṛtimān sukhaṃ viharitīti niṣprītikaṃ tṛtīyaṃ dhyānam upasampadya viharati.* T: *dga' ba'i 'dod chags dang bral bas / btang snyoms la gnas shing dran pa dang shes bzhin can yin te / bde ba lus kyis myong la / 'phags pa rnams kyis gang de dran pa dang ldan pa bde ba la gnas pa / btang snyoms pa'o zhes brjod pa te / dga' ba med pa bsam gtan gsum pa bsgrubs te gnas so.*

674 Again, this is the equanimity that is evenness of mind, not the neutral feeling that is neither pleasant nor unpleasant.

675 *ŚB*, p. 453. It should be noted that the term translated as "ease" (S: *sukham*, T: *bde ba*) in the first and second meditative absorptions is the same one that is translated here as "pleasure" in relation the third meditative absorption.

676 S: *saumanasyam*, T: *yid bde ba*.

677 S: *sukhasya ca prahāṇād duḥkhasya ca prahāṇāt pūrvam eva saumanasyadaurmanasyayor astaṃgamād aduḥkhāsukham upekṣāsmṛtipariśuddhaṃ caturthaṃ dhyānam upasampadya viharati*. T: *bde ba yang spangs te / snga nas sdug bsngal yang spangs shing yid bde ba dang / yid mi bde ba yang nub pas bde ba yang ma yin / sdug bsngal yang ma yin / btang snyoms dang / dran pa yongs su dag pa bsam gtan bzhi pa sgrubs te gnas so*.

678 S: *sa sarvaśo rūpasaṃjñānāṃ samatikramāt pratighasaṃjñānāṃ astaṃgamān nānātrasaṃjñānām amanasikārād anantam ākāśam ityākāśānantyāyatanam upasampadya viharati*. T: *de rnam pa thams cad du gzugs kyi 'du shes rnams las yang dag par 'das te / thogs pa'i 'dus shes rnams nub par gyur cing / sna tshogs kyi 'du shes rnams yid la mi byed pas / nam mkha' mtha' yas so snyam nas / nam mkha' mtha' yas skye mched bsgrubs te gnas so*.

679 S: *sa sarvaśo ākāśānantyāyatanaṃ samatikramyānantaṃ vijñānam iti vijñānānantyāyatanam upasampadya viharati*. T: *de rnam pa thams cad du nam mkha' mtha' yas skye mched las yang dag par 'das te / rnam shes mtha' yas so snyam nas / rnam shes mtha' yas skye mched bsgrubs te gnas so*.

680 S: *sa sarvaśa vijñānānantyāyatanaṃ samatikramya nāsti kiṃcid ity ākiṃcanyāyatanam upasampadya viharati*. T: *de rnam pa thams cad du rnam shes mtha' yas skye mched las yang dag par 'das te / ci yang med do snyam nas ci yang med pa'i skye mched bsgrubs te gnas so*.

681 S: *sa sarvaśa ākiṃcanyāyatanaṃ samatikramya naiva saṃjñā nāsaṃjñāyatanam upasampadya viharati*. T: *de rnam pa thams cad du ci yang med pa'i skye mched las yang dag par 'das nas / 'du shes med 'du shes med min skye mched bsgrubs te gnas so*.

682 *ŚB*, p. 470.

683 See above, pp. 125–134.

684 S: *niścayaḥ*, T: *nges pa*.

685 An understanding of the full extent of the range of the truths (S: *yāvatbhāvikatā*, T: *ji snyed yod pa nyid*) means the realization that the Four Noble Truths encompass all entities that [followers of the Listeners' path] need to know (S: *sarvajñeyavastusaṃgraha āryasatyair*, T: *'phags pa'i bden pa rnams kyis shes bya'i dngos pa thams cad bsdus pa*; *ŚB*, p. 196). An understanding of the true nature of their being (S: *yathāvadbhāvikatā*, T: *ji lta ba bzhin du yod pa nyid*) means the realization of the correctness of their true and actual nature on the basis of the four kinds of reasoning: (1) reasoning about dependence (S: *apekṣāyuktiḥ*, T: *ltos pa'i rigs pa*); (2) reasoning about the performance of an action (S: *kāryakāraṇayuktiḥ*, T: *bya ba byed pa'i rigs pa*); (3) reasoning about valid evidence (S: *upapattisādhanayuktiḥ*, T: *'thad pas grub pa'i rigs pa*); and (4) reasoning about the nature of things (S: *dharmatāyuktiḥ*, T: *chos nyid kyi rigs pa*). Gyeltsab Je (*Chos mngon rgya mtsho'i snying po*, f. 175a) identifies these forms of reasoning as "the methods for developing the wisdom derived from reflection on the basis of [examining the instruction contained in] the scriptures." Reasoning about dependence recognizes that the arising of conditioned entities is dependent upon specific causal factors. Reasoning about the performance of an action recognizes that entities with distinct essential characteristics carry out their own individual actions. Reasoning about valid evidence reveals that the essential nature or other attributes of the object to be established are not inconsistent with such valid forms of knowledge as direct perception and inference. Reasoning about the nature of things recognizes that the general and unique characteristics that entities have possessed since beginningless time represent their true nature.

686 S: *aparyantaṃ jñānam*, T: *shes pa mtha' yas pa*.

687 S: *asmi mānaḥ*, T: *nga'o snyam pa'i nga rgyal.* See Part Two, pp. 293–294.

688 S: *abhisamayāya vibandhakaraḥ*, T: *mngon par rtogs pa'i bar du gcod par byed pa.*

689 This particular statement is a reference to the three "doors to liberation" (S: *trīṇi vimokṣamukhāni*, T: *rnam thar sgo gsum*). Asaṅga describes them as follows in his *Listeners' Level:* "There are three doors to liberation: emptiness, that which is not to be desired, and the signless. How are these three doors to liberation set forth? There are two [types of entities to be distinguished]: the conditioned and the unconditioned. 'Conditioned [entities]' refers to the five heaps that are related to the three realms; 'the unconditioned' refers to nirvana. These two, the conditioned and the unconditioned, do exist. That which is referred to as 'soul' (S: *ātman*, T: *bdag*), 'sentient being' (S: *sattvaḥ*, T: *sems can*), 'spirit' (S: *jīvaḥ*, T: *srog*) or 'living being' (S: *jantuḥ*, T: *skye ba po*) does not exist. By perceiving the faults and disadvantages of the conditioned, one does not long for them. Thus, the door to liberation of that which is not to be desired is established through this absence of longing [for conditioned entities]. However, nirvana is something that should be longed for, because it possesses qualities that make it worthy of being desired. It is perceived as a state of peace, goodness, and deliverance. Thus, the door to liberation of the signless is established through the fact that [nirvana] is perceived as being a state of deliverance. One does not develop longing for that which is unreal and nonexistent. Thus, the door to liberation of emptiness is established through knowing and perceiving exactly how that which does not exist is nonexistent. This is how the three doors to liberation are established" (*ŚB*, pp. 267–268).

690 S: *āryasatyānyavatīrṇaḥ*, T: *'phags pa'i bden pa dag la zhugs pa.*

691 S: *samasamālambyālambakajñānam*, T: *dmigs par bya ba dang dmigs par byed pa mnyam zhing mtshungs pa'i ye shes.*

692 S: *mṛdukṣāntisahagatam*, T: *bzod pa chung ngu dang ldan pa.* "Forbearance" is a reference to the fact that the mind accepts in a favorable manner the nature of the truths.

693 S: *mūrdhānaḥ*, T: *rtse mo dag.*

694 S: *kṣāntiḥ*, T: *bzod pa.*

695 S: *nirvikalpacittam*, T: *rnam par mi rtog pa'i sems.*

696 See above, note 650.

697 S: *laukikā agradharmāḥ*, T: *'jig rten pa'i chos kyi mchog.*

698 Sanskrit, pp. 503–506; Tibetan, ff. 192a–193a.

699 *ŚB*, p. 503.

700 *ŚB*, p. 506.

701 S: *vajropamaḥ samādhiḥ*, T: *rdo rje lta bu'i ting nge 'dzin.*

702 *ŚB*, p. 506.

703 *ŚB*, p. 510.

704 *ŚB*, p. 510. "Absolute completion" (S: *atyantaniṣṭhā*, T: *shin tu mthar thug pa nyid*) is meant to be understood as the state of having attained the ultimate result of the Hīnayāna path.

705 S: *cārasahagatam*, T: *rgyu ba dang ldan pa.* The Sanskrit noun suggests the activity of walking about, such as when monks go out from their residence to request their daily food alms, or when the walk about their compound observing mindfulness.

706 S: *vihāragatam*, T: *spyod par gtogs pa.* The original Sanskrit *vihāra* has a range of meanings, of which the most familiar Buddhist one is that of the monks' residence. However, the Tibetan equivalent here is *spyod pa*, which means "practice," suggesting that in this context it refers to an inner contemplative state. The actual list that appears below supports this interpretation.

707 See above, p. 150.

708 S: *ārakṣitasmṛtiḥ*, T: *dran pa kun tu bsrungs pa.*

709 S: *nipakasmṛtiḥ*, T: *dran pa rtag 'grus byed pa.*

710 S: *smṛtyā ārakṣitamanasaḥ*, T: *dran pas yid kun tu bsrungs pa.*

711 S: *samāvasthāvacārakaḥ*, T: *gnas skabs mnyam pa 'jog par byed pa.*

712 S: *nimittagrahī*, T: *mtshan mar 'dzin pa.* "Grasping at a sign" is described as the activity in which each of the six forms of consciousness takes hold of the objects that represent their respective "field of action." The spiritual exercise of not being one who grasps at signs means not to allow oneself to indiscriminately engage the objects of the six forms of consciousness that, because of improper attention, will cause one to develop the mental afflictions. In other words, the practitioner should cultivate restraint and discipline with regard to the objects that are allowed to enter his or her field of awareness.

713 S: *anuvyañjanagrahī*, T: *mngon rtags su 'dzin pa.* "Grasping at secondary marks" refers to the activity in which the objects that are engaged by any of the six forms of consciousness subsequently become a "field of action" for the type of deliberative mind consciousness that generates desire, hatred, or ignorance. The effort to avoid allowing this type of deliberative thought to occur is what it means to avoid being one who grasps at secondary signs.

714 *ŚB*, pp. 64–67.

715 S: *saṃkṣiptacittam*, T: *sems kun tu bsdus pa. AKB* (p. 396) records that the Western Sarvāstivādins (S: *pāścāttyāḥ*, T: *nub phyogs pa*; i.e., those who are from Gandhara, which lies to the west of Kashmir) interpret a "contracted mind" as one that is accompanied by sleep (S: *middhasaṃprayuktam*, T: *gnyid dang mtshungs par ldan pa*). The Vaibhāṣikas disagree, citing a passage from the *Jñānaprasthānam* (T: *Ye shes la 'jug pa*) which declares "A contracted (i.e., focused or concentrated) mind perceives things as they truly are." *AKB* goes on to note that the Sautrāntikas disagree with the Vaibhāṣikas, citing the sutra passage that states: "How does the mind become inwardly contracted? [It occurs with] the mind that is associated with torpor and sleep and that is associated with inward suppression [of thought] but that is not accompanied by insight." It would appear that the term "contracted" can be taken in at least two senses. Asaṅga takes it here in the positive sense to mean a mind that is well focused and concentrated in a one-pointed manner. Other scholars and traditions interpret the term as referring to a mind that is enervated and inwardly drawn to such a degree that it becomes dull, clouded, and unable to grasp an object with any clarity. Indeed, both Vasubandhu and Asaṅga define sleep as "a contraction of the mind" (S: *cetaso 'bhisaṃkṣepaḥ*, T: *sems sdud pa*).

716 S: *vikṣiptacittam*, T: *sems rnam par g.yengs pa.*

717 S: *līnaṃ cittam*, T: *sems zhum pa.*

718 S: *pragṛhītaṃ cittam*, T: *rab tu bzung ba.*

719 S: *uddhataṃ cittam*, T: *rgod pa*

720 S: *auddhatyam*, T: *rgod pa.* This is one of the twenty secondary mental afflictions; see Part Two, p. 308.

721 S: *anuddhataṃ cittam*, T: *rgod pa ma yin pa.*

722 S: *vyupaśāntaṃ cittam*, T: *sems nye bar zhi ba.*

723 S: *nivaraṇāni*, T: *sgrib pa rnams.* The following seven qualities are recognized as comprising five obstacles to the attainment of a state of composure: (1) longing for sense objects; (2) malice; (3) torpor and sleep; (4) regret and excitation; and (5) doubt.

724 S: *avyupaśāntaṃ cittam*, T: *sems nye bar zhi ba ma yin pa.*

725 S: *samāhitaṃ cittam*, T: *mnyam par bzhag pa'i sems.*

726 S: *asamāhitaṃ cittam*, T: *mnyam par ma bzhag pa'i sems.*

727 S: *subhāvitaṃ cittam*, T: *sems legs par bsgoms pa.*

728 S: *asubhāvitaṃ cittam*, T: *sems legs par bsgoms pa ma yin pa.*

729 S: *suvimuktaṃ cittam*, T: *sems shin tu rnam par grol ba.*

730 S: *asuvimuktaṃ cittam*, T: *sems shin tu rnam par grol ba ma yin pa.*

731 *ŚB*, pp. 297–298.

732 S: *nivaraṇaviśuddhibhūmim ārabhya vihāragatāni cittāni*, T: *sgrib pa rnam par dag pa'i sa las brtsams pa'i spyod par gtogs pa'i sems.*

733 S: *kleśaviśuddhim ārabhya vihāragatāni cittāni*, T: *nyon mongs pa rnam par dag pa las brtsams pa'i spyod par gtogs pa'i sems.*

734 S: *layaḥ*, T: *zhum pa*. In other texts where this Sanskrit term occurs, it is also rendered in Tibetan as *bying ba.*

735 S: *pragrahaḥ*, T: *rab tu 'dzin pa*. This is the form of effort that is applied to overcome languor.

736 S: *auddhatyam*, T: *rgod pa*. As mentioned above, this mental factor is one of the twenty secondary mental afflictions and also forms an aspect of one of the five hindrances to one-pointed concentration.

737 *ŚB*, pp. 294–295.

738 *ŚB*, p. 298.

739 The twelve bases consist of the six inner bases of the eye, ear, nose, tongue, body, and mind, and the six outer bases of [visible] form, sound, smells, tastes, tangible objects, and entities (i.e., the objects of mind consciousness). These two sets of bases are the inner and outer conditions, respectively, that cause the six primary forms of consciousness to arise. As Vasubandhu's *Summary* notes, they called "bases" (S: *āyatanam*, T: *skye mched*) "because they are the sources for the appearance of consciousness" (S: *vijñānāyadvāratvāt*, T: *rnam par shes pa'i skye ba'i sgo'i phyir*; Part Two, p. 241). For additional remarks, see also Part Two, p. 353.

740 S: *saṃyojanam*, T: *kun tu sbyor ba*. Each of the entities in this group of mental afflictions is called a fetter because it causes the grasping heaps to become reborn in samsara, thereby perpetuating one's suffering. In Asaṅga's words, "it binds one to suffering by causing suffering to come into being in the future." (S: *tena āyatyāṃ duḥkhābhinivṛttau duḥkhena saṃyujyate*, T: *des phyi ma la sdug bsngal mngon par 'grub par byed pas sdug bsngal dang kun du sbyor ro*; *AS*, p. 44). Of the nine fetters, the first one, "attachment" (S: *anunayaḥ*, T: *rjes su chags pa*), is identical with the root mental affliction "desire" (S: *rāgaḥ*, T: *'dod chags*). The "fetter of views" (S: *dṛṣṭisaṃyojanam*, T: *lta ba'i kun tu sbyor ba*) refers to the first three of the five views that are mental afflictions: (1) the perishable collection view (S: *satkāyadṛṣṭiḥ*, T: *'jig tshogs la lta ba*), (2) the view that grasps an extreme (S: *antagrāhadṛṣṭiḥ*, T: *mthar 'dzin par lta ba*), and (3) wrong view (S: *mithyādṛṣṭiḥ*, T: *log par lta ba*). The "fetter of supreme considerations" (S: *parāmarśasaṃyojanam*, T: *mchog tu 'dzin pa'i kun tu sbyor ba*) refers to the remaining two views: (1) the consideration that views are supreme (S: *dṛṣṭiparāmarśaḥ*, T: *lta ba mchog tu 'dzin pa*), and (2) the consideration that morality and asceticism are supreme (S: *śīlavrataparāmarśaḥ*, T: *tshul khrims dang brtul zhugs mchog tu 'dzin pa*; *AS*, p. 44). For more on the five views, see Part Two, pp. 296–302.

741 *ŚB*, pp. 298–299.

742 S: *saptasaṃbodhyaṅgāni*, T: *byang chub yan lag bdun*. The seven entities that make up this group are recollection, discrimination of entities (S: *dharmapravicayaḥ*, T: *chos rnam par 'byed pa*; i.e., wisdom), joy, effort, agility, concentration, and equanimity. They are recognized as being achieved when one reaches the Seeing Path.

743 *ŚB*, p. 299.

744 *ŚB*, p. 299.

745 T: *rigs can gsum*. That is, those beings who are of the lineage of the Listeners' Vehicle, the Solitary Realizers' Vehicle, and those of the Mahāyāna or Great Vehicle.

746 T: *Byang chub sems 'grel*, v. 38. T: *rang nyid nges bzhin gzhan dag la / nges pa bskyed par 'dod pa yis / rtag tu 'khrul pa med par ni / mkhas rnams rab tu 'jug pa yin*. See listing in Bibliography under Nāgārjuna.

747 *PV*, ch. 2, v. 133. S: *parokṣopeyataddhetos tadākhyānam hi duṣkaram*, T: *thabs byung de rgyu lkog gyur pa / de 'chad pa ni dka' ba yin*. The "aims" are the ultimate goals of liberation and Buddhahood, and their "causes" are the respective paths of the three vehicles.

748 S: *ajitaḥ*, T: *ma pham pa*. An epithet of the future Buddha Maitreya.

749 *Abhisamayālaṃkāraḥ*, ch. 1, v. 1. S: *yā mārgajñatayā jagatdhitakṛtāṃ lokārthasaṃpādikā*, T: *'gro la phan par byed rnams lam shes nyid kyis 'jig rten don sgrub mdzad pa gang*. The complete verse states: "I bow to that Mother of [both] the Buddha and the assembly of Listeners and Bodhisattvas, / Which, through the knowledge of all entities, leads to Peace those Listeners who desire peace; / Which, through the knowledge of the path, accomplishes the aim of the world for those who aid beings; /And which endows the Munis with the ability to teach this entire multiplicity of modes." The phrase "those who aid beings" is a reference to Bodhisattvas. The knowledge of the path (S: *mārgajñatā*, T: *lam shes pa nyid*) is one of three principal forms of knowledge that are taught in the Perfection of Wisdom sutras. It is defined in monastic study manuals (T: *yig cha*) as "the knowledge of a Mahāyāna Ārya that is supported by the direct realization of emptiness and great compassion." It has three main aspects: (1) knowledge of the path that relates to the Listeners' path; (2) knowledge of the path that relates to the Solitary Realizers' path; and (3) knowledge of the path that relates to the Mahāyāna path.

750 S: *jinajananī*, T: *rgyal ba'i yum*. An epithet of the Perfection of Wisdom sutras. These sutras, and the wisdom that is conveyed in them, are also referred to simply as "the Mother" (S: *mātā*, T: *yum*). This passage is part of a larger citation that appears in both Ārya Vimuktisena's *Abhisamayālaṃkāravṛttiḥ* (T: *rNgon rtogs rgyan gyi 'grel pa*) and Haribhadra's *Sphuṭārtham* (T: *'Grel pa don gsal*). Haribhadra attributes it to the middle-length version of the *Mother of the Conquerors*—which is to say, the *Twenty-five-Thousand-Line Perfection of Wisdom Sutra*. While the entire passage is taken word for word from the sutra, the sentences are not cited in precisely the same order as they appear there, and some of the intervening rhetorical questions are left out.

751 The remainder of this statement declares, "but he [or she] should not manifest the summit of reality (S: *bhūtakoṭir na sākṣāt kartavyā*, T: *yang dag pa'i mtha' mngon sum du mi bya*) without having fulfilled the power of prayer (S: *aparipūrya praṇidhānam*, T: *smon lam yongs su rdzogs par ma byas par*), perfected the ability to ripen sentient beings (S: *aparipācya sattvān*, T: *sems can yongs su smin par ma byas par*), and purified a Buddha field (S: *apariśodhya buddhakṣetram*, T: *sangs rgyas kyi zhing yongs su ma sbyang par*). In the present context, the phrase "should not manifest the summit

of reality" is an admonition to Bodhisattvas not to enter irreversibly into the realm of peace that terminates the suffering of conditional existence until they have perfected these three activities. Of the three, "fulfillment of prayer" means to perfect the power of virtuous prayers so that one can accomplish the welfare of beings effortlessly and spontaneously, without the need to generate any discriminative thought and while remaining in a state of one-pointed meditation on the true nature of reality. "Perfecting the ability to ripen sentient beings" means to complete the virtuous practices that will enable one to manifest emanations in a billion worlds. Each of these emanations should have the power to lead countless sentient beings to the transcendent path of Āryas with the teaching of a single verse of dharma. "Purifying a Buddha field" means to complete the virtuous causes that will enable one to create two kinds of location. One is a site where a Buddha's emanation body will give the appearance of achieving Buddhahood; the other is the extraordinary Buddha field where a great tenth-stage Bodhisattva actually does achieve complete enlightenment. Gyeltsab Darma Rinchen provides a comprehensive analysis of this topic in his *Ornament of Essential Explanations* (T: *rNam bshad snying po'i rgyan*), ff. 24b–30b.

752 *LC*, f. 9a–9b.

Chapter Four

753 *RA*, ch. 2, vv. 73cd–74. T: *bdag nyid dang ni 'jig rten 'dis / bla med byang chub thob 'dod na / de yi rtsa ba byang chub sems / ri dbang rgyal po ltar brtan dang / phyogs mthas gtugs pa'i snying rje dang / gnyis la mi brten ye shes lags*. The "you" in this verse is a reference to a king of the Sātavāhana dynasty to whom Nāgārjuna addressed the poem. The two extremes that should be avoided are those of realism and nihilism. The original Sanskrit of these lines is not extant.

754 T: *theg chen gyi 'jug sgo sems bskyed kho nar bstan pa*.

755 *MA*, ch. 1, v. 2. T: *gang phyir brtse nyid rgyal ba'i lo tog phun tshogs 'di'i / sa bon dang ni spel la chu 'dra yun rin du / longs spyod gnas la smin pa lta bur 'dod gyur pa / de phyir bdag gis dang por snying rje bstod par bgyi*.

756 S: *kaṃ ruṇaddhi*, T: *bsod nyams bsrel ba*. The first syllable of *karuṇā*, *ka*, is identified with a noun that means "ease" or "happiness." The latter two syllables (*ruṇā*) are identified with the third person present singular form of a verbal root that means "to obstruct" or "to prevent" (*rudh*). See Part Two, p. 304.

757 S: *avihiṃsā*, T: *rnam par mi 'tshe ba*.

758 S: *adveśaḥ kuśalamūlam*, T: *zhe sdang med pa'i dge ba'i rtsa ba*. See Part Two, p. 286. There are three roots of virtue. The other two are avoidance of attachment and avoidance of ignorance.

759 In addition to immeasurable compassion (S: *apramāṇakaruṇā*, T: *snying rje tshad med*), the remaining three immeasurable meditations are immeasurable equanimity (S: *apramāṇopekṣā*, T: *btang snyoms tshad med*), immeasurable loving-kindness (S: *apramāṇamaitrī*, T: *byams pa tshad med*), and immeasurable joy (S: *apramāṇamuditā*, T: *dga' ba tshad med*). They are called immeasurable states because they focus on an immeasurable number of beings and because they generate an immeasurable quantity of virtue.

760 T: *sdug bsngal dang bral 'dod kyi snying rje*.

761 T: *skyobs 'dod kyi snying rje chen po*.

762 S: *adhyāśayaḥ*, T: *lhag pa'i bsam pa*.

763 Their Sanskrit and Tibetan equivalents are, in the same order: (1) S: *sattvālambanā karuṇā*, T: *sems can la dmigs pa'i snying rje*; (2) S: *dharmālambanā karuṇā*, T: *chos la dmigs pa'i snying rje*; and (3) S: *anālambanā karuṇā*, T: *dmigs pa med pa'i snying rje*.

764 S: *ākāraḥ*, T: *rnam pa*. Tibetan commentaries often discuss mental factors in terms of their "aspect" and "object" (S: *ālambanam*, T: *dmigs pa*). The aspect of a mental factor refers to the subjective manner or form in which it apprehends its object. For instance, the "aspect" of anger refers to the quality of hostility that is felt toward some object.

765 T: *gang zag rang rkya thub pa'i rdzas yod kyis stong pa*.

766 T: *rang bzhin gyis med pa*.

767 *Elucidation of the True Intent: An Extensive Commentary on the Introduction to the Middle Way* (T: *dBu ma la 'jug pa'i rgya cher bshad pa dgongs pa rab gsal*), f. 15a.

768 *Prathamaḥ Bhāvanākramaḥ*, p. 198. S: *yadā ca duḥkhitabālapriyeṣviva duḥkhoddharaṇecchākārā svarasavāhinī sarvasattveṣu samapravṛttā kṛpā bhavati tadā sā niṣpannā bhavati mahākaruṇāvyapadeśaṃ labhate*. T: *gang gi tshe yid du 'ong ba'i bu mi bde ba bzhin du sems can thams cad la'ang sdug bsngal gtan nas byang bar 'dod pa'i rnam pa'i snying rje rang gi ngang gis 'jug pa bdag nyid kyis mtshungs par 'jug par 'gyur ba de'i tshe de rdzogs pa yin pas snying rje chen po'i ming 'thob ste*. The Tibetan translation of this passage is the one that appears in Je Tsongkapa's *Great Treatise* (*LC*, ff. 199b–200a). The version in the Tg. translation of Kamalaśīla's text differs slightly.

769 S: *araghaṭṭaḥ*, T: *zo chun rgyud*. There are several Sanskrit terms that refer to this type of machine.

770 *MA*, ch. 1, v. 3. T: *dang por nga zhes bdag la zhen gyur cing / bdag gi 'di zhes dngos la chags bskyed pa / zo chun 'phyan ltar rang dbang med pa yi / 'gro la snying rjer gyur gang de la 'dud*.

771 The twelve limbs of dependent origination are classified as forming three aspects of afflicted existence: (1) the first, eighth, and ninth limbs of ignorance, craving, and grasping, respectively, represent the mental afflictions; (2) the second and tenth limbs, called "formations" and "existence," represent two phases of karma; and (3) the remaining seven limbs—ranging from the third limb of consciousness through the seventh of feeling, along with the last two limbs of birth, and old age and death—are the result limbs that occur in samsaric rebirth. As Nāgārjuna states in his *Verses on the Essence of Dependent Origination* (S: *Pratītyasamutpādahṛdayakārikā*, v. 3), "From the three, two arise. From the two / There come seven; from the seven again / Come the three. So does this very wheel / Of existence turn round and round again" (S: *tribhyo bhavati dvandvaṃ dvandvāt prabhavanti sapta saptabhyaḥ / traya udbhavanti bhūyo bhramati tad eva tu bhavacakram*; T: *gsum po dag las gnyis 'byung ste / gnyis las bdun 'byung bdun las kyang / gsum 'byung srid pa'i 'khor lo de / nyid ni yang dang yang du 'khor*). Thus, the three limbs that are mental afflictions cause the two limbs of karma to arise. The two limbs of karma, in turn, bring about the seven that represent the suffering of samsaric existence. Those seven limbs then bring about the three mental affliction limbs again, causing the cycle to be repeated endlessly, without beginning, middle, or end.

772 *Elucidation of the True Intent: An Extensive Commentary on the Introduction to the Middle Way* (T: *dBu ma la 'jug pa'i rgya cher bshad pa dgongs pa rab gsal*), f. 12b.

773 *LC*, ff. 206b–207a. T: *byams pa dang snying rje sbyong mi shes pa'i byang chub sems dpa' bod kyis shes pa*.

774 Ibid, f. 207a. T: *dang po nas go rim du bslabs nas byed pa zhig dgos*. The annotated

edition of Je Tsongkapa's *Great Treatise* (T: *Lam rim mchan bzhi sbrags ma*, vol. 1, pp. 514–517) contains two lengthy comments on this passage that elaborate what it means to cultivate loving-kindness and compassion in a step-by-step or systematic manner. See listing in Bibliography under Ba so Chos kyi rgyal mtshan et al.

775 S: *dharmāyatanam*, T: *chos kyi skye mched*. Vasubandhu's *Summary* describes both the entity basis and the entity constituent as containing five types of object: (1) feelings, (2) conceptions, (3) the formations, (4) noninformative form, and (5) unconditioned entities. The root text also identifies four types of unconditioned entities: (1) space, (2) the nonanalytic cessation, (3) the analytic cessation, and (4) suchness (i.e., the insubstantiality of entities). Noninformative form is special type of form included in the form heap. It is further explained in Sthiramati's *Commentary*, Part Two, pp. 262–266.

776 S: *dharmadhātuḥ*, T: *chos kyi khams*

777 S: *tathatā*, T: *de bzhin nyid*. See Part Two, p. 241.

778 S: *paramārthasatyam*, T: *don dam pa'i bden pa*.

779 S: *śūnyatā*, T: *stong pa nyid*.

780 S: *tattvam*, T: *de kho na nyid*.

781 S: *bhūtakoṭiḥ*, T: *yang dag pa'i mtha'*.

782 S: *dharmadhātuḥ*, T: *chos kyi dbyings*.

783 S: *ālayavijñānam*, T: *kun gzhi rnam par shes pa*.

784 S: *kliṣṭamanas*, T: *nyon mongs pa can gyi yid*.

785 S: *pañca sarvatragāḥ*, T: *kun 'gro lnga*. The five are (1) contact, (2) attention, (3) feeling, (4) conception, and (5) volition.

786 Part Two, p. 353.

787 T: *mKhan chen byang chub sems dpa'*.

788 T: *lTa ba'i khyad par*, in *sNa tshogs* section of Tg., vol. 208 (*jo*), f. 213b.

789 *bDen pa gnyis la 'jug pa*, vv. 15–16ab. T: *stong nyid gang gis rtogs she na / de bzhin gshegs pas lung bstan zhing / chos nyid bden pa gzigs pa yi / klu sgrub slob ma zla grags yin // de las brgyud pa'i man ngag gis / chos nyid bden pa rtogs par 'gyur*.

790 T: *bka' gdams gzhung drug*. The six are (1) *Śikṣāsamuccayaḥ*, (2) *Bodhicaryāvatāraḥ*, (3) *Jātakamālā*, (4) *Udānavargaḥ*, (5) *Mahāyānasutrālaṃkāraḥ*, and (6) *Bodhisattvabhūmiḥ*.

791 T: *Bla ma gser gling pa*. The name is a reference to his homeland, which in ancient times was known as Suvarṇadvīpa or "Isle of Gold" (T: *gser gling*). The region lies within the greater Malay archipelago. It is believed that this teacher lived on the island of Sumatra, where the center of the Buddhist kingdom of Śrī Vijaya was located. This teacher's ordination name was Dharmakīrti (T: Chos kyi grags pa), not to be confused with the renowned Indian epistemologist of the same name. Lord Atiśa traveled to Suvarṇadvīpa to study with him and stayed for some twelve years.

792 *MMK*, ch. 24, vv. 8–11. S: *dve satye samupāśritya buddhānāṃ dharmadeśanā / lokasaṃvṛtisatyaṃ ca satyaṃ ca paramāthataḥ // ye 'nayor na vijānanti vibhāgaṃ satyayor dvayoḥ / te tattvaṃ na vijānanti gambhīraṃ buddhaśāsane // vyavahāram anāśritya paramārtho na deśyate / paramārtham anāgamya nirvāṇaṃ nādhigamyate // vināśayati durdṛṣṭā śūnyatā mandamedhasam / sarpo yathā durgṛhīto vidyā vā duṣprasādhitā*. T: *sangs rgyas rnams kyis chos bstan pa / bden pa gnyis la yang dag brten / 'jig rten kun rdzob bden pa dang / dam pa'i don gyi bden pa'o // gang dag bden pa de gnyis kyi / rnam dbye rnam par mi shes pa / de dag sangs rgyas bstan pa ni / zab mo'i de nyid rnam mi shes // tha snyad la ni ma brten par / dam pa'i don ni bstan mi nus / dam*

pa'i don ni ma rtogs par / mya ngan 'das pa thob mi 'gyur // stong pa nyid la lta nyes na / shes rab chung rnams phung bar 'gyur / ji ltar sbrul la gzung nyes dang / rig sngags nyes par bsgrubs pa bzhin.

793 S: *niṣprapañcasvabhāvaḥ*, T: *spros pa dang bral ba'i rang bzhin. MMK,* ch. 18, v. 9 describes one of ultimate truth's five attributes as being that which is "unelaborated by elaborations" (S: *prapañcair aprapañcitam*, T: *spros pa rnams kyis ma spros pa*). Candrakīrti (*PP,* p. 159) notes about this: "elaboration is speech, since that is what causes entities to be elaborated upon." As it is used here, *prapañca* seems to mean "an inappropriate and excessive verbal amplification of meaning"—hence, [inappropriate verbal] "elaboration."

794 *PP*, p. 215.

795 *YṢ*, v. 35. T: *mya ngan 'das pa bden gcig pur / rgyal ba rnams kyis gang gsungs pa / de tshe lhag ma log min zhes / mkhas pa su zhig rtog par byed.*

796 *dBu ma la 'jug pa'i bshad pa*, ff. 275b–276a.

797 *MMK*, ch. 24, v. 14. S: *sarvaṃ ca yujyate tasya śūnyatā yasya yujyate / sarvaṃ na yujyate tasya śūnyaṃ yasya na yujyate.* T: *gang la stong pa nyid rung ba / de la thams cad rung bar 'gyur / gang la stong nyid mi rung ba / de la thams cad rung mi 'gyur.*

798 In the opening six verses of this same chapter, Nāgārjuna portrays Buddhist realists as arguing that acceptance of the doctrine of emptiness leads necessarily to a repudiation of the Four Noble Truths, the Three Jewels, and indeed all conventional description of ordinary experience. In his commentary on these verses, Candrakīrti provides a lengthy description of the nature of these topics. At this later point in the chapter, the rejoinder is made that, on the contrary, it is only the Mādhyamika School that can give a coherent account of these topics.

799 *PP*, p. 218.

800 S: *śūnyaṃ ca śāntam anutpādam ayaṃ avijānad eva jagad udbhramatī / teṣām upāyanayayuktiśatair avatārayasyapi kṛpālutayā*; T: *stong pa zhi ba skye ba med pa'i tshul / mi shes pas ni 'gro ba 'khyam gyur pa / de dag thugs rje nga' bas thabs tshul dang / rigs pa brgya dag gis ni 'dzud par mdzad.* This verse is quoted in *PP*, p. 193.

801 S: *neyārtham*, T: *drang ba'i don.*

802 S: *nītārtham*, T: *nges pa'i don.*

803 S: *rathī*, T: *shing rta'i srol 'byed.* The term literally means "charioteer," and by extension suggests a champion or hero. In the present context, the term means something like "philosophical innovator," and is generally applied to Nāgārjuna and Asaṅga, who are recognized as the two major innovators of Mahāyāna Buddhist philosophy.

804 *Drang nges legs bshad snying po*, f. 2a–2b. The verse cited at the end of this passage is found in the *Śrī Mahābalatantrarāja*. Śāntarakṣita also quotes it in his survey of Indian philosophy, *Tattvasaṃgrahaḥ* (v. 3,587). S: *tāpāc chedāc ca nikaṣāt suvarṇam iva paṇḍitaiḥ / parīkṣya bhikṣavo grāhyaṃ madvaco na tu gauravāt.* T: *dge slong dag gam mkhas rnams kyis / bsregs bcad brdar ba'i gser bzhin du / legs par brtags la nga yi bka' / blang bar bya yi gus phyir min.* In another verse (v. 3,343), Śāntarakṣita again refers to the analogy of testing gold by means of the three actions of burning, cutting, and rubbing, and, in his commentary on the verse, Kamalaśīla makes a correlation between these three techniques and the three forms of investigation that enable one to determine the authoritativeness of the Buddha's word (see above, pp. 84–89). He compares the act of testing gold by burning it to the exercise of examining Buddha's teachings on the objects of direct perception; the technique of rubbing gold to the type of inference that is based on the nature of entities (S: *vastubalapravṛttānu-*

mānam, T: *dngos po stobs zhugs kyi rjes dpag*); and the act of cutting gold to the examination of the overall consistency of the Buddha's teachings on "extremely hidden" objects that lie beyond ordinary comprehension.

805 This parenthetical phrase does not appear in the Tibetan translation.

806 *PP*, p. 152.

807 *CŚ*, ch. 8, v. 15. S: *vāraṇaṃ prāg apuṇyasya madhye vāraṇam ātmanaḥ / sarvasya vāraṇaṃ paścād yo jānite sa buddhimān.* T: *bsod nams min pa dang por bzlog / bar du bdag ni bzlog pa dang / phyi nas lta zhig kun bzlog pa / gang gis shes de mkhas pa yin.*

808 *PP*, p. 153. The final three verses are from *RA*, ch. 4, vv. 94–96. S: *yathaiva vaiyākaraṇo mātṛkām api pāṭhayet / buddho 'vadat tathā dharmaṃ vineyānāṃ yathākṣamam // keṣāṃ cid avadad dharmaṃ pāpebhyo vinivṛttaye / keṣāṃ cit puṇyasiddhyarthaṃ keṣāṃ cid dvayaniśritam // dvayāniśritam ekeṣāṃ gambhīraṃ bhīrubhīṣaṇam / śūnyatākaruṇāgarbham ekeṣāṃ bodhisādhanam.* T: *brda sprod pa dag ji lta bur / yi ge'i phyi mo'ang klog 'jug ltar / de bzhin sangs rgyas gdul bya la / ji tsam bzod pa'i chos ston to // kha cig la ni sdig pa las / rnam par bzlog phyir chos ston te / kha cig bsod nams 'grub bya'i phyir / kha cig la ni gnyis brten pa // kha cig la ni gnyis mi brten / zab mo khu 'phrigs can 'jigs pa / stong nyid snying rje'i snying po can / byang chub bsgrub pa kha cig la.*

809 This is a reference to a passage from the *Sutra on the Ten Levels* (S: *Daśabhūmisūtram*, T: *Sa bcu pa'i mdo*).

810 That is, the first level Bodhisattva Ārya would not merely surpass the Hīnayāna Arhats on the basis of the spirituality that is represented by his or her aspiration to achieve supreme enlightenment.

811 S: *anuśayaḥ*, T: *phra rgyas*. This is a technical term that is synonymous with the more familiar "mental affliction" (S: *kleśaḥ*, T: *nyon mongs*). The verbal root from which it derives means "to adhere closely" to something. The Tibetan translation, literally "that which grows in a subtle manner," was formulated on the basis of several classical interpretations of the term (see verse cited below). Thus, as it is being used here, "attachment" should not be viewed as a synonym for the specific mental affliction of desire (S: *rāgaḥ*, T: *'dod chags*). Vasubandhu describes the term in his *Treasury of Higher Learning* (*AK*, ch. 5, v. 39): "They are called 'attachments'/ Because they are minute and follow closely after,/ Because they grow stronger in two ways,/ And because they attach themselves." (S: *aṇavo 'nugatāś caite dvidhā cāpyanuśerate / anubadhnanti yasmāc ca tasmād anuśayāḥ smṛtāḥ.* T: *gang phyir de dag phra ba dang / rjes 'brel rnam gnyis rgyas 'gyur dang / rjes su 'brang bas de yi phyir / phra rgyas dag tu bshad pa yin.*) In his subcommentary (vol. 1, p. 17), Yaśomitra glosses *anuśerate* ("[they] grow stronger") as meaning "to obtain growth" (S: *puṣṭim labhante*) or to "obtain a stable resting place" (S: *pratiṣṭhāṃ labhante*).

812 f. 226b.

813 See above, pp. 100–102.

814 *Śikṣāsamuccayaḥ*, p. 37.

815 Ibid., p. 41. S: *śūnyatāyāś ca kathanāt sattveṣvakṛtabuddhiṣu*, T: *blo sbyangs ma byas sems can la / stong pa nyid ni brjod pa dang.*

816 *CŚ*, ch. 8, v. 18. S: *śūnyatā puṇyakāmena vaktavyā na hi sarvadā / nanu prayuktam asthāne jāyate viṣam auṣadham.* T: *bsod nams 'dod pas stong pa nyid / kun tshe brjod par bya min te / gnas ma yin par sbyar ba'i sman / dug tu 'gyur ba ma yin nam.*

817 *AA*, ch. 1, vv. 4–5. S: *prajñāpāramitāṣṭābhiḥ padārthaiḥ samudīritā / sarvākārajñatā mārgajñatā sarvajñatā tataḥ // sarvākārābhisaṃbodho mūrdhaprāpto 'nupūrvikaḥ /*

ekakṣaṇābhisaṃbodho dharmakāyaś ca te 'ṣṭadhā. T: *shes rab pha rol phyin pa ni / dngos po brgyad kyis yang dag bshad / rnam kun mkhyen nyid lam shes nyid / de nas thams cad shes pa nyid // rnam kun mngon rdzogs rtogs pa dang / rtse mor phyin dang mthar gyis pa / skad cig gcig mngon rdzogs byang chub / chos kyi sku dang de rnam brgyad.*

818 *AAA*, p. 277.

819 See pp. 190–192.

820 S: *sarvavastujñatā*, T: *gzhi thams cad shes pa nyid.*

821 T: *don bdun bcu.*

822 *Droplets of Nectar: An Explanation of the Seventy Topics* (T: *Don bdun bcu'i rnam bshad brdud rtsi'i gzegs ma*), first wood-block edition published in Tibet in 1950.

823 T: mKhas grub bstan pa dar rgyas (1493–1568).

824 ff. 2b–3a.

825 T: *rnal sbyor spyod pa'i dbu ma rang rgyud pa.*

826 S: *vipakṣikā sarvavastujñatā*, T: *mi mthun phyogs kyi gzhi shes.*

827 S: *prātipakṣikā sarvavastujñatā*, T: *gnyen po'i phyogs kyi gzhi shes.*

828 *AA*, ch. 3, v. 1. S: *nāpare na pare tīre nāntarāle tayoḥ sthitā / adhvanāṃ samatājñānāt prajñāpāramitā matā.* T: *tshu rol pha rol mtha' la min / de dag bar na mi gnas pa / dus rnams mnyam pa nyid shes phyir / shes rab pha rol phyin par 'dod.*

829 S: *bhavāntaḥ*, T: *srid pa'i mtha'.*

830 S: *śamāntaḥ*, T: *zhi ba'i mtha'.*

831 The general definition of "Perfection of Wisdom" is a Mahāyāna form of knowledge that realizes emptiness and is supported by the Mahāyāna enlightenment mind. Of the various uses of term, one is the threefold formulation of (1) scriptural Perfection of Wisdom (T: *gzhung sher phyin*), (2) path form of Perfection of Wisdom (T: *lam sher phyin*), and (3) result form of Perfection of Wisdom (T: *'bras bu sher phyin*). The first is defined as the collection of Mahāyāna scriptures that unerringly teach the Mahāyāna path and its result as their principal topic. This includes all the versions of the *Perfection of Wisdom Sutras*—especially the extensive, medium, and short versions in 100,000, 25,000, and 8,000 lines, respectively—as well as other Mahāyāna scriptures. The path form of Perfection of Wisdom is defined as a Bodhisattva's knowledge that is supported by the two qualities of extraordinary wisdom and means. The result form of Perfection of Wisdom is defined as the ultimate knowledge that is qualified by three characteristics. The three characteristics are (1) it is present only in the mind of a fully enlightened Buddha; (2) its essence is transcendent nondual wisdom; and (3) it is illusory in the sense that it is not self-existent. This third form is the actual Perfection of Wisdom; the scriptural and path forms are only nominal forms of Perfection of Wisdom, because they do not constitute ultimate wisdom. As Dignāga states in his *Essence of Perfection of Wisdom* (*Prajñāpāramitāpiṇḍārthaḥ*, v. 1): "Perfection of Wisdom is the nondual / Awareness that is the Tathāgata. / Scripture and path receive that term / Because that goal is their purpose." (S: *prajñāpāramitā jñānam advayaṃ sā tathāgataḥ / sādhyā tādarthyayogena tācchabdyaṃ granthamārgayoḥ.* T: *shes rab pha rol phyin gnyis med / ye shes de ni de bzhin gshegs / bsgrub bya don de dang ldan pas / gzhung lam dag la de sgra yin.* The debate manuals observe a number of distinctions in seeking to establish the precise sense of these three forms of Perfection of Wisdom.

832 S: *apratiṣṭhitanirvāṇam*, T: *mi gnas pa'i mya ngan las 'das pa.* Buddhahood is referred to by this term because it does not abide in either of the extremes of samsaric existence or Hīnayāna nirvana.

833 *rNam bshad snying po'i rgyan*, f. 181a–181b.
834 S: *vastu*, T: *dngos po*.
835 S: *avastu*, T: *dngos pa med pa*.
836 *rNam bshad snying po'i rgyan*, f. 182a–182b.
837 S: *dhīman*, T: *blo ldan*. This is a reference to skillful and knowledgeable Bodhisattva practitioners.
838 "Others" here is primarily a reference to Hīnayāna followers of the Listeners' Vehicle.
839 *MSA*, ch. 18, vv. 43–45. S: *caturdaśabhir ākāraiḥ smṛtyupasthānabhāvanā / dhīmatām asamatvāt sā tad anyebho viśiṣyate // niśrayāt pratipakṣāc ca avatārāt tathaiva ca / ālambanamanaskāraprāptitaś ca viśiṣyate // ānukūlyānuvṛttibhyāṃ parijñotpattito 'parā / mātrayā paramatvena bhāvanāsamudāgamāt*. T: *blo ldan dran pa nyer bzhag pa / bsgom pa rnam pa bcu bzhi yis / mtshungs pa med pa'i phyir na de / de las gzhan las khyad par 'phags // rten dang gnyen po dag dang ni / de bzhin rjes su 'jug pa dang / dmigs pa dang ni yid byed dang / thob pas bsgom pa khyad par 'phags // mthun dang rjes su 'jug pa dang / yongs su shes dang skye ba dang / chen po dang ni mchog nyid dang / bsgom pa yang dag 'grub pas gzhan*.
840 This is a reference to the verse that was discussed earlier; see pp. 143–147. What distinguishes the Mahāyāna form is that this knowledge is also used to teach others how to gain an understanding of the Four Noble Truths.
841 That is, the Bodhisattva considers not only his or her own condition but that of all sentient beings as well.
842 *MSV*, pp. 135–136.
843 This passage occurs in the *Twenty-five-Thousand-Line Perfection of Wisdom Sutra;* see above, p. 148.
844 S: *Dharmasaṃgītisūtram*, T: *Chos yang dag par sdud pa'i mdo*. Quoted in Śāntideva's *Compendium of Training* (*Śikṣāsamuccayaḥ*), p. 124.
845 S: *prāptitaḥ*, T: *thob pas*.
846 "Separation" (S: *visaṃyogaḥ*, T: *bral ba*) here refers to the nirvana that represents liberation from samsaric existence.
847 S: *phenapiṇḍaḥ*, T: *dbu ba'i gong bu*.
848 In other words, while the Bodhisattva does not renounce the body as something to be abandoned categorically and does willingly continue to take birth in samsara, he or she still does also recognize that one must sacrifice the body repeatedly and in myriad ways for the sake of sentient beings as part of the effort to accumulate the merit that is required to achieve a Buddha's three bodies.
849 *mDo sde rgyan gyi 'grel bshad*, in *Sems tsam* section of Tg., vol. 126 (*tsi*), f. 15a–15b.
850 S: *ānukūlyam*, T: *rjes su mthun pa*.
851 These are two of the "four qualities that make one a spiritual ascetic" (S: *catvāraḥ śramaṇakārakadharmāḥ*, T: *dge sbyong du byed pa'i chos bzhi*). The other two are not to respond to anger with anger, and not to respond to criticism with criticism. Monks and nuns accept these four principles when they take ordination.
852 *mDo sde rgyan gyi 'grel bshad*, f. 15b.
853 S: *paramatvam*, T: *mchog nyid*.
854 S: *miśropamiśrākāraḥ*, T: *dres pa dang nye bar dres pa'i rnam pa*.
855 *mDo sde rgyan gyi 'grel bshad*, ff. 16b–17a.
856 In *dKon rtsegs* section of the Kg, vol. 44 (*cha*), ff. 225b–226a. This passage is also quoted in Śāntideva's *Śikṣāsamuccayaḥ*, ch. 13, which is devoted to the four closely placed recollections.

857 S: *akṣaṇam*, T: *mi khom pa*. See above, note 148, where the eight inopportune states are described in verses from Nāgārjuna's *Letter to a Friend*.

858 *Blo gros mi zad pas bstan pa'i mdo*, in *mDo sde* section of Kg., vol. 60 (*ma*), f. 157a.

Part Two

A Summary of the Five Heaps

1 Sthiramati (see Part Two, p. 343) reports the existence of Sanskrit editions of the root text that have a variant reading for the second reason that appears here. That reading is: "[That very consciousness is called the 'storehouse consciousness' because of . . .] its quality of being the storehouse and cause of belief in a self."

A Detailed Commentary on the Summary of the Five Heaps

2 S: *prakaraṇam*, T: *rab tu byed pa*. It is difficult to find a single term that precisely captures the sense of this type of composition. Vasubandhu wrote several texts in this genre. Only those written in prose, like the present work and his *Summary That Establishes the Nature of Karma* (S: *Karmasiddhiprakaraṇam*, T: *las grub pa'i rab tu byed pa*) include the term in their title; however, Sthiramati also refers to Vasubandhu's *Thirty Verses* (S: *Triṃśikā*, T: *Sum cu pa*) as a *prakaraṇam*, so the same would also seem to apply to his *Twenty Verses* (S: *Viṃśatikā*, T: *Nyi shu pa*). Their main characteristic is that of being a very concise, even aphoristic, presentation of a specific subject. The Buddhist logician Dharmakīrti also wrote several works in this style, such as his *Drop of Reasoning* (S: *Nyāyabinduḥ*, T: *Rigs pa'i thigs pa*).

3 S: *Yogācārabhūmiḥ*, T: *rNal 'byor spyod pa'i sa*. This is Asaṅga's master work on all aspects of Buddhist doctrine and practice. The Tibetan tradition refers to this work along with other related texts by Asaṅga as the Five Sections on Levels (T: *sa sde lnga*). For a list of the five divisions of this collection and a description of their contents, see Part One, Chapter One, note 28.

4 S: *udghāṭitajñaḥ*, T: *mgo smos pas go ba*. Such persons would find detailed explanations unnecessary and perhaps even tedious. They are contrasted with "one who learns by elaboration" (S: *vipañcitajñaḥ*, T: *spros pas go ba*)—that is, a person who learns best when presented with a detailed explanation of a subject.

5 S: *grantham*, T: *le'u grangs rgya cher byas pa*.

6 S: *pravrajitaḥ*, T: *rab tu byung ba*. The terms means literally, "one who has gone forth"—that is, one who has left the householder state and entered that of a homeless ascetic. More specifically, it refers to a person who has taken the vows of a Buddhist monk or nun.

7 S: *ācāryaḥ*, T: *slob dpon*. This is a title that means "learned teacher"; in this instance it refers to Vasubandhu.

8 S: *vaiśāradyam*, T: *mi 'jigs pa*. While this is the same term that is used to describe four kinds of fearlessness that a Buddha possesses, here it refers to the self-confidence of a learned scholar. The last chapter of Asaṅga's *Compendium of Higher Learning* (S: *Abhidharmasamuccayaḥ*, T: *mNgon pa kun las btus pa*) investigates the topic of proper discourse (S: *sāṃkathyam*, T: *'bel ba'i gtam*) and includes this quality among those that represent "ornaments of public speaking" (S: *vādālaṃkāraḥ*, T: *smra ba'i rgyan*). Jinaputra's commentary to the *Compendium of Higher Learning* (S: p. 153;

T: vol. 56 [*li*], f. 289a) explains the term with this statement: "Fearlessness is a person's ability to speak without apprehension or uneasiness even in the presence of a group of learned individuals who are intent on hearing numerous illustrative statements" (S: *vaiśāradyam anekodāhārābhiniviṣṭavidvajjanasamāvarte 'pi bruvato nirāsthāgatavyathatā*, T: *mi 'jigs pa ni dper brjod du ma la mngon par zhen pa can mkhas pa 'dus par yang smra zhing bag tsha ba med la zhum pa med pa'o*).

9 The terms "impure" and "pure" are somewhat loose translations of a pair of technical Buddhist expressions that literally mean "related to the outflows" (S: *sāsravaḥ*, T: *zag bcas*) and "unrelated to the outflows" (S: *anāsravaḥ*, T: *zag pa med pa*). "Outflow" (S: *āsravaḥ*, T: *zag pa*) is a synonym for mental affliction (S: *kleśaḥ*, T: *nyon mongs*). The Vaibhāṣika description that appears in the *Commentary to the Treasury of Higher Learning* (S: *Abhidharmakośabhāṣyam*, in explanation of ch. 5, v. 40 of the root text) is that the mental afflictions are outflows in the sense that they flow out through the "wounds" of the six inner bases (S: *āyatanam*, T: *skye mched*) of the eye, etc., reaching everywhere from the Peak of Existence down to Avīci Hell. Vasubandhu then presents an alternative explanation that he considers preferable: "The mental afflictions are called 'outflows' because they cause the mind continuum to flow along—that is, go forth (S: *gaccanti*, T: *'gro ba*)—toward objects." He also explains that the expression "related to the outflows" applies to all conditioned entities (S: *saṃskṛtadharmāḥ*, T: *'dus byas kyi chos rnams*), with the exception of the Truth of the Path, because of their capacity to cause the mental afflictions to become stronger (*Treasury of Higher Learning*, S: *Abhidharmakośakārikā*, ch. 1, v. 4). See also below, pp. 360-361.

Asaṅga (*AS*, p. 49) presents the following description of the term "outflow": "There are three types of outflows: the desire-outflows (that is, all the mental afflictions of the desire realm with the exception of ignorance), the existence-outflows (all the mental afflictions of the form and formless realms with the exception of ignorance), and the ignorance-outflows (the ignorance of all three realms). They are called 'outflows' because they cause the mind to flow out—that is, go forth (S: *visāram*, T: *'phro ba*)—[toward various kinds of objects]. How, then, do they do this? The desire-outflows cause a going forth that occurs in an outward manner; the existence-outflows cause a going forth that occurs in an inward manner; and the ignorance-outflows constitute the basis for both types of going forth."

The expression "pure entities" (S: *anāsravadharmāḥ*, T: *zag pa med pa'i chos rnams*) refers principally to the Truth of the Path and the Truth of Cessation; however, only the Truth of the Path forms part of the classification of the five heaps. The Truth of Cessation is not included in the five heaps because it is not a conditioned entity; however, it is included in the formulation of the twelve bases and the eighteen constituents. See below, pp. 351-352, where it is referred to by the expression "analytic cessation."

10 S: *bālaḥ*, T: *byis pa*. This term and several others, like "ordinary person" (S: *pṛthagjanaḥ*, T: *so so skye bo*), refer to beings who have not achieved the transcendent realization that defines one as having become a Buddhist saint or Ārya (S: *āryaḥ*, T: *'phags pa*).

11 S: *ātmātmīyagrāhaḥ*, T: *bdag dang bdag gir 'dzin pa*. This phrase describes the mistaken belief that one's personal being constitutes a real self and that other entities pertain to that self. Because it is identified as the source of samsaric existence, this belief is also a fundamental error that the Buddha's teaching seeks to remove. The technical term for this root mental affliction is the "view of the perishable assemblage" (S:

satkāyadṛṣṭiḥ, T: *'jig tshogs la lta ba*). See the discussion of this mental affliction below, pp. 296–301.

12 "Inner form" refers to the five sense faculties of the eye, etc.; they are the agents for the activities of seeing, hearing, and so forth. "Outer form" refers to the objects perceived by the senses. Both objects are considered "mine" in that they are associated with the concept of a subjective self, as in "I perceive with 'my' eyes," and "That object is 'mine.'"

13 S: *ālayavijñānam*, T: *kun gzhi rnam par shes pa*. Asaṅga's Mind Only School (S: *cittamātra*, T: *sems tsam pa*) holds the doctrine that there are eight types of consciousness. The storehouse consciousness, in particular, is discussed below, pp. 328–344. In this school, only neutral feelings accompany the storehouse consciousness.

14 S: *vyavaharati*, T: *tha snyad 'dogs pa*. In his commentary to Asaṅga's *Compendium of Higher Learning*, Jinaputra (*ASB*, p. 2) glosses this phrase as: "to make known by means of expressions" (S: *abhilāpaiḥ prāpayati*, T: *brjod pas go bar byed pa*). This mental factor can be said to "name" objects in the sense that it identifies what they are. When a blue object is perceived, the action of this mental factor is to generate the thought, "This is blue."

15 S: *saṃskārāḥ*, T: *'du byed rnams*. This is principally a reference to the virtuous and nonvirtuous mental factors that are included in the formations heap. See below, pp. 273–326.

16 S: *sapratighaḥ*, T: *thogs pa dang bcas pa*. See discussion of this term below, pp. 359–360.

17 S: *āśrayaḥ*, T: *gnas*. This is a reference to the five sense faculties of the eye, etc.

18 S: *pracāraḥ*, T: *rgyu ba*. This term has a range of meanings, including "roaming" and "wandering," which the Tibetan seems to mirror. However, here the meaning is more that of the manner in which the mental states become apparent or make themselves evident.

19 S: *nimittodgrahaḥ*, T: *mtshan mar 'dzin pa*. See explanation of this phrase below, p. 271.

20 S: *saṃskāralakṣaṇam*, T: *'du byed pa'i mtshan nyid*. Yaśomitra (*AKV*, p. 66) illustrates this quality in terms of such thoughts as "May I be happy," and "May I not be unhappy."

21 Yaśomitra (*AKV*, p. 66) identifies this subtlety as "the mere perception or apprehension [of an object]" (S: *upalabdhimātralakṣaṇam*, T: *dmigs pa tsam gyi mtshan nyid*).

22 These two terms each refer to a class of Sanskrit compound. The Sanskrit expression *rūpaskandhaḥ* ("form heap") is a compound and the present discussion is an investigation of what type of compound it represents. Because the text relies on principles of Sanskrit grammar, I have retained the original terms. The term *samānādhikaraṇa* (T: *gzhi mthun pa*) here denotes an appositional compound. *Tatpuruṣa* (T: *de'i skyes bu*) literally means "that [person's] man" and is the name for a determinative compound.

23 T: *phung po*. This is the original Sanskrit for the Buddhist technical term that is being translated as "heap," as in the phrase "five grasping heaps." See below, p. 346 and note 563, for a discussion of several views on its meaning.

24 S: *rāśiḥ*, T: *spungs pa*. This is the classic explanation of what the term *skandha* literally means.

25 S: **devadattamātulaḥ, T: lhas byin gyi zhang po*. The original Sanskrit is a compound consisting of two nouns in which there is no explicit indication of the grammatical

relation between them. The reader should recognize that this phrase and all those set in quotes in this paragraph and the next one are also compounds in the original Sanskrit text.

26 The sixth grammatical case is the genitive or possessive case.

27 S: **rūpakṛtadehaḥ*, T: *gzugs su byas pa'i lus.*

28 S: **rūpāpūrvaḥ*, T: *gzugs kyi snga na med pa.*

29 S: *upādāya rūpam*, T: *rgyur byas pa'i gzugs.*

30 S: *audārikatvam*, T: *gtos che ba. AKB* (p. 8) has a phrase that parallels the one that appears here, which allows the following tentative reconstruction: **bhūtānāṃ mahattvaṃ sarvopādāyarūpāśrayatvenaudārikatvāt.* The Sanskrit adjective *audārikam* often means "coarse" (T: *rags pa*) as opposed to "fine" or "subtle" (S: *sūkṣmam*, T: *phra ba*); however, Yaśomitra (*AKV*, p. 42) glosses it here in the form of a substantive noun as being equivalent to "greatness" (S: *mahattvam*, T: *che ba nyid*). Thus, the term as being used here seems to suggest the "great consequence" of the elements.

31 Hardness, fluidity, heat, and motility are recognized as the essential attributes of earth, water, fire, and air, respectively. See discussion below.

32 T: *'byung ba rnams.* This is the plural form of the word for "element" (S: *bhūtaḥ*).

33 The past participle of the Sanskrit verbal root *bhū*, which means variously "to come into being," "to exist," "to be," etc., is the same word as the Sanskrit noun for the word "element" (S: *bhūtaḥ*).

34 This interpretation alludes to the Buddhist doctrine that the physical world is produced by the collective karma of sentient beings, not the act of a divine creator. This explanation again centers on the Sanskrit root *bhū*. In short, it states they are called "elements" because they have always existed.

35 Sthiramati's point seems to be that there should be no disagreement over what the elements are since their names are well known, as evidenced by their occurrence in a variety of ordinary expressions like the example presented here.

36 S: *dhṛtiḥ*, T: *brten pa.* That is, support in the sense of holding up an object or keeping it from falling.

37 S: *saṃgrahaḥ*, T: *sdud pa.* Cohesion in the sense of holding together a mass or not allowing it to separate and scatter.

38 S: *paktiḥ*, T: *smin pa.* The action of fire is not simply that of heating; in fact, the basic signification of the verbal root from which the term is derived literally means "to cook." This root also includes a range of other meanings, such as "burn," "bake," "digest," "ripen," or "mature," as well as "develop" or "transform." Thus, the fire constituent is recognized as the principal agent or catalyst in chemical reactions that bring about a change in physical properties. In combination with the air constituent, it is also a principal factor in the growth and development of the bodies of animate beings and of plant life. In this paragraph, the action of the fire constituent in ordinary rocks, water, and wind, respectively, is described as causing dryness and the development of a lotus blossom.

39 S: *vyūhanam*, T: *skyod par byed pa.* See below where this action is described as having two forms.

40 S: *avakāśam dadāti*, T: *go 'byed pa.* The suggestion here is that space performs the action of providing the locus in which physical things can exist.

41 S: *upādāya.* This Sanskrit term is translated into Tibetan as *rgyur byas pa* ("serving as a cause") when describing how derivative form arises from the great elements. In other contexts it is rendered in Tibetan as *brten nas* ("in dependence on"). The analogy

that is translated here as "fire is derived from fuel" appears in the Tibetan text as *shing rgyur byas nas me byung ba*. Elsewhere this same phrase is translated into Tibetan as *shing la brten nas me byung ba*, which means literally "fire arises in dependence on fuel." This analogy is used by both Vasubandhu and Candrakīrti to describe the relationship between the nominal self and the five heaps. Thus, it is said that the existence of the nominal self "is ascribed in dependence on the heaps" (S: *skandhān upādāya prajñāptiḥ*, T: *phung po la brten nas btags pa*).

42 S: *jananahetuḥ*, T: *bskyed pa'i rgyu*. The elements are the cause from which derivative form arises.

43 S: *niśrayahetuḥ*, T: *rten gyi rgyu*. Yaśomitra explains this cause by saying that, once derivative form has arisen, it conforms to the elements, as a student does when relying on a teacher, etc. (*AKV*, p. 39).

44 S: *pratiṣṭhāhetuḥ*, T: *gnas pa'i rgyu*. Yaśomitra explains this cause as constituting the nature of a substratum, like a wall on which a painting has been drawn (*AKV*, p. 39).

45 S: *upastambhahetuḥ*, T: *rton pa'i rgyu*.

46 S: *upabṛṃhaṇahetuḥ*, T: *'phel ba'i rgyu*. The strengthening of the elements simultaneously brings a strengthening of derivative form.

47 S: *dhātuḥ*, T: *khams*. Based on a similar phrase in *AKB* (p. 8), this statement can be tentatively reconstructed as **svalakṣaṇopādāyarūpadhāraṇād pṛthvyādīnyeva dhātavaḥ*.

48 See the traditional classification of all entities into eighteen constituents that appears below, pp. 353–355.

49 *AKB* (p. 9): "That is, those who are pointing out the earth [element] are [in fact] pointing to color and shape" (S: *tathā hi pṛthvīṃ darśayanto varṇaṃ saṃsthānaṃ darśayanti*).

50 S: **kharatvam*, T: *sra ba nyid*, based on *AK*; *AS* has *kaṭhiṇatā*; *MVy* has *khakkhaṭatvam*.

51 T: *mkhrang ba*.

52 T: *'thas pa*.

53 S: **snehatvam*, T: *gzher ba nyid*. Sanskrit is conjectural; the Tibetan term is variously used to translate such Sanskrit words as *dravatvam*, *snehatvam*, and even *nisyandatā*.

54 This is a reference to the action (S: *karma*, T: *las*) exerted by the water constituent. Cohesion (S: *saṃgrahaḥ*, T: *sdud pa*) is meant in the sense of resisting dispersion.

55 S: *uṣṇatā*, T: *tsha ba*.

56 S: *laghusamudīraṇatvam*, T: *yang zhing g.yo ba nyid*. Vasubandhu quotes this phrase in *AKB* (p. 8) and asserts that it appears in both the original Abhidharma treatises and the sutras.

57 This is a reference to the fact that one of the derivative forms in the category of tangible qualities is lightness.

58 In other words, the fact that a plant can develop in water is an indication of the fire constituent's action (S: *paktiḥ*, T: *smin pa*). *AKV* (p. 42) states that the fact water can be heated indicates the presence of the fire constituent.

59 Vasubandhu's *AKB* (p. 130) describes five stages of embryonic development. The first four are associated with each of the first four weeks of gestation. During the first stage (S: *kalalam*, T: *nur nur po*), the fetus is the consistency of whey; in the second (S: *arbudam*, T: *mer mer po*) it is like curds or coagulated oil; in the third (S: *peśī*, T: *ltar ltar po*), it is shaped like a tiny spoon; and in the fourth (S: *ghanaḥ*, T: *mkhrang gyur*), it is like a pestle. The fifth stage (S: *praśākhā*, T: *rkang lag 'gyus pa*), which begins

during the fifth week, marks the point at which the body begins to form limbs and develop into a human form. Asaṅga's *YB* (p. 28) adds three more stages to these five: (1) the stage during which hair and nails are formed, (2) the stage during which the sense faculties begin to develop, and (3) the stage during which the seats of the sense faculties become formed.

60 The two forms of expansion are meant to differentiate between growth in all directions (S: *vṛddhiḥ*, T: *'phel ba*) or movement in only one direction (S: *prasarpaṇam*, T: *'gyur bar byed pa*).

61 S: *svabhāvaḥ*, T: *ngo bo nyid.*

62 S: *varṇaviṣayaḥ*, T: *yul kha dog.* The original Sanskrit phrase is actually a *bahuvrīhi* (T: *'bru mang po*) compound that has the form "color-object," and which can be glossed as "(an entity) whose object is a color." Since the noun ("clear form") that this compound modifies also appears in the root text as part of the definition of the eye faculty, I have rendered the compound as the adjectival phrase "that has color as its object."

63 S: *prasādaḥ*, T: *dang ba* (sometimes also spelled *dwang ba*).

64 In Buddhist literature, the term "form" (S: *rūpam*, T: *gzugs*) can refer either to all instances of physical matter, in which case it means the entire form heap, or it can refer just to visible form. If the sense is ambiguous, sometimes the phrase "form basis" (S: *rūpāyatanam*, T: *gzugs kyi ske mched*) or "form constituent" (S: *rūpadhātuḥ*, T: *gzugs kyi khams*) will be used to indicate that the term is being restricted to "visible form." In this commentary when the sense is clearly "visible form" but only the term "form" appears, I have added the adjective in brackets.

65 That is, the sense faculties must be distinguished from those external objects that are clear and transparent, like glass, crystal, water, and the like.

66 S: *manas*: T: *yid.* The mind faculty is not a physical entity; it is discussed in the context of the fifth and last heap, that of consciousness. See below, p. 345.

67 S: *prasādaḥ*, T: *dang ba.* This term is also used to define one of three main types of faith, which is described as a "clarity of mind" (S: *cetasaḥ prasādaḥ*, T: *yid dang ba*). See below, pp. 283–284.

68 S: *indantītīndriyāṇi*, T: *dbang byed pas na dbang po rnams.* This is the so-called "etymology" or literal interpretation (S: *nirvacanam*, T *nges tshig*) of the term translated as "faculty" (S: *indriyam*, T: *dbang po*). Abhidharma literature identifies some twenty-two types of "faculty." In this root text, only six of the twenty-two are mentioned—that is, the five sense faculties that are explained here and the mind faculty that is mentioned later within the consciousness heap. All twenty-two are discussed in chapter two of Vasubandhu's *Treasury of Higher Learning.* The remaining sixteen are (1) the male sex faculty (S: *puruṣendriyam*, T: *pho'i dbang po*), (2) the female sex faculty (S: *strīndriyam*, T: *mo'i dbang po*), (3) the faculty of a life force (S: *jīvitendriyam*, T: *srog gi dbang po*); the five faculties that are feelings—(4) the faculty of pleasure (S: *sukhendriyam*, T: *bde ba'i dbang po*), (5) the faculty of suffering (S: *duḥkhendriyam*, T: *sdug bsngal gyi dbang po*), (6) the faculty of mental ease (S: *saumanasyendriyam*, T: *yid bde ba'i dbang po*), (7) the faculty of mental discomfort (S: *daurmanasyendriyam*, T: *yid mi bde ba'i dbang po*), and (8) the faculty of equanimity (S: *upekṣendriyam*, T: *btang snyoms kyi dbang po*); the five spiritual faculties—(9) the faculty of faith (S: *śraddhendriyam*, T: *dad pa'i dbang po*), (10) the faculty of effort (S: *vīryendriyam*, T: *brtson 'grus kyi dbang po*), (11) the faculty of recollection (S: *smṛtīndriyam*, T: *dran pa'i dbang po*), (12) the faculty of

concentration (S: *samādhīndriyam*, T: *ting nge 'dzin gyi dbang po*), and (13) the faculty of wisdom (S: *prajñendriyam*, T: *shes rab kyi dbang po*); and the three pure faculties—(14) the faculty in which one reflects, 'I shall gain full knowledge of what is not yet fully known' (S: *anājñātamājñāsyāmīndriyam*, T: *kun shes par byed pa'i dbang po*), (15) the faculty of full knowledge (S: *ājñendriyam*, S: *kun shes pa'i dbang po*), and (16) the faculty of possessing full knowledge (S: *ājñātavīndriyam*, T: *kun shes pa dang ldan pa'i dbang po*).

69 *S: ādhipatyam*, T: *bdag po byed pa* or *dbang byed pa*.

70 S: *viṣayī*, T: *yul can*. Literally, "that which has an object"; here it is a synonym for "faculty."

71 That is, the present topic is the form heap, and the mind faculty is not included in this heap. One reason for this statement is the recognition that the mind faculty can hold any of the six external bases (S: *āyatanam*, T: *skye mched*) as its object. Thus, the statement that visible form is exclusively an object of the eye faculty is made in the context of the five sense faculties.

72 This statement seems to be Sthiramati's way of introducing his investigation into the precise status of color, shape, and informative visible form. As the discussion indicates, there were different opinions among Buddhist schools about what constitutes the unique object of the eye faculty. A summary of Vasubandhu's own position, as it accords with the Yogācāra School, appears at the end of Sthiramati's presentation.

73 Following early Sanskrit Abhidharma texts, Vasubandhu's *AKB* (p. 6) identifies form and shape as the two basic types of visible form and then presents twenty varieties, which include four primary colors, eight shapes, and the first eight of the ten items that appear in this list. This list of twenty types of visible form presumably represents the view of the Kashmir Vaibhāṣika School, which holds that the latter eight items include both shape and form. In his *Ornament of Higher Learning* (T: *mNgon pa'i rgyan*, ff. 21b–22a), the thirteenth-century Tibetan scholar Chim Namkha Drak (T: mChims nam mkha' grags) states: ". . . ordinary persons consider the first four items—cloud, [smoke, dust, and mist]—not to have any substance and the next four—shadow, [sunshine, light, and darkness]—not to exist separately from the surface of the earth or wherever else [they are perceived]. Therefore, in order to dispel these misconceptions, the Sutras mention these [eight phenomena] within the classification of [visible] form. No other [ordinary] phenomena [like water, fire, pillars, pots, etc.] are mentioned [in the Sutras], because there is no [similar] need [for doing so]." Vasubandhu also notes several alternative views in *AKB*. Asaṅga's *AS* presents a longer list of twenty-five varieties that includes the last two that are mentioned here—"openings" and the "sky"—as well as "atoms," "coarse form," and "[bodily] informative form." As is evident from the discussion below, the Yogācāra view being presented in this *Summary of the Five Heaps* is that shape is not a distinct type of visible form that exists apart from color, nor is it exclusively an object of the eye faculty.

74 S: *paricchinnaviṣayaḥ*, T: *yul yongs su chad pa*. That is, they can occur in a form that has a well-defined outline or shape.

75 S: *abhyavakāśaḥ*, T: *mngon par skabs yod pa*.

76 S: *nabhas*, T: *nam mkha'*.

77 S: *anumānajñānam*, T: *rjes su dpag pa'i shes pa*. In other words, there is a conceptual component in the notion of a shape.

78 See *AKB*, pp. 194–195. The distinction is made that the connection between a par-

ticular flower's smell and its color is infallible (assuming, of course, that it is a species of flower that has only one color); therefore, it is a case of association of the two qualities. However, no such relation exists between tangible sensations and shape; therefore, the determination of a shape based on the sense of touch is not one that is based on establishing in the mind an inferential link between the two.

79 That is, you can determine that an object such as a pot has a long shape both by seeing its shape with the eye faculty and by feeling the pot with the body faculty (i.e., by touching it with your hands).

80 S: *paramāṇuḥ*, T: *rdul phra rab*. According to the Buddhist realists, atoms are the smallest particles of physical matter that are both indivisible and partless. This particular discussion centering on the nature of atoms seems to be between two realist schools—the Vaibhāṣikas, who hold that shapes are real external substances, and the Sautrāntikas, who refute this claim.

81 S: **asammukhībhāvaḥ*, T: *mngon sum du ma gyur pa*. This phrase seems to suggest separateness in the sense of not occupying the same spatial locus.

82 S: *vijñaptiḥ*, T: *rnam par rig byed*. There are two kinds of informative form: bodily informative form and verbal informative form. In this case, the discussion is limited to bodily informative form because only that kind is the object of the eye faculty.

83 S: **tadupalabdhicittajaḥ*, T: *de la dmigs pa'i sems las skyes pa*.

84 The movement of the lips in speech is a physical action that is largely automatic; it is not necessary for the mind to be principally focused on performing the actions that will give voice the words one intends to utter. By contrast, when one makes a prostration, the mind is deliberately focused on carrying out the bodily action that is expressive of a gesture of homage.

85 S: *praṇidhānajaḥ*, T: *smon lam las skyes pa*. *NgG* (f. 186b) states: "The Master [Lord Buddha's physical qualities of] lips that are red like a bilva fruit, and so forth, are excluded [from the category of bodily informative form].... [The Vaibhāṣika School] holds that the Master's lips [are not bodily informative form] because they are produced by [the power] of prayer and not by a mind that is [consciously] holding that [part of the body in the mind]."

86 S: *śāstā*, T: *ston pa*. Here the term "Master," the original of which literally means "Teacher," refers to Buddha Śākyamuni.

87 This phrase is somewhat obscure. A mind that is a cause of a karmic ripening (S: *vipākahetuḥ*, T: *rnam par smin pa'i rgyu*) is one that is either nonvirtuous in nature or an impure virtue (*AK*, ch. 2, v. 54cd). The point here may be that while the mind that is the motivation for uttering some form of speech may be virtuous or nonvirtuous in nature, the mere shape of a person's lips during the act of speaking does not convey the virtuous or nonvirtuous nature of that mind.

88 "Treatises" here should be understood in the sense of Buddhist philosophical literature.

89 S: *śabdāyatanam*, T: *sgra'i skye mched*. See pp. 347–353 for a discussion of the twelve bases.

90 S: *upāttaḥ*, T: *zin pa*. *AKB* (p. 23) states that nine of the eighteen constituents (S: *dhātuḥ*, T: *khams*) can be either retained or unretained: "the eye, ear, nose, tongue, and body [constituents] of the present are retained. Those of the past and future are unretained. The constituents of [visible] form, smell, taste, and tangible objects that are of the present and do not exist apart from the faculties are retained. All others are unretained." "All others" means the remaining nine constituents—

namely, the seven mental constituents, the dharma constituent, and sound. While sound itself is classified as being unretained, its cause, the four elements, can be either retained or unretained. The four elements are classified within the tangible-object constituent (S: *spraṣṭavyadhātuḥ*, T: *reg bya'i khams*). See also Vasubandhu's *Summary*, p. 244.

91 S: **adhiṣṭhānam*, T: *rten*.

92 More specifically, this example refers to sound generated by beating a drum with the hand. The drum represents an object composed of unretained elements and the hand represents an object composed of retained elements.

93 That is, in the case of sound it was explained that sound is exclusively the object of the ear faculty.

94 S: *samagandhaḥ*, T: *dri mnyam pa*. This term does not occur in the root text. It is found, however, in both *AKB* (p. 7) and *AS* (p. 4). Two different opinions are expressed in the literature concerning the meaning of a moderate smell. One states that it means either a moderately pleasant smell or a moderately unpleasant smell, and therefore does not constitute a third category of smell. The second view is that a moderate smell is a neutral odor that is different from those that are pleasant or unpleasant. Sthiramati seems to intend the term to be taken as synonymous with what the root text describes as "those that are other than that"—which is to say, smells that are not identifiable as either pleasant or unpleasant.

95 This classification appears in *AS* (p. 4); the Sanskrit and Tibetan equivalents are (1) S: *sahajaḥ*, T: *lhan skyes*; (2) S: *sāṃyogikaḥ*, T: *sbyar ba las byung ba*; and (3) S: *pāriṇāmikaḥ*, T: *gyur pa las byung ba*, respectively.

96 S: *bhūtaḥ*, T: *'byung ba*. That is, all four of the great elements—earth, water, fire, and air—are classified as tangible objects, even though they are not the topic under discussion here.

97 S: *bhautikaḥ*, T: *'byung ba las gyur pa*. That is, the type of derivative form that is a tangible object.

98 S: **mūrtiḥ*, T: *gong bu*.

99 That would contradict the thesis that atomic particles are partless and indivisible.

100 That is, the desire for warmth.

101 This is a reference to the list in Asaṅga's *Compendium of Higher Learning* of tangible objects that are derivative form. The examples that do not appear in Vasubandhu's root text are slipperiness (S: *picchilatvam*, T: *mnyen pa*); softness (S: *mandatvam*, T: *lhod pa nyid*); hardness (S: *amandatvam*, T: *lhod pa ma yin pa*); satiety (S: *tṛptiḥ*, T: *tshim pa*); strength (T; *balam*, T: *nyam yod pa*); weakness (S: *daurbalyam*, T: *nyam med pa*); fainting (S: *mūrcchā*, T: *brgyal ba*); itching (S: *kaṇḍūtiḥ*, T: *gya' ba*); putrefaction (S: *pūtiḥ*, T: ?); illness (S: *vyādhiḥ*, T: *na ba*), agedness (S: *jarā*, T: *rga ba*), death (S: *maraṇam*, T: *'chi ba*); fatigue (S: *klāntiḥ*, T: *ngal ba*), rest (S: *viśramaḥ*, T: *ngal sos pa*); and vigor (S: *ūrjjā*, T: *spungs che ba*). The Sanskrit for the term that occurs between "itching" and "illness" means "putrefaction" or "purulence." One might expect *rul ba* or *myags pa* as the Tibetan equivalent. The Tibetan term that appears in this place is *'gred pa*, which means "slipperiness." I am not sure how best to explain this anomaly.

102 S: *anidarśanam*, T: *bstan du med pa*. See below, p. 359, and especially notes 609 and 610, for a description of the meaning of this term. Of all the different types of form, only the form that is the object of eye consciousness is described as "capable of being indicated" (S: *sanidarśanam*, T: *bstan du yod pa*).

103 S: *avyākṛtaḥ*, T: *lung du ma bstan pa*. Indeterminate literally means those entities that were not "declared" or "explained" by Buddha as being either virtuous or nonvirtuous in nature.

104 S: *anāsaravaḥ*, T: *zag pa med pa*. See note 9 above.

105 S: *saṃvaraḥ*, T: *sdom pa*. This term is often translated as "vow"; however, Vasubandhu describes its literal meaning as follows (*AKB*, p. 205): "that which restrains or stops ongoing immorality" (S: *dauḥśīlyaprasarasya saṃvaraṇaṃ saṃrodhaḥ saṃvaraḥ*, T: *'chal ba'i tshul khrims kyi rgyun sdom zhing 'gog pas na sdom pa*).

106 S: *asaṃvaraḥ*, T: *sdom pa ma yin pa*. Vasubandhu glosses this term in the following way (*AKB*, p. 211): "It is negative discipline because it fails to restrain one in body and speech" (S: *kāyavācor asaṃvaraṇād asaṃvaraḥ*, T: *lus dang ngag mi sdom pa'i phyir sdom pa ma yin pa*). It is possible for a person to "acquire" negative discipline by adopting a form of livelihood that is harmful to other beings—for example, those who slaughter animals for a living, fishermen, hunters, thieves, and the like. Such persons continually accrue nonvirtuous karma, even when they are not directly engaged in committing misdeeds, until they completely renounce that lifestyle.

107 S: *prātimokṣaḥ*, T: *so sor thar pa*. The Kadampa Vinaya Master Tsonawa Sherab Sangpo (T: mTsho sna ba Shes rab bzang po, fl. late thirteenth–fourteenth centuries) presents three explanations of the term "individual liberation" in his commentary *Light Rays of the Sun* (T: *Nyi ma'i 'od zer*). All three are based on different interpretations of the prefix *prāti*. The first takes it to mean "individual" (T: *so sor*) and thus *prātimokṣa* discipline is a "discipline of individual liberation" in the sense that each individual person who observes morality is able to gain his or her own liberation from the lower realms and samsara, but no one can gain liberation through someone else's observance of morality. According to a second interpretation, *prāti* means "first" (T: *dang por*) and, hence, *prātimokṣa* discipline is a "vow of first liberation" because in the first moment that the *prātimokṣa* discipline is achieved one is liberated from whatever form of negative discipline one may have possessed before. A third interpretation uses Sanskrit grammatical theory to derive the sense of being a "means" (T: *thabs*) and thus *prātimokṣa* discipline is a "discipline that provides a means [to the attainment] of liberation."

108 They are (1) fully ordained monk (S: *bhikṣuḥ*, T: *dge slong*); (2) fully ordained nun (S: *bhikṣuṇī*, T: *dge slong ma*); (3) probationary nun (S: *śikṣamāṇā*, T: *dge slob ma*); (4) novice monk (S: *śramaṇeraḥ*, T: *dge tshul*); (5) novice nun (S: *śramaṇerikā*, T: *dge tshul ma*); (6) layman (S: *upāsakaḥ*, T: *dge bsnyen*); (7) laywoman (S: *upāsikā*, T: *dge bsnyen ma*); and (8) one-day fasting vow (S: *upavāsaḥ*, T: *bsnyen gnas*).

109 The original is usually rendered "in every way" (S: *sarvathā*, T: *rnam pa thams cad du*); however, that expression doesn't seem appropriate to the present context.

110 In general, the expression "discipline that arises from meditative absorption" (S: *dhyānasaṃvaraḥ*, T: *bsam gtan gyi sdom pa*) describes a quality that accompanies the attainment of any of the various states of one-pointed concentration that are associated with the form realm. This quality is said to be a kind of "discipline" in that the person who attains any of those states of one-pointed concentration naturally becomes indisposed to committing nonvirtuous actions. The "four meditative absorptions" are the main levels that are identified with the form realm, and they are known as the first, second, third, and fourth meditative absorptions, respectively. See Part One, pp. 174–178 for further description of these meditative levels. "All-powerful" (S: *anāgamyam*, T: *mi lcogs pa med pa*) is the name of a level of

one-pointed concentration that occurs prior to attainment of the first meditative absorption. It is called "all-powerful" because it can serve as the basis for destroying all the mental afflictions of the three realms. The "superior meditative absorption" (S: *dhyānāntaram*, T: *bsam gtan khyad par can*) is associated with the first level of the form realm but is more subtle than the ordinary first meditative absorption in that, of the two types of examination called deliberation (S: *vitarkaḥ*, T: *rtog pa*) and reflection (S: *vicāraḥ*, T: *dpyod pa*), only reflection is active there; however, both types of examination occur in the ordinary first meditative absorption. The term "impure" (S: *sāsravaḥ*, T: *zag pa dang bcas pa*) technically refers to all impermanent and causally produced entities with the exception of the Truth of the Path because they have the potential to strengthen the mental afflictions. In this case, these levels of one-pointed concentration as said to be "impure" when they are not accompanied by the wisdom that directly perceives the true nature of reality. These states are also called "mundane" in that when they lack the wisdom just mentioned, they cannot directly and permanently eliminate any portion of the mental afflictions and ultimately lead to complete liberation from samsara.

111 S: *anāsravasaṃvaraḥ*, T: *zag pa med pa'i sdom pa*. This form of discipline is possessed only by someone who has attained the transcendent path (See Part One, pp. 179–184). Such a person is known as an Ārya or a "Noble One" (S: *āryaḥ*, T: *'phags pa*). Vasubandhu provides the following interpretation of this term (*AKB*, p. 157): "Who are the Noble Ones? [This term refers to] those who have given rise to the pure [i.e., transcendent] path. They are called 'Noble Ones' because they have reached [a state] that is far removed from evil qualities through having attained the 'acquirement' (S: *prāptiḥ*, T: *thob pa*; see below, pp. 313–314) that is a permanent separation from them" (S: *āryāḥ katame / yeṣām anāsravo mārga utpannaḥ / ārād yātāḥ pāpakebhyo dharmebhya ityāryāḥ / ātyantikavisaṃyogaprāptilābhāt*. T: *'phags pa rnams gang zhe na / gang dag la zag pa med pa'i lam skyes pa'o / sdig pa'i chos rnams las ring du song bas na 'phags pa rnams te / gtan du bral ba'i thob pa rnyed pa'i phyir ro*). "Permanent separation" is a reference to the Truth of Cessation. By contrast, all beings who have not attained the transcendent path are known as "ordinary beings" (S: *pṛthagjanaḥ*, T: *so so skye bo*).

112 S: *nidarśanam*, T: *bstan pa*. See also below, note 609.

113 S: *pratighātaḥ*, T: *thogs pa*. Three kinds of resistance are described in the *Commentary to the Treasury of Higher Learning*. The one presented here is the type called obstruction-opposition (S: *āvaraṇapratighātaḥ*, T: *sgrib pa'i thogs pa*). See below, pp. 359–360.

114 S: *dharmāyatanam*, T: *chos kyi skye mched*. This is one of the twelve types of basis; see below, p. 348. The five types of form that are included in the entity basis are mentioned in Asaṅga's *Compendium of Higher Learning* (*AS*, p. 4).

115 S: *ābhisaṃkṣepikam*, T: *bsdus pa las gyur pa*.

116 S: *ābhyavakāśikam*: T: *mngon par skabs yod pa*.

117 S: *sāmādānikam*, T: *yang dag par blangs pa las byung ba*. It is called "undertaken" because it refers to the noninformative form that is generated when a practitioner adopts any of the vows. This is, therefore, another name for noninformative form, the eleventh and last type of form that is presented in Vasubandhu's root text.

118 S: *parikalpitam*, T: *kun brtags pa*.

119 S: *vaibhūtikam*, T: *dbang 'byor pa*.

120 The expression "undertaken form," which appears in Asaṅga's *AS*, is synonymous with

the "noninformative form" that is mentioned in Vasubandhu's *Summary*.

121 S: *pratibimbaḥ*, T: *gzugs bsnyan*. This "[mental] image" refers to an image of form that is visualized in the mind. For instance, a skeleton is used as a visualization object to overcome attachment to one's own body as well as attachment to the bodies of others, through a particular form of the practice that is called "meditation on [the body's] unattractiveness" (S: *aśubhabhāvanā*, T: *mi sdug pa sgom pa*; see Part One, pp. 157–160).

122 S: *vimokṣaḥ*, T: *rnam par thar pa*. Eight deliverances are described in canonical literature. They are cultivated in order to attain mastery of the states of mental composure associated with the form and formless realms. The first three, in particular, are associated with the four meditative absorptions of the form realm and involve developing the ability to emanate attractive and unattractive forms at will, in order to achieve mastery over this process as well as to gain other extraordinary spiritual attributes.

123 S: *vikalpaḥ*, T: *rnam par rtog pa*.

124 This description is identical to the one that appears in Vasubandhu's *Treasury of Higher Learning* (ch. 1, v. 11). The root text of that work presents the doctrine of the Vaibhāṣika School (T: *bye brag tu smra ba*), which claims that noninformative form is a real substance. In the next paragraph, Sthiramati presents the Yogācāra School's (T: *rnal 'byor spyod pa*) position that noninformative form is only nominally existent.

125 S: *ālayavijñānam*, T: *kun gzhi'i rnam par shes pa*. This type of consciousness is a unique doctrine of Asaṇga's Mind Only School. It is discussed at some length below in the section on the consciousness heap (see below, pp. 328–344).

126 S: *lajjā*, T: *'dzem pa*. The meaning of this term is central to the Buddhist explanation of morality. It is the essential nature of the pair of virtuous mental factors called "shame" (S: *hrīḥ*, T: *ngo tsha shes pa*) and "abashment" (S: *apatrāpyam*, T: *khrel yod pa*), which are explained below, pp. 284–285. The Sanskrit term carries a range of meanings that include "shame," "embarrassment," or "shyness"; the Tibetan literally means "avoidance." In both languages the respective terms are used in situations that do not strictly fall in the province of morality. However, the relevant meaning in the present context is that of a strong sense of apprehension about the consequences of wrongdoing that has the effect of restraining one from engaging in such actions.

127 S: *kāraṇe kāryopacāraḥ*, T: *rgyu la 'bras bu'i ming gis btags*. Traditional Abhidharma literature formulates a distinction between the intention to observe a system of vows, which is formed at the time that the vows are accepted, and the discipline which results from that mental act, which is described as constituting a unique type of form. The physical and verbal form that is present at the time that the vows are being taken is called informative, because it has the capacity to make known the mental act that produced it. The ritual itself is also said to have the capacity to generate in its wake the noninformative form that maintains the discipline over time, even when the individual is not consciously thinking of the vows that he or she took. However, Sthiramati's explanation essentially reduces noninformative form to a mental propensity to keep one's commitment to the vows. He suggests a similar explanation for pure discipline, the discipline that arises from meditative absorption, and negative discipline. Thus, the noninformative "form" that is referred to as a result is explained as constituting the continuum of an act of volition that is its cause. Various other issues are raised in connection with this controversy, such as the relationship between the primary elements and noninformative form; however, as these are beyond the scope of this work,

the interested reader is urged to consult the relevant works of the different Buddhist philosophical schools.

128 Only the Vaibhāṣika and Prasaṅgika schools consider the form that is present during physical and verbal acts to be virtuous in nature; all the other schools explain virtuous physical and verbal deeds in terms of the volition that generates them. Thus Sthiramati is saying that the form that is present during physical and verbal acts is the object and result of the subjective volition that generates them. Hence, it is virtuous only in a figurative sense; the precise meaning is that such form is considered virtuous because of the volition that caused it to be produced.

129 S: *rūpaṇam*, T: *gzugs su rung ba*. This is the classic description of the essential characteristic of form. *AKB* (p. 9) glosses it to mean that form is "capable of being damaged" (S: *bādhyate*, T: *gnod par bya rung ba*). The damage that form undergoes is further described as meaning that it can be "caused to undergo a transformation" (S: *vipariṇāmotpādanā*, T: *yongs su 'gyur ba bskyed pa*) or to undergo "a deteriorating change" (S: *vikriyā*, T: *rnam par 'gyur ba*). *AS* (p. 2) gives two interpretations of the phrase "displaying [the quality of] form." One is the quality of being tangible (S: *sparśena rūpaṇam*, *reg pas gzugs su yod pa*), which Asaṅga describes as "the injury [that can be caused] through being touched with such things as a hand, foot, rock, sword (or weapon), club, [the sensations of] cold, heat, hunger, thirst, mosquito, stinging insect, snake, or scorpion." (The list of causes in the Tibetan translation differs slightly.) The second interpretation is that "displaying [the quality of] form means an entity that is capable of being pointed out (S: *pradeśena rūpaṇam*, T: *yul dpyad pas gzugs su yod pa*). Asaṅga describes this as the quality by which "a person who is either in a composed or an uncomposed state can determine through deliberation (*vitarkaḥ*, T: *rtog pa*) about an image [of some object] that [is present] in some physical location, 'It is this or that form' or 'It is a form of this or that kind.'"

130 This passage is quoted in *AKB* (p. 9): S: *rūpyate rūpyata iti bhikṣavaḥ tasmād rūpopādānaskandha ityucyate / kena rūpyate / pāṇisparśenāpi spṛṣṭo rūpyata iti vistaraḥ*. T: *dge slong dag gzugs su yod cing gzugs su rung bas / de'i phyir gzugs nye bar len pa'i phung po zhes bya'o / ci gzugs su rung zhe na / lag pas 'dus te reg pas reg na yang gzugs su rung ngo zhes rgyas par gsungs so*. The Tibetan translations of this passage that appear in *AKB* and *PSV* differ slightly.

131 S: *anubhavaḥ*, T: *myong ba*.

132 S: *sparśānubhavaḥ*, T: *reg pa myong ba*. *AKV*, p. 48. Saṃghabhadra (T:'Dus bzang), a contemporary and rival of Vasubandhu, wrote a treatise in defense of the Vaibhāṣika views.

133 S: *sākṣāt karaṇam*, T: *mngon sum du byed pa*.

134 This criticism of Saṃghabhadra's view also appears essentially verbatim in *AKT* (Tg., vol. 211, f. 61a–61b).

135 The original Sanskrit of this paragraph appears in *TB*, p. 56.

136 S: *yasmin utpanne 'viyogecchā jāyate*, T: *gang 'byung na mi bral bar 'dod pa skyes ba*. See Tibetan translation of Vasubandhu's *Pratītyasamutpādādivibhaṅgabhāṣyam* (Tg., vol. 115 [*chi*], f. 33b). The original Sanskrit of this phrase appears in Sthiramati's *TB*, p. 56.

137 Vasubandhu presents this example in his *Pratītyasamutpādādivibhaṅgabhāṣyam*, f. 34a.

138 S: **āśrayaḥ*, T *gnas*. This term is also often translated in Tibetan as *rten* or "support"; here the reference is to the faculty (S: *indriyam*, T: *dbang po*) through which not only

feelings but all the other mental entities as well, including consciousness, arise. These six types of feeling are known as "the six collections of feelings" (S: *ṣaḍvedanākāyāḥ*, T: *tshor ba'i tshogs drug*).

139 S: *saṃcitaḥ*, T: *bsags pa*. They are aggregates in the sense of being a composite of atomic particles.

140 S: *vipakṣaḥ*, T: *mi mthun phyogs*.

141 S: *pratipakṣaḥ*, T: *gnyen po*.

142 These two pairs of terms are listed in *AS* (p. 4) as part of the description of the feeling heap. They also appear in Asaṅga's *Collection of Determinations* (T: *rNam par btan la dbab bsdu ba*) at the end of the section that pertains to the eleventh chapter of the *Yogācārabhūmi*, entitled "The Stage on Wisdom That Arises From Contemplation" (S: *cintāmayībhūmiḥ*, T: *bsams pa las byung ba'i sa*), Tg., vol. 130 (*zhi*), f. 207b, where they are explained in terms of five factors: locus, basis, essential nature, accompaniment, and consequences. See also Part One, pp. 167–169.

143 S: *āmiṣam*, T: *zang zing*. The original Sanskrit term can mean variously "flesh," "an object of enjoyment," "desire," or a "gift." In Buddhist literature, the term frequently appears in the phrase *āmiṣadānam* (T: *zang zing gi sbyin pa*), where it generally means a gift of a physical object having material value, as opposed to, for instance, a gift of the Dharma or spiritual knowledge. As the commentary indicates, here the term refers to the form of desire that is attachment to one's own samsaric existence.

144 S: *ātmabhāvatṛṣṇā*, T: *lus la sred pa*.

145 See p. 346, where the expression "inner heaps" is identified as those that are "included within your own continuum."

146 S: *sāmiṣam*, T: *zang zing dang bcas pa*. See Asaṅga's *rNam par btan la dbab bsdu ba*, f. 207b.

147 S: *nirāmiṣam*, T: *zang zing med pa*.

148 S: *gredhaḥ*, T: *zhen pa*.

149 S: *gredhāśritaḥ*, T: *zhen pa brten pa*.

150 S: *vairāgyam*, T: *'dod chags dang bral ba*. Complete absence of attachment for the sense objects means to overcome all attachment for the desire realm. This occurs when one attains the first meditative absorption (S: *dhyānaḥ*, T: *bsam gtan*) of the form realm.

151 S: *naiṣkramyāśritaḥ*, T: *mngon par 'byung ba brten pa*.

152 The Sanskrit original of this paragraph can be easily reconstructed as it is virtually identical with the description found in *TB*, p. 56.

153 S: *nirvikalpaḥ*, T: *rtog pa med pa*. As a form of direct perception, sense consciousness is by definition free of ideation.

154 S: *paricchedaḥ*, T: *yongs su gcod pa*.

155 S: *mandaḥ*, T: *zhan pa*. That is, raw sense consciousness and the conception that accompanies it are undiscerning and not able to identify or distinguish specific characteristics.

156 This statement simply asserts that sensory consciousness must be accompanied by some form of conception, without stating precisely what specific sort of action that type of conception carries out. Presumably it is a pre-linguistic capacity to isolate, detect, or delimit an object from among the possible range of sense data that can enter through a particular sense faculty. For instance, Yaśomitra notes in *AKV* (Skt., p. 209, Tib., f. 129b) that when consciousness perceives a blue or yellow entity, the accompanying conception literally "delimits it" or "fixes its boundaries" (S: *vijñānaṃ*

hi nīlaṃ pītaṃ vā vastu vijānāti / upalabhata ityarthaḥ / tad eva tathālambanaṃ vastu vedanānubhavati saṃjñā parichinatti cetanābhisaṃskarotītyevam ādi. T: *rnam par shes pas ni sngon po'am ser po'i dngos po rnam par shes te / dmigs par 'gyur ro zhes bya ba'i tha tshig go / de ltar dmigs pa'i dngos po de nyid ni tshor bas nyams su myong go / 'du shes kyis ni yongs su gcod do / sems dpas ni mngon par 'du byed do zhes bya ba de lta bu la sogs pa yin no*). He also provides an alternate description: "Consciousness grasps the general essence of the object; . . . conception grasps that particular form that is capable of being delineated" (S: *atha vā tasyaivālambanasya vijñānaṃ sāmānyarūpeṇopalabhyatārūpaṃ gṛhṇāti viśeṣarūpeṇa tu vedanānubhavanīyatārūpaṃ gṛhṇāti saṃjñā paricchedyatārūpaṃ gṛhṇatītyevam ādi,* T: *yang na dmigs pa de nyid la rnam par shes pas ni spyi'i ngo bor dmigs par bya ba'i tshul du 'dzin la / bye brag gi ngo bo ni tshor bas ni myong bar bya ba'i tshul du 'dzin to / 'du shes kyis ni yongs su gcad par bya ba'i tshul du 'dzin to zhes bya ba de lta bu la sogs pa yin no*).

157 S: *ṣaḍsaṃjñākāyāḥ,* T: *'du shes kyi tshogs drug.*

158 The following six types of conception are presented and described briefly in Asaṅga's *AS* (p. 5). Vasubandhu mentions the third, fourth, and fifth types in his *Summary.*

159 S: *sanimittam,* T: *mtshan ma dang bcas pa.*

160 S: *animittam,* T: *mtshan ma med pa.*

161 S: *parīttam,* T: *chung ngu.*

162 S: *mahadgatam,* T: *rgya chen por gyur pa.*

163 S: *apramāṇam,* T: *tshad med pa.*

164 S: *ākiṃcanyāyatanam,* T: *ci yang med pa'i skye mched.* This is the name of the third of the four states of composure that occur in the formless realm.

165 S: *bhavāgraḥ,* T: *srid pa'i rtse mo.* This is a mental state associated with the fourth level of the formless realm. It is called "the Peak of Existence" because it is the highest and most subtle level of samsaric existence. It is also known as "the Sphere in Which There Is Neither Conception nor Absence of Conception" (S: *naiva saṃjñā nāsaṃjñāyatanam,* T: *'du shes med 'du shes med min gyi skye mched*).

166 Newborn infants are cited as examples of beings who form concepts but do so without the aid of language. For example, when a nursing infant sees its mother's breast it can recognize it as a source of milk without resorting to language. This represents an example of a signless concept.

167 S: *saṃskṛtaḥ,* T: *'dus byas.* This is the Buddhist term for any entity that is impermanent and produced by causes. The five heaps are a formulation that encompasses all conditioned entities. Nirvana, space, emptiness, and the Truth of Cessation are examples of uncaused entities. *AKB* (p. 449) identifies ten signs that are not present in the "signless concentration" (S: *ānimittasamādhiḥ,* T: *mtshan ma med pa'i ting nge 'dzin*): the five sense objects, the quality of being male or female, and the three characteristics of conditioned entities—birth, continuing to exist [for only a moment], and destruction.

168 S: S: *ākāśānantyāyatanam,* T: *rnam mkha' mtha' yas skye mched.* This is the name of the first of the four states of composure that occur in the formless realm.

169 S: *vijñānānantyāyatanam,* T: *rnam shes mtha' yas skye mched.* This is the name of the second level of the formless realm.

170 See Part One, p. 178, for a description of this state of composure that is associated with the formless realm.

171 This statement is virtually identical with one that occurs in Vasubandhu's *AKB*, p. 4 (S: *sametya sambhūya pratyayaiḥ kṛtā iti saṃskṛtāḥ,* T: *rkyen rnams 'dus shing phrad*

nas byas pa dag ni 'dus byas rnams te) with the exception that it describes "conditioned entities" (S: *saṃskṛtāḥ*, T: *'dus byas rnams*) rather than "formations" (S: *saṃskārāḥ*, T: *'du byed rnams*), which suggests that, in some instances at least, the two terms can be considered interchangeable.

172 S: *caittaḥ* or *caitasikaḥ*, T: *sems las byung ba.*

173 S: **upabhogabhāvaḥ*, T: *nye bar spyod pa'i dngos po.*

174 S: **abhilāpavastu*, T: *tha snyad 'dogs pa'i gzhi.*

175 An alternative explanation for why feelings and conceptions are classified within separate heaps is given in *AK* ch. 1, v. 21: "Feeling and conception were placed in heaps / Apart from the [other] mental factors / Because they are the root of argument, / Samsara's cause, and for reasons of order." *AKB* (p. 14) explains: "There are two roots of argument (S: *vivādamūlaḥ*, T: *rtsod pa'i rtsa ba*): attachment to sense objects and attachment to views. Feeling and conception, respectively, are the principal causes of these two [forms of attachment]. Through the relishing of feelings, [beings] develop attachment for the sense objects and, through erring conceptions, [they develop attachment] for [mistaken] views. Therefore, these two [mental factors—i.e., feelings and conceptions] are principal causes of samsara, as it is the person who craves [pleasurable] feelings and who has mistaken views that [is forced to] wander [in samsara]. In addition, it is to be understood that for reasons of order . . . these two [mental factors] were classified into separate heaps." One explanation for the order of the heaps—their relative coarseness—was cited earlier by Sthiramati in the opening portion of his commentary. See above, p. 247.

176 *AKV*, p. 48. S: *saṃskāraskandhaḥ katamaḥ / ṣaṭcetanākāyāḥ*, T: *'du byed kyi phung po gang zhe na / sems dpa'i tshogs drug.*

177 This description follows *AK*, ch. 2, v. 34. That is, whatever faculty and object serve as the "basis," or causes, for the arising of a particular consciousness also serve as the same faculty and object for the feeling, conception, volition, etc., that accompany that consciousness. To have the same "aspect" means that if an eye consciousness arises in the form of a blue object that it has perceived, then the accompanying mental factors will also have that same blue aspect. "Sameness of time" means that consciousness and its accompanying factors arise simultaneously. "Sameness of substance" means that just as each moment of consciousness can only arise in a single form (i.e., two or more distinct forms of eye consciousness cannot exist simultaneously), each of the mental factors accompanying that moment of consciousness also can only arise in a single distinct form.

178 S: *sarvatragaḥ*, T: *kun tu 'gro ba.*

179 S: *pratiniyataviṣayaḥ*, T: *yul so sor nges pa.*

180 S: *kuśalamūlam*, T: *dge ba'i rtsa ba.* Three of the eleven virtues—avoidance of desire, avoidance of hatred, and avoidance of ignorance—are each known as a "root of virtue." See below pp. 285–287.

181 In other words, only the twenty mental factors that range from anger to lack of vigilance are always secondary mental afflictions. Nevertheless, the phrase "the remaining ones" does also refer to the final four mental factors of regret, sleep, deliberation, and reflection, since they too can be secondary mental afflictions, depending on the circumstances.

182 S: **kleśāṃśikāt cittakliṣṭakaraṇāt kleśasamīparūpāt*; T: *nyon mongs pa'i char gtogs pa dang / sems nyon mongs par byed pa dang / nyon mongs pa dang nye ba'i phyir.*

183 See note 103, above.

184 The main source for the actions of the mental factors is Asaṅga's *AS*.

185 This sentence is somewhat problematic. The text literally says: "Because the essential nature is presented first, it will be explained first." In fact, as Sthiramati just noted, the root text *only* presents the essential nature of each mental factor; it is he who adds the actions. The point seems to be simply that he will begin his explanation of each mental factor with a clarification of the description that appears in the root text.

186 Of the five universal mental factors, feeling and conception have already been explained.

187 In other words, the "convergence" of faculty, object, and consciousness should not be taken to mean that these three entities exist simultaneously, since the faculty and object are the causes of a particular consciousness. Therefore, the consciousness that is produced by a specific moment of a faculty and an object must follow them in time.

188 S: *vikāraḥ*, T: *'gyur ba*.

189 S: *vedanāsaṃniśrayatvam asya karma*, T: *'di'i las ni tshor ba'i rten byed pa*.

190 S: *ābhogaḥ*, T: *'jug pa*.

191 S: *ālambane cittadhāraṇakarmakaḥ*, T: *dmigs pa la sems 'dzin pa'i las can*.

192 Sthiramati is saying that his explanation should not be thought of as suggesting that this mental factor continues to exist over time, exerting its action on multiple moments of consciousness. He clarifies this in his commentary to the *Thirty Verses* by saying, "The operation (of this mental factor) only occurs within each individual moment; it does not carry over to any other moment." This is an affirmation that his description does not contradict the Buddhist doctrine of impermanence.

193 S: *cittābhisaṃskāraḥ*, T: *sems mngon par 'du byed pa*.

194 S: *manaskarma*, T: *yid kyi las*.

195 *AS*, p. 6: "Its action is to direct the mind toward virtuous, nonvirtuous, and indeterminate [entities]" (S: *kuśalākuśalāvyākṛteṣu cittapreraṇakarmikā*, T: *dge ba dang mi dge ba dang lung du ma bstan pa rnams la sems 'jug bar byed pa'i las can*).

196 S: *tṛṣṇā*, T: *sred pa*. Craving is synonymous with the root mental affliction of desire (S: *rāgaḥ*, T: *'dod chags*). The question being asked is not an idle one; for instance, the question might be phrased this way: Is the desire to attain liberation or Buddhahood a mental affliction? While this form of desire or aspiration is not a mental affliction, there are many for whom this question can be confusing. Strictly speaking, the mental factor of aspiration is morally neutral; however, the aspiration to pursue a virtuous object is by definition *not* a nonvirtue. Nevertheless, the topic is further complicated by the fact that a virtuous activity can remain a cause of samsaric existence if it does not directly promote the attainment of liberation or Buddhahood.

197 S: **abhiṣvaṅgaḥ*, T: *mngon par chags pa*.

198 S: *vīryārambhasaṃniśrayadānakarmakaḥ*, T: *brtson 'grus rtsom pa'i rten byed pa'i las can*.

199 S: *niścitam*, T: *nges pa*.

200 S: *asaṃhāryatākarmakaḥ*, T: *mi 'phrogs pa nyid kyi las can*.

201 S: *saṃstutam*, T: *'dris pa*.

202 S: *asaṃpramoṣaḥ*, T: *mi brjed pa*. The Tibetan translation of the Sanskrit original literally means "[the quality of] not being forgetful." This does not seem to accurately capture the intended sense of the original Sanskrit term. The primary meaning of the Sanskrit verbal root *muṣ* is "to steal" or "to carry off," in the sense of theft of property. A secondary meaning that relates to the mind or intellect is "to be clouded" or "to be obscured." However, as Sthiramati's gloss of *asaṃpramoṣaḥ* clearly indicates, the pre-

cise sense of the term here is "the avoidance of loss [of a mental object]," which led us to render the term as "avoidance of inattentiveness."

203 S: *pūrvagṛhītasya vastunaḥ punaḥ punar ālambanākārasmaraṇam*; T: *sngon bzung ba'i dngos po la dmigs pa'i rnam par yang dang yang du dran pa'o*. In *TB* (p. 74), Sthiramati presents this very same description to gloss the meaning of "[mental] discourse" (S: *abhilapanam*, T: *mngon par brjod pa*). The activity of repeatedly recalling an object is not meant to be limited to meditation; nevertheless, it clearly has a direct relevance to that subject. "An entity that was previously understood" can be interpreted to mean an understanding of spiritual instruction that was gained with any of the three types of wisdom—the wisdom derived from hearing, the wisdom derived from reflection, or the wisdom derived from meditation. See also Asaṅga's description of how one becomes a practitioner who has developed "well-guarded recollection" (S: *ārakṣitasmṛtiḥ*, T: *dran pa kun tu bsrungs pa*; Part One, pp. 184–185). The Sanskrit original of the term translated here as "mental object" (S: *ālambanam*, T: *dmigs pa*) literally means "that which [the mind] rests upon." It is also the term that Asaṅga uses to describe the four main categories of meditation object that are discussed at great length in his *ŚB*. Therefore, "to recall [some entity] again and again as a mental object" can certainly be explained within the context of any number of contemplative exercises.

204 S: *avikṣepakarmikā*, T: *mi g.yeng ba'i las can*.

205 S: *upaparīkṣyam*, T: *brtag pa*.

206 S: *jñānasaṃniśrayadānakarmikā*, T: *shes pa'i rten byed pa'i las can*.

207 S: *samāhite citte yathābhūtaparijñānāt*; T: *sems mnyam par bzhag na yang dag pa ji lta ba bzhin du yongs su shes pa'i phyir ro*.

208 S: *śāntam*, T: *zhi ba*. Each of the four truths is described as having four aspects. The other three aspects of the Truth of Cessation are that it is a state of cessation (S: *nirodham*, T: *'gog pa*), goodness (S: *praṇītam*, T: *gya nom pa*), and deliverance (S: *niḥsaraṇam*, T: *nges par 'byung ba*). See Part One, p. 82.

209 S: *nairyāṇikaḥ*, T: *nges par 'byin ba*. The other three aspects of the Truth of the Path are that it is a path (S: *mārgaḥ*, T: *lam*), a system possessing rightness (S: *nyāyaḥ*, T: *rigs pa*), and a means of attainment (S: *pratipad*, T: *sgrub pa*). See Part One, pp. 82–83.

210 S: *anityam*, T: *mi rtag pa*. The other three aspects of the Truth of Suffering are that the five grasping heaps are characterized by a state of suffering (S: *duḥkham*, T: *sdug bsngal ba*), that they are void (S: *śūnyam*, T: *stong pa*) of any governing self that is distinct from them, and that they do not constitute a self (S: *anātmam*, T: *bdag med*). See Part One, p. 81.

211 S: *hetuḥ*, T: *rgyu*. The other three aspects of the Truth of Origination are that (1) impure deeds and craving constitute the origination (S: *samudayaḥ*, T: *kun 'byung ba*) of samsaric suffering; (2) they are the source (S: *prabhavaḥ*, T: *rab skyes*) from which the impure heaps arise; and (3) they are the contributing factor (S: *pratyayaḥ*, T: *rkyen*) in the arising of the impure heaps. See Part One, pp. 81–82.

212 S: *nava bhūmayaḥ*, T: *sa dgu*. The nine levels are the desire realm, the four meditative absorptions of the form realm, and the four levels of the formless realm. This statement is a reference to the so-called "mundane path" (S: *laukikamārgaḥ*, T: *'jig rten pa'i lam*), a system of meditative practice in which one overcomes attachment for a lower level of consciousness by regarding it as coarse and flawed, and by also regarding a higher level as tranquil and superior. It is called "mundane" because it does not

have the capacity to permanently eradicate the seeds of mental afflictions. That result can only be accomplished through the "transcendent path" (S: *lokottaramārgaḥ*, T: *'jig rten las 'das pa'i lam*) See Part One, pp. 169–184, for a discussion of both paths.

213 S: *pravicayaḥ*, T: *rab tu rnam par 'byed pa.*

214 S: *vivekāvabodhaḥ*, T: *so sor rtogs pa*. This description identifies the principal quality of wisdom to be that of making distinctions or clearly discerning specific and discrete qualities that would otherwise remain indistinct or muddled. The discussion also reveals that this mental attribute does not always function accurately. Thus, it is, in fact, imprecise always to refer to it as "wisdom."

215 S: *vairāgyam*, T: *'dod chags dang bral ba*. This "absence of attachment" represents a temporary state that is achieved through the mundane path (see also Part One, note 645). Here it refers more specifically to the detachment that is achieved by non-Buddhist "heretics" (S: *tīrthakaḥ*, T: *mu stegs pa*) who are still under the influence of mistaken views regarding the self.

216 S: *saṃśayavyāvartanakarmikā*, T: *som nyi bzlog pa'i las can.*

217 With the exception of the explicit reference to the Sāṃkhya and Vaiśeṣika schools, the original Sanskrit of this entire description of wisdom appears verbatim in Sthiramati's *TB*, p. 74.

218 S: *abhisaṃpratyayaḥ*, T: *mngon par yid ches pa*. This is the first of three types of faith to be described. Below, Sthiramati describes this type of faith as the belief in an entity that exists and has either good qualities or bad qualities. This type of faith also would apply toward belief in the first two of the Four Noble Truths.

219 S: *abhilāṣaḥ*, T: *mngon par 'dod pa*. This is the second of the three types of faith. Below, Sthiramati describes it as an aspiration in which it is believed either, "I can achieve an entity that exists and has good qualities," or "I can develop an entity that exists and has good qualities."

220 In Buddhist cosmology, a kalpa or eon is the vast period of time during which a section of the universe comprising a billion solar systems passes through four phases of equal duration: voidness, formation, stability, and destruction. In his *Commentary to the Treasury of Higher Learning* Vasubandhu explains the term "countless" (S: *asaṃkhyam*, T: *grangs med*) to mean one times ten raised to the power of fifty-nine. See text relating to ch. 3, vv. 89–93 of the root text. Thus, three such intervals of "countless" kalpas is the length of time required to achieve unsurpassed Buddhahood in the non-tantric Mahayana path.

221 In Buddhist mythology, the flower is said to bloom only once every several thousand years and thus it is a symbol for the rare appearance of the Buddha in the world.

222 S: **prākāmyaniṣṭhāpadam*, T: *'dod dgu mthar phying pa'i gnas thob pa*. This term is a reference to Buddhahood.

223 S: *puṇyasaṃbhāraḥ*, T: *bsod nams kyi tshogs*. Based on *MSA*, ch. 18, v. 40, Vasubandhu explains the term "accumulation" (S: *saṃbhāraḥ*) as follows (*MSV*, p. 134): "The syllable *sam* means 'continually.' The syllable *bhā* means 'having attained [proficiency at] meditation.' The syllable *ra* means the 'acquisition [of virtue] to a greater and greater degree'" (S: *sam iti saṃtatyā / bhā iti bhāvanām āgamya / ra iti bhūyo bhūya āhāraḥ*; T: *sam zhes bya ba ni rgyun du'o / bhā zhes bya ba ni sgom pa thob nas so / ra zhes bya ba ni yang dang yang du sgrub pa'o*). Sthiramati augments this interpretation in his subcommentary (*Sems tsam* section of Tg., vol. 126 [*tsi*], f. 102b): "In short, "accumulation" means [those activities that bring about] the *acquistion* of a Buddha's three bodies through *continually* meditating upon [the perfections of] generosity and the

rest and by *meditating* upon the virtues of the six perfections *to a greater and greater degree*."

224 S: *jñānasaṃbhāraḥ*, T: *ye shes kyi tshogs*.

225 These lines appear in the following two verses (vv. 94, 95) of Mātṛceṭa's *One Hundred and Fifty Verses of Praise*: "Celebration [of you] takes away sin; / Remembrance of you brings joyfulness; / Seeking [you] out brings wisdom; / Full knowledge [of you] brings purity. // Approaching you brings fortune; / Serving [you] brings supreme wisdom; / Worshipping [you] frees one from fear; / Honoring [you] brings happiness" (S: *kīrtanaṃ kilbiṣaharaṃ smaraṇaṃ te pramodanam / anveṣaṇaṃ matikaraṃ parijñānaṃ viśodanam // śrīkaraṃ te 'bhigamanaṃ sevanaṃ dhīkaraṃ param / bhajanaṃ nirbhayakaraṃ śamkaraṃ paryupāsanam.* T: *bsgrags pas sdig pa 'phrog par mdzad / khyod dran pas ni rangs par 'gyur / btsal bas blo gros skye 'gyur te / yongs su shes pas rnam par 'dag // khyod la bsu bas dpal du byed / brten pas blo gros mchog tu 'gyur / bsten na 'jigs pa med par mdzad / bsnyen bkur bgyis pas bde bar 'gyur*).

226 See *Supreme Banner Sutra* (S: *Dhvajāgrasūtram*, T: *mDo chen po rgyal mtshan dam pa*. The full passage states: "O monks, when you are staying in a forest, at the foot of a tree, or in an abandoned building, if you should develop fear, apprehension, or terror, then recollect me in this form: 'He is the Lord, the One who has gone thus, a Worthy One, the One who has attained true and complete enlightenment, the One who is endowed with wisdom and its foundation, the One who has gone to happiness, the Knower of the world, the unsurpassed Leader for those who are spiritually disciplined, the Teacher of gods and men, the Enlightened One, the Lord' (S: *sa bhagavāṃs tathāgato 'rhan samyaksaṃbuddho vidyācaraṇasaṃpannaḥ sugato lokavid anuttaraḥ puruṣadamyasārathiḥ śāstā devamanuṣyāṇāṃ buddho bhagavān*. T: *bcom ldan 'das ni de bzhin gshegs pa dgra bcom pa yang dag par rdzogs pa'i sangs rgyas rig pa dang zhabs su ldan pa / bde bar gzhegs pa / 'jig rten mkhyen pa / skyes bu 'dul ba'i kha lo sgyur ba bla na med pa / lha dang mi rnams kyi ston pa sangs rgyas bcom ldan 'das so*). When you recollect my qualities in this manner, your fear, apprehension, or terror will disappear."

227 This a reference to the twelve divisions of scripture (S: *dvādaśāṅgapravacanam*, T: *gsung rab yan lag bcu gnyis*). They are (1) discourses (S: *sūtram*, T: *mdo'i sde*); (2) mixed prose and verse (S: *geyam*, T: *dbyangs kyis bsnyad pa'i sde*); (3) explanatory responses (S: *vyākaraṇam*, T: *lung du bstan pa'i sde*); (4) verses (S: *gāthā*, T: *tshigs su bcad pa'i sde*); (5) uplifting sayings (S: *udānam*, T: *ched du brjod pa'i sde*); (6) statements of theme or subject matter (S: *nidānam*, T: *gleng gzhi'i sde*); (7) narratives of spiritual lives (S: *avadānam*, T: *rtogs par brjod pa'i sde*); (8) accounts of past events (S: *itivṛttakam*, T: *de lta bu byung ba'i sde*); (9) stories of the Buddha's past lives (S: *jātakam*, T: *skyes pa'i rabs kyi sde*); (10) extensive discourses (S: *vaipulyam*, T: *shin tu rgyas pa'i sde*); (11) marvels (S: *adbhūtadharmaḥ*, T: *rmad du byung ba'i chos kyi sde*); and (12) instruction (S: *upadeśaḥ*, T: *gtan la phab pa'i sde*). A similar grouping of the scriptures lists only nine categories, leaving out numbers 7–9. For a brief description of the twelve categories, see *ASB*, pp. 95–96 (T: *mNgon pa kun las btus pa'i rnam par bshad pa*, ff. 233a–234b), listed in Bibliography under *Jinaputra*.

228 S: *sopadhiśeṣanirvāṇam*, T: *lhag bcas kyi mya ngan las 'das pa*.

229 S: *nirupadhiśeṣanirvāṇam*, T: *lhag med kyi mya ngan las 'das pa*.

230 There are four fruits of asceticism: (1) Stream Enterer (S: *srota āpannaḥ*, T: *rgyun zhugs pa*); (2) Once Returner (S: *sakṛdāgamī*, T: *lan gcig phyir 'ong ba*); (3) Nonreturner (S: *anāgamī*, T: *phyir mi 'ong ba*); and (4) Arhat (S: *arhat*, T: *dgra bcom pa*); see

also Part One, note 649. The eight types of sangha are (1) the one who is striving after the fruit of a Stream Enterer; (2) one who is abiding in the fruit of a Stream Enterer; (3) one who is striving after the fruit of a Once Returner; (4) one who is abiding in the fruit of a Once Returner; (5) one who is striving after the fruit of a Nonreturner; (6) one who is abiding in the fruit of a Nonreturner; (7) one who is striving after the fruit of an Arhat; and (8) one who is abiding in the fruit of an Arhat. Thus, four are individuals who are "pursuing a fruit" (S: *phalapratipannakaḥ*, T: *'bras bu la zhugs pa*) and four are individuals who are "abiding in a fruit" (S: *phalasthaḥ*, T: *'bras bu la gnas pa*). Each fruit is achieved as a practitioner progressively abandons an ever greater portion of the mental afflictions connected with the three realms—the desire realm, the form realm, and the formless realm. See also Part One, p. 172.

231 I.e., the Truth of Cessation, and especially nirvana itself. This was referred to earlier as the "ultimate Dharma" (S: *paramārthadharmaḥ*, T: *don dam pa'i chos*).

232 I.e., the Truth of the Path. This was referred to earlier as "the Dharma of practice" (S: *pratipattidharmaḥ*, T: *sgrub pa'i chos*); it is also known as the "Dharma of realization" (S: *adhigamadharmaḥ*, T: *rtogs pa'i chos*).

233 This is a reference to the form of the Dharma that was described above as the "Dharma of instruction" (S: *deśanādharmaḥ*, T: *bstan pa'i chos*); it is also known as the "scriptural Dharma" (S: *āgamadharmaḥ*, T: *lung gi chos*).

234 S: *rūpaprasādaḥ*, T: *gzugs dang ba*. This phrase is used to describe the five sense faculties; see above, p. 230.

235 S: *chandasaṃniśrayadānakarmikā*, T: *'dun pa'i rten byed pa'i las can*.

236 S: *avadyam*, T: *kha na ma tho ba*.

237 S: *lajjā*, T: *'dzem pa*.

238 S: *duścaritasaṃyamasaṃniśrayadānakarmikā*, T: *nyes par spyod pa yang dag par sdom pa'i rten byed pa'i las can*.

239 S: *alobhaḥ*, T: *ma chags pa*. The original Sanskrit term is simply the term "attachment" with a negative prefix. However, this prefix does not indicate the mere absence of attachment or an entity that is distinct from attachment; it is meant to identify a positive mental attitude that has the power to counteract attachment.

240 S: *nirvidanāgrahaḥ*, T: *yid 'byung zhing len pa med pa*.

241 S: *upakaraṇam*, T: *longs spyad*. The Sanskrit term means such things as "instrument" or "anything that supports life." The Tibetan translation of the Sanskrit subcommentary written by an Indian scholar whose name is translated into Tibetan as Sa'i rtsa lag ("Earth-Friend") glosses the term as meaning "food and drink." The Tibetan term generally means "objects of enjoyment" or "wealth." In the present context, the sense is certainly more broad than just food and drink, and should be taken as including any and all things that are capable of eliciting ordinary desire.

242 S: *duścaritāpravṛttisaṃniśrayadānakarmakaḥ*, T: *nyes par spyod pa la mi 'jug pa'i rten byed pa'i las can*.

243 S: *āghātaḥ*, T: *kun nas mnar sems pa*.

244 S: *jñānam*, T: *shes pa*.

245 This point is taken directly from Asaṅga's *AS* (p. 6); the commentary to this work identifies the four as knowledge possessed from birth, and that which derives from listening, reflection, and meditation, respectively.

246 S: *pratisaṃkhyā*, T: *so sor rtog pa*.

247 S: *dhairyam*, T: *brtan pa*. "Firmness" seems to suggest a mental factor that provides support for wisdom.

248 S: *kliṣṭe tūtsāhaḥ kutsitatvāt kausīdyam eva*, T: *nyon mongs pa can la spro ba ni smad pa yin pa'i phyir le lo nyid do.*

249 These five types of effort are mentioned in Asaṅga's *AS* (p. 6). *ASB* (p. 5) states that they correspond to terms in sutras which describe a practitioner who develops effort as "stalwart" (S: *sthāmavān*, T: *mthu dang ldan pa*); "courageous" (S: *vīryavān*, T: *brtson 'grus dang ldan pa*); "mighty" (S: *utsāhī*, T: *spro ba dang ldan pa*); "firmly bold" (S: *dṛḍhaparākramaḥ*, T: *brtul ba brtan pa*); and "unceasing" (S: *anakṣipadhuraḥ*, T: *brtson pa mi 'dor ba*) in his or her drive to accomplish virtue.

250 S: *kuśalapakṣaparipūraṇaparinispādanakarmakam*, T: *dge ba'i phyogs yongs su rdzogs par byed pa dang / yongs su sgrub pa'i las can.*

251 S: *parikarma*, T: *yongs su sbyong ba*. See, for example, chapter one, vv. 49–71 of the *Abhisamayālaṃkāraḥ*, which identifies a particular group of spiritual practices that are associated with each of the various Bodhisattva levels. These are also enumerated in the *Twenty-five-Thousand-Line Perfection of Wisdom Sutra.*

252 S: *dauṣṭhulyam*, T: *gnas ngan len*. See also Part One, note 408.

253 S: *sāṃkleśikadharmabījāni*, T: *kun nas nyon mongs pa'i chos kyi sa bon rnams*. The term "afflicted entities" refers to three aspects of samsaric existence: (1) birth, (2) karma, and (3) the mental afflictions. These three have a correspondence with the twelve limbs of dependent origination. The first, eighth, and ninth limbs of ignorance, craving, and grasping, respectively, represent the mental afflictions; the second and tenth limbs, called "formations" and "existence," represent two phases of karma; and the remaining seven limbs—ranging from the third limb of consciousness through the seventh of feeling, along with the last two limbs of birth, and old age and death—are the result limbs that occur in all samsaric rebirth. See also Part One, note 771.

254 S: *karmaṇyatā*, T: *las su rung ba nyid.*

255 S: *samyaṅmanasikārasaṃprayuktasya cittasyāhlādalāghavanimittaṃ*, T: *yang dag pa'i yid la byed la zhugs pa'i sems kyi sim pa dang yang bar 'gyur pa'i rgyu.*

256 S: *prītimanasaḥ kāya praśrabhyate*. This passage is introduced to suggest that agility of body represents a change that the body undergoes. The instruction on mental quiescence (S: *śamathaḥ*, T: *zhi gnas*) describes the role of agility in achieving this important state of one-pointed concentration.

257 S: *praśrabdhibodhyaṅgam*, T: *shin tu sbyangs pa byang chub kyi yan lag*. Vasubandhu's *Commentary to the Treasury of Higher Learning* (in explanation of ch. 2, v. 25) records some debate about the nature of agility of body. The Vaibhāṣika School, in particular, maintained that there is an agility of body that is mental in nature, in the sense that it accompanies sensory consciousness just as the feeling that accompanies sensory consciousness is called corporeal sensation. An important aspect of the discussion centers around the fact that agility constitutes one of the seven "limbs of enlightenment," and in that context it is understood to be a mental factor. Nevertheless, Sthiramati asserts here that agility of body is physical in nature since he identifies it as "a particular tangible object of the body" (S: *kāyasya spraṣṭavyaviśeṣaḥ*, T: *lus kyi reg bya'i khyad par*).

258 S: *iyam tad vaśenāśrayaparāvṛttito 'śeṣakleśādyāvaraṇaniṣkarṣaṇakarmikā*, T: *'di ni de'i dbang gis gnas 'gyur bas nyon mongs pa la sogs pa'i sgrib pa ma lus pa sel ba'i las can.* Agility plays an important role in the attainment of quiescence (see Part One, pp. 165–166). Without attaining quiescence, one cannot achieve the transcendent awareness that eradicates both the seeds of the mental afflictions and the more subtle obscurations to objects of knowledge. Agility brings about "a transformation of one's

being" in that it has the power to eliminate the state of indisposition that the mental afflictions impose on one's mind and body.

259 Sa'i rtsa lag's *PSB* (f. 58a) glosses "overcome" (S: **nirvāpaṇam*, T: *sel ba*) as meaning to remove the mental afflictions by means of the mundane path; "destroy" (S: **vikramaṇam*, T: *rnam par gnon pa*) as meaning to abandon them by means of the Seeing Path; and "eradicate" (S: **bījasamuddharaṇam*, T: *sa bon yang dag par 'don pa*) as meaning to abandon all remaining traces of the mental afflictions by means of the Meditation Path.

260 S: *laukikalokottarasampattiparipūraṇakarmakaḥ*, T: *'jig rten dang / 'jig rten las 'das pa'i phun sum tshogs pa thams cad yongs su rdzogs par byed pa'i las can.*

261 S: *bhavopakaraṇaviśeṣalābhaḥ*, T: *srid pa dang / longs spyod kyi khyad par rnyed pa.* See also note 241, above.

262 S: *cittasamatā*, T: *sems kyi mnyam pa nyid.*

263 S: *praśaṭhatā*, T: *rnal du 'dug pa.*

264 S: *anabhogatā*, T: *lhun gyis grub pa.*

265 S: *saṃkleśānavakāśasaṃniśrayadānakarmikā*, T: *kun nas nyon mongs pa'i skabs mi 'byed pa'i rten byed pa'i las can.*

266 The two Sanskrit nouns *vadhaḥ* and *bandhanam* are rendered unambiguously in the Tibetan here as "killing" (T: *gsod pa*) and "binding" (T: *'ching ba*), respectively. While the original terms certainly carry these two meanings, they can convey a broader sense as well. The first term, *vadhaḥ*, can also mean "striking" or "beating"; in fact, Sa'i rtsa lag's commentary translates it as "beating" (T: *brdeg pa*). Similarly, the second term, *bandhanam*, can mean such things as "confinement" or "imprisonment," and sometimes even more broadly "chastisement" or "punishment." Therefore, the first term could be taken to mean the inflicting of direct physical harm in a broad sense, including the extreme act of killing, while the second term should be taken as referring mainly to the restriction of a person's freedom of movement through some form of confinement.

267 S: *karuṇā*, T: *snying rje.*

268 S: *kaṃ ruṇaddhi*, T: *bsod nyams bsrel ba.*

269 S: *kam*, T: *bsod nyams.*

270 S: *aviheṭhanakarmikā*, T: *tho mi 'tshams pa'i las can.*

271 S: *tṛṣṇā*, T: *sred pa.* This term is used here as a synonym for the root mental affliction of desire.

272 This description is taken directly from Vasubandhu's *Commentary to the Treasury of Higher Learning* in connection with his explanation of ch. 1, v. 8. The text there states: "'Grasping' refers to the mental afflictions. The impure heaps are called 'grasping heaps' because they originate from grasping (S: *tatsambhūtatvāt*, T: *de dag las byung ba'i phyir*) as in the expression 'grass fire' and 'straw fire.' Or, they are so designated because they are governed by grasping (S: *tadvidheyatvāt*, T: *de dag la rag lus pa'i phyir*), as (a person who is subject to a king's rule) is called a 'king's man.' Or, they are so designated because grasping arises from the impure heaps (S: *upādānāni tebhyaḥ sambhavanti*, T: *de dag las nye bar len pa rnams 'byung bas*) as in the expressions 'flower tree' and 'fruit tree.'" For comments on the expression "impure heaps," see note 9 above.

273 S: *snehaḥ*, T: *zhen pa.*

274 S: *snehaḥ*, T: *'jen pa*, also *snum pa.*

275 S: **adhyavasānam*, T: *lhag par chags pa.*

276 S: *duḥkhasaṃjananakarmakaḥ*, T: *sdug bsngal bskyed pa'i las can.*
277 The three types of suffering are (1) the suffering of suffering (S: *suḥkhaduḥkhatā*, T; *sdug bsngal gyi sdug bsngal nyid*); (2) the suffering of change (S: *pariṇāmaduḥkhatā*, T: *'gyur ba'i sdug bsngal nyid*); and (3) the suffering of conditioned existence (S: *saṃskāraduḥkhatā*, T: *'du byed kyi sdug bsngal nyid*). See Part One, pp. 105–133.
278 S: *āghātaḥ*, T: *kun nas mnar sems pa.*
279 See above, note 266, for a discussion of the terms "killing" and "binding."
280 S: *asparśavihāraduścaritasaṃniśrayadānakarmakaḥ*, T: *reg par mi gnas pa dang / nyes par spyod pa'i rten byed pa'i las can.*
281 S: *sparśaḥ*, T: *reg pa*. The original Sanskrit term *sparśa* generally means "touch" or "making contact"; in the present context it has the special sense of a "pleasant feeling." Hence I translate the term here somewhat more broadly as "contented state." The phrase "to remain in a contented state" (S: *sparśavihāraḥ*, T: *reg par gnas pa*) has many applications.
282 This is the mistaken belief in a real self. See discussion of this view within the topic of the five views, below.
283 S: *cittasyonnatilakṣaṇaḥ*, T: *sems khengs pa'i mtshan nyid.*
284 S: *agauravaduḥkhotpattisaṃniśrayadānakarmakaḥ*, T: *mi gus pa dang / sdug bsngal 'byung ba'i rten byed pa'i las can.*
285 The original Sanskrit of these three paragraphs appears verbatim in *TB*, p. 86.
286 In addition to its occurrence in the compound "grasping heaps," the term "grasping" (S: *upādānam*, T: *nye bar len pa*) is also the name of the ninth limb in the twelvefold teaching on dependent origination. See Part One, note 454.
287 S: *chandaḥ*, T: *'dun pa.*
288 S: *rāgaḥ*, T: *'dod chags.*
289 S: *dhyānaḥ*, T: *bsam gtan*. These are the four meditative absorptions of the form realm. See Part One, pp. 174–178.
290 S: *samāpattiḥ*, T: *snyoms par 'jug pa*. These are the four states of composure associated with the formless realm. For a brief description, see Part One, p. 178.
291 This second statement is taken verbatim from Vasubandhu's *AKB* (p. 285): S: *asti sadṛśo yo 'bhiprete vare sattvarāśau nihīnam apyātmānam bahu manyate*. T: *gang dag sems can mchog dam pa'i tshogs kyi nang na dbag dma' bar 'gyur na'ang tha gi'o snyam du sems khengs pa dag yod do.*
292 S: *sahajaḥ*, T: *lhan cig skyes pa.*
293 S: *parikalpitaḥ*, T: *kun brtags pa*. See also below, p. 303.
294 Sthiramati's description of these three examples of contrived ignorance seems to be based on the following passage from Vasubandhu's *rTen cing 'brel bar 'byung ba dang po'i rnam par dbye ba bshad pa* (**Pratītyasamutpādādivibhaṅgabhāṣyam*), Tg., vol. 115 (*chi*), f. 9a: "What is absence of knowledge with regard to karma? It is [the absence of knowledge] that is uncertain about the good and bad [karma] that do exist and [the absence of knowledge] that denies [that good and bad karma exist]. It is also [the absence of knowledge possessed by] those who conceive of what is virtuous as nonvirtuous and engage in such practices as animal sacrifice and suicide by fire, as well as the opposite of that—[which is to say, the absence of knowledge possessed by] those who conceive of what is nonvirtuous as virtuous and engage in such practices as animal sacrifice and suicide by fire." Guṇamati's subcommentary on this passage (S: **Pratītyasamutpādādivibhaṅganirdeśaṭīkā*, T: *rTen cing 'brel bar 'byung ba dang po'i rnam par dbye ba bstan pa'i rgya cher bshad pa*, Tg., vol. 115 (*chi*), f. 91a–91b) states

the following about the third form of contrived ignorance: "The lack of knowledge possessed by those who conceive of what is virtuous as nonvirtuous is [a form of ignorance] that can be concomitant with the view that one's conduct and asceticism are supreme and one that can also be concomitant with wrong view. How is that? If [the person who possesses this lack of knowledge] regards the virtuous [karma] that is the cause of a favorable result as nonvirtuous, then [his or her lack of knowledge] is concomitant with the view that one's conduct and asceticism are supreme. On the other hand, if [the person who possesses this lack of knowledge forms the determination] that virtuous [karma] is not a cause of any favorable result at all, then [his or her lack of knowledge] is concomitant with wrong view. How does [a person] conceive of what is virtuous as nonvirtuous such that he [or she] is said to engage in such practices as animal sacrifice and suicide by fire? [Such persons] do so because they regard engaging in such practices as animal sacrifice and suicide by fire as virtuous. Therefore, because [the truth] is the opposite of [what they believe], the lack of knowledge possessed by those who conceive of what is virtuous as nonvirtuous and [the lack of knowledge] possessed by those who conceive of what is nonvirtuous as virtuous constitute [forms of] ignorance that are both concomitant with the view that one's conduct and asceticism are supreme and concomitant with wrong view."

295 S: *dharmeṣu mithyāniścayavicikitsāsaṃkleśikotpattisaṃniśrayadānakarmikā*; T: *chos rnams la log par nges pa dang / the tshom dang / kun nas nyon mongs pa 'byung ba'i rten byed pa'i las can*. *TB* (p. 84) provides the following additional remarks about the meaning and nature of this action. "'States of affliction' (S: *saṃkleśaḥ*, T: *kun nas nyon mongs pa*) are of three types: the mental afflictions, karma, and birth. Their 'arising' means that each prior state of affliction serves as the condition for the next state of affliction to come into being. The action of 'providing support for their arising' means that only someone who is bewildered [by ignorance] gives rise to wrong understanding, doubt, the mental afflictions of desire and the rest, the karma that brings rebirth, and rebirth itself; someone who is not bewildered [by ignorance] does not give rise to them."

296 S: *dṛṣṭiḥ*, T: *lta ba*. *AKB* (p. 29) identifies judgment (S: *santīraṇam*, T: *nges par rtog pa*) as an essential characteristic of a view, both those that are correct and those that are mental afflictions. Judgment, in turn, is described (*AKV*, S: p. 113; T: f. 74a) as [a cognitive state that is] preceded by close consideration of its object (S: *viṣayopadhyānapūrvakam*, T: *yul la nges par dpyad pa sngon du 'gro ba*) and [one that] elicits a determination [in relation to that object] (S: *niścayākarṣaṇam*, T: *nges pa 'dren pa*).

297 The text is noting the fundamental distinction between correct views and views that constitute mental afflictions. The worldly correct view (S: *laukikasaṃyagdṛṣṭiḥ*, T: *'jig rten pa'i yang dag pa'i lta ba*) is the belief that virtuous karma carried out in this life leads to a favorable rebirth in future lives and nonvirtuous karma carried out in this life leads to unfavorable rebirths (see also Part One, pp. 34–35 and 40–42). Thus, it implies belief both in the doctrine of karma and in the existence of past and future lives. The transcendent correct view (S: *lokottarasaṃyagdṛṣṭiḥ*, T: *'jig rten las 'das pa'i yang dag pa'i lta ba*) denotes a view of ultimate reality and the nature of that view would vary according to the particular Buddhist philosophical school. For Hīnayāna schools, it would represent the view that realizes the insubstantiality of the person (S: *pudgalanairātmyam*, T: *gang zag gi bdag med*); for Mahayanists it would also represent the view that realizes the insubstantiality of entities (S: *dharmanairātmyam*, T: *chos kyi bdag med*).

298 S: *sad*, T: *'jig*.
299 S: *sīdati*, T: *'jig pa*.
300 S: *kāyaḥ*, T: *'tshogs pa*.
301 S: *cayaḥ*, T: *bsags pa*.
302 S: *buddhiḥ*, T: *blo*.
303 T: *gcer bu pa*. This is another name for the Jain tradition.
304 S: **rūpāvabhāsaḥ*, T: *gzugs su snang ba*.
305 S: *vastumātram*, T: *dngos pa tsam*. Momentary consciousness itself is the only thing that can be identified as constituting a cognizer in a nominal sense.
306 S: **kāritram*, T: *byed pa*.
307 S: **ātmalābhaḥ*, T: *bdag thob pa*.
308 This is the central thesis of the Buddhist doctrine of impermanence. In essence, it is that all causally produced entities without exception perish in the very next moment immediately following their appearance, because no external cause is required to occur at some later time in order to bring about their destruction. See also Part One, pp. 126–129.
309 S: *vināśaḥ*, T: *'jig pa*. The quality of "destruction" or "perishability" is a condition that characterizes real entities, but it has no distinct reality or independent substance of its own.
310 S: **prāgabhāvaḥ*, T: *snga na med pa*. For example, Kumarila's *Ślokavarttika* states: "The absence of yogurt, etc., in milk is called 'prior nonexistence.'" This term can also be rendered as a "nonexistence which may yet come to be."
311 S: **pradhvaṃsābhāvaḥ*, T: *zhig nas med pa*. Kumarila's *Ślokavarttika* states: "The nonexistence of milk in yogurt is the quality of nonexistence by destruction."
312 S: **kriyā*, T: *bya ba*.
313 That is, if an entity is an agent, it must always have the property of being associated with an action.
314 This would seem to be one of the several explanations of the agent-object relation. That is, it is one in which the object is produced (S: *utpādanam*, T: *bskyed pa*) by the agent. It is described, for example, in the statement, "Devadatta makes a mat."
315 That is, in the circumstance where there is an agent and an object.
316 The sDe dge edition reads *gnas pa med par 'gyur ro*, which seems to be a corruption. An early hand-written manuscript edition states *gsal ba med par 'gyur ro*. The translation is based on the latter reading. The intended meaning seems to be that the result of the rice becoming cooked would not occur.
317 S: **adhikaraṇavikārahetuḥ*, T: *gzhir 'gyur ba'i rgyu*.
318 S: **vikāraḥ*, T: *'gyur ba*.
319 S: **anyathābhāvaḥ*, T: *gzhan du 'gyur ba*.
320 S: **antaḥkaraṇapuruṣaḥ*, T: *nang na byed pa'i skyes bu*.
321 That is, this phrase distinguishes the perishable collection view from the view that holds an extreme, because the latter view does not [merely] regard the five heaps as "I" and "mine"; rather, it views the self that is mistakenly assumed to be real as undergoing extinction or as existing permanently.
322 Sthiramati seems to cite here the term that appears in Asaṅga's *AS*, p. 7 (S: *samanupaśyato*, T: *yang dag par rjes su lta ba*), rather than the simpler form that appears in Vasubandhu's root text (S: *paśyato*, T: *lta ba*); however, I assume the meaning of both to be the same.
323 S: *kliṣṭaprajñā*, T: *shes rab nyon mongs pa can*.
324 S: **viparyastaḥ*, T: *phyin ci log tu gyur pa*.

325 The term *ātman* (T: *bdag*) can be translated as "self" or as the personal pronoun "I." The sense of this statement is that an individual can only form the notion of a subjective self in relation to the five heaps that make up his or her own continuum.

326 S: *anupāttaḥ*, T: *ma zin pa*. In the present context, "unretained" refers to those entities that are not part of a sentient being's heaps. For a more literal explanation of the term "retained," see above, p. 258, and below, pp. 367–368.

327 S: *sarvadṛṣṭisaṃniśrayadānakarmikā*, T: *lta ba thams cad kyi rten byed pa'i las can*.

328 The verb "regards" and the expression "afflicted wisdom" were just discussed in relation to the perishable collection view.

329 S: *madhyamāpratipanniryāṇaparipanthakarmikā*, T: *dbu ma'i lam gyi nges par 'byung ba'i bar du gcod pa'i las can*.

330 The sixth section of the *Yogācārabhūmiḥ* identifies sixteen types of faulty doctrines. The description of wrong view here is based entirely on points that appear in the description of nihilism (S: *nāstikavādaḥ*, T: *med par smra ba*). To "deny causes" means to believe and profess that charity, sacred rites (S: *iṣṭam*, T: *mchod sbyin*), and fire offerings (S: *hutam*, T: *sbyin sreg*) are not efficacious, that good deeds don't necessarily lead to a higher rebirth and bad deeds don't necessarily bring rebirth in the lower realms. To "deny results" is to reject the notion that the actions just mentioned necessarily bring the karmic consequences that religious adherents believe they do. *ASB* (p. 6) identifies "denial of actions" as the series of beliefs that "this world does not exist; the next world does not exist; mothers do not exist; fathers do not exist; and sentient beings are not born in superhuman states (S: *upapādukam*, T: *rdzus te skye ba*)." Again, *YB* provides clarification of what these beliefs are: "On the basis of a mundane meditative absorption . . . certain individuals see that a Kṣatriya is reborn in a Brahman, Vaiśya, or a Śudra caste. Or they see that a Brahman is reborn in a Kṣatriya, Vaiśya, or a Śudra caste. And the same is true for a Vaiśya and a Śudra. Because of this they think to themselves: 'This world does not exist in such a way that those who were born as Kṣatriyas and the rest in another world are reborn into this one as a Kṣatriya, and the rest. Nor does the next world exist in such a way that those who were born as Kṣatriyas, and the rest, in this world are reborn in the next world as a Kṣatriya, and the rest.' . . . They also see that a mother can be reborn in the state of a daughter; a daughter can be reborn in the state of a mother; a father in the state of a son; and a son in the state of a father. Seeing the indefinite nature of the status of father and mother, they think to themselves, 'mothers do not exist,' 'fathers do not exist.' . . . Certain individuals, who seek to learn the rebirth of a particular person, fail to perceive where he [or she] was reborn. That person may have been reborn among the deities that lack any conception (S: *asaṃjñikaḥ*, T: *'du shes med pa*), among the beings of the formless realm, or he [or she] may have attained nirvana. Not realizing the nature of those states, they think to themselves, 'sentient beings are not born in superhuman states.'" Finally, the rejection of entities that exist is explained in relation to someone who wrongly believes himself or herself to have attained the status of an Arhat. When such a person realizes that he or she will be reborn again, he or she concludes that there is no such thing as an Arhat who has attained complete liberation from samsara. With the exception of the last example, all of these erroneous beliefs represent confusion about the workings of karma. The full significance of the denial of this world, the next world, and father and mother is somewhat ambiguous. They seem to be misunderstandings about the nature of cosmic order and negative reactions to what are perceived to be violations of that cosmic order. Asaṅga explains that

the denial of causes, results, and this and the next world can be corrected by understanding the type of karma that is called "that which is experienced at some later occasion" (S: *aparaparyāyavedanīyam*, T: *lan grags gzhan la myong bar 'gyur ba*). The "denial of father and mother" seems to hinge on the notion that if someone is the father or mother of some particular individual, it is improper that he or she should ever become the son or daughter of that individual. Perhaps the idea that the person who was your father or mother could become your own child contradicts some sensibility or principle relating to the validity of ancestor worship. Asaṅga's response to this form of wrong view seems to confirm such an interpretation. He writes: "What do you believe: Is the person who gives birth to someone their mother or not? Is the person from whose seed someone originates their father or not? If father and mother do exist [in this sense], then it is wrong to declare that mother and father do not exist. If [you insist that] they are not father and mother even though they gave birth to you and you sprang from their seed, again it is wrong to deny that mother and father do not exist. On the particular occasion when someone is your mother or father, they are not your son or daughter; and on the particular occasion when someone is your daughter or son, they are not your mother or father."

331 S: *kuśalamūlsamucchedakarmikā / akuśalamūladṛḍhatāsaṃniśrayadānakarmikā*, T: *dge ba'i rtsa ba gcod pa'i las can dang / mi dge ba'i rtsa ba dam du 'dzin pa'i rten byed pa'i las can*.

332 The point is that this view is not limited to the notion that one's beliefs are supreme when in fact they are not. This view can also occur in relation to one's own impure heaps as a whole. Thus, one can mistakenly regard ones impure grasping heaps as pure or as constituting a state of happiness, etc., and regard that condition as excellent.

333 S: *asaddṛṣṭyabhiniveśasaṃniśrayadānakarmakaḥ*, T: *lta ba ngan pa la mngon par zhen pa'i rten byed pa'i las can*.

334 As examples of "outer appearance" (S: **veṣaḥ*, T: *cha byad*), *PSB* (f. 68a) indicates shaving the head and going about naked. For conduct (S: **cāritraḥ*, T: *tshul*), the same text indicates fasting, and adopting the behavior of a cow or dog.

335 S: *prajñā*, T: *shes rab*. The root text describes all five of the views as "afflicted wisdom." In this context, it does not seem appropriate to translate this term, where it is appearing alone, as "wisdom." See above, p. 280, where *prajñā* is described as sometimes constituting an incorrect discrimination.

336 S: *śramavaiphalyasaṃniśrayadānakarmakaḥ*, T: *ngal ba 'bras bu med pa'i rten byed pa'i las can*. *ASB* (p. 6) explains that this view has this action "because [misguided conduct and asceticism] are not conducive to deliverance" (S: *tenāniryāṇāt*, T: *des nges par mi 'byung ba'i phyir*). The terms "morality and asceticism," as they are being used here, refer to codes of conduct that are affiliated with erroneous belief systems—which is to say, those found in religious traditions that fall outside the domain of Buddhism. Since this kind of conduct and asceticism will not lead to deliverance, whatever exertion you make in cultivating them will prove fruitless. By contrast, the Buddhist training of morality and its related ascetic practices are conducive to liberation when they are cultivated in combination with the superior trainings of concentration and wisdom.

337 S: *vimatiḥ*, T: *yid gnyis za ba*.

338 S: *kuśalapakṣāpravṛttisaṃniśrayadānakarmikā*, T: *dge ba'i phyogs la mi 'jug pa'i rten byed pa'i las can*.

339 Contrived forms of the mental afflictions are abandoned by the Seeing Path. *AS* (p.

52) identifies 112 forms of the ten root mental afflictions that are abandoned by the Seeing Path. Forty are associated with the desire realm. That is, each of the ten root mental afflictions has a form that relates to each of the Four Noble Truths that are associated with the desire realm. Because there is no hatred in the form or formless realms, there are only thirty-six forms that relate to the Four Noble Truths associated with each of these two realms. As Sthiramati notes here, the three latter views and doubt only have contrived forms. That is because these four mental afflictions are generated solely on the basis of mistaken judgments and bad reasoning. Once a practitioner achieves a direct realization of selflessness on the Seeing Path, he or she is no longer subject to such error and, therefore, will no longer develop any of these four mental afflictions. The other six mental afflictions—desire, hatred, ignorance, pride, the perishable collection view, and the view that grasps an extreme—also have "innate" forms that are more deeply ingrained and arise on the strength of habitual predispositions rather than flawed conceptual thought. These forms of the mental afflictions can only be abandoned by the Meditation Path. All six of these mental afflictions have innate forms that are associated with the desire realm; the five other than hatred also have innate forms that are associated with the form and formless realms. Hence there are sixteen basic forms of these six mental afflictions that are innate and must be abandoned by the Meditation Path.

340 S: *upakleśāḥ*, T: *nye ba'i nyon mongs pa rnams*. *YB* (p. 167): "The secondary mental afflictions are [the mental factors that] agitate the mind to a lesser degree [than the root mental afflictions], due to [the various forms of] error" (S: *viparyāsaiś cittopakleśakatvād upakleśāḥ*, T: *phyin ci log rnams kyis sems nye bar nyon mongs par byed pas na nye ba'i nyon mongs pa rnams so*). In the same place, Asaṅga describes seven kinds of "error" (S: *viparyāsaḥ*, T: *phyin ci log*): (1) error of conception, (2) error of view, (3) error of mind, (4) the error that [mistakenly] regards what is impure as pure, (5) the error that [mistakenly] regards what is impermanent as permanent, (6) the error that [mistakenly] regards what is unsatisfactory (i.e., suffering) as a state of well-being, and (7) the error that [mistakenly] regards what is not a real self as constituting a real self. Error of conception is the conception that affirms the last four types of error. Error of view is the strong belief in and adherence to any of those errors of conception. Error of mind is the state in which [the mind] becomes afflicted by desire, etc., because of those errors of view.

341 S: *āghātaḥ*, T: *kun nas mnar sems pa*. This is the same essential nature as that of the root mental affliction of hatred. *AKB* (p. 312) makes the observation that anger is an animosity toward sentient beings and inanimate objects that does not include malice (S: *vyāpādaḥ*, T: *gnod sems*) and harmfulness (S: *vihiṃsā*, T: *rnam par 'tshe ba*). The purpose of this distinction, apparently, is to indicate that anger is a generalized animosity that occurs before any determination has been made to engage in violence. *AKV* (p. 845) gives these two illustrations of anger: (1) the mental agitation felt by a monk who is desirous of cultivating spiritual training and (2) the agitation that is felt toward a thorn and the like. Presumably, in the first instance the agitation is felt toward someone who is disturbing the monk that wishes to cultivate spiritual training.

342 S: *daṇḍādānādisaṃniśrayadānakarmakaḥ*, T: *dbyug pa len pa la sogs pa'i rten byed pa'i las can*. As the Tibetan suggests, the action includes a phrase that literally means "taking up a club." However, while the Sanskrit *daṇḍa* does mean "rod," "staff," or "club," the term is also a symbol of judicial authority and punishment, and can stand for all

forms of punishment—corporal, verbal, and fiscal; as well as for chastisement, imprisonment, and fines. This same phrase is rendered in the Tibetan translation of *AS* as *chad pas gcod pa*, which means "to punish." *AS* also includes "taking up a weapon" (S: *śastrādānaḥ*, T: *mtshon cha len pa*) as part of the action of anger, and this expression states more directly the notion of resorting to physical violence. Butön's commentary to *AS* summarizes the action of anger as initiating all manner of harm to a person's body, life, or wealth.

343 S: *akṣāntisaṃniśrayadānakarmakaḥ*, T: *mi bzod pa'i rten byed pa'i las can*.

344 Although the meaning of this secondary mental affliction is not limited to the act of confession, that seems to be the context in which it is being described here.

345 S: *kaukṛtyāsparśavihārasaṃniśrayadānakarmakaḥ*, T: *'gyod pa dang reg par mi gnas pa'i rten byed pa'i las can*.

346 S: *dāśitā*, T: *sher 'debs pa nyid*.

347 S: *caṇḍavacodāśitā*, T: *tshig brlang pos zher 'debs pa*. Vasubandhu's description of this mental factor relies on the Sanskrit root *dās* or *dāś*, which means "to injure," or, when combined with the prefix *abhi*, "to treat as an enemy." Sthiramati also draws on the root *daṅs* ("to bite") in his explanation of Vasubandhu's phrase. The Tibetan phrase *zher 'debs pa* is based mainly on the first root, as it means "to upset [i.e., harm] the mind [of others by criticism or reproach]." Sthiramati glosses Vasubandhu's substantive noun *dāśitā* with a passage that is difficult to render literally into English in a way that ably captures these different verbal allusions. *Daśanasīlo*, which I render as "to have an acrimonious nature" literally means "a biting nature." The Tibetan renders this as *zher 'debs pa'i ngang tshul*, which translates as "a nature that injures the minds [of others]." The adjective *dāśī* ("injurious" or even "fiendish") is translated in the Tibetan with the same phrase *zher 'debs pa*. *Tadbhāvo dāśitā* translates literally as "that quality [i.e., of being fiendish] is injuriousness." Sthiramati glosses Vasubandhu's original phrase a second time with the phrase *caṇḍena vacasā pradaśati*, "[spite is a mental factor that] bites by means of heated words." Here the Tibetan does approach the Sanskrit more closely with *tshig brlang pos za ba dang 'dra bar*, which can be rendered literally as "[spite is a mental factor that] appears to devour [i.e., harm or destroy] by means of heated words." Neither *AKB* nor Nāgārjuna's *RA* refer to harsh speech in their descriptions of this mental factor. The former (p. 313) states: "Spite is the quality of grasping firmly to blameworthy matters; it is [the mental factor] that causes one to refuse good advice" (S: *sāvadyavastu dṛḍhagrāhitā pradāśo yena nyāyasaṃjñāptiṃ na gṛhṇāti*, T: *kha na ma tho ba'i dngos po dam du 'dzin pa ste gang gis rigs par gtams pa mi 'dzin pa*). *AK* (ch. 5, v. 50) also states that "spite arises from the consideration that views are supreme" (S: *dṛṣṭyāmarśāt pradāśas . . . utthitam*, T: *'tshig pa lta ba mchog 'dzin las / . . . kun nas bslang*). Nāgārjuna's *RA* (ch. 5, v. 3) gives the simple description that "spite is attachment to evil" (S: *pradāśaḥ pāpasaṅgitā*, T: *'tshig pa sdig la zhen pa'o*). Drawing on all these sources, Yongzin Yeshe Gyeltsen offers this summary description in his *Elucidation of Mind and Mental Factors*: "It is a mental state that, instead of reacting with remorse or a sense of acknowledgment when someone tells you that you have done something wrong, is moved by anger and resentment to develop the enmity that wishes to utter harsh speech."

348 This is virtually a repetition of Asaṅga's description in *AS* (p. 5).

349 S: *vāgduścaritaprasavakarmakaḥ / asparśavihārakarmakaś ca*; T: *ngag gi nyes par spyod pa skyed pa'i las can dang / reg par mi gnas pa'i las can*. Asaṅga describes its actions as threefold: (1) to provide support for loud and exceedingly harsh speech; (2) to

engender nonvirtuous deeds; and (3) [to cause others] to remain in a discontented state.

350 *TB* (p. 92) has *svam āśrayam* (T: *rang gi gnas*), which would translate as "one's being," rather than the phrase *svam āśayam* (T: *rang gi bsam pa*) as is suggested here.

351 S: *daurmanasyāsparśavihārakarmikā*, T: *yid mi bde ba dang / reg par mi gnas pa'i las can.*

352 S: *asaṃlekhasaṃniśrayadānakarmikam*, T: *yo byad ma bsnyungs pa'i rten byed pa'i las can.* "Simplicity" (S: *saṃlekhaḥ*, T: *yo byad bsnyungs pa*) represents the virtuous principle by which an individual seeks to keep desire in check by avoiding the accumulation of possessions that are not necessary for the pursuit of a spiritual life. While "simplicity" is not entirely satisfactory as a translation of the original term, it carries a less negative connotation than words like "temperance," "frugality," "austerity," "abstinence," and the like, which all touch on this quality but either suggest puritanical self-denial or are related too narrowly to the avoidance of improper indulgence in food, drink, or sexual activity. While this quality is certainly meant to be followed by monks and nuns, who adhere to the twin virtues of "having few desires" (S: *alpecchā*, T: *'dod pa chung ba*) and "being satisfied with what one has" (S: *saṃtuṣṭaḥ*, T: *chog shes pa*), it should not be considered as exclusive to that life-style. It is also to be distinguished from the frugality that is the adherence to economy, since that can lead easily to stinginess rather than absence of desire.

353 S: *mithyājīvasaṃniśrayadānakarmikā*, T: *log pas 'tsho ba'i rten byed pa'i las can.*

354 S: *anyenānyatpratisaran*, T: *gzhan nas gzhan du bsgyur ba*. Literally, "one who replaces one thing with another." *PSB* (f. 72a): "If someone asks you, 'Did you commit this wrongful act?' you might respond by saying something like, 'I had gone from Madura to Rajagir,' thereby misleading the questioner or keeping the matter uncertain."

355 S: *samyagavavādalābhaparipanthakarmakam*, T: *yang dag pa'i gdams ngag rnyed pa'i bar du gcod pa'i las can.*

356 S: *yoniśomanaskāraḥ*, T: *tshul bzhin yid la byed pa*. In a broad sense, this expression means "to properly engage an object in the mind." However, in this context it clearly refers more specifically to the cultivation of states of meditative concentration, a result that can be attained by practicing the instruction received from a spiritual teacher.

357 S: *cetasaḥ paryādānam*, T: *sems yongs su 'dzin pa*. The Tibetan translations of *AK*, *AKB*, and *AKV* all render *paryādānam* as *yongs su gtugs pa*. The meaning of the term as it is being used here is clearly indicated by Sthiramati; however, its literal sense apparently can include "to be overcome" (T: *yongs su 'dzin pa*) as well as "to be exhausted" (T: *yongs su gtugs pa*). This difference seems to be reflected in the variant Tibetan equivalents.

358 S: *tṛṣṇā*, T: *sred pa*. Often translated as "thirst" or "craving"; "attachment" seems more appropriate in this context. In the root text description, the person who possesses this form of attachment is described as being "infatuated" (S: *raktaḥ*, T: *chags pa*) with his or her own well-being.

359 S: *sarvakleśopakleśasaṃniśrayadānadarmakaḥ*, T: *nyon mongs pa dang nye ba'i nyon mongs pa thams cad kyi rten byed pa'i las can.*

360 S: *sattvaviheṭhaṇakarmikā*, T: *sems can rnams la rnam par tho 'tshams pa'i las can.*

361 *TB* (p. 94): "Absence of abashment [is the mental factor that] constitutes the antithesis of abashment—which is to say, it is the lack of embarrassment about doing an evil act, even if it should become known that you did something that is opposed by the world [at large] and [philosophical] treatises."

362 S: *sarvakleśopakleśasāhāyyakarmakam*, T: *nyon mongs pa dang nye ba'i nyon mongs pa thams cad kyi grogs byed pa'i las can*. While the Tibetan literally means "to accompany" the mental afflictions, the original Sanskrit term (S: *sāhāyyam*) means "helping" or "giving assistance"—hence, I have rendered the action as "facilitating" all the other root and secondary mental afflictions, in the sense of making it more likely that they will occur.

363 S: *jaḍībhavam*, T: *blun par gyur pa*. The original Sanskrit has a range of meanings, including "stiff," "motionless," "senseless," "dull," "inanimate," "stupid," and "lifeless." While the Tibetan equivalent literally means "stupid," it is probably more correctly a lack of vitality and alertness.

364 S: *śamathaḥ*, T: *zhi gnas*. This is the same term that is used to describe a specialized form of one-pointed concentration that is practiced jointly with insight (S: *vipaśyanaḥ*, T: *lhag mthong*) to gain transcendent realization (see Part One, pp. 162–166). While excitation is one of the main obstacles to the attainment of that form of quiescence, in the present context the term should be understood in a much broader sense as well.

365 S: *śamathaparipanthakarmakam*, T: *zhi gnas bar du gcod pa'i las can*.

366 See earlier description of the three types of faith, pp. 281–284.

367 S: *kausīdyasaṃniśrayadānakarmakam*, T: *le lo'i rten byed pa'i las can*.

368 S: *kutsite sīdyata iti kausīdyam*, T: *ngan pa la sbyor bas ni le lo'o*. This is an explanation of the literal meaning (S: *nirvacanam*, T: *nges tshig*) of the term.

369 S: *kuśalapakṣaprayogaparipanthakarmakam*, T: *dge ba'i phyogs la sbyor ba'i bar du gcod pa'i las can*.

370 S: *akuśalavṛddhikuśalaparihāṇisaṃniśrayadānakarmakaḥ*, T: *mi dge ba 'phel ba dang dge ba 'grib pa'i rten byed pa'i las can*.

371 *PSB* (f. 75a–75b): "Just as those individuals who are accustomed to eating honey and sugar are unable to eat bitter foods, those whose recollection is accompanied by a mental affliction such as desire are only able to recall objects of desire such as [attractive] women; they cannot maintain any clarity of mind with regard to virtuous objects. Therefore, clouded recollection is the failure to maintain a state of recollection in the mind of such virtuous objects as excellent spiritual instruction, and thus the mind becomes clouded with regard to [that type of] object."

372 S: *vikṣepasaṃniśrayadānakarmikā*, T: *g.yeng ba'i rten byed pa'i las can*.

373 S: *vividhaṃ kṣipyate 'nena cittam iti vikṣepaḥ*, T: *rnam par g.yeng ba ni 'dis sems sna tshogs su g.yeng bar byed pa'o*. In fact, Sthiramati does not directly address the wording of Vasubandhu's root text, which describes the essential nature of this mental factor as a "flowing outward" or "flowing away" (S: *visāraḥ*, T: *'phro ba*) of the mind from some object. Asaṅga describes six kinds of distraction in his *AS* (pp. 9–10): (1) innate distraction; (2) outward distraction; (3) inner distraction; (4) distraction caused by an [improper] motive; (5) distraction caused by indisposition; and (6) distraction due to [application of a different form of] attention.

374 S: *vairāgyaparipanthakarmakaḥ*, T: *'dod chags dang bral ba'i bar du gcod pa'i las can*.

375 For a comprehensive treatment of vigilance (S: *saṃprajānyam*, T: *shes bzhin*), see Asaṅga's discussion in *ŚB* (Sanskrit text: pp. 121–127, a portion at the end is missing; Tibetan text: ff. 44a–52a) on maintaining a state of vigilance (S: *saṃprajānyadvihāritā*, T: *shes bzhin to spyod pa nyid*). Vigilance is also counted among the eight factors (S: *aṣṭasaṃskārāḥ*, T: *'du byed brgyad*) that must be practiced in order to overcome the five faults (S: *pañcadoṣāḥ*, T: *nyes pa lnga*) that prevent one from achieving the state

of one-pointed concentration known as "quiescence" (S: *śamathaḥ*, T: *zhi gnas*). Vigilance is addressed in this latter context in a number of important works, particularly the *Madhyāntavibhāgaḥ* and Je Tsongkapa's *Lamrim Chenmo.*

376 S: *āpattisaṃniśrayadānakarmakam*, T: *ltung ba'i rten byed pa'i las can.*

377 This paragraph represents a derivation of the literal meaning of the word "regret" (S: *kaukṛtyam*, T: *'gyod pa*) based on the expression "bad deed" (S: *kukṛtam*, T: *ngan pa byas pa*). I include the original Sanskrit term for regret in the text, in order to retain the double meaning that is conveyed by both the state of having acted badly and the feeling of regret (S: *kutsitaṃ kṛtam iti kukṛtam / tadbhāvaḥ kaukṛtyam / iha tu kukṛtaviṣayaś cetaso vilekhaḥ kaukṛtyaṃ caitasikādhikārāt.* T: *ngan pa byas pas 'gyod de de'i ngos po ni 'gyod pa nyid do / ngan pa byas pa'i yul la sems mi dga' ba ste / sems las byung ba'i skabs yin pas 'gyod pa zhes bya'o*).

378 S: *cittasthitiparipanthakarmakam*, T: *sems gnas pa'i bar du gcod pa'i las can.* "Mental stability" refers to a state in which the mind remains stationary or fixed upon a particular meditation object. The instruction for cultivating quiescence describes a process in which a practitioner progressively develops nine levels of mental stability. See Part One, pp. 163–165.

379 S: *kṛtyātipattisaṃniśrayadānakarmakam*, T: *bya ba shor ba'i rten byed pa'i las can.*

380 S: *sparśāsparśvihārasaṃniśrayadānakarmikau*, T: *reg par gnas pa dang / reg par mi gnas pa'i rten byed pa'i las can. TB* (p. 100) describes afflicted and unafflicted deliberation and reflection as follows: "Deliberation about such things as the sense objects, malice, and the wish to do harm is afflicted; deliberation about departure (S: *naiṣkramyam*, T: *mngon par 'byung ba*) and the like is unafflicted (see above, pp. 172–173, for a description of the term "departure"). Similarly, reflection about ways of harming others is afflicted; reflection about ways of benefiting others is unafflicted." *PSB* (ff. 78a, 79a) adds that unafflicted deliberation and reflection "give support to remaining in a contented state because they represent a cause of happiness." Similarly, afflicted deliberation and reflection "give support to remaining in a discontented state because they represent a cause of suffering."

381 This represents the view of the Yogācāra School. The view expressed in the *AK* represents that of the Kashmir branch of the Vaibhāṣika School. According to the followers of the latter school, the formations that are not associated with consciousness are real entities that are distinct in nature from form, consciousness, and the mental factors.

382 S: *avasthā*, T: *gnas skabs.*

383 S: **adhiṣṭhānam*, T: *gnas.*

384 S: **avasthāyī*, T: *gnas skabs can.* In the present context, this term refers to the form, consciousness, or mental factor that represents the basis for ascribing the particular type of formation that is not associated with consciousness.

385 Uncertain reading: *gnas skabs can la 'bras bu rtag par thal bar 'gyur ba'i phyir ro.* Perhaps this statement represents the argument that if the state were distinct from the entity that is its basis, it would no longer possess the characteristics of a conditioned entity and that would mean it must have a permanent nature. In any case, a permanent result is a logical absurdity. Therefore, the formations that are not associated with consciousness must be nominally existent entities that are ascribed to states of form, consciousness, and mental factors; and those states are not something that is distinct from them.

386 These nine additional entities are not mentioned in either *PS* or *AK*; however, all of them are presented in Asaṅga's *AS* (p. 11).

387 S: *pratilambhaḥ*, T: *rnyed pa.*
388 S: *samanvāgamaḥ*, T: *ldan pa.*
389 S: *prāptiḥ*, T: *thob pa.*
390 S: **vaśitvam*, T: *dbang.*
391 S: **sammukhībhāvaḥ*, T: *mngon du gyur pa.*
392 S: *asaṃjñisamāpattiḥ*, T: *'du shes med pa'i snyoms par 'jug pa.* This state of composure is not meant to be cultivated, because it leads to rebirth among those long-lived deities who have no opportunity for further spiritual development and who are destined to fall back to the desire realm in their next life. It is only developed by those who mistakenly consider it a means of attaining liberation.
393 S: *asaṃjñisattvaḥ*, *'du shes med pa'i sems can.* As a result of having generated this state of composure, a being is reborn in a level of the form realm associated with the fourth meditative absorption (S: *dhyānam*, T: *bsam gtan*) where the worldly gods are called Those of Great Fruit (see description below of "[the quality of] having no conception"). These beings manifest a conception only at the time of their birth and their death. As a sutra declares: "And after having lived for a very extensive period of time, in conjunction with the arising of a conception, those beings fall away (i.e., die) from that place." Without exception, they are reborn in the desire realm, like an arrow that falls to the earth after its momentum has been exhausted.
394 S: *śubhakṛtsnaḥ*, T: *dge rgyas.*
395 S: *niḥsaraṇam*, T: *nges par 'byung ba.*
396 S: *vidūṣaṇākāram*, T: *rnam par sun 'byin pa'i rnam pa. PSB* (f. 82a) provides the following clarification of this phrase: "The ordinary person (i.e., non-Ārya) who desires to enter the state of one-pointed concentration that lacks conception begins [his or her practice] by discrediting conceptions with such thoughts as 'conception is a sharp pain' (S: *śalyaḥ*, T: *zug rngu*), 'conception is a disease' (S: *rogaḥ*, T: *nad*), 'conception is a boil' (S: *gaṇḍaḥ*, T: *zhu ba* also *'bras*), and contrasts that with such thoughts as 'the absence of conception is peaceful' (S: *śāntā*, T: *zhi ba*), '[the absence of conception] is excellent' (S: *pranītā*, T: *gya nom pa*), and '[the absence of conception] is deliverance.' Because [the practitioner] enters this state of composure after having disparaged conceptions in this way, [the root text states that this state of composure is] 'preceded by a form of attention that conceives of deliverance.'"
397 S: *pravṛttivijñānāni*, T: *'jug pa'i rnam par shes pa rnams.* This is a term used in the Mind Only School to differentiate six forms of consciousness—those that range from eye consciousness to mind consciousness—from the storehouse consciousness (S: *ālayavijñānam*, T: *kun gzhi rnam par shes pa*) and the afflicted mind (S: *kliṣṭamanas*, T: *nyon mongs pa'i yid*).
398 Two examples of unconscious states (S: *acittakam*, T: *sems med pa*) are identified in *TB* and *PSB* as deep sleep and fainting. *PSB* (f. 82b) further clarifies the sense in which the six active forms of consciousness are "not always present during conscious states": "When [these six forms of consciousness and their associated mental factors] are directed toward a virtuous object, the nonvirtuous and indeterminate forms of these minds are not present; when they are directed toward a nonvirtuous object, virtuous and indeterminate minds are not present; and when they are directed toward an indeterminate object, virtuous and nonvirtuous minds are not present. This is why the six active forms of consciousness are described as 'inconstant' minds and mental factors."
399 Of the two states of awareness described as constant, the afflicted mind is not present

in any of the three situations mentioned here; however, it is present in all other conscious and unconscious states, as well as the state of composure without conception. For its part, the storehouse consciousness only disappears when one reaches the stage that is beyond training (S: *aśaikṣaḥ*, T: *mi slob pa*), which is gained when one becomes an Arhat.

400 S: *nirudhyate 'neneti nirodhaḥ*, T: *'dis 'gag par byed pas na 'gog pa*. This statement is a literal explanation of the term "cessation."

401 S: **āśrayasyāvasthāviśeṣaḥ*, T: *lus kyi gnas skabs kyi bye brag*. The Tibetan makes clear that "basis" (S: *āśrayaḥ*) here refers to the physical body.

402 In other words, this part of the description is meant to indicate that only Āryas can enter this state of composure. In general, the phrase "one who has overcome desire for the Sphere of Nothingness" (S: *ākiṃcanyāyatanavītarāgaḥ*, T: *ci yang med pa'i skyes mched la 'dod chags dang bral ba*) can refer either to an ordinary being (S: *pṛthagjanaḥ*, T: *so so skye bo*) or to an Ārya, depending on whether the practitioner has overcome desire for this level by the mundane path (S: *laukikamārgaḥ*, T: *'jig rten ba'i lam*) or by the transcendent path (S: *lokottaramārgaḥ*, T: *'jig rten las 'das pa'i lam*). The second part of the description, "one who has set out to rise above the Peak of Existence" (S: *bhavāgrād uccalitaḥ*, T: *srid pa'i rtse mo las gyen du bskyod pa*) could only refer to an Ārya, since a practitioner cannot rise above this level except by the transcendent path. For a discussion of these two paths, see Part One, pp. 169–184.

403 See above, note 230, where these two phrases are explained. See also Part One, note 649.

404 This part of the explanation is meant to indicate that the first six of the eight Ārya practitioners cannot enter this state of mental composure. Because the Sphere of Nothingness refers to the third of the four levels of the formless realm, even the Nonreturner who enters this state of composure must be one who has overcome desire for three of the four levels of the formless realm and, therefore, he or she would also be known as "one who is striving after the fruit of an Arhat."

405 This statement is deceptively simple; a detailed investigation of all the possible ways in which the mental afflictions can be abandoned is quite complex in nature. An excellent summary of this topic is Je Tsongkapa's *The Staircase for the Clear-Minded to Climb: An Explanation of the Great Spiritual Beings Who Strive After and Abide in the Four Fruits* (T: *Zhugs pa dang gnas pa'i skyes bu chen po rnams kyi rnam par bzhag pa blo gsal bgrod pa'i them skas*). See listing in Bibliography under author's name. *PSB* (f. 83b) identifies the Ārya who is abiding in the fruit of a Stream Enterer and the Ārya who is abiding in the fruit of a Once Returner as practitioners who have set out to rise above the Peak of Existence because they have abandoned the mental afflictions associated with the Peak of Existence that are abandoned by the Seeing Path. It is in this limited sense that both of these Āryas can be said to have at least partially overcome their attachment for the Peak of Existence. Although there are many ways in which an Ārya can abandon the remaining innate mental afflictions that are abandoned by the Meditation Path, all attachment for the Peak of Existence is not permanently and completely abandoned until one attains the status of an Arhat.

406 S: *vihārasaṃjñāpūrvakeṇa manasikāreṇa*, T: *gnas pa'i 'du shes sngon du btang ba'i yid la byed pas*. Vasubandhu's description doesn't include the word "peace" that appears in Asaṅga's description of this state of composure (*AS*, pp. 10–11). Sthiramati cites Asaṅga's phrase in his remarks here: "conceives of abiding in [a state of] peace" (see following note). The Sanskrit noun *vihāraḥ* itself includes such meanings as "walking about for pleasure or amusement," "roaming," "sport," "play," "diversion," "enjoyment,"

and also refers to Buddhist monasteries and temples in the sense of a place to meet in or where there are places to walk about. Vasubandhu seems to be using the noun in the sense of "abiding in a state of ease." The Tibetan equivalent, *gnas pa*, suggests the bare action of "spending time" or "abiding." Given Asaṅga's more expanded phrase and the Tibetan translation, I have translated Vasubandhu's phrase as "conceives of abiding [in a state of ease]." Sthiramati's remarks below also support the notion that "ease" is implied in the present use of the term.

407 S: *śāntavihārasaṃjñā*, T: *zhi bar gnas pa'i 'du shes.*

408 S: **vihārasaṃjñā hi samasthasaṃjñā*, T: *gnas su mnyam pa'i 'du shes ni gnas pa'i 'du shes.*

409 S: *viharatyaneneti vihāraḥ*, T: *'dis gnas par byed pas gnas pa.*

410 S: **sūkṣmatamam*, T: *phra ba'i phra ba*. The Peak of Existence is the most subtle level of all samsaric states of mind; yet this state of composure is even more subtle than the general form of the Peak of Existence.

411 S: *vipākavijñānam*, T: *rnam par smin pa'i rnam par shes pa*. This is a synonym for the storehouse consciousness (S: *ālayavijñānam*, T: *kun gzhi rnam par shes pa*). See *TK*, v. 2. During this state of composure, the storehouse consciousness is not suspended.

412 Earlier, Sthiramati specified that the afflicted mind is also not active "when [a practitioner who has attained] the transcendent path enters a state of composure with regard to the [Four Noble] Truths"; however, as the passage indicates, that is not an "impure" state (S: *sāsravaḥ*, T: *zag pa dang bcas pa*).

413 The form realm is made up of four meditative absorptions. Each of the first three absorptions is described as consisting of three levels. The fourth meditative absorption consists of eight levels, of which the first three are inhabited principally by ordinary beings. The deities called Those of Great Fruit (S: *bṛhatphalaḥ*, T: *'bras bu che*) reside in the highest of these three levels. The remaining five levels of the fourth absorption are inhabited exclusively by Āryas; hence they are also known as "pure abodes" (S: *śuddhāvāsāḥ*, T: *gnas gtsang ma*).

414 The Buddhist doctrine of karma makes a fundamental distinction between karma that is "definite" (S: *niyatam*, T: *nges pa*) and karma that is "indefinite" (S: *aniyatam*, T: *ma nges pa*). Definite karma (whether virtuous or nonvirtuous) is that for which a consequence must be experienced. It is classified into three types: (1) [karma for which the consequence is] experienced in the same birth that it was performed (S: *dṛṣṭadharmavedanīyam*, T: *mthong ba'i chos la myong bar 'gyur ba*); (2) [karma for which the consequence is] experienced in the very next birth (S: *upapadyavedanīyam*, T: *skyes nas myong bar 'gyur ba*); and (3) [karma for which the consequence is] experienced in some other future birth (S: *aparaparyāyavedanīyam*, T: *lan grangs gzhan la myong bar 'gyur ba*). The nature of indefinite karma is such that a consequence does not necessarily have to be experienced.

Definite karma also has three main types of result: (1) maturation result (S: *vipākaphalam*, T: *rnam smin gyi 'bras bu*), (2) corresponding result (S: *niṣyandaphalam*, T: *rgyu mthun gyi 'bras bu*), and (3) governing result (S: *adhipatiphalam*, T: *bdag po'i 'bras bu*). The maturation result refers to the type of rebirth that one experiences because of the deed. For instance, the maturation result of killing another living being is to be born in the hells, as a hungry ghost, or as an animal, depending on the gravity of the deed. The corresponding result is to undergo an experience that is similar in nature to the deed. For instance, the corresponding result of killing another being is for oneself to die at an early age in a future life. The governing result refers to the outer environmental conditions that are experienced because of a past deed. For instance, the governing result of killing is to be born in a land where food, crops, and medicine are of poor quality, likely to cause illness, and so forth. *AK* (ch. 2, v. 42c) indicates that the being who generates the state of composure without conception necessarily will be reborn in this realm in the very next life. Thus, not only does it represent a form of definite karma, it is exclusively the kind for which the consequence is experienced in the very next birth.

415 S: **svādhiṣṭāne*, T: *rang gi gnas*. This seems to be a reference to the storehouse consciousness where the seeds of all forms of consciousness reside.

416 S: **sthitikālatā*, T: *gnas kyi dus nyid*.

417 S: *jīvitam*, T: *srog*.

418 S: *nikāyasabhāgaḥ*, T: *ris mthun pa*. I translate the term here as "class affiliate," because it refers to the continuum of a particular sentient being's heaps. See description in next paragraph. However, when it refers to the non-mental formation that is to be described next I render it as "class affiliation," because in that context the term refers to the similarity that is shared by members of a class of sentient beings. See note 428, below.

419 S: *nikāyaḥ*, T: *ris*. The Sanskrit term can also mean a "collection"; however, as the Tibetan equivalent indicates, the meaning here is that of a "class" or "type."

420 S: *sabhāgaḥ*, T: *mthun pa*.

421 S: *samāno bhāgaḥ*, T: *skal ba mtshungs pa*.

422 S: *gatiḥ*, T: *'gro ba*. Buddhist literature describes five or six states of existence. The five are (1) worldly god, (2) human, (3) animal, (4) tormented spirit, and (5) hell being. The formulation of six states adds that of a demigod.

423 S: *ekajanmikaḥ skandhasaṃtānaḥ*, T: *tshe gcig gi phung po'i rgyun*.

424 S: *sthitiḥ*, T: *gnas pa*.

425 S: *kālaniyamaḥ*, T: *dus nges pa*.

426 S: *āyuḥ*, T: *tshe*. This term is a synonym for life force.

427 S: *sāmarthyaviśeṣaḥ*, T: *nus pa'i bye brag*. That is, the efficacy to continue existing within a single class affiliate for some fixed period of time.

428 S: *nikāyasabhāgaḥ*, T: *ris mthun pa*. This term occurs in canonical literature and is recorded in the original Sanskrit Abhidharma works, such as *Jñānaprasthānam* (T: *Ye shes la 'jug pa*), among the various non-mental formations. Its philosophical importance is to explain how we identify a similarity among all sentient beings—whether human, animal, god, spirit, hell being, etc.—that allows us to recognize them all as sharing the quality of a "sentient being." Likewise, this same entity allows us to recognize a commonality within various categories of sentient beings, such as their being of a particular realm, spiritual level, class of being, type of birth state, male or female, etc. Adherents of the Vaibhāṣika School not only claimed that it is a distinct and real substance, they also sought to extend its meaning beyond animate life. Both views were rejected by other Sanskrit Buddhist philosophical traditions, Hīnayāna and Mahāyāna alike. Vasubandhu's *AKB* (p. 68) records that the Sautrāntika School accused the Vaibhāṣikas of maintaining a doctrine tantamount to the universals (S: *sāmānyam*, T: *spyi*) posited by the Indian realist Vaiśeṣika School.

429 S: *pañcagatāni*, T: *'gro ba lnga*. These are (1) gods, (2) humans, (3) animals, (4) hungry ghosts, and (5) hell beings. Sometimes, a sixth class, that of demigods (S: *asuraḥ*, T: *lha ma yin*), who are in perpetual conflict with the gods, is identified separately.

430 S: *sattvānām ātmabhāvaḥ*, T: *sems can rnams kyi lus*. The Sanskrit term *ātmabhāvaḥ* is typically translated into Tibetan as "body" (T: *lus*), which can be its meaning. This

same Sanskrit term is rendered a second time more literally in Tibetan in this sentence as *bdag gi dngos po*. Since the term is identified in the present context with all four or all five of an individual's heaps and not just the form heap, it represents the entire makeup or being of an individual. I translate it here variously as "composition" and "individual existence."

431 Beings of the desire and form realms are composed of all the five heaps; however, those of the formless realm are only composed of four heaps, because they lack physical bodies.

432 As stated in the discussion of the faculty of a life force, the term "class affiliate" means "the continuum of heaps that occurs within a particular [sentient being's] single birth."

433 *ASB* (p. 10) remarks that outer formations are governed by the characteristics of appearance (S: *saṃvarttam*, T: *'byung ba*) and disappearance (S: *vivarttam*, T: *'jig pa*), which is a reference to the cosmic formation and destruction of the physical universe. Inner formations—that is, those associated with animate beings—are governed by the four characteristics of birth, duration, aging, and impermanence. Sthiramati makes the same point at the end of his discussion of "impermanence."

434 S: *abhūtvābhāvaḥ*, T: *ma byung ba las byung ba*.

435 These two beliefs are attributed to followers of the Vaibhāṣika School, who maintained that each of the four characteristics of formations are distinct and real entities, and that all four of them are associated with each and every momentary occurrence of the formations. In fact, they further posited four secondary characteristics: the birth of birth, the duration of duration, the aging of aging, and the impermanence of impermanence. They also described the actions (S: *kāritram*, T: *byed pa*, also sometimes *bya ba*) of these characteristics as integral to how we distinguish the past, present, and future. For instance, the characteristic of birth causes formations to move from the future into the present; likewise, those of aging and impermanence cause them to move from the present into the past. The action of duration is to maintain their existence in the present, albeit for only an instant. The Yogācāra views regarding these four characteristics that Sthiramati is explaining here appear to be essentially the same as those of the Sautrāntika School that Vasubandhu outlines in *AKB* (pp. 75–79). Both these schools describe the characteristics as being meant only to describe aspects of the continua that make up sentient beings. Thus, "birth" is a nominally existent characteristic that refers only to the first moment in which the continuum of the heaps that make up a particular sentient being comes into existence.

436 S: *tatra teṣāṃ*, T: *de ltar de dag gi*. The structure of the Sanskrit phrasing in the root text that describes "aging," "duration," and "impermanence" parallels the description of "birth." That is, the pronoun "their" (S: *teṣāṃ*, T: *de dag gi*) and the locative singular of the pronoun "that" (S: *tatra*, T: *de ltar*) in the succeeding three descriptions mirror the possessive plural of the noun "formations" and the locative singular of the noun "class affiliate" in the description of "birth." The noun "class affiliate" and the pronoun "that" are in the locative to show that the four characteristics of birth, etc., apply only in relation to those formations that make up a class affiliate. This use of the locative case carries such meanings as "with reference to," "regarding," "in relation to," etc., which Whitney's *Sanskrit Grammar* (p. 102) describes as "touching upon dative and genitive constructions."

437 S: *prabandhaḥ*, T: *rgyun*.

438 S: *anyathātvam*, T: *gzhan du 'gyur ba*.

439 See above, note 59.

440 See above, p. 258, and related note 90, as well as p. 367 below, for explanations of the term "retained."

441 Appearance (S; *saṃvarttam*, T: *'byung ba*) and disappearance (S: *vivarttam*, T: *'jig pa*) are the terms that are used to describe the cosmic formation and destruction of the physical universe.

442 S: *nāman*, T: *ming*.

443 S: *abhidhānam*, T: *brjod pa*.

444 S: *abhidheyam*, T: *brjod par bya ba*.

445 S: *vyañjanam*, T: *yi ge*. I translate this term as "syllable" rather than "letter" because it is understood as having the nature of sound and does not refer to written characters. However, "phoneme" might be more accurate, since the term as it is used here is intended to designate the basic units of speech.

446 S: *adhivacanam*, T: *tshig bla dags*.

447 S: *svalakṣaṇam*, T: *rang gi mtshan nyid*.

448 S: *viśeṣaḥ*, T: *khyad par*.

449 S: *padam*, T: *tshig*. *AKB* (p. 80) gives two explanations of the term *padam* ("assertion") as it is to be understood in the present context: (1) "a statement (S: *vākyam*, T: *ngag*) of whatever length [that allows] a meaning to be fully expressed"; and (2) "a statement [that enables] a logical connection with [such] properties [as those of] action, quality, and time to be understood." The first of these descriptions is represented by such assertions as "All formations are impermanent." As relates to the second description, *AKV* (p. 270) cites an aphorism from Pāṇini's *Aṣṭādhyāyī* (I, 4, xiv) that states, "That which ends in *sup* (i.e., a case ending for a declined noun) or *tiṅ* (i.e., the tense ending of a conjugated verb) is called a *padam*." In this grammatical sense, *padam* means an "inflected word." This grammatical reference is left out of the Tibetan translation of Yaśomitra's *AKV*. *AKV* (p. 270) then further clarifies the second description with such assertions as "[he or she] cooks" (S: *pacati*, which links an action with a subject); "it is red" (S: *raktaḥ*, which links a subject and a quality); and "[he or she] cooked" (S: *apākṣīt*, which links the property of past time with a subject).

450 *PSB* (f. 80a) further clarifies this point by saying that, according to the everyday sense of the word *padam* (S: *laukikapadam*, T: *'jig rten pa'i tshig*), the statement "Devadatta cooked rice" (T: *lhas byin 'bras tshos*) is made up of three *pada* (i.e., words); but in the philosophical sense, a statement such as "All formations are impermanent" constitutes a single *pada* (i.e., assertion).

451 S: *viśeṣyam*, T: *khyad par gyi gzhi*.

452 I.e., this description was introduced before the one that states, "the expressions [that describe] the distinguishing characteristics of entities." In other words, this is the reason for presenting the topic of the collection of names before that of the collection of assertions.

453 This statement refers to the last paragraph in the explanation of names, which addressed the ineffability of the ultimate nature of things.

454 S: **vyanaktyanenaiti vyañjanam*, T: *'dis gsal bar byed pas yi ge'o*.

455 The phrase "and the rest" presumably is meant to indicate other synonyms for "syllable" (S: *vyañjanam*), such as the word "phoneme" (S: *akṣaram*) that appears here. Both of these Sanskrit terms are rendered in Tibetan by the single word *yi ge*. The Sanskrit *vyañjanam* also is used to refer just to those "syllables" that are formed with

the thirty-four consonants—i.e., *ka, kha, ga, gha, nga*, etc. In that context, the term is rendered in Tibetan as *gsal byed*. Similarly, the term translated here as "sound" (S: *varṇaḥ*) also is used to refer just to the sixteen Sanskrit "vowel" phonemes: *a, ā, i, ī, u, ū, ṛ, ṝ, ḷ, ḹ, e, ai, o, au, aṃ*, and *aḥ*. In that usage, the term is rendered in Tibetan as *dbyangs*.

456 S: **varṇo 'pi te*, T: *brjod pa yang de dag yin te*.

457 S: *akṣaram*, T: *yi ge*.

458 S: *cakṣuḥ*, T: *mig*.

459 S: *netraḥ*, *'dren byed*. That is, the word "guide" is a synonym for the eye in the sense of being the sense organ that guides us.

460 These first two sentences appear verbatim in *ASB*, p. 10.

461 S: *pṛthagjanatvam*, T: *so so skye bo nyid*.

462 This literal explanation of the term is virtually identical to one that appears in *AKB* (see above, note 111).

463 S: *aśaikṣamārgaḥ*, T: *mi slob pa'i lam*. This third "path" actually represents the ultimate goal of the path. In the case of the Hīnayāna path, it is synonymous with the status of an Arhat who has achieved liberation from samsara. In the Mahāyāna system, it represents the attainment of a Buddha's complete enlightenment. See also Part One, note 385.

464 S: *pravṛttiḥ*, T: *'jug pa*.

465 S: *pratiniyamaḥ*, T: *so sor nges pa*.

466 S: *yogaḥ*, T: *'byor ba*.

467 S: *javaḥ*, T: *mgyogs pa*.

468 S: *anukramaḥ*, T: *go rims*.

469 S: *kālaḥ*, T: *dus*.

470 S: *deśaḥ*, T: *yul*.

471 S: *saṃkhyā*, T: *grangs*.

472 S: *sāmagrī*, T: *tshogs pa*.

473 *ASB* (p. 11) notes: "For example, the conditions of cause and effect that relate to consciousness are (1) an unimpaired faculty, (2) an object that has comes into view, and (3) the proximity of the attention that can generate a particular consciousness. A similar analysis can be applied to other situations."

474 S: *ālambanam*, T: *dmigs pa*. Literally, the term means "that which is rested upon," and it is used with reference to objects of the mind.

475 The term *dharmaḥ* (T: *chos*), in the sense of an "entity," is used when referring to the objects of mind consciousness.

476 S: *vijñaptiḥ*, T: *rnam par rig pa*.

477 S: *prativijñaptiḥ*, T: *so sor rnam par rig pa*. This term, with the additional prefix, appears in both *AK* and *AS*. *AKV* (p. 50) explains the prefix *prati* (T: *so sor*) here as meaning the "successive" or "repeated" (S: *vīpsārthaḥ*, T: *zlos pa'i don*) perception of a variety of objects.

478 S: *cittam*, T: *sems*.

479 S: *citratvāt*, T: *sna tshogs pa'i phyir*. Compare this interpretation with the one that appears in *AKB* (pp. 61–62): "Thought is where the elements of virtue and nonvirtue are collected" (S: *citam śubhāśubhair dhātubhir iti cittam*; T: *dge ba dang mi dge ba'i khams dag gis bsags pas na sems so*). The word "elements" in this description refers to the traces or imprints (S: *vāsanā*, T: *bag chags*) of karma and the mental afflictions. As the root text notes below, the Yogācāra School preferred this latter interpretation;

nevertheless, both interpretations seem to have been accepted.

480 S: *manas*, T: *yid*. Although "mind" is represented as being a synonym for consciousness, it also has the more restricted sense of the faculty that serves as the support for mind consciousness.

481 Cf. *AK* (ch. 1, v. 17ab): "Mind is that which is the immediate past of the six forms of consciousness" (S: *ṣaṇṇām anantarātītaṃ vijñānām yad dhi tan manaḥ*; T: *drug po 'das ma thag pa yi / rnam shes gang yin de yid do*).

482 S: *ālayavijñānam*, T: *kun gzhi rnam par shes pa*.

483 S: *sāsravaḥ*, T: *zag bcas*. See note 9 above for clarification of this term.

484 S: *catur pratyayāḥ*, T: *rkyen bzhi*. See Part One, note 458, for a description of the four types of condition.

485 S: *hetupratyayaḥ*, T: *rgyu'i rkyen*.

486 S: *vāsanā*, T: *bag chags*.

487 S: *adhipatipratyayaḥ*, T: *bdag po'i rkyen*.

488 S: *samanantarapratyayaḥ*, T: *de ma tag rkyen*.

489 S: *ālambanapratyayaḥ*, T: *dmigs pa'i rkyen*.

490 S: *paryeṣakam manovijñānam*, T: *kun tu tshol ba'i yid kyi rnam par shes pa*. The discussion presented in this paragraph and the one preceding it is a distillation of the first two sections of Asaṅga's *Yogācārabhūmi*.

491 S: *vipākavāsanā*, T: *rnam par smin pa'i bag chags*. "Maturation imprint" means the kind of seed that will ripen as a continuum of a future life's storehouse consciousness.

492 S: *niṣyandavāsanā*, T: *rgyu mthun pa'i bag chags*. "Consequence imprint" means the kind of seed that will bring about a consequence or result that is similar in nature to the cause.

493 That is, maturation imprints generate a new continuum of the storehouse consciousness in a being's future existence.

494 That is, when formations cease, that event creates the seeds from which formations have the capacity to arise in the future.

495 S: *vipākavijñānam*, T: *rnam par smin pa'i rnam par shes pa*. This is a reference to storehouse consciousness. *ASB* (p. 11) states: "[The storehouse consciousness] is called 'maturation consciousness' because it is created by past karma."

496 Both the active forms of consciousness and their objects are "discernible" (S: *paricchinnam*, T: *yongs su chad pa*) in the sense that a person is able to introspectively observe and recognize them.

497 S: *aparicchinnālambanākāram*, T: *dmigs pa dang rnam pa yongs su ma chad pa*.

498 In other words, the storehouse consciousness perceives both an individual's inner being and the outer world. However, an ordinary being is not capable of recognizing that it does; therefore, he or she cannot perceive the storehouse consciousness itself.

499 S: *adhyātmam upādānam*, T: *nang gi nye bar len pa*.

500 S: *parikalpitasvabhāvaḥ*, T: *kun brtags pa'i ngo bo nyid*.

501 S: *sādhiṣṭhānam indriyarūpam*, T: *gnas dang bcas pa'i dbang po'i gzugs*. The five sense faculties themselves are subtle form that ordinary beings cannot perceive. The physical eyeballs represent the seat (S: *adhisthānam*, T: *gnas*) of the eye faculty, in that they are the place where the eye faculty resides. A similar description applies for the other faculties and their seats. *TB* (p. 52) adds that "inner grasping" includes name (S: *nāma*, T: *ming*) as well as form. "Name" is a synonym for the mental heaps.

502 S: *ekajātīyam*, T: *rigs gcig pa*.

503 S: **saṃtānānuvṛttiḥ*, T: *rgyun chags par 'jug pa'o*. Cf. *MVy*, 2124. *TB* (p. 60): "It pro-

ceeds uninterruptedly" (S: *avyuparatam pravartate*, T: *rgyun ma chad par rgyun du 'byung ngo*).

504 S: *pratisaṃdhiḥ*, T: *nyin mtshams sbyor ba*. This term literally means "reunion," in the sense of reentering one of the four birth states at conception. The four birth states are (1) womb birth, (2) egg birth, (3) birth from moisture and heat, (4) and spontaneous birth. See Part One, p. 106.

505 That is, the form realm.

506 That is, the formless realm.

507 S: *anādikāliko dhātuḥ sarvadharmasamāśrayaḥ / tasmin sati gatiḥ sarvā nirvāṇādhigamo 'pi vā*. T: *thog ma med pa'i dus kyi dbyings / chos rnams kun gyi gnas yin te / de yod pas na 'gro kun dang / mya ngan 'das pa'ang thob par 'gyur*.

508 S: *ādānavijñānam*, T: *len pa'i rnam par shes pa*. *ASB* (p. 11) states: "[The storehouse consciousness] is called 'the acquiring consciousness' because it takes on, again and again, a [new] embodied existence at the moment of reentry [into a birth state]" (S: *punaḥ punaḥ pratisaṃdhibandhe ātmabhāvopādānād ādānavijñānam*. T: *yang dang yang nying mtshams sbyor ba'i lus len pa'i phyir kun du len pa'i rnam par shes pa'o*).

509 S: *oghavat*, T: *chu bo bzhin*. *TB* (p. 60) explains this simile as follows: "Just as a river flows carrying along grass, sticks, cow dung, and the like, so too, the storehouse consciousness, endowed with the imprints of virtuous, nonvirtuous, and invariable karma, flows on continuously and without interruption for as long as samsara exists, carrying with it the mental factors of contact, attention, etc."

510 S: *ādānavijñānagaṃbhīrasūkṣmo ogho yathā vartati sarvabījo / bālā naiṣo mayi na prakāśi mā haiva ātmā parikalpayeyuḥ*; T: *len pa'i rnam par shes pa zab cing phra / sa bon thams cad chu bo'i rgyun bzhin 'bab / bdag tu rtog par gyur na mi rung te / 'di ni byis pa rnams la ngas ma bstan*.

511 Primordial matter and a self are nonexistent entities that are posited by non-Buddhist philosophical traditions. They are mentioned here as concordant examples (S: *sapakṣaḥ*, T: *mthun dpe*) of nonexistent entities that are incapable of producing a result.

512 This section is a presentation of several explanations of the tenet for which the Sarvāstivāda School receives its name, which is that all the entities of the three times are real. See *AK*, ch. 5, vv. 24–27.

513 S: *kāritram*, T: *byed pa*. The actions of the eye, etc., are identified as those of seeing, etc.; the action of consciousness is that of becoming aware; and the actions of visible form, etc., are those actions serving as the objects of their respective faculties.

514 *PSB* (f. 101b) identifies this position as that of the Sautrāntika School.

515 S: *sendriyarūpa*, T: *dbang po dang bcas pa'i gzugs*.

516 This paragraph reflects points that Vasubandhu makes in the opening portion of his commentary to the *Pratītyasamutpadādivibhaṅganirdeśa sūtra* (T: *rTen cing 'brel bar 'byung ba dang po dang rnam par dbye ba bstan pa zhes bya ba'i mdo*, f. 5a). There he reviews a series of explanations of the two phrases: "when this is present, that comes into being" (S: *asmin sati idam bhavati*, T: *'di yod na 'di 'byung*) and "From the arising of that, this arises" (S: *tasyotpadāt idam utpadyate*, T: *'di skyes pas 'di skye ste*). The final position that he considers is identified as being that of the followers of Asaṅga's *Yogācārabhūmi*. According to this view, the first phrase is meant to indicate that the process of dependent origination occurs because the twelve limbs of ignorance and the rest have not been abandoned. The second phrase is explained as indicating that the causal conditions from which phenomena arise are impermanent. Several sutras are quoted in support of this position, including one referred

to as *Astitvādiviśeṣavibhaṅgeti dharmaprayāyaḥ* (T: *Yod pa nyid la sogs pa'i bye brag rnam par 'byed pa zhes bya ba'i chos kyi rnam grangs*), which states that the doctrine of dependent origination has three essential characteristics: (1) the characteristic of arising from a motionless condition; (2) the characteristic of arising from an impermanent condition; and (3) the characteristic of arising from an efficacious condition. The phrase "when this is present, that comes into being" is said to represent the first characteristic, in the sense that the mere presence or existence of a condition is sufficient to bring about its result, without the need for that condition to carry out some particular action. The phrase "from the arising of that, this arises" is represented by the second characteristic, in the sense that the arising of an impermanent condition is what generates a result. The twelve individual limbs of dependent origination represent the third characteristic in the sense that their fixed order indicates the nature of their efficacy.

517 In other words it cannot be argued that, in special circumstances like these states of composure, it is possible for the mental factor of contact to occur without it being accompanied by the arising of the mental factors of feeling and conception.

518 This statement applies to the grammatical form of the original Sanskrit. The term *upādāya* in combination with the accusative of a substantive noun is a construction that indicates a reason. In Vasubandhu's root text, the particle only appears once at the end of the statement that contains three separate reasons, of which this is the first.

519 S: *ālambanapratyayaḥ*, T: *dmigs pa'i rkyen*. See Part One, note 458, for a description of the four conditions.

520 S: **anyākāravṛttitām*, T: *rnam pa gzhan 'byung ba nyid*.

521 These are two more of the four conditions.

522 See note 9 above.

523 S: *vipākavāsanāvijñānam*, T: *rnam par smin pa'i bag chags kyi rnam par shes pa*. This phrase is a reference to the storehouse consciousness. See description of "maturation imprints" above. That is, the arising and cessation of the active forms of consciousness occur simultaneously with the storehouse consciousness that accompanies them.

524 That is, by "storing" the imprints of former occurrences of the active forms of consciousness, the maturation consciousness has the capacity to generate similar instances of those forms of consciousness at a later time.

525 S: *pravṛttiḥ*, T: *'jug pa*.

526 S: *nivṛttiḥ*, T: *ldog pa*.

527 See above, p. 283, where these two expressions are explained.

528 S: *saṃskārapratyayam vijñānam*, T: *'du byed kyi rkyen gyis rnam par shes pa*. This is a reference to the third of the twelve limbs of dependent origination.

529 *PSB* (f. 107a–107b) identifies this as the position held by the Vaibhāṣika School. While the Tibetan translation has *nyan thos rnam par smra ba pa* and not the more familiar *bye brag tu smra ba*, it is clear that the reference is to adherents of the Vaibhāṣika School.

530 *PSB* (f. 107b) attributes this latter alternative to the Sautrāntika School and explains Sthiramati's description as follows: "The mental factor known as 'volition' urges the active forms of consciousness to generate virtuous, nonvirtuous, and invariable formations. [These formations] then impregnate the very next moment of the active forms of consciousness with their imprints. This is [the Sautrāntika School's] explanation of the phrase 'consciousness is conditioned by the formations.'"

531 *PSB* (f. 108a) identifies this as the Vaibhāṣika School's response to the criticism that Sthiramati has just raised against them.

532 This paragraph is Sthiramati's defense against the criticism raised by the Vaibhāṣikas in the preceding paragraph.

533 This is the second alternative that was identified earlier as being the position that is held by the Sautrāntika School. Sthiramati's criticism of that position begins here.

534 This is a reference to the fifth limb, which is that the six bases are conditioned by name and form (S: *nāmarūpapratyayaṃ ṣaḍāyatanam*, T: *ming dang gzugs kyi rkyen gyis skye mched drug*).

535 This sentence requires some elaboration for its full significance to be appreciated. First of all, it is not stating that those Āryas other than Arhats will no longer be reborn in samsara, since clearly they will be as long as they have not eradicated all the innate forms of the mental afflictions, and the innate forms of the mental afflictions are abandoned by the Meditation Path, not by the Seeing Path. The key element of the statement is that "the karma [accumulated] by those who have [directly] perceived the [Four Noble] Truths does not *project* a rebirth." *PSB* (f. 110a–110b) explains this statement as making two points: (1) an Ārya will continue to be reborn in samsara but only for, at most, seven lifetimes, and (2) an Ārya will not be reborn in the lower realms, even though he or she does still possess karmic seeds that could otherwise cause him or her to be born there. As Je Tsongkapa also describes in the *Great Treatise* (*LC*, f. 155a–155b), Āryas no longer accumulate any new "projecting karma" (T: *'phen byed kyi las*): "In general, Āryas do carry out and accumulate [impure] virtuous karma; moreover, Stream Enterers and Once Returners can even accumulate nonvirtuous karma. However, it is impossible for an Ārya to accumulate karma that will project [him or her] into either an inferior or a happy state of samsara. As the *Root Treatise on the Middle Way* (*MMK*, ch. 26, v. 10) states: 'Because the unwise [person] creates / The formations that are samsara's root, / Therefore, the unwise [person] is a [karmic] agent. / [However,] the wise [person] is not [an agent], through having seen reality' (S: *saṃsāramūlān saṃskārān avidvān saṃskarotyataḥ / avidvān kārakas tasmān na vidvāṃs tattvadarśanāt*. T: *'khor ba'i rtsa ba 'du byed de / de phyir mkhas rnams 'du mi byed / de phyir mi mkhas byed po yin / mkhas min de nyid mthong phyir ro*). Master Vasubandhu also writes (*Pratītyasamutpādādivibhaṅgabhāṣyam*, f. 52b): 'One who has seen Truth does not project.' Therefore, as long as you are still subject to [the belief that] grasps at the existence of a [real] personal self, you will [continue to] accumulate projecting karma. But once you have gained a direct realization of the insubstantiality of the person you will no longer accumulate any new projecting karma, even though you will still undergo rebirth in samsara by the power of karma and the mental afflictions. As the *Levels of Spiritual Practice* (*YB*, p. 18) states, a Stream Enterer and a Once Returner no longer acquiesce to attachment to a self but rather reject attachment to a self, in the manner that a strong person overpowers a weaker one."

536 To paraphrase *PSB* (f. 111a): Only an impure (S: *sāsravam*, T: *zag pa dang bcas pa*) form of consciousness can be present at the time that the mental afflictions are active. Therefore, the pure mind that is the antidote to the mental afflictions cannot abandon the mental afflictions when they are active, because the antidote that is the agent and the mental afflictions that are the object that it acts upon cannot both be present at the same time.

537 *PSB* (f. 111a) explains Sthiramati's argument as saying that, according to the

Sautrāntika School, among the forms of consciousness that are impregnated by the seeds of the mental afflictions are the five sensory forms of consciousness. Because these forms of consciousness cannot be present at the time that the antidote to the seeds of the mental afflictions is active, that antidote could not abandon the seeds that are associated with the sensory forms of consciousness.

538 The Tibetan equivalent of this suffix is the particle *nyid*; thus, the term becomes *kun gzhi rnam par shes pa nyid.*

539 S: *vastumātra*, T: *dngos pa tsam*. That is, the awareness that is the essence of consciousness is identified as the knowing agent.

540 S: *sthānam*, T: *gnas*. Cf. *TB*, p. 50.

541 *TB* (p. 50): *atha vālīyante upanibadhyante 'smin sarvadharmāḥ kāryabhāvena tad vālīyate upanibadhyate kāraṇabhāvena sarvbadharmeṣvityālayaḥ*. The term "storehouse" is explained using the passive of the Sanskrit verbal root *ālī*, which means literally "to come close to" or "to settle down upon." I translate it here as "reside." Sthiramati glosses the verb with another root *upanibandh*, which has many senses, but here—where it is rendered in the passive—it can be understood to mean "to be fixed upon" or "to be located in."

542 S: *ātmabhāvaḥ*, T: *lus*. The Sanskrit term *ātmabhavaḥ* is almost universally translated into Tibetan as *lus*, which has the unambiguous meaning of "physical body." While the Sanskrit term can mean the physical body alone, it literally means "existence of the self" and thus is also used to refer to a "soul" or "self." Given the Buddhist doctrine of selflessness, the latter would never be its intended meaning. However, Sthiramati does gloss the term here as "name and form," which indicates that in this context its meaning is not limited to the body. "Name and form" (S: *nāmarūpam*, T: *ming dang gzugs*) is a term that in Buddhist usage is identified with the five heaps, and thus represents the totality of an individual's being—both mental and physical—not just the body. Therefore, I have translated it here as "individual existence." Note that the term is also used again in the root text with a meaning that Sthiramati identifies as being limited to the physical body.

543 In other words, this interpretation states that the totality of a sentient being's existence—that is, the five heaps—arises from the storehouse consciousness; therefore, it is the storehouse of one's individual existence.

544 S: *ātmamānālāyanimittatām upādāya*, T: *bdag tu nga rgyal gyi gzhi dang / rgyu nyid kyi phyir ro*. Sthiramati is reporting the existence of a variant reading of this compound in Vasubandhu's root text. This alternate wording has the word *ātmamānaḥ* (T: *bdag tu nga rgyal*) in place of *ātmabhāvaḥ* (T: *lus*). The Tibetan *nga rgyal* should not be taken here in the ordinary sense of "pride," but rather in the sense of a "mistaken opinion"; therefore, I have translated it simply as "belief," since it is the nature of the afflicted mind to mistakenly regard the storehouse consciousness as constituting a real personal self.

545 S: *ātmamānālayaḥ*, T: *bdag tu nga rgyal gyi kun gzhi*. In this context *ālayaḥ* might be rendered more accurately as "basis" rather than "storehouse."

546 S: *ālīyate*, T: *sbyor ba*. This is the same verb that was used earlier to explain the term "storehouse" (see note 541 above).

547 The second reason for its being called the "storehouse consciousness"—"[because of the quality of being] the cause [of belief in a self]"—should be explained in the same manner as was stated above. That is to say, the storehouse consciousness is the cause of the belief in a self in the sense that when the seeds of that belief are "acti-

vated" or caused to ripen, it will arise or come into existence from the storehouse consciousness.

548 S: *kāyaḥ*, T: *lus*. As Sthiramati notes, in this instance the meaning of the term is limited to the physical body.

549 S: *ādānavijñānam*, T: *len pa'i rnam par shes pa*.

550 S: *kāyaḥ*, T: *lus*. Here the term refers to the collection of four or five heaps that are taken on with each samsaric rebirth.

551 This discussion of the formations as the cause of consciousness should be understood as a reference to the third limb in the twelve-part process of dependent origination, which states that "consciousness is conditioned by the formations." As discussed earlier (see above, pp. 338–340), the Yogācāra School maintains that "consciousness" in this context refers to the storehouse consciousness.

552 This sentence is a reference to the way in which an intermediate state being (S: *antarābhāvaḥ*, T: *bar srid pa*) takes birth in a new class of sentient being. It assumes rebirth in a womb or an egg. The loss of consciousness marks the death of the intermediate state being. See Part One, pp. 206–207, for a fuller description of this process.

553 S: *ādatte*, T: *len pa*. This is a form of the same root that is being translated as "acquire" in the expression "acquiring consciousness."

554 It is a postulate of the theory of karma that the result of a virtuous or nonvirtuous entity, which is also referred to as a "maturation" (S: *vipākam*, T: *rnam par smin pa*) is itself morally neutral or "indeterminate" (S: *avyākṛtam*, T: *lung du ma bstan pa*) in nature. In this case, the term "maturation" is a reference to the storehouse consciousness, which, as mentioned earlier, is also known as the "maturation consciousness."

555 S: *kliṣṭamanas*, T: *nyon mongs pa can gyi yid*.

556 S: *sadā mananātmakatvān manas*, T: *rtag par rlom sems pa'i bdag nyid yin pas yid do* (cf. *TB*, p. 62). The Tibetan equivalent of *mananam* is also rendered as *ngar sems pa*. Both of these Tibetan translations of the same Sanskrit term hint at the fact that the original refers to a form of understanding in which the subject is aware that he/she is thinking. This awareness of one's subjective state of thinking indicates its close connection with the process by which we form the notion of a self, hence the Tibetan *ngar sems pa*. The alternate translation *rlom sems pa* apparently comes from the sense in which the Sanskrit root from which the term is derived also means "to think highly of," especially as in when one has an unwarranted high opinion of oneself or one's beliefs.

557 S: *āśrayaḥ*, usually T: *rten*. This term is used to refer to the faculties that are the inner basis for the six active forms of consciousness; thus, this second interpretation of the term "mind" is describing the mind faculty (S: *mana indriyam*, T: *yid kyi dbang po*).

558 See above, p. 327, and related note 480.

559 S: *ātmamohaḥ*, T: *bdag tu rmongs pa*.

560 *TB* (p. 54) identifies "the view that believes in a self" (S: *ātmadṛṣṭiḥ*, T: *bdag tu lta ba*) as the perishable collection view (S: *satkāyadṛṣṭiḥ*, T: *'jig tshogs la lta ba*); "pride toward a self" (S: *ātmamānaḥ*, T: *bdag tu nga rgyal*) as egoistic pride (S: *asmi mānaḥ*, T: *nga'o snyam pa'i nga rgyal*); and "attachment toward a self" (S: *ātmasnehaḥ*, T: *bdag la chags pa*) as love of self (S: *ātmapreman*, T: *bdag la dga' ba*).

561 More precisely, there are two categories of mental afflictions: nonvirtuous and obstructive-indeterminate (S: *nivṛtāvyākrtaḥ*, T: *sgrib lung ma bstan*). Only the mental afflictions that operate in the desire realm are nonvirtuous; those of the form

and formless realms are obstructive-indeterminate entities. An obstructive-indeterminate entity is afflicted in the sense that it constitutes a form of obscuration (S: *āvaraṇam*, T: *sgrib pa*). The mental afflictions that are obstructive-indeterminate entities serve as causes for the suffering of continued samsaric existence, but not that of overt pain. The afflicted mind is thus an obstructive-indeterminate entity, not a nonvirtuous mind, by virtue of its association with the four mental afflictions that are obstructive-indeterminate entities. There are also unobstructive-indeterminate entities (S: *avṛtāvyākrtaḥ*, T: *ma sgrib lung ma bstan*), which means that they do not constitute a form of obscuration. Examples include the ordinary physical activities of walking, sitting, standing, and reclining, as well as the activity of working at various arts and crafts (see also note 625, below). So when the text states here that the afflicted mind is neither virtuous nor indeterminate, it really means that it is not an unobstructive-indeterminate entity. This distinction is stated explicitly in *TK*, v. 6ab.

562 This is an indirect way of saying that the afflicted mind does occur when one is absorbed in the state of composure without conception.

563 S: *rāśiḥ*, T: *phung po*. While this is the most common interpretation of the term *skandhaḥ* (T: *phung po*), *AS* (p. 15) mentions two more: "[Form and the rest] are also referred to as a '*skandhaḥ*' (i.e., 'branch' or 'limb') in the sense that [they possess] the characteristic of [comprising] extensive suffering, as in [the expression] 'great tree limb.' As the sutras declare, 'Thus does the origination of this sole and great *skandhaḥ* of suffering come about.' [Form and the rest] are also referred to as a '*skandhaḥ*' (i.e., 'shoulder') in the sense that they carry the burden of being afflicted (S: *saṃkleśabhāravahanam*, T: *kun nas nyon mongs pa'i khur khyer ba*), as one carries a burden with the shoulder." *AKB* (p. 13) mentions the second of these two additional interpretations, and adds another: "Alternatively, [others state that the meaning of *skandhaḥ* is] that of a 'portion' (S: *pracchedaḥ*, T: *yongs su chad pa*), as when speakers say, "We shall give a gift [in the form] of three portions (*skandhaḥ*)."

564 S: *sapratighaḥ*, T: *thogs pa dang bcas pa*. See below, pp. 359–360.

565 S: *āśrayavaśāt*, T: *gnas kyi dbang gis*. *AKV* (p. 59): "Feelings and the rest [are near and far] 'on the strength of their source,' because they are not situated in any physical location since they do not possess physical form. Therefore, the following explanation is given: 'far' feelings, etc., are those whose source cannot be seen; 'near' ones are those whose source can be seen."

566 S: *avakāśaḥ*, T: *go 'byed pa*.

567 The Sanskrit and Tibetan equivalents for these terms are, respectively, (1) S: *saṃkhyā*, T: *brtags pa*; (2) S: *pramā*, T: *gzhal ba*; (3) S: *pravicayaḥ*, T: *rnam par 'byed pa*; and (4) S: *prajñā*, T: *shes rab*.

568 T: *so sor*.

569 S: **pratyayavaikalyam*, T: *rkyen ma tshang ba*.

570 S: **na visaṃyogaḥ*, T: *bral ba ma yin pa*. "Separation" refers to the Truth of Cessation, which is a state of separation from at least some portion of the seeds of the mental afflictions. Another name for this separation is "analytic cessation." There is also a state of separation from any portion of the obscurations to objects of knowledge (S: *jñeyāvaraṇam*, T: *shes bya'i sgrib pa*). A Hīnayāna Arhat possesses a state of separation from the seeds of all the mental afflictions. A Buddha possesses a state of separation from the totality of the obscurations to objects of knowledge, in addition to a state of separation from the seeds of all the mental afflictions.

571 Although this description does not say so explicitly, it applies to the way in which the direct realization of selflessness brings about the attainment of the Truth of Cessation by destroying the seeds of the mental afflictions.

572 That is, the phrase "related to the antidote to the mental afflictions."

573 S: *anāsravamārgaḥ*, T: *zag ma med pa'i lam*. "Pure path" is a synonym for transcendent path (S: *lokottaramārgaḥ*, T: *'jig rten las 'das pa'i lam*), which includes the Seeing Path and the Meditation Path.

574 S: *samanantarapratyayaḥ*, T: *mtshungs pa de ma thag rkyen*. See Part One, note 458, for a discussion of the four conditions.

575 S: *ālambanapratyayaḥ*, T: *dmigs rkyen*.

576 In other words, because the mind can only perceive one particular entity at any given moment, there occurs a nonanalytic cessation in relation to all the other entities that existed at that same moment in the sense that one is forever prevented from having directly experienced any of them. One way of understanding this is that while each individual is presented with a myriad number of possible experiences with each passing moment, such factors as where we choose to direct our interest at that moment and the capacity of our awareness at that time necessarily determine and limit the course that our lives will take in the future. Thus, each moment that our five heaps take on one specific form they are irreversibly precluded from having been formulated in a different manner and, therefore, incapable of having followed some other path of experience.

577 S: *ānantaryamārgaḥ*, T: *bar chad med lam*. Noninterruption paths occur only on the two transcendent paths—that is, the Seeing Path and the Meditation Path. They constitute the wisdom that is a direct realization of ultimate truth, and they can only occur during a state of one-pointed meditative absorption. The development of this wisdom represents the direct antidote that destroys the seeds of the mental afflictions. When this action of destroying some aspect of the mental afflictions has been completed, the practitioner achieves a particular form of the Truth of Cessation and simultaneously achieves what is referred to as the "liberation path" (S: *vimuktimārgaḥ*, T: *rnam grol lam*). These two types of realization represent the most important elements of the Truth of the Path.

578 See note 570 above.

579 The main point is that each succeeding moment of the path only removes the seeds of a portion of the mental afflictions.

580 S: **ananyathārthena tathatā*, T: *gzhan ma yin pa'i don gyis na de bzhin nyid do*. Cf. *MVṬ*, p. 36. Sthiramati further explains there, "This means that because [suchness] always [remains] an unconditioned entity, it does not undergo any change."

581 S: *dharmatā*, T: *chos nyid*.

582 S: *dharmanairātmyam*, T: *chos kyi bdag med pa nyid*.

583 S: *śūnyatā*, T: *stong pa nyid*.

584 S: *āyadvāraḥ*, T: *skye ba'i sgo*. This is the first of a number of interpretations that appear in the *Mahāvibhāṣaśāstram* (see Part One, n. 514). It seems to be widely followed by other Buddhist schools. Cf. *AS*, p. 15.

585 S: **kāraṇahetuḥ*, T: *byed rgyu*.

586 S: **nimittam*, T: *rgyu mtshan*.

587 S: *cittacaittānām āyaṃ tanvanti vistṛṇvantītyāyatanāni*. T: *sems dang sems la byung ba rnams kyi 'byung ba mched par byed cing rgyas par byed pas skyes mched rnams te*. Cf. *AKB*, p. 13.

588 S: *sapta cittadhatavaḥ*, T: *sems khams bdun*. The seven mental constituents are made up of the six consciousness constituents and the mind constituent.

589 S: **āśrayaḥ*, T: *rten*. In this context the word "basis" is synonymous with "faculty" (S: *indriyam*, T: *dbang po*).

590 This is a reference to Sthiramati's introductory remark relating to the explanation of the term "basis" that since the term is applied to entities with distinct essential natures, it is necessary to discern what quality they have in common such that they can all be referred to by that term. Here the same point should be made with regard to the term "constituent."

591 S: **nirvyāparatvāt*, T: *byed pa med pa'i phyir*. See description above (pp. 297–300) of the Vaiśeṣika view regarding the self that appears as part of the explanation of the perishable collection view. One element of the Buddhist theory of causation states that the mere existence of a cause brings about the arising of its result, and that the cause does not exercise any action that is separate from its essential nature. Also see discussion below that the constituents were taught as an antidote for the belief in an agent.

592 S: *svalakṣaṇadhāraṇatvāt*, T: *rang gi mtshan nyid 'dzin pa'i phyir*. This is one of four interpretations that appear in Asaṅga's *AS* (p. 15). It suggests that the meaning of the term *dhātuḥ* is derived from the verbal root *dhṛ*, which means "to hold" or "to retain," as it is translated here. In Vasubandhu's *Treasury of Higher Learning*, the principal interpretation of the term *dhātuḥ* is that of a "class" of entity (S: *gotram*, T: *rigs*). This represents the first in a series of interpretations that is found in the *Mahāvibhāṣaśāstram*. *AKB* (p. 13) cites the explanation of this first interpretation from the *Mahāvibhāṣaśāstram* as follows: "Just as the many classes (S: *gotrāṇi*, T: *rigs*) of [ore, such as] iron, copper, silver, gold, and the like, [that are found] on a single mountain are called "constituents" (S: *dhātavaḥ*, T: *khams*), the eighteen classes [of entities] that exist within a single support or continuum are called the 'eighteen constituents.'" In *AKB* (p. 13), Vasubandhu adds that this interpretation of "class" (*gotram*) is understood by some to mean "source" (S: *ākaraḥ*, T: *'byung gnas*), in the sense that each type of entity is the cause from which its future instances arise. This adds a causal dimension to the meaning of the term, which is that the continuum of prior instances of the eye, etc., are the source and "like cause" (S: *sabhāgahetuḥ*, T: *skal ba mnyam pa'i rgyu*) from which their subsequent forms arise.

593 S: **ekatvagrāhaḥ*, T: *gcig tu 'dzin pa*. *MVṬ* (p. 104): "'Belief in a unity' is [a belief that is] formed by apprehending the five grasping heaps as a self that is a [single] mass" (S: *ekatvagrāha iti pañcopādānaskandheṣu piṇḍātmagrahataḥ*. T: *gcig pur 'dzin pa zhes bya ba ni nye bar len pa'i phung po lnga po dag la ril po'i bdag tu 'dzin pa te*).

594 S: **bhoktṛtvagrāhaḥ*, T: *za bar 'dzin pa*. *MVṬ* (p. 104): "'Belief in an experiencer' is [the belief that] the self is an experiencer, because [the self possesses the quality of being] intelligent. On the other hand, [both objects that are] perceptible [by the senses] and [objects that are] imperceptible are [considered to be] an object of experience (S: *bhojanam*, T: *bza' ba*), because they do not [possess the quality of being] intelligent. Alternatively, belief in an experiencer is the thought that an experiencer is the entity, [i.e., the self, that experiences] the favorable and unfavorable results that are caused to arise by karma" (S: *bhoktṛtvagrāha iti ātmā bhoktā cetanatvāt / vyaktāvyaktaṃ tu bhojanam acetanatvāt / atha vā yasya śubham aśubhaṃ karmabhir utpadyate sa eva tat phalānāṃ bhokteti bhoktṛtvaghrāhaḥ*. T: *za bar 'dzin pa zhes bya ba ni sems yin pa'i phyir bdag ni za ba'o / gsal ba dang mi gsal ba ni sems med pa'i phyir*

bza' ba'o // yang na dge ba dang mi dge ba'i las rnams kyi bar du skye ba gang yin pa de nyid de'i 'bras bu la za bar byed do snyam pa na za bar 'dzin pa'o).

595 S: **kartṛtvagrāhaḥ*, T: *byed par 'dzin pa*. *MVṬ* (p. 104): "Belief in an agent is the belief that the self is the agent of good and bad deeds. Alternatively, it is the belief that the self is that entity which, by virtue of possessing [a number of] active properties (S: *karaṇaḥ*, T: *byed pa*, e.g., the organs of thought, perception, speech, etc.), performs a variety of actions" (S: *ātmaiva sukṛtaduṣkṛtānām karmaṇām kartteti yo grāhaḥ yo vā karaṇādyupetas tās tāḥ kriyāḥ karoti sa ātmeti kartṛtvagrāhaḥ*. T: *byed par 'dzin pa zhes bya ba ni legs par byas pa dang / nyes par byas pa'i las rnams bdag nyid kyis byed par 'dzin pa gang yin pa'o // yang na byed pa dang ldan pa gang zhig bya ba de dang de dag byed pa ni bdag go zhes byed par 'dzin pa'o*).

596 S: **ātmabhāvaḥ*, T: *lus*. See above, notes 430, 542, 548, and 550 for various instances where this term is used.

597 S: **upalabdhiḥ*, T: *dmigs pa*.

598 S: **apasphoṭanam*, T: *sprugs bsigs pa*.

599 "These [entities]" refers to the ten constituents that are identified in the next paragraph.

600 See above, note 129, for a description of the quality of exhibiting form. *AKV* (p. 79): S: *rūpaṇaṃ rūpaṃ tad eṣām astīti rupinaḥ*. *AS* (p. 17) also describes twenty criteria for classifying entities as material. This corresponds to the first one, which states that certain entities "have that nature" (S: *tadātmataḥ*, T: *de'i bdag nyid*)—i.e., they have the nature of exhibiting the quality of form.

601 This description corresponds to the second of Asaṅga's twenty criteria, that of being "based in the elements" (S: *bhūtāśrayataḥ*, T: *'byung ba'i rten du gyur pa*). *ASB* (p. 22) explains this second reason as being meant to point out two facts: (1) that all derivative form is dependent upon—that is, based upon—the four great elements, and (2) that the four elements are mutually dependent—that is, each one is dependent on the other three and they always occur in combination. Thus, Sthiramati's phrase "the form that constitutes a basis" (S: *āśrayarūpam*, T: *rten gyi gzugs*) refers to the four elements and "the form that is dependent [on that basis]" (S: *āśritarūpam*, T: *brten pa gzugs*) refers to derivative form.

602 This objection is also raised in *AKB*, p. 9. As Sthiramati explains here, *AKB* also records a view that the term "basis" (S: *āśrayaḥ*, T: *rten*) has a different meaning when it refers to the faculties than when it is being used to describe the relation between the elements and derivative form (S: *cakṣurvijñānādīnām āśrayo bhedam gataḥ*. T: *mig gi rnam par shes pa la sogs pa'i rten ni tha dad du gyur pa te*).

603 The six faculties are also referred to as the "bases" (S: *āśrayaḥ*, T: *rten*) for the six active forms of consciousness.

604 S: *ādharaḥ*, T: *gzhi*. That is, the faculty for each consciousness is the support for the arising of its respective consciousness, but that consciousness does not reside in its faculty the way derivative form resides in the elements.

605 That is, the entity constituent does not contain any form that is either a great element or a type of derivative form that is dependent on the great elements in the sense of being inseparably attached to them. In other words, this reason excludes noninformative form.

606 This refers to the remaining seven types of entity that make up the entity constituent: the feeling, conception, and formation heaps, as well as the four types of unconditioned entities.

607 This third reason is similar to the following explanation that appears in the *AKV* (p. 79): "Why is the entity constituent excluded [from the group of constituents that is material]? It should also be described as material, since it contains noninformative form. It is excluded because [the designation "material"] is restricted to those constituents that are exclusively material. Thus, only those constituents that are exclusively material in nature are meant [by that designation]; whereas the entity constituent includes both entities that have a material nature and entities that do not have a material nature."

608 S: *arupī*, T: *gzugs med.*

609 S: **nidarśanam*, T: *bstan pa. AKV* (p. 78): "The quality that enables an entity to be pointed to is called *nidarśanam*. Alternatively, *nidarśanam* is the quality that enables an eye consciousness to be generated in another person by means of speech."

610 S: *sanidarśanam*, T: *bstan du yod pa. AS* describes this term as referring simply to "the objects of the eye" (S: *cakṣurgocaraḥ*, T: *mig gi spyod yul*). *AKV* (p. 79) notes that this term and its opposite, "not capable of being indicated" (S: *anidarśanam*, T: *bstan du med pa*), appear in sutras in conjunction with two other pairs of terms—"having resistance" (S: *sapratighaḥ*, T: *thogs pa dang bcas pa*) and "lacking resistance" (S: *apratighaḥ*, T: *thogs pa med pa*) along with "material" (S: *rupī*, T: *gzugs bcas*) and "not material" (S: *arupī*, T: *gzugs med*)—to clarify and differentiate among phenomena. The following passage is cited: "O monks, the eye [faculty] is an inner basis. It is clear form that is derived from the four great elements. It is material, not capable of being indicated, and has resistance." (A similar description applies for the other four sense faculties.) "O monks, the mind [faculty] is an inner basis that is not material, is not capable of being indicated, and lacks resistance. O monks, forms are an outer basis that is derived from the four great elements. They are material, capable of being indicated, and have resistance. O monks, sounds are an outer basis that is derived from the four great elements. They are material, not capable of being indicated, and have resistance." (A similar description applies for the remaining sense objects.) "O monks, entities are an outer basis that consists of those things not included in the other eleven bases. They are not material, not capable of being indicated, and lack resistance."

611 S: *sālambanam*, T: *dmigs pa dang bcas pa*. The term *ālambanam* (T: *dmigs pa*) literally means "apprehended object" and refers to any object of consciousness. When the topic is forms of meditation practice, this term can be translated as "meditation object." The prefix *sa* indicates such things as "conjunction" or "possession," and when combined with nouns forms adjectives that can be translated as "accompanied by," "having," "possessing," etc. Thus, *sālambanam* could be translated as "having an apprehended object," and that is how it is rendered below. I have translated it here as "capable of apprehending [an object]" in order to convey the similarity of construction that it shares with the term *sanidarśanam*.

612 S: *sapratighaḥ*, T: *thogs pa dang bcas pa*.

613 S: *viṣayapratighātaḥ*, T: *yul gyi thogs pa. ABK*, (p. 19): "object-opposition is that of entities that hold objects—[namely,] the eye [faculty], etc.—[and it occurs] in relation to the objects of [visible] form, etc." In this context, "obstruction" means for any of the five sense faculties to engage its particular object. Vasubandhu then quotes a passage from the *Prajñaptiśāstram*, which says in part: "There are instances in which an eye [faculty] experiences obstruction in water but not on land, such as [the eyes] of fish. There are instances [in which obstruction occurs] on land but not in water, such

as [the eyes] of most humans. There are instances [in which obstruction occurs] in both places, such as crocodiles, frogs, demons, and fishermen. There are instances [in which obstruction] does not [occur] in both places, such as [beings] other than those types." *AKV* (p. 80) glosses the last category as follows: "[such as the eyes] of beings that are certain to die in the womb."

614 S: *ālambanapratighātaḥ*, T: *dmigs pa'i thogs pa*. *AKB* (p. 19): "Apprehension-opposition is that of mind and the mental factors [and it occurs] in relation to the objects that they apprehend. What is the difference between an object (S: *viṣayaḥ*, T: *yul*) and an apprehended object (S: *ālambanam*, T: *dmigs pa*)?" An object is that [entity] in relation to which an action [is carried out]. An apprehended object is that [entity] which is grasped by mind and mental factors. Why, then, is the occurrence [of an action by a faculty or a mental entity] in relation to its object or its apprehended object called "obstruction"? [Because when a faculty or a mental entity engages some particular object] it is unable to engage any [object] other than that one."

615 S: *āvaraṇapratighātaḥ*, T: *sgrib pa'i thogs pa*.

616 S: *sāsravaḥ*, T: *zag pa dang bcas pa*. See above, note 9.

617 S: **pratyakṣagocaraḥ*, T: *mngon sum gyi spyod yul*. Asaṅga's *VS* (f. 205b) identifies this term as follows: "the field of experience of the forms of consciousness that are based on clear [form] (i.e., the sense faculties) constitute direct fields of experience." This is one of three types of objects that are identified there as being related to the outflows.

618 S: *kāmāḥ*, T: *'dod pa rnams*. The sense objects are also referred to as "the qualities of desire" (S: *kāmaguṇāḥ*, T: *'dod pa'i yon tan rnams*).

619 S: *kavaḍīkārāhāraḥ*, T: *kham kyi zas*. Buddhist literature defines food as that which causes the world to continue to exist. This is meant both in the sense of maintaining life and in the sense of perpetuating samsaric existence. There are four types: (1) food that is taken in morsels, (2) contact, (3) volition, and (4) consciousness. The first kind, which nourishes the physical body, is also of two types: coarse and fine. The type that is fine is explained in a number of ways. For instance, it is the food that is consumed by beings that are in the intermediate state, since they consume odors as food. A second interpretation is that it refers to the food of certain deities and of humans who live at the beginning of a kalpa, since their food is absorbed into the body entirely without producing any residual waste. Food that is taken in morsels is only present in the desire realm and, for those who crave it, it also serves as a cause of rebirth there. The mental factor called "contact" nurtures consciousness and the other mental factors in the sense that it is a necessary condition for the continued occurrence of perception and experience. These first two types of food are thus identified as the main factors that sustain beings in this life. Volition and consciousness are also considered to help sustain this life, but in a less obvious way. Volition (i.e., mental karma) is the propelling force that brings about rebirth. A being who is propelled by karma is brought into being through the karmic seeds that are implanted in [his or her] consciousness. Thus, volition and consciousness are the principal types of food that bring about future existence. Scriptures also compare the first two types of food to a wet nurse, in that they nurture beings who have already been born. The latter two are said to be like a mother, because they are what cause beings to be born. These remarks are based on the *AKB*, pp. 152–155.

620 These are the same ten constituents as the ones that are described above as being "material."

621 S: *kuśalaḥ*, T: *dge ba*. As a masculine noun, the term means "a virtuous person." The neuter noun (S: *kuśalam*, T: *dge ba*) refers to the quality of being virtuous. The original Sanskrit term can mean variously "good," "healthy," "prosperous," "skillful," and even "clever." The first interpretation turns on the meanings of "skillful" or "clever" in the sense of overcoming evil. The middle two interpretations introduce the term *kuśa* grass with the sense of being "skillful." The descriptions that appear here all constitute the Sanskrit literary convention of devising literal interpretations that might be called artificial etymologies (S: *nirvacanam*, T: *nges tshig*). These explanations typically incorporate most, if not all, of the actual syllables of the term being explained. A more straightforward explanation appears in the *AKB* (p. 203): "[The impure entity] that has a favorable maturation is called 'virtuous'" (S: *yat sāsravam . . . iṣṭavipākaṃ kuśalam ityucyate*, T: *zag pa dang bcas pa gang zhig . . . rnam par smin pa yid du 'ong ba can ni dge ba can zhes bya'o*).

622 Cf. *AKV* (p. 82): "The virtuous are those who have driven away what is contemptible—that is, they have escaped from the lower realms" (S: *kutsitāścalitā gatā apakrāntā iti kuśalāḥ*. T: *smad pa las 'das shing ngan song las rgal pas na dba ba'o*). The Sanskrit and Tibetan do not coincide precisely; the English translation is based on the Tibetan version.

623 Cf. *AKV* (p. 82) "Alternatively, the term *kuśa* stands for wisdom in that it is sharp like *kuśa* grass. The virtuous ones, then, are those who acquire that [quality of being sharp]." (S: *prajñā vā kuśa iva tīkṣṇeti kuśaḥ tam lānti ādādata īti kuśalāḥ*. T: *rnam pa gcig tu na shes rab ni rtswa ku sha dang 'dra bar rno bas ku sha zhes bya ste / de len cing kun tu len pas na dge ba'o*.)

624 S: *avyākṛtaḥ*, T: *lung du ma bstan pa*.

625 These four categories also appear in the *AK* (ch. 4, vv. 8b–9). Sthiramati's remarks here do not, however, mirror that formulation precisely. *AK* describes nirvana as virtue in an ultimate sense (S: *paramārthataḥ*, T: *don dam par*), because it is the supreme state of well-being. Similarly, samsara is nonvirtuous in the ultimate sense, because it is the supreme form of ill in that it is the source of all suffering. The three roots of virtue, together with shame and abashment, are virtuous by their very nature (S: *svabhāvataḥ*, T: *ngo bo nyid kyis*), because that quality does not depend either on being associated with or being generated by other mental factors. By this same principle, the three roots of nonvirtue, together with shamelessness and absence of abashment, are nonvirtuous by their very nature. Those entities that are associated with the three roots of virtue, as well as shame and abashment, are virtuous by concomitance (S: *samprayogataḥ*, T: *mtshungs par ldan pas*), because they would not be virtuous unless they were associated with any of those five mental factors. The opposite of this explanation applies to being nonvirtuous by concomitance. *AS* (pp. 22–24) presents many more categories than just these four and identifies all eleven virtuous mental factors as virtuous by their very nature. Those entities that are nonvirtuous by their very nature are described as all the root and secondary mental afflictions that produce misdeeds, with the exception of the mental afflictions that are associated with mind consciousness in the form and formless realms. This is because only the mental afflictions that operate in the desire realm are nonvirtuous; those of the form and formless realms are obstructive-indeterminate entities (S: *nivṛtāvyākṛtaḥ*, T: *sgrib lung ma bstan*; see note 561 above). Both *AK* and *AS* describe space and the nonanalytic cessation as indeterminate in an ultimate sense. The paradigmatic examples of unobstructive-indeterminate entities (S: *anivṛtāvyākṛtaḥ*, T: *ma sgrib lung ma bstan*) are the following four types: (1) entities that arise from the cause of a karmic maturation (S:

vipākajam, T: *rnam smin las skyes pa*; i.e., a virtuous or nonvirtuous deed); (2) entities that are related to physical deportment (S: *airyāpathikam*, T: *spyod lam pa*; e.g. standing, sitting, walking, and reclining); (3) entities that are related to skill in various manual arts or crafts (S: *śailpasthānikam*, T: *bzo yi gnas pa*); and (4) the mind that produces emanations (S: *nirmāṇacittam*, T: *sprul pa'i sems*; i.e., a mental power that can manifest physical objects and that stems from having attained one-pointed concentration.)

626 S: **ahaṃkāraḥ*, T: *ngar 'dzin pa*. This refers to the sense or notion of one's subjective individuality. Its "basis" (S: **nidānam*, T: *gzhi*) is its cause or its object.

627 *Udānvargaḥ*, ch. 23, v. 17. S: *ātmanā hi sudāntena svargaṃ labhati paṇḍitaḥ*. T: *bdag ni legs par dul gyur na / mkhas pas mtho ris thob par 'gyur.*

628 Ibid., ch. 31, v. 1. S: *cittasya damanaṃ sādhu cittaṃ dāntaṃ sukhāvaham*; T: *sems 'dul ba ni legs pa ste / sems 'dul bde ba thob par byed.*

629 Except for a few additional phrases, this entire discussion on the nature of being inner or outer is taken verbatim from *AKB* as part of the explanation of ch. 1, v. 39ab of the root text. The last sentence recorded here is followed in the *AKB* (p. 27) with these remarks: "Otherwise, only the mind constituent of the past would be [a support of mind], not that of the future or the present. And it is maintained that the eighteen constituents pertain to all three times."

630 S: *sālambanaḥ*, T: *dmigs pa dang bcas pa*. See above, note 611, where the same term is translated as "capable of apprehending [an object]. *AKB* (p. 23) states: "These seven mental constituents [as well as a part of the entity constituent] have apprehended objects because they grasp an object."

631 S: *viṣayaḥ*, T: *yul.*

632 S: *gocaraḥ*, T: *spyod yul.*

633 S: *ālambanam*, T: *dmigs pa*. An "apprehended object" means an object that is grasped by consciousness or a mental factor.

634 S: *anusmaraṇavikalpaḥ*, T: *rjes su dran pa'i rnam par rtog pa.*

635 S: *abhinirūpaṇavikalpaḥ*, T: *mngon par dpyod pa'i rnam par rtog pa*. The Tibetan translation of *AKB* renders this term *nges par rtog pa'i rnam par rtog pa.*

636 These descriptions do not appear in Asaṅga's root text; however, they are found in Jinaputra's commentary in more or less the same language as Sthiramati presents here. "Hidden entities" means those that are not directly evident to the senses. (*ASB*, p. 16: *anusmaraṇavikalpo yo anubhūtapūrvasaṃskārākāraḥ / abhinirūpaṇāvikalpo yo atītānāgatapratyutpanneṣu viparokṣeṣvabhyūhanākāraḥ vikalpaḥ.*)

637 In the Tibetan translation of Sthiramati's commentary the original Sanskrit compound is interpreted as having a locative relation between the term "formation" (S: *samskāraḥ*, T: *'du byed*) and "former experience" (S: *anubhūtapūrvaḥ*, T: *sngon myong ba*). The Sanskrit compound could just as easily be interpreted as follows: "[A recollective concept is a concept] that occurs in relation to a previously experienced formation." In fact, that is how the phrase is rendered in the Tibetan translation of *ASB* (f. 13a): *gang sngon myong ba'i 'du byed rnams kyi rnam par rtog pa.*

638 Cf. *AKB*, p. 23.

639 S: *sacetanam*, T: *sems dang bcas pa*. More literally, this term means to be "sentient"; however, *AKV* (p. 91) glosses the term as meaning to be "alive" (S: *sajīvam*, T: *srog dang bcas pa*), which is a more common expression in ordinary speech than "sentient."

640 That is, it is those instances of these four constituents that *do* exist separately from the five sense faculties.

641 S: *sabhāgaḥ*, T: *bsten pa mtshung pa*. The literal sense of the term *sabhāgaḥ* is that of "having a share" in something. *AKB* (p. 28) gives the following description: "What does the term *sabhāgaḥ* mean? 'Share' (S: *bhāgaḥ*, T: *bsten pa*) is the mutual efficacy (S: *anyonyabhajanam*, T: *phan tshun brten pa*) that occurs among faculty, object, and consciousness; or, it is the sharing of an action (S: *kāritrabhajanam*, T: *byed pa la brten pa*). Because an entity possesses this quality, it is described as 'having a share'; or [an entity is described as 'having a share'] because [the mental factor] contact is a shared result." *AKV* (f. 71a) gives this analysis of the term: "[Those entities] that act in a shared manner are described as 'having a share.' Or, those [entities] that have the same allotment are [described as] 'having a share'" (S: *saha bhāgena vartante sabhāgā iti / samāno vā bhāga eṣāṃ te ime sabhāgāḥ*. T: *rten pa dang lhan cig 'dug pas rten pa dang bcas pas sam 'di dag la rten pa 'dra ba yod pas 'di dag ni rten pa mtshungs pa dag yin no*). Regarding the related term *tatsabhāgaḥ*, *AK* (ch. 1, v. 39d) describes *tatsabhāgaḥ* as meaning "that which does not carry out its action" (S: *yo na svakarmakṛt*, T: *gang rang gi las mi byed*). *AKB* (p. 28) further explains the literal meaning of *tatsabhāgaḥ* (T: *de dag dang mtshungs pa*) as follows: "By contrast, those [entities] that do not have a share are [described as] 'resembling those [that have a share]' because they share with those [entities] that *do* have a share the quality of being the same type [of entity]." The significance of this pair of terms is to contrast instances in which an entity does carry out its common action with those in which it does not. I translate the pair of terms as "having a shared [action]" and "resembling those [that have a shared action]."

In this work, Vasubandhu follows the position expressed in *AS*, which is that these terms apply only to the five sense faculties. Asaṅga takes the term *sabhāgaḥ* to refer to those instances of the five sense faculties in which they operate in conjunction with their respective forms of consciousness in the sense of engaging the same object. When any of the sense faculties does not engage its respective object, it is termed *tatsabhāgaḥ*. An example of the latter would be when a person is asleep. Reflecting the view of the Sarvāstivāda School, Vasubandhu's *AK* identifies all eighteen constituents as capable of being referred to with one or both of these terms.

642 S: *tatsabhāgaḥ*, T: *de dag dang mtshungs pa*.

643 S: *niyataḥ*, T: *nges pa*. In other words, no instance of the eye, etc., is ever described as "having a shared [action]" for one person, but "resembling those [that have a shared action]" for someone else. Cf. *AKB* (p. 28).

644 That is, according to the Mind Only School, the constituents other than those of the five sense faculties are not described with either of these two qualities. The restrictive view of these two terms is also affirmed in *VS*, f. 78b. However, in the *AKB* (cf. pp. 27–28), Vasubandhu presents the view of the Sarvāstivāda School, which identifies the distinctions in relation to all eighteen constituents: ". . . Therefore, the entity constituent always [possesses only the quality of] having a shared [action].

". . . Whatever eye has seen, is seeing, or will see forms is said to "have a shared [action]." The same should be said [for the other five faculties] up to the mind [faculty]. [That is,] they are described [as having a shared action] on the basis of the action of their respective objects. According to the Vaibhāṣikas of Kashmir, the eye that resembles those [that have a shared action] is of four types: (1) that which has ceased without having seen form; (2) that which is in the process of ceasing [without having seen form]; (3) that which will cease in the future [without having seen form] and (4) that which is incapable of arising. . . . The same [description] should be understood [for the other four sense faculties] up to the body [faculty]. In the case of the mind [faculty], only that which is incapable of arising constitutes [the mind faculty that] resembles those [that have a shared action].

"Those [visible] forms that have been seen by the eye, are being seen, or will be seen constitute [visible form that] has a shared [action]. [The visible forms that] resemble those [that have a shared action] are of four types: (1) those that cease without having been seen; (2) those that are ceasing [without having been seen]; (3) those that will cease [without having been seen]; and (4) those that are incapable of arising. The same [description] should be understood for [the other four sense objects] ranging up to tangible objects. [That is, they are classified] as having a shared [action] or as resembling those [that have a shared action] on the basis of the action of their respective faculties.

". . . In the case of eye consciousness, etc., the qualities of having a shared [action] or of resembling those [that have a shared action] are distinguished on the basis of whether they are capable of arising or not, as was the case with the mind constituent."

645 S: *upādhyāyaḥ*, T: *mkhan po*. The Tibetan is usually translated as "abbot," since it applies to the administrative head of a monastery. This title also refers to the functionary who presides over the ordination rituals for monks and nuns. The usage in this context probably is meant to convey the sense of a senior teacher or scholar.

646 T: *lo tsā ba*. A title given to those Tibetan scholar-translators who rendered Sanskrit Buddhist scriptures into Tibetan. The term is said to mean literally "eyes of the world," suggesting that it is derived from a contraction of the Sanskrit expression *lokacakṣuḥ*.

Abbreviations

AA	*Abhisamayālaṃkāraḥ* (Maitreya Nātha)
AAA	*Abhisamayālaṃkārālokaḥ* (Haribhadra)
AK	*Abhidharmakośakārikā* (Vasubandhu)
AKB	*Abhidharmakośabhāṣyam* (Vasubandhu)
AKV	*Sphuṭārthābhidharmakośavyākhā* (Yaśomitra)
AKT	*Abhidharmakośabhāṣyaṭīkā Tattvārthaḥ* (Sthiramati)
AS	*Abhidharmasamuccayaḥ* (Asaṅga)
ASB	*Abhidharmasamuccayabhāṣyam* (Jinaputra)
BB	*Bodhisattvabhūmiḥ* (Asaṅga)
BCA	*Bodhicaryāvatāraḥ* (Śāntideva)
CŚ	*Catuḥśatakam* (Āryadeva)
CŚṬ	*Catuḥśatakaṭīkā* (Candrakīrti)
LC	*Byang chub lam gyi rim pa chen mo* (Tsong kha pa)
MA	*Madhyamakāvatāraḥ* (Candrakīrti)
MMK	*Mūlamadhyamakakārikā* (Nāgārjuna)
MSA	*Mahāyānasūtrālaṃkāraḥ* (Maitreya Nātha)
MSV	*Mahāyānasūtrālaṃkāravyākhyā* (Vasubandhu)
MV	*Madhyāntavibhāgakārikā* (Maitreya Nātha)
MVB	*Madhyāntavibhāgabhāṣyam* (Vasubandhu)
MVṬ	*Madhyāntavibhāgaṭīkā* (Sthiramati)
MVy	*Mahāvyutpatti* (T: *Bye brag tu rtogs pa chen po*)
NgG	*Chos mngon mdzod kyi tshig le'ur byas pa'i 'grel pa mngon pa'i rgyan* (Nam mkha' grags)
PP	*Prasannapadā* (Candrakīrti)
PS	*Pañcaskandhaprakaraṇam* (Vasubandhu)
PSB	*Pañcaskandhaprakaraṇabhāṣyam* (Sa'i rtsa lag)

PSV	*Pañcaskandhaprakaraṇavibhāṣyaṃ* (Sthiramati)
PV	*Pramāṇavārttikakārikā* (Dharmakīrti)
PVS	*Pañcaviṃśatisāhasrikāprajñāpāramitāsūtram*
PVṬ	*Pramāṇavārttikavṛttiṭīkā* (Karṇakagomī)
PVV	*Pramāṇavārttikavṛttiḥ* (Dharmakīrti)
RA	*Ratnāvalī* (Nāgārjuna)
RG2	*Tshad ma rnam 'grel gyi rgya cher bshad pa rigs pa'i rgya mtsho las tshad ma grub pa'i le'u'i rnam bshad* (mKhas grup dGe legs dpal bzang)
ŚB	*Śrāvakabhūmiḥ* (Asaṅga)
TB	*Triṃśikābhāṣyam* (Sthiramati)
TK	*Triṃśikākārikā* (Vasubandhu)
VS	*Viniścayasaṃgrahaṇī* (Asaṅga, T: *rNam par btan la dbab pa bsdu ba*)
YB	*Yogācārabhūmiḥ* (Asaṅga)
YṢ	*Yuktiṣaṣṭikākārikā* (Nāgārjuna)
YṢV	*Yuktiṣaṣṭikāvṛttiḥ* (Candrakīrti, T: *Rigs pa drug cu pa'i 'grel pa*)

Bibliography

The bibliography is divided into four sections, of which only the first, "Canonical Works," lists the entries by title. The other three sections (with a few exceptions) are arranged by author or translator. The order follows the roman alphabet, with both Tibetan authors and titles presented according to the capitalized "main" letter of the first word.

Wherever a Sanskrit edition is known to have survived, I have listed that first. To accommodate readers with little or no facility in either Tibetan or Sanskrit, I have also tried to include information for any English translations that may be available.

For works in the Kangyur and Tengyur, folio numbers (abbreviated "f." or "ff.") refer to the Derge edition. The volume numbers follow the system used in the digital editions of these collections by the Tibetan Buddhist Resource Center. I have also provided the reference numbers for those works that are listed in the well-known catalogues published by Tohoku University.

Please note the following abbreviations:

Kg. Kangyur

Tg. Tengyur

Toh. Tohoku catalogue numbers from *A Complete Catalogue of the Tibetan Buddhist Canons* (#1–#4569) and *A Catalogue of the Tohoku University Collection of Tibetan Works on Buddhism* (#5001–#7083); see separate listings below in last section of Bibliography.

Canonical Works

Avadānaśatakam. Buddhist Sanskrit Texts, no. 19. Darbhanga, India: Mithila Institute, 1958. Tibetan translation: *Gang po la sogs pa'i rtogs pa brjod pa brgya pa.* In *mDo sde* section of Kg., vol. 75 (*am*), ff. 1–286b (Toh. #343).

(*'Phags pa*) *Blo gros mi zad pas bstan pa zhes bya ba theg pa chen po'i mdo* (Tibetan translation of *Akṣayamatinirdeśasūtram*). In *mDo sde* section of Kg., vol. 60 (*ma*), ff. 79a–174b (Toh. #175). English translation: *Akṣayamatinirdeśasūtra.* 2 vols. Tr. Jens Braarvig. Oslo: Solum Forlag, 1993.

(*'Phags pa*) *Chos yang dag par sdud pa zhes bya ba theg pa chen po'i mdo* (Tibetan translation of *Dharmasaṃgītisūtram*). In *mDo sde* section of Kg., vol. 65 (*zha*), ff. 1b–99b (Toh. #238).

(*'Phags pa*) *Dam pa'i chos dran pa nye bar bzhag pa* (Tibetan translation of *Saddharmasmṛtyupasthānasūtram*). In *mDo sde* section of Kg., vol. 68 (*ya*), f. 82a–vol. 71 (*sha*), f. 229b (Toh. #287).

Daśabhūmikasūtram. Buddhist Sanskrit Texts, no. 7. Darbhanga, India: Mithila Institute, 1958. Tibetan translation: *Sa bcu pa'i mdo* (ch. 30 of *Sangs rgyas phal po che zhes bya ba shin tu rgyas pa chen po'i mdo*). In *Phal chen* section of Kg., vol. 37 (*ga*), ff. 67a–234b (Toh. #44). English translation in *Flower Ornament Scripture.* Tr. Thomas Cleary. Boston: Shambhala Publications, 1984, ch. 26, pp. 695–811.

(*'Phags pa*) *De bzhin gshegs pa'i gsang ba bsam gyis mi khyab pa bstan pa zhes bya ba theg pa chen po'i mdo.* (Tibetan translation of *Tathāgatācintyaguhyanirdeśasūtram*). In *dKon brtsegs* section of Kg., vol. 39 (*ka*), ff. 100a–203a (Toh. #47).

Dhvajāgrasūtram. In *Kleine Bhrāmī-Schriftrolle.* Ed. E. Waldschmidt. Gottingen: Nachrichten der Akademie der Wissenschaften in Göttingen, 1959, nr. 1, pp. 8–18. Tibetan translation: *mDo chen po rgyal mtshan dam pa.* In *mDo sde* section of Kg., vol. 71 (*sha*), ff. 265b–267a (Toh. #293).

mDzangs blun zhes bya ba'i mdo (Tibetan translation of *Damamūkasūtram*). In *mDo sde* section of Kg., vol. 74 (*a*), ff. 207b–476b (Toh. #341). English translation: *Sutra of the Wise and the Foolish.* Tr. Stanley B. Frye. Dharamsala: Library of Tibetan Works and Archives, 1981.

Las brgya tham pa (Tibetan translation of *Karmaśatakam*). In *mDo sde* section of Kg., vol. 73 (*ha*)–vol. 74 (*a*), f. 128b (Toh. #340).

Pañcavimśatisāhasrikāprajñāpāramitāsūtram. (Recast version of the original sutra that conforms to the sections of the *Abhisamayālaṃkāraḥ.*) 3 vols. Bibliotheca Indo-Tibetica Series, 61. Ed. Dr. Vijay Raj Vajracharya.

Sarnath, India: Central Institute of Higher Tibetan Studies, 2006–2008. Tibetan translation: *Shes rab kyi pha rol tu phyin pa stong phrag nyi shu lnga pa*. In *Sher phyin stong phrag nyi shu lnga pa* section of Kg., vols. 26–28 (*ka–ga*) (Toh. #9). English translation: *The Large Sutra on Perfect Wisdom*. Tr. Edward Conze. Berkeley: University of California Press, 1975.

Pratītyasamutpādādivibhaṅganirdeśasūtram. In *Ārya Śālistamba Sūtra Pratītyasamutpādavibhaṅga Nirdeśa Sutra and Pratītyasamutpādagāthā Sūtra*. Adyar Library Series 76. Ed. N. Aiyaswami Śastri. Adyar, India: Adyar Library, 1950. Tibetan translation: *rTen cing 'brel bar 'byung ba dang po'i rnam par dbye ba bstan pa zhes bya ba'i mdo*. In *mDo sde* section of Kg., vol. 62 (*tsha*), ff. 123b–125a (Toh. #211).

(*'Phags pa*) *gTsug na rin po ches zhus pa zhes bya ba theg pa chen po'i mdo* (Tibetan translation of *Ratnacūḍaparipṛcchāsūtram*). In *dKon brtsegs* section of the Kg., vol. 44 (*cha*), ff. 210a–254b (Toh #91).

Udānavargaḥ. Ed. Franz Bernhard. Gottingen: Vandehoeck and Ruprecht, 1965. Tibetan translation: *Ched du brjod pa'i tshoms*. In *mDo sde* section of Kg., vol. 72 (*sa*), ff. 209a–253a (Toh. #326). English translation: *Udānavarga*. Tr. W. Woodville Rockhill. 1884; reprinted Amsterdam: Oriental Press, 1975.

(*Mūlasarvāstivāda*) *Vinayavastu*. Buddhist Sanskrit Texts, no. 16 (2 vols.). Darbhanga, India: Mithila Institute, 1970. Tibetan translation: *'Dul ba gzhi*. In *'Dul ba* section of Kg., vols. 1–4 (*ka–nga*) (Toh. #1).

Indian Treatises

Āryadeva. *Catuḥśatakaśāstrakārikā*. Extant and reconstructed verses in *Catuḥśatakam*. Ed. P.L. Vaidya. Nagpur, India: Alok Prakashan, 1971. Tibetan translation: *bsTan bcos bzhi brgya pa zhes bya ba'i tshig le'ur byas pa*. In *dBu ma* section of Tg., vol. 97 (*tsha*), ff. 1b–18a (Toh. #3846). English translation: in *Aryadeva's Four Hundred Stanzas on the Middle Way with Commentary by Gyel-tsap*. Tr. Ruth Sonam with Geshe Sonam Rinchen. Ithaca, N.Y.: Snow Lion Publications, 2008.

Asaṅga. *Abhidharmasamuccayaḥ*. Ed. Prahlad Pradhan. Shantiniketan, India: Visva-Bharati, 1950. Tibetan translation: *Chos mngon pa kun las btus pa*. In *Sems tsam* section of Tg., vol. 134 (*ri*), ff. 44a–120a (Toh. #4049). English translation: *Abhidharmasamuccaya: The Compendium of the Higher Teaching*. Tr. Sara Boin-Webb (from Walpola Rahula's French translation). Berkeley: Asian Humanities Press, 2001.

______. *Bodhisattvabhūmiḥ*. Ed. Nalinaksha Dutt. Patna: K. P. Jayaswal

Research Institute, 1978. Tibetan translation: (*rNal 'byor spyod pa'i sa las*) *Byang chub sems dpa'i sa*. In *Sems tsam* section of Tg., vol. 129 (*wi*), ff. 1b–213a. (Toh. #4037).

———. *rNam par gtan la dbab pa bsdu ba* (Tibetan translation of *Viniścayasaṃgrahaṇī*). In *Sems tsam* section of Tg., vol. 130 (*zhi*), ff. 1b–289a (Toh. #4038).

———. *Śrāvakabhūmiḥ*. Tibetan Sanskrit Works Series vol. XIV. Ed. Karunesha Shukla. Patna: K.P. Jayaswal Research Institute, 1973. Tibetan translation: (*rNal 'byor spyod pa'i sa las*) *Nyan thos kyi sa*. In *Sems tsam* section of Tg., vol. 128 (*dzi*), ff. 1b–195a (Toh. #4036).

———. *Yogācārabhūmiḥ* (incomplete). Parts 1-5 in *The Yogācārabhūmi of Ācārya Asaṅga*. Ed. Vidhushekhara Bhattacharya. Calcutta: University of Calcutta, 1957, pp. 1–232. Parts 8, 9, 11, and 14 in *Buddhist Insight*. Delhi: Motilal Banarsidass, 1984, pp. 327–331 and pp. 333–352. See separate listings for *Śrāvakabhūmiḥ* (part 13) and *Bodhisattvabhūmiḥ* (part 15). Tibetan translation: Parts 1-12, 14, 16–17, referred to as *Sa mang po pa*, in *Sems tsam* section of Tg., vol. 127 (*tshi*), ff. 1–283a (Toh. #4035).

Atiśa (Dīpaṃkāra Śrījñāna). *Bodhipathapradīpaḥ* (restored from Tibetan by Losang Norbu Shastri; also contains Tibetan, Hindi, and English texts). Bibliotheca Indo-Tibetica Series 7. Revised 2nd edition. Sarnath, India: Central Institute of Higher Tibetan Studies, 1994. Tibetan translation: *Byang chub lam gyi sgron ma*. In *dBu ma* section of Tg., vol. 111 (*khi*), ff. 242a–245a (Toh. #3947).

———. *bDen pa gnyis la 'jug pa* (Tibetan translation of *Satyadvayāvatāraḥ*). In *dBu ma* section of Tg., vol. 109 (*a*), ff. 72a–73a (Toh. #3902).

Bhavya. *Madhyamakahṛdayam*. In *Madhyamakahṛdayam of Bhavya*. Ed. Chr. Lindtner. Chennai, India: The Adyar and Research Library and Research Centre, 2001. Tibetan translation: *dBu ma'i snying po'i tshig le'ur byas pa*. In *dBu ma* section of Tg., vol. 98 (*dza*), ff. 1b–40b (Toh. #3855).

Candragomī. *Śiṣyalekhaḥ*. In *Invitation to Enlightenment*. Tr. Michael Hahn. Berkeley: Dharma Publishing, 1999, pp. 51–131. Tibetan translation: *Slob ma la springs pa'i spring yig*. In *sPring yig* section of Tg., vol. 173 (*nge*), ff. 46b–53a (Toh. #4183). English translation in *Invitation to Enlightenment*. Tr. Michael Hahn. Berkeley: Dharma Publishing, 1999, pp. 51–131.

Candrakīrti. *dBu ma la 'jug pa* (Tibetan translation of *Madhyamakāvatāraḥ*). In *dBu ma* section of Tg., vol. 102 (*'a*), ff. 201a–219a (Toh. #3861).

———. *dBu ma la 'jug pa'i bshad pa* (Tibetan translation of *Madhyamakāva-*

tārabhāṣyam). In *dBu ma* section of Tg., vol. 102 (*'a*), ff. 220b–348a (Toh. #3862).

______. *Bodhisattvayogācāracatuḥśatakaṭīkā* (fragments). Ed. Haraprasad Shastri. In *Memoirs of the Asiatic Society of Bengal*, vol. 3, no. 8, pp. 449–514. Calcutta: The Asiatic Society, 1914. Also reconstructed Sanskrit text of portions of chapters 7–16 in *Catuḥśatakam*. P.L. Vaidya. Nagpur, India: Alok Prakashan, 1971. Tibetan translation: *Byang chub sems dpa'i rnal 'byor spyod pa bzhi brgya pa'i rgya cher 'grel pa*. In *dBu ma* section of Tg., vol. 103 (*ya*), ff. 30b–239a (Toh. #3865).

______. *Prasannapadā*. In *Madhyamakaśāstra of Nāgārjuna*. Buddhist Sanskrit Texts, no. 10. Darbhanga, India: Mithila Institute, 1960, pp. 1–259. Tibetan translation: *dBu ma rtsa ba'i 'grel pa tshig gsal ba zhes bya ba*. In *dBu ma* section of Tg., vol. 102 (*'a*), ff. 1a–197a (Toh. #3860).

______. *Rigs pa drug cu pa'i 'grel pa* (Tibetan translation of *Yuktiṣaṣṭikāvṛttiḥ*). In *dBu ma* section of Tg., vol. 103 (*ya*), ff. 1a–30b (Toh. #3864). English translation: *Nāgārjuna's Reason Sixty* (*Yuktiṣaṣṭikā*), *with Candrakīrti's Commentary* (*Yuktiṣaṣṭikāvṛtti*). Tr. Joseph Loizzo. New York: Columbia University Press, 2007.

Dharmakīrti. *Pramāṇavārttikakārikā*. In *Pramāṇavārttika The Kārikās with Manorathanandi's Vṛtti*. Varanasi: Bauddha Bharati, 1968. Tibetan translation: *Tshad ma rnam 'grel gyi tshig le'ur byas pa*. In *Tshad ma* section of Tg., vol. 174 (*ce*), ff. 94b–151a (Toh. #4210).

______. *Pramāṇavārttikavṛttiḥ*. *The Pramāṇavārttikam of Dharmakīrti* (the first chapter with the autocommentary). Text with critical notes. Serie Orientale Roma 23. Ed. Raniero Gnoli. Rome: Istituto Italiano per il Medio ed Estremo Oriente, 1960. Tibetan translation: *Tshad ma rnam 'grel gyi 'grel pa*. In *Tshad ma* section of Tg., vol. 174 (*ce*), ff. 261b–365a (Toh. #4216).

Dignāga. *Tshad ma kun las btus pa* (Tibetan translation of *Pramāṇasamuccayaḥ*). In *Tshad ma* section of Tg., vol. 174 (*ce*), ff. 1b–13a (Toh. #4203).

______. *Prajñāpāramitāpiṇḍārthaḥ*. In *Aṣṭasahasrikā Prajñāpāramitā* (see entry for *Abhisamayālaṃkārālokaḥ* under listing for Haribhadra), pp. 263–266. Tibetan translation: *'Phags pa shes rab kyi pha rol tu phyin ma sdus pa'i tshig le'ur byas pa*. In *Sher phyin* section of Tg., vol. 93 (*pha*), ff. 292b–294b (Toh. #3809).

Guṇamati. *rTen cing 'brel bar 'byung ba dang po'i rnam par dbye ba bstan pa'i rgya cher bshad pa* (Tibetan translation of *Pratītyasamutpādādivibhaṅganirdeśaṭīkā*. In *mDo 'grel* section of Tg., vol. 114 (*ci*), ff. 61b-234a (Toh. #3996).

Guṇaprabha. *Phung po lnga'i rnam par 'grel pa* (Tibetan translation of *Pañcaskandhavivaraṇam*). In *Sems tsam* section of Tg., vol. 137 (*si*), ff. 1b–31b (Toh. #4067).

Haribhadra. *Abhisamayālaṃkārakārikāśāstravivṛttiḥ* (*Sphuṭārtham*). Ed. Hirafuso Amano. In 6 parts. *Hijiyama Joshi Tankdaigaku Kiyō* [*Bulletin of the Hijiyama Women's Junior College*] 17 (1983): 1–15; *Shimane Daigaku Kyōiku Gakubu Kiyō* [*Bulletin of the Faculty of Education of Shimane University*] 19 (1985): 124–138; 20: 67–86; 21: 39–51; 22: 10–25; 23: 1–7. Tibetan translation: *Shes rab kyi pha rol tu phyin pa'i man ngag gi bstan bcos mngon par rtogs pa'i rgyan zhes bya ba'i 'grel pa* (*'Grel pa don gsal*). In *Shes phyin* section of Tg., vol. 86 (*ja*), ff. 78b–140a (Toh. #3793).

———. (*Āryāṣṭasāhasrikāprajñāpāramitāvyākhyā*) *Abhisamayālaṃkārālokaḥ*. In *Aṣṭasahasrikā Prajñāpāramitā*. Buddhist Sanskrit Texts, no. 4. Darbhanga, India: Mithila Institute, 1960, pp. 267–558. Tibetan translation: (*'Phags pa shes rab kyi pha rol tu phyin pa brgyad stong pa'i bshad pa*) *mNgon par rtogs pa'i rgyan gyi snang ba*. In *Shes phyin* section of Tg., vol. 85 (*cha*), ff. 1–341a (Toh. #3791).

Jinaputra. *Abhidharmasamuccayabhāṣyam*. Ed. Nathmal Tatia. Patna, India: K.P. Jayaswal Research Institute, 1976. Tibetan translation: *mNgon pa chos kun las btus pa'i rnam par bshad pa*. In *Sems tsam* section of Tg., vol. 135 (*li*), ff. 119a–296a (Toh. #4054).

Kamalaśīla. *Tattvasaṃgrāhapañjikā* (2 vols.). Ed. Swami Dwarikadas Shastri. Varanasi: Bauddha Bharati, 1968. Tibetan translation: *De kho na nyid bsdus pa'i dka' 'grel*. In *Tshad ma* section of Tg., vol. 191 (*ze*), f. 133b–vol. 192 (*'e*) (Toh. #4267). English Translation: *The Tattvasaṅgraha of Śāntarakṣita with the Commentary of Kamalaśīla*. 2 vols. Baroda, India: Oriental Institute, 1937.

Karṇakagomī. *Pramāṇavārttikavṛttiṭīkā*. Ed. Rahula Samkrtyayana. In *Karṇakagomin's Commentary on the Pramāṇavārttikavṛtti of Dharmakīrti*. Kyoto: Rinsen Book Co., 1982. Reprint of the original 1943 Allahabad edition. No Tibetan translation.

Maitreya Nātha. *Abhisamayālaṃkāraḥ* (Sanskrit and Tibetan texts). Ed. T. Stcherbatsky and E.E. Obermiller. Leningrad: Bibliotheca Buddhica, 1929. Tibetan translation: (*Shes rab kyi pha rol tu phyin pa'i man ngag gi bstan bcos*) *mNgon par rtogs pa'i rgyan zhes bya ba'i tshig le'ur byas pa*. In *Shes phyin* section of Tg., vol. 80 (*ka*), ff. 1b–13a (Toh. #3786). English translation: *Abhisamaya Alaṃkāra*. Tr. Edward Conze. Rome: Serie Orientale Roma, 1954.

______. *Madhyāntavibhāgakārikā*. Contained in *Madhyānta Vibhāga Śāstra*. Ed. by Ramchandra Pandeya. Delhi: Motilal Banarsidass, 1971. Tibetan translation: *dBus dang mtha' rnam par 'byed pa'i tshig le'ur byas pa*. In *Sems tsam* section Tg., vol. 123 (*phi*), ff. 40b–45a (Toh. #4021).

______. *Mahāyānasūtrālaṃkāraḥ*. In Buddhist Sanskrit Texts, no. 13. Darbhanga, India: Mithila Institute, 1970. Tibetan translation: *Theg pa chen po mdo sde'i rgyan zhes bya ba'i tshig le'ur byas pa*. In *Sems tsam* section Tg., vol. 123 (*phi*), ff. 1–39a (Toh. #4020).

Manorathanandī. *Pramāṇavārttikavṛttiḥ*. Ed. Swami Dwarikadas Shastri. Varanasi: Bauddha Bharati, 1968. No Tibetan translation.

Mātṛceṭa. *Śatapañcāśatkastotram*. In *The Śatapañcāśatka of Mātṛceṭa*. Ed. D. R. Shackleton Bailey. Cambridge: Cambridge University Press, 1951. Tibetan translation: *brGya lnga bcu pa zhes bya ba'i bstod pa*. In *bsTod pa* section of Tg., vol. 1 (*ka*), ff. 110a–116a (Toh. #1147). English translation: In *The Śatapañcāśatka of Mātṛceṭa*, pp. 152–180.

Nāgārjuna. *bShes pa'i spring yig* (Tibetan translation of *Suhṛllekhaḥ*). In *sPring yig* section of Tg., vol. 173 (*nge*), ff. 40b–46b (Toh. #4182). English translation with commentary in *Nāgārjuna's Letter*. Tr. Geshe Lobsang Tharchin and Artemus B. Engle. Dharamsala, India: Library of Tibetan Works and Archives, 1979.

______. *Byang chub sems kyi 'grel pa* (Tibetan translation of *Bodhicittavivaraṇam*). In *rGyud* section of Tg., vol. 35 (*ngi*), ff. 38a–45a (there are two separate versions of the same text translated by different scholars (Toh. #1800, 1801).

______. *mDo kun las btus pa* (Tibetan translation of *Sūtrasamuccayaḥ*). In *dBu ma* section of Tg., vol. 110 (*ki*), ff. 148b–215a (Toh. #3934).

______. *Lugs kyi bstan bcos skye bo gso ba'i thigs pa* (Tibetan translation of *Nītiśāstrajantupoṣaṇabinduḥ*). In *Thun mong ba lugs kyi bstan bcos* section of Tg., vol. 203 (*ngo*), ff. 109a–112b (Toh. #4330).

______. *Mūlamadhyamakakārikā*. In *Mūlamadhyamakaśāstra of Nāgārjuna*, Buddhist Sanskrit Texts, no. 10. Darbhanga, India: Mithila Institute, 1960. Tibetan translation: *dBu ma rtsa ba'i tshig le'ur byas pa shes rab ces bya ba*. In *dBu ma* section of Tg., vol. 96 (*tsa*), ff. 1b–19a (Toh. #3824). English translation: *The Fundamental Wisdom of the Middle Way: Nagarjuna's Mulamadhyamakakarika*. Tr. Jay L. Garfield. New York: Oxford University Press, 1995.

______. *Pratītyasamutpādahṛdayakārikā* (restored from Tibetan translation). In *Pratītya-samutpādahṛdaya and Āryadharmadhātugarbhavivaraṇa of Ācārya Nāgārjuna*. Bibliotheca Indo-Tibetica Series 39.

Sarnath, India: Central Institute of Higher Tibetan Studies, 1997. Tibetan translation: *rTen cing 'brel bar 'byung ba'i snying po'i tshig le'ur byas pa*. In *dBu ma* section of Tg., vol. 96 (*tsa*), ff. 146b (Toh. #3836).

———. *Ratnāvalī* (incomplete text). In *Nāgārjuna's Ratnāvalī*, ed. Michael Hahn. Bonn: Indica et Tibetica Verlag, 1982. Tibetan translation: *rGyal po la gtam bya ba rin po che'i phreng ba*. In *sPring yig* section of Tg., vol. 172 (*ge*), ff. 116a–135a (Toh. #4158). English translation in *The Precious Garland and the Precious Song of the Four Mindfulnesses*. Tr. Jeffrey Hopkins and Lati Rinpoche with Anne Klein. New York: Harper and Row, 1975.

———. *bSam gyis mi khyab par bstod pa* (Tibetan translation of *Acintya-stavaḥ*). In *bsTod tshogs* section of Tg., vol. 1 (*ka*), ff. 76b–79a (Toh. # 1128).

———. *Rigs pa drug cu pa'i tshig le'ur byas pa* (Tibetan translation of *Yuktiṣaṣṭikākārikā*). In *dBu ma* section of Tg., vol. 96 (*tsa*), ff. 20b–22b (Toh. #3825). English translation in *Nāgārjuna's Reason Sixty (Yuktiṣaṣṭikā), with Candrakīrti's Commentary Yuktiṣaṣṭikāvṛtti*. Tr. Joseph Loizzo. New York: Columbia University Press, 2007.

Prajñākaragupta. *Pramāṇavārttikālaṃkāraḥ*. Ed. Rāhula Sāmkṛtyāyana. Patna, India: Kashi Prasad Jayaswal Research Institute, 1953. Tibetan translation: *Tshad ma rnam 'grel gyi rgyan*. In *Tshad ma* section of Tg., vols. 178–179 (*te–the*) (Toh. #4221).

Prajñāvarman. *Ched du brjod pa'i tshoms kyi rnam par 'grel pa* (Tibetan translation of *Udānavargavivaraṇam*). In *mNgon pa* section of Tg., from vol. 148 (*tu*), f. 46b, to vol. 149 (*thu*), f. 221a (Toh. #4100).

Sa'i rtsa lag (original Sanskrit name uncertain). *Phung po lnga'i bshad pa* (Tibetan translation of *Pañcaskandhabhāṣyam*). In *Sems tsam* section of Tg., vol. 137 (*si*), ff. 32a–139a (Toh. #4068).

Śāntarakṣita. *Tattvasaṃgrāhakārikā*. Verses contained in *Tattvasaṃgrāhapañjikā* (2 vols.). Ed. Swami Dwarikadas Shastri. Varanasi: Bauddha Bharati, 1968. Tibetan translation: *De kho na nyid bsdus pa'i tshig le'ur byas pa*. In *Tshad ma* section of Tg., vol. 191 (*ze*), ff. 1b–133a (Toh. #4266). English translation of root text contained in *The Tattvasaṅgraha of Śāntarakṣita with the Commentary of Kamalaśīla*. 2 vols. Baroda, India: Oriental Institute, 1937.

Śāntideva. *Bodhicaryāvatāraḥ* (Sanskrit and Tibetan texts). Ed. Vidushekhara Bhattacharya. Calcutta: The Asiatic Society, 1960. Tibetan translation: *Byang chub sems dpa'i spyod pa la 'jug pa*. In *dBu ma* section of Tg., vol. 105 (*la*), ff. 1–40a (Toh. #3871). English translation: *A Guide to the*

Bodhisattva's Way of Life. Tr. Stephen Batchelor. Dharamsala: Library of Tibetan Works and Archives, 1979.

______. *Śikṣāsamuccayaḥ*. Buddhist Sanskrit Texts, no. 11. Darbhanga, India: Mithila Institute, 1960. Tibetan translation: *bSlab pa kun las btus pa*. In *dBu ma* section of Tg., vol. 111 (*khi*), ff. 3a–194b (Toh. #3940). English translation: *Śikṣā Samuccaya, A Compendium of Buddhist Doctrine*. Tr. Cecil Bendall and W.H.D. Rouse. Reprint edition, Delhi: Motilal Banarsidass, 1971.

Sthiramati. *Chos mngon pa mdzod kyi bshad pa'i rgya cher 'grel pa don gyi de kho na nyid* (Tibetan translation of *Abhidharmakośabhāṣyatīkā Tattvārthaḥ*. In *sNa tshogs* section of Tg., vols. 209–210 (*tho–do*) (Toh. #4421).

______. *mDo sde rgyan gyi 'grel bshad* (Tibetan translation of *Mahāyānasūtrālaṃkāravṛtti-bhāṣyam*). In *Sems tsam* section of Tg., vols. 125–126 (*mi–tsi*) (Toh. #4034).

______. *Triṃśikābhāṣyam*. In *Sthiramati's Triṃśikāvijñaptibhāṣya*. Ed. Hartmut Buescher. Vienna: Österreichische Akademie der Wissenschaften, 2007. Tibetan translation: *Sum cu pa'i bshad pa*. In *Sems tsam* section of Tg., vol. 136 (*shi*), ff. 146b–171b (Toh. #4064).

______. *Madhyāntavibhāgaṭīkā*. In *Madhyānta-Vibhāga-Śāstra*. Ed. Ramchandra Pandeya. Delhi: Motilal Banarsidass, 1971. Tibetan translation: *dBu dang mtha' rnam par 'byed pa'i 'grel bshad*. In *Sems tsam* section of Tg., vol. 124 (*bi*), ff. 189b–318a (Toh. #4032).

______. *Phung po lnga'i rab tu byed pa bye brag tu bshad pa* (Tibetan translation of *Pañcaskandhaprakaraṇavibhāṣyam*). In *Sems tsam* section of Tg., vol. 136 (*shi*), ff. 195b–250a (Toh. #4066).

Vasubandhu. *Abhidharmakośakārikā*. Ed. G.V. Gokhale. Journal of the Royal Asiatic Society, vol. 22. Bombay: Royal Asiatic Society, 1946. Tibetan translation: *Chos mngon pa mdzod kyi tshig le'ur byas pa*. In *mNgon pa* section of Tg., vol. 140 (*ku*), ff. 1–25a (Toh. #4089). English translation in *Abhidharmakośabhāṣyam*. 4 vols. Tr. Leo M. Pruden. Berkeley: Asian Humanities Press, 1988.

______. *Abhidharmakośabhāṣyam*. Ed. Prahlad Pradhan. Patna: K. P. Jayaswal Research Institute, 1975. Tibetan translation: *Chos mngon pa'i mdzod kyi bshad pa*. In *mNgon pa* section of Tg., vol. 140 (*ku*), f. 25a–vol. 141 (*khu*), f. 97b. (Toh. #4090). English translation: *Abhidharmakośabhāṣyam*. 4 vols. Tr. Leo M. Pruden (from Louis de La Vallée Poussin's French translation). Berkeley: Asian Humanities Press, 1988.

______. *Mahāyānasūtrālaṃkāravyākhyā*. Buddhist Sanskrit Texts, no. 13.

Darbhanga, India: Mithila Institute, 1960. Tibetan translation: *mDo sde'i rgyan gyi bshad pa*. In *Sems tsam* section of Tg., vol. 123 (*phi*), ff. 129b–260a (Toh. #4026). English translation: *The Universal Vehicle Discourse Literature*. Tr. L. Jamspal et al. New York: American Institute of Buddhist Studies, 2004.

———. *Madhyāntavibhāgabhāṣyam*. In *Madhyānta-Vibhāga-Śāstra*. Ed. Ramchandra Pandeya. Delhi: Motilal Banarsidass, 1971. Tibetan translation: *dBu dang mtha' rnam par 'byed pa'i 'grel pa*. In *Sems tsam* section of Tg., vol. 124 (*bi*), ff. 1b–27a (Toh. #4027). English translation in *Seven Works of Vasubandhu*. Stefan Anacker. Delhi: Motilal Banarsidass, 1998 (corrected edition), pp. 191–286.

———. *Pañcaskandhaprakaraṇam*. Tibetan translation: *Phung po lnga'i rab tu byed pa*. In *Sems tsam* section of Tg., vol. 136 (*shi*), ff. 11b–17a (Toh. #4059).

———. *Pratītyasamutpādādivibhaṅgabhāṣyam*. Fragments in *Journal of the Royal Asiatic Society of Great Britain and Ireland*, July 1930, pp. 611-623. Tibetan translation: *rTen cing 'brel bar 'byung ba dang po'i rnam par dbye ba bshad pa*. In *mDo 'grel* section of Tg., vol. 115 (*chi*), ff. 1b-61a (Toh. #3995).

———. *Triṃśikākārikā*. In *Sthiramati's Triṃśikāvijñaptibhāṣya*. Ed. Hartmut Buescher. Vienna: Österreichische Akademie der Wissenschaften, 2007. Tibetan translation: *Sum cu pa'i tshig le'ur byas pa*. In *Sems tsam* section of Tg., vol. 136 (*shi*), ff. 1b–3a (Toh. #4055). English translation: in *Seven Works of Vasubandhu*. Stefan Anacker. Delhi: Motilal Banarsidass, (Corrected edition) 1998, pp. 181–190.

(Ārya) Vimuktisena. *Abhisamayālaṃkāravṛttiḥ*. Sanskrit of the first chapter only is available in *Abhisamayālaṃkāravṛtti di Ārya Vimuktisena: Primo Abhisamaya*. Rome: Istituto Italiano per il Medio ed Estremo Oriente, 1967. Tibetan translation: *mNgon par rtogs pa'i rgyan gyi 'grel pa*. In *Shes phyin* section of Tg., vol. 80 (*ka*), ff. 14b–212a (Toh. #3787).

Yaśomitra. *Sphuṭārthābhidharmakośavyākhyā*. 4 vols. Ed. by Swami Dwarikadas Shastri. Varanasi: Bauddha Bharati, 1970. Tibetan translation: *Chos mngon pa'i mdzod kyi 'grel bshad*. In *mNgon pa* section of Tg., vols. 142–143 (*gu–ngu*) (Toh. #4092).

Tibetan Works

(Gro lung pa) Blo gros 'byung gnas. *bDe bar gshegs pa'i bstan pa rin po che la 'jug pa'i lam gyi rim pa rnam par bshad pa* (*bsTan rim chen mo*). Mundgod, India: Library of Trijang Labrang, 2001.

Ba so Chos kyi rgyal mtshan et al. *mNyam med rje btsun tsong kha pa chen pos mdzad pa'i byang chub lam rim chen mo'i dka' ba'i gnad rnams mchan bu bzhi'i sgo nas legs par bshad pa theg chen lam gyi gsal sgron* (*Lam rim mchan bzhi sbrags*). (2 vols.) Mundgod, India: Drepung Gomang Library, 2005 (Toh. # 6977).

Bu ston Rin chen grub. *Chos mngon pa kun las btus pa'i rnam bshad nyi ma'i 'od zer*. In vol. 20 (*wa*) of *The Collected Works of Bu-ston* (28 vols.), pp. 79–747. New Delhi: International Academy of Indian Culture, 1966 (Toh. #5183).

______. *bDe bar gshegs pa'i bstan pa'i gsal byed chos kyi 'byung gnas gsung rab rin po che'i mdzod* (*Bu ston chos 'byung*). In vol. 24 (*ya*) of *Collected Works*, pp. 633–1055 (Toh. #5197). English translation: *History of Buddhism by Bu-ston*. Tr. E.E. Obermiller. Originally published Heidelberg: O. Harrassowitz, 1931. Reprint edition, Tokyo: Suzuki Research Foundation.

rGyal Tshab Dar ma Rin chen. *mNgon pa kun las btus pa'i rnam bshad legs par bshad pa'i chos mngon rgya mtsho'i snying po*. In vol. 3 (*ga*) of *The Collected Works (gSuṅ 'bum) of The Lord rGyal-tshab rJe Dar-ma-rin-chen*, pp. 463–892. New Delhi: Mongolian Lama Gurudeva, 1982 (Toh. #5435).

______. *Shes rab kyi pha rol tu phyin pa'i man ngag gi bstan bcos mngon par rtogs pa'i rgyan gyi rtsa ba 'grel pa dang bcas pa'i rnam bshad snying po'i rgyan* (*rNam bshad snying po'i rgyan*). Vol. 2 (*kha*) of *Collected Works* (Toh. #5433).

______. *Tshad ma rnam 'grel gyi tshig le'ur byas pa'i rnam bzhad thar lam phyin ci ma log par gsal bar byed pa*. Vol. 6 (*cha*) of *Collected Works* (Toh. #5450).

(Khams stong bskor) 'Jam dpal dge 'dun rgya mtsho. *Don bdun bcu'i rnam bshad brdud rtsi'i gzegs ma*. Handwritten photo-reprint edition. Bylakuppe, India: Sera Mey College, 1969.

Jo bo rje dpal ldan mar me mdzad ye shes kyi rnam thar rgyas pa. In vol. 1 of *bKa' gdams rin po che'i glegs bam* (2 vols.), pp. 4–279. Reprinted as *Biography of Atisha and His Disciple Hbrom Ston*. New Delhi: Lokesh Chandra, 1982.

mKhas grub bsTan pa dar rgyas. *bsTan bcos mngon par rtogs pa'i rgyan rtsa 'grel gyi spyi don rnam bshad snying po rgyan gyi snang ba* (*Phar phyin spyi don*). New Delhi: Geshe Lobsang Tharchin, 1980.

mKhas grub dGe legs dpal bzang. *rGyas pa'i bstan bcos tshad ma rnam 'grel gyi rgya cher bshad pa rigs pa'i rgya mtsho las rang don le'u'i rnam bshad*. In vol. 10 (*tha*) of the *Collected Works of the Lord Mkhas-grub Rje*

Dge-legs dpal bzaṅ-po (12 vols.), pp. 619–1001. New Delhi: Mongolian Lama Gurudeva, 1980 (Toh. #5505A).

———. *rGyas pa'i bstan bcos tshad ma rnam 'grel gyi rgya cher bshad pa rigs pa'i rgya mtsho las tshad ma grub pa'i le'u'i rnam bshad.* In vol. 11 (*da*) of *Collected Works*, pp. 3–218 (Toh. #5505B).

———. *Tshad ma sde bdun gyi rgyan yid kyi mun sel.* In vol. 10 (*tha*) of *Collected Works*, pp. 3–449 (Toh. #5501).

(Sa skya Paṇḍi ta) Kun dga' rgyal mtshan. *sDom pa gsum gyi rab tu dbye ba.* In vol. 5 of *The Complete Works of the Great Masters of the Sa Skya Sect of Tibetan Buddhism*, pp. 297–320. Tokyo: The Toyo Bunko, 1968.

Legs par bshad pa bka' gdams rin po che'i gsung gi gces btus nor bu'i bang mdzod (*bKa' gdams bces btus*). Compiled by Ye shes don grub bstan pa'i rgyal mtshan. Delhi: D. Tsondu Senghe, 1985 (Toh. #6971).

(mChims) Nam mkha' grags (mChims 'Jam pa'i dbyangs). *Chos mngon mdzod kyi tsig le'ur byas pa'i 'grel pa mngon pa'i rgyan.* sBag sa, India: n.p., 1967 (Toh. #6954).

(sKyabs rje) Pha bong kha pa (Rin po che) Byams pa bstan 'dzin 'phrin las rgya mtsho (sKyabs rje bDe chen snying po). *rNam grol lag bcangs su gtod pa'i man ngag zab mo tshang la ma nor ba mtshungs med chos kyi rgyal po'i thugs bcud byang chub lam gyi rim pa'i nyams khrid kyi zin bris gsung rab kun gyi bcud bsdus gdams ngag bdud rtsi'i snying po* (*rNam grol lag bcangs*). Vol. 11 of *The Collected Works of Pha-boṇ-kha-pa* (11 vols.). New Delhi: Chophel Legdan, 1973. English translation: *Liberation in Our Hands.* 3 vols. Tr. Sermey Khensur Lobsang Tharchin with Artemus B. Engle. Howell, New Jersey: Mahayana Sutra and Tantra Press, 1990–2001.

———. *Byang chub lam gyi rim par myong khrid gnad du bkar te skyong tshul gyi man ngag phal tshig dmar rjen lag len mdzub btsugs kyi tshul du bkod pa.* In vol. 5 (*ca*) of *Collected Works*, pp. 338–358. English translation: *How to Meditate on the Stages of the Path to Enlightenment: A Teaching with Special Emphasis on the Methods of an Experiential Instruction, Expressed Openly and in Plain Words as if Pointing with a Finger to Each Element of Practice.* In *Liberation in Our Hands*, Part Two, pp. 323–344 (see preceding entry).

Red mda' ba gZhon nu blo gros. *bShes pa'i springs yig gi 'grel pa don gsal.* Thimbu, Bhutan: Mani Dorje, 1981. English translation: *Nāgārjuna's Letter.* Tr. Sermey Khensur Geshe Lobsang Tharchin and Artemus B. Engle. Dharamsala, India: Library of Tibetan Works and Archives, 1979.

mTsho sna ba Shes rab bzang po. *'Dul ba mdo rtsa'i 'grel pa legs bshad nyi ma'i 'od zer*. Beijing: Krung go'i bod kyi shes rig dpe skrun khang, 1993 (Toh. #6850).

(rJe) Tsong kha pa (Blo bzang grags pa'i dpal). *Bla ma dBu ma pa la mdo khams su phul ba('i springs yig)*. In vol. 2 (*kha*) (item #65 of *bKa' 'bum thor bu*) of *The Collected Works of the Incomparable Lord Tsongkhapa blo bzang grags pa* (18 vols.), pp. 334–337. New Delhi: Mongolian Lama Guru Deva, 1978–1983 (Toh. #5275).

———. *Byang chub lam gyi rim pa chen mo* (*Lam rim chen mo*). Vol. 13 (*pa*) of *Collected Works* (Toh. #5392). English translation: *The Great Treatise on the Stages of the Path to Enlightenment.* 3 vols. Ithaca, N.Y.: Snow Lion Publications, 2000–2004.

———. *dBu ma la 'jug pa'i rgya cher bshad pa dgongs pa rab gsal*. In vol. 16 (*ma*) of *Collected Works*, pp. 3–535 (Toh. #5408).

———. *dBu ma lta ba'i khrid yig.* In vol. 15 (*ba*) of *Collected Works,* pp. 723–776 (Toh. #5405).

———. *Drang ba dang nges pa'i don rnam par 'byed pa'i bstan bcos legs bshad snying po* (*Drang nges legs bshad snying po*). In vol. 14 (*pha*) of *Collected Works*, pp. 443–669 (Toh. #5396). English translation: *The Central Philosophy of Tibet*. Tr. Robert A. F. Thurman. Princeton: Princeton University Press, 1984.

———. *Lam mchog sgo 'byed*. In vol. 2 (*kha*) of *Collected Works* (item #1 of *bKa' 'bum thor bu*), pp. 202–206 (Toh. #5275).

———. *Lam gyi gtso bo rnam gsum*. In vol. 2 (*kha*) of *Collected Works* (item #85 of *bKa' 'bum thor bu*), pp. 584–586 (Toh. #5275). English translation with commentary in *The Principal Teachings of Buddhism*. Tr. Geshe Lobsang Tharchin and Michael Roach. Howell, New Jersey: Mahayana Sutra and Tantra Press, 1988.

———. *rGyal tshab chos rjes rje'i drung du gsan pa'i tshad ma'i brjed byang chen mo*. In vol. 14 (*pha*) of *Collected Works*, pp. 809–895 (Toh. #5400).

———. *bSam gzugs zin bris*. In vol. 18 (*tsha*) of *Collected Works*, pp. 799–817 (Toh. #5417).

———. *Yid dang kun gzhi'i dka' ba'i gnas rgya cher 'grel pa*. In vol. 18 (*tsha*) of *Collected Works*, pp. 623–735 (Toh. #5414). English translation: *Ocean of Eloquence: Tsong kha pa's Commentary on the Yogācāra Doctrine of Mind*. Tr. Gareth Sparham. Albany, N.Y.: State University of New York Press, 1993.

———. *Zhugs pa dang gnas pa'i skyes bu chen po rnams kyi rnam par bzhag pa blo gsal bgrod pa'i them skas*. In vol. 18 (*tsha*) of *Collected Works*, pp. 539–621 (Toh. #5413).

(sNa snam) Ye shes sde. *lTa ba'i khyad par*. In *sNa tshogs* section of Tg., vol. 206 (*jo*), ff. 213b–228a (Toh. # 4360).

(Tshe mchog gling yongs 'dzin) Ye shes rgyal mtshan. *Sems dang sems byung gi tshul gsal bar ston pa blo gsal mgul rgyan*. In vol. 16 of *The Collected Works (gsuṅ-'bum) of Tshe-mchog-gliṅ Yoṅs-'dzin Ye-śhes-rgyal-mtshan* (25 vols.), pp. 1–101. New Delhi: Tibet House Library, 1974–1977 (Toh. #6100).

Reference Works

A Catalogue of the Tohoku University Collection of Tibetan Works on Buddhism. Ed. Y. Kanakura et al. Sendai, Japan: Tohoku Imperial University, 1953.

A Complete Catalogue of the Tibetan Buddhist Canons. Ed. Hakuju Ui et al. Sendai, Japan: Tohoku Imperial University, 1934.

Aṣṭādhyāyī of Pāṇini. 2 vols. Ed. Śrīśa Chandra Vasu. 1st edition, 1891. Reprint edition, Delhi: Motilal Banarsidass, 1962.

Bod rgya tshig mdzod chen mo. Beijing: Mi rigs dpe skrun khang, 1985.

Buddhist Hybrid Sanskrit Dictionary. 2 vols. Ed. Franklin Edgerton. 1st edition, New Haven: Yale University Press, 1953. Reprint edition, Delhi: Motilal Banarsidass, 1970.

History of Buddhism by Bu-ston. Tr. E.E. Obermiller. Heidelberg: O. Harrassowitz, 1931; reprint edition, Tokyo: Suzuki Research Foundation [1964].

Jackson, Roger R. *Is Enlightenment Possible? Dharmakīrti and rGyal tshab rje on Knowledge, Rebirth, No-Self and Liberation*. Ithaca: Snow Lion Publications, 1993.

L'Abhidharmakośa de Vasubandhu. 6 vols. Translation and annotations by Louis de La Vallée Poussin. New edition by Étienne Lamotte. Brussels: Institut Belge des Hautes Études Chinoise, 1980.

Mahāvyutpattiḥ. (Tibetan title: *Bye brag tu rtogs pa chen po*). In *sNa tshogs* section of Tg., vol. 204 (*cho*), ff. 1b–131a (Toh. #4346). References to this text are based on the numbering system used in the 2 vol. reprint edition with Sanskrit and Tibetan indices. Tokyo: Suzuki Gakujutsu Zaidan, 1962.

Sanskrit-English Dictionary. Sir Monier Monier-Williams. 1st edition, London: Oxford University Press, 1899. Reprint edition, Delhi: Motilal Banarsidass, 1963.

Sanskrit Grammar. William Dwight Whitney. 1st edition, London: Oxford University Press, 1879. Reprint edition, Cambridge, Massachusetts: Harvard University Press, 1973 (thirteenth issue).

Seven Works of Vasubandhu. Stefan Anacker. Delhi: Motilal Banarsidass, 1998 (corrected edition).

Tāranātha's History of Buddhism in India. Tr. by Lama Chimpa and Alaka Chattopadhyana. Simla, India: Indian Institute of Advanced Study, 1970.

Tibetan-Sanskrit Dictionary. 16 vols. Ed. J.S. Negi. Sarnath, India: Central Institute of Higher Tibetan Studies, 1993–2005.

Index

abashment (T: *khrel yod pa*), 233, 285; one of five mental factors that is virtuous by its very nature, 510 (n. 625); one of seven spiritual riches, 27; key mental factor in cultivation of morality, 73, 469 (n. 126)

Abhidharma literature, xii, xiii, 6, 7, 12, 60, 72, 96, 103, 104, 105, 182, 201, 330, 385, 425 (n. 413), 426 (n. 425), 430 (n. 458), 431 (n. 475), 432 (n. 497), 437 (n. 563), 462 (n. 56), 463 (n. 68), 464 (n. 73), 469 (n. 127), 494 (n. 428)

Abhidharma School, 114, 120, 198

absence of abashment (T: *khrel med pa*), 236, 307–308; one of eight "perturbations," 426 (n. 424)

accumulation(s), two, 282; literal meaning, 476 (n. 233); merit, 282; wisdom, 282

acquirement (T: *thob pa*), 238, 313–314, 468 (n. 111)

afflicted entities (T: *kun nas nyon mongs pa'i chos*), 233, 290, 424 (n. 408), 479 (n. 253); correspondence with three states of affliction, 452 (n. 771), 482 (n. 295)

afflicted mind (T: *nyon mongs pa can gyi yid*), 344–346; always accompanied by four mental afflictions, 344–345; three situations in which it does not occur, 240, 345–346

agility (T: *shin tu sbyangs pa*), 151, 162, 163, 175, 177, 233, 288, 424 (n. 408), 479–480 (n. 258); an "attendant" of untainted wisdom, 422 (n. 379); of the mind, 162, 165, 166, 288; of the body, 162, 165, 166, 288; ease (T: *bde ba*) associated with two types of, 165–166; one of the seven limbs of enlightenment, 190, 288, 450 (n. 742)

aging (also "old age," T: *rga ba*), 106, 108, 109, 112, 121, 131, 136, 180, 239, 320–321, 322, 495 (n. 433)

Ākāśagarbha Sūtra, 210

analytic cessation (T: *so sor brtag pas 'gog pa*), 103–104, 240, 241, 351–352, 364, 453 (n. 775), 459 (n. 9), 504 (n. 570)

analytic meditation (T: *dpyad sgom*), 24, 29–30, 47, 399–400 (n. 47)

anger (T: *khro ba*), 235, 303–304, 486 (n. 341)

Annotated Edition of the Great Treatise on the Stages of the Path to Enlightenment (T: *Lam rim mchan bzhi sbrags ma*), 452–453 (n. 774)

Anthology of Precious Kadampa Writings (T: *Legs par bshad pa bka' gdams rin po che'i gsung gi bces btus nor bu'i bang mdzod*), 402 (n. 78), 406 (n. 130)

Aphorisms on Individual Liberation (S: *Prātimokṣasūtram*), 426 (n. 425)

Aphorisms on Knowledge (T: *Tshad ma mdo*), 70, 414 (n. 246). *See also* Compendium of Knowledge.

Aphorisms on the System of Morality

Six-armed Mahākāla